Sustainable Agriculture

Editor:
Christine Jakobsson

Editorial Board
Arne Gustafson
Allan Kaasik
Alexander Fehér
John Sumelius

D1719974

Editor: Christine Jakobsson
© The Baltic University Programme, Uppsala University, 2012
Cover Photo: Christine Jakobsson
Layout: Magnus Lehman
Print: Elanders
ISBN 978-91-86189-10-5

CONTENTS

Preface

The Baltic Sea and the North American Great Lakes are influenced by many different and similar problems affecting its environmental status. The Baltic Sea was classified by the United Nations International Maritime Organization (IMO) as a Particularly Sensitive Sea Area (PSSA) in April 2004. Both the Baltic Sea and the Great Lakes are of ecological, socioeconomic, cultural or scientifically importance. Discharge of nutrients from agriculture and waste-water treatment plants, as well as from industries, transportation and other human activities leads to eutrophication and other forms of pollution. The Ecosystem Health and Sustainable Agriculture project aims at updating knowledge in the field of rural development, sustainable agriculture and animal health pertaining to the Baltic Sea Region and to some degree also the Great Lakes region.

The agricultural activities are often based on individual producer´s decisions and on their attitudes, knowledge and level of technology. It is however also based on political and economic considerations, attitudes and opinions from the society. Thus, continuously updated scientifically based knowledge, both from an environmental, social and economic view, need to be disseminated and applied with a much increased ambition. Technological facts may be well known, but still strong social and economic reasons and pressure from outside to make short term profits hinders the appropriate application of relevant measures. This is the reason why we have all parts of the sustain-ability concept covered in our texts: the ecological, the social, the economical, and the institutional/juridical.

The books produced as part of this project include:

1. Sustainable Agriculture
2. Ecology and Animal Health
3. Rural Development and Land Use

These three books are based on experience from the Baltic Sea and Great Lakes Regions and written by prominent experts and scientists from the two regions. Two networks have been involved in the production of the books, The Baltic University Programme (BUP) and the Envirovet Baltic Networks. The BUP is a network of approximately 220 universities in the drainage basin to the Baltic Sea that cooperates on sustainable development, studies of the region, its environment and its political changes. The program, founded in 1991 at Uppsala University, Sweden, operates by producing courses, holding conferences and seminars. In 2010, the BUP network delivered courses at more than 100 universities serving nearly 9,500 undergraduate and graduate students. The Envirovet Baltic, a network of environmental health scientist/ educators from USA and the nine countries bordering the Baltic Sea, was founded in 2001 on an initiative of the College of Veterinary Medicine, University of Illinois and the Centre for Reproductive Biology in Uppsala,

Swedish University of Agricultural Sciences with scientists from universities in the Baltic Sea Region (BSR). Courses are delivered separately by each university in the networks in both cases. Preferably all the three books should be studied to give a comprehensive overview on actual experience and research findings. We have chosen to use the ecosystem health concept to understand and prevent problems for the future. It is our aim that the books will strengthen knowledge on ecosystems and its interaction with human activities in a wider sense. The texts presented in this book should deepen and update our knowledge on all aspects of rural development and sustainable agriculture. Our aim is furthermore to provide explanations of the problem complexity and examples of problem solving.

Target groups are students, teachers, experts and people working in government offices, ministries, municipalities and as agricultural advisors and managers of different natural resource based activities in rural areas.

The Baltic Sea Watershed with its population of more than 85 million people contributes to an ongoing environmental disaster. The disaster is well documented and can be summarized as:

1) Eutrophication from heavy contamination of excess Nitrogen and Phosphorus – sources are diffuse sources, point sources and atmospheric downfall
2) Excess fishing, distorting the marine ecosystem; diminishing cod population being the most drastic example
3) Contaminants other than nutrients, mainly PCB, heavy metals, oil spill, human and animal drugs, etc.
4) Distortions of the biodiversity of the sea, e.g extinction of many indigenous species, and introduction of alien species which distort the ecological balance drastically
5) Threats connected to climate change

Sustainable Agriculture and Sustainable Rural Development

"Sustainable agriculture" has become a popular way of expressing that what society wants is an environmentally sound, productive, economically viable, and socially desirable agriculture. However, the concept of agricultural sustainability does not lend itself to precise definition. Agriculture is practiced in so many climates and in different cultural contexts, so "sustainable agriculture" cannot possibly imply a special way of thinking or of using farming practices.

Sustainable agriculture is an approach to securing the necessary resources for safeguarding global food production, biodiversity reserves, recreation needs, water quality and well developed rural areas and wildlife areas. It can also be an effective means of poverty reduction and of achieving the Millennium Development Goals, as well as means of mitigating climate change. It is also about health, welfare, respect and ethics regarding animals and man, as well as quality of food and feed. In other words they are truly transdisciplinary and represent a new holistic outlook on ecosystem health and sustainable agriculture.

We have chosen to give agriculture a wider meaning than the traditional. It is common to understand agriculture as being the activity which is securing food supply. But as we shall see in the chapters on historical trends, activities on the countryside have always been complex and integrated with other activities in rural areas, such as small business, forestry, fishing, and other activities. Also several hundred years ago, the farmer combined biological and technical knowledge with economical and organisational skill, and very often he or she made money from different other jobs like carpentry, timber and coal production, horse- and oxen driving, cheese production, food conservation etc. Today the diversity in income generation is even higher and in fact, every farming enterprise has at least one or two side activities. Our definition of agriculture as main activity would today be: to produce and manage biomass. Some examples, explained in more detailed in our books, are (besides food production):

- public goods in the form of natural and cultural amenities to benefit the ecosystem (such as management national parks and of landscape for a certain type of desired biodiversity)
- fish production
- biomass for timber and fibre products
- biomass for energy production

- social caretaking of, for instance, sick people or people who needs rehabilitation from criminal or other lives
- tourism (including views, maintenance of tracks, camping sites, buildings, etc)
- recreation (such as horseback riding and horse racing, golf- and soccer fields, fishing sites, hunting etc)
- animal raising and caretaking (dog- and cat kennels etc)

A widespread definition of sustainability of agriculture, with which we sympathise, is the FAO (Food and Agricultural Organisation of the UN) statement:

> *"Overall objectives of technological interventions for sustainable agriculture can be summarized as food security and risk resilience, environmental compatibility, economic viability, and social acceptability."*

An addition to the FAO definition would need, as we see it, the following phrasing: *Sustainable agriculture is not linked to any particular technological practice. Sustainable agriculture should have adaptability and flexibility over time to respond to demands for biomass production but it should also have ability to protect the soil, the genetic resources and the waters.*

We also want to recall the definition done for the specific Baltic Sea Region, as expressed by the Baltic Agenda 21:

Sustainable agriculture is the production of high-quality food and other agricultural products and services in the long run, with consideration taken to economy and social structure in such a way that the resource base of non-renewable and renewable resources is maintained. Important sub goals are:

- *The farmers` income should be sufficient to provide a fair standard of living in the agricultural community;*
- *The farmers should practice production methods which do not threaten human or animal health or degrade the environment, including biodiversity, and a the same time minimise the environmental problems that future generations must assume responsibility for;*

- *Non-renewable resources gradually have to be replaced by renewable resources, and that re-circulation of non-renewable resources is maximized;*
- *Sustainable agriculture will meet the needs of food and recreation, and preserve the landscape, cultural values and historical heritage of rural areas, and contribute to the creation of stable, well-developed and secure rural communities;*
- *The ethical aspects of agricultural production are secured.*

It is our firm belief that agriculture and related activities can, if well managed, be positive for the ecosystems and for biodiversity. Contrary, agricultural activities can also give disastrous effects to the environment including humans living in the area. Often national goals are not only to sustain a food security of the country, but also to keep an open landscape and rural lifestyle. A sustainable rural development has its backbone in a sustainable agriculture.

The books were produced with the main financing from the Swedish International Development Authority, SIDA. Additional funding was received from the Swedish Environmental Protection Agency, the Swedish Institute, the University of Illinois, the Hewlett Foundation and some private donors, as well as within the networks of the Baltic University Programme and Envirovet Baltic.

Authors have to a great degree contributed with unpaid work. All these contributions are gratefully acknowledged.

Uppsala August 2011

Christine Jakobsson, Leif Norrgren, Ingrid Karlsson, and Jeffrey Levengood

Part A

Definitions
and Prerequisites

Authors: Angelija Bučiene, Yariv Cohen, Patrik Enfält, Christine Jakobsson, Holger Kirchmann, Evgeny Krasnov, Piotr Prus, Torbjörn Rydberg, Staffan Steineck and Hava Zaburaeva

Coordinating Author: Christine Jakobsson

Definitions of the Ecosystems Approach and Sustainability

1

Christine Jakobsson
Uppsala University, Uppsala, Sweden

Sustainable agriculture is dependent on many different factors and intervening systems. It is dependent on environmental, social and economic decisions as well as on individuals and on society in general. During later years it has become more obvious that it is important to implement the ecosystem approach to be able to reach good results. What is the ecosystem approach and how can it be implemented? To find a good definition of the ecosystem approach, the report "Ocean- time for a new strategy", SOU 2003:72 was consulted.

more adaptive and instructive with clear links between implemented measures, environmental monitoring and research. Management must be based more on the obligations of the sectors and less on their rights. The environmental requirements placed on the sectors must be founded on the limitation of the ecosystems. The aim is to preserve the structure and function of ecosystems and hence maintain their capacity to provide us with goods and services ("Ocean – time for a new strategy", SOU 2003:72).

Definition of the Ecosystem Approach

Ecosystems consist of different components, flora, fauna, other organisms and of the surrounding environment. These various organisms in an ecosystem are all part of a food chain, with interconnections and with the different levels influencing each other as the result of complex and dynamic relationships. If a critical species decreases in number or disappears, these relationships can break down. The ecosystem can then take on a completely different state after the breakdown. Sustainable management must be based on this perspective and consider the impact of proposed measures in a holistic manner.

The ecosystem approach places more far-reaching demands on protection measures than is the case with the current 'sectorised' method. Management must be

Definition of Ecosystem Health

In Ecosystem Health two concepts are joined together. First we have the Ecosystem concept which is described above and secondly we add the concept of health. In today's world the effects of ecosystem decline are becoming more and more evident. At the same time, health is an important indicator of the systems function. Ecosystem health is a comprehensive and integrated approach, which reflects the health of the living and non-living components of the land and marine world. It expands the traditional definitions of health, and implies the links between human activity, ecological change and health. Ecosystem health is transdisciplinary by nature, as it brings together the natural, social and health sciences and incorporates ecological, social, and economic perspectives with human health. Health ultimately depends upon ecosystem services e.i. availability of fresh water, food, fuel, pollination etc.

Definition of Sustainable Agriculture

Sustainable agriculture has been defined in several different contexts. The FAO definition can be found in the preface. It was defined for the Baltic Sea Region in 1997-1998 in connection with Baltic 21 – An Agenda 21 for the Baltic Sea Region. Baltic 21 was initiated by the Prime Ministers of the Baltic Sea Region in 1996 and is a regional Agenda 21 working towards regional sustainable development. Baltic 21 consists of stakeholders, government ministries and agencies from the Baltic Sea states, the European Commission, numerous intergovernmental and non-governmental organisations, academic and financial institutions, as well as local, city and business networks. The Baltic 21 Agriculture Sector was requested to give a definition and goal for sustainable agriculture. This was discussed during an international process of approximately one year and all ten participating countries (Denmark, Estonia, Finland, Germany, Latvia, Lithuania, Norway, Poland, NW Russia, and Sweden) were active in the process.

The Baltic 21 Definition of Sustainable Agriculture
"Agriculture contributes significantly to the society of the future. Sustainable agriculture is the production of high quality food and other agricultural products/services in the long run with consideration taken to economy and social structure, in such a way that the resource base of non-renewable and renewable resources is maintained. Important sub-goals are:

1. Farmers' income should be sufficient to provide a fair standard of living in the agricultural community.
2. Farmers should practise production methods which do not threaten human or animal health or degrade the environment, including biodiversity, and at the same time minimise our environmental problems for which future generations must assume responsibility.

Non-sustainable Issues

The most urgent non-sustainable issues for sustainable agriculture are:

Production
- Contaminants and residues in food.
- Unfavourable market conditions for agricultural production.
- Excessive livestock density.

Natural resources
- Dependence on fossil energy.
- Low efficiency of energy use in agricultural production.
- Dependence on non-renewable phosphorus deposits.
- Lack of water and deteriorating water quality.
- Nutrient losses (N and P) to the environment.
- Decrease in soil fertility (acidification, carbon content, nutrient status, structure, compaction, salinisation).
- Erosion.
- Pesticide residues in soil, water and non-target organisms.
- Accumulation of heavy metals and nuclides.
- Soil contamination with persistent organic and inorganic substances.
- Loss of biodiversity and genetic resources.
- Air pollution (NH_3, CH_4, N_2O, pesticides).

Human and animal welfare
- Occupational threats to farmers' and consumers' health.
- Dependence on growth promoters and antibiotics in animal production.
- Unfavourable animal welfare and threats to animal health.
- Diseases that can spread from animals to humans, e.g. BSE, avian influenza.

Socio-economic criteria
- Poor profitability of farming.
- Lack of food security and food production security.
- Unfavourable social infrastructure in rural areas.
- Lack of preservation of nature and historical values.
- Urbanisation.

Expertise – Education
- Lack of education, information and management skills.

Agenda 21 for the Baltic Sea Region, Sustainable Development of the Agricultural Sector in the Baltic Sea Region, Baltic Sea Environment Proceedings No. 74, Helsinki Commission 1998

3. Non-renewable resources have to gradually be re-placed by renewable resources and recirculation of non-renewable resources maximised.
4. Sustainable agriculture will meet society's needs of food and recreation and preserve the landscape, cultural values and the historical heritage of rural areas and contribute to create stable, well-developed and secure rural communities.
5. The ethical aspects of agricultural production are secured." (Helsinki Commission, 1998)

Problems or Non-sustainable Issues for the Agricultural Sector

There are many different types of farms and agriculture throughout the Baltic Sea Region, all with various sustainability impacts. Regions and farms with a high livestock density and/or high inputs of fertilisers, as well as inappropriate agricultural management, can often be a serious environmental threat. This varies within the Baltic Sea Region. The main challenges are to reduce the negative effects of agriculture on the Baltic Sea by reducing the pollution by nutrients, which to a large extent originates from animal production and improper use of fertilisers, and through reducing the risks associated with the use of plant protection products, as well as developing and maintaining bio-diversity. Great differences exist between EU15 member countries (the 15 countries that were members in 1994) and the new members of EU27 (EU member countries in 2004 e.g.Estonia, Latvia, Lithuania, Poland, Slovakia) and Russia. In the EU15 countries, point sources in connection with manure handling have been the focus for environmental action programmes for more than a couple of decades, with diffuse sources also considered more recently. On the other hand, in the new EU27 member countries and Russia, an immediate problem today is nutrient point sources, due to insufficient or non-existent manure storage and often large animal holdings. Diffuse pollution is also a problem here. The development within this area is in some countries still too slow.

Nitrogen losses are basically correlated to the total turnover of nitrogen in the system and different correc-tive measures in crop production practices have so far not proven sufficient to reduce the nitrate losses to acceptable levels for the water environment. Efficient tools to effect such a reduction are important. EU legislation such as the Nitrate directive and the Water framework directive are such tools among many others (see the chapter on Nitrogen losses from Agricultural Soils in the Baltic Sea Area page 78-81).

Modern agriculture also relies on imported feed and non-renewable fossil fuel and finite phosphorus resources. The specialisation of agriculture has greatly increased the transportation of commodities and agricultural products. In addition, large differences exist between countries and regions in economic conditions and infrastructure in rural areas. This means that measures necessary for sustainable development are not always the same within the entire Baltic Sea Region. As there is a great lack of education and knowledge on sustainable agriculture, education, advisory services and training are needed in the whole region, but particularly for the new family farms in the new EU27 member countries. Throughout the whole Baltic Sea Region, there is a need for development and demonstration of more sustainable agricultural systems. A well functioning agricultural extension service has an important role to play and demonstrate to the farmers the best ways to implement changes towards sustainable development. Appropriate monitoring systems and the proposed indicators of sustainable development are indispensable tools to evaluate the progress towards the established goals of sustainable agriculture.

In the context of the Baltic 21 Agricultural Sector in 1998 the task on identifying what sustainable agriculture was started when the sector defined the non-sustainable issues in agriculture. This list was used as a starting point also for the planning of this project and only a few issues were added in 2006 by the group of researchers involved in producing these three books in the Ecosystem Health and Sustainable Agriculture series. The updated version is provided in this book.

Land is a Prerequisite for Food Production

Torbjörn Rydberg
*Swedish University of Agricultural Sciences,
Uppsala, Sweden*

Direct Use of Arable Land

Humans exist in ecosystems and are part of these ecosystems. We depend on ecosystems for all our activities. We need a steady supply of basic requirements such as food, water, energy in terms of fuels, fibres, building materials, waste sinks and all other ecosystem services that directly and indirectly make life possible.

It has been estimated that the acreage of arable land could theoretically be doubled in the future, but there are potential problems due to competition for land for other purposes and difficulties with freshwater supplies for irrigation. If more area can be taken into production, this new land may require more resources, not only for irrigation, but also for increased fertilisation and mechanical work, etc. to produce the same volume of crops.

Since arable land is a limited resource, there will be less land per capita as the global population grows. In 1960 there was 0.48 hectare arable land per capita, but by 2000 this had declined to 0.23 hectare per capita. It is estimated that there will be only 0.18 hectare per capita in 2025 as the global population grows.

The direct land area used to support food consumption in Sweden in the period 1997-2000 was on average approximately 3.7 million ha, or 0.41 ha per capita (Johansson, 2005). This direct area for Swedish food production required not only domestic land but also the land used for imported food products, see Figure 2.1.

Ecological Footprint

Besides arable land to grow our food we also need land for energy crops, land for timber production, land to capture the water we drink and land for assimilation of the waste we generate in society. The ecological footprint measures how fast we consume resources and generate waste compared with how fast nature can absorb our waste and generate new resources. The ecological footprint keeps track of these uses to some extent. If we know how much resources we are consuming and how much waste we are generating, most of these resources and waste streams can be converted to biologically productive area.

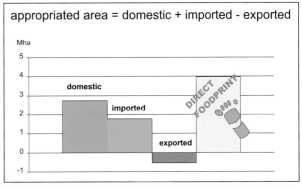

Figure 2.1. Appropriated area for Swedish food production = domestic + imported − exported area (Johansson, 2005).

Six areas are considered in an ecological footprint evaluation: 1) Crop; 2) Pasture (livestock production); 3) Sea (fish and aquatic plants); 4) Forest (timber and firewood); 5) Building area (living and dam areas) and 6) Area for carbon fixation.

Using this assessment, it is possible to estimate how much of the Earth (or how many Earths) it would take to support humanity if everybody lived a given lifestyle. In 2010, humanity's total ecological footprint was estimated at 2.23 Earths – in other words, humanity uses ecological services 2.23 times as fast as Earth can renew them (Figure 2.2). Every year, this number is recalculated – with a three-year lag due to the time it takes for the UN to collect and publish all the underlying statistics.

Ecological footprint can be measured for an individual, a city, a business, a nation or all of humanity. It can also be used to assess the footprint of food consumption ('foodprint'). The ecological footprint of Swedish food consumption is in the range 7.4-14.5 million, hectares according to Johansson (2005). The ecological footprint is one indicator that can be used to estimate the indirect land needed to support a specific activity.

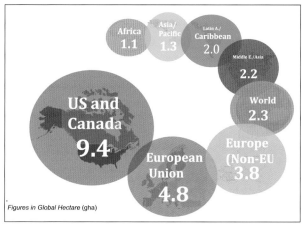

Figure 2.2. Ecological footprint (in 2010) for the World, US and Canada, European Union, Europe (non-EU), Middle East/Central Asia, Latin America/Caribbean, Asia/Pacific, and Africa (Data from WWF, 2008).

Emergy Footprint

Recognition of the relevance of energy for the growth and dynamics of different complex systems has resulted in increased emphasis on methods of environmental evaluation that can account for and interpret the effects of matter and energy flows at all scales in systems of humanity and nature.

Another method used for calculation of the interdependence of human activities with their environment is emergy synthesis. Emergy accounting uses the thermodynamic basis of all forms of energy, resources and human services, and converts them into equivalents of one form of energy, usually solar emergy. It takes into account all the free environmental inputs (sunlight, wind, rain), as well as the indirect environmental support embodied in human labour and services often associated with monetary transactions. It is a quantitative measure of all the resources required to make something, whether those resources are mineral deposits resulting from biogeological processes, renewable resources such

as wood, fuel sources used directly, or goods or services resulting from industrial processes offered on the market. For further explanations of the concept, see Odum (2007). This method is more comprehensive than the ecological footprint methodology. Therefore the calculation of indirect land use needed to support the Swedish food consumption gives larger values than the ecological footprint method. The emergy footprint for Swedish food production system is an estimated 147 million hectares (Johansson et al., 2000). This is about 40 times the direct area used for cropping and 3.6 times the total land area of Sweden.

Summary

The direct use of agricultural land is a limiting factor for food production. Some of the major problems today are land degradation, competition with other land use issues, the increasing global population and associated growing demand for food, the need to maintain yield levels by use of non-renewable inputs and uneven access to arable land and the output of food production systems. All these factors need to be given high priority in research, education and the policy-making process if we are to achieve a more sustainable future.

Methods are available that reveal the interrelationship between human activities and their environment. The results of such analyses show that the indirect environmental support is large. Higher yields per hectare have so far been achieved in modern agriculture and food production systems by increasing inputs of high quality resources of a non-renewable character. The development of agro-ecological principles and their implementation in agriculture is necessary to meet the future in a more sustainable way. Food production systems need to be based to a much higher degree than today upon renewable energy sources rather than non-renewable inputs.

Plant Nutrient Supply in Agriculture

Abundance Today and Shortage Tomorrow?

3

Holger Kirchmann and Yariv Cohen
Swedish University of Agricultural Sciences, Uppsala, Sweden

Patrik Enfält
EasyMining Sweden AB

Christine Jakobsson
Uppsala University, Uppsala, Sweden

Introduction

The production of sufficient food for a growing population is a major challenge for agriculture. Since agricultural land can only be expanded at the expense of deforestation, crop production must be increased mainly on existing agricultural land. However, higher yields per area require greater input of nutrients. It is therefore essential that limited resources of plant nutrients are used in an efficient way.

This chapter provides an overview of nutrient reserves and a summary of recent associated information. Knowledge about the amounts and limits of nutrient reserves is vital for decisions on how to utilise resources in an appropriate manner. In order to conserve resources and secure production of food, nutrients must be recycled. The potential and conditions to achieve functioning nutrient recycling to secure food supply over the long term are discussed.

Influential Trends

Population Growth, Urbanisation and Decline in Arable Land Area Per Capita

It is possible to identify certain significant trends worldwide that will affect agricultural production and nutrient use in future. Population growth and urbanisation are increasing (Figure 3.1). Between 1950 and 2009, the global population increased from 2.5 billion to 6.8 billion and is expected to reach 9.1 billion by 2050 (United Nations, 2009). Furthermore, population growth is expected to occur mainly in urban areas (Table 3.1). Statistics show that 1.4 billion people are now living in 600 cities with a mean population of 2.3 million per city, excluding suburban areas with a population greater than 0.75 million inhabitants (GeoHive, 2010). These scenarios will have some foreseeable effects.

Population growth will not be accompanied by an increase in agricultural land, as the total area of agricultural land can only be marginally expanded. In most cases, only forests are at hand for conversion, as pointed out by Gregory et al. (2002), and other areas cannot be trans-

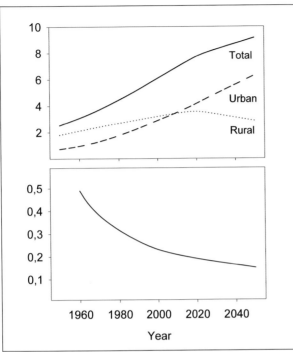

Figure 3.1. Projected urban and rural population growth and arable land area available per capita. Data from United Nations (2010) and FAO (2008).

Table 3.1. Predicted population growth for some large cities. Cities ranked after expected size in 2025. Data from GeoHive (2010).

Population (million)	2000	2010	2025
Tokyo, Japan	34.4	36.7	37.1
Delhi, India	15.7	22.2	28.6
Mumbai (Bombay), India	16.1	20.0	25.8
São Paulo, Brazil	17.1	20.3	21.7
Dhaka, Bangladesh	10.3	14.6	20.9
Ciudad de México, Mexico	18.0	19.5	20.7
New York-Newark, USA	17.8	19.4	20.6
Kolkata (Calcutta), India	13.1	15.6	20.1
Shanghai, China	13.2	16.6	20.0
Karachi, Pakistan	10.0	13.1	18.7
Lagos, Nigeria	7.2	10.6	15.8
Beijing, China	9.8	12.4	15.0
Manila, Philippines	10.0	11.6	14.9
Buenos Aires, Argentina	11.8	13.1	13.7
Los Angeles, USA	11.8	12.8	13.7
Al-Qahirah (Cairo), Egypt	10.2	11.0	13.5
Rio de Janeiro, Brazil	10.8	11.9	12.7
Istanbul, Turkey	8.7	10.5	12.1

formed into agricultural land. In fact, arable land area per person has decreased, from 0.38 hectares in 1970 to 0.23 hectares in 2000, with a projected decline to 0.15 hectares per person by 2050 (FAO, 2008; Figure 3.1). There will be less agricultural land available per capita in future and consequently crop production on existing arable land must be intensified in order to produce sufficient food.

The demographic trend for increasing urbanisation will make towns and cities hot-spots for accumulation of plant nutrients (Grimm et al., 2008). Food transported to cities results in wastes, from which plant nutrients must be recycled and redistributed. To avoid overloading arable land with recycled nutrients, long-distance transportation from cities back to remote arable land is necessary. However, municipal organic wastes typically have high water and low nutrient contents. For example, dewatered sewage sludge contains 70-80% water and the total content of nitrogen or phosphorus does not exceed 3% of

dry matter. The volume of urban wastes to be handled is three- to five-fold larger than the volume of most harvested crops (Kirchmann et al., 2005).

In summary, two aspects of nutrient management can be identified as being central tasks: Firstly, to intensify crop production, which includes use of more plant nutrients to increase yields without causing negative environmental side-effects; and secondly, to redistribute nutrients in wastes from large urbanised areas back to arable land in an equitable manner.

Yield Increase and Efficiency of Nutrient Use

Two significant developments can be identified in Swedish crop production systems. Crop yields have increased at an average rate of 0.5% per year. Furthermore, this enhancement has not been achieved through larger inputs of fertiliser, as fertiliser input has remained constant. Instead, use efficiency of inputs has improved by about 10% over 20 years (Table 3.2). Increasing the ef-

Table 3.2. Crop yield and efficiency of N fertiliser use in Swedish agriculture (data from SCB, 1982-2010).

Crop	Mean yield 1980-1990 (kg)	Yield per N input (kg kg-1 N)	Mean yield 2000-2010 (kg)	Yield per N input (kg kg-1 N)	Yield increase (%)	Efficiency increase (%)
Winter wheat	5,500	50	6,200	56	11	11
Barley	3,600	45	4,200	52	14	13
Oats	3,600	45	3,900	49	7	8

ficiency in crop production systems through inputs, farm operations, etc. is a central and driving force in agricultural research. In order to improve the use of organic and mineral fertilisers, detailed knowledge to fine-tune soil and crop management is needed.

Nutrient Reserves for Fertiliser Production

A critical question often raised is how long global reserves used for the production of mineral fertilisers will last. Although there are different opinions on what appropriate use of non-renewable nutrient reserves means, it is necessary to summarise data on known reserves to forecast possible scenarios.

Nitrogen
Nitrogen fertiliser production is based on ammonia synthesis, requiring hydrogen gas (H_2) and nitrogen gas (N_2). Nitrogen gas is taken from the atmosphere (air contains 78% N_2) and hydrogen gas is produced from fossil energy, mainly natural gas or through gasification of coal according to the following reactions:

$$CH_4 + H_2O \rightarrow CO + 3\ H_2$$
$$CO + H_2O \rightarrow CO_2 + H_2$$

Hydrogen gas reacts under high pressure and temperature to form ammonia gas according to the Haber-Bosch reaction, which is an energy-demanding process.

$$N_2 + 3\ H_2 \rightarrow 2\ NH_3$$

Roughly 5% of annual gas consumption in the world is used for ammonia production, of which more than 90% is used in agriculture for the production of different nitrogen fertilisers. Natural gas (CH_4) accounts for about 70% of ammonia production, coal and petroleum coke for the remaining 30%. Hydro-electric power has also been used in some fertiliser plants in the past. Globally, we are using 3.2 trillion cubic metres of natural gas per year of proven reserves of 175 trillion cubic metres (Energy Information Administration, 2010). This would mean a life-time of about 50 years.

The dependence of N fertiliser production on fossil fuels is often questioned. Instead, biological nitrogen fixation by legumes is proposed to replace nitrogen fertiliser application (e.g. Watson et al., 2002). It is also argued that N fertiliser production is too large, threatening the ecological functions of our planet (Rockström et al., 2009). However, hydrogen gas can be produced from renewable resources.

There are different ways to produce hydrogen gas from biomass, such as (i) anaerobic digestion providing methane; (ii) combustion to form electricity for electrolysis of water; and (iii) thermochemical conversion through pyrolysis and gasification. The last alternative - gasification of biomass - has been investigated by Ahlgren et al. (2009) from a life-cycle perspective using straw or short-rotation willow as feedstock for an ammonia plant. The results indicate that 1 kg of N can be produced from 2.6 kg dry salix or 2.7 kg dry straw.

In the straw alternative, no extra land was set aside and the straw was removed from 1 hectare arable land cropped with wheat. Assuming an average winter wheat yield for Sweden, straw from 1 ha would allow net production of 1,615 kg N. In the salix alternative, net production of 3,914 kg N per ha plantation was derived. This clearly shows that biomass-based production of nitrogen fertiliser from straw or salix is not only self-supporting but provides N fertiliser for an additional 20 or 49 ha, respectively, assuming an application rate of 80 kg per ha

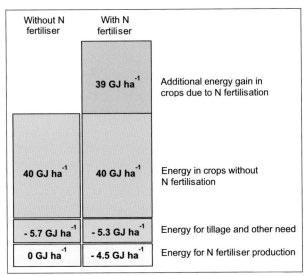

Without N fertiliser	With N fertiliser	
	39 GJ ha^{-1}	Additional energy gain in crops due to N fertilisation
40 GJ ha^{-1}	40 GJ ha^{-1}	Energy in crops without N fertilisation
- 5.7 GJ ha^{-1}	- 5.3 GJ ha^{-1}	Energy for tillage and other need
0 GJ ha^{-1}	- 4.5 GJ ha^{-1}	Energy for N fertiliser production

Figure 3.2. Energy input in relation to energy gain through crops and residues in crop production systems with N fertiliser (right) compared with systems replacing N fertiliser with biological N fixation (left) (data from Bertilsson et al., 2008).

Table 3.3. Total mineable rock phosphate reserves according to USGS (2011).

Ranking of countries according to reserve size	Total mineable reserves		Proportion of total production
	(billion ton)	Proportion of reserves (%)	(%)
Morocco + Western Sahara	50	77	15
China	3.7	5.6	37
Algeria	2.2	3.4	1
Syria	1.8	2.8	1.6
South Africa	1.5	2.3	1.3
Jordan	1.5	2.3	3.4
USA	1.4	2.1	15
Russia	1.3	2.0	5.7
Brazil	0.34	0.5	0.3
Israel	0.18	0.3	1.7
Senegal	0.18	0.3	0.04
Tunisia	0.1	0.2	4.3
Egypt	0.1	0.2	1.7
Australia	0.08	0.1	1.6
Togo	0.06	0.1	0.04
Other countries	0.62	0.9	10
Total	65	100	100

of arable land. This shows that nitrogen fertilisers can be produced with renewable energy in the future.

Ammonia production according to the Haber-Bosch reaction is an energy-demanding process. However, application of nitrogen fertiliser to crops results in a positive energy balance (Figure 3.2). Nitrogen is the plant nutrient that has the greatest impact on crop yields. Application of N fertiliser enhances crop production, whereby more solar energy is captured through a larger biomass, increasing photosynthesis. As a result, more energy is bound in N-fertilised than unfertilised crops. The energy gain through enhanced photosynthesis is 5 to 10 times higher than the energy required for N fertiliser production (Bertilsson et al., 2008). This means that the energy-demanding production of N fertiliser is greatly compensated for by the much higher energy yield, which is a strong argument for producing nitrogen fertiliser.

Renewable energy can replace natural gas as an energy source for N fertiliser production. It is therefore possible to produce N fertilisers from renewable biomass even if fossil energy becomes scarce. This is important because of the crucial role of nitrogen fertiliser for food supply in the world. Smil (2001, 2002) concluded that the Haber-Bosch process for industrial fixation of atmospheric ni-

trogen provides the very means of survival for 40% of humanity and that only half the current population in the world could be supported by pre-fertiliser farming, even with a mainly vegetarian diet. Thus one has to recognise the immense role of nitrogen fertiliser for human welfare and why fertiliser production will not stop even if fossil resources may be depleted.

Phosphorus

World reserves of phosphate rock are large, but most of these reserves are found in Saharan Africa (Table 3.3). About 80% of the rock phosphate currently mined is used to manufacture mineral fertilisers. Use for detergents, animal feeds and other applications (metal treatment, beverages, etc.) accounts for approximately 12.5%, 5% and

3%, respectively (Heffer et al., 2005). The global production of rock phosphate amounted to 174 million tonnes in 2008 (IFA, 2010a). Depending on its origin, phosphate rock can have widely differing mineralogical, textural and chemical characteristics. Igneous deposits typically contain fluorapatites and hydroxyapatites, while sedimentary deposits typically consist of carbonate-fluorapatites collectively called francolite. Sedimentary deposits account for about 80% of the global production of phosphate rock (Stewart et al., 2005). As high-quality deposits have already been exploited, the quality of the remaining sedimentary phosphorus reserves is declining and the cost of extraction and processing is increasing, mainly due to a lower phosphorus content in the ore (Driver et al., 1999). Associated heavy metals such as cadmium and uranium substituting for calcium in the apatite molecule are often present at high levels in phosphate rock, especially that of sedimentary origin. Rock phosphate may contain up to 640 mg cadmium per kg phosphorus and only a minor proportion of phosphorus reserves have a low cadmium content (McLaughlin et al., 1996) (Table 3.4, Figure 3.3). Most (85-90%) of the cadmium in rock phosphate ends up in fertilisers (Becker, 1989).

Table 3.4. Cadmium concentrations in rock phosphate reserves (McLaughlin et al., 1996).

Country and mine	Cadmium concentration (mg Cd kg^{-1} P)
Russia (Kola), Finland (Sillinjärvi)	1.0
South Africa (Phalaborwa)	23
China (Yunan)	35
Syria (Eastern and Khneifiss)	35
Australia (Duchess)	50
Egypt (Quseir)	61
Morocco (Khouribga)	80
Israel (Arad)	85
Tunisia (Gafsa)	108
Israel (Zin)	228
Morocco (Boucraa)	240
Christmas Island	275
USA (North Carolina)	311

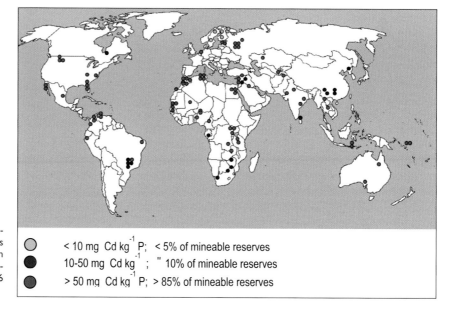

Figure 3.3. Locations of phosphorus deposits, mapping out cadmium contents and proportion of mineable reserves in relation to cadmium contamination (combined data from McLaughlin et al., 1996 and USGS, 2011a).

○ < 10 mg Cd kg^{-1} P; < 5% of mineable reserves
● 10-50 mg Cd kg^{-1} ; " 10% of mineable reserves
● > 50 mg Cd kg^{-1} P; > 85% of mineable reserves

Phosphate Rock Reserves

It is difficult to forecast how long the existing phosphorus reserves will last. Earlier estimates vary between 50 to 100 years and peak phosphorus is a foreseeable scenario (Stewart et al., 2005; Buckingham and Jasinski, 2006; Cordell et al., 2009). Including reserve bases would prolong the life-time to around 350 years, based on the current production capacity and excluding an increased demand for phosphorus (IFDC, 2010; USGS, 2011a).

Cadmium Problem

A new standard for low cadmium content in phosphorus fertilisers may be required, since the European Food Safety Authority recently reduced the recommended tolerable weekly intake of cadmium from 7 to 2.5 µg per kg body weight, based on new data regarding the toxicity of cadmium to humans (EFSA, 2009). The reasons given by EFSA (2009) are as follows: Cadmium is efficiently retained in the kidney and liver in the human body, with a very long biological half-life ranging from 10 to 30 years. Cadmium is primarily toxic to the kidney, especially to the proximal tubular cells, where it accumulates over time and may cause renal dysfunction. Cadmium can also cause bone demineralisation, either through direct bone damage or indirectly as a result of renal dysfunction. After prolonged and/or high exposure, the tubular damage may progress to decreased glomerular filtration rate, and eventually to renal failure. Cadmium has been classified as a human carcinogen by the International Agency for Research on Cancer and there is evidence that it mimics the function of steroid hormones and can function biologically as an oestrogen and an androgen (Bryne et al., 2009; Joseph, 2009). However, the extent to which exposure to metalloestrogens could explain increased rates of breast and prostate cancer in developed countries is still being discussed (Järup and Åkesson, 2009).

Several countries already restrict cadmium levels in phosphate fertilisers and there is a need for exclusion of cadmium from phosphorus fertilisers to ensure safe food production. Based on a balance calculation, we calculated the maximum cadmium concentrations in fertilisers and amendments not leading to an increase of cadmium concentrations in soil (Box 1). This calculation is based on Swedish conditions.

Box 1.
Assessment of a safe cadmium threshold concentration for phosphorus sources applied to Swedish agricultural soils

The new recommendation by the European Food Safety Authority (EFSA, 2009) to reduce cadmium intake through food from the previous 7 to only 2.5 µg per kg body weight and week requires strategies to reduce the cadmium content in food. Cadmium is considered a human carcinogen (Bryne et al., 2009; Joseph, 2009; Järup and Åkesson, 2009) and requires whole-hearted attention. This implies that the cadmium content of agricultural soils should not be enriched with cadmium through manures, organic wastes and fertilisers.

Using soil and environmental conditions in Sweden as an example and applying the principal of nutrient replenishment - phosphorus removed through harvest is replaced through an equivalent input - a critical threshold concentration of 10 mg cadmium per kg phosphorus was estimated to avoid accumulation in soil. This critical concentration is valid for phosphorus fertilisers and different types of wastes recycled to agricultural soils.

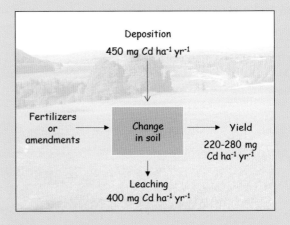

Current annual flows of cadmium (Cd) to and from Swedish agricultural soils per hectare (data from Eriksson, 2009) were used to calculate the threshold concentration:

With deposition and leaching being roughly in balance, minimum crop removal of 220 mg Cd allows a maximum application of 160-210 mg Cd to avoid enrichment in soil.

If 20 kg of phosphorus are applied, the cadmium mass is equal to the amount of phosphorus x concentration of cadmium.

160 mg Cd = 20 kg phosphorus x X mg Cd/kg; 8 mg Cd per kg phosphorus
210 mg Cd = 20 kg phosphorus x X mg Cd /kg; 10.5 mg Cd per kg phosphorus

The estimated threshold concentration for cadmium in phosphorus sources is about 10 mg Cd per kg phosphorus in order not to enrich Swedish agricultural soils.

Box 2. Non-utilised P reserves from iron ore – An example from Sweden

Short History of Europe's Largest P Deposits

In 1889, the Swedish Parliament commissioned the geologist Hjalmar Lundbohm to explore technically useful rocks and in particular apatite reserves in the North of Sweden (Åslund, 1965). In the following years, he investigated 'Gällivare Malmberg', Kiirunavaara, Luossavaara and Svappavaara. The main conclusions in his report were that significant apatite reserves existed, but that they were associated with iron ore. No isolated apatite was present and magnetic or metallurgic separation was necessary in order to use the reserves. During renewed prospecting in 1897, he found another iron ore deposit in Tuollavaara that was low in apatite and could be used without difficulties by the Swedish iron and steel industry. History tells us that despite the original aim to mine apatite for fertiliser production, so far only iron ore low in phosphorus has been mined and apatite-rich iron ore deposits have been excluded.

The Swedish Kiruna mine (Photo: LKAB).

Potential Reserves

The iron content in the Kiruna ore amounts to 50-60%, while phosphorus amounts to 1-5%. Phosphorus is present as apatite associated with haematite, quartz, actinolite and hornblende. Apatite is separated from iron ore through a chain of extraction steps in order to produce high quality iron ore. Separation of phosphorus produces about 100 000 tons per year. Over time, about 5 million tons of extracted phosphorus have been deposited. Total reserves of phosphorus in iron ore amount to 15-20 million tons, equivalent to 100 million tons of apatite (Swedish EPA, 2002), which ranks Sweden among the top 10 countries with significant reserves (Table 3.3 refers to apatite reserves). The P-content in apatite usually varies between 11-15%. The P content in apatite-

enriched deposits, which are already ground into fine particles with a P concentration of around 2.75%, can easily be enhanced to higher concentrations by flotation. In comparison, the Finnish apatite ore at Siilinjärvi contains only approx. 1.7% P (Kemira Oy, 1980).

Trace and Rare Earth Elements in Apatite Deposits

The apatite from Kiruna is as low in cadmium as the Kola apatite (Russia), but the material is natively contaminated with arsenic at a level of 60 ppm. Removal of arsenic from apatite is necessary in order to use this resource for fertiliser production. In addition, the material contains about 0.5% rare earth elements (Zhang and Muhammed, 1990).

Potassium

Major potassium reserves that are economically feasible to mine include evaporated salt deposits from ancient inland seas, salt lakes and natural brines. According to US Geological Survey (2008), the largest deposits are found in Saskatchewan (Canada), Russia, Belarus and Germany, which together hold 92% of all reserves. Other significant reserves are found in Spain, England, Brazil, Chile and Israel (see Figure 3.4).

Potassium salts are mined in two different ways: 1) solution mining, which means that water is used to dissolve deposits, pumped up and evaporated in basins on the surface, and 2) mining of underground deposits through cutting/drilling followed by removal and transport. The main minerals are potassium chloride (sylvite) and mixtures with sodium chloride (sylvinite), magnesium sulphate (kieserite) and magnesium chloride (carnallite).

The life-time of potassium reserves based on the current production rate is about 250 years for currently mined reserves and 500 years if the reserve base is included.

Sulphur

Sulphur is the 10th most common element on earth and many minerals occur as sulphides. Gypsum is a common sulphur-containing mineral, with thick and extensive deposits, but sulphur is also found as a pure element. Today, the demand for sulphur is covered from extraction of crude oil containing about 0.1-0.28% sulphur, from which it is obtained mainly as hydrogen sulphide by-product. The gas is converted into elemental sulphur through the Claus Process.

Global production of sulphur amounted to 48 million tons in 2009 (IFA, 2010a). Only around 14% of the world's sulphur production is used as a plant nutrient

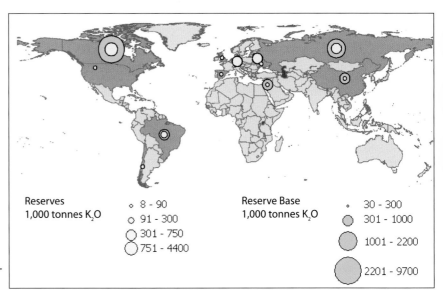

Figure 3.4. Locations of potassium deposits and size of reserves (USGS, 2008).

(ammonium sulphate or superphosphate fertiliser) (IFA, 2010a, 2010b). The main use of sulphur is as a raw material for production of sulphuric acid for industrial uses (80-85%). Roughly half the sulphuric acid produced is used by the fertiliser industry to process phosphate rock into water-soluble phosphorus fertiliser. However, nitric acid and hydrochloric acid can replace sulphuric acid for that purpose.

Large amounts of sulphur (more than 600 billion tons) are contained in coal, natural gas, crude oil and oil shale. Sulphur in gypsum and anhydrite is almost limitless (USGS, 2011b). Sulphur can be extracted from gypsum in the form of pure ammonium sulphate according to the Merseburg process (William et al., 1996). Processing gypsum into ammonium sulphate is not economically justifiable as long as sulphur is obtained as a cheap by-product from processing of oil, gas and coal. Sulphur can also be recovered from renewable bio-fuels. In other words, sulphur will not be a limited element for agriculture in the foreseeable future.

Remarks

It must be borne in mind that assessments of the life-time of nutrient resources are based on assumptions. In the estimates given above, it was assumed that current fertiliser use will remain constant over time. However, if increasing demand for fertiliser due to population growth is taken into consideration, the life-time of reserves will be shortened and the figures given are overestimates. On the other hand, if technical development allows nutrient recycling to be improved so that the majority of fertiliser use is based on recycled nutrients, the life-time of reserves will be prolonged. Such development is discussed below.

Recycling of Plant Nutrients

All forms of agriculture remove plant nutrients from fields via the harvest of crops. The nutrients removed from fields flow through one or more of three cycles: the fodder cycle, the food cycle, and the industrial cycle (Figure 3.5). The fodder cycle is the flow through housed animals, on or off the farm, which results in manures, slurries, urine, feed-lot wastes and deep-litter wastes. The food cycle concerns human consumption of food of plant or animal origin, and the resulting wastes. The industrial cycle concerns the industrial residues from processing of animal and vegetable food products.

Description of Major Problems

In the past, the fodder cycle was more or less closed, since manures were normally recycled to arable land except for a proportion used for nitrate production for gunpowder. Today, however, transfer of fodder to a livestock farm can result in nutrient accumulation that far exceeds the absorption capacity of nearby farmland. Manure surpluses occur in many regions of Europe, Asia and the USA. For example, Haygarth et al. (1998) calculated that a typical intensive dairy farm of 57 ha in the UK with 129 lactating cows results in a net annual accumulation of approximately 26 kg phosphorus per hectare. On a national level, the Netherlands reported an estimated national surplus of about 8000 tons of phosphorus per year (Greaves et al., 1999). Incineration of manure to minimise the logistical difficulties of handling surplus manure and to recover energy is now practised in regions with a high animal density (Kuligowski and Poulsen, 2010).

The food cycle suffers from severe problems regarding return of nutrients from cities back to arable land. Urban growth has resulted in centres of consumption, and hence accumulation of human wastes containing nutrients, that are far away from areas of agricultural production. Nutrients removed from the fields enter cities in the form of food of plant or animal origin, resulting in the production of municipal wastes such as toilet waste in the form of sewage sludge, and organic household waste in the form of compost or biogas residues. The proportion of plant nutrients removed through harvest ending up in municipal waste amounts to about 25%, while the remaining 75% are present in animal manure (Kirchmann, 1998).

Waste accumulation around cities leads to logistical difficulties in re-distributing human waste to arable land. Lack of available arable land for organic waste application within a reasonable distance from cities requires strategies and technologies for reducing the volume of urban wastes. In many cities sewage sludge is incinerated, whereby the volume can be reduced by approx. 90%.

Conditions Necessary to Achieve Efficient Recycling

An environmental target in modern societies is to recycle nutrients back to agricultural land in a sustainable way, which presupposes 'safe and clean' products. In order to achieve this target, a number of actions have already been taken. For example in EU countries, landfilling of organ-

Table 3.5. Outline of conditions to achieve sustainable recirculation of nutrients.

Conditions for sustainable recycling of plant nutrients
No adverse effect on food quality and the environment
Low levels of unwanted metals
Low levels of organic pollutants
Low levels of pharmaceuticals
Low levels of pathogens
Efficient nutrient supply
High plant availability
Low nutrient losses
Application according to crop demand
Equitable redistribution on arable land
Concentrated fertilisers enabling long-term transportation
Less energy demand for redistribution than production of mineral fertilisers

ic material has been prohibited. The use of certain metals (e.g. cadmium, mercury) has been prohibited or is highly restricted to reduce contamination of wastes. Industries connected to sewage treatment plants must keep discharge of pollutants at a minimum to avoid contamination of sewage sludge. Source-separation of household wastes has been introduced to produce composts without contaminants. These efforts have improved the quality of municipal wastes. For example, the cadmium level in sewage sludge in Sweden has declined from rather high concentrations to only 20-40 mg per kg phosphorus (Eriksson, 2009).

However, it is questionable whether these commendable improvements will result in long-term use of municipal wastes on arable land, considering that a number of conditions must be fulfilled for sustainable recycling. Table 3.5 summarises the most important conditions that must be fulfilled to achieve sustainable recycling of municipal wastes back to soil, including: (i) 'safe and clean' wastes that have a negligible effect on the soil and environment (refers to their possible content of metals, organic contaminants and pathogens); (ii) high plant availability of nutrients in wastes to give a significant fertiliser effect (i.e. if nutrients in wastes are bound in less soluble or insoluble form, recycling will not replace inorganic fertilisers); and (iii) redistribution of nutrients on arable land must be related to nutrient removal by crops (i.e. the 'law of nutrient replacement' should be followed).

Nutrients removed from soil through harvest and losses should be replenished with equivalent amounts. Application of excessive amounts to arable land is unacceptable and long-distance transportation would be required to achieve equitable redistribution while avoiding accumulation of nutrients in arable land surrounding cities. It seems that all these conditions can only be achieved if nutrients from organic wastes rather than whole wastes are recycled.

Recycling Alternatives

As toilet waste contains most of the nutrients present in municipal wastes (Kirchmann, 1998), this fraction is most important to recycle. There are four main options available for recycling of nutrients in toilet wastes: a) spreading sewage sludge on arable land; b) separating human urine from faeces in special toilets and using the urine as a fertiliser; c) recovering phosphorus from sewage water in wastewater treatment plants; and d) recovering phosphorus from the ash of incinerated sewage sludge. Each option has advantages and disadvantages and the best choice depends on the conditions present, as discussed by Cohen et al. (2011).

As outlined in the paragraph 'Influential trends', a dominant future trend will be accumulation of nutrients in cities (Grimm et al., 2008). Applying recycled organic wastes may not be a viable option, as the required land area will not be available within a reasonable distance. There is currently a trend for more sewage sludge to be incinerated, not only in mega-cities but also in cities and towns, which means that spreading of sewage sludge will decrease in future. Ash may become the main waste product from increasing urbanisation. Processing of ash from combusted municipal wastes for nutrient extraction may be an important step to close nutrient cycling in society (Figure 3.5). The approach of not recycling urban organic wastes as such but producing inorganic fertilisers from nutrients present in wastes has been proposed earlier (Kirchmann et al., 2005).

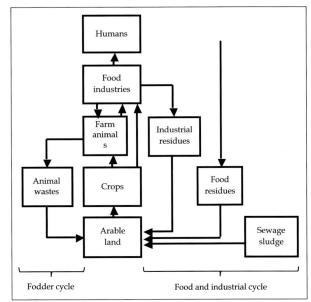

Figure 3.5. Plant nutrient cycling in society divided into fodder, food and industrial cycles.

Outlook and Conclusions

Assessments of global reserves for fertiliser production have changed over time. In fact, reserve capacities have been upgraded several times and previous surveys indicating 'peak nutrients' in coming decades seem less likely. Over the long-term, recirculation of nutrients is the key to achieving more sustainable nutrient management.

Rather than shortage of rock phosphate, cadmium contamination of existing reserves is the most critical issue, due to serious health risks associated with cadmium intake through food. There is a need to implement a technical step for removal of cadmium from phosphorus fertilisers in order to avoid an enrichment of the cadmium content in soil.

It should be remembered that the application of nitrogen, phosphorus and potassium fertilisers to agricultural soil over the last 100 years has increased nutrient levels and improved soil fertility. However, in other parts of the world such as sub-Saharan Africa, arable soils are still nutrient-poor and there is a need to increase their nutrient status.

As pointed out in this chapter, it is necessary to increase the use of recycled instead of mined nutrients for fertilisation in future. This requires new approaches and technologies for handling municipal organic wastes. Only nutrients recovered from wastes, and not whole wastes, should be redistributed on arable land. This transformation is necessary in order to achieve efficient nutrient flows back from cities to remote arable land. In addition, recycled nutrients should have the same fertiliser value as mineral fertilisers, i.e., the same water solubility.

Based on the information given in this chapter, it can be concluded that there will not be a shortage of nutrients for fertiliser production in coming generations. Important points are:

- Nitrogen fertiliser produced with fossil energy can be based on renewable energy in the future
- Reserves of rock phosphate have been upgraded again. However, low-cadmium rock phosphates are highly limited.
- Cadmium-related health problems seem to be more serious than previously assumed
- Sulphur, the 10th most abundant element in the world, will not become a limited element for crop production due to copious amounts of sulphate and sulphide mineral reserves
- Nutrient recirculation from organic to inorganic forms may be the way forward.

We believe that further development of waste treatment techniques will lead to sustainable nutrient recycling in society, characterised by efficient processes and high quality products.

Plant Nutrient Management, Livestock Density, Agricultural Structure and the Environment

4

Christine Jakobsson
Uppsala University, Uppsala, Sweden
Staffan Steineck
previously JTI and SLU, Uppsala, Sweden

Plant Nutrients and Plant Nutrient Pathways

A Short Historical Outlook

In earlier days, when the majority of people were occupied in agriculture, plant nutrient resources remained largely within agriculture and were recycled. Plant nutrients in the form of manure from animal husbandry, household and slaughter waste etc. were returned to arable land. This made it possible to maintain the production level of the arable land but at a restricted level. At the same time, there was a shortage of plant nutrients which limited the production of food and thus the population. Not so seldom, people were starving.

At the beginning of the nineteenth century, the cultivation of clover in grasslands became common. Through its nitrogen fixing capacity, it could supply the pasture with nitrogen, which also could be used by the following crops. The farming systems that developed in the middle of the 19th century were to last about a century, until the end of the Second World War. Crop and animal production were tightly inter-connected in systems of production which were distinguished by fairly good biological balance. Different crops replaced each other at regular intervals in the crop rotation, where clover and other legumes provided a basis for nitrogen supply.

This development led to yield increases of more than 50% by the 1930s compared with the beginning of the 19th century. The insignificant use of fertilisers limited further increases in production and did not even compensate for the flux of plant nutrients in agricultural produce to cities and urban areas.

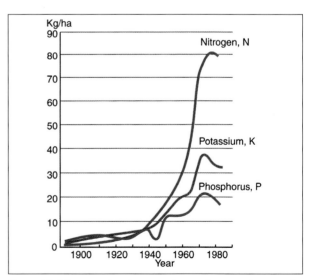

Figure 4.1. Nitrogen, phosphorus and potassium use. Averages for Sweden in kg per hectare arable land. (Claesson and Steinek, 1996).

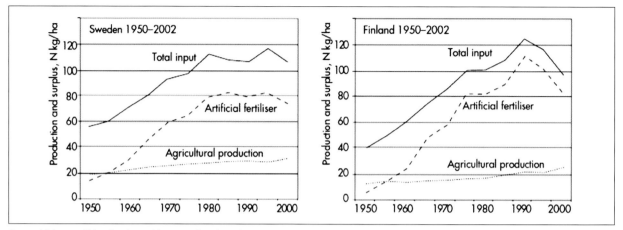

Figure 4.2. Input of N in fertilisers, N in agricultural production and surplus (difference between total input and production) of nitrogen in Sweden and in Finland 1950-2002. The difference between total input and agricultural production shows an increasing surplus, i.e. losses of reactive nitrogen (Granstedt et al., 2004).

At the end of World War II, the most dramatic and rapid change in our agricultural history occurred. The rise of a modern industrial society brought a rapidly increasing stream of people from rural to urban areas. This gigantic reallocation of people and the implemented methods of waste management led to plant nutrient losses, as the nutrients in waste were not recycled to arable land anymore. Instead inputs of mineral fertiliser, produced from cheap energy, became necessary. This, in combination with society's demands for rationalisation and increased yields, led to the specialisation of agricultural production. The earlier balance between cattle, pastures and grain production was in large broken.

The plant nutrients in manure became unevenly distributed between different agricultural businesses. Intensive animal production gave a supply of plant nutrients in manure that was larger than arable soil and crop nutrient requirements. This led to negative effects on the environment, in the form of increasing leakage of nitrogen and phosphorus to the water and losses of nitrogen to the air. At the same time, pure plant husbandry farms had a lack of manure and consequently of plant nutrients that had to be replaced with mineral fertilisers. Manure was considered to be a waste instead of a resource!

A study of statistics on the use of manure and fertiliser during the years illustrates the change of use of plant nutrients in manure. Until the 1950s the use of mineral fertilisers was still very limited. In the 1960s and 70s, the agricultural extension service was still recommending that farmers consider manure a waste and instead use mineral fertilisers.

In the middle of the 1980s, a new awareness started to grow in Sweden on the importance of using the plant nutrients in manure as a resource for growing crops. Soil mapping regarding the amount of phosphorus and potassium was relatively common. Analysis of soil nitrogen content early in spring in order to predict the amount of nitrogen fertiliser needed started at the end of the 1980s and early 1990s. It was important to teach the farmers to once again first use the plant nutrients in manure in the best way possible and after that add mineral fertilisers to compensate for crop needs.

Farm-gate Nutrient Balance

In farm-gate plant nutrient balances the amounts of nitrogen, phosphorus and potassium accumulated on the farm are calculated and compared with the amounts that leave the farm. The usual nutrient inputs are: fertilisers, imported or purchased fodder, purchased animals, purchased seed, the deposition of nitrogen from the air and the amount of nitrogen fixed by leguminous bacteria. The

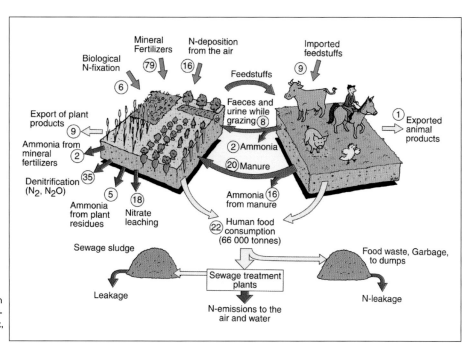

Figure 4.3. Nutrient fluxes in Sweden expressed as kg N per hectare and year (Claeson & Steineck, 1996).

amounts of plant nutrients leaving the farm are usually contained in agricultural produce such as grain, milk, meat, potatoes, etc. but can also be in sold animals or gaseous losses of ammonia from fertilisers, manure or crop residues or leakage and surface run-off and denitrification. Manure, slurry, urine, as well as crop roots and harvest residues e.g. straw are usually only recycled on the farm and therefore are neither an input to the farm nor a product that leaves the farm and are not included in the farm-gate balance calculation. Special cases exist when manure is brought from one farm to another, where it is used as a fertiliser to crops, and in that case manure must also be considered to be an input of nutrients. The same thing applies when manure leaves one farm to be spread on another farm. In that case the manure must be considered to be a product leaving the farm and included in the farm-gate balance calculation. The same applies to straw if it leaves one farm to be used on another farm, when it must be included in the farm-gate nutrient balance.

To make the results of the farm-gate nutrient balance clear for implementation on the farm, the next step is to consider the results in comparison to the general status of the farm. Here comparisons are made to soil maps of phosphorus and potassium to see which fields are in the greatest need of nutrients. These are usually the fields farthest away from the barns and manure storage. Then a plant husbandry plan is elaborated where the results from the farm-gate balance are included when deciding which crops to grow on which fields, how to spread the manure/slurry/urine in suitable amounts considering the plant requirements, as well as the best timing and technology for spreading manure. Here consideration must be given to the crops, the soil type and risk for soil compaction and the weather. The next step is to add the fertilisers to the plan, to choose suitable fertilisers or combinations of fertilisers, suitable timing and technology for applying fertilisers and also to calculate appropriate amounts according to crop requirements and the soil maps and the previous crops and manure spread in earlier years.

Livestock Density

To ensure that manure is not produced in excess in comparison to the amount of arable land on the farm, it is important that there is a balance between the amount of animals on the farm and the amount of land available for spreading manure. The maximum number of animals has been specified with consideration given to the amount of phosphorus and nitrogen in manure and normal crop requirements and removal of plant nutrients. The limiting factor for Swedish legislation on livestock density is phosphorus, with a maximum amount of 22 kg phosphorus per hectare. As the amount of manure per area will be moderate, the risk of nutrient leaching of both nitrogen and phosphorus should be substantially smaller. It also means that it is possible to produce feed for the animals using the land on which manure is spread as a fertiliser. The nutrients only change phase from nutrients in crops as they pass through the animal intestine and become nutrients in manure to be used as a fertiliser for producing more feed. One other advantage with using phosphorus instead of nitrogen is that the figures on phosphorus content in manure are more reliable, as phosphorus losses in the animal house and during storage are almost non-existent.

Table 4.1. Livestock density in Sweden.

Type of animal	Animals/ha
Dairy cows	1.6
Cows for breeding calves	2.3
Heifers, bulls, steers > 1 year old	4.6
Calves < 1 year old	5.8
Sheep and goats	15.0
Sows in production	2.2
Fattening pigs, places	10.5
Laying hens, places	100.0
Young hens, places	250.0
Broilers, places	470.0
Turkeys, ducks, geese, places	140.0
Horses	3.0
Mink, breeding females	50.0

In Sweden the main rule is that the supply of phosphorus from manure and organic fertilisers may not exceed 22 kg per hectare available land (with certain exceptions), counted as a five-year average. Until 31 December 2012, farms with livestock may spread the same amounts of manure as these livestock density regulations permit (See table 4.1). The supply of nitrogen via number of animals

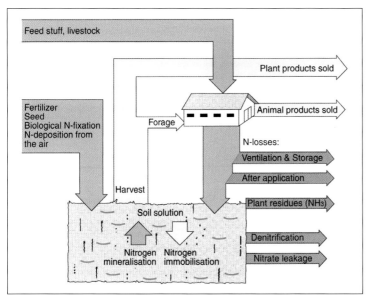

Figure 4.4. Plant nutrient pathways on a farm.

per hectare may not be larger than what is shown in table 4.1.

Accessible land for spreading manure can consist of:

- Suitable arable land used for crop production on the farm.
- Arable land elsewhere if there is a contract on manure spreading for at least a 5-year period.
- Grazing land, pastures on farms with grazing livestock.

At most 50% of the area that grazing animals need for spreading livestock manure on can consist of pasture. Normally only 30% is used, as this corresponds to the livestock waste production during a 4-month grazing period. The animal density requirements apply to all farms with more than 10 animal units (1 animal unit: 1 cow, 3 sows, 10 fattening pigs, 100 poultry or 1 horse) in Sweden.

Agricultural Production Structure Sets the Framework for the Success of Measures on Farm Level

Progress towards sustainable agriculture has up to now mainly been characterised by agricultural adjustments in terms of 'good agricultural practice' at farm level. However, the results achieved have not reached the established goals, especially regarding nutrient losses. In spite of this fact, some improvements have been noticed.

Issues such as production levels, total input of nutrients in crop production, total numbers of animals and the degree of net export of agricultural products have to be further analysed with respect to sustainability concepts. Some fundamental prerequisites concerning the overall production structure of the farm sector have to be fulfilled if sustainability is to be improved through modifications of practices at farm level.

The distribution pattern of animal production very much sets the base level for nutrient losses to water, as well as to the atmosphere. High **livestock density** in relation to available land for spreading of manure often causes severe nitrate leaching and inefficient recycling of the phosphorus in manure. This is true on farms, as well as for regions. **Animal production concentrated to cer-**tain regions creates heavy emissions and local negative impacts of ammonia per land unit.

Differences in environmental impact can also be identified in relation to the **types of animals**. Grazing animals such as cattle, horses and sheep provide opportunities to preserve old natural permanent grazing land and thus maintain biodiversity. The amount of permanent pastures is most likely one of the most important factors for biodiversity. The existence of grazing animals also has a positive effect on soil fertility, due to favourable crop rotations with a high proportion of perennial crops. Crop rotations with leys also require less pesticides than rotations consisting of annual crops only, which dominate on farms with pigs and poultry and on grain farms. However, animal products from ruminants cause greater losses of nutrients per unit produced than products based on pigs and poultry, due to the less concentrated feed and the use of roughage, which needs greater areas for production than grain feeds. This is one of the difficulties with measures that can be positive for one part of sustainability but negative for another.

Biodiversity, the characteristic of biological systems to be different from each other, is manifested at the level of genes, species, populations, communities and ecosystems. The main sources of threat are loss of landraces and old species, as well as destruction of habitats due to intensive, mechanical agriculture, land-use changes and abandonment of land, as well as polluting emissions. New niches for successor species can be created through adapted, extensive forms of land management, thus enhancing species diversity. Placing areas under protection within the framework of nature conservation treaties is an important but expensive instrument to preserve extensive areas as habitats and to protect the species that remain. Promotion of organic farming could also be a way to maintain biodiversity as no pesticides or artificial fertilisers are used.

Large farms are often regarded to be less favourable with respect to resource and environmental maintenance than small ones. Except for very large animal holdings, such a statement is not scientifically proven and good opportunities to afford better techniques for farm buildings, storage and spreading of manure on larger farms may even change the situation completely. It can be difficult for the farmer to check all the fields on a large farm and therefore the use of herbicides and pesticides can increase on large farms. Machinery pools can improve farm finances on all types of farms except the extremely large animal complexes existing today in the countries in transition, Poland, Russia, Belarus and Ukraine. Where there usually is no balance between the amount of animals and arable land for spreading of manure and a lack of techniques for correct manure storage and spreading.

Organic farming, meaning the use of no commercial fertilisers and pesticides, is in many aspects in agreement with the sustainability concept, but not in all aspects. Due to widespread growing of nitrogen fixing crops and use of organic wastes, nitrate leaching can often be unacceptably high, although often not as high as in conventional agriculture. As it is always more difficult to steer the mineralisation and uptake of organic nitrogen than compared to nitrogen in mineral fertilisers, this affects the problems with nitrate leaching negatively. Furthermore, continuous phosphorus export from the farm with agricultural products may lead to a phosphorus deficit in the soil, if not compensated for in some way. This could be the case even with respect to other nutrients depending on the soil type and origin. Compared with conventional agriculture, yields are usually lower in organic farming systems, which means that the production per hectare or production unit is usually smaller than for conventional agriculture. Organic farming with dual purpose milk/meat production seems to have the best market competitiveness in comparison with other types of commercial farming.

During previous decades, people were more closely integrated with agriculture and arable land. Animal feed was mainly produced on the farm and the amount of purchased necessities was small at that time. Today most people live in urban areas and the production of food relies heavily on purchases of necessities, including those from other countries. Transportation has thus increased to a large extent during the 20th century, as well as the environmental impact due to increased fossil fuel consumption and related pollution. Urban development and the increased dependency of farms on necessities from other countries has exaggerated the linear elemental flow. Nutrients, as well as non-biotic elements e.g. heavy metals and rest substances from pharmaceuticals accumulate in urban vicinities and on animal-dense farms and regions. Large distances between food producers and consumers not only create long transport of food but also constitute an obstacle for the recirculation of nutrients.

Farming under less competitive conditions is prevalent for holdings on less fertile land, mainly situated on the outskirts of agricultural plains and for enterprises situated far from urban districts. A lack of social infrastructure, e.g. availability of services such as education, health care, public transport and shops, may be a determining factor for the running of such farms. There usually also is a lack of complementary employment as well and it is common that the younger generation leaves the region to find opportunities in urban areas. Lack of competitiveness may also be a consequence of insufficient funds for investment in appropriate farm equipment or for purchases of essential means of production. When valuable areas are threatened, such holdings and regions may need special policy actions to survive. This applies to farming in Western countries and can be very important for farming in the Baltic States, Poland, Russia, Belarus and Ukraine.

Conclusions for Sustainable Agricultural Structure

Integration
- Crop and animal production should be more integrated in all countries.
- Very large non-sustainable animal holdings should reduce the number of livestock or be split up into smaller, more evenly distributed animal holdings.

Biodiversity
- The number of ruminants should locally correspond to the amount of old permanent grazing land to preserve biodiversity. In some countries it may not be possible to retain all such land, so selected valuable grazing areas may need special policies to maintain these.
- Remains of natural biotopes such as wetlands, islands in field etc. should preferably be saved.
- On-farm conservation of landraces and old species.

Transport
- Transport of feed, food and wastes should be minimized by promoting local alternatives before centralized ones when this is deemed profitable by life cycle analysis.

Less competitive farming

- All countries in the Baltic Sea Region should support remote and less market-competitive farming and the development of essential services and complementary employment, in order to preserve a viable countryside all around the Baltic Sea.

Co-operation within watersheds

- Co-operation between neighbouring farms should be promoted to overcome negative effects of extensive specialisation on individual farms by mutual care for the arable resources, such as permanent grazing land, exchange of feed and manure etc. This can be a way to achieve sustainability for the total area without jeopardising the benefits of specialisation of individual farms.

Organic farming

- Society should promote organic farming wherever it contributes to sustainable development.

Factors Regulating Nutrient Losses from Farms

Drainage and cultivation of wetlands and old grasslands may cause extensive nitrate leaching due to increased mineralisation of stored organic matter. Nutrient losses may also occur as a consequence of wind and water erosion, due to inappropriate soil management. In all other cases of unacceptable nutrient losses from arable land, the losses are related to the **degree of fertiliser/nutrient input** e.g. mineral fertilisers and manure. Heavy leaching of nitrogen can only occur in relation to intensive fertilization but not necessarily as a result of the fertiliser input in an individual year, but as a consequence of long-term use of high inputs. The purchase of feed and feed concentrates to the farm is often an underestimated or forgotten component of the farm nutrient balance. The ratio between total nutrient input and product output is a key factor directing the long-term losses. A goal should be to have as efficient use as possible of the nutrients on the farms, which should in many cases lead to reduced fertiliser input. This means that on livestock farms that the nutrients in manure should be used first before adding complementary mineral fertilisers.

As already mentioned, the use of **animal manure in crop production** is often a main contributor to nutrient losses to the atmosphere as well as to water. A lot of research has been performed with the aim of improving the utilisation of nutrients in manure but there is still more to be done in this field. If no other possible short-term measures are applicable to prevent excessive negative effects on the environment for regions and individual farms with an excessive production of manure compared with available spreading land, it could be of interest to develop methods to concentrate the valuable nutrients in manure through some sort of technical manure processing. That would make it possible to transport the nutrients in manure over greater distances, but at the same time these types of processes have a high energy input. Such research is underway and may provide one possible solution to leaching problems in animal-dense areas. This type of solution should only be used as an emergency measure during the time that it can take to implement other structural measures with a greater potential for long-term sustainability, such as adjustments of the livestock density.

Ammonia emissions are strongly correlated to the **number of animals** and also to the housing and ventilation system used, manure storage practices and spreading procedure. A less protein-rich animal feed diet decreases the amounts of ammonia in the manure that can be lost to the atmosphere. The same is true if the ventilation air is cleaned, the manure storage tank is covered and the manure is incorporated into the soil during or immediately after application. Efficient use of manure in crop production requires sufficient manure storage capacity in relation to optimal timing of spreading and suitable spreading technology as well as spreading amounts that are dimensioned according to the crops nutrients requirements.

Cropping practices such as soil tillage, choice of crop, crop rotation, timing and equipment for spreading manure are all factors influencing nutrient turnover and flow in the soil-crop system. In addition to more appropriate total fertiliser use, these are the main tools for minimizing the nutrient losses at farm level. Nutrient leaching and surface run-off may be reduced in systems with direct drilling, a high proportion of winter-green fields and manure spreading mainly during spring. Slurry seems to give better opportunities for efficient handling and nutrient recycling than solid manure systems, due to recent developments in techniques. Slurry in Western countries commonly has a dry matter content of 5-10%. The slurry that commonly existed previously in countries in transition, Poland and Russia, with a dry matter content of approx. 0.5%, would lead to large problems as the amounts are so large that building suitable manure storage would be economically non-viable. Furthermore, problems with soil compaction are common when spreading large amounts of dilute slurry.

Point pollution sources of urine or leakage from manure storage are not acceptable in a sustainable production system. Furthermore, wastewater from households and farm buildings should be collected, stored and applied to farmland as a nutrient.

Conclusions for Sustainable Farm Management Concerning Nutrient Losses

Nitrogen input
- Application rates for nutrients should not exceed the crop nutrient requirements. National guidelines should be developed with fertilising recommendations and they should refer to:
  a) soil conditions, soil nutrient content, soil type and slope
  b) climatic conditions, precipitation and irrigation
  c) land use and agricultural practices, including crop rotation systems
  d) all external potential nutrient sources.
- Nitrogen nutrient balances should be performed on the farm to show the size of the nitrogen surplus and should be used when planning fertilisation.

Phosphorus input
- The available phosphorus content of arable topsoils should not exceed the requirements of acceptable crop production.
- The annual phosphorus input should be calculated in relation to:
  - the phosphorus content in the field
  - the crop requirements.

- Good monitoring data on the phosphorus status of arable land is needed in every country, as well as nutrient balances to show whether the supply of phosphorus in the soils is increasing or being depleted.
- At farm level the phosphorus input should be of the same size as the phosphorus removed. Phosphorus nutrient balances should be prepared for the farm to show the size of the phosphorus surplus and should be used when planning fertilisation.

Livestock density and manure handling
- In regions with high average livestock density, and preferably also on individual farms, the total number of animals should be reduced to a level consistent with efficient recycling of nitrogen and phosphorus.
- Efficient circulation of nutrients on animal farms in combination with a high degree of self-sufficiency in feed is a prerequisite for limited losses of plant nutrients.
- The utilisation efficiency of the nutrient content in animal manure should be improved as much as technically feasible. That can be achieved by:
  - building sufficient storage capacity for manure for optimal timing of spreading
  - covering slurry and urine stores to reduce the odour and the emissions of ammonia nitrogen
  - improving manure spreading techniques and maintenance of manure spreaders
  - incorporating slurry, urine and solid manure into the soil immediately after spreading on open soils to minimise ammonia nitrogen losses.

Nutrient point sources
- Nutrient point sources on the farm, such as from manure storage, milking parlours, silage storage etc., should be identified and eliminated.

Crops and crop rotations
- Choose crops and crop rotations with a minimum need for soil cultivation and keep a high proportion of arable land covered by crops during autumn and winter.
- In areas with more than 50% annual crops, the proportion of perennial crops or green cover crops should be increased. This is most urgent in areas with

sandy soils and in areas that are used for drinking water purposes and also on land sensitive to erosion.

New technology
- Promote the development and implementation of new technology that can reduce nutrient losses, such as precision farming with site-specific crop management by use of global positioning systems.

Criteria for surplus land
- The farmers should take environmental considerations into account when removing land from food production in a situation of surplus agricultural land for food production:
  - soils poor in phosphorus
  - organic soils on previously drained wetlands
  - soils sensitive to erosion
  - soils sensitive to nitrate leaching

Nutrient traps
- Create buffer zones and wetlands to reduce nutrient losses and increase biodiversity.

Additional Measures to Meet other Sustainability Issues

Soil fertility is determined by chemical, physical and biological soil conditions. Mineral fertilisers may be contaminated with pollutants due to the process by which they are manufactured, or depending on the origin of the raw materials. Phosphate fertilisers in particular display high levels of polluting elements, above all cadmium. Depending on the system of land use and fertilisation methods, these pollutants enter agricultural soils by fertilisers. Cadmium and chromium are the main contaminants, with lesser quantities of lead, nickel and arsenic being deposited. Recycling of urban waste may also contribute to the input of heavy metals, persistent toxic substances and rest substances from pharmaceuticals to arable land. However for most of the Baltic region, atmospheric deposition is the main pollutant source.

Soil erosion in the strictest sense refers to degradation processes exceeding natural dimensions. It is caused by water and wind and increased by intensive soil cultivation and bare soils. Soil erosion due to non-sustainable land management leads not only to loss of soil fertility, but also to water pollution through phosphates, plant protection products and nitrogen compounds deposited along with soil material.

Cropping methods in intensive farming, especially soil tillage and the use of heavy farming equipment, cause **structural damage to both the topsoil and subsoil**, especially compaction, with subsequent negative impacts on the regulatory functions and fertility of the soil. Structural damage leads to yield reductions. Topsoil compaction is repairable, but greater weights can lead to subsoil compaction, which is extremely serious, as subsoil compaction is irreparable. In recent years there has been a trend towards heavier farm machinery and at the same time better wheel equipment has become more common, but cannot always solve the problems caused by the large weights. Consideration must be given to total weight, wheel pressure and wheel equipment when developing or purchasing farm machinery for sustainable agriculture.

The inadequate **use of plant protection products** is always related to health and environmental risks. The utmost goal is to minimise those risks. To reach this goal it is necessary to improve the registration and handling and to reduce the overall use. Point-source pollution in connection with pesticides arises e.g. when filling or cleaning sprayers and with careless handling of plant protection products. Diffuse pollution is mainly associated with leaching or surface run-off, erosion or as wind-driven dispersal of pesticides. Pesticide residues are found in products as well as in water. On the other hand, the introduction of pesticides into crop production some decades ago led to a more reliable yield level and also to healthier harvests with respect to naturally produced toxins. In most countries work is currently taking place on minimizing the use of pesticides in agriculture and on replacing risky products with less toxic and easy degradable alternatives. Educating farmers in handling pesticides and requiring a certificate or license for all those handling pesticides and sprayers is important. The measures are well known and the work towards minimal or even zero-use has to continue. How close to zero we will come without jeopardizing essential benefits from proper pesticide use will be seen in the future.

The introduction of **genetically modified organisms (GMO)** is exponentially increasing in agriculture. Such new crops are often linked to the use of specific pesticides. Through gene insertion techniques, the crop can be made resistant to specific pesticides for combating weeds and fungi. Knowledge is still very restricted about the risks for genetic pollution of wild species but it now seems impossible to completely prohibit the introduction of these new seeds. In aquaculture, there is a risk of genetically modified material spreading to wild fish species. Use of GMO in animal husbandry is mainly a question of ethics. What can be done, and has to be done, is to adopt a restrictive policy for accepting and introducing GMO. At the same time, the use of GMO in crop production should not lead to an increased use of herbicides.

Intensive and increasing use of **veterinary drugs** e.g. use of antibiotics for animal medication and as **growth promoters** creates a serious human and animal health problem for the future. A number of bacteria have become increasingly resistant to antibiotics, restricting future possibilities of combating diseases. The use of antibiotics can be reduced if the breeding intensity, feed and housing conditions are suitable for the biological production potential of the individual species. Animal welfare concerns should be taken seriously.

An important step to achieve sustainability in agricultural production is to develop efficient **recirculation of urban bio-waste/human effluents** into cropping systems. For that purpose, appropriate waste collecting urban systems have to be established, where contamination with non-biotic pollutants can be avoided. The main purpose is to keep phosphorus in human food in circular flows in the soil-crop-consumer-soil system and also to stop urban pollution to water bodies. In many places the need for urban investment to enable the development of circular elemental flow will be enormous within the next few decades.

Fossil energy has to be successively replaced, due to the greenhouse effect and air pollution as well as the fact that it is a non-renewable resource. According to several sources, we have already passed peak oil. Agriculture can produce **bio-energy**. Some possible crops are willow (*Salix*), grass, oilseed rape and wheat. Among these, willow and grass seem to be the most favourable for the environment and also for soil fertility. Harvest residues such as straw can also be used for energy purposes. Consequently, using environmentally sensitive land for production of energy can improve the environment. To get the bio-energy sector to expand, bio-energy has to be efficiently and profitably produced and techniques for converting bioenergy to electricity and heat must be improved. Another way of producing energy that is becoming more and more interesting in the Baltic Sea region is through the production of bio-gas from e.g. manure and fermentation of some other waste products from agriculture. Production of renewable energy is usually area dependent and as such competes with food production.

The availability of **clean groundwater** is rapidly decreasing in most countries. Agriculture plays a role in this development, as nitrate and pesticide residues in water mainly originate from agriculture. Powerful measures have to be implemented if the present negative trends are to be broken and the remaining waters of high quality are to be preserved.

Agriculture produces nitrous oxides (N_2O), methane (CH_4), and carbon dioxide (CO_2) that are of substantial importance for **the greenhouse effect** with global warming as the ultimate result. These emissions are mainly attributable to livestock farming and combustion from heating and agricultural machinery. About three-quarters of the methane emissions from agriculture come from animal digestion. Agricultural machinery and mineral fertilisers account for about 60% of the fossil fuel consumption on cash crop farms. It has been calculated that the global emissions of greenhouse gases could be balanced if the soil organic matter content were to be increased by 0.01% per annum by implementing careful land use practices. This situation will not continue in the long run, but could be a solution during a transition period, while the emissions are measured.

Maintaining a **high degree of employment** is an essential component of a sustainable society. Employment is of fundamental importance to enhance social stability and personal finances and health. However, in the future it will most likely be difficult to sustain employment in most countries. In that perspective a general commitment for the agricultural sector, as for all sectors, should be to develop new profitable services and products based on farm assets and produce. This is really a challenge. In Sweden it has been calculated that employment in

Swedish agriculture will be reduced by approximately 40% up to 2021, mainly due to the implementation of more efficient production methods and increased yields in both crop and animal production.

In most countries **farmers' income** is often insufficient for necessary investments on the farm. Lack of time and income restrains farmers from finding and implementing new production methods. On the other hand, implementation of sustainable farming systems could in the short run lead to economic losses for farmers, in particular when the total output per land unit is reduced. To some extent, their income is linked to their degree of **education**. Extended education, demonstrations and advisory activities can no doubt improve farmers' finances and their understanding of sustainable issues and willingness to change practices on the farm. Research and extension service can be of great importance not only for the financial outcome of the farm but also for the effects on the environment and for the sustainability of agriculture.

Conclusions on Additional Measures Towards Sustainability

Finances
- Farmers' income should be sufficient to provide a fair standard of living and consist of reasonable compensation for products and other services.

Water quality
- Long-term water quality should be secured by suitable land use within potential and existing pumping areas for high quality groundwater. This usually corresponds to less intensive forms of land use.

Soil fertility
- Soil fertility should be maintained and improved with respect to soil organic matter, soil structure, nutrient status and contents of non-biotic elements and chemicals by use of only non-polluted means of production, non-compacting machinery and cultivation practices promoting increased soil organic matter.
- Nutrient balances, soil analysis and monitoring programmes should be established as a basis for appropriate use of arable land.

Animal health and welfare
- To promote animal health and welfare, animals should:
  - be fed a balanced diet
  - not be subjected to long distance transportation
  - preferably have outdoor access and be kept in loose housing systems.
- The use of antibiotics in animal medication should decrease and the use of growth promoters should be terminated.

Genetically modified organisms, GMO
- The introduction of GMO into food production should be subjected to a very restrictive approval procedure and any increase in the use of plant protection products should not be allowed.

Bio-energy
- Bio-energy production should be increased on excess arable land. Present land use must not jeopardise possibilities in the future to produce high quality food on the same land.

Recirculation
- The recirculation of nutrients and organic matter in urban bio-waste to the production of biomass on arable land should be promoted. Efficient administrative systems for waste quality assessment are necessary in every country.

Plant protection products
- The use and risks of plant production products must be reduced in the future. This can be achieved by:
  - selecting crops and cropping systems with less need for plant protection products
  - improving spraying techniques and maintenance of sprayers
  - making certificates obligatory after participation in courses on safe handling practices for all farmers handling plant protection products and sprayers
- All plant protection products must be registered and approved by national or international authorities.

Climate change
- Promote cropping systems that increase the soil organic matter content e.g. increase permanent grassland, perennial crops and reduced soil tillage.
- Promote farming with a reduced use of mineral fertilisers and imported feed.
- Introduce CO_2 energy taxes on non-renewable energy.
- Reduce ruminant livestock numbers and/or increase production level.

Employment
- Emphasise a sector commitment to developing new profitable services and products based on farm assets and production.

Expertise
- Implement action programmes for extended education, demonstrations and advisory activities for sustainable agriculture.
- Initiate and support research for sustainable agriculture and to mitigate and adapt to climate change.

Conclusions

For sustainable agriculture it is important to take into consideration the ecosystem concept and how all parts of the ecosystem are dependent on one another. Measures must be taken and plans made so that problems will not be created for the future. A holistic view on agriculture must be adopted. This means that it is important to use all nutrients such as those in manure as a resource in the most optimal way, but also that all inputs and resources should be used most effectively. Improved technology and combining the best from all farming systems is one of the keys. Consideration must be given to producing food and feed of high quality while minimising transport. The welfare and health of both man and beast should also be high on the agenda. Climate change must be combated and it will most likely lead to new crops, pests and diseases on plants, animals and humans, as well as a longer growing season. Good products should also lead to fair prices that make it possible to farm with a reasonable standard of living comparable to that in other parts of society. Here education and training, as well as the advisory service, will play an important role. Arable land will be become more and more important to feed the world population and produce renewable energy.

On the Sustainability of Conventional, Organic and Integrated Farming Systems

5

CASE STUI
Lithua

Angelija Bučiene
Klaipeda University, Klaipeda, Lithuania

Concepts and Groups

Agriculture operates on the interface of two complex, hierarchically organised systems: the socio-economic system and the ecosystem (Hart, 1984; Lowrance et al., 1986; Conway, 1987; Ikerd, 1993; Giampietro, 1994a; Giampietro, 1994b; Wolf and Allen, 1995; Giampietro, 1997, Gomiero et al., 2006). Prior to discussing the sustainability of different farming systems, it is worth remembering the place and relations of key concepts such as agroecosystem and farming system, from the point of agroecological science. Implicit in agroecological research is the idea that by understanding these ecological relationships and processes, agroecosystems can be manipulated to improve production and to produce more sustainably, with fewer negative environmental or social impacts and fewer external inputs (Altieri, 1995). As illustrated in Figure 5.1, the agroecosystem (agri-ecosystem) can be described as a system arising at the intersection of natural and social-agrarian components and maintaining its homogeneity while various natural and anthropogenic components within its boundaries are in mutual systemic relationships. The farming system is then considered to be a complex of measures and actions of an agrarian character affecting the ecosystem, and managing the regimes of agroecosystem. Both are coupled in a dynamic relationship: The farming system determines the regime and functional conditions of the agroecosystem, while the agroecosystem influences the farming system's structure, cultivation methods, techniques, etc.

Around the beginning of the 21st century, due to increased environmental concern in the world, many dif-

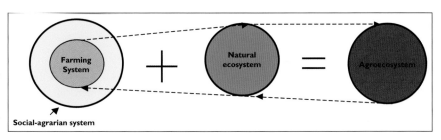

Figure 5.1. Agroecosystem as a result of the influence of the farming system, the component of social-agrarian system, on the natural ecosystem, with feedback. Adapted from Bučiene (2003).

ferent farming systems were introduced or remained after some changes in agricultural practices, although all these can be grouped into three main groups. These are: 1) Conventional (high input, intensive); 2) alternative (moderate or low input; organic, ecological, biological, biological-organic, etc); and 3) integrated (with a combination of elements from low and high input systems).

It is not easy to make a sustainability assessment of different farming systems due to the complexity of structural elements and their intricate relations. However, let us try to do this looking from the two main points: (i) nutrient flows and soil fertility status and (ii) nutrient leaching losses with drainage runoff.

Impact of Different Farming/Cropping Systems on Soil Fertility

Some Soil Properties Affected

Some soil properties, including mobile fractions of organic matter, available phosphorus (P) and potassium (K), microbial and enzyme activity, react quickly to changes in land use and management, whereas passive pools of soil organic matter, notably their organic nitrogen (N) and humus contents, are more stable (Bučiene et al., 2003). In many countries with various soil types, some essential plant nutrients in soil are declining in low-input systems as well as under continuous conventional cropping of monocultures (Scow et al., 1994; Liu et al., 1997; Askergaard, 1999; Løes and Øgaard, 1999; Krauss, 2000; Friedel and Gabel, 2001). In Central Norway, plant available phosphorus decreased in the soil of four of five organic farms (Askergaard, 1999), whereas research in Latvia and Russia (Zarina, 2000; Mishina, 1984) has shown that the crop rotation is among the crucial factors within farming systems, influencing the content of available P and K even in the reference treatments with zero input. The rotations with abundant crop residues are not only improving the physical properties of soil, but are also making more soil P (30-50%), Ca (14-19%) and Zn (13-17%) available to plants due to the larger amount of live roots penetrating deeper into the soil with retained plant residues (Mishina, 1984). However, investigations on organic farms on different

soil types in Lithuania have shown a more marked reduction in the contents of organic carbon, humus, available phosphorus and potassium in crop rotations involving legumes compared with crop rotations receiving organic fertiliser (Mažvila et al., 2003). Thus, it seems that crop rotations with abundant crop residues, particularly rich with legumes, still have to be studied more attentively in order to use all their advantages and avoid any disadvantages.

Importance of Soil Types

Soil type is also an important factor in this regard. The plant-available P_2O_5-AL on Luvisols with a loamy texture increased in intensive cropping systems during two crop rotations, while it declined in the organic and integrated systems (Baltramaityte, 2001) or did not decline during 4 years of further investigations of these cropping systems on plot level (Pupaliene and Stancevičius, 2003). However on gleic Planasols with medium loam texture at the organic farm of the Lithuanian Agricultural University, available P decreased by 16.5-37.1 mg kg^{-1} and available K by 44.0-47.3 mg kg-1 in the topsoil under the same crop rotation and management conditions as on Luvisols (Pekarskas, 2005).

Research on Albeluvisols in western Lithuania showed that available K did not change from the initial status for any crop management regime, but on Luvisols there was a significant increase in available P and K contents of topsoil under winter wheat, sugar beet, barley and ley in the rotation (Gužys, 1999). On the Luvisols in eastern Lithuania, the content of available P and K decreased in the organic management system, while it increased in the integrated and conventional systems growing winter wheat, maize, barley and ley in the rotation (Bundiniene, 2003). On the gleic Cambisols, one of the most fertile soil types in Lithuania, after 8 years of growing winter wheat, potatoes/rapeseed, barley with undersown ley, a statistically significant increase in content of available P and K was determined in both high input crop management systems (conventional and integrated) (Table 5.1).

The humus content was noticeably higher (by 0.72-0.99%) after four years of crop rotation in western Lithuania on Luvisols, Cambisols and particularly on Albeluvisols at any crop management regime (Gužys, Arlauskiene, 2001).

Table 5.1. Average topsoil nutrient status in the different crop management treatments in two rotations (I: 1995-1999 and II: 2001-2003) on Cambisols, Dotnuva, Lithuania.

Treatments	Humus%		N tot%		P-AL mg kg[-1]		K-AL mg kg[-1]	
	I	II	I	II	I	II	I	II
CON	2.8-2.7	2.7-2.7	0.16-0.17	0.17-0.16	51-61	68-74	64-81	102-95
INT	2.6-2.7	2.7-2.8	0.18-0.17	0.17-0.18	47-86**	59-62	90-110**	99-91
ORG1	3.2-2.8	2.8-2.8	0.17-0.19	0.17-0.18	51-62	57-58	51-76	123-103
ORG2	3.4-3.4	-	0.19-0.21	-	66-66	-	76-76	-
REF	3.4-3.0	2.9-3.0	0.15-0.18	0.18-0.20	65-77	67-80	60-78*	102-85

* tact>t_{05} ; ** tact>t_{01} Note: The first figure shows the value at the beginning of rotation, the second that at the end. Explanation: CON – conventional with high rates of commercial fertilisers; INT – integrated with high rate (about 50 t ha[-1]) of farmyard manure (FYM) as basic fertiliser supplemented with moderate rates of commercial fertilisers; ORG1 – with moderate rate of FYM (25-30 t ha[-1]) and green manure; ORG2 – with moderate rate of compost of sewage sludge and straw (about 35 t ha[-1]); REF- zero fertilisation or reference treatment (Bučienė et al., 2003; Bučienė et al., 2007).

Table 5.2. Mean percentage of water-stable aggregates (WSA) in the topsoil of the cropping systems on Cambisols in 1996 and 1999.

Treatment[a]	WSA *			
	> 1 mm		> 0.25 mm (including >1mm)	
	1996	1999	1996	1999
CON	8.2±0.02	10.2±1.55	50.7±0.35	43.6*±0.65
INT	7.5±0.04	15.2**±0.02	38.5±0.62	51.0**±0.42
ORG1	12.0±0.24	17.6**±0.23	51.3±0.43	52.3±0.15
ORG2	13.9±0.22	25.2*±1.48	57.3±0.72	64.2*±0.62
REF	11.3±0.17	15.8*±0.22	48.1±0.62	51.9*±0.07

*tact>t_{05} ; ** tact>t_{01}
For treatment descriptions see Explanation below Table 5.1. (Bučienė et al., 2003).

On the gleic Planasols organic carbon decreased by 0.22-0.25% (Pekarskas, 2005), and a decrease was also recorded on Luvisols in all cropping system treatments (Baltramaitytė, 2001). However, on Cambisols organic carbon content did not change in the topsoil, but increased significantly in the subsoil horizon of different crop management regimes (Bučienė et al., 2003). The total nitrogen content did not change during both rotations in the topsoil of all treatments on Cambisols (see Table 5.1).

In eastern Lithuania on Luvisols with different topsoil texture, the organic matter content remained the same after a four-year rotation under the different crop management regimes (Bundinienė, 2003).

Implications for Soil's Physical Properties
Soil physical properties such as structural composition and content of water-stable aggregates have changed in the treatments with different crop management systems on Cambisols (Table 5.2 and Figure 5.2).

The structure of these sandy loam Cambisols was typically good, with abundant aggregates 0.25-5 mm in diameter under the ORG1, INT and CON treatments (Figure 5.2 for explanation on treatments, see text under Table 5.1). The largest increase in aggregates in this size range was in the soil of the ORG2 treatment. The INT treatment showed little difference over the study period. The content of water-stable aggregates >1 mm by the end of the rotation had increased significantly in all treatments except CON (Table 5.2). The largest increase was in the INT system. The water-stable aggregates >0.25 mm increased most under the INT treatment, but they decreased substantially under the CON treatment, whereas there was no change in the ORG1 system. Thus, in general structural characteristics of the soil under the INT and ORG2 treatments showed most improvement.

Implications for Humus Fractional Composition

Qualitative changes in humus fractional composition take place due to the crop rotation and cropping system. Research on the Luvisols (Baltramaitytė, 2001) has shown that after two crop rotations, the best humus composition was found in the integrated system and the worst in the conventional cropping system. On the Cambisols after the first rotation, the content of all humic acid fractions in the CON system decreased, and there was a trend towards an increase in the INT, ORG1 and REF treatments (Table 5.3). The HA1 fraction (the most mobile fraction of humic acids) remained fairly constant in all systems, while the HA2 fraction (bound with Ca) increased by 0.9% and by 0.5% in the INT and ORG1, respectively, but decreased by 0.5% in the CON treatment. The HA3 fraction (bound with clay particles) increased by 0.3% in the INT and REF systems and decreased by 0.4% in the CON system (Bučienė et al., 2003).

The sum of fulvic acids decreased over time in all treatments. By the end of the rotation there was a trend towards an increase in the mobile FA1 fraction in the INT and REF treatments. The FA2 (bound with Ca) and FA3 (bound with clay particles) fractions decreased in all the treatments, and the aggressive FA1a fraction remained the same. The HA/FA ratio changed, with the organic matter in general becoming richer in humic acids in all cropping systems. This in accordance with results obtained in Russia showing that when organic fertilisers had been applied for many years at high rates, the organic matter con-

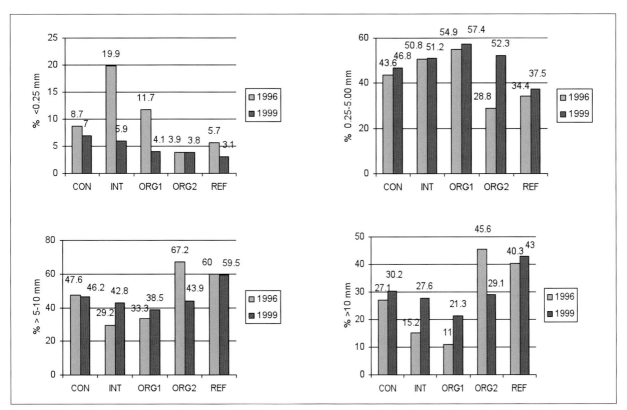

Figure 5.2. Distribution by size of topsoil aggregates in 1996 and 1999. For treatment descriptions see Explanation below Table 5.1. (Bučiene et al., 2003).

Table 5.3. Sum of fulvic acid (FA) and humic acid (HA) fractions and ratio (HA/FA) as a percentage of total soil in the different cropping systems on Cambisols, 1991-1999 (Bučienė et al., 2003).

	CON	INT	ORG1	ORG2	REF
∑ HA 1991	0.54	0.30	0.54	0.56	0.41
1999	0.46	0.44	0.58	0.56	0.50
∑ FA 1991	0.67	0.52	0.76	0.76	0.62
1999	0.49	0.44	0.54	0.62	0.50
HA/FA 1991	0.81	0.58	0.71	0.74	0.66
1999	0.94	1.00	1.07	0.90	1.00

For the treatment description see Explanation below the Table 5.1.

tent increased, as did the HA2 content, the most valuable fraction, while the total amount of fulvic acids decreased (Shatokhina and Khristenko, 1998).

Implications for Soil Microorganisms

The number and activity of different microorganisms in the soil varied little among the different cropping systems on Luvisols, Albeluvisols and Gleysols in Western Lithuania, but there was a tendency for higher numbers in the conventional system with higher inputs of fertilisers (Gužys and Arlauskienė, 2001). The same tendency was observed on Luvisols in eastern Lithuania (Bundinienė, 2003). Research on Cambisols in Central Lithuania showed that comparatively higher numbers of ammonifying microorganisms as well as spore-forming bacteria occurred in the CON system, while other groups of mi-

croorganisms were most numerous and the content of enzymes higher in the REF or ORG2 system (Table 5.4).

Summarising the results above, it can be stated that different low and high input crop management systems influence soil fertility elements (physical, chemical and microbiological) differently, depending on the initial soil nutrient status, soil type (horizons, texture, organic matter content, etc.), crop rotation and local climate specifics. In order to understand this impact, many site-specific conditions and factors have to be studied and analysed as background using integrated data processing and system analysis methods in each individual case.

Impact of Different Farming/Cropping Systems on Nutrient Leaching

There are different opinions concerning the impact of fertilisation and farming intensity on the amount of main nutrient leaching. Some researchers (Tyla et al., 1997; Eželinskas, 1998; Bokhorst, 1989; Mažvila et al., 1992; Jankauskas, 1989) confirm that more intensive fertilisation enhances migration and leaching of ions such as Ca^{2+}, NO_3^-, K^+, Cl^-, SO_4^{2-}, while others (Švedas, 1990; Švedas and Antanaitis, 2000) disagree about nitrogen. From data obtained with ^{15}N isotopes, it is evident that nitrogen in commercial fertilisers only contributes to a very small part of the leached amount of soil mineral nitrogen. However, almost all researchers agree that the leaching

Table 5.4. Impact of different cropping systems on the parameters of soil microbial activity on Cambisols by the end of rotation I, 1998-1999 (Bučienė et al., 2003).

Parameters	CON	INT	ORG1	ORG2	REF	LSD05
Ammonifying microorganisms mln g^{-1}	14.2	10.8	13.0	11.2	13.4	3.6
Mineral N assimilating bacteria mln g^{-1}	15.2	13.5	12.8	12.0	16.2	4.5
Actinomycetes mln g^{-1}	5.9	6.6	5.9	4.8	7.2	1.8
Spore-forming bacteria ths g^{-1}	460	397	306	375	318	155
Micromycetes ths g^{-1}	47.8	45.6	44.1	61.4	50.0	15.1
Urease mg NH_3 g^{-1} 24 h^{-1}	1.8	2.0	1.8	1.7	2.0	0.6
Invertase mg glucose g^{-1} 48 h^{-1}	69.1	65.8	76.0	80.0	74.0	16.9
Nitrate reductase* mg NO_3 100g^{-1}	40.6	44.5	41.5	46.0	42.8	8.1

*in 1999. For treatment descriptions see Explanation below Table 5.1.

occurs when the nutrients are in surplus in the soil and mainly not during the vegetation period when they are taken up by plants. Thus crops are responsible for nutrient uptake and leaching amounts. Investigations on Cambisols on a watershed scale revealed that the largest quantities of nitrogen were leached from fields under row crops (22.4 kg ha^{-1} year^{-1}), whereas leaching from spring and winter cereals was 18.9 and 16.5 kg ha^{-1} year^{-1}, respectively, and the lowest N leaching was from fields under pastures (10.5 kg ha^{-1} year^{-1}) (Kutra et al., 2006). This analysis also revealed that the fertilisation rate was not higher than the plant requirements (considering plant-available nutrient storage in the soil) and that minimal tillage systems are more effective in reducing leaching than changes in crop rotation. In other studies on Cambisols where different crop rotations were compared, the highest average DIN (dissolved inorganic nitrogen) concentration in drainage water and total leaching was determined in cereals and row crop rotations (Aksomaitiene et al., 2004), but there was no major impact of these crop rotations on phosphate concentration in drainage water and leaching.

Green manure crops or leys before winter cereal sowing will not always catch the available soil mineral nitrogen, as in wet autumns it might migrate to deeper horizons and leach with drainage runoff (Romanovskaja and Tripolskaja, 2003). In addition, FYM spread before winter wheat sowing on sandy loamy Haplic Dystric Cambisols adds to N_{min} leaching in the autumn (Tripolskaja and Romanovskaja, 2001).

Research with lysimeters on Luvisols has revealed that systematic fertilisation only with FYM or with FYM and mineral fertilisers can change soil acidity and nutrient content, not only in the ploughed horizon but also in the El and B horizons. Application of farmyard manure and mineral NPK fertilisers changes the intensity and character of phosphate migration, resulting in more intensive leaching of phosphates bound to organic compounds. Leaching of the soil fine dispersion fraction from the upper horizons and accumulation in an arenaceous quartz filter has been reported (Tripolskaja, 2004). According to Barrow (1979), the ions Na^+, K^+, NH_4^+ desorb more P than Ca^{2+} and Mg^{2+}. Since the first group of ions is more abundant in FYM, their occurrence in soil might provoke P desorption and increase P leaching (Marcinkonis and Karmaza, 2007).

Kirchmann and Bergström (2001) analysed the available literature and concluded that the average leaching of NO_3-N from organic farming systems over a crop rotation period was somewhat lower than in conventional agriculture, but the authors stressed that a proper comparison of leaching between two types of systems should take the yield into account.

Relatively few studies have been done on the losses of P by leaching in respect of different crop management practices (Breeuwsma et al., 1995; Sharpley et al., 1994; Bahman, 2003) though it is considered a problem in coarse-textured soils high in organic matter (Sharpley et al., 1994) and areas of intensive livestock farming (Breeuwsma et al., 1995; Bahman, 2003).

To determine the effects of low and high-input agriculture on nutrient leaching, several forms of arable land management were compared in a rotation experiment lasting 8 years on drainage plots on Cambisols and 4 years on Luvisols, Albeluvisols and Cambisols of western Lithuania (Bučiene et al., 2007; Gužys, 1999; Gužys, 2001). The aim of this experiment was to compare different crop management systems on a few soil types in respect of the major nutrients N, P and K and some micronutrient flows and balances, in order to reveal the most problematic points and to reduce the leaching losses. The results on the main nutrients are presented in Tables 3.5-6.

Mean N_{min}, P_{tot} and K losses during rotation I (1995-1999) with normal and extremely high discharge conditions by leaching in the CON treatment were significantly greater than in the REF treatment, and mean N_{min} and K losses were greater than in the ORG2 treatment (Table 5.5). Means P_{tot} leaching losses were similar in all treat-

Table 5.5. Leaching of major nutrients with drainage runoff (kg ha^{-1} year^{-1}) from the different crop management treatments in two rotations on Cambisols, Dotnuva (Bučiene et al., 2007).

	CON	INT	ORG1	ORG2	REF	LSD$_{05}$
1995-1999						
Nmin	53.4	47.7	40.1	17.9	33.2	22.3
Ptot	0.286	0.280	0.205	0.271	0.192	0.105
K	3.8	3.1	2.3	2.2	1.9	1.45
2001-2003						
Nmin	13.4	8.8	14.4	-	11.8	14.0
Ptot	0.071	0.054	0.108	-	0.055	0.043
K	0.7	0.7	0.8	-	0.8	0.44

Table 5.6. Mean leaching of major nutrients with drainage runoff (kg ha^{-1} year^{-1}) from the different crop management treatments on Albeluvisols, Luvisols and Gleysols,Vežaičiai, 1995-1998 (Gužys, 2001).

	Albeluvisols		Luvisols		Gleysols
	ORG	CON	ORG	CON	CON
K$^+$	4.2±0.6	4.7±0.8	3.4±0.4	2.2±0.4	2.6±0.4
NO$_3^-$	63.1±16.6	100.7±27.9	101.3±13.5	82.4±10.8	69.2±22.2
PO$_4^{3-}$	0.108±0.016	0.078±0.004	0.162±0.008	0.145±0.014	0.155±0.005

ments and thus there was no cropping system impact here. However during dry weather and under low discharge conditions (during rotation II, 2001-2003) there was no discernible difference in impact between high and low input systems on main nutrient leaching.

In western Lithuania, with the highest annual precipitation rate, leaching of the main nutrients was different on the various soil types under the same treatment and crop rotation (Table 5.6).

In general, the highest K leaching was determined on Albeluvisols, irrespective of the crop management system, and the highest PO$_4$ leaching on Luvisols and Gleysols. The lowest nitrate leaching was in the organic treatment on Albeluvisols, while on Luvisols it was higher in the organic treatment than in the conventional. On the Gleysols one treatment was studied, conventional cropping, where nitrogen leaching was also not among the highest values. Correlation-regression analysis of the experiment data revealed that nitrate leaching mostly depended on the organic matter/humus content of the topsoil (equation 1):

$$y = 483.2 + 239.31x_1 - 32.608x_1^2 \qquad (1)$$

where y is nitrate content in kg ha^{-1} per year leached with drainage runoff and x_1 is humus content of topsoil in% (Gužys, 2001).

These results showed that differences in nutrient leaching were not always apparent in the crop management treatments studied, and therefore an attempt was made to search for factors other than crop management that affected nutrient leaching. Studies under Swedish conditions (Bergström and Johnsson, 1988; Larsson and Johnsson, 2003) revealed that soil textural class and organic matter content, crops and climate conditions are among the crucial factors influencing N leaching. Another study, conducted in Dotnuva experimental site with regression-cor-

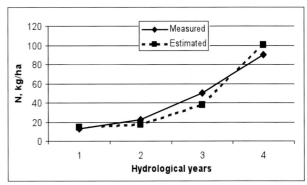

Figure 5.3. Comparison of measured annual leaching of mineral N and that calculated by equation (2) with drainage runoff during different hydrological years with low (1,2) normal (3) and high (4) discharge (Bučiene et al., 2007).

relation analysis (Švedas and Antanaitis, 2000; Bučiené et al., 2003) showed that the leached mineral nitrogen was a function of soil humus content, total nitrogen content, drainage discharge and amounts of active ingredients in mineral and organic fertilisers. Correlation-regression analysis of data obtained in this management study showed that nitrogen leaching mostly depended on crop characteristics (undisturbed permanent pasture or field crops established on arable land), drainage runoff/discharge magnitude and soil organic matter/humus, and was less well related to the amount of fertiliser applied (see equation 2). The N mineral leaching values estimated by equation (2) are in good agreement with the measured values (Figure 5.3):

$$y = (6.50x_1 + 65.01x_2 + 51.3x_3 + 0.01072x_4 + 0.05002x_5 - 4.35)\,0.01x_3 \qquad (2)$$

where y is N$_{min}$ in kg ha^{-1} year^{-1} leached with drainage runoff; x_1 is humus content of topsoil,%; x_2 is soil N$_{tot}$ content in topsoil,%; x_3 is yearly runoff, mm; x_4 is active

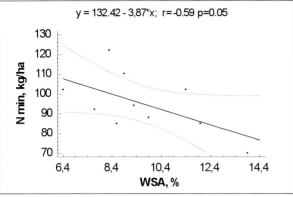

Figure 5.4. Correlation between N$_{min}$ leached with drainage runoff and content of water-stable aggregates > 1 mm in topsoil of Cambisols (Bučiene et al., 2007).

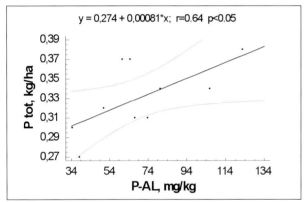

Figure 5.5. Correlation between P$_{tot}$ leached with drainage runoff and available P$_2$O$_5$-AL in the topsoil of Cambisols (Bučiene et al., 2007).

ingredients in N mineral fertilisers, kg ha^{-1} year^{-1} and x$_5$ is N in organic fertilisers, kg ha^{-1} year^{-1}.

A close negative correlation was determined between annual N$_{min}$ leaching and the content of water-stable aggregates (WSA) in the topsoil of crop management systems on Cambisols in Dotnuva (Figure 5.4). Increasing the WSA content from 6.4 to 14% decreased mean annual leaching of N$_{min}$ from 108 to 76 kg ha^{-1}.

Leaching of P$_{tot}$ in this experiment was positively correlated to the amount of available P$_2$O$_5$-AL in the topsoil (Figure 5.5).

With an increase in available P$_2$O$_5$-AL from 79 to 279 mg kg^{-1} leaching increased by almost 0.100 kg P$_{tot}$ ha^{-1}. This corresponds to other findings (Raupp, 1995; Indiati

and Sequi, 2004; Daniel et al., 1994; Sharpley et al., 1994) that P leaching is potentially higher with enrichment of soil with phosphorus.

Soil type and particularly the textural composition and organic matter content are other important factors that have to be considered when the impact of different cropping or farming systems on nutrient leaching are studied and compared. Long-term lysimeter studies with different types of soil in Lithuania (Tyla et al., 1997) have shown that particularly large amounts (75-90%) of the main nutrients leached from light-textured (loams, sandy loams), intensively cultivated carbonate soils.

Conclusions

1. Different low and high input crop management systems influence soil fertility elements (physical, chemical and microbiological) differently, depending on the initial soil nutrient status, soil type (horizons, texture, organic matter content, etc.), crop rotation and local climate specifics. Thus in order to understand this impact, many site-specific conditions and factors have to be studied and analysed as background using integrated data processing and system analysis methods in each individual case.

2. On Cambisols, organic cropping with moderate additions of compost (ORG2) caused the largest increase in aggregates in the 0.25-5 mm range and gave a high water-stable aggregate content in the topsoil. This may reduce N$_{min}$ leaching in this treatment during years with normal and high discharge. Of the low-input systems, this organic regime seemed the most sustainable.

3. Integrated cropping (INT) gave rise to the largest proportion of water-stable aggregates due to the high FYM rate. It also increased the available P and K in the topsoil and the total nitrogen and organic matter content in both topsoil and subsoil. The HA2 fraction increased most in this treatment, but much mineral nitrogen was leached in years with normal and high discharge.

4. Under conventional cropping (CON) there was a significant increase in the available K content of the topsoil.

The sum of all humic acid fractions including HA2 decreased. The microbial content and activity in this treatment were not significantly less than in the other treatments at the end of the rotation, but the loss of mineral nitrogen by leaching was the largest in years with normal and high discharge.

5. In the reference (REF) treatment the leaching of all nutrients was low, but not always significantly lowest.

6. Different cropping regimes did not influence the main nutrient leaching during dry conditions with low discharge on Cambisols.

7. Organic farming (ORG1) with moderate rates of FYM and green manure caused an increase in the most valuable HA2 fraction in the topsoil, but showed comparatively high N_{min} leaching in the years with normal and high discharge.

8. A close negative correlation was determined between the annual amount of N_{min} leached and the content of water-stable aggregates >1 mm in the topsoil of Cambisols.

9. Leaching of P_{tot} on Cambisols was positively correlated to the amount of available P_2O_5-AL in the topsoil.

10. The regression equations (1) and (2) can be used for N leaching and balance calculations if there are data available on drainage discharge, the content of soil organic matter/humus, soil N_{tot} content, fertilisation rate and fertiliser chemical composition.

Perspectives for Sustainable Development of Agricultural and Rural Areas

6

CASE STUDY
Poland

Piotr Prus
University of Technology and Life Sciences,
Bydgoszcz, Poland

Introduction

Rural areas and agriculture play a significant role in the Polish national economy and throughout the European Union, of which Poland became a member in May 2004. The countryside is the home and workplace of a large part of society and produces food and raw materials used in industry. Unfortunately, past experiences with rural development and agriculture show that these sectors generate many problems associated with lack of balance between economic, social and environmental factors.

The rapid growth of industrial agriculture in developed countries has led to the emergence of environmental threats. Agriculture has in many cases become the site of application and accumulation of pollutants. The intensive use of e.g. fertiliser and plant protection chemicals as production inputs has resulted in accumulation of residues in the entire food chain, including food intended for human consumption. The release of nitrogen into groundwater, rivers and lakes has led to eutrophication. The introduction of monoculture on arable land has resulted in an impoverishment of biological diversity. Labour-saving production techniques and technologies undermine the economic viability of small farms and there has been a deterioration in economic conditions and quality of life among rural communities, leading to a negative balance of migration and depopulation of many rural areas.

The Polish experience has been slightly different. In many regions industrial agriculture has developed, as in other countries of the European Union. However, because of the many restrictions and difficulties, mainly economic, the majority of Polish agriculture continues to be based on extensive production methods and low capital intensity, but high labour intensity. The consequence is overcrowding of some rural areas and impoverishment of communities living primarily on agriculture.

The contemporary image of agriculture and rural areas will be subject to further change. The evolutionary nature of their development is a natural thing, due to the need for adapting to a changing reality and economic and social environment (Hunek, 2004). It is important, therefore, owing to the close links between agriculture and natural resources, to design a model for rural development and agriculture that can guarantee economic development in balance and harmony with social expectations and the requirements of the environment (Lantinga and Rabbinge, 1997; Oomen Ormowski et al., 1998).

Objectives

The principles of sustainable agriculture define an appropriate system of production on a farm to ensure the wise and rational use of natural resources, protect the environment and allow for the preservation of its biological diversity (De Buck et al., 2001; Helander, 1997; Oomen Ormowski et al., 1998). This can be achieved by selecting the appropriate species and varieties of plants and species and breeds of animals for the prevailing conditions, and by using appropriate technologies to sustain soil fertility. A major component in farm management is the replacement of expenditure on inputs with investments in highly skilled farmers' knowledge. Their theoretical knowledge and experience are necessary for appropriate planning of agricultural production on a farm, allowing them to gain a good position in the market and in their social surroundings.

This sub-section examines the possibilities for sustainable development of family-run farms, where farmers using appropriate methods of production would be able to respect the environmental requirements and satisfy the needs of their economic and social conditions. For this analysis, it was necessary to find answers to the following questions:

Figure 6.1. Sustainable development of rural areas goes hand in hand with the idea of multifunctional rural development. It consists in diversifying the rural economy by moving away from treating rural areas as monofunctional areas where agriculture and production of agricultural raw materials are the dominant or sole functions. Multifunctional rural development is the skilful incorporation of additional non-agricultural functions into rural areas. An example of non-agricultural income is producing renewable energy - a windmill on a farm in Kujawsko-Pomorskie Region. Photo: P. Prus.

- What is the state of knowledge of farmers on the principles of sustainable development?
- What factors determine the choice of enterprise and method of production?
- Can farmers use the principles of sustainable development or is there scope for their input?
- To what extent are natural resources used in a manner that does not distort their sustainability?
- What are the prospects for transition towards sustainable agriculture at the present stage of development of rural areas in Poland?
- Is the current use of funds from the European Union to support agricultural production in line with the principles of sustainable development by Polish farmers?

The identification of factors and the state of readiness to implement the concept of sustainable development was particularly interesting, especially taking into account the state of agriculture in Poland and other European countries. There is an excess on the food market and farmers have difficulties in disposing of their produce. It is extremely important to determine how the survival of agriculture can be ensured. On the one hand, Polish agriculture faces competition from other member states

through membership of the European Union, but on the other hand, the European market is open to Polish goods. Whether Polish farmers seize this opportunity depends on the price level and to a large extent on the quality of their produce. High quality agricultural commodities can be produced by applying appropriate manufacturing technologies, in accordance with the principles of sustainable development, during their production (Oomen Ormowski et al., 1998; Prus, 2008). Exploration of the use of EU funds supporting sustainable agricultural production in the first years after integration allows for a comparison of the actual behaviour of Polish farmers and their declared attitudes.

This topic is multifaceted and interdisciplinary. It requires an analysis of different components of farming practices that make up the development of rural areas. Therefore a field study was carried out to identify and analyse factors affecting agricultural production and the viability of farms within three main groups of variables: environmental, economic and social change. These factors are interrelated and conditional.

Methods

The basic method used for collecting the empirical material was the diagnostic method of a questionnaire-based survey. The questionnaire was distributed to a target group, owners of agricultural holdings, and directly to a selected test group of farmers who at the time of the survey were participating in training courses organised by the Agricultural Advisory Centre in Kujawsko-Pomorskie province.

The survey was conducted from October 2002 to May 2003 among the owners of agricultural holdings in the following provinces: Zachodniopomorskie, Pomorskie, Kujawsko-Pomorskie, Wielkopolskie, Warmia and Mazury, Mazovia and Lodz. In total 1,000 questionnaires were sent out, 714 of which were returned.

Among the farmers who took part in the survey, many were fairly young people with a long period of professional activity ahead of them (Figure 6.2). According to the stated level of education (Figure 6.3), the largest group was made up of graduates of vocational schools and secondary schools, which may have meant that most of the farmers in the study were well prepared professionally. There were fewer respondents with only primary education or with university education. It was mainly farmers owning large farms by Polish standards that took part in the study (Figure 6.4). The largest group was composed of owners of farms of 15 ha or larger, the second larg-

---

Fact Box

- Agriculture in Poland has great significance in a social and economic context, although it accounts for only 2.6% of GDP.
- Rural areas in Poland occupy an area of 2,914,000 km^2 and make up 93% of total land in Poland.
- Rural areas are home to 38.2% of the entire Polish population, with 14,600,000 inhabitants. Of these, 44.4% live on individual farms, but only 18.6% live mainly or only on the income from their own farm.
- Agriculture in Poland occupies about 2.2 million people or 16.6% of the total workforce in the country. About 2.0 million people live on individual farms.
- There are about 16.2 million ha of agricultural land in Poland and it occupies 51.7% of the whole area of Poland. The total area of agricultural land in Poland makes it one of the largest farming countries in the EU. Only France, Spain and Germany have a larger area.
- The average area of farms in Poland is 10.23 ha (in 2010). In previous years it was: 10.15 ha in 2009, 10.02 ha in 2008 and 9.91 ha in 2007, showing a tendency for increasing average farm area in Poland.
- The overall land use on Polish farms is: arable land 65.8%, meadows 13.4%, pastures 3.9%, orchards 1.8%, forests and forested land 6.4% and other land 8.7%.
- The total area of arable land in Poland is about 11.6 million ha. The main crops are: cereals 73.9%, feed crops 9.2%, industrial crops 8.9%, potatoes 4.2%, leguminous edible plants 0.2% and other crops 3.6%.
- The proportion of various cereal crops in the total area of cereals is: wheat 27.3%, rye 16.3%, barley 13.5%, oats 6.1%, triticale 17.1%, cereal mixtures 15.6%, maize 3.2%, buckwheat, millet and other cereals 0.9%.
- The total area of industrial crops consists of: rape and turnip 78.6%, sugar beet 19.4% and other industrial crops 2.0%.
- The total area of sown feed crops consists of: forage legumes and other forage and grass 47.9%, feed maize 39.3%, feed legumes 10.1% and feed root crops 2.7%.
- The livestock population in Poland is made up of: poultry 140,826,000, pigs 14,278,600, cattle 5,700,000, sheep 286,400, horses 297,900, goats 118,900.
- The households in rural areas usually consist of five or more inhabitants. Such households make up 24.5% of the total number of rural households.
- In a demographic sense, the rural population in Poland is quite young in comparison with other European countries, with 58% of rural inhabitants being less than 40 years old.
- Rural places are very diverse in terms of population density:
  + 15% have less than 100 inhabitants,
  + 66% have between 100 and 500 inhabitants,
  + 13% have between 500 and 1,000 inhabitants,
  + 6% have more than 1,000 inhabitants.

Source: Own study on the data published by Polish Central Statistical Office (http://www.stat.gov.pl/gus)

est group was owners of 7.0-14.9 ha farms, the smallest group was owners of farms smaller than 6.9 ha.

In addition to the survey data, statistical data were obtained from the Central Statistical Office in Poland on the size of individual farms in Poland and the age and education level of agricultural holdings owners in Poland and of the public in general. The current level of uptake of EU funds and the national budget to support agricultural production in line with the principles of sustainable development were also studied, using data published by the Ministry of Agriculture and Rural Development on the basis of information supplied by the Agency for the Restructuring and Modernisation of Agriculture. Due to the enormous breadth of the research topic, the study focused on usage of funds allocated under the Rural Development Plan for the period 2004-2006, which was the first period after the entry of Poland into the European Union.

Results

The vast majority of surveyed farmers declared that they fulfilled most of the criteria for compliance with the principles of sustainable development (De Buck et al., 2001; Helander, 1997; Lantinga and Rabbinge, 1997). Most respondents reported implementing the following actions (Figure 6.5): practising mixed agricultural production (crop and livestock production; 86.6% of respondents); balanced use of mineral and organic fertilisers (NPK amounts in organic fertilisers as a proportion of the whole dosage of fertilisers; 70.0%); taking care to preserve the fertility of soils (the introduction of 'green fields'; 79.5%); enriching soil through ploughing in straw (53.8%); using plant protection chemicals at the most suitable time (71.1%); selection of resistant plants to diseases (59.0%); and using relevant subsequent crops (67.2%). In livestock production the vast majority of the respondents reported (Figure 6.5): taking into account animal welfare issues when providing farm animals with living conditions and housing (amount of space per animal; 77.0%); maintaining natural bedding (84.0%); appropriate light exposure (72.0%); adequate humidity and air temperature (60.1%); ventilation (62.9%); outdoor grazing in summertime (52.4%); favouring the use of fodder produced on their

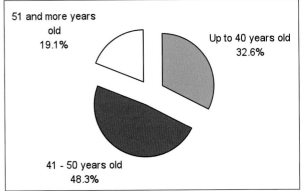

Figure 6.2. Proportions of surveyed farmers in the age groups < 40 years, 41-50 years and > 51 years.

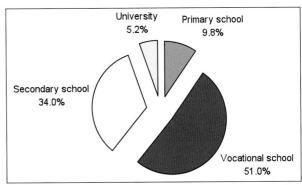

Figure 6.3. Proportions of surveyed farmers with primary, secondary, vocational college and university education.

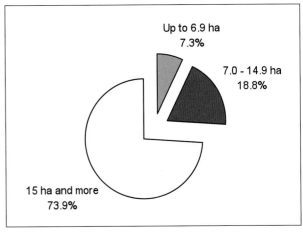

Figure 6.4. Proportions of surveyed farmers with holdings within the size classes < 6.9 ha, 7.0-14.9 ha and >15 ha.

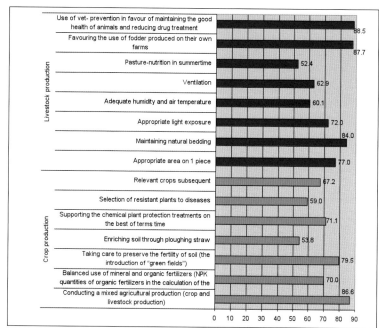

Figure 6.5. Criteria for carrying out production in accordance with the principles of sustainable development fulfilled by the surveyed farmers (%). AMEND DIAGRAM 'Outdoor grazing' 'Applying plant protection chemicals at the best time' 'ploughing in straw' 'NPK amounts in organic fertilisers as a proportion of the whole dosage of fertilisers' 'Practising mixed'.

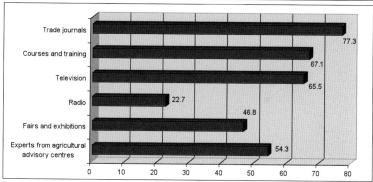

Figure 6.6. The main sources of information about production techniques and technologies mentioned by the surveyed farmers (%).

own farms (87.7%); and frequent consultation with veterinary surgeons in order to maintain the good health of animals and reduce treatment with drugs (88.5%).

The majority of surveyed farmers increased their knowledge and professionalism by looking for specialist information about production techniques and technologies (Figure 6.6). Their main sources of information were: agricultural journals/magazines (77.3%); courses and training (67.1%); television (65.5%); radio (22.7%); and fairs and exhibitions (46.8%). The results also showed that respondents highly valued the wide array of experts at agricultural advisory centres (54.3%).

The surveyed farmers were aware of their impact on the environment (85.3%) and showed a belief in the need to maintain its high quality (96.1%). They also reported increasing knowledge and skills in the field of ecology (61.1%). However, very often in practice this was limited to organising field roads (67.1%), and unfortunately not the introduction of large-scale ecological utilities (43.6%), or a suitable way of dealing with waste (42.4%). Only slightly more than half the surveyed farmers (54.4%) indicated that their holdings had tanks to store animal manure and to prevent the leakage of fluids directly into the ground (Figure 6.7).

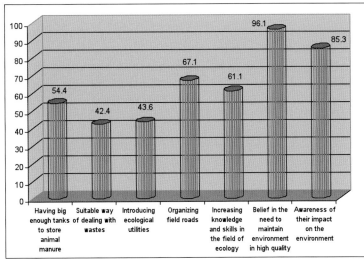

Figure 6.7. Awareness of surveyed farmers of their impact on the environment and their ecological actions (%).

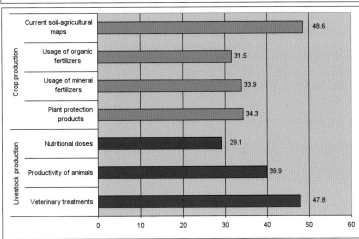

Figure 6.8. Proportion of surveyed farmers with documentation regarding the usage of production inputs (%).

The respondents identified a number of shortcomings in the process of planning, organisation and production when monitoring in accordance with the principles of sustainable development (Figure 6.8) (Helander, 1997). Most of them did not have current soil maps with information about pH and abundance of soil nutrients (51.4%), or documentation of individual fields regarding the usage of plant fertilisers (organic compounds 68.5%, mineral fertilisers 66.1%) and plant protection products (65.7%). Similarly, in livestock production, the majority of respondents did not record nutritional inputs (70.9%), the productivity of animals (60.1%), or veterinary treatments (52.2%).

The survey showed that most respondents did not attach importance to the keeping of accounts (57.9%; 1.8% did not answer this question), and did not acknowledge the importance of this in the process of effective planning of production and monitoring of cash flow (Figure 6.8). Farmers owning a computer were in the minority (40.9%), and even among them, very few used it as a tool for planning their agricultural production (9.5%).

Most of the farmers surveyed were not satisfied with the income derived from agricultural production (75.2%), while many were dissatisfied with their agricultural machinery and tools (56.3%). Around one-third did not see

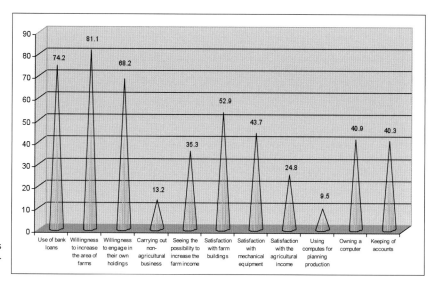

Figure 6.9. Proportions of surveyed farmers reporting different economic and social aspects of farms sustainability (%).

any possibility to increase their farm income (64.7%). Only a small group of respondents sought to improve their situation by carrying out non-agricultural activities (13.2%) (Figure 6.9).

Despite the negative opinions about their current economic situation and how to improve it in the immediate future (Figure 6.9), most respondents indicated willingness to engage in their holdings and to transfer them to their heirs (68.2%). The majority of farmers involved in the studies were satisfied with the quantity of technical and farm buildings (52.9%). In addition, the overwhelming majority of respondents planned to increase the area of their holdings (81.1%).

The vast majority of farmers declared the use of bank loans (74.2%), with a much more pointed use of preferential loans (70.2%) than commercial (15.8%). This behaviour should be regarded as legitimate and beneficial, as it demonstrates the ability to use external sources of financing for investments.

The surveyed farmers reported the existence of a number of barriers to the development of agricultural holdings (Figure 6.10). The main obstacles included: volatile prices of agricultural raw materials (84.0%) and manufacturing inputs (64.3%); lack of resources for investments (55.5%); and uncertainty of markets and lack of contract agreements (39.9%).

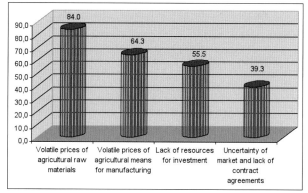

Figure 6.10. Proportions of surveyed farmers citing different barriers to the development of agricultural holdings (%).

The analysis of measures to support agricultural activities conforming with the principles of sustainable development revealed a correlation between the responses obtained on ecological attitudes and the behaviour of Polish farmers before Poland joined the European Union. The proof of this was the submission of applications and the uptake of grants for agri-environmental schemes. The uptake of these grants was very high, as they were used to 100% until the end of 2008, which was the deadline for allocation.

SWOT Analysis of Polish Agriculture and Rural Areas Development

STRENGTHS	WEAKNESSES
• Large, under-utilised agricultural land area • Large resources of relatively cheap labour (low cost of labour unit) • Favourable age structure of rural residents (high percentage of young people) • Low level of specialisation, giving great flexibility to change the direction of production • Relatively good natural environment conditions • Favourable conditions for agri-tourism development • Modernised food processing industry • Proximity to large markets (e.g. the EU, Russia) • Experience of raising EU funding	• High unemployment rate • Low mobility of the rural population • Poor education level of rural residents • Lack of capital in agriculture and in rural areas • Low credit rating in agricultural sector • Limited opportunities for employment outside agriculture • Poorly developed social infrastructure (schools, cultural institutions) and technical infrastructure (water, sewer, gasification) • Low investment attractiveness of rural areas • Weak vertical and horizontal integration in the agri-food sector and low propensity for joint action • Poor marketing and managerial staff in small processing enterprises • Unfavourable structure of farms • Widening disparity in profitability between small and large farms • Diversity of regional development
OPPORTUNITIES	**THREATS**
• Polish agriculture joining the Common Rural Policy, which gives the opportunity to compete in the common European market in relatively equal conditions • Development of non-agricultural activities in rural areas • Diversification of agricultural activities • Large internal market in rural areas related to the potential increase in purchasing ability • Large and uniformed EU market • Changing expectations of the population in the EU about social functions of agriculture and the benefits of sustainable rural development • Changing consumer expectations on food production methods and growing awareness of the benefits of extensive and environmentally friendly agriculture • Transfer of economic activities into rural areas • Increased interest in rural areas as places of residence and leisure • Projected growth of agri-tourism • Opening of the EU market for Polish producers of organic, traditional and regional food • Development of cultural infrastructure and cultural heritage, which will contribute to meeting social needs and enhancing the attractiveness of rural areas	• Conflicting priorities for rural development and agricultural policy among developed countries in the EU and Poland • Reduction of support for European agriculture as a result of WTO negotiations • Limited opportunity to improve education level in poor rural populations in connection with poor social infrastructure • Rapid development of agricultural production in countries with low production costs • The necessity to incur large expenses in a short time to adapt to EU standards • The expanding global economic crisis • Falling prices for agricultural products on the EU and global market • Price increases for raw materials and means used in agricultural production • Climate change and extreme weather events (droughts, floods, etc.)

Source: on the basis of "The strategy of rural areas and agriculture development in 2007-2013 (with some elements of foreseeing until 2020)." A document accepted by the Council of Ministers on 29 June 2005, Warsaw.

Summary

On the basis of the above results, it can be concluded that the surveyed farmers were on track to fulfil the terms of sustainable agricultural production. Most of them reported proper use of environmental resources and thus maintenance of the long-term equilibrium. A negative finding was that a significant proportion of respondents did not have adequate storage tanks for animal manure, whether or not they correctly handled municipal waste and packaging from plant protection chemicals. Many shortcomings in the planning of production were noted, with a lack of current soil maps, plans and documentation on the use of fertilisers and plant protection chemicals and a reluctance to use agricultural accounting or computers, which can be important tools for effective management of holdings.

According to the respondents, their economic and social needs were not satisfied to the expected extent. However, it should be noted that due to the complexity of the issue of sustainable development of agricultural holdings, it is very difficult in practice to be a fully sustainable farm that satisfies all the requirements and criteria. Bearing in mind that many of the surveyed farmers had already implemented many elements of environmentally-friendly production, it can be concluded that there is a real opportunity for sustainable development of individual agricultural holdings. However, this requires time. It is difficult to change all former habits and practices at once. This can be done gradually, by changing the rules for subsequent production over several years. Admittedly, this requires broad knowledge and skills among farmers, but this may lead to an improvement in their economic situation and provide non-quantifiable benefits, e.g. better environmental living conditions in rural areas and the satisfaction of a production-friendly environment.

The survey also showed that the sustainability of agricultural holdings was influenced by their owner's educational level. In many cases, an increase in overall education level increased the percentage of responses to questions and declared actions complying with sustainable development. There was also a significant effect of farm size, with more declarations attesting to sustainable farming activities on larger farms. The factor with the smallest impact on the way farms were run was the farmer's age, with only a few significant differences between respondents in different age groups.

The key to sustainable rural development and agricultural holdings in Poland seems to be to generate greater awareness among farmers of the environmental problems already identified and to increase knowledge and skills in this area (Prus, 2008). A frequent reason for erroneous decisions on production that had a negative impact on the environment was the lack of knowledge, and not the greed of farmers. A very significant role will also be played by the financial support from the national budget and the European Union. This will promote activities related to improving the environment and rural areas, as well as the quality of life and the economic diversification of rural areas. This is provided in the Rural Development Program for 2007- 2013.

Sustainable Development and Sustainable Agriculture

Russian Definitions

7

Evgeny Krasnov and Hava Zaburaeva

Immanuel Kant State University of Russia,
Kaliningrad, Russia

The concept of sustainable development is a modern, prevalent concept about the interaction of society and nature that is widely supported by the world community. The term 'sustainable development' was first founded in the report 'Our common future' (1987) by the International Commission on Environment and Development, headed by G.H. Brundtland. Sustainable means such a development, which fills the needs of the present and does not endanger the abilities of future generations to fill their own needs. The term was translated in Russia to a 'stable development'.

Most people consider this translation to be not successful, using as a model the words of B. Shaw: 'Development is continual, death is sustainable', and also assuming that the words 'sustainable' and 'development' are contradictory to each other, so development essentially cannot be sustainable, 'something should be abandoned: either development or sustainable' (Valyansky and Kaljuzhny, 2002). Even the mathematical dictionary states: 'Stability – term, which does not have a fixed content...' (Mathematics Encyclopaedic Glossary, 1988). N.N. Moiseev translated this concept as 'admissible development', 'unexhausting development' or 'keeping integrity development'. The philosopher P.V. Malinovski holds to the understanding of 'sustainable development' as 'self-sustained development'.

Economists usually consider everything from the point of their own indices and notions. P.G. Oldak offers the concept of a balanced usage of nature supposing that 'humanity has the necessary knowledge and techno-economic potential for assuring a consistent motion to higher and higher levels of equilibration of natural management' (Oldak, 1983: p.28).

Nevertheless, in spite of the variety of definitions, it is important to understand what scientists mean when using this term (Danilov-Daniljan and Losev, 2000).

The Brundtland Commission's definition is criticised in Russia for different reasons. Some critics claim it is too imprecise and anthropocentric and should include the concept of saving the environment as well. Others completely deny the possibility of decision problems on the ways of technical progress and consider that any energy used by humans is directed at destroying the environment, so it is necessary to reduce its very consumption (Danilov-Daniljan and Losev, 2000).

Essential contents of the sustainable development concept are expounded as general principles at the 'Rio Declaration of Environment and Development' which should be used as rules by countries, business and public organisations (Rudsky and Sturman, 2007). In spite of the importance and value of the sustainable development ideas, N.N. Moiseev claims that Rio de Janciro's conception and documents, which were approved, generated a dangerous illusion about the regulation of global processes and attainment of some stability in terms of it.

According to the 'Conception of Russian Federation crossing to the sustainable development' (Decree of the President of the Russian Federation from 1.04.1996, №

Table 7.1. Western and russian models.

Sustainable Development	Balanced Development
(G.H. Brundtland)	(P.G. Oldak)
1. Needs notions (particularly those, which are necessary for the existence of the poorest population layers)	1. Resource-saving production
2. Notions of the limitations which are conditional upon technological status and society organisation, applying to the ability of the environment to fulfil the needs of the present and future generations.	2. New level of social development management (creating rational needs)

440) 'sustainable development is a stable socioeconomic development, which does not destroy its natural basis.' This version of the sustainable development concept for Russia has also been criticised, mostly for temporary disruption between solving socioeconomic and ecological problems' (Rudsky and Sturman, 2007), as it means that socioeconomic stabilisation actions, without which we cannot speak about ecological stabilisation, are 'insufficient'.

The structure of the Western model of 'sustainable development' by definition is not so different from the Russian model of 'equilibration or balanced development' (Table 7.1).

On a national scale, transition to sustainable development, also in Russia, is rather difficult, including durable and multiple processes, intending an attainment of an equilibrium interaction between society and environment, a harmonisation of their relations in terms of abidance by rules of biosphere development, which means natural management system adaptation, particularly of agricultural production.

Passing to the sustainable development of agriculture, one of the necessary conditions is eradication of any contradictions between human activity and the function of the agrosystems, which are controlled by humans to different extents.

Sustainable development of Russian agriculture should provide food and ecological safety of the country, while obtaining environmentally safe and biologically active bioproducts under environmental conditions significantly changed by humans and influenced by different stresses. Furthermore, sustainable agriculture means to secure the open air, drinking water sources, irrigation water and soil saving measures.

Important factors in sustainable development in arable farming, which takes a leading position in the structure of Russian agriculture, should be obviation of drought and soil erosion and real reduction in CO_2 emissions by the agrosphere. According to this, agro-ecological monitoring of park lawns, which are classed as agricultural areas, is also very important. It is necessary to consider the food chains which exist in every specific agrocenosis when planning and implementing crop protection against agricultural pests and other threats and their aftermath, both near and distant.

According to the Western model (Sundström and Rydén, 2003) for sustainable development, agricultural systems should be:

1. Objective (fair).
2. Effective.
3. Flexible, i.e. less prone to natural changes and periodical infestations by pests.
4. Independent (self-sufficient).
5. Integrated in synergetic functions, when national, regional and local systems complete each other, so the production of waste and cooperative products can be used together (inside one region) with minimal harm.

'Organic farming' is becoming more and more popular in Russia, but it is not wide-spread. Organic farming is an integrated system based on the natural ecosystem, which does not consider cattle breeding and crop growing to be separate fields. It is developing, for example, on some Kaliningrad private farms, but currently only 1-2% of agricultural land is used for organic farming. The government gives grants to organic farming, which are needed to stimulate its development and expansion and to compensate for the high risks and conceivably low productivity levels compared with conventional farming.

Part B

Reducing Nutrient Losses from Agriculture

Authors: Angelija Bučiene, Stefan Bäckman, Thomas E. Davenport,
Faruk Djodjic, Arne Gustafson, Vytas Mašauskas, Audrone Mašauskiene,
Gregory McIsaac and Barbro Ulén

Coeditor and Coordinating Authors: Arne Gustafson and Christine Jakobsson

Leaching Losses of Nitrogen from Agricultural Soils in the Baltic Sea Area

8

Arne Gustafson
Swedish University of Agricultural Sciences, Uppsala, Sweden

Background

Eutrophication by nitrogen of coastal zones and seas is a major and growing water problem for the Baltic Sea. Both point sources and diffuse sources contribute to the problems. This is fully clear from the results of pollution load compilation PLC5 of HELCOM- the Helsinki Commission (Figure 8.1)

In a wider European perspective analysis of source apportionment of nitrogen load in selected regions and catchments shows the importance of diffuse load to the water bodies. Agriculture is also a very significant contributor to this diffuse load (Figure 8.2).

In Sweden and other countries there is and has been an ongoing work to reduce the nitrogen contribution from large sewage treatment plants, by introducing tertiary treatment, a programme that seems to be successful. However in transition countries there is still substantial potential for reduction of these point sources (Table 8.1). This is especially important since point sources are emitted directly into stream waters in contrast to emissions from diffuse sources (as arable land) which are significantly subject to retention before entering the water bodies.

However the efforts to reduce the impact from arable land on the water bodies have so far, in spite of considerable efforts, shown only emerging evidence of **substantially** decreasing the nitrogen-loads in small streams. This is a tendency both in Sweden and in other countries around the Baltic Sea. Evaluation of this statement can be made

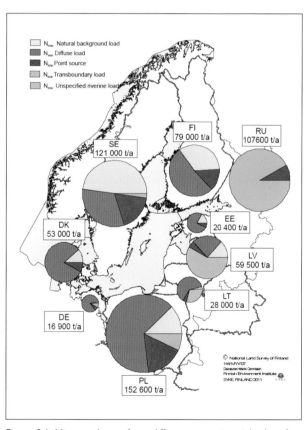

Figure 8.1. Nitrogen losses from diffuse sources into inland surface waters within the nine Contacting Parties' Baltic Sea catchment areas in 2006 based on the source-orientated approach (HELCOM, SYKE, Finland. PLC5, 2011).

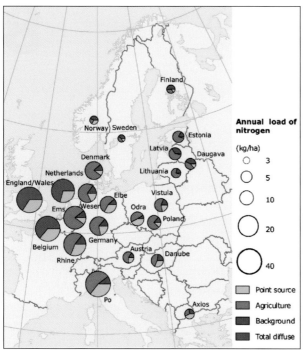

Figure 8.2. Source apportionment of nitrogen load in selected regions and catchments. The area of each pie chart indicates the total area-specific load. Mixed approaches. (European Environment Agency, EEA 2005)

Table 8.1. Levels of sewage treatment by country in 2004. Percentage of population connected to treatment plants of different levels.(from Humborg et al., 2007).

Country	Primary	Secondary	Tertiary
Belarus	0	50	0
Czech republic	0	61	0
Denmark	2	5.2	81
Estonia	2.2	34	34
Finland	0	0	80
Germany	0	9	85
Lithuania	33	6	18
Latvia	1.8	35	33
Norway	0	5.8	86
Poland	2.2	23	34
Russia	0	50	0
Sweden	0	5.8	86

FACT BOX 1

Overland flow:
The water flow takes place at the soil surface.

Preferential flow:
The water flow takes place in cracks and worm-holes.

Matrix flow:
The water percolates the whole soil profile.

through a network of small agricultural catchments in the Baltic Sea region. In Sweden a downward trend for nitrate nitrogen was found only in seven out of 24 agricultural catchments (Kyllmar et al., 2006) and downward trends in several minor rivers in Estonia and Denmark have also been reported (Iital et al., 2005; Kronvang et al., 2005).

Furthermore there are large differences in the leaching magnitude as shown by measurements made at the outlet of the catchments (Figure 8.3). There are lots of factors regulating the final leaching magnitude, such as soil types, farming practices, climatic conditions and denitrification rates in the plough layer and also deeper in the soil profile. Dominating water flow pathways are also important – i.e. *overland flow* or *subsurface flow*, the latter can be divided into *matrix flow* and *preferential flow*. We have also to take into account the interaction with the deeper groundwater system. (Gustafson, 1983; Vagstad et al., 2001). It is the interaction between agricultural practices and basic catchment characteristics, including the

hydrological processes, that determines the final losses of nitrogen to the water bodies. It is necessary to stress that we need both a nutrient source and a transport mechanism to create a nutrient leaching situation.

Intensity of crop production increased after the Second World War. The breeding of high-yielding varieties of cereals and other crops, and chemical control of pests and diseases, required a higher input of mineral nitrogen, principally in the form of synthetic fertilisers. The amounts applied per hectare reached a plateau in the 1980s (Figure 8.4).

The largest outputs are normally in the form of crop off-take, but quantities of readily mineralisable nitrogen in the form of crop residues are also considerable in spite of greater percentage crop uptake in harvested products at actual fertilisation levels.

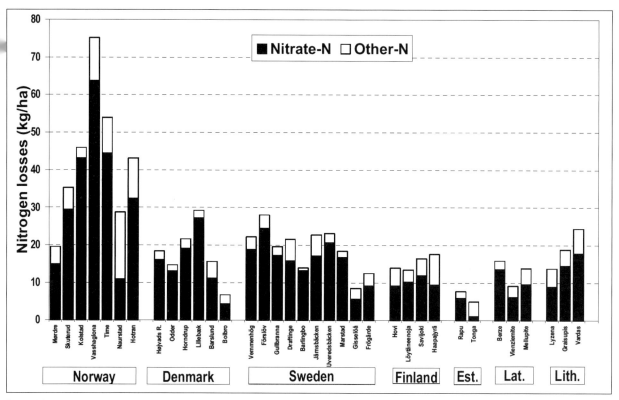

Figure 8.3. Mean annual losses of nitrogen from 35 agricultural catchments in the Nordic and Baltic countries (from Vagstad et al., 2001).

Animal-based systems have also been intensified over the same period, and large applications of nitrogen to arable land in the form of manure have become common. Losses of nitrogen from livestock-based agriculture have also increased with intensification, and contribute to a very significant part of the total losses from soils.

Gas losses are also important but little is known in detail of how to manage these losses under field conditions. It is also necessary to optimise the agricultural system in such a way that a decrease in losses in one way does not increase losses in another way. Thus a holistic knowledge of causes for nitrogen losses to water and air is of the utmost importance to be able to manage an environmentally friendly food production system.

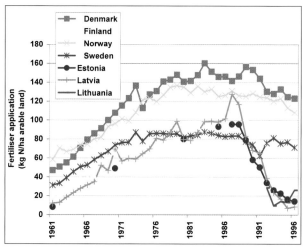

Figure 8.4. Changes in application of mineral nitrogen fertilisers (kg N ha^{-1} arable land) in the Nordic and Baltic countries from 1961 to 1996 (FAO, Statistics).

The Complexity of Nitrogen Losses to Water and Air – *Some Processes and Management Factors Involved*

Mineralisation/Immobilisation

As has been indicated earlier, fluxes of nitrogen through the soil by drainage water vary greatly. Only a part of available nitrogen is removed with the harvest and thus in spite of successful cropping, the losses might be high due to mineralisation of crop residues and easily decomposable organic material in the soil during the autumn period. Climatic conditions, pedological conditions, type of production and tillage management influence the mineralisation conditions. Soil disturbance through cultivation also increases the rate of mineralisation. The result is an increased amount of mineral nitrogen in the soil profile, which is vulnerable to leaching and /or denitrification.

Of major importance for the balance between mineralisation and immobilisation is the C:N ratio in the decomposing organic substances. Although there is a general trend relating net immobilisation to the C:N ratio, there is no precise critical value which marks the point at which reversal from immobilisation to mineralisation occurs (See page 129 for more information on immobilisation and C/N ratio). This is because other aspects of substrate quality have a major impact on the rate of decomposition. The rate of mineralisation of nitrogen from soil organic matter generally increases with increasing moisture content between permanent wilting point and field capacity. As the soil moisture content is raised above field capacity, however, mineralisation rates fall because of limited aeration.

It is not only moisture content that is important; temporal changes in content, i.e. cycles of drying and wetting, have a profound effect on the rate of mineralisation. There is evidence that rewetting of a dried soil results in a burst of microbial activity associated with an expansion in microbial populations. The substrate responsible for the stimulation is partly microbial cells killed during the drying phase, with a low C:N ratio, and partly soil organic matter newly exposed to microbial attack as a result of physical disruption of aggregates due to swelling and shrinking of the soil.

Freezing and thawing have comparable effects to those initiated by drying and rewetting. The freezing process kills a substantial part of the soil microbial biomass, which is then available for decomposition by the surviving population, once the temperature increases to allow the resumption of microbial activity. In conditions such as those of a Swedish winter, the effects of freezing and thawing may exceed those of drying and rewetting.

Rates of organic matter decomposition generally rise rapidly with increasing temperature, above the range normally found in soils in the field. This may result in large differences in the rate of nitrogen mineralisation between typically cool conditions in early spring, especially in the north of Sweden, and conditions in midsummer. This is of special interest because of the possible implications for organic farming systems.

In conclusion, mineralisation/immobilisation of nitrogen in soil is a complex process dependent on many factors. Much is known from laboratory experiments and much less from field experiments, especially for cold (autumn, winter, and early spring) conditions. The conditions during the cold period, however, play an important role in the leaching of nitrate to the water bodies. More should be known about the effect of catch crop management and the tillage regimes and more attention should be paid to this so that nitrogen leaching can be managed by proper control of the mobilisation/immobilisation processes.

Denitrification

Denitrification – the microbial reduction of nitrate to NO, N_2O and N_2 – is the major biological process by which the nitrogen cycle is completed and fixed nitrogen returned to the atmosphere. The environment in which the greatest quantities of nitrate, the essential substrate for denitrification, are likely to be found is agricultural land receiving substantial inputs of nitrogenous fertilisers or manure. Estimates of the quantities of nitrogen lost by denitrification from agricultural land differ widely; more than 50% of the applied nitrogen has been reported. There are concerns about N_2O since this gas is one of the more important contributors to the greenhouse effect and is also considered to be a partial cause of the depletion of the Earth's stratospheric ozone layer.

Recent research related to denitrification confirms greater losses in the presence of manure. Increased soil carbon content after long-term manure applications also promotes the process, as does straw incorporation. It appears to be a readily decomposable fraction of the organic matter that affects the capacity of soil to denitrify.

Denitrification rates are to some extent correlated with concentrations of nitrate in the soil. Where fertilisers containing nitrogen in the nitrate form are applied, much of the loss due to denitrification occurs in the period immediately following the application. This usually means that the maximum losses from cereal-growing land and grassland occur in spring, under Swedish conditions, with a tendency towards another peak in autumn from arable land, following the release of nitrate from the mineralisation of crop residues, and an increase in soil water content.

The effects of plants on denitrification are complex. On the one hand, they can promote it by providing carbon in the form of exudates and root cell material. On the other hand, water demand by the plants dries the soil and improves aeration; plant uptake of nitrate removes it from the danger of loss by denitrification.

Many studies have shown that denitrification activity in soils is correlated with water content. This dependence on water content is a direct consequence of the fact that the diffusion rate of oxygen through a water-filled pore is only one ten-thousandth of that through an air-filled pore. The potential for the development of anaerobic zones is thus to a greater degree dependent on water content than any other variable.

Agricultural land is a significant source of emissions of N_2O. Normally, but not always, increased fertiliser rates correspond to greater emissions. Several studies have shown that very high rates of N_2O emissions may occur when peat soils are drained and cultivated.

Soil pH is another factor affecting the ratio of N_2O to N_2 in the gaseous products of denitrification. Inhibition of N_2O reduction to N_2 occurs at all concentrations of nitrate at low pH, resulting in an increased proportion of the emissions occurring as N_2O. Studies have shown that the effect of acidity on N_2O is an immediate one, and thus not due to a change in the balance of microbial population.

The conclusion is that the possible risk for formation of N_2O lends great importance to the denitrification process and the manipulation strategies to avoid both major denitrification of a valuable N resource and the formation of N_2O. Not much is done under Nordic conditions concerning this issue and even less when it comes to interactions between mineralisation/denitrification and coun-

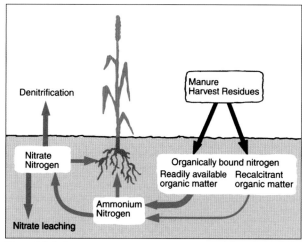

Figure 8.5. Soil nitrogen types, turnover, storage and losses (Claesson and Steineck, 1996).

termeasures against nitrogen leaching through different field management strategies. This must be an important field for research in the future.

Ammonia Volatilisation

Nitrogen can be lost from agricultural soils by the release of gaseous ammonia, NH_3, into the atmosphere. The predominant source of the ammonia in the farming systems is urea in the faeces and urine of livestock, either voided directly onto land by grazing animals or spread as slurry or farmyard manure. Ammoniac fertilisers also contribute to the release, when applied to calcareous soils. The ammonia lost to the atmosphere is a major contributor to acid deposition. Some of the NH_3 deposition is very local, within a few hundred metres of the source; at the other extreme, some is dispersed over large areas. Ammonia volatilisation contributes to acidification of land and in some limited areas even to nitrogen saturation in forest soils, as well as to eutrophication in lakes, rivers and the sea. It can also affect biological diversity negatively.

When urea is added to a soil, the urease enzyme rapidly hydrolyses it to ammonium and bicarbonate ions. The latter tends to raise the soil pH near the surface, and promote the loss of NH_3 by volatilisation. The amounts of ammonia lost are influenced by a number of factors, such as aerodynamic factors affecting the transfer of NH_3

from the soil surface to the atmosphere, the amount of urea applied, the rate of hydrolysis, the initial pH and the buffer capacity of the soil, the soil moisture level and the depth of application.

There exists rather good and detailed knowledge concerning individual processes regulating losses of NH_3 from arable soil but on the combined effect of all simultaneous ongoing processes there is still a considerable lack of knowledge. Research must therefore be directed towards a more complete understanding of the combined effect of all ongoing processes to reach the final goal of better utilisation of the nitrogen resource and thereby save the surrounding environment.

How Nitrate Moves in the Soil
Influence of Soil Texture
Of the various combined forms of nitrogen present in soils or added as fertiliser, only the nitrate ion is leached out in appreciable amounts by water passing through the soil profile. This is because there is no significant adsorption of nitrate onto soil surfaces, and there are no common insoluble nitrates. Thus nitrate in the soil solution is displaced downwards by rainfall or irrigation water and if sufficient water is added it can be carried beyond the root zone and eventually to the groundwater and/or to a tile drainage system if present.

The water content of the soil affects the rate of downward movement of nitrate during leaching. The depth of displacement by a given quantity of rainfall is generally greater for sandy soils than for clays, making sandy soils more vulnerable to leaching than clay soils (Figure 8.6). However, nitrate movement in the field is a complex process, and the effect of soil structure increases as clay content increases. Variations in pore size, in the spatial distribution of pores and their continuity all contribute to irregular movement of water down the soil profile. The effect of this is to spread out the front between the resident soil solution and the displacing rainfall, a phenomenon known as hydrodynamic dispersion. Superimposed on this effect is diffusive dispersion of nitrate in the soil solution, due to differences in concentration within the soil profile.

Recognition of the high hydrodynamic dispersion in structured soils has led to the concept of mobile and immobile water. The immobile water is retained in the aggregates, from which nitrate can only be transferred to

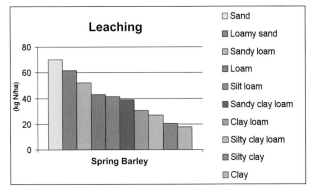

Figure 8.6. Leaching after spring barley in southern Sweden in relation to different soil textures. (Calculated values with the SOILNDB, Johnsson et al., 2002).

the mobile water phase by diffusive transfer across the mobile-immobile water interface. This concept has been used with good effects in improving simulation of solute transport in structured soils. However, under intensive rainfall snow melt, water and solute may completely bypass the mobile pore system and move via large macro pores. The description of water movement under these conditions is being developed (Larsson and Jarvis, 1999), but detailed analysis of solute transport under these conditions is still not complete. One problem with improving the description of bypass transport is the highly transient nature of this type of transport. Time steps during simulation need to be the same order as rainfall events (i.e. hours rather than days), and data with such high time resolution are often lacking.

Sources of Leachable Nitrogen
Obviously, the size of the sources of nitrogen available for leaching will vary as regards both place and time. An example from a 9-year-old experiment on a clay-till in Skåne (southern Sweden) may serve as an example of the relative size of the sources in this part of the country (Table 8.2).

The amount of residual nitrogen and mineralisation during the winter in this example were of about the same magnitude. Atmospheric deposition was by far the smallest component. Almost half of the nitrogen available for leaching was in fact leached. Discharge was, on average, 237 mm. A larger discharge would have increased the leaching, while a smaller discharge would have decreased the leaching. Since the size of the discharge depends

Table 8.2. Sources of available nitrogen for leaching. Results from a 9-year investigation on clay till in southern Sweden. The dominant crops were spring wheat, barley and sugar beet. (from Gustafson, 1987)

Nitrogen source	Time or period of the year	N(kg/ha)
Nitrate in the soil, residual-N down to a depth of 1 m in the soil	1 Sept.	31
From mineralisation of litter and other organic material in the soil	1 Sept. – 31 March	34
Atmospheric deposition	1 Sept. – 31 March	6
Total available		71
Leached through drain pipes		31

largely on the amount of precipitation and its distribution, we are unable to influence the factor that regulates leaching apart from using irrigation. However, the amount of nitrogen available for leaching can be controlled to some extent. In the short-term, attempts can be made to reduce the amount of residual nitrogen by better dosing of the fertiliser in both amount and time. The amount of organic material available for mineralisation can also be influenced. This is particularly important in a long-term perspective. It is essential to attack both sources in order to achieve a sustainable reduction of leaching. Another possibility is to make use of catch crops during the winter so that the mineral nitrogen becomes incorporated into the plant material instead of being leached out; this is discussed in greater detail below.

The Role of Soil Organic Material

The availability of relatively easily mineralised organic nitrogen in the soil is, as has been shown, of major importance for the magnitude of the leaching. Soils given large amounts of organic material will, in the long-term perspective, have a larger capacity for net mineralisation. Agriculture with different lines of production and cropping systems will therefore, when "equilibrium" is finally reached after a fairly long period (decades), have clearly different contributions of net mineralisation from the soil. Both Swedish and foreign studies confirm this. It is mainly the semi-stable young humus pool in the soil that contributes to increased nitrogen mineralisation. This contributes to the nitrogen supply of the crops during the growing season but also to the formation of nitrate outside the growing season, which is less desirable from the leaching viewpoint.

Naturally, a good organic content has many positive effects on the soil, when regarded as an environment in which plants grow, but from the leaching viewpoint, the formation of organic material must not proceed too far. It is important to find an optimal situation. In a monoculture of grain crops where only fertilisers are applied there may, in the long run, be a reduction in the organic content, leading to undesirable effects on the soil structure, which may cause reduced crop growth and a decreased ability to utilise supplied and mineralised nitrogen. This should lead to increased leaching but if the monoculture is balanced with the ploughing-in of straw, the system can, nonetheless, survive for a long period and leaching losses may probably be kept at an acceptable level.

Mineralisation has been found to be greater on fields that are regularly treated with organic manure. Manure

Table 8.3. Mean annual losses and concentrations of nitrogen during a five-year period on sandy soils in southern Sweden when growing spring cereals with fertilization according to crops nutrient requirements and without manure for a long period of time (from Gustafson et al., 1990).

Site	Discharge(mm)	Losses N (kg/ha)			Concentrations N (mg/l)		
		NH_4	NO_3	Tot. N	NH_4	NO_3	Tot. N
		Fertiliser					
1	239	0.09	31	33	0.04	13	14
2	263	0.06	31	35	0.02	12	13
3	232	0.06	31	35	0.03	14	15
		Fertiliser and manure					
4	291	0.10	41	44	0.03	14	15
5 *	290	0.31	62	67	0.11	22	23

*Large application rates of manure

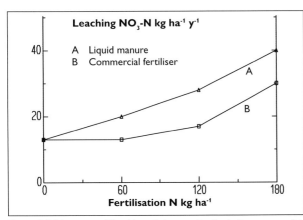

Figure 8.7. Mean annual leaching of nitrogen in tile drainage water following different fertilisation rates of commercial fertiliser and liquid pig slurry.

Table 8.4. Mean nitrate losses by tile drainage water on a sandy soil in southern Sweden during (1991-94).

Fertilisation (N kg ha⁻¹ y⁻¹)	0	50	100	150
Losses (N kg ha⁻¹ y⁻¹)	34	36	45	66

of water is fairly unusual and then it is the availability of heat and oxygen that mainly restricts mineralisation. A warm autumn and early soil tillage, which increases the availability of oxygen in the soil at a time when its temperature is relatively high, will increase the autumn mineralisation and thereby the availability of nitrate and, consequently, possibly lead to increased leaching.

The colder conditions prevailing in the north of the Baltic area cause the formation of nitrate between the time of harvesting and the arrival of winter to decrease. Quite simply, there is insufficient time during autumn for particularly large quantities of nitrate to be formed, and as a result the leaching will be less the further to the north we proceed.

Another reason for the smaller leaching in the north is the different flow patterns of water as a result of frequently frozen ground. When the ground is frozen, a larger proportion of the water leaves as surface runoff and thus the soil is not leached of nitrate.

The increasing share of grassland in the north, where the soil has a crop cover during winter, together with late nitrogen uptake, also contributes to the leaching of nitrate in northern areas being relatively moderate. Consequently, there are considerable differences in leaching pattern and amount depending on the geographical location as can be demonstrated from the results from observation fields located from south to north in Sweden (Figure 8.8).

contains both mineral and organic nitrogen and the latter contributes to the enrichment of organic material in the soil. As a consequence, leaching under otherwise similar conditions will be greater on fields spread with manure or other organic fertilisers (Table 8.3).

Thus, it is important from a leaching point of view to take into account the organic part of manure when fertilising. In a five-year experiment, the impacts on leaching from commercial fertiliser and liquid manure were compared when adding equal amounts of inorganic nitrogen. The organic part in the liquid manure clearly contributed to elevated leaching magnitude at all fertilisation levels used (Figure 8.7). When using manure, a combination of manure and commercial fertilisers could be good, just to avoid to high losses from the organic part of the manure outside the growing season.

Climate-related Factors

Temperature and availability of water, oxygen and suitable nutrients control microbial processes. The longer the period between completed nitrogen uptake and the formation of frozen soil, the better the possibilities for enrichment of nitrogen in the soil. Both mineralisation and conversion to nitrate are favoured by good access to oxygen, heat and soil water. During summer, drought is often an inhibiting factor. Rainfall will then favour nitrogen mineralisation. In autumn, however, a shortage

Overdoses of Fertilisers

Experiments illustrating the massive increases in leaching following excessive applications of fertiliser have been conducted in many countries. Results from a sandy soil in southern Sweden may illustrate this (Figure 8.9). Cereals were grown except in 1988 when the land was under set-aside and no fertilisers applied. In spite of this the leaching was high, illustrating the capacity of the soil to deliver mineralised nitrogen from the organic N-pool. Modern methods of predicting nitrogen requirement are available to ensure that excessive applications of fertiliser

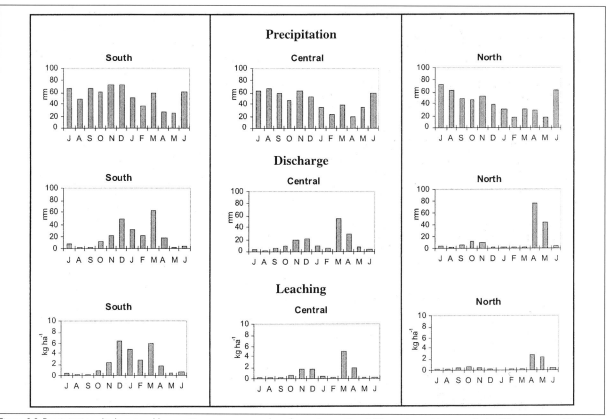

Figure 8.8. Precipitation, discharge and losses nitrogen, as mean values, from observation fields on clay and loamy soils in different parts of Sweden.

Figure 8.9. Effect of fertilisation levels on nitrogen concentrations in tile drainage effluent from a sandy soil. Recommended dose is 100 N kg ha^{-1} and 150 N kg ha^{-1} is an excessive dose. The crop rotation was : Barley (84), winter rye (85), oats (86), winter rye (87), fallow (88), winter rye (89), potatoes (90).

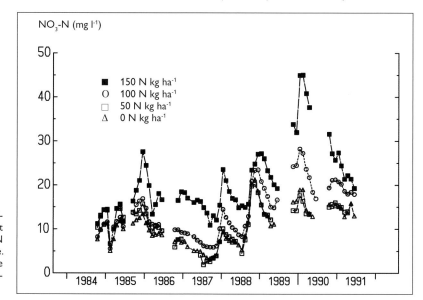

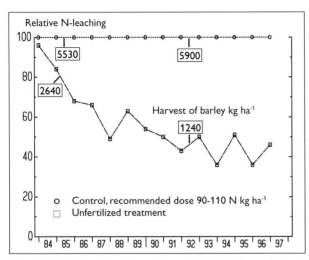

Figure 8.10. Relative N-leaching and harvest of barley (kg per hectare) in a treatment with recommended dose of fertiliser (yield=100) and a treatment without any N-fertiliser.

Figure 8.11. A well established ryegrass catch crop in the stubble of the main crop. Photo: A. Gustafson.

FACT BOX 2

Precision Farming

is an agricultural concept relying on the existence of in-field variability. It is about doing the right thing, in the right place, in the right way, at the right time. It requires the use of new technologies, such as global positioning (GPS), sensors, satellites, aerial images, and information management tools (GIS) to assess and understand variations. Collected information may be used to more precisely evaluate optimum sowing density, estimate fertilisers and other input needs, and to more accurately predict crop yields. It seeks to avoid applying inflexible practices to a crop, regardless of local soil/climate conditions, and may help to better assess local situations of disease or lodging.

---

are not made. The importance of finding the right fertilisation level on every field each year must be stressed. Today precision farming techniques are also available so that farmers can automatically allocate the right dose within each field.

The results also clearly demonstrate that a reduction of the recommended dose by half, or avoiding the use of fertilisers, does not reduce the losses very much, at least in the short term (Table 8.4).

However, if fertilisers are not used, the yield will drop drastically (by half) in the second year and even more in the long run, since the nitrogen delivery capacity of the soil will decrease with time. A field trial in the Laholm Bay area in Sweden illustrates this. In the second year the yield of barley dropped by half in a zero-fertilised treatment compared with the control with a recommended dose of 90-10 N kg ha⁻¹. After 8 years the barley yield was only 20% of the control and the leaching 40% of the control (Figure 8.10).

The results demonstrate that the farmer cannot reduce the nitrogen level too much since yields will decrease. This is also meaningless from the leaching point of view. However the leaching magnitude from an environmental point of view might still be too high, even when using recommended fertilisation levels. In such cases the use of catch crops, and in some cases increased use of winter crops, can constitute possibilities for further decreasing the leaching magnitude.

Catch Crops

Many times not even optimal amounts of fertilisers or manure give an acceptable concentration in the tile drainage water. The nitrogen mineralised outside the cropping season must be utilised. Introduction of catch crops and increased use of winter crops can in such cases further reduce the leaching. A catch crop is grown over the winter or late in the autumn for no other purpose than to take up nitrate. The catch crops themselves have to be killed off by cold temperatures or ploughed in late in the autumn or the following spring. A typical undersown catch crop such as ryegrass is normally well established after the harvest of the main crop and ready to pick up available nitrate (Figure 8.11).

In an eight-year Swedish experiment, acceptable leaching losses were obtained, both after fertiliser applied

Table 8.5. Mean annual leaching for an eight year period on a sandy soil in southern Sweden.

Time of application for liquid manure	Winter state	NO$_3$-N kg ha^{-1}	NO$_3$-N mg l^{-1}
Commercial fertiliser 90 N (kg ha^{-1}) in the spring			
	ploughed	44	16
	ryegrass catch crop	15	5
Pig slurry 90-110 Tot.N (kg ha^{-1}) and 45-55 N (kg ha^{-1}) commercial fertiliser in the spring			
Autumn	ryegrass catch crop	27	10
Spring	ploughed	49	15
Spring	ryegrass catch crop	19	8
Pig slurry 180-220 Tot.N (kg ha^{-1})* and 45-55 N (kg ha^{-1}) commercial fertiliser in the spring			
Autumn	ryegrass catch crop	46	18
Spring	ploughed	63	23
Spring	ryegrass catch crop	40	16

*Overdose

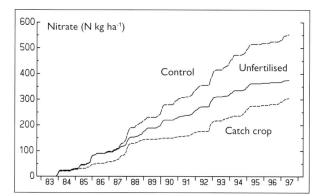

Figure 8.12. Cumulative monthly leaching of nitrate in a cropping system with mainly spring-sown grain crops. Two treatments received normal fertiliser doses (commercial fertilisers and manure, spring applications). One of these had a catch crop during the winter season, either winter rye (1984/89) or ryegrass (1989/96), ploughed in before sowing in the spring. The unfertilised treatment had no catch crop. In the first year (1983/84) all treatments were similar, with normal fertilisation rates and no catch crop.

in spring and autumn or spring application of pig slurry in combination with fertiliser at normal doses, when growing ryegrass as catch crop (Table 8.5). The grass was sown in the main crop in the spring and remained during the winter before being tilled during the spring operations. However when an overdose of liquid manure was used in combination with fertiliser the leaching became too high, in spite of the ryegrass and time of application.

A long-term experiment (14 years) of continuous catch crop treatment (mainly rye grass) showed the sustainability of the catch crop system to decrease the leaching losses in a cereal-potato crop rotation (potatoes every fifth year) on a light soil in southern Sweden (Figure 8.12).

N-leaching in Organic Farming

In addition to what has been mentioned earlier as efficient countermeasures to reduce N-leaching, whole farming concepts have also been introduced as organic farming (see fact box).

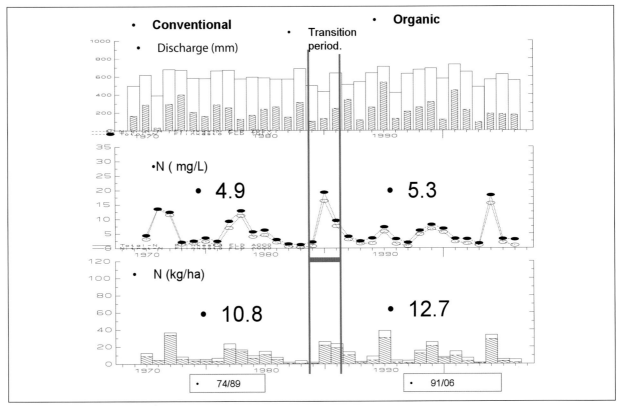

Figure 8.13. Leaching of nitrogen from an observation field in central Sweden before and after conversion from conventional to organic farming. Mean annual values as well as long-term mean values (15 years) for both the conventional and organic farming period. A transition period of three years is not included in the long-term values. (after Johansson and Gustafson, 2008).

Organic farmers use manures to dress crops with nitrogen or they use methods of supplying nitrogen in crop rotation. Growing a legume crop such as peas or beans brings nitrogen into the soil because bacteria living in association with these crops fix atmospheric nitrogen. Clover has the same benefit, so a field may be put down to grass with clover in it for a year or two at a time. Not all organic farmers have animals to supply manure and those that do not, rely heavily on crop rotations.

Plants must take up mineral nitrogen whether they are grown conventionally or organically. The ready availability of nitrogen from chemical fertilisers encourages fast growth and, if other conditions are favourable, large yields. Organic farmers usually produce less yield of what is perceived to be a higher quality and for which people may be prepared to pay a higher price. Arable organic farms may lose less nitrate by leaching than conventional ones but this is probably only when they are less productive. A long-term study from an observation field in central Sweden can confirm the small differences in leaching before and after transition from conventional to organic production on a dairy farm (Figure 8.13). Therefore, claims about water quality benefits associated with the use of animal or green manures should be viewed with great caution. This is especially critical for N due to the often poor synchronicity between release of inorganic nitrogen from animal or green manures and N uptake by the crop (Torstensson et al., 2006). Yields of cereal crops in organic systems can also be considerably lower than in conventional systems, which means that leaching losses per harvested crop unit can be significantly higher in the organic systems. (Aronsson et al., 2007)

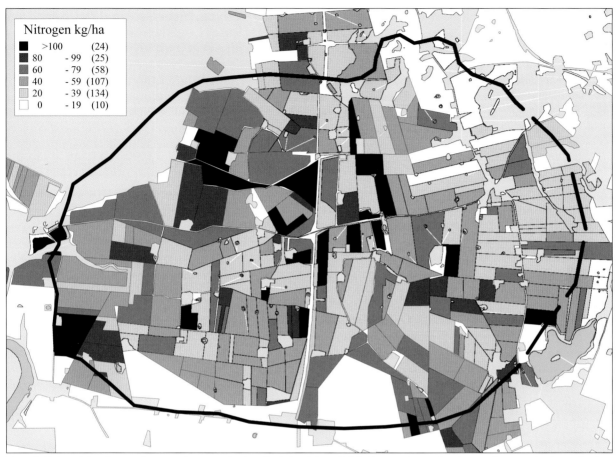

Figure 8.14. Spatial distribution of estimated nitrogen leaching (kg ha^{-1} yr^{-1}) from 331 fields in south-west Sweden as a function of soil type, fertilisation rate, crop type and soil tillage (within brackets = number of fields) (from Gustafson et al., 2000).

Perspectives of Counter-measures on the Farm and Local Watershed Level

Watershed Perspective

To be effective, the watershed perspective requires development and utilisation of more effective tools in water quality management work. Such tools include creation of a comprehensive watershed database concerning governing factors for nutrient losses on a suitable GIS media, indexing procedure to locate critical pollution areas within the watershed, and interaction between the GIS media and predictive mathematical modelling of nutrient losses to prescribe cost-effective and sustainable best management practices for pollution reductions. Without knowing the critical areas of concern, money and efforts may be spent wastefully or in the wrong order and non point source pollution may be hard to reduce. The advisory service in a region should have access to a GIS tool to be able to convince the farmer about necessary measures. An example of an analysis of leaching losses using a comprehensive database and a GIS tool for spatial distribution on a watershed level is demonstrated in Figure 8.14.

Ecotechnological Measures

Even if the farm is managed according to best management practices there still will be a need to do things close to or in water courses to achieve good water quality. One of these measures does not decrease leaching or emissions from soil, but increases removal of nutrients during runoff, i.e. restoration of ponds and wetlands.

The upper limit for N-removal is set by the hydrological conditions (Fleischer et al., 1994). Sedimentation of organic material must be favoured in order to obtain adequate conditions for denitrification at the sediment-water interface. In the long run, channel flow should be avoided by appropriate management.

Creation/restoration of wetlands has now become a part of the Swedish agro-environmental programme. One problem is, however, that ponds should be located at strategic sites in the watershed, rather than at sites identified by farmers. An inventory of optimal sites for a pond must therefore be made for each watershed subject to pond/wetland restoration. This can be included in the GIS tool and presented to the farmer.

Advisory Service and Co-operation Among Farmers

With an effective GIS tool, a programme for effective measures to be included in an environmental plan for good and sustainable farming and water quality can be set up for any watershed. The advisor and the farmer must cooperate in a positive way and the farmers can also work together to achieve the goals of the plan.

For water quality purposes the plan must as a minimum include proposals of measures to:

- Avoid overdoses of fertilisers.
- Improve manure management.
- Increase cultivation of winter crops, especially catch crops.
- Reduce soil tillage in autumn.
- Reduce erosion losses by leaving uncultivated strips of land alongside watercourses.
- Restoration or construction of ponds/wetlands in the watercourses to trap nutrients.

EU Directives, International Agreements and National Legislation and Regulations to Minimise Agricultural Leaching

Nitrate Directive 91/676/EEC

The aim of the Nitrate Directive (EU, 1991) is to reduce and prevent water pollution caused by nitrates from agricultural sources. The Directive obliges EU member states to monitor the nitrate concentration and trophic status of bodies of water. Member states must identify the bodies of water with a eutrophic level above 50 mg/l or those that might reach this eutrophic level if no action is taken.

Under the Directive, member states must designate vulnerable zones which include polluted waters. They must carry out measures to reduce nitrate pollution in these zones and also monitor water quality. Member states also need to draw up codes of good agricultural practices that can be taken up by farmers on a voluntary basis. Several member states did not fully comply with the Directive's requirements in time (mid-1990s).

Member states must submit implementation reports every four years. Based on these reports the Commission publishes a summary of the information received. If the reports show that the objectives have not been achieved, remedial action must be taken by member states.

The implementation of the Nitrate Directive is essential to achieving good water status. The Water Framework Directive has incorporated several aspects of the Nitrate Directive in its provisions. For example, the nitrate vulnerable zones became protected areas under the Water Framework Directive and the measures under the Nitrate Directive became the measures of the River Basin Management Plan.

EU Water Framework Directive 2000/60/EC

The EC Water Framework Directive, which came into force on 22 December 2000, establishes a new, integrated approach to the protection, improvement and sustainable use of Europe's rivers, lakes, estuaries, coastal waters and groundwater.

The Directive introduces two key changes to the way the water environment must be managed across the European Community. The first relates to the types of environmental objectives that must be delivered. Previous European water legislation set objectives to protect particular uses of the water environment from the effects of pollution and to protect the water environment itself from especially dangerous chemical substances. These types of objectives are taken forward in the Directive's provisions for Protected Areas and Priority Substances respectively.

However, the Directive also introduces new, broader ecological objectives, designed to protect and, where necessary, restore the structure and function of aquatic ecosystems themselves, and thereby safeguard the sustainable use of water resources. Future success in managing Europe's water environment will be judged principally by the achievement of these ecological goals.

The second key change is the introduction of a river basin management planning system. This will be the key mechanism for ensuring the integrated management of: groundwater; rivers; canals; lakes; reservoirs; estuaries and other brackish waters; coastal waters; and the water needs of terrestrial ecosystems that depend on groundwater, such as wetlands.

The planning system will provide the decision-making framework within which costs and benefits can be properly taken into account when setting environmental objectives and proportionate and cost-effective combinations of measures to achieve the objectives can be designed and implemented. It will also provide new opportunities for anyone to become actively involved in shaping the management of river basin districts – neighbouring river catchments, together with their associated stretches of coastal waters. The key dates for delivery of the requirements of the directives as listed in Table 8.6.

Table 8.6. The Water Framework Directive (WFD) past and future key dates for delivery of the requirements of the Directive.

Year	Requirement
Dec 2000	Directive comes into force
By Dec 2003	Transpose requirements to Member State Law; Identify River Basin Districts (RBD) and competent authorities
By Dec 2004	**Undertake RBD characterisation**: Pressures and impacts upon water status; Economic analysis of water use; Identify heavily modified and artificial waters; Monitoring programmes operational; Register of protected areas
By 2006	Monitoring programmes operational; Publish, for consultation, a work programme for River Basin Management Plan (RBMP) production;
By 2007	Publish, for consultation, interim overview of significant water management issues in river basin district (RBD)
By 2008	Publish full draft RBMP for consultation
By 2009	Publish final first RBMP; Designate heavily modified water bodies; Environmental objectives; Programme of measures; Monitoring networks
By 2010	Introduce pricing policies
By 2012	Programme of measures operational
By 2013	**Review, for the first RBMP**: Characterisation assessments; Economic analysis; Publish, for consultation, interim overview of significant water management issues for second RBMP
By 2015	Achieve environmental objectives of first RBMP; Publish second RBMP
By 2021	Achieve environmental objectives of second RBMP; Publish third RBMP
By 2027	Achieve environmental objectives of third RBMP; Fourth RBMP

Baltic Sea Action Plan – BSAP

The HELCOM Baltic Sea Action Plan is an ambitious programme to restore the good ecological status of the Baltic marine environment by 2021. The final version of the Baltic Sea Action Plan was complete in the beginning of November 2007. It was adopted at the HELCOM Ministerial meeting which was held on 15 November 2007 in Krakow, Poland.

The Baltic Sea Action Plan addresses all the major environmental problems affecting the Baltic marine environment. However of the many environmental challenges, the most serious and difficult to tackle with conventional approaches is the continuing eutrophication of the Baltic Sea. Clear indicators of this situation include

problems with algal blooms, dead sea-beds, and depletion of fish stocks. Such problems call for immediate wide-scale action to put an end to the further destruction of the Baltic Sea environment. Failure to react now would undermine both the prospects for the future recovery of the sea and its capability to react to the projected stress by the climate change. Furthermore, inaction will affect vital resources for the future economic prosperity of the whole region and would cost tenfold more than the cost of action.

Concerning inputs of nutrients which are responsible for eutrophication, HELCOM has already achieved a 40% reduction in nitrogen and phosphorus discharges (from sources in the catchment area) and likewise a 40% decrease as regards emissions of nitrogen to the air. But in order to achieve "clear water", which is one of the main objectives of the HELCOM Baltic Sea Action Plan, phosphorus and nitrogen inputs to the Baltic Sea must be further cut by about 42% and 18%, respectively.

However, further progress cannot be achieved using only the old administrative measures of equal reductions in pollution loads. A completely different approach and new tailor-made actions are required to reach the goal of good ecological status. Moreover, the remaining challenges are more difficult than earlier obstacles. Reductions in nutrient inputs have so far mainly been achieved through improvements at major point sources,

Table 8.7. Country-wise provisional nutrient reduction burden in 2007.

Country	Phosphorus (tonnes)	Nitrogen (tonnes)
Denmark	16	17,210
Estonia	220	900
Finland	150	1,200
Germany	240	5,620
Latvia	300	2,560
Lithuania	880	11,750
Poland	8,760	62,400
Russia	2,500	6,970
Sweden	290	20,780
Transboundary Common pool	1,660	3,780

FACT BOX 4

The HELCOM system of vision, strategic goals and ecological objectives

VISION

A healthy Baltic Sea environment, with diverse biological components functioning in balance, resulting in a good ecological status and supporting a wide range of sustainable human economic and social activities

GOALS

Baltic Sea unaffected by eutrophication	Baltic Sea life undisturbed by hazardous substances	Favourable conservation status of Baltic Sea biodiversity	Maritime activities in the Baltic Sea carried out in an environmentally friendly way

OBJECTIVES

Concentrations of nutrients close to natural levels	Concentrations of hazardous substances close to natural levels	Natural marine and coastal landscapes	Enforcement of international regulations -No illegal pollution
			Safe maritime traffic without accidental pollution
Clear water	All fish safe to eat		Efficient emergency and response capability
Natural level of algal blooms	Healthy wildlife	Thriving and balanced communities of plants and animals	Minimum sewage pollution from ships
			No introductions of alien species from ships
Natural distribution and occurrence of plants and animals			Minimum air pollution from ships
			Zero discharges from offshore platforms
Natural oxygen levels	Radioactivity at pre-Chernobyl level	Viable populations of species	Minimum threats from offshore installations

National legislations and code of good agriculture practice
A comprehensive review of these issues in the European context has been published earlier (De Clercq et al., 2001) and is highly recommended to those interested in this matter.

such as sewage treatment plants and industrial wastewater outlets. Achieving further reductions will be a tougher task, requiring actions to address diffuse sources of nutrients such as run-off from agricultural lands.

The innovative approach is that the BSAP is based on a clear set of 'ecological objectives' defined to reflect a jointly agreed vision of 'a healthy marine environment, with diverse biological components functioning in balance, resulting in a good ecological status and supporting a wide range of sustainable human activities'. Example objectives include clear water, an end to excessive algal blooms, and viable populations of species. Targets for 'good ecological status' are based on the best available scientific knowledge.

HELCOM's plan is a cornerstone for further action in the Baltic Sea region, emphasising that the plan is instrumental to the successful implementation of the proposed EU Marine Strategy Directive in the region. The proposed EU Marine Strategy Directive foresees such an action plan for each eco-region, including the Baltic. HELCOM is in a unique position to deliver this already, given its embracing of all the countries in the Baltic Sea catchment area. HELCOM is also in a unique position to ensure that the special characteristics of the Baltic Sea are fully accounted for in European policies.

In order to reach the goal towards a Baltic Sea unaffected by eutrophication the BSAP includes an agreement on the principle of identifying maximum allowable inputs of nutrients in order to reach good environmental status of the Baltic Sea and further an agreement that there is a need to reduce the nutrient inputs and that the needed reductions shall be fairly shared by all Baltic Sea countries.

To identify maximum allowable input and the reductions needed, the Baltic Nest decision support system, including the MARE NEST model, was used (Johansson et al., 2007; Baltic Nest Institute; Mare model). This is believed to be the best scientific information available, and thus stressing the provisional character of the data. The conclusion is that the maximum nutrient input to the Baltic Sea that can be allowed and still reach good environmental status with regard to eutrophication is about 21,000 tonnes of phosphorus and 600,000 tonnes of nitrogen. Furthermore, based on national data or information from 1997-2003 in each sub-region of the Baltic Sea, the maximum allowable nutrient inputs to reach good envi-

ronmental status and the corresponding nutrient reductions that are needed in each sub-region were calculated. In addition, country-wise provisional nutrient reduction burdens for each country were decided (Table 8.7).

Actions should be taken not later than 2016 to reduce the nutrient load from waterborne and airborne inputs aiming at reaching good ecological and environmental status by 2021.

According to the adaptive management principles, all figures relating to targets and maximum allowable nutrient inputs should be periodically reviewed and revised using a harmonised approach and updated information to be made available by the Contracting Baltic Sea countries. This should start in 2008, taking into account the results of the Fifth Pollution Load Compilation (PLC-5) and national river basin management plans.

In order to reach the above country-wise provisional reduction targets the countries must develop and to submit for HELCOM's assessment national programmes by 2010 with a view to evaluate the effectiveness of the programmes at a HELCOM Ministerial Meeting in 2013 and whether additional measures are needed.

The countries must also identify and, where appropriate include the required and appropriate measures into national programmes/River Basin Management Plans of the EU Water Framework Directive (Directive 2000/60/EC) for HELCOM Contracting States that are also EU member states.

Phosphorus Load from Agricultural Land to the Baltic Sea

9

Barbro Ulén and Faruk Djodjic
Swedish University of Agricultural Sciences, Uppsala, Sweden

Angelija Bučiene and Audrone Mašauskiene
Klaipeda University, Klaipeda, Lithuania

Introduction

Phosphorus losses from agricultural land may occur as point sources, diffuse pollution or in an intermediate form (Table 9.1). Transport of phosphorus from agricultural land may occur by channel flow through the soil profile. Since large agricultural areas of the Nordic and Baltic regions are artificially drained, this pathway is most important being both a diffuse source from the entire field and a point source at the outlet of the drain system to the water course. The factors with the greatest impact on phosphorus losses are the hydrology of the site and intrinsic characteristics of the soil: the texture and chemistry of the entire soil profile down to drainage depth. However local transport by more shallow water flows may also be important and in this case top soil characteristics down to the plough pan are most important.

Beside hydrology and soil chemical and physical processes, a range of other processes are involved in phosphorus turnover and mobilisation. Manure, mineral fertilisers, soil, crops, crop residues and weeds are all potential phosphorus sources for water transport of phosphorus. The mobilisation also occurs in several ways and for instance Lithuanian studies have demonstrated phosphorus in manure to be more mobile than in mineral fertiliser (Triposkaja, 2004; Marcinkonis and Karmaza, 2007).

Table 9.1. Losses of phosphorus by different water pathways in the agricultural landscape.

Sources	Water flows		Phosphorus
	Dependency on precipitation	Flow pattern	Concentration
Point sources			
Wastewater from single houses	Low	Partly episodic	High
Diffuse sources			
Surface water	High	Episodic	High
Groundwater	Low	Continuously	Low
Intermediate sources			
Tile drain water	High	Episodic	High/Low

Phosphorus Losses from Arable Catchments

In the Baltic Sea drainage area, phosphorus losses from arable land are monitored in small agricultural catchments (see fact box 2). The total transport from such monitored catchments offers a relatively acceptable prediction of the diffuse phosphorus losses from arable land, since contributions from scattered households and non-arable land are estimated to be of minor quantitative importance (Figure 9.1). Several countries have problematic areas with high phosphorus losses from agricultural catchments, as well as areas with low losses (Figure 9.2). In Sweden the agricultural areas on the East Coast and the Östgöta Plain are of special concern, since phosphorus retention in streams, rivers, and lakes has been estimated to be very small and the majority of phosphorus transported from agricultural land is lost to the Baltic Sea Proper (Brandt et al., 2006).

Phosphorus Forms in Water and Soil Types

High concentrations of dissolved reactive phosphorus (DRP) (see fact box 1) in streams can derive from private wastewater systems, an effect that is usually more obvious in summer, when water flow is low. High concentrations of dissolved phosphorus can also be the result of desorption of phosphorus from the soil, especially at snowmelt and in connection with heavy rain. A further source is phosphorus from the actual plant material, especially if the plant cells have been damaged by e.g. frost.

In the Baltic area, there is great variation estimated in the contribution of drainage loss of total phosphorus. This, together with the wide variation in the proportion of dissolved phosphorus lost by drainage, indicates that

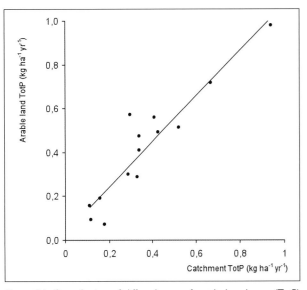

Figure 9.1. Contribution of diffuse losses of total phosphorus (TotP) from arable land compared with total transport from all sources in small agriculture-dominated catchments in Denmark, Estonia and Sweden. The figures represent annual averages for 1994-2006. The line represents a regression coefficient of 87%.

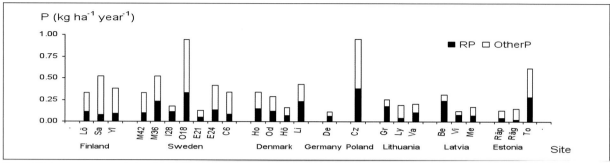

Figure 9.2. Average measured phosphorus losses: (usually dissolved) reactive phosphorus (RP) and other P (total phosphorus minus RP) (kg ha⁻¹ yr⁻¹) from small agricultural catchments in countries bordering the Baltic Sea and Kattegat in 1994-2006 (or shorter periods). Germany and Poland are each represented by a single research catchment and six other countries by several monitored catchments (Own research by Barbro Ulén).

in some fields soil erosion causes a large influx, while in other fields leaching of dissolved reactive phosphorus is the main problem. Soil profiles with silt and clay generally have a high risk of erosion (Ulén and Jakobsson, 2005). Many Nordic and Baltic silt and clay soils are drained, which allows for good agricultural production. The drainage system can be an advantage if the aim is to achieve a low level of phosphorus leaching, since it contributes to more uniform and better infiltration. On the other hand, it means that drainage water can run directly to the watercourse. In situations with high concentrations of particulate phosphorus in the drainage water, the drainage system can therefore make an effective contribution towards carrying high concentrations of such phosphorus to recipient waters. Distinct silty soils are found along the Finnish and Swedish river valleys. Clay soils are mainly concentrated to the central part of Sweden and eastern Finland. The clay particles transported through the drains are partly in very fine colloidal form and this phospho-

rus can therefore be transported great distances (Ulén, 2004). In some areas with silt and clay soils, the subsoil has a very low infiltration capacity and the particles can be transported horizontally over the soil surface or above a dense plough pan (Lundekvam and Skøien, 1998). In contrast, soddy podsolic soils and podsols are the main soil type in the Leningrad oblast (NW Russian), where the majority of soils have a sandy loam texture. Poland is predominantly a lowland. Central and northern parts have glacigenic deposits with both bolder clay and sand. About 52% of the Lithuanian relief is undulating hills where the soil is erodible. Here on very acid soils (pH<4.7), the phosphorus content increased significantly when moderate rates of phosphorus mineral fertilisers were applied (17 P kg ha⁻¹). At higher pH (5.2-5.7 and 6.2-6.7), the

FACT BOX 3

Characteristic of phosphorus losses via drain water

In the Swedish part of the Baltic area, drainage losses via subsurface drainage systems contribute 10-90% of total phosphorus losses by water. 22-86% of the total phosphorus lost from individual Swedish fields is in dissolved reactive form (DRP). The fields are situated in different parts of the country and are not affected by wastewater. (Johansson & Gustafson, 2008).

FACT BOX 4

Phosphorus sorption capacity in soils

Physically phosphorus may attach both on the outside and inside of the soil particles. It is usually impossible to separate the different processes and they may both be named sorption. Through desorption phosphorus is released back into the soil water. Important factors for the soil's ability to sorb phosphorus (sorption capacity) are the contents of aluminium and iron. Aluminium may exist as amorphous oxides without structure and also as hydroxides that may cover clay particles as a film. In contrast, iron oxides and iron hydroxides usually occur as clods.

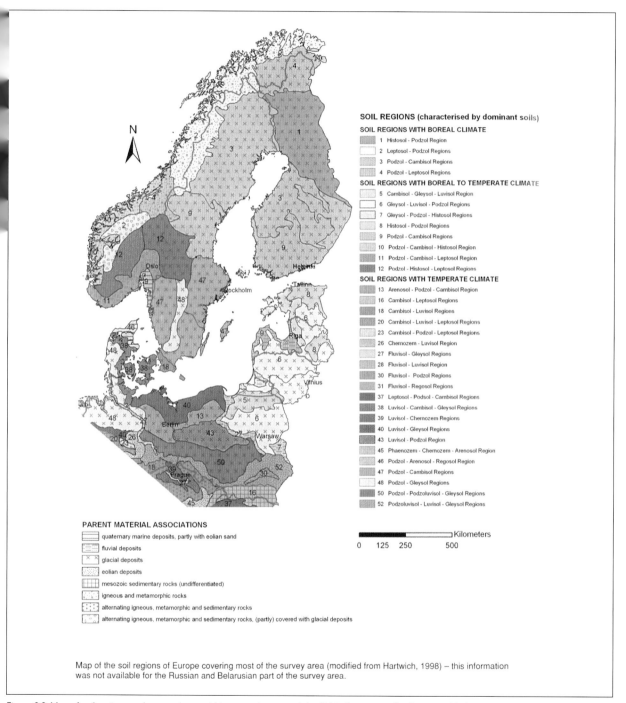

SOIL REGIONS (characterised by dominant soils)

SOIL REGIONS WITH BOREAL CLIMATE
1 Histosol - Podzol Region
2 Leptosol - Podzol Regions
3 Podzol - Cambisol Regions
4 Podzol - Leptosol Regions

SOIL REGIONS WITH BOREAL TO TEMPERATE CLIMATE
5 Cambisol - Gleysol - Luvisol Region
6 Gleysol - Luvisol - Podzol Regions
7 Gleysol - Podzol - Histosol Regions
8 Histosol - Podzol Regions
9 Podzol - Cambisol Regions
10 Podzol - Cambisol - Histosol Region
11 Podzol - Cambisol - Leptosol Region
12 Podzol - Histosol - Leptosol Regions

SOIL REGIONS WITH TEMPERATE CLIMATE
13 Arenosol - Podzol - Cambisol Region
16 Cambisol - Leptosol Regions
18 Cambisol - Luvisol Regions
20 Cambisol - Luvisol - Leptosol Regions
23 Cambisol - Podzol - Leptosol Regions
26 Chernozem - Luvisol Region
27 Fluvisol - Gleysol Regions
28 Fluvisol - Luvisol Region
30 Fluvisol - Podzol Regions
31 Fluvisol - Regosol Regions
37 Leptosol - Podsol - Cambisol Regions
38 Luvisol - Cambisol - Gleysol Regions
39 Luvisol - Chernozem Regions
40 Luvisol - Gleysol Regions
43 Luvisol - Podzol Region
45 Phaenozem - Chernozem - Arenosol Region
46 Podzol - Arenosol - Regosol Region
47 Podzol - Cambisol Regions
48 Podzol - Gleysol Regions
50 Podzol - Podzoluvisol - Gleysol Regions
52 Podzoluvisol - Luvisol - Gleysol Regions

PARENT MATERIAL ASSOCIATIONS

quaternary marine deposits, partly with eolian sand
fluvial deposits
glacial deposits
eolian deposits
mesozoic sedimentary rocks (undifferentiated)
igneous and metamorphic rocks
alternating igneous, metamorphic and sedimentary rocks
alternating igneous, metamorphic and sedimentary rocks, (partly) covered with glacial deposits

Kilometers
0   125   250   500

Map of the soil regions of Europe covering most of the survey area (modified from Hartwich, 1998) – this information
was not available for the Russian and Belarusian part of the survey area.

Figure 9.3. Map of soil regions and parental material in countries around the Baltic Sea, except for Russia and Belarus (Reinmnann et al., 2003). Used with permission (BZ8-shub/jb) from Bundesanstalt für Gewissenschaften und Rohstoffe, © 2003 BGR, Hannover.

Table 9.2. Agricultural phosphorus (P) balance in recent years (2000-2005) in countries bordering the Baltic Sea according to the soil surface gross method, mainly based on Csathó et al. (2007); average livestock density index in 2005 as livestock units per unit area utilised (LIU UUA⁻¹)(ESO, 2007), livestock units per unit area total arable land including pasture (LIU TAL⁻¹) (Henriksson, 2006 and internet sources) and actual animal density (AU) per capita (Isermann, 2007).

Country	Soil P balance	LIU UUA^{-1}	LIU TAL^{-1}	LIU TAL
	kg P ha^{-1} year^{-1}	units ha^{-1}	units ha^{-1}	per capita
Denmark	+13	1.75	0.92	0.85
Estonia	-4	0.38	0.3	0.24
Finland	+8	0.51	0.35	0.23
Germany	+4	1.08	<0.5*	0.23
Latvia	0	0.27	0.2	0.20
Lithuania	+3	0.46	0.2	0.34
Poland	+3	0.72	0.45	0.29
Russia NW	-10	-	0.2	-
Sweden	+2	0.57	0.40	0.21

* The federal state Mecklenburg-Vorpommern, which loads the Baltic Sea together with Schleswig-Holstein.

soil accumulated phosphorus only after higher loads of P fertilisation (51 P kg ha^{-1}) (Končius, 2007).

There are a variety of soils around the Baltic Sea. Figure 9.3 shows the soil regions and the parent material in the different countries neighbouring the Baltic Sea. The soils in northern Sweden are mainly Podsols and Cambisols, while in central Sweden postglacial deposits of heavy clay dominate. In the Baltic States glacial tills and glaciofluvial sediments are found, with a more or less clear gradient from the south to the north-west. Gleysols rich in humus are also quite common in central parts of Lithuania and Latvia (Reimann et al., 2003).

Use of Phosphorus Fertilisers and Livestock Density

From the beginning of the 1950s and up until the beginning of 1990s, large amounts of mineral phosphorus fertiliser were applied to farmland to increase yields. In addition, the soil received farmyard manure relatively often without any consideration being given to its value as a phosphorus fertiliser. After 1975, the amount of mineral fertiliser used in Sweden decreased rapidly. In Poland, the Baltic States and Russia, the use of mineral fertilisers decreased later, during the economically turbulent years in the early 1990s. In recent years the use of manure has decreased in several parts of the Baltic region with the decline in livestock farming. Total phosphorus fertilisation is now down to the same level as it was a hundred years ago. Substantial surplus addition of phosphorus by fertilisers and manure is still taking place in Denmark and Finland (Table 9.2). In contrast Poland, the Baltic States and NW Russia have a low or even negative soil phosphorus balance. This is also the situation in Belarus, a country not bordering the Baltic Sea but covering a substantial part of the drainage area. According to EU statistics (ESO, 2007), livestock density is lower in all countries surrounding the Baltic Sea than in the EU as a whole. The only exception is Denmark. In the German federal states of Mecklenburg-Vorpommern and Schleswig-Holstein, which border the Baltic Sea, livestock density is also low, although Germany on average has a relatively high livestock density (Table 9.2).

Agronomic testing of the topsoil (see fact box 5) is used as a tool to decipher information on the phosphorus status of the soil which can be used when decreasing phosphorus sources and improving the phosphorus balance. Different extraction methods for soil phosphorus tests have been selected in the different countries (Table 9.3). This selection depends on soil pH and other criteria in order to interpret the results to the actual soil properties. Thus unifying the phosphorus test method all over the area may not prove very efficient. The acid extraction methods are generally adapted to the relatively acidic soils in many parts of the Nordic and Baltic region and may result in higher soil concentrations than the common

Table 9.3. Commonly used extraction methods for analysing plant-available phosphorus (P) in agricultural soil, average topsoil P concentration (Soil P) and average soil P class in Roman numerals (number of classes in brackets) in countries bordering the Baltic Sea. In the last column, average soil P values are related to fertiliser recommendations.

Country	Extraction and soil P method		Soil P (mg kg⁻¹)	Soil P class	Soil P and fertilisation
Denmark	Sodium bicarbonate	P-Olsen	40	II (3)	Acceptable[a]
Estonia	Double lactate	P-DL *	50	III (5)	Acceptable[b]
Finland	Ammonium acetate	P-AAC	12[$]	IV (7)	High[c]
Germany	Calcium lactate	P-CAL**	100[#]	IV (5)	Acceptable[d]
Latvia	Double lactate	P-DL	60	III (5)	Acceptable[b]
Lithuania	Ammonium lactate	P-AL	125[£]	III (4)	Acceptable [e]
Poland	Double lactate	P-DL	-	III (5)	Acceptable [b]
Russia NW	HCl-solution	P-HCl	20-40[&]	-	Low[f]
Sweden	Ammonium lactate	P-AL	106	IV (5)	High[g]

*Since 2004, Mechlich 3 extraction has been implemented as the soil P method in the national survey
**The double lactate method is also used
$ Expressed as mg L⁻¹
# The federal states Mecklenburg-Vorpommern and Schleswig-Holstein
£ Weight average in topsoil (Mažvila et al., 2005)
& Extraction with 0.2 N HCl. The results have been recalculated from P_2O_5
a At this level annual phosphorus is allowed to increase by up to 4 kg ha⁻¹
b Acceptable, but attention to negative soil balances also needed (Astover et al., 2006; Kopinski et al., 2006)
c At this level only low input is recommended in order to reach phosphorus balance
d Even above this level a surplus of 8.7 kg P ha⁻¹ yr⁻¹ is tolerated
e At this level the recommendation for phosphorus fertilisation rates is zero balance
f 25-60% of the soils have low P concentrations (< 10 mg kg⁻¹)
g Soil class III should be obtained

extraction methods used in southern and Western Europe (Neyrod and Lischer, 2003). This is due to some calcium-bound phosphorus being dissolved out of soils even if the soil has very low lime content. In particular, the HCl solution used for soil phosphorus tests in Russia is quite acid (pH 0.7).

Conversion factors between the analytical methods are site-specific and consequently no general comparisons between the different countries can be made. A measured soil phosphorus concentration may be attributed to several status and fertility classes depending on the practice of the country (Neyrod and Lischer, 2003). The mean value of P-AL in Sweden is 106 mg P per kg soil (Eriksson et al., 1997), which corresponds to the second highest (4) of five classes used to categorise available phosphorus in soil. Similarly average phosphorus status is regarded as high in many countries, although there is also concern about the long-term effects of imbalanced soil phosphorus applications (Table 9.3).

FACT BOX 5

Agronomic Phosphorus Soil Tests

Seven different extraction agents are used for an estimation of plant-available soil phosphorus concentrations in countries bordering the drainage basin of the Baltic Sea: Mechlich 3 extraction (Mechlich, 1984) in Estonia since 2004, sodium bicarbonate (Olsen et al., 1954) in Denmark, double lactate (Riehm, 1943) in Latvia and Poland, ammonium acetate in Finland (Vuorinen and Mäkitie, 1955), calcium lactate (Schüller, 1969) in Germany, HCl-solution (Kirsanov, 1935) in NW Russia, ammonium lactate according to Ivanov (1984) in Lithuania and according to Egnér et al. (1960) in Sweden. Some of the countries use two of these methods.

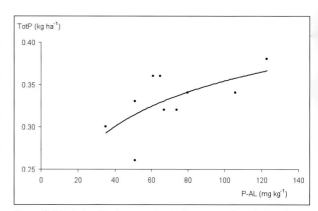

Figure 9.4. Relationship between leached amount of total phosphorus (TotP kg ha^{-1}) and concentration of soil available phosphorus extracted in ammonium-lactate (P-AL, mg kg soil^{-1} according to Ivanov (1984)) from 10 experimental plots in Lithuania. This relationship was based on one year with high discharge (Bučienė et al., 2007). The logarithmic relationship has a coefficient of determination R^2 = 39%.

Although a relationship may occasionally be found between the test and phosphorus loss by drainage water (Figure 9.4) this is not general. At low or medium discharge from experimental plots (Figure 9.4) the relationship was very weak (Bučienė et al., 2007). However, the agronomic tests may be more useful in combination with evaluations of the sorption capacity of the soil (see fact box 4). In contrast, the relationship between phosphorus accumulation zones and phosphorus sorption was found to be weak in Lithuanian soils loaded with dirty water or cleaning water from pigs. In addition there are a number of problems with using different types of soil tests. They do not take account of the way the fertiliser is applied, transport processes linking the field with surface water, or the sensitivity of the recipient waters.

Livestock-intensive Areas

In several countries in the Baltic area, there are production areas with intensive livestock farming. In Sweden, these are located e.g. in the south-east (Blekinge) and south-west (Halland). Current phosphorus fertilisation in Sweden is generating a surplus (see fact box) of on average 2 kg P ha^{-1}. In Poland, agriculture and the associated management of nutrients are very heterogeneous. Higher livestock densities are found in Wielkopolskie province west of Warsaw (3 LIU/UUA) and in Pomorskie province close to the shores of the Baltic Sea, where the soil phosphorus surplus is +8 kg ha^{-1} (Kopinski et al., 2006). This surplus is similar to those in common livestock-intensive areas in other countries (Table 9.4), whereas in cereal growing areas without livestock there is often a deficit. In an experiment in Lithuania, 50 ha of a natural grass-land were irrigated by the slurry from pig units without taking into account the natural diversity (Marcinkonis and Karmaza, 2007). As a result of intensive anthropogenic influence and natural spatial variability of the area (0.36-18.9% organic C level), in these zones P-AL differed up to 26-fold (from 12-200 mg kg^{-1}) and the phosphorus sorption potential up to 53-fold (2-106 mg kg^{-1}). Generally in areas with extremely intensive livestock farming, soil build-up is still very high, at least 20 kg P ha^{-1} yr^{-1} in some of the countries.

Risk Assessments as an Abatement Strategy

Phosphorus flows from the soil are complex and difficult to predict. The relative importance of the mechanisms involved must be known, at least conceptually, before appropriate preventive measures can be selected. To focus prevention efforts, a so-called risk index for phosphorus has been drawn up in which each individual field is assessed (Djodjic and Bergström, 2005). The strategy can be to reduce the problem by either controlling the source of the losses or the actual transport. These two strategies can also be combined. For example, frequent attempts have been made to adjust fertilisation so that the phosphorus supplied corresponds to phosphorus removed with the harvested crop (control of source), while other attempts have focused on reducing the cause of erosion or on establishing buffer zones along waterways (primarily control of transport). In areas of the USA, there are examples of strategies where the emphasis has been on one or other of these strategies (Baker and Richards, 2002). However, the concept of a risk index for phosphorus losses represents a combination of both strategies (Djodjic and Bergström, 2005). In the Baltic region, many countries have focused on controlling the source of the phosphorus losses but are also attempting to reduce the actual transport to some extent (Table 9.5).

Regulations

Regulations on stocking density and application of slurry usually take the form of laws specifying the permitted time of spreading (Table 9.5). In addition, slurry and fertilisers are not allowed to be applied to waterlogged or heavily snow-covered soils in most of the countries. In Sweden the regulations are stricter in southern coastal areas and thus to a certain extent take account of the Baltic Sea Proper as the recipient. However, the regulations do not take the actual soil characteristics into account, although it is known that different soil textural classes have different soil hydrological properties and affect the dissolved/bound phosphorus relationship. In contrast the actual type of soil is considered in extension services. Spring ploughing of certain clay soils is not recommended, since they can be severely damaged by soil compaction. Finland has similar subsidies to Sweden (Table 9.5) but also provides subsidies for edge buffer zones with lime-sand and for controlled drainage. Lime filter drains and controlled drainage have also been subsidised in the past.

Table 9.4. Proportion of agricultural land in relation to total area of the country (%), amount of phosphorus (P) supplied (mean P to agricultural land in the form of manure, artificial fertiliser, sewage sludge and atmospheric deposition), mean soil P balance for all agricultural land in livestock-intensive (LI) areas in recent years, phosphorus losses, annual climate, annual number of days with snow cover and typical runoff in the countries Finland, Sweden, Poland and Lithuania. Source: Based on Antikainen et al., 2005 and other sources.

Country	Finland	Lithuania	Poland	Sweden
Agricultural area				
Total agricultural area (%)	8	43	58	8
Ploughed agricultural area (%)	4	29	40	6
Average P input				
Farmyard manure (kg P ha^{-1} yr^{-1})	6	3	6	7
Mineral fertiliser (kg P ha^{-1} yr^{-1})	13	3	8	5
Sewage sludge, seeds and tubers (kg P ha^{-1} yr^{-1})	-	0	0.6	0.2
Atmospheric deposition (kg P ha^{-1} yr^{-1})	0.2	0.3	-	0.3
Average total supply (kg P ha^{-1} yr^{-1})	20	6	15	13
Soil balance in relatively livestock-intensive areas				
Soil surplus LI areas (kg P ha^{-1} yr^{-1})	+10-15	+10-15	+8	+8
Phosphorus losses based on national publications				
Total phosphorus (kg P ha^{-1} yr^{-1})	0.8	0.3	0.2	0.4
Average total phosphorus concentration (mg L^{-1})	0.5	0.1	0.2	0.2
Proportion of dissolved phosphorus (%)	20-80	-	40[e]	20-80[d]
Climate/region	*Turku*	*Central Lithuania*	*Warsaw*	*Stockholm*
'Hardiness zone' (scale 1-11)	5	5	6	5-6
Days with snow cover (%)	28	19-29	17	20
Runoff from agricultural land (mm yr^{-1})	150	210	130	220

b Assuming 3% phosphorus in the sludge
c Maximum tolerated level
d Analysed after filtration
e Average

Table 9.5. Methods to reduce phosphorus losses at farm level in Finland, Sweden, Poland and Lithuania.

Country	Finland	Sweden	Poland	Lithuania
Measures to reduce contributions at source				
Permissible livestock density (P kg ha^{-1})	25-50*	22	25-50*	25-50*
Required manure storage capacity (months)	12[a]	6-10	4-6[f]	6-8[h]
Ban on spreading farmyard manure	15/10-15/4	1/1-15/2[c]	1/12-28/2	1/12-1/4
Ban on spreading farmyard manure	>10% slopes	-	>10% slopes	-
Manure has to be incorporated:	always	within 4 hrs[d]	-	
Ban on loading fertilisers and manure on waterlogged or snow-covered soils	X	-	-	X
Fertiliser planning based on:	Soil P tests	Soil P tests	-	Soil P tests
Subsidised measures to reduce phosphorus transport				
Decreased autumn ploughing	-	X[e]	-	-
Buffer zones/set-aside along watercourses	X	X	X[g]	X[g]
Establishment of wetland	X	X	-	-
Set-aside, EU fallow	(earlier)	X	-	-
Grassed water pathways	-	-	-	-
Catch crop	-	X[e]	-	-
Other subsidised measures	X[b]	-	-	-

* Based on the EU Nitrate Directive and a P/N ratio of 0.2-0.4 in stocking of cattle and pigs
a Less for grazing animals; b Precision farming, lime-sand filters, controlled drainage; c Refers to sensitive areas along the coast; d Only in nitrate-sensitive areas; e Catch crop only in southern Sweden and aimed at decreasing nitrogen leaching; f Only for big farms and in vulnerable zones, 6 months; g Legislation on buffer zones; h 8 months for pigs and poultry

Best Management Practice at Farm Level

Cultivation practices to optimise phosphorus utilisation in agriculture (Best Management Practice BMP) should aim to achieve efficient and safe use of any phosphorus applied in order to maintain satisfactory levels of yield, while keeping the phosphorus levels in the soil within acceptable limits. In other words, soil depletion or unacceptable accumulation should be avoided and the aim should instead be to achieve a balance between inflows and outflows in the system. Calculation of general farm phosphorus balances, appropriate storage of manure and additives for animal feed that increase uptake of phosphorus are practical measures at farm level.

Farm Phosphorus Balances

A good starting point for minimising phosphorus losses from agriculture is to have a farm system in balance, i.e. to have inflows and outflows of phosphorus balancing each other. A positive balance indicates that there is a risk of phosphorus accumulation in the system and environmental impacts, while a negative balance indicates a risk of depletion and agronomic concerns. A significant and positive correlation between plant available P-AL content in topsoil and leaching of total P with drainage runoff has been demonstrated on Lithuanian Cambisols (Bučienė et al., 2007).

Manure Storage

There are a number of tried and tested measures to reduce phosphorus losses during storage and application of manure. The most important of these is to have sufficient storage capacity, which provides better opportunities for ensuring that the manure is spread when the risk of phosphorus losses to the environment is small. This also increases the value of manure as a source of nutrients. It requires a good manure container with a storage capacity corresponding to the amount of manure stored during periods when spreading is not permitted. The container dimensions should also be designed with regard to extreme weather conditions and other factors that can hamper manure spreading. In most countries bordering the Baltic Sea, the storage capacity for manure must be at least half a year

(Table 9.5). In practice, problems still arise in view of the fact that there are few opportunities during the year when conditions for spreading are good. This is particularly true in the case of slurry spreading on clay soils.

Feed Additives

It is a well-known fact that phosphorus utilisation in animal feed is poor, since 80-90% of the phosphorus in cereal grain is stored as phytate (inositol hexakisphosphate) (Jongbloed and Kemme, 1990). This substance is stable and poorly digestible for most species of animals, particularly monogastrics (pigs and poultry), which do not possess the advantage of having a rumen containing microbes that can release phytate-P. Because e.g. pigs have a very low utilisation rate of phytate, inorganic phosphorus is often added to pig feed. This further increases the risk of phosphorus losses, since the amount of phosphorus in the manure increases. There is a distinct correlation between pig intake and excretion of phosphorus. Studies have shown that the amount of phosphorus in pig manure increases to levels between 20 and 40 g P kg^{-1} dry material with relatively high rates of phosphorus addition to the feed , while the levels are generally below 20 g P kg^{-1} dry material with low or no additives .

There are currently two ways to counteract the problem of low phosphorus utilisation in feed. One is simply to use feed that contains phosphorus in a more available form (smaller amounts of phytate-P), while the other is to add the enzyme phytase. Phytase is produced by microorganisms (e.g. *Aspergillus niger*), and the enzyme catalyses the hydrolysis of phytate in the digestive tract of animals to produce orthophosphate, which can be taken up by monogastrics. Addition of phytase means that the animals can utilise the phosphorus in the feed more efficiently and the phosphorus content can therefore be lowered. This in turn has been shown to decrease the amount of phosphorus in manure and thereby the risk of losses to the environment. The cost of adding phytase is usually lower than that of adding extra phosphorus to the feed. In other words, phytase (Figure 9.5) additives are a good measure to reduce phosphorus losses to surface waters and groundwater in a cost-effective way. Furthermore, phytase additives have a number of other positive effects, such as increased availability of nutrients such as Ca and Zn.

Best Management Practice at Field Level

Best management practice at field level should contribute to a system in balance at field level, restricting the transport of phosphorus to surface waters and groundwater from every field. Figure 9.6 shows a flow diagram describing preventive measures aimed at minimising phosphorus losses at field level. These measures have been divided into those that decrease the release of phosphorus from soil and fertilisers and those that affect the actual transport of phosphorus on the soil surface or in the soil.

Field Phosphorus Balance and Soil Testing

Accumulation of phosphorus in a field is usually revealed when a soil test is performed. Therefore the risk of phosphorus losses from agricultural land is currently often based on soil test values determining phosphorus available to crops to be similar to that available for leaching. A number of studies have shown that the risk of phosphorus losses is better predicted by determining the concentration of dissolved phosphorus in the soil (Leinweber et al., 1999), which may therefore be decisive for fertilisation recommendations aimed at avoiding overapplication of phosphorus. Table 9.6 shows a matrix indicating the relationship between phosphorus balances and soil test values. The risk of large excesses within a system is naturally greatest when large quantities of feed are bought in for an animal production unit. A more flexible approach to livestock density can be justifiable, but it is difficult to implement in practice.

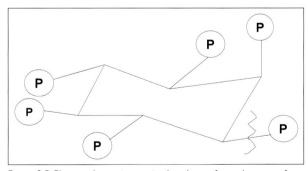

Figure 9.5. Phytase cleaves inorganic phosphorus from phytate to form orthophosphate, which can be taken up in the digestive tract of monogastrics.

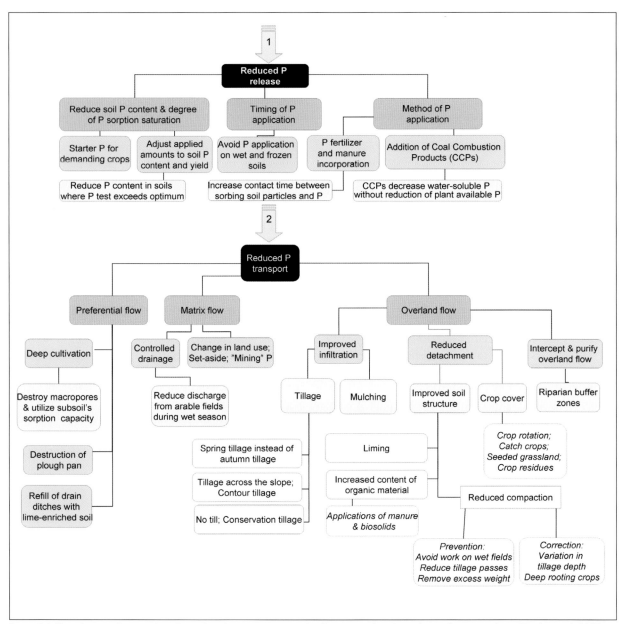

Figure 9.6. Flow diagram showing the relationships between measures for decreasing phosphorus losses from agriculture (Djodjic et al., 2005).

Fertiliser Placement

What can be done to improve the use efficiency of applied phosphorus and thereby decrease the risks of losses? A well-proven method is to apply fertiliser phosphorus in bands in the soil instead of broadcasting it on the soil surface. This applies equally to artificial fertiliser and manure. It decreases the risk e.g. of surface runoff losses and for manure also the risk of ammonia losses to the atmosphere. It has also been shown that a marked reduction in leaching losses of phosphorus can be achieved by incorporating fertiliser at the time of application (Djodjic et al., 2002). In soils with a low phosphorus content and a high phosphorus binding capacity, good crop growth is generally obtained if mineral fertiliser phosphorus is placed in bands beside the seed through combi-drilling (starter P). This also allows the fertiliser dose to be decreased. However, the disadvantage of band placement is that the root volume coming into contact with the phosphorus applied is often smaller. It has been demonstrated that maize (Richards et al., 1985), linseed and rapeseed can even be damaged by placement in seed rows of amounts of phosphorus fertiliser granules corresponding to the optimal dose. In such cases, it is important that the fertiliser granules are placed somewhat below the seed.

Manure Spreading

As mentioned before, phosphorus in manure is mobile and reduced manuring has been indicated to reduce phosphorus migration within the soil profile in central Lithuania (Tripolskaja, 2004). There are several measures that can be adopted to decrease phosphorus losses and to increase the efficiency of phosphorus use from manure, some of which concern the time of application and incorporation requirements. The first measure is to analyse the nutrient content of the manure so that the correct amount of phosphorus is applied. Simply relying on standard values given in various books and other literature is not enough. For solid manure, which varies most, it is recommended that samples be taken from the manure spreader, while slurry samples can be taken from the storage tank. There are a range of chemical methods used to determine the total phosphorus content of manure (Peters et al., 2003). There are also examples of cases where the phosphorus content is stated in terms of water-soluble phosphorus in order to emphasise that it is the amount of phosphorus that can either run off the soil surface or be leached out that is important, i.e. to give an indication of the potential environmental load.

Another important factor for good phosphorus use efficiency is that the correct amount of manure is spread on fields, which requires a reliable manure spreader that is calibrated at regular intervals. If the spreader is not calibrated there is a risk of excessive amounts being applied, which in the long term can lead to unnecessary phosphorus losses to water courses. When calibrating a manure spreader it is important to check both the amount emitted and the area over which this amount is applied. There are a number of methods used for calibration, from those based on individual loads of manure to those based on the contents of the slurry tank on the farm. It is important to bear in mind that regardless of the calibration method used, the spreader must be re-calibrated after every effective change in the composition of the manure. In comparison with many other methods to decrease phosphorus losses from agricultural soil, it is very cost-effective to have a well-calibrated manure spreader.

Limiting the Release of Phosphorus

Even if the supply of phosphorus to agricultural land is in balance with its removal, high losses can still occur due to the fact that they are often concentrated to short episodes. To decrease the effect of these episodic losses, great attention should be given to the time of phosphorus application and the method of fertiliser application.

Infiltration of water into frozen soil is mainly governed by the soil structure and the water content of the soil at the time of freezing. When the soil freezes at a

Table 9.6. Matrix indicating the relationship between phosphorus balances and soil test values based on Beegle and Lanyon (2006) but modified for Baltic Sea conditions with need of high environmental concern.

	Phosphorus balance		
	Annual supply – Annual removal		
Soil test value	–	0	+
Low	Agronomic concern		Acceptable
Medium	Desirable	Optimal	Environmental concern
Excess	Desirable	Environmental concern	

high water content or at saturation, it becomes practically impermeable to water, which means that meltwater or rain falling during the winter often gives rise to severe surface runoff, which in turn increases the risk of high phosphorus losses. This risk is particularly great if manure is applied in late autumn or during the winter (Sharpley et al., 1994). However, air-filled macropores in frozen soil can also pose a risk of phosphorus losses, since water with its content of dissolved or particle-bound phosphorus can be rapidly transported downwards in the soil. Ulén (1995) demonstrated that considerable leaching losses can occur in such conditions. In contrast, liming was indicated to reduce phosphorus migration within the soil profile in central Lithuania (Tripolskaja, 2004).

Reduction of Phosphorus Losses by Influencing Transport pathways

As mentioned above, measures to reduce phosphorus losses must take account of the dominant transport pathway in phosphorus flow, which can occur through surface runoff, macropores in the soil or more slow flow through the soil matrix (so-called piston flow). The type of flow that dominates is dependent on a number of factors such as soil sorption capacity and rain intensity. Leaching of phosphorus through the soil profile by piston flow is strongly affected by the sorption capacity of the soil, while surface runoff is completely unaffected by this parameter. When suitable preventive measures are being sought to decrease phosphorus losses in an area or from a field, it is therefore essential to identify the dominant transport pathway.

Reducing Phosphorus Losses by Surface Runoff

In some regions of the Baltic Sea area a large proportion of the phosphorus losses from agricultural soils may occur through surface runoff. In some areas, such losses are considered to be completely dominant, which means that remediation strategies to decrease phosphorus emissions have been linked to a greater extent to methods designed to prevent and reduce erosion. Surface runoff losses can occur both in the form of dissolved reactive phosphorus and phosphorus bound to soil particles. In general, phosphorus losses decrease with increasing soil infiltration capacity and thus decreasing runoff (Turtola

and Jaakola, 1995). Knowledge based on research into the dependency of erosion on rain intensity, soil characteristics, topography and soil tillage has been used to rectify problems relating to surface runoff losses of phosphorus. Tillage and mulching methods have since been developed to improve soil infiltration capacity and decrease the release of particles from soil, while various measures have been designed to control the transport of phosphorus (Figure 9.6).

The prevention of erosion demands systematic and often comprehensive efforts. However, it is important to take action in fields where erosion causes phosphorus losses, not just where erosion occurs, since erosion is not necessarily associated with losses of phosphorus (Sharpley et al., 1994). The fact is that large phosphorus losses can occur even during periods with low rainfall intensity and small erosion losses. However, knowledge within this area needs to be improved and to encompass not only particle-bound phosphorus but also phosphorus bound to colloidal material (Ulén, 2003).

Soil Tillage

A number of soil tillage strategies to decrease the velocity of water flow during surface runoff events, and thereby the transport of soil particles and any phosphorus bound to these, have been developed over the years. These include carrying out tillage operations perpendicular to the slope of the field and contour ploughing, which are methods applied in a number of countries where sloping fields are a commonly occurring feature. However, there is little experience of these in the Baltic area. Reduced soil tillage is also used to decrease surface runoff losses of phosphorus. Leaving harvest residues on the soil surface increases infiltration and decreases soil drying and thus more water is retained in the soil for the following crop. A problem is that not all erosion control measures decrease phosphorus losses. Plant residues left on the soil surface can act as a phosphorus source (Gaynor and Findlay, 1995) and increase the losses of dissolved reactive phosphorus. Dissolved phosphorus creates considerably greater problems in most water ecosystems than particle-bound phosphorus due to its high bioavailability.

Spring tillage, which is normally better than autumn tillage as regards reducing phosphorus losses, can destroy the soil structure and thereby decrease infiltration capacity

Figure 9.7. A cultivator for shallow soil tillage. Photo: B. Ulén.

and increase runoff, if carried out when the soil has a high degree of hydraulic saturation. If soil tillage operations are not carried out, the macropore flow in certain soils can increase, which in turn often contributes to greater phosphorus losses (Petersen et al., 1997). In the US, McDowell and McGregor (1984) also found that even though losses of total phosphorus were considerably reduced when no soil tillage was performed, the losses of dissolved phosphorus were eight-fold higher compared with after conventional tillage operations. Generally, the effects of cultivation on phosphorus mobilisation are highly dependent on soil type, and reduced cultivation must be linked to improved crop and nutrient management to achieve lasting environmental benefits (Withers et al., 2007).

Buffer Zones
Other measures that have been proven to significantly decrease surface runoff losses of phosphorus in the agricultural landscape include vegetation filters along watercourses, often referred to as buffer zones (Leinweber et al., 2002). The mechanisms that control phosphorus retention in vegetation filters are sediment deposition, infiltration capacity and uptake of phosphorus by the vegetation. The efficiency of vegetation filters along watercourses is strongly linked to filter width, while vegetation type and density of the vegetation cover have been shown to be of secondary importance. In a Nordic study, the total phosphorus content was reduced by between 27 and 97% depending on filter width, which was equivalent to 0.24-0.67 kg P ha^{-1} yr^{-1} (Uusi-Kämppä et al., 2000).

There is often a greater accumulation of particles in a vegetation filter than of phosphorus. Vegetation filters have also been used to decrease phosphorus losses from different types of wastewater generated in agriculture, e.g. wastewater from dairy units. Such wastewater, which contains large amounts of phosphorus, can be spread on a vegetated area that captures up to 90% of the phosphorus. Several international studies (e.g. Timmons et al., 1970; Miller et al., 1994) mention that with vegetation filters in cold regions there is a risk of the plant material in the filter freezing. This can lead to increased losses of phosphorus since freezing bursts the cell membranes and releases the phosphorus in the plant cells, which is then carried away by runoff water. Increased phosphorus losses as a result of freezing of plant material have also been demonstrated in Swedish studies.

Catch Crops
It can be assumed that the introduction of a catch crop, which is a proven method of decreasing nitrogen leaching from lighter soils in southern Sweden, also has a decreasing effect on phosphorus losses. This would occur through decreased surface runoff and erosion, phosphorus uptake by the catch crop and improved infiltration. Studies have shown that a catch crop that is allowed to grow for several months can bind 10-30 kg P ha^{-1} in aboveground biomass. However, freezing-out of the phosphorus in plant cells, and thus the potential for increased losses, is also a risk with catch crops under Baltic climatic conditions. However, in a study in south-west Sweden this effect was demonstrated to be of minor importance as long as the surface runoff was low (Ulén, 1997).

Reducing Phosphorus Losses from Drained Soils
Large losses of phosphorus occasionally occur through water, and the dissolved or particle-bound phosphorus contained therein, is transported through large pores in the soil profile. During such transport, the phosphorus usually does not have time to react with the soil material, but bypasses sorption surfaces in the soil and continues to deeper layers in the profile. The effect on phosphorus losses is then similar to that described above for surface runoff. This type of loss is often referred to as internal erosion, since particles and their bound phosphorus are ripped from the pore walls when the water

Figure 9.8a. Buffer zone on a field outside of Västerås, Sweden in March 2009. Photo: B. Ulén.

Figure 9.8b. The same site but without a buffer zone. The direct effect of surface water can be seen. Photo: B. Ulén.

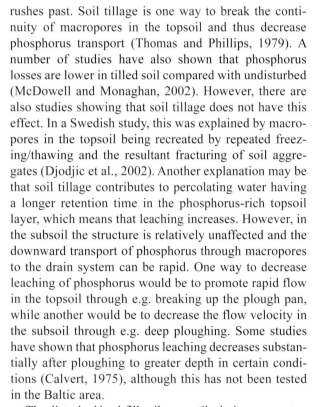

rushes past. Soil tillage is one way to break the continuity of macropores in the topsoil and thus decrease phosphorus transport (Thomas and Phillips, 1979). A number of studies have also shown that phosphorus losses are lower in tilled soil compared with undisturbed (McDowell and Monaghan, 2002). However, there are also studies showing that soil tillage does not have this effect. In a Swedish study, this was explained by macropores in the topsoil being recreated by repeated freezing/thawing and the resultant fracturing of soil aggregates (Djodjic et al., 2002). Another explanation may be that soil tillage contributes to percolating water having a longer retention time in the phosphorus-rich topsoil layer, which means that leaching increases. However, in the subsoil the structure is relatively unaffected and the downward transport of phosphorus through macropores to the drain system can be rapid. One way to decrease leaching of phosphorus would be to promote rapid flow in the topsoil through e.g. breaking up the plough pan, while another would be to decrease the flow velocity in the subsoil through e.g. deep ploughing. Some studies have shown that phosphorus leaching decreases substantially after ploughing to greater depth in certain conditions (Calvert, 1975), although this has not been tested in the Baltic area.

The disturbed backfill soil over a tile drain represents a good pathway for generating rapid phosphorus transport in the soil similar to the flow through macropores, especially in the first few years after drain installation. A method of backfilling developed for clayey soils in Finland (the FOSTOP method, Nordkalk Oy Ab) involves incorporating burnt (i.e. unslaked) lime (CaO) with the backfill material in drains. The result is a stable and porous backfill that efficiently binds the phosphorus in percolating water. The lime requirement has been determined in trials to be 3-8% of soil wet weight. The method has been tested in a number of experiments and has been found to reduce the phosphorus concentrations in running water by more than 80% in most cases. In addition to phosphorus removal, the lime filter drain can also lead to improved drainage in impervious clay soils and can thus contribute towards decreasing erosion. The average lifetime for the lime filter drain has been shown to exceed 10 years without any loss in treatment effect. The method has only been tested at one experimental site in Sweden and the long-term effects have not been monitored.

Large leaching losses of phosphorus have been measured from sandy soils with a low sorption capacity for phosphorus, particularly in combination with large phosphorus doses in the form of manure or artificial fertiliser. The highest phosphorus losses occur from sandy soils with distinctly low sorption capacity and a high degree of phosphorus saturation (Djodjic and Bergström, 2005). There can be no doubt that such soils are very susceptible to high phosphorus leaching and will probably give rise to considerable leaching losses over a long period even if they are not fertilised. Mining phosphorus by taking away large amounts of phosphorus by fast-growing grass

Figure 9.9. Spreading of unslaked lime. Photo: B. Ulén.

or other crops seems to be the only way to reduce phosphorus losses from such soil profiles

Crop Rotation

Another option to reduce the risk of phosphorus leaching is to grow crops such as lucerne, which due to their deep root system have the capacity to take up large amounts of phosphorus from the soil without any being added, a process usually referred to as mining. At harvest, the phosphorus is then removed from the field. However, the difficulties in establishing a dense lucerne crop can decrease the effect (Ulén and Mattsson, 2003). Perennial ley crops are generally better suited to mining than cereal crops and the practice works best on soils with high phosphorus levels. Maize has been demonstrated to decrease the phosphorus level in the soil by 150 kg P ha-1 during a period of 10 years, which markedly lowers the risk of phosphorus leaching.

Conceptual Evaluations of Countermeasures

For sandy soils there may be limited possibilities to bind dissolved reactive phosphorus (DRP) especially when the soil already contains much phosphorus. Suggested effective measures to reduce leaching are relatively few (Table 9.7). Reducing losses of DRP, which is usually the main problem from this type of soil, is most urgent. Mining of phosphorus, i.e. growing crops that can accumulate high amounts of phosphorus from the soil and at the same time generate large biomass, has been proposed as an attractive measure to reduce P. However, in several Baltic States ac-

cumulated uptake and transport of phosphorus by biomass is limited due to the moderate mean annual temperatures and this measure will probably have limited effects.

Silty soils usually suffer from surface erosion and several measures to reduce erosion may be highly effective (Table 9.7). Structured clay soils are also often characterised by rapid fluxes of water. Agricultural production on such soils means that they are tilled, usually in autumn, which always includes a risk of much transport of phosphorus bound to particles (Part P) in the following winter. Reduced ploughing means shallow tilling with a cultivator or disc harrow. One should bear in mind that reduced ploughing is a complex measure and experiences from Canada, have brought it into question regarding phosphorus losses (Gaynor and Findlay, 1995). The tile drainage losses of P may increase, probably as a result of increased P on the soil surface and transport of P through macropores. Surface water inlets may be regarded as point sources for P emissions to rivers and lakes. On the other side, conducting surface water to the tile drain system by such inlets may offer a better alternative than ponding water or pure surface runoff above the clay soil. The hydrological impact of water from ponded depressions is reduced by such a measure. Grassed buffer strips around the surface water inlets should reduce P losses significantly in certain areas. However, in general surface water inlets should be regarded as an emergency measure and they should, under acid soil conditions, be dug under the soil surface with limed backfill in order to avoid negative effects such as a direct conduit to tile drains.

Improved Drain Systems

Sub-surface drainage systems may be fundamental for rapid water flow out of the root zone, especially on clayey soil with dense structure in the near-surface horizon. Efficient sub-surface drainage is thus essential for achieving the full yield potential in the Baltic climate with excess rainfall. Drain trenches are very conductive and form routes for water which would otherwise flow as surface, near surface or plough pan runoff towards the lowest end of the field. Less surface runoff means lower erosive risk, especially at the lower end of the fields. Further water infiltration increases the potential for sieving of surface-eroded soil particles in soil pores and of sorption of surface-derived dissolved reactive phosphorus in the drained water.

Table 9.7. Measures and mechanisms to reduce the phosphorus losses of dissolved reactive phosphorus (DRP) and particulate phosphorus (PartP) from sandy soil, silt soil and clay soil . The effects are usually conceptual, and are indicated by 0, +, ++ or +++ so that more plus signs mean a better effect.

Measure	Mechanism	Sand		Silt		Clay	
		DRP	PartP	DRP	PartP	DRP	PartP
Balance and soil P testing							
Adding balanced manure/fertilisation	No increased surplus P in the soil	+++	+	+++	+	+++	+
Fertiliser placement							
Combi drill or instant incorporation (not only ploughing)	Improved contact with soil at application	+++	++	+++	++	+++	++
Grass/reduced erosion							
Densely vegetated winter soil: permanent grass, ley or catch crops	Filtration of particles	0	+	0	+++	0	+++
Spring ploughing	Less detachment and P desorption	++	+	++	+++	+	+
Improved water infiltration							
Reduced soil compaction	Less water channel flow	++	++	++	+++	++	+++
Trapping in artificial drainage							
Limed backfills in the tile drain system	Improving water infiltration and chemical precipitation of SRP	++	++	++	+++	+	++
Buffer zones							
Buffer zones including zones around surface water inlets	Intercepting surface-runoff P and improving water infiltration	-	+	-	+++	-	+++
Grassed strips within the field	Intercepting surface-runoff P and improving water infiltration	-	+	-	+++	-	+++

By improving infiltration and percolation, subsurface drainage systems will decrease the proportion of surface run-off. In addition, improvement of soil structure and better root growth after the operation are likely to be followed by a rise in yield level and effective use of phosphorus in soil and added fertilisers. A short-term reduction of 15-25% for soil erosion and dissolved reactive phosphorus has been measured (Turtola and Paajanen, 1985), but on the other hand, nitrogen leaching may slightly increase. With increased yield, phosphorus soil balance may improve markedly, with long-term positive effects on phosphorus loss potential.

Reducing the Amount of Polluted Water at Farm Level and Protection of Slurry Stores
Options for minimising the amount of phosphorus-containing water at farm level include: covering slurry stores (regulated in many countries); avoiding excessive use of water in washing down yards and buildings; roofing over yard areas; minimising unnecessarily dirty yard areas and

avoiding accidents with slurry stores. Spreading of slurry is restricted in time in most countries and slurry may not be applied towater-saturated soil. Reducing the amount of water means less risk of slurry stores becoming over-filled and slurry or urine having to be spread at times when more P losses may occur. In Denmark, more restrictions and rules were introduced for functional pumps in summer 2008. By 2009, farmers must arrange some form of barrier to prevent any spill water reaching the surface water. If the store is placed more than 100 m away from a lake or river, an earthen mound must be constructed with dimensions to keep the entire volume of the slurry store (Danish Ministry of Environment, 2008).

Controlled Drainage for Reducing the Amount of Water Leaving the Field
Preferential flow of phosphorus through cracks may be enhanced after a dry season or a drought period in clayey soil. By controlled drainage, soil wetting from "the bottom" occurs, and in addition, the amount of drainage

Figure 9.10. Missing ditch and poor drainage in the county of Östergötland, SE Sweden. Photo: B. Ulén.

water may be somewhat reduced. The site must have groundwater with up-pressure. In addition, the groundwater must not be too high in periods when the field is managed and the water level has to be controlled. There is very little experience of this kind of measure in the Baltic region.

Mitigation of Phosphorus Losses by Improved Land Infrastructure

Manage Downslope Field Boundaries, Re-site Gateways and Avoid Tramlines

Downslope boundaries (hedges, fences, banks, vegetative buffers) represent a change in the hydrological and biogeochemical properties. If properly managed they can buffer water quality of surface and subsurface flow. If field boundaries are located so as to force run-off flow across them in sheet flow, they may trap and filter sediment and phosphorus. Gateways, livestock and tractor pathways represent a network of preferential pathways that connects fields situated up-slope to down-slope. Moving the gate is a simple way to decrease any surface runoff of phosphorus that may occur.

Tramlines are semi-permanent wheel-ways for farming machines to travel down during spraying and fertilising operations without causing wheel damage to the rest of the field, a practice sometimes referred to as 'con-

trolled traffic'. Thus tramlines are important vectors of runoff, causing increased mobilisation of sediment and phosphorus. Uncultivated wheel tracks have a very low infiltration rate and are effective paths for sediment and P transport via surface run-off, especially after multiple tractor passes. Avoiding their use in the winter reduces run-off volumes while mechanical disruption of tramlines can minimise their negative effect. Compacted tramlines can further result in channelling of surface water into rills and gullies on erosion-susceptible soil. The reason is the critical shear stress of water flow created by the channelling effect and subsequent encroachment on surrounding soil. In addition, tramlines can act as a flow pathway during periods of snow melt and avoiding tramlines over the winter is therefore a highly significant option to prevent soil erosion under Baltic climate conditions. The solution could be either to delay the establishment of tramlines until crop cover has been established (or alternatively until the spring), or to shallow cultivate them using a simple goose-foot tine.

Improved Placement of Grazing Land within the Farm and in Connection to Streams

Through grazing, phosphorus is distributed in patches which increase the losses by surface runoff and drainage. The pattern for grazing land around the farm centre has an impact on which grazing system that is used. Few animals per hectare and rotation between the grazed fields will reduce this point source for water. The feeding and drinking site could also be moved and not be at the same place from year to year.

Free access to water has an impact on water quality by direct defecating and urination into the water course. In addition, trampling can lead to erosion of riverbanks and resuspension of river sediment. Modifying or restricting the access of livestock to the stream may reduce such phosphorus losses that follow. Measures may include; fences along the stream, bridging the necessary crossing areas instead of wading across the stream and avoiding gateways close to the stream but keeping the grazing cattle higher up in the watershed.

Constructed Wetlands

Constructed wetlands are designed to remove nitrogen and may in addition store phosphorus. Nitrogen is re-

Figure 9.11. A reversible plough for conventional ploughing to the depth of 23 cm. Photo: B. Ulén.

duced by denitrification and phosphorus by sedimentation and adsorption. The wetland may include overflow zones for oxygenation of water and sedimentation of fine particles under small runoff situations and shallow vegetative filters for sedimentation of phosphorus enriched particles (Braskerud et al., 2005). Constructed wetlands can be made up of a combination of sedimentation basins and infiltration basins with horizontal flow through the soil matrix for sorption of P. Another type of wetland is installed in open ditches and has an initial sedimentation pond area for capturing sediment-associated phosphorus. A certain hydraulic retention time is important for any retention. The phosphorus retention is more certain for particulate phosphorus than for dissolved phosphorus. The experience from some constructed wetlands is even net leaching of dissolved reactive phosphorus. This is a serious risk when the wetlands are constructed on former agricultural land, since this is usually rich in phosphorus. The sedimentation ponds may have to be emptied now and then and if sorption material is included it may have to be changed at time intervals.

Re-establishment of Riparian Wetlands at the Flood Plain

Low-lying organic soils along lowland rivers have usually been drained and used as agricultural land. Re-establishment of such wetland may reduce the flood risk, increase denitrification and, in addition, sedimentation of particulate suspended sediments and phosphorus may take place in the flood plain. Biomass should be removed

since phosphorus from the former agricultural land and iron-bound phosphorus may desorb from the riparian soil for some years and the biomass should be removed. Buffers have been indicated to be more effective if planted with trees.

Streambank and Shoreline Protection

Structural or vegetative measures may be used to protect streambank and shoreland from erosion. These include vegetative planting, and structural measures as sock riprap, piling revetments, jacks and gabion. Such measures avoid the detachment of soil particles. However, this cannot be considered a long-term strategy since phosphorus accumulated in the soil bank can reach the saturation level, or the hydrological conditions can change.

Summary and Conclusions

Phosphorus concentrations in the arable soils and phosphorus losses to waters are high in certain areas around the Baltic Sea. Even though phosphorus losses, apart from soil chemistry, also are controlled by hydrological conditions and soil physics, such losses can be decreased through cultivation practices. Of the measures introduced to decrease phosphorus losses, restriction of manure doses based on the phosphorus concentration in the soil has been the most effective, at least in the short term. Some of the problems with manure have decreased in recent years due to extensive regulation of storage and spreading. However, the problem will never be completely solved as long as manure continues to be applied to soils in the high soil phosphorus classes. Manure treatment at farm level by both simple and more complicated methods should be prioritised so that the manure can be transported at a reasonable price, as should technology for spreading and mobile grazing (moving animals around). All phosphorus fertilisers should be applied in such a way that the phosphorus has as good soil contact as possible while at the same time being available to the crop.

Soil hydrology can be affected by surface water management through good drainage tillage and liming to produce good, uniform infiltration into the soil, while all forms of channel flow must be avoided. Appropriate preventive measures must be adapted to the local soil type and cropping system. Functioning strategies and sufficiently advanced tools for this local adaptation of preventive measures within agriculture are currently lacking but need to be developed.

Agricultural Nutrient Management in the Great Lakes Region

10

Gregory McIsaac
University of Illinois at Urbana Champaign
Urbana, Illinois, USA

Nitrogen (N) and phosphorus (P) are essential macro-nutrients for all living organisms. In natural terrestrial ecosystems, there tends to be a relatively intense competition for nutrients, which become incorporated into living biomass and decomposing organic matter. As organic matter decays, inorganic N and P become available to plants and soil microbes, but also become susceptible to being moved out of the root zone by water movement. Furthermore, surface runoff mobilizes soil, detritus and attached nutrients. The normal movement of water through and over soils transports N and P from the land to groundwater and surface water. In natural ecosystems, the availability and mobility of N and P are relatively low and consequently movement to water bodies is also low (Smith et al., 2003).

In contrast there are many aspects of modern agricultural systems that increase nutrient availability and mobility. In many settings, annual cultivation increases surface runoff, erosion and transport of surficial nutrients and organic matter. In order to increase agricultural production per unit of land area, the availability of N and P in soils may be increased by applications of fertiliser and/or manure, and/or growing legumes and/or tilling the soil. While these measures can increase crop productivity, they often lead to increased movement of nutrients from the landscape to water bodies (Smith et al., 1997; Carpenter et al., 1998). Additionally, consumption of agricultural products by humans and livestock produces municipal wastewater and livestock manure that have

relatively high concentrations of N and P, which can also contaminate surface waters depending on how these wastes are treated and managed.

In general, runoff and drainage waters from agricultural lands tend to have higher concentrations of nitrogen (N) and phosphorus (P) than water draining from natural lands (Smith et al., 1997; Clark et al., 2000; Smith et al., 2003). Increased P in freshwaters can contribute to increased algal growth, which can alter aquatic food webs and result in algal blooms, eutrophication, seasonal oxygen depletion known as hypoxia, which can kill fish and other organisms (Carpenter et al., 1998). Nitrate-N is a drinking water concern when concentrations exceed 10 mg N L^{-1} in water supplies. Microbes can also convert nitrate to nitrous oxide (N_2O), a potent greenhouse gas. Fertilisers also require energy for manufacture, transport and application. Thus, managing agricultural nutrients to optimize their benefits and minimize their harms can promote sustainability by reducing energy use, greenhouse gas emissions and water pollution.

Agricultural Nutrients in the Great Lakes Basin

About 35% of the land in the Great Lakes Basin is devoted to agriculture and most of this agricultural land is concentrated in the southern and eastern portions of the

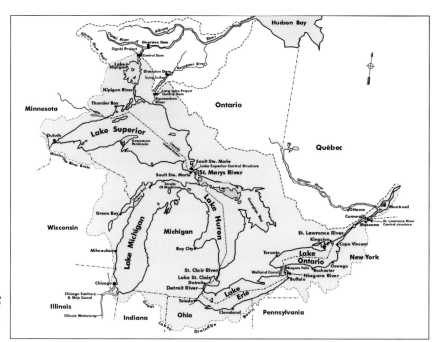

Figure 10.1. Map of the Great Lakes Basin, produced by the US Army Corps of Engineers. http://en.wikipedia.org/wiki/File: Great_lakes_basin.jpg

Basin. Approximately 67% of the Lake Erie Basin is used for agriculture, while 44% of the Lake Michigan Basin, 39% of the Lake Ontario Basin, 27% of the Lake Huron Basin and only 3% of the Lake Superior Basin is classified as agricultural. The effects of agriculture are most pronounced in Lake Erie because of the high percentage of agricultural land in its basin, and because Lake Erie is the smallest of the Great Lakes (Fuller et al.,1995).

Much of the cropland land in the Great Lakes Basin is used for maize and soybean production. Maize requires significant quantities of N and P fertiliser (typically 100-175 kg N ha^{-1} and 20-30 kg P ha^{-1} depending on soil properties and other factors) while soybean require only P fertiliser (typically 20-30 kg P ha^{-1}). N transport from the land to surface waters in agricultural basins ranges from 5 to 40 kg N ha^{-1} yr^{-1}, with the larger values occurring in regions with artificial subsurface (tile) drainage and about 300 mm yr^{-1} of drainage (McIsaac and Hu, 2004). P losses typically range from 0.5 to 2 kg ha^{-1} yr^{-1}. Baker and Richards (2002) reported average values of 1.4 kg P ha^{-1} yr^{-1} during 1975-95 in rivers draining agricultural areas in northwest Ohio and which flow into Lake Erie.

Except for in Lake Erie, P concentrations in the open waters of all the Great Lakes were assessed as being acceptably low in 2007 (Dove and Warren, 2008). However, P concentrations in open waters of Lake Erie and some nearshore waters of all the assessed Lakes periodically exceed concentrations that promote algal growth (nearshore waters of Lake Superior were not assessed). In addition to extensive agricultural land, the Lake Erie Basin has a high population density which is a source of P. Fortunately, P concentrations in Lake Erie and Lake Ontario have declined from the 1970s to the 1990s. A portion of this decline is attributable to the introduction of the invasive and prolific zebra mussel (*Dreissena polymorpha*), which filters large quantities of algae out of the water.

Efforts to reduce P loading into Lake Erie date back to the 1970s and include reduction in point-source discharges (primarily municipal wastewater) as well as agricultural conservation practices (Richards and Baker, 2002). Richards and Baker (2002) reported a significant decline in sediment and P loads in the northwest Ohio Rivers which appeared to be associated with adoption of conservation tillage and decreased application of P fertiliser. Since P tends to be strongly adsorbed to sediment, much of the P carried in surface waters is attached to eroded soils. Reducing soil erosion often reduces total P transport. In spite of this decline, Myers et al., (2000) reported that rivers sampled in the Lake Erie Basin in 1996-98 tended to have P and N concentrations that were greater than the U.S. average. One river draining a forest and pasture land in western New York had an annual average P yield of nearly 3 kg P ha^{-1} yr^{-1}, although observations over a three-year period may not reflect the long-term average.

The adoption of conservation tillage is a national and international trend enabled by the availability of cost effective herbicides. Additionally, reduction in P fertiliser application rate is a trend that has been observed throughout the U.S. (Fixen and West, 2002) and Ontario (International Plant Nutrition Institute 2008). There has been a shift away from applying fertiliser in order to "build" soil P levels in favor of applying fertiliser to replace P removal in crop harvest. Crop yields have increased substantially, while the amount of P fertiliser applied has declined and N fertiliser application has remained constant or increased at a relatively slow rate. This has partly been a result of characteristics of newer maize hybrids which have more robust production under a wider variety of environmental conditions (such as drought) but lower grain protein concentrations (Duvick, 2005). There has been greater attention to development of nutrient management plans for croplands as well as installing and maintaining buffer strips and wetlands adjacent to water bodies. In Ontario, farmers are required to develop nutrient management plans (Roberts et al., 2008). In the U.S., funds are available to provide farmers an incentive for voluntarily adopting recommended nutrient management practices.

While these trends represent steps in the direction of sustainability, there is still need for improvement and the impacts of these trends and activities on water quality are difficult to document quantitatively. There has been little long-term, systematic monitoring of nutrient use on the landscape and riverine flow in tributaries to the Lakes, except at relatively large scales, where it becomes difficult to separate out the effects of agricultural management practices from other influences such as climatic fluctuation, urbanization and changes in municipal waste treatment. Additionally, some changes in agricultural practices may reduce nutrient losses, while other practices may

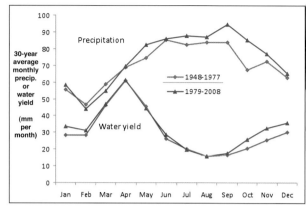

Figure 10.2. Thirty-year average monthly precipitation (top) over the land surface in the Great Lakes Basin and estimated monthly water yields (bottom) from the land surface for 1948-77 and 1979-2008 (Data from NOAA, 2010).

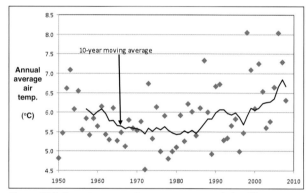

Figure 10.3. Annual average air temperatures and the 10-year moving average over land in the Great Lakes Basin 1950-2008 (Data from NOAA, 2010).

increase losses. Hence, it becomes difficult to quantify the effects of specific practices on nutrient fluxes within large scale basins where multiple changes are occurring simultaneously.

Variations in precipitation and temperature may affect the quantity and timing of N and P transported to surface water and groundwater. Precipitation and water yield from the Great Lakes Basin (and throughout eastern North America) increased in the early 1970s (Figure 10.2). Average air temperatures decreased slightly from 1945 to 1980, and have tended to increase since 1980 (Figure 10.3). Precipitation in many regions of North America follows decadal oscillations that appear to reflect the influence of oscillations in sea surface temperatures (McCabe et al., 2004) and may be additionally influenced by anthropogenic climate change. The increased precipitation in the Great Lakes Basin has been greatest in September and October and this appears to produce increased water yield during the dormant season. This is likely to increase nutrient flows because it occurs at a time of year with little or no vegetative uptake of nutrients. Water yield is greatest in the spring as a consequence of snow melt and soil saturation. Nutrient fluxes are typically greatest during this period, primarily because of the high water flows.

Potential Improvements in Nutrient Management

Synchronizing Nutrient Availability with Crop Needs

To be most efficient and minimize losses to the environment, nutrient availability should be timed to match the nutrient uptake characteristics of the crop. This type of spoon feeding can be accomplished with irrigation, but irrigation is relatively rare in the Great Lakes Basin. There are considerable economic challenges to applying commercial fertilisers to extensive acres of maize and soybean during the growing season. Other field operations (weed control, field preparation and planting) create a high demand for labor during the early growing season. Many farmers apply manure and fertiliser in the fall and winter when there is less demand for labor, and when fertiliser companies offer discounted prices. This practice tends to produce greater nutrient losses, however, because nutrients are exposed to water movement during a greater share of the dormant season and long before crop uptake is possible. In European Union Countries in the Baltic Sea region this practise is not allowed according to the Nitrate Directive.

Under careful management, nutrients derived from the decomposition of organic matter (animal manures, compost, crop residues) may become available to crops in synchrony with crop demands. This can occur because rates of crop growth and microbial decomposition of organic matter vary similarly with temperature and soil moisture. Manures can have a highly variable nutrient composition, however, which adds to the challenge of nutrient management. Analysis of the manure for nutri-

ent composition adds to the cost of its use as a fertiliser. Manures often have a low N to P ratio for crop nutrition, but this ratio can be increased by altering feed rations and using supplements that improve P adsorption by the livestock (Sharpley et al., 2003).

Cover Crops

There has been considerable experimentation with cover crops, i.e. crops grown primarily to provide ground cover during the dormant season. It has been shown that these cover crops can reduce losses of nutrients by their capacity to absorb nutrients and to increase evapotranspiration, and thereby reduce the quantity of drainage, runoff and erosion. Little direct benefit to the grower has been demonstrated, however, and consequently there has been little use of this practice.

Perennial Crops

Because of a long dormant period between annual crops, and because of slow root development early in the growing season, annual crop rotations tend to be more leaky of water and nutrients than systems that include perennial crops (Randall and Mulla, 2001). Many perennial crops can store nutrients in their root systems over winter and usually start growth earlier in the spring and maintain growth later in the fall compared to annual crops. This can reduce drainage, runoff, erosion and nutrient loss.

Limited market demand for perennial crops has been the main limitation to their inclusion in the Great Lakes cropping systems. Organic production systems rely on perennial legumes to fix nitrogen, and although the market for organic foods has been growing it is still a relatively small portion of the world and US food market. If and when the production of energy from biomass becomes more economically attractive, there could be greater use of perennial grasses in agricultural regions of the Great Lakes (Figure 10.4). This could reduce nutrient flows, and may also reduce water flows (McIsaac et al. 2010).

Targeted Conservation

Research has demonstrated that surface runoff may be disproportionately generated from specific areas within a landscape such as areas where bedrock or groundwater is close to the soil surface, thereby limiting the water-holding capacity of the soil profile (Sharpley et al., 2003).

Figure 10.4. *Miscanthus x. giganteus* (taller green grass) and switchgrass (*Panicum virgatum*) growing in experimental plots in central Illinois. These perennial grasses are being evaluated for the production of biomass energy (Photo: L. Brian Stauffer, University of Illinois).

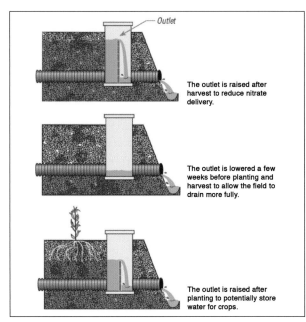

The outlet is raised after harvest to reduce nitrate delivery.

The outlet is lowered a few weeks before planting and harvest to allow the field to drain more fully.

The outlet is raised after planting to potentially store water for crops.

Figure 10.5. The use of a tile drain outlet control structure to manipulate the water table and reduce nitrate delivery to from agricultural fields to surface waters (adapted from Frankenberger et al. 2006).

These areas can produce high quantities of P in runoff if they receive high quantities of P fertiliser or manure. The potential for P losses can be reduced by minimizing P input to these critical areas and maintaining vegetative cover to minimize erosion.

Drainage Water Management

In fields that are naturally flat and swampy, artificial subsurface drainage systems remove water from the root zone and allow for more timely management operations and greater crop growth. This drainage water is typically high in nitrate N where maize and soybean are grown. However, the drainage systems can be managed to manipulate the water-table to promote denitrification during the dormant season and provide irrigation water to the root zone during the growing season (Figure 10.5). The latter practice can increase crop yields and both practices reduce N loss to drainage waters (Elmi et al., 2002). However, by creating reducing conditions in the soil, this practice can mobilize phosphate, which is a more common water quality concern throughout the Great Lakes Basin (Valero et al., 2007).

Conclusions

Agricultural production is highly variable in the Great Lakes Basin and is most heavily concentrated in the Lake Erie Basin, although there are some tributaries to the oth-er Lakes that are also heavily agricultural. N and P are a necessary aspect of agricultural production and drainage waters from agricultural lands are often enriched with these nutrients. Water quality problems from N in the Great Lakes Basin have been limited to a few local water supplies. P concentrations in Lake Erie and in some coastal waters of the other Lakes periodically reach levels that can promote eutrophication. P concentrations in Lakes Erie and Ontario declined between 1970 and 1990, which may be attributable to a variety of factors that include reduced fertiliser P application, conservation tillage, improved municipal waste treatment, and introduction of the zebra mussel. P losses from agriculture are also influenced by precipitation and drainage, which have increased over much of the Basin after 1970. Additional monitoring, research and conservation are needed to further reduce N and P losses from agriculture in areas where these losses cause water quality impairments. Conversion of large areas from maize-soybean production to perennial biomass crops for energy has some potential to reduce P losses from croplands, depending on the practices employed.

Regulations for Protection of Groundwater and Surface Waters in Agricultural Areas

11

CASE STUDY USA

Thomas E. Davenport
US Environmental Protection Agency, Chicago, Illinois, USA

In the US there is no single law that specifically addresses pollution in agricultural areas. In the US, regulations are established to carry out legislation (laws) and guidance is written to help in carrying out and/or complying with regulations and sometimes legislation. Protecting and managing water quality in agricultural areas requires an effective management framework. This framework must be based upon various provisions of Federal and State laws and regulations, and local efforts. However, there are a number of federal laws affecting water quality issues in agricultural areas. The five principal laws are the Clean Water Act (CWA), Safe Drinking Water Act (SDWA), Farm Bill (FB), Coastal Zone Management (CZM) and the Federal Insecticide, Fungicide and Rodenticide Act. Most tools and programs not under direct federal authorization are not uniformly available throughout the Great Lakes Basin under state and local authority.

Federal Programs

CWA, as amended, is the primary law in the United States to protect the quality of water resources (originally named the Water Quality Act of 1965). CWA has been around for over 40 years and has expanded and refocused several times. However, the goal of the Act has remained constant; 'to restore and maintain the chemical, physical, and biological integrity of the Nation's waters and where at-tainable, to achieve a level of water quality that provides for the protection and propagation of fish and shellfish, wildlife, and recreation in and on the water.'

The United States Environmental Protection Agency (EPA) is responsible for carrying out the Act nationwide, States and Tribes can assume authority to manage within their jurisdictions portions of the Act provided they meet the appropriate legal and program criteria. Water quality standards establish the foundation for most activities carried out under the Act. The Water Quality Act of 1965 relied on violations of water quality standards as a basis for pollution control. This approach was not uniformly successful in limiting water pollution, therefore the 1972 amendments (Federal Water Pollution Control Act) established the first comprehensive national framework for improving the quality of the nation's waters. This framework resulted in a dual system being established that consisted of: 1) a technology-based approach that sets national discharge limits on point sources of pollution, and 2) a water quality-based approach that focuses on achieving and maintaining the specific quality of a water body (defined as water quality standards) that supports its designated uses. The water quality-based approach requires a Total Maximum Daily Load plan for managing both point and non-point source pollution (NPS) of pollution for those water bodies not meeting its water quality standards. Generally, States adopt water quality standards to protect the following six standard designated uses of surface water bodies: aquatic life support, fish consumption, primary contact recreation, (e.g. swimming and diving), secondary contact recreation, (e.g. boating), drinking water supply, and agricultural use. At a minimum, a water resource's designated use must include secondary contact and propagation of fish and wildlife (NALMS, 1992).

Clean Water Act

There are two CWA pollution control programs linked to achievement of the management of water quality in agricultural areas. The Federal government established the National Pollutant Discharge Elimination System (NPDES) system to regulate point source discharges. The backbone of the system are permits to regulate the amount and/or concentration of pollutants that can be legally discharged into a water body. These regulatory limits are set for each permit so as not to violate water quality in the receiving water. Section 502(14) of the Act defines point sources to include pipes, ditches and other discernible, confined and discrete conveyance from which pollutants are or may be discharged. Agricultural storm water discharges are explicitly excluded as point sources, except concentrated animal feeding operations (CAFOs). CAFOs are point sources, as defined by the CWA [Section 502(14)], must first be defined as an Animal Feeding Operation (AFO). AFOs are agricultural operations where animals are kept and raised in confined situations.

AFOs generally congregate animals, feed, manure, dead animals, and production operations on a small land area. Feed is brought to the animals rather than the animals grazing or otherwise seeking feed in pastures. Animal waste and wastewater can enter water bodies from spills or breaks of waste storage structures (due to accidents or excessive rain), and non-agricultural application of manure to crop land.

An AFO is a lot or facility (other than an aquatic animal production facility) where the following conditions are met:

- Animals have been, are, or will be stabled or confined and fed or maintained for a total of 45 days or more in any 12-month period, and
- Crops, vegetation, forage growth, or post-harvest residues are not sustained in the normal growing season over any portion of the lot or facility.

AFOs that meet the regulatory definition of a CAFO may be regulated under the NPDES permitting program. Previous EPA regulations based the definition of CAFOs on the number of 'animal units' confined. EPA no longer uses the term 'animal unit,' but instead refers to the actual number of animals at the operation to define a CAFO. See the summary in Table 11.1.

A Large CAFO confines at least the number of animals described in the table below. A Medium CAFO falls within the size range in the table below and either:

- has a manmade ditch or pipe that carries manure or wastewater to surface water; or
- the animals come into contact with surface water that passes through the area where they are confined.

If an operation is found to be a significant contributor of pollutants, the permitting authority may designate a medium-sized facility as a CAFO.

A Small CAFO confines fewer than the number of animals listed in Table 11.1 and has been designated as a CAFO by the permitting authority as a significant contributor of pollutants.

Considerable progress has been made in remediating and preventing point source discharges. However, after three decades of increasingly stringent controls on point source discharges, much of the remaining pollution impacting water quality comes from NPSs.

The 1987 amendments to the Act established the first comprehensive national NPS pollution program. NPSs are defined as water pollution sources not meeting the definition of a point source. NPSs are generally episodic in nature, originating from diffuse sources at divergent locations making them inherently difficult to measure and manage. NPSs are not regulated at the Federal level nor are they traditionally regulated at the State and local level. The 1987 amendment (Section 319) required States to develop a NPS Assessment Report that documents the type of NPSs and locations that were threatening, or causing, water quality problems, or impairing uses. Based upon the Assessment Report findings, States were to develop a comprehensive management program to address the problems identified and prevent future problems. When the EPA approves both the assessment report and the management program (or portions of) the State is eli-

Table 11.1. Regulatory definitions of Large, Medium and Small CAFOs.

Animal Sector	Size Thresholds (number of animals)		
	Small CAFOs[2]	Medium CAFOs[1]	Large CAFOs
Cattle or cow/calf pairs	less than 300	300-999	1,000 or more
Nature dairy cattle	less than 200	200-699	700 or more
Veal calves	less than 300	300-999	1,000 or more
Swine (weighing over 55 pounds)	less than 750	750-2,499	2,500 or more
Swine (weighing less than 55 pounds)	less than 3,000	3,000-9,999	10,000 or more
Horses	less than 150	150-499	500 or more
Sheep or lambs	less than 3,000	3,000-9,999	10,000 or more
Turkeys	less than 16,500	16,500-54,999	55,000 or more
Laying hens or broilers (liquid manure handling systems)	less than 9,000	9,000-29,999	30,000 or more
Chickens other than laying hens (other than liquid manure handling systems)	less than 37,500	37,500-124,999	125,000 or more
Laying hens (other than liquid manure handling systems)	less than 25,000	25,000-81,999	82,000 or more
Ducks (other than liquid manure handling systems)	less than 10,000	10,000-29,999	30,000 or more
Ducks (liquid manure handling systems)	less than 1,500	1,500-4,999	5,000 or more

[1] Must also meet one or two "method of discharge" criteria to be defined as a CAFO or may be designated.
[2] Never a CAFO by regulatory definition, but may be designated as a CAFO on a case-by case basis.

gible for financial assistance to implement the approved portions of the management program. Specifically, State management programs were required to include, as a minimum, six components to be approved by EPA.

Two components are extremely important for managing water quality in agricultural area lake management. These are:

1) Identification of best management practices and measures that will be undertaken to reduce NPS loadings (taking into impacts on ground water).
2) Identification of programs (including, as appropriate, non-regulatory or regulatory programs for enforcement, technical assistance, financial assistance, education, training, technology transfer, and demonstration projects) to achieve implementation of the best management practices (Section 319(b)).

Section 319 did not establish a permit program or numerical discharge requirements applicable to NPSs. The basic mechanism for controlling NPS pollution is a voluntary incentive-driven process to implement best management practices jurisdiction-wide, or on a watershed basis.

If management efforts are not sufficient to achieve and maintain water quality standards in a particular wa-ter body, the Act provides for the States to impose more stringent requirements on the discharger, based on the approved Total Maximum Daily Load (TMDL) for that water body. The TMDL for a particular pollutant is the sum of the point source loadings, NPS loadings, background loadings and a margin of safety that allows for the water quality standards in a water body to be met. As appropriate, the implementation of the TMDL is to include both point sources and NPS measures and actions. Depending upon the pollutant, one of the most efficient ways to implement a TMDL is through what is known as the Watershed Approach. In short, the Watershed Approach is designed to effectively implement control and restoration actions that mitigate or eliminate specific problems not otherwise addressed by the Clean Water Act. Because watersheds are the hydrological units through which our surface waters flow, there are several linkages among water quality/ habitat conditions, problems, and solutions.

The Watershed Approach (Terrene, 1996) is flexible and geographically customized; consequently there is no single definition that encompasses all the programs and activities that it can include. Since it is an approach or a general strategy, it is best defined by describing the common steps for successful watershed management that it contains. For the watershed approach to be successful, there needs to be active local involvement; opportunities for participation by all 'stakeholders' who may be interested in, or affected by, decisions about the water resources; an active effort to engage the public to participate at all stages, throughout the watershed management process; and an effective project manager. The typical steps in watershed management are:

- Collecting and evaluating information to characterize the existing condition of the water resources in the watershed.
- Identifying key issues and problems associated with the area's water resource.
- Setting goals for the watershed's aquatic resources.
- Identifying alternative ways to meet watershed goals; assessing the advantages and disadvantages of each; selecting the optimal alternatives; and developing an action-oriented implementation plan
- Putting the plan in place; monitoring its implementation; and making adjustments as lessons are learned.

With a targeted geographic focus, watershed management enables an efficient concentration of scare resources that then builds upon the foundation of protection provided by the regulatory point source programs and undertakes additional actions (controls & restoration) to address specific problems in each watershed.

The four principles that provided the foundation for the Clean Lakes Program (U.S. EPA, 1993) have been embedded in many new initiatives (e.g.: Watershed Approach, community based environmental protection) and programs (e.g. NPS Program, National Estuary Program).

Safe Drinking Water Act

Many water bodies in the US are designated as public drinking water supplies. The Safe Drinking Water Act (SWDA) delegates the EPA authority to establish and enforce standards for protection of drinking water supplies. Regulations addressing nitrates and turbidity have been promulgated by EPA under this authority. SDWA regulations are geared toward ensuring that the public receives safe drinking water. With this focus, SDWA regulations have concentrated on what remains in the water after it has undergone treatment and is ready for distribution to the general public, rather than on what pollutants and

in what quantity may be present prior to treatment. The 1996 SDWA amendments introduced provisions addressing source protection. Source Water Protection is a community-based approach to protecting sources of drinking water contamination. The approach is based on three principles' commonly known as the '**Three R's**':

- 'Restore the public's right and responsibility to protect their drinking water and their health through community-based pollution prevention efforts and by that:
- Raise public confidence in their drinking water supply; and
- Reduce the costs of providing safe drinking water – essential to a community's sustainable development' (U.S. EPA, 1995).

Source water protection needs to be viewed as the SDWA counterpart to watershed management to achieve Clean Water Act objectives. EPA and the States are just beginning to put in place the guidance and programs to carry out the source water provisions of the 1996 amendments. In Ohio they are developing joint watershed management plans and source water protection plans so the management of pollution and source water protection is a comprehensive approach for managing drinking water on a watershed basis.

Federal Insecticide, Fungicide and Rodenticide Act

In October 1991, EPA published the *Pesticides and Ground Water Strategy*. This strategy provides a basis for Pesticides and Ground Water Management Plans (PMP). Because of the diverse, localized nature of water quality, states are in a better position to manage pesticides to maintain groundwater quality than a national pesticide label program.

The state lead agency for pesticides has been designated by the EPA to coordinate the development and implementation of PMPs. PMPs are for the entire state and require input from and cooperation with other state, federal, and local agencies, and private organizations. There are two types of PMPs: generic and pesticide-specific. Generic PMPs are voluntary. They are considered a blueprint for developing pesticide-specific PMPs. Generic PMPs have no regulatory authority. Pesticide-specific

PMPs can only be required by developing and publishing federal regulations in the Federal Register. Pesticide-specific PMPs affect how a pesticide is used. If the EPA determines a pesticide requires more management, states are required to develop a pesticide-specific PMP or lose use of the pesticide in their state.

Both the generic and specific PMPs contain twelve components. They are:

1. The state's philosophy and goals.
2. Roles and responsibilities of state agencies.
3. Legal authority.
4. Resources.
5. Basis for assessment and planning.
6. Monitoring.
7. Preventative actions.
8. Response to detections.
9. Enforcement mechanisms.
10. Public awareness and participation.
11. Information dissemination.
12. Records and reporting.

In June 1996, EPA published the proposed PMP rule in the *Federal Register*. The proposed rule lists atrazine, alachlor, metolachlor, simazine and cyanazine as the first five pesticides that will require PMPs. Due to the agreement to withdraw the cyanazine registration, cyanazine was dropped from the final rule. The final rule was issued in 2000.

Coastal Zone Management Act

The Coastal Nonpoint Pollution Control Program falls under Section 6217 of the Coastal Zone Act Reauthorization Amendments (CZARA). The Program is unique in that it establishes a set of management measures for states to use in controlling polluted runoff and is jointly administered by EPA and NOAA. The measures are designed to control runoff from six main sources including agriculture. These measures are backed by enforceable state policies and actions – state authorities that will ensure implementation of the program. All Great Lakes States (except Illinois) participating in the Coastal Zone Management Program are required to develop coastal nonpoint pollution control programs. The Coastal Nonpoint Program focuses on pollution prevention, minimizing the creation of polluted runoff rather than cleaning up already contaminated water – a very difficult and expensive process. The program encourages pollution prevention efforts at a local level, particularly improvements to land use planning and zoning practices to protect coastal water quality.

Farm Bill

The United States Department of Agriculture (USDA) is the other leading federal agency with water clean-up programs in agricultural areas. USDA's Natural Resources Conservation Service (NRCS) allocates technical and financial assistance to private landowners and farmers to implement conservation practices that can protect and/or improve water quality through five programs. The Environmental Quality Incentive Program (EQIP) promotes over 200 conservation practices with cost-sharing and incentive payments. The Conservation Stewardship Program (CSP) provides financial rewards to farmers and landowners for the environmental benefits their conservation efforts provide. The Wetland Reserve Program (WRP) provides technical and financial assistance to farmers and landowners to restore non-tidal wetlands. WRP also provides funding to farmers to restore and/or enhance wetlands on agricultural lands for the length of 5-15 years or as a permanent easement. NRCS through the Wildlife Habitat Incentives Program (WHIP) provides technical and financial assistance to farmers to convert land or improve land to develop high-quality wildlife habitats on their property. The Farmland Protection Program (FPP) helps farmers and ranchers keep their land in agriculture through the purchase of other interests. The remaining two USDA Programs are the Conservation Reserve Program (CRP) and the Conservation Reserve Enhancement Program (CREP) under the Farm Services Agency (FSA), which encourage farmers to convert environmentally sensitive farmland to vegetative cover through annual rental payments.

With the exception of CREP and CSP, these USDA programs provide farmers and landowners with piecemeal assistance rather than integrated environmental management plans for their agricultural operations. Additionally, USDA is institutionally constrained by law, regulation and guidance to implement its programs from the perspective of individual producer on a discrete piece of land – so it means funds are not targeted and made available on a first come, first served basis for those farmers and landowners that meet the eligibility requirements. The majority funding is contained within the EQIP, WRP, CRP and CREP.

State and Local Efforts

As noted earlier, the key to effective water quality management, protection and restoration is the establishment of a management framework that combines State and local authorities and programs in a comprehensive approach. The management framework must include natural resource management programs besides the water quality programs mentioned earlier. The greatest strength and simultaneously the greatest weakness are local ordinances and zoning. Local support and involvement are some of the keys to effective water quality management. Land use decisions are primarily made at the local level by a combination of elected, appointed, and volunteer officials serving on land use commissions such as planning and zoning. The strength of the approach is locals solving their own problems for the good of the community, its weakness is one vote and it can all be undone. In agricultural areas, zoning is the principal tool locals use to manage the location of production facilities and animal feeding operations. The Terrene Institute (1995) provides excellent examples of what needs to be in an ordinance to make it work. Public education provides the foundation for local support and leadership in using zoning tools. In addition to zoning, some States and locals have:

- Nutrient management laws (including banning use of phosphorus).
- Abatement and corrective action orders for farming operations.
- Erosion and sediment controls (based soil loss tolerance limits).
- More stringent pollutant discharge controls for permitted facilities (siting laws for animal operations).
- Nuisance and misdemeanour laws (location to schools, etc.).

Conclusions

The EPA and USDA Programs provide limited funding and direction to States and locals to manage, restore and protect water quality in agricultural areas. These largely voluntary programs do not go far enough in themselves to solve and prevent agricultural water quality problems. Local leadership and programs are needed to ensure the resources are there to manage agricultural production while ensuring water quality.

Soil Sulphur Problems and Management

12

CASE STUDY
Lithuania

Audrone Mašauskiene and Vytas Mašauskas
Lithuanian Institute of Agriculture, Akademija, Lithuania

Relevance of the Subject

A problem which has emerged in modern plant production and requires new scientific solutions is the decrease in sulphur in the soils of most European countries during the last 20-30 years. According to the predictions of scientists from the USA Sulphur Institute, the deficit of sulphur as a nutritional element will have increased to over 11 million tonnes worldwide by 2010 (Zhao et al., 2003). Problems with the sulphur nutrition of agricultural plants have also been observed in Lithuania and are associated with a decrease in sulphur in atmospheric pollution, as the average concentration of sulphates in precipitation has decreased more than by half (Kairiūkštis and Rudzikas, 1999). At the same time, fertilisers containing less sulphur are being used. As a result, less sulphur reaches the soil (Velička et al., 2001). An increase in crop yields in agriculture leads to increased uptake of plant nutrients, including sulphur. In recent years in Lithuania, there has been a considerable increase in the area covered by winter and spring rapeseed crops, which have a high demand for sulphur for growth. The area cropped with rapeseed in 2007 had doubled from 60,000 ha in 2002 and has a tendency to increase in the future. Rapeseed occupies 10.1% of arable land and is one of the most promising oilseed crops in Lithuania (Lietuvos žemės ir maisto ūkis, 2008). Currently, rapeseed is used for vegetable and engine oil, an ecologically clean fuel. Conditions for spring rapeseed growing in Lithuania are favourable because of the suitable texture of many soils, and a sufficient amount of moisture and warmth. Spring rapeseed can tolerate a moderate soil acidity and can therefore be cultivated not only on heavy, but also on light soils (Velička, 2002; Šidlauskas and Bernotas, 2003).

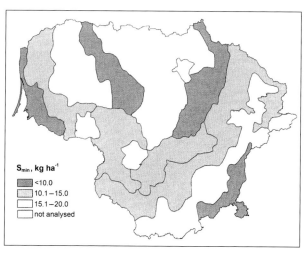

Figure 12.1. Available sulphur content in 0-60 cm layer in Lithuania's soil at spring-time in year 2008. The soils of very low (<10.0 kg ha-1), low (10.1-15.0 kg ha-1) and moderate (15.1-20.0 kg ha-1) content of sulphur prevailed (Staugaitis et al., 2009).

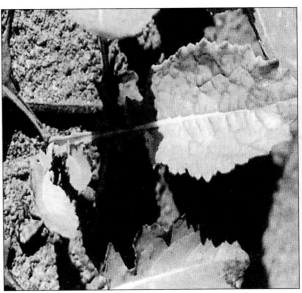

Figure 12.2. The symptoms of sulphur shortage for winter wheat and winter rape are similar to that of nitrogen shortage - yellowish leaves.

Sulphur Contents in Soil

In Lithuania, 45.4% of soils are very low and low (content of mobile sulphur less than 6.0 mg kg^{-1}) in mobile sulphur (S-SO$_4$ determined in 1 M KCl extract turbidimetrically). There are moderate contents of sulphur (6.1-12.0 mg kg^{-1}) on 33.2% of soils and sufficient contents (more than 12.0 mg kg^{-1}) on 21.4% (Mažvila, 1998). Regular application of sulphur-containing fertilisers has a significant effect on sulphur content in the 0-20, 21-40, 41-60 and 61-90 cm layer of soils. When mineral fertilisers were applied in four crop rotations (winter wheat, sugar beet, spring barley and perennial grasses) in the period 1976-2005 at annual rates of 96 kg ha^{-1} P$_2$O$_5$ (simple superphosphate, which contains gypsum – 13% of sulphur), 96-192 kg ha^{-1} K$_2$O and 114-228 kg ha^{-1} N, the content of mobile sulphur in the 0-90 cm soil layer increased by on average 9.7 mg kg^{-1} (5.8-fold) (Mažvila et al., 2007). The content of sulphur in the soil depends on the sequence of crops in the crop rotation. A higher content of mobile sulphur (22.0 mg kg^{-1}) was determined when spring or winter rapeseed was cultivated three years in a row (75% rapeseed in the crop rotation), compared with 17.9 mg kg^{-1} of mobile sulphur when rapeseed occupied 25% of the crop rotation

(Velička et al., 2001). The content of mobile sulphur in soil before these trials was low (5.6 mg kg^{-1}) and sulphur was released from gypsum (single superphosphate was applied) and from the soil organic material. After the first four-year rotation, the humus content in soil decreased by 10-16% and the content of total sulphur tended to decrease by 10-27%.

Effect on Crop Yield

A positive effect of sulphur on crop yield was revealed in long-term investigations. A single superphosphate was used as a source of sulphur during 1971-2004. The effect of gypsum containing single superphosphate was compared with that of ammonium phosphate (ammophos). The yield of potato tubers and spring barley grain increased when sulphur was applied at a rate of S 23-35 kg ha^{-1} as gypsum together with single superphosphate annually on NPK background, but the effect of sulphur on yield of red clover and winter wheat was insignificant (Mašauskas and Mašauskienė, 2005). The data indicating that sulphur effects on wheat grain yield are minor and

Table 12.1. Effect of mineral fertilisation on the concentration of sulphates in lysimeter water over different periods. Lithuania, LIA (Mažvila et al., 2007).

Fertiliser	rate kg ha^{-1}		1976-1985	1976-1995	1976-2005 (n 671)
N	P_2O_5 (single superphosphate)	K_2O	SO_4^{2-} mg l^{-1}	In lysimeter water	
			At 40 cm depth		
0	0	0	53±30	39±25	39±20
0	96	96	199±120	128±94	134±90
114	0	96	52±29	44±24	33±16
114	96	0	252±88	167±110	176±103
114	96	96	128±76	115±62	129±67
0	192	192	213±106	202±100	232±125
228	0	192	53±29	36±23	34±16
228	192	0	194±131	198±119	235±110
228	192	192	224±151	212±118	222±115
				At 80 cm depth	
0	0	0	67±28	45±27	43±19
114	96	96	127±64	115±52	130±64
0	192	192	300±131	293±118	291±117
228	192	192	178±81	218±100	223±102

are in good agreement with the results of trials conducted in 2003-2005 (Šiaudinis, 2007). The experiments were performed in soil which according to the classification used in Lithuania was sufficient in total, but low in mobile sulphur. Despite the low content of mobile sulphur in the soil, spring wheat did not show any sulphur deficiency – the measured sulphur concentrations in plants at different growth stages were higher than critical values mentioned in the literature (Spencer and Freney, 1980). Therefore the influence of 15 and 30 kg ha^{-1} sulphur (S) applied as potassium sulphate on top of NPK (40 kg ha^{-1} of P_2O_5, 100 kg ha^{-1} K_2O and 90-150 kg ha^{-1} N) for wheat grain yield was insignificant. However the moderate rate (20 kg ha^{-1}) of sulphur significantly increased the number of pods per spring rapeseed plant, number of secondary branches and rape seed yield. However, the N/S ratio in rape seeds varied from 7.67 to 9.61 and exceeded the critical (10/1) value (Šiaudinis, 2007).

New nitrogen fertilisers which contain natural sulphur minerals have been developed. Their effect is 0.53-0.55 t ha^{-1} for winter wheat (at a total 7-8 t ha^{-1} grain yield on Cambisols), 0.03-0.05 t ha^{-1} for spring rapeseed (at total rapeseed yield of 2 t ha^{-1}on Albeluvisols), and 3.8-4.2 t ha^{-1} for potato tubers (at 40-50 t ha^{-1} tuber yield on Luvisols) compared with the effect of nitrogen fertiliser without sulphur (Mažeika et al., 2008).

Uptake and Leaching

In recent trials, sulphur (S) uptake per hectare by plant production was found to be 30.9 kg for sugar beet roots, 16.5 kg for annual grasses, 14.9 kg for spring barley and 12.3 kg for winter wheat grain (Mažvila et al., 2007). The uptake by rapeseed was much more – 60-80 kg ha^{-1} for 2-3 t ha^{-1} seed production. Therefore in soil where rapeseed was a pre-crop, shortage of sulphur for other crops in the rotation markedly increased.

The essential source of sulphur losses is leaching. The amount of leached sulphur ranged from 33.1-202.9 kg ha^{-1} and depended on weather conditions and management (Tyla et al., 1997). Up to 80% of sulphur is leached over the warm growth period. Long-term experiments conducted on sandy and silty loam Cambisol soils showed that the variation in amount of leached sulphur was high and was influenced by the fertilisation, crop type and meteorological conditions. The average concentration of sulphates in lysimeter water at 40 cm depth amounted to

39-53 mg l^{-1} in plots where mineral fertilisers were not applied and to 115-252 mg l^{-1} in fertilised plots (Table 12.1) (Mažvila et al., 2007). However in a few cases the concentration at 40 cm depth was up to 133 mg l^{-1} when no fertilisers were applied and up to 288 and 507 mg l^{-1} when fertiliser in doses of $N_{114}P_{96}K_{96}$ and $N_{228}P_{192}K_{192}$ were applied, respectively. Sulphur leaching was closely related to the single superphosphate rate and thus to the sulphur rate. At the end of a 35-year period (1976-2005) the concentration of SO_4 in lysimeter water at 40 cm depth was 176 mg l^{-1} when P_{96} of single superphosphate (with 56 kg of pure S in gypsum) was applied annually to crops in a rotation of winter wheat-sugar beet-spring barley-annual grasses, and 235 mg l^{-1} when P_{192} was applied. Based on the average data for 1976-2005, it was concluded that crop fertilisation with 96 kg ha^{-1} resulted in a 95 mg l^{-1} increase in sulphate concentration in lysimetric water to a level of 176 mg l^{-1}, while 192 kg ha^{-1} phosphorus fertilisation rate resulted in a 189 mg l^{-1} increase to a level of 235 mg l^{-1}.

Although a lot of research has been done at a global scale, the optimal rate between nitrogen and sulphur has still not been finally estimated, since the potential of cultivars is changing as well as cultivation management and environmental conditions. The phenomenon is that much more sulphur is leached when the cropping system is extensive. For example, the five-year average amount of leached SO_4 with drainage water was 554 kg ha^{-1} per season in organic cropping systems and 349 kg ha^{-1} of SO_4 in intensive systems (Gužys, 2001). This could be related to the evidence that lack of sulphur in the environment is caused by slower nitrate reduction and utilisation. Correlation analyses show the dependency of nutrient leaching on crop yield, with the amount of the leached elements increasing when crop yield decreases. Application of fertiliser to soils is required for economically viable plant production, although leaching of elements contributes to eutrophication of streams and lakes. However, decreasing the inputs of fertilisers will not automatically result in decreasing nutrient losses (Šileika et al., 2003), so sulphur leaching is not possible to predict if good agricultural practice is maintained. The management measures implemented to reduce levels of leached elements in drainage water and groundwater must include balanced fertilisation required for target yield, taking ac-

count of sulphur. An increasing proportion of grasses on arable land can also decrease sulphur leaching.

Soil Potassium Problems and Management

13

CASE STUDY
Lithuania

Audrone Mašauskiene and Vytas Mašauskas

Lithuanian Institute of Agriculture, Akademija, Lithuania

Relevance of the Subject

Lithuania is located in the vulnerable Baltic Sea drainage basin. This is important for people involved in research, farming, trade and monitoring of the environment. Farmers face a highly competitive global market. In order to survive in such a situation, farm production has to be cost/price driven. Average fertiliser use efficiency is estimated to be 20-50% for NPK fertilisers. Compared with the effect on plant productivity of nitrogen fertilisers, the effectiveness of potassium is relatively low. Therefore farmers pay less attention to the proper application of potassium fertiliser and the potassium balance mostly tends to be in deep deficit. Data on soil surface and farm gate nutrient balances (NPK) from representative farms in Central and Eastern Europe monitored through the years 1999 and 2000 show surpluses of nitrogen and deficits of potassium for most countries (Bujnovsky and Igras, 2001). The deficits in soil surface balances were explained by fertiliser consumption and by the intensity of plant and animal production expressed in cereal units and animal units per hectare of agricultural land.

Content in Soil

In 1995-2005, the area of soils with sufficient and high contents of available potassium was higher than in 1985-1990 (Table 13.1).

Inorganic potassium fertilisers containing K_{60-90} (potassium calculated as K_2O) accounted for 37.8-50.4% of the potassium removed with the harvested crop. In an experiment on light loam soils with moderate potassium content, soil testing indicated that for over 24 years the soil remained within the same testing group (Mašauskas and Mašauskiene, 2006). Over that time period, potassium could have been released from the interlayers of micas. The content of available potassium in soil increased when K_{90} and large rates were used in long-term experi-

Table 13.1. Quantity (%) of soils according to available potassium (K_2O by A-L method) content.

Years	Investigated area	Very low (lower than 50 mg kg⁻¹)	Low (51-100 mg kg⁻¹)	Moderate (101-150 mg kg⁻¹)	Sufficient (151-200 mg kg⁻¹)	High (more than 150 mg kg⁻¹)
	ha	%				
1985-1990	636,702	6.2	32.2	33.7	18.0	9.9
1995-2005	625,368	2.2	15.2	38.7	26.1	17.8

ments. The fertilisation systems that are effective for crop yield did not secure any positive changes in available potassium content in the soil, since crops removing large amounts of potassium, especially with by-products, had been grown (Mažvila et al., 2007; Maikštėnienė et al., 2008). Investigations revealed that the negative balance of potassium led to exhaustion of the soil potassium reserves, although soil testing showed only a slight decrease.

Comparison of Available K Analysis Methods

The most suitable analytical method for measuring available potassium in soil differs between countries as a result of soil type. Lithuanian soils were formed during the last ice age from glacial deposits, which covered the territory to different thickness and were later affected by various soil formation factors. Therefore the types and properties of soils differ in different areas. The greatest amount of acidic soils is in Western Lithuania, where the carbonated layer is deeper than in Eastern Lithuania. From 1961, the Egner-Riehm method was used for soil testing but this method was inadequate for acidic soils. Therefore in 1970 the Egner-Riehm-Domingo (A-L) method, which is suitable for a range of soils, was adopted. For measuring available potassium in soils of moraine, fluvial and glacial lacustrine origin, the A-L extract method should be used, although extraction with $CaCl_2$ 0.01M and $MgSO_4$ (0.03%) can also be used. The concentration of available potassium in all these extracts has been found to be well correlated with the crop yield increase obtained due to potassium fertilisation (Mažvila et al., 2004).

Leaching

Run-off of drainage water and migration of elements and matter depends on the amount of precipitation and cropping intensity. However, the results of a comparison of organic and intensive cropping systems showed that cropping intensity had no influence on potassium concentration in drainage and groundwater (Gužys, 2001). The balance of potassium in both cropping systems was negative and the average amounts of K^+ leached were 3.5-3.8 kg

Table 13.2. Content of available potassium and crop yield (Matusevičius 2005).

Content of available potassium in arable layer	Very low	Low	Moderate	Sufficient	High
The extra grain yield for 1 kg K_2O	3.5 kg	2.8 kg	1.4 kg	0.6 kg	0.0 kg

ha^{-1}. The fluctuation from year to year was 0.5-7.5 kg ha^{-1}. The amounts of leached potassium depend on the yield obtained, with leaching decreasing as yield increases.

Potassium Uptake and Effect on Crop Yield

The yield of crops is likely to increase and potassium (K_2O) uptake in 2010 could be as follows: for cereals 95-110 kg ha^{-1} (yield 4.6-5.0 t ha^{-1}), for sugar beet 240 kg ha^{-1} (yield 48 t ha^{-1}), for potato tubers 180 kg ha^{-1} (yield 30 t ha^{-1}). Per kg of K_2O applied, the extra grain yield (kg) obtained is described in Table 13.2 (Matusevičius, 2005).

Manure is an important source of soil nutrients, including potassium, but the amount of manure used on conventional farms in Lithuania is only 6.09 t ha^{-1}. Therefore mineral potassium fertilisers have been applied, despite their effectiveness on Lithuanian soils being only moderate. Moderate rates of fertilisers, including K_{70} and K_{36}, increased the yield of metabolisable energy by 31% in a six-crop rotation on soils of high fertility (217 mg kg^{-1} of A-L K_2O) and by 29% on soils of moderate fertility (131 mg kg^{-1} of A-L K_2O) (Feizienė et. al., 2007). This led to the conclusion that the effect of potassium fertilisers is moderate. Therefore it is recommended to recalculate potassium fertiliser rates according to potassium uptake by the coefficients described in Table 13.3.

Table 13.3. Recalculation rates of potassium fertilisers (Šileika, 2001).

Content of available potassium in arable layer	Very low	Low	Moderate	Sufficient	High
Coefficient for recalculation of K rates	1.3	1.2	1.0	0.8	0.5

Positive effects of mineral fertilisers are more evident for new crop varieties compared with older varieties (Mažvila et al., 2007). A previous attitude on safe fertilisation requirements prevalent in Lithuania was that the application of mineral PK fertilisers is necessary only if soil potassium (K_2O) and phosphorus (P_2O_5) level is below 150 mg kg[-1]. Nowadays fertilisation recommendations suggest using fertiliser rates according to the expected yield, while paying attention to plant uptake and to soil properties.

Reduced Input of Nutrients on Farms

14

Stefan Bäckman
University of Helsinki, Finland.

Efficiency is a relative measure of performance between farms or within the same farm over time. Considering all elements of production, the measure refers to technical efficiency. It is important to distinguish between productivity and efficiency, since if a farm is productive then it is also technically efficient but not necessarily economically efficient, as this depends on prices. To be efficient the farm does not need to be at maximum production, since the intensity and scale of the business also plays an important role. In an environmental sense, productivity and input-specific efficiency are both crucial measures. From a nutrient point of view farms should have as high productivity as possible. It is also important to realise that high productivity is not equivalent to high intensity. Although this all sounds confusing, the elements can be clarified in a diagram (Figure 14.1).

The system boundary is the extreme observation. Typically the boundary is determined by parametric or non-parametric econometric methods such as stochastic boundary or data envelopment analysis. The relative efficiency value of the observations can vary between one and zero, with one indicating technical efficiency (TE) or simply that the observation is on the boundary. Low TE values indicate that the relationship between outputs and inputs is worse than on other farms or in other years, indicating either too high inputs or too low outputs. Moving vertically in the diagram gives increasing technical efficiency and moving

horizontally gives increasing input-specific efficiency, or environmental efficiency as it is also called.

When it comes to actually measuring efficiency and productivity, we often have to rely on farm accountancy data or experimental data. The benefit of farm accountancy data is that the economic activities are all handled similarly. However production possibilities, e.g. soil types, are not distinguished from management. The benefit of experimental data is that it eliminates the management component, as well as including a range of intensities for the same type of production.

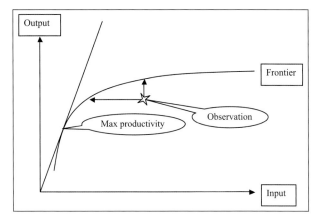

Figure 14.1. Relation between productivity and efficiency (Coelli et al., 1999).

Nutrient management is important for productivity, since appropriate fertilisation of crops increases output considerably. The use of crop protection chemicals also increases the uptake of nutrients that will end up as outputs. Clearly the maximum biological output is not the same as the highest productivity. In most cases the intensity of nutrient use has the following sequence: the biological maximum requires the highest amounts of inputs, then follows the economically efficient production level, which is dependent on prices and is close to the economic optimum and thereafter the level of input that is at the most productive level. Reducing inputs even further decreases output even more and therefore productivity. The environmental efficiency or the input specific efficiency might be anywhere on the boundary but on average is probably close to the most productive output level.

In a study by Bäckman (2008), livestock density was shown to increase technical efficiency using results based on aggregation of products with 2004 prices (Increased cereal prices in relation to intermediates could change this interdependency since the competitiveness of self-sufficient farms would increase). However, this increased efficiency is associated with an increase in nutrient management problems. Having high livestock units per hectare (LU/ha) creates a need to export fertilisers (manure) from farms. In cases with regionally intensive livestock production there is a need to process organic fertilisers. In Sweden, for example, there is a LU/ha density upper limit, while in organic farming there is an indirect livestock density restriction in that only a certain degree of feed is allowed to be imported to livestock production on the farm.

Part C

Recycling of Nutrients

Authors: Ann Albihn, Tujana Burkhieva, Albert E. Cox, Bettina Eichler Löbermann, Thomas C. Granato, Christine Jakobsson, Allan Kaasik, Louis Kollias, Julia Nikulina, Karin Nyberg, Jakob Ottoson, Ola Palm, Mikhail Ponomarev, Staffan Steineck, Vladimir Surovtsev and Björn Vinnerås

Coordinating Author: Christine Jakobsson

Management of Manure on the Farm

One of the Keys to the Future

15

Christine Jakobsson
Uppsala University, Uppsala, Sweden

Staffan Steineck
previously Swedish University of Agricultural Scieces and JTI, Uppsala, Sweden

Economy and the Environment

The economy of the farm is very important. One resource that is always available on animal farms and that can be utilised more or less well is manure/slurry/urine. Another factor of great importance for the future of agriculture on the farm is the environmental status of the farm. In the concept environmental status, serious problems can be included such as elevated levels of nitrate in the groundwater which renders the water non-drinkable for people and animals on the farm, pesticide residues in the groundwater, elevated levels of heavy metals or radioactive isotopes or unwanted waste substances in the soil that can affect the quality of the agricultural produce from the farm.

Manure

Manure is the common name for faeces, urine, bedding, spilt feed and water from various sources. The latter includes precipitation during storage and water from leaking water cups, washing of animal houses and equipment, etc. Manure is either handled and stored as solid farmyard manure (FYM), semi-solid manure or slurry according to the dry matter content (Figure 15.1). Poultry manure differs from other types as it can only be heaped if the dry matter content exceeds 25%. The type of bedding also influences the properties of the manure. If finely chopped straw is used instead of longer straw, manure can retain semi-solid properties even when the dry matter content is above 20%.

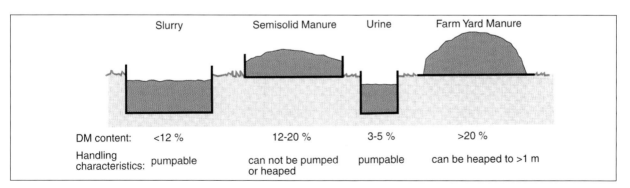

Figure 15.1. Types of manure, dry matter content and handling characteristics. Deep straw litter has a dry matter content of >25% and can be stacked >1.5 metres.

Plant Nutrient Content in Manure

As it is important to know the approximate amounts of nutrients in manure in order to use it efficiently as a fertiliser and not risk polluting the environment, the nitrogen (Total-N and NH_4-N), phosphorus and potassium contents can be calculated using norms. This involves step-by-step calculation of:

- Gross nitrogen, phosphorus and potassium content in the manure.
- The amount of plant nutrients which are added to the soil after losses during handling.
- The amount of manure produced.
- The storage requirements.

The norms for the gross plant nutrient content and manure produced account for the per animal or per pen place production over a period of 12 months. By multiplying the norms by the correct number of animals or pen places and the occupation coefficient, the number or pen places used and for how long, the amount of nitrogen, phosphorus and potassium produced is calculated as well as the amount of manure.

Total-N is included mainly to be able to follow the situation of a specific field over time. The amounts of phosphorus and potassium do not need to be reduced due to storage and handling, as long as these take place according to acceptable standards. The gross amount of nitrogen must be reduced to account for losses during storage and handling.

The individual farm can calculate with this method:

- The total annual nitrogen, phosphorus and potassium available.
- The amounts of these nutrients which are added to the soil corrected for losses according to the farm's storage and handling method.
- The amount of manure to be stored and spread.

On a farm with slurry it is easier to determine the annual amount of manure and the nitrogen content at spreading through chemical analysis. However, the amount of nitrogen left for the crop must be reduced by a factor in order to account for spreading losses.

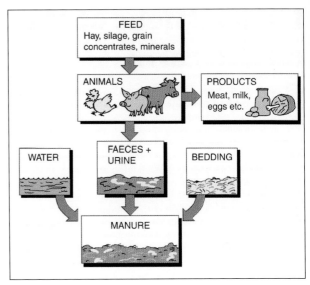

Figure 15.2. Principles for determining the plant nutrient content in manure via the plant nutrients in the feed rations minus the content in the product.

No animal can produce plant nutrients, they only transform feed to products – milk, meat, eggs, etc. In the process, plant nutrients in their faeces and urine are 'waste products' (Figure 15.2).

The production level also affects the amount of nutrients in manure. With rising milk production, the plant nutrient content in manure increases considerably. When straw is used as bedding, the nutrient content in manure is increased, especially the potassium content. As mentioned before under farm-gate balances (page 31), if normal amounts of straw and manure are used on the farm, they may be discounted in the balance, except if straw is purchased or when manure is sold.

Cattle

Table 15.1 shows the norms for fresh manure nitrogen, Total-N, phosphorus and potassium content per dairy cow and 12 months for different production levels and normal feed rations.

Variations exist in the nutrient content even at the same level of production. For nitrogen the variation can be up to 10-12% due to excessive feed rations, year-round housing and pasturing. For phosphorus and potassium the variations are mainly due to the great range of levels of these plant nutrients depending on ley productivity, fertilisation and the ability of the soil to deliver these nutrients. In hay the phosphorus content can vary between 0.2-0.4% of the dry matter and potassium between 1.5-5%. If most of the manure is spread on the pasture or grasslands, these variations will not be important. In that case the manure will contain the same amounts of phosphorus and potassium as the roughage and the elements will just be recycled.

Swine

Swine rations are more uniform than those for cattle and therefore the plant nutrient content in their faeces and urine is more uniform. The norm for pig meat production is based on 2.5 batches per year, i.e. 2.5 pigs per pen place and year. Norms for replacement animals are not given, as their rations and growth are similar to those of fattening pigs in meat production. The norms for a sow are based on 2.2 litters per year of 17 piglets each for six weeks, plus one twenty-fifth of a boar. The sow's requirements during gestation are included.

Storage and Spreading of Manure

Nutrient Losses

The plant nutrients in manure must be stored in the best possible way so that the manure can be spread at the time when the crop needs it. This is usually in connection with spring sowing or in a growing crop. Some exceptions exist, e.g. it can be wise to spread farmyard manure FYM (solid manure) on heavier clay soils late in the autumn and plough it in so that the nitrogen is available for plant uptake in the spring (Jakobsson and Lindén, 1991). Otherwise spreading FYM on heavy clay soils in spring can ruin the seedbed and emergence of the crop. As much as possible of the plant nutrients that have been purchased to the farm as fodder etc. should be left in the manure to be used by the crops after spreading.

Losses in the Stables

It is mainly nitrogen in manure that is at risk of being lost in the house. In both faeces and urine, the nitrogen is organically bound at excretion. In the faeces nitrogen is comparatively firmly bound and the transformation to

Table 15.1. Norms for dairy cows for nitrogen, N, phosphorus, P, and potassium, K, contents in fresh faeces and urine at various levels of production, kg per animal and year.

	5,000 kg/year			7,000 kg/year			9,000 kg/year		
	N	P	K	N	P	K	N	P	K
Faeces	37	13	27	46	15	30	56	18	35
Urine	38	-	63	49	-	70	59	-	80
Total	75	13	90	95	15	100	115	18	115

Table 15.2. Norms for replacement animals for nitrogen, N, phosphorus, P, and potassium, K, contents in fresh faeces and urine at various levels of production, kg per animal and year.

	Replacement animal < 1 year			Replacement animal > 1 year		
	N	P	K	N	P	K
Faeces	14	3	8	18	6	14
Urine	16	-	22	20	-	31
Total	30	3	30	38	6	45

Table 15.3. Norms for beef cattle for nitrogen, N, phosphorus, P, and potassium, K, contents in fresh faeces and urine at various levels of production, kg per animal and year.

	Beef cattle animal < 1 year			Beef cattle animal > 1 year		
	N	P	K	N	P	K
Faeces	16	4	10	24	8	15
Urine	18	-	23	26	-	35
Total	34	4	33	50	8	50

Table 15.4. Norms for a sow with piglets for nitrogen, N, phosphorus, P, and potassium, K, contents in fresh faeces and urine at various levels of production, kg per animal and year.

	Sow incl. piglets and 1/25 boar		
	N	P	K
Faeces	11	8	3
Urine	15	2	9
Total	26	10	12

Table 15.5. Norms for pig meat production for nitrogen, N, phosphorus, P, and potassium, K, contents in fresh faeces and urine at various levels of production, kg per animal and year.

	2,5 fattening pigs per pen place and year		
	N	P	K
Faeces	4	1.6	1
Urine	5	0.4	3
Total	9	2	4

mineral form is slow. The nitrogen in urine is primarily bound as urea and when the urine leaves the animal, the urea begins to split up into ammonia and carbon dioxide. The enzyme urease aids the process.

As fresh urine has a high pH value, the ammonia evolved has a tendency to evaporate from the urine. The general environment of the house – temperature, humidity, air flows etc. – promotes this tendency. These losses are closely related to how long the urine remains in the house and can be called ventilation losses. Quick and effective urine separation can reduce these losses. The degree and type of separation are affected by the amount and type of bedding used, see Table 15.6. Generous amounts of bedding with a high absorption rate cause larger ammonia losses than sparing use in combination with effective urine separation. This is not true for peat-based bedding.

Poultry Pens
Birds, unlike cattle and pigs, discharge their urine in a semi-solid form together with the faeces. Another difference is that the nitrogen is in the form of uric acid instead of urea. Uric acid also breaks down to ammonia and carbon dioxide. In this case it is the enzyme uricase that effects the decomposition, which is considerably slower than for urea.

Measures to Prevent Losses
Effective urine separation and daily cleaning are the most important measures in limiting nitrogen losses in the houses. Since ammonia evaporation increases with higher temperatures, the houses should be kept as cool as possible. Poultry manure should be dried as quickly as possible to avoid the breakdown of uric acid into ammonia and carbon dioxide. Only little nitrogen is lost during drying. After drying, the nitrogen content is constant as the reaction requires water. Heated floors and conditioned ventilation air can lead to reduced ammonia evaporation and smells from the house. Peat as bedding reduces the nitrogen evaporation by lowering the pH of the manure and by binding the nitrogen in strong chemical bonds. The addition of chemicals and additives to lower the pH of manure or to reduce ammonia emissions is usually not recommended due to unwanted side-effects or to not being able to deliver the wanted effects.

As some ammonia is bound to leave the house by the ventilation, this can be captured either in a biofilter or a scrubber. A biofilter can be made of different materials, one type is made from a mixture of peat and heather through which the ventilation air is forced. In a scrubber, ammonia is washed out of the air by a wet filter and is dissolved in a suitable acid to be used later on as a plant nutrient. Both biofilters and scrubbers can be expected to remove approximately 50% of the ammonia. Biofilters require careful maintenance and both methods require substantial investments.

Storage Losses
It is primarily nitrogen that is lost during manure storage. Losses of phosphorus only occur when manure spills from insufficient or poorly designed storage facilities and leaky canals. Potassium is water-soluble and can therefore be lost due to leaks in manure pads and tanks. Losses of both phosphorus and potassium are due to inadequate storage facilities.

Storage in Aerobic Conditions
During storage, manure is subject to both aerobic (access to oxygen in air) and anaerobic (absence of air) degradation. In aerobic conditions microorganisms break down

Table 15.6. Absorbency of bedding materials. The variation is due to differences in initial water content.

Bedding type	Absorption ability, number of times its own weight
Chopped straw	3-4
Whole straw	1-2
Peat	3-12
Saw dust	2-3

Table 15.7. Norms for nitrogen losses from the house, ventilation losses, for different types of animals and handling systems. Percentage of manure gross content.

	Nitrogen loss,% of the crop's gross content		
House type	FYM	Semisolid manure	Slurry
Cow stable	7	7	7
Swine stable	12	12	12
Laying hens	-	10	3

most of the organic material in the manure to simple inorganic compounds. The material is mineralised into ammonia, carbon dioxide and water and a smaller part is transformed into humus, a biologically more stable material. In favourable conditions, well-aerated manure rich in straw, the oxygen-requiring organisms multiply very quickly as plenty of available energy is available in the carbohydrates from the straw. The carbon is 'combusted' in the organisms and given off as carbon dioxide. Water and heat are produced at the same time in the respiratory process:

Carbohydrates + oxygen = carbon dioxide + water + heat

If enough heat is produced to raise the temperature to 60-70°C, the manure is composted (see Figure 15.3) and the energy in the manure is consumed. Most pathological organisms die and weed seeds lose their ability to germinate at such high temperatures. After composting, manure is almost odourless. To achieve such composting, mixing is necessary.

Immobilisation

A very high straw content in manure may elevate the carbon content to 40 times the nitrogen content, i.e. the carbon-nitrogen ratio (C/N) is 40. This material is low in nitrogen but high in energy for the microorganisms and in the beginning no nitrogen will be released as ammonia. The microorganisms need all nitrogen for their protein synthesis and nitrogen is immobilised. This can also happen in the soil. Eventually, as the energy is being used, the C/N ratio will diminish and when it reaches 20, more nitrogen is released as ammonia than the microorganisms require. The environment will be alkaline, as pH will be higher than 7 and in the presence of oxygen, gaseous ammonia will evaporate. If the composting process continues until only humus is left, the C/N ratio will be around 10 and about 50% of the original nitrogen will be lost and the rest bound to humus and dead organisms.

Loss of Dry Matter (Energy) and Nitrogen

When carbohydrates decompose, the dry matter diminishes. The evaporation of ammonia and other volatile substances also contributes to this reduction. In well-composted manure the losses of dry matter and nitrogen are approximately 50% (Figure 15.4). For the climate in the

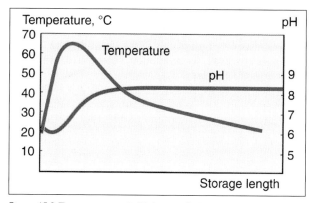

Figure 15.3. Temperature and pH changes during composting.

Baltic Sea Region, 3-12 months are needed for complete decomposition if the composted manure is rich in straw.

Storage in Anaerobic Conditions

In anaerobic circumstances decay takes place. The losses of nitrogen and dry matter will be considerably smaller than for aerobic degradation. The lower loss of dry matter is a consequence of the limited production of carbon dioxide. Much of the energy remains in the manure in the form of organic acids. No increase in the temperature takes place. Methane, hydrogen sulphide and various foul gases are produced and the process is termed 'fermentation'. The number of microorganisms is much lower, only 10% of that in aerobic degradation.

Nitrogen Losses

Nitrogenous compounds in the manure are again broken down into ammonia, which is dissolved in the manure's water phase. The pH is neutral or about 7 and ammonia is transformed into ammonium. Only about 0.5% remains as dissolved ammonia and it is in equilibrium with the ammonia trapped within the manure in gaseous form. Should the amount of gaseous ammonia above the manure heap decline due to an exchange of air with the atmosphere, it will be replaced by ammonia from the solution until equilibrium is reached.

When ammonia evaporates from the manure, new ammonia is formed from the ammonium until equilibrium is also achieved here. The more intensive the gaseous exchange at the manure surface, the larger the evaporation of ammonia nitrogen, reducing the remaining amount of ammonium (Figure 15.5). These losses will seldom amount to much more than 8-10% of the nitrogen content in the manure because the ammonia content is low. These are common circumstances in slurry pits.

To minimise nitrogen losses to the air as ammonia, urine and slurry stores should be covered and filling should take place beneath the covering (Figure 15.6). In the house, the losses should be minimised by actions such as using suitable bedding material, e.g. chopped straw, peat or sawdust, and also by regularly mucking out the houses. It is important to remember that all the nitrogen that is saved throughout the manure management chain can be lost in connection with spreading. Therefore it is important when spreading manure/slurry/urine to incorporate it as soon as possible, preferably within 4 hours.

Type of Manure Handling System

As regards the type of manure handling system that is preferable both from an economic and environmental point of view, slurry handling has most benefits. It is more economical to build a system for one type of manure, slurry, instead of for two different kinds, FYM and urine. Only one storage container and only one spreader are needed instead of two of each. Suitable measures exist to minimise the losses at all stages when handling manure. It is also easier to get better plant nutrient effect from slurry than from FYM. Another benefit is that slurry is easier to spread evenly and in the right amounts. In the case of deep-straw bedding in loose housing, the environment for the animals is better but the deep-straw bedding manure is difficult to use as a fertiliser in crop husbandry and large nitrogen losses are common. It has been shown that mixing in peat when establishing a deep-straw bed can reduce nitrogen losses.

Environmental Concerns with Manure Handling

When planning manure handling systems, consideration should be given to feeding and medication of the animals. The majority of what the animals are fed will appear in the manure and then be spread on the soil as a fertiliser.

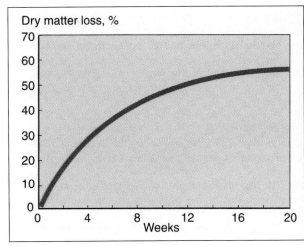

Figure 15.4. Loss of dry matter during composting.

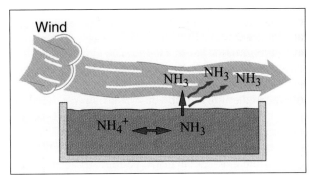

Figure 15.5. Air exchange above the manure surface causes increased ammonia evaporation.

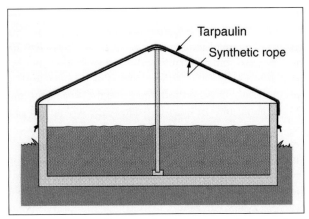

Figure 15.6. Example of how a roof can be constructed to cover slurry or urine pits.

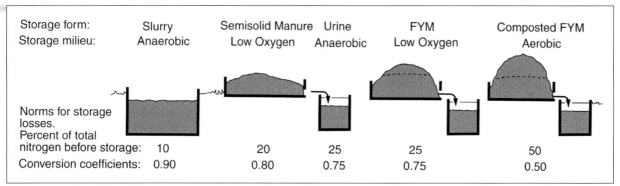

Storage form:	Slurry	Semisolid Manure	Urine	FYM	Composted FYM
Storage milieu:	Anaerobic	Low Oxygen	Anaerobic	Low Oxygen	Aerobic
Norms for storage losses. Percent of total nitrogen before storage:	10	20	25	25	50
Conversion coefficients:	0.90	0.80	0.75	0.75	0.50

Figure 15.7. Norms for storage losses for different storage forms, the 'coefficients' and characteristics of the storage environment. The indicated losses for urine concern covered containers with an opening for the pump.

A better balance should be provided when feeding with protein and phosphorus to avoid getting large amounts of nitrogen and phosphorus in the manure. Heavy metals and other waste products in manure must also be avoided and consideration taken to this when planning animal feed rations and medication, i.e. treating piglets with zinc in connection with weaning to reduce diarrhoea and also to reduce the usage of antibiotics for this. Another important issue is to reduce the usage of antibiotics and all medication that is not absolutely necessary. Other actions such as good hygiene and care of animals can be taken, as farms do exist that manage weaning without zinc and antibiotics. Research can be an important strategy to find alternative methods. Delivery of cadmium through imported concentrates and fertilisers can also be a problem for manure quality.

On the farm it is important to minimise all losses in all stages of manure handling. It is much easier to minimise losses from point sources, e.g. by having fully functioning manure storage containers or wells and good handling of sewage from households and milking parlours. It is much more difficult to reduce losses from diffuse sources, e.g. leaching from arable land through spreading excessive amounts of manure or fertilisers, spreading at incorrect timing or poor management of the farm. These types of losses can lead to negative effects on surface water and groundwater and eutrophication of lakes and rivers, coasts and oceans.

Techniques for Application of Manure to Land

16

Allan Kaasik

Estonian University of Life Sciences, Tartu, Estonia

Solid manure can be spread in spring or in autumn. In the Baltic countries and Scandinavia, application (spreading) of solid manure in spring is currently a problematic issue. Manure spreading is not allowed on land that is frozen or snow-covered. As in spring soil properties are altering swiftly and the optimum sowing time is short, the period for proper spreading and incorporation of solid manure into the soil remains too short. One possibility for using solid manure in spring is its application and incorporation into newly established grasslands.

Solid manure is widely used for fertilising fallows. During the period of fallow cultivation the average diurnal air temperature is still relatively high, therefore manure should be incorporated rapidly in order to reduce nutrient losses, especially these of ammonia.

It is most appropriate to use solid manure in autumn. Nutrient losses are minimal when solid manure is incorporated as late as possible before autumn ploughing but before November 1st (Figure 16.1) (Jakobsson and Lindén, 1991; Claesson and Steineck, 1996).

The importance of liquid manure/slurry in manure management is continuously increasing. Compared with solid manure, there are more possibilities for using it. Depending on technology, it is possible to spread liquid manure in spring and autumn before ploughing the soil, or on already growing plants (max. height of plants 25-30 cm).

In order to get precise results of fertilisation, manure must be analysed for its content of essential nutrients before application to land. The samples of liquid manure should be taken from homogenised (stirred) manure as the nutrient content of unstirred liquid manure in different layers varies in a wide range.

Before application, liquid manure must be homogenised (stirred). Stirring of stored manure with a small amount of sediment should begin at least four hours before the start of application. The thicker the sediments, the longer the period of stirring needed.

Solid Manure Application Systems

The dry matter content of manure applied with a solid manure spreading device should be at least 15%. A common disadvantage of different solid manure spreaders is

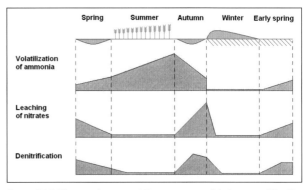

Figure 16.1. Nitrogen losses in different seasons (Jakobsson and Lindén, 1991; Claesson and Steineck, 1996).

Figure 16.2. Rotaspreader. Photo: IPPC.

Figure 16.4. Dual purpose spreader. Photo: IPPC.

Figure 16.3. Rear discharge spreader. Photo: IPPC.

Table 16.1. Nitrogen (ammonia) emissions from liquid manure spread by different methods Source: Claesson and Steineck, 1996.

Method	Ammonia emissions,%	
	6 h after spreading	96 h after spreading
Broadcast spreading	55.2	65.6
Band spreading	10.7	20.4
Injection (open slot)	4.0	9.4
Injection (closed slot)	0.8	0.9

their relatively low capacity due to quite narrow spreading width. Accurate dosing of solid manure is difficult due to its uneven consistency.

Three main types of solid manure spreaders are commonly used:

a) *Rotaspreaders* (Figure 16.2). A rotaspreader is a side-discharge spreader which features a cylindrical body and a power take-off-driven shaft fitted with flails running along the centre of the cylinder. As the rotor spins, the flails throw the solid manure out to the side.

b) *Rear discharge spreaders* (Figure 16.3). The spreader has a trailer body fitted with a moving floor or other mechanism which delivers solid manure to the rear of the spreader. The spreading mechanism can have two or four either vertical or horizontal beaters. The modern spreaders of this type which allow exact dosing have spinning discs as well.

c) *Dual purpose spreaders* (Figure 16.4). Such spreaders are capable of handling both liquid manure and solid manure. The spreader is a side discharge machine with a

V-shaped body. A fast-spinning rotor throws manure from the side of the machine. The rotor is fed with manure by a special mechanism (an auger etc.).

Liquid Manure Application Systems

The advantages of liquid manure application are high capacity (spreading width can be 8-24 m, depending on the machine), less intensive trafficking of soil, especially if tramlines are established in the field, and precision dosing. Disadvantages are the higher transportation cost and intensive odour and ammonia emissions (Table 16.1).

The main types of liquid manure application systems:

a) *Broadcast spreaders* (Figure 16.5). These combine a tractor and a tanker with a liquid manure spreading device at the rear. The liquid manure is forced under pressure through a discharge nozzle, onto an inclined splash plate to increase the sideways spread.

Broadcast spreading of manure has a number of disadvantages:
- High nitrogen loss due to ammonia emissions.
- High odour emissions.
- Uneven spreading, inconvenient dosing.
- Problems in application to growing plants, especially grasslands – it is not possible to prepare a high quality silage (hay) from plants polluted with manure, and the intake of such herbage is reduced in grazing or as a green fodder.

Figure 16.5. Broadcast spreader with a splash plate. Photo: IPPC.

There is a specific type of broadcasting system for liquid manure with very low dry matter content (dilute) – a hose-reel irrigator with 'rain gun' (Figure 16.6). The area to be irrigated or fertilised must be located near the manure storage (maximum distance 300 m). Liquid manure of sufficiently low dry matter content is usually stored in large lagoons open to rainfall or in tanks into which the cleaning water from barn equipment and facilities and rainfall collected from the farmyard are directed.

Figure 16.6. Broadcasting of liquid manure with 'raingun'. Photo: IPPC.

b) *Band or trailing hose spreaders* (Figure 16.7). Band spreaders consist of a liquid manure tank and hose system, a series of hanging or trailing pipes attached to a boom. The width of a band spreader is typically 12 m, with about 30 cm between bands. Band spreaders discharge liquid manure just above ground level and rapid contact with the soil significantly reduces ammonia emissions. The technique is applicable to grass and arable land (growing crops). Band spreaders are less suitable for fertilising grasslands intended for silage making or grazing, as contamination of grass by liquid manure may occur. Because of the width of the machine, the technique is not suitable for small, irregularly shaped fields or steeply sloping land.

Figure 16.7. Band or trailing hose spreader. Photo: IPPC.

c) *Trailing shoe spreaders* (Figure 16.8). This is a similar configuration to the band spreader with or without a shoe added to each hose allowing the liquid manure to be deposited directly into the soil surface, reducing the pollution risk of the vegetative parts of plants. The technique is applicable to grass and arable land (growing crops). The standard width of a trailing shoe spreader is 7 to 8 m. The technique is not suitable for small, irregularly shaped fields or steeply sloping land. Stones on the soil surface should be avoided.

Figure 16.8. Trailing shoe spreader. Photo: IPPC.

d) *Open slot injectors* (Figure 16.9). The system injects liquid manure into the soil at a depth of 50 to 150 mm. Special knives and disc coulters are used to cut vertical slots in the soil. The spacing between the slots is typically 20 to 40 cm, with a working width of 6 m. The application rate must be adjusted so that excessive amounts of liquid manure do not spill out of the open slots onto the soil surface. The injectors are mainly used for fertilising pasture and grassland (growing plants). With proper dosing the plants are not polluted with manure. Ammonia emission is not high. The technique is not applicable on very stony soil or on very shallow or compacted soils, where it is impossible to achieve uniform penetration of the knives or disc coulters to the required working depth. Injectors have a larger need of tractive power and at the same time have a smaller working width.

Figure 16.9. Open-slot shallow injector. Photo IPPC.

d) *Closed slot injectors*. This system injects liquid manure into the soil at a depth of 50 to 200 mm. Liquid manure is covered after injection by closing the slots with press wheels or rollers fitted behind the injection tines. Tine spacing is typically 25 to 50 cm. Closed slot injectors are the most environmentally friendly liquid manure spreading devices as ammonia and odour emission is minimal. The use of deep injection increases the risk of nitrate leaching, while crop productivity may decrease because of mechanical damage to underground parts of herbage grasses. The use of deep injection is restricted mainly by the soil conditions. It is not applicable on soils with high clay and stone content. The injectors need a high draught force, requiring a large tractor and higher fuel consumtion.

Sanitisation Treatment Reduces the Biosecurity Risk when Recycling Manure and Biowaste

17

Ann Albihn and Karin Nyberg
National Veterinary Institute, Uppsala, Sweden
Jakob Ottoson and Björn Vinnerås
National Veterinary Institute, Uppsala, Sweden
Swedish University of Agricultural Sciences, Uppsala, Sweden

Introduction

Manure and biological waste (biowaste) from households, the food industry, restaurants, slaughterhouses, toilets, etc. can be a valuable resource when used as a fertiliser on arable land. The flow of nutrients is currently linear, as the excess nutrients in food mainly end up in water recipients. This causes a net loss from productive land that is commonly compensated for by application of virgin mineral fertilisers. Redirecting this linear flow back into food production could benefit society in several ways, by decreasing the use of natural resources and lowering environmental pollution. However, manure and biowaste may contain disease-causing microorganisms (pathogens) such as bacteria, viruses and parasites. Since recycling of biowaste creates new ways of disease transmission between humans and animals, a particular area of concern is zoonoses, disease that can be transmitted between humans and animals. Although pathogens occur naturally in the environment, in many cases there is a man-made reason for their presence. One way for pathogens to be introduced into ecosystems is when biowaste of agricultural, mu-

nicipal or industrial origin is recycled to agriculture or forestry (Albihn, 2009). Once contamination has taken place, it is often impossible to control the spread of the infective agents either in time or space. Infections may be transmitted to grazing animals or by feed and water to indoor animals. In addition, if zoonotic infections are introduced into the food chain there is a potential health risk for humans. Therefore, to minimise the biosecurity risk when using manure and biowaste on arable land, treatment of the material to reduce the load of pathogens before spreading is highly recommended.

Disease-causing Microbes in Manure and Biowaste

Huge numbers of species and subtypes of bacteria, viruses and parasites are found in manure and different kinds of biowaste. Some of these microorganisms are pathogens and some are also zoonoses, for example *Salmonella* and EHEC (enterohaemorrhagic *E. coli*) (Table 17.1). Zoonotic parasites such as *Toxoplasma* and some subspecies of *Cryptosporidium* and *Giardia* are expected to cause increasing problems in the developed world in the near future (Gajadhar and Allen, 2004; Mas-Coma et al., 2008).

Some pathogens can cause serious animal contagious (epizootic) diseases that spread quickly over regions, for example classical swine fever (Table 17.1). Many epizootic diseases are characterised by being highly infectious, so transmission via contaminated surfaces or transport vehicles within and between farms may be possible. In such cases, the animals in the infected holding are culled and their carcases destroyed to interrupt further spread of the disease as quickly as possible. According to EU legislation, the disinfection process must also include treatment of the accumulated manure and biowaste.

Spore-forming bacteria such as *Bacillus* and *Clostridia* species are often present in manure and biowaste, but most of these species are common soil bacteria and non-pathogenic. However, some pathogen species of spore-forming bacteria may be present, for example *B. anthracis*, which causes the zoonotic and epizootic disease anthrax,

Table 17.1. Examples of zoonotic* and epizootic[†] agents that can be transmitted via manure and biowaste.

Agent	Disease	Primary reservoir/host
Bacteria		
Bacillus anthracis[*,†]	Anthrax	Ruminants, horses
Brucella spp.[*,†]	Brucellosis	Ruminants, swine
Campylobacter spp[*]	Campylobacteriosis	Multiple[‡]
Coxiella burnetii[*,†]	Q-fever	Small ruminants
Escherichia coli[*]	EHEC (Enterohaemorrhagic *E. coli*)	Ruminants
Listeria monocytogenes[*]	Listeriosis	Multiple[‡]
Mycobacterium bovis[*,†]	Tuberculosis	Cattle
Mycobacterium avium subsp. paratuberculosis[†]	Tuberculosis	Ruminants
Salmonella spp.[*]	Salmonellosis	Multiple[‡]
Yersinia enterocolitica[*]	Yersiniosis	Swine
Viruses		
African swine fever virus[†]	African swine fever	Swine
Aujeszky's disease virus[†]	Aujeszky's disease	Swine
Bovine herpes virus type 1[†]	Infectious bovine rhinotracheitis	Cattle
	Infectious pulmonary vulvovaginitis	Cattle
Classical swine fever virus[†]	Classical swine fever	Swine
Foot-and-mouth disease virus[†]	Foot-and-mouth disease	Cattle, swine
Goat pox virus[†]	Goat pox	Goat, sheep
Hepatitis E virus[*]	Hepatitis	Swine
Influenza A virus[*,†]	Avian influenza	Poultry
Newcastle disease virus[†]	Newcastle disease	Poultry
Porcine reproductive and respiratory syndrome virus[†]	Porcine reproductive and respiratory syndrome	Swine
Rinderpest virus[†]	Rinderpest	Cattle, goat, sheep, Asian pig
Sheep pox virus[†]	Sheep pox	Sheep
Swine vesicular disease virus[†]	Swine vesicular disease	Swine
Parasites		
Cryptosporidium parvum[*]	Cryptosporidiosis	Cattle
Giardia spp.[§]	Giardiasis	Multiple[‡]
Toxoplama gondii[*]	Toxoplasmosis	Cat
Trichinella spp.[*]	Trichenillosis	Swine

[‡] Most warm-blooded animals can be infected
[§] Transmission between animals and humans not clear

Figure 17.1. Pathogens can enter a farm environment via incoming manure and biowaste to be used as a fertiliser or from other sources such as purchased live animals, feedstuff or equipment. Also, vector animals may transmit pathogens from neighbouring farms. Grazing animals can pick up pathogens and further transmit them directly to other animals, humans or into the food chain. Photo: M. Löhmus, SVA.

and *C. chauvoie*, which causes black-leg in ruminants. Both these diseases may result in high mortality. In addition to the listed pathogens (Table 17.1), there are several non-listed organisms that can be present in manure and biowaste, and new disease-causing agents will always be found. In developing countries, infectious diseases of both animals and man are more frequent than elsewhere, causing a heavy load of pathogens in manure and biowaste.

Exposure Pathways

The use of biowaste from society creates new routes for the spread of pathogens between animals, humans and the environment. Pathogens can enter a farm environment via incoming manure and biowaste, or via other sources such as purchased live animals, feedstuffs or equipment. There is also a risk of pathogen transmission from neighbouring farms via vector animals, e.g. birds, rodents or insects. Humans can also spread pathogens, e.g. if toilet waste is added to slurry tanks. In high-density livestock areas, excess manure may have to be transported to other regions, a practice involving a risk of long-distance spread of pathogens.

On-farm spread of pathogens can occur via storage, transport and use of manure. From fertilised land, fur-

ther spread may occur via surface runoff, leakage to groundwater, dust particles and harvested crops. Grazing animals can pick up pathogens and further transmit them directly to other animals, humans or into the food chain. Recycling of manure and biowaste may also affect water quality if freshwater recipients are contaminated, e.g. after heavy rainfall or flooding. The highest risk of humans acquiring zoonotic infections is via consumption of infected food or water (Bemrah et al., 1998; Cassin et al., 1998), but humans can also be infected directly through contact with live animals or the environment.

Survival and Proliferation of Microbes in the Environment

The survival and proliferation of pathogenic microorganisms in the environment varies depending on differences between species, but also on factors such as agricultural management strategy and climate conditions (Mitscherlich and Marth, 1983; Hutchison et al., 2004). It is well known that bacterial endospores, from species such as *Bacillus* and *Clostridia*, can survive for decades in soil. However, survival for over one year is also possible for some vegetative bacteria, if conditions are favourable (Mitcherlich and Marth, 1983). Different soil types affect microbial survival owing to the combined effects of soil texture, pore space, surface activity and moisture-holding characteristics. The presence of manure or biowaste also affects pathogen survival in soil due to availability of essential nutrients and organic material to which the pathogens can adhere (Nyberg et al., 2010). Survival of pathogens on crops has also been reported. Bacteria may be incorporated into biofilm on plant surfaces or even colonise internal structures (Heaton and Jones, 2008). Zoonotic parasites such as *Toxoplasma* and some subspecies of *Cryptosporidia* and *Giardia* can also survive for long periods of time in the environment, and their ability to resist many natural and artificial conditions makes them most difficult to control (Feachem et al., 1983).

The method used for application of manure or biowaste to land is another important factor for the survival of pathogens. Due to the ammonia emissions from field-applied manure, incorporation directly after application by tillage

Figure 17.2. One way of studying the survival and proliferation of pathogens under outdoor conditions is by the use of lysimeter systems, which consists of soil-filled polyvinyl tubes lowered into the ground with separate collection of drainage water. Photo: K. Nyberg, SVA.

is mandatory. This procedure reduces animal exposure, but persistence is considerably prolonged within soil compared with on the soil surface, partly because the pathogens are protected against deteriorating UV-light (Hutchison et al., 2004). The reliability of natural inactivation factors on plant surfaces, in soil and in feed and foodstuffs should not be overestimated. In addition, some pathogenic bacteria such as *Salmonella, E. coli* and *Bacillus* can multiply in favourable circumstances, such as in warm and humid weather (Mitscherlich and Marth, 1983).

Other Unwanted Organic Material in Manure and Biowaste

Apart from pathogens, hormones, antibiotics and other pharmaceutical residues are also found in manure and biowaste (Vinnerås et al., 2008). Antibiotic-resistant bacteria that end up in the environment may spread their resistance genes to better-adapted indigenous bacteria, thereby increasing the environmental resistance reservoir (Kühn et al., 2005).

Unwanted organics in soil can affect plant growth but the higher density of microorganisms in soil than in water probably results in higher degradation of unwanted organics in the soil. The main negative effect of pharmaceutical residues is reported to be on aquatic life, e.g. reproductive disorders in fish (Sumpter and Johnsson, 2005).

Treatment and Handling of Manure and Biowaste to Reduce the Biosecurity Risk

Current large-scale livestock production, epizootic diseases and globalisation increase the need for biosecurity. Practices that have been considered adequate for decades may not be sufficient any longer. By introducing a barrier to disease transmission early in the food chain, food safety can be increased. Manure treatment differs depending on tradition and local conditions and, in general, large farms have more opportunities for treatment. Some examples of treatment methods for producing hygienically safe end products are described below, and some of these methods offer opportunities to co-treat manure with biowaste. Effective treatment can prevent ecosystem contamination and dissemination of pathogens. In order to be sustainable, suitable treatment methods must combine biosecurity aspects with environmental, economic and nutrient recycling aspects. As an extra safety precaution, the use of a particular end-product on farmland may be restricted, or there may be a quarantine period between spread of the end-product and crop harvest or grazing.

Composting
Composting can be used for both small-scale household kitchen waste and large-scale solid waste treatment, e.g. in windrow composting. Both open and closed systems are used, or a combination in different steps. During composting, bacterial activity in the treated material generates heat and, if well managed, temperatures up to 70°C can be obtained. If a high temperature can be maintained for long enough, an adequate reduction in pathogens can be achieved. However, studies have shown that there is a risk of pathogen re-growth in cold outer zones of the compost pile, especially if the material is relatively fresh (Elving et al., 2010).

Anaerobic Digestion

In biogas plants, manure and biowaste can be co-treated. According to European legislation, heat treatment is compulsory when animal by-products, e.g. from slaughter houses, are being processed (EC 1774/2002). Pasteurisation at 70°C for 60 min gives a sufficient reduction for most pathogens (Mitscherlich and Marth, 1983; Sahlström et al., 2008). However, the reduction in heat-resistant viruses is limited, and bacterial endospores and prions are not reduced at all (Bagge et al., 2005). Outside the EU, heat treatment before digestion is not as common and the reduction in pathogens through the digestion process is limited, most often 1-3 $\log_{10}$, although with higher reduction rates at longer hydraulic retention times (Yen-Phi et al., 2009).

Ammonia Treatment

Ammonia treatment involves application of either ammonia in solution or urea, which upon being dissolved are degraded by the naturally occurring enzymes in manure. The resulting increase in pH (to approximately 9) increases the concentration of uncharged ammonia, which is the active substance. Ammonia has shown to be an efficient bactericide, irrespective of temperature, starting from concentrations of 10mM. The effect on the parasite *Ascaris* spp. has been shown to be considerably greater at temperatures above 20°C and ammonia concentrations above 40mM (Nordin, 2010). The reduction effect on enveloped ssRNA viruses such as avian flu is also reported to be sufficient at a range of temperatures (Emmoth, 2010).

Formic Acid

Formic acid is used in Sweden for stabilisation of milled slaughter house waste intended for incineration. Addition of approximately 1% formic acid decreases the pH below 5 and the material is then stabilised and safer to handle during transport and storage. This treatment has been shown to sufficiently decrease pathogenic enterobacteriases, e.g. *Salmonella*. However, it has only a limited effect on viruses.

Liming

Increasing the pH by application of hydrated lime (calcium hydroxide) to a value over 11 effectively reduces the numbers of pathogenic bacteria present, although a pH

Figure 17.3. Manure slurry is relatively convenient to handle, but sanitation during storage is not reliable. A proper hygiene treatment before spread on arable land is recommended, e.g. by composting, anaerobic digestion or treatment with ammonia or lime. Photo: B. Ekberg, SVA.

above 12 is required for a long time to remove the highly chemically resistant *Ascaris* spp. Faecal coliforms and *Salmonella* are rapidly inactivated after liming, reaching no-detection levels within periods shorter than 24 hours (Bennet et al., 2003; Bean et al., 2007). However, there is a risk of re-growth of pathogens and therefore the pH value needs to be kept high for a certain amount of time. In addition, liming is most effective in materials with a high water content, as the inhibitory effect is dependent on free ions in aqueous solution. When treating manure with lime the high pH induces formation of carbonates, e.g. $CaCO_3$, which precipitate and form a thick sludge in the manure tank.

Storage

Manure slurry is relatively convenient to handle, but sanitisation through storage is not reliable (Himathongkham et al., 1999). Levels of indicator organisms vary over time during storage, indicating that pathogen levels may follow a similar pattern. In addition, a long period of storage without adding fresh material is generally impossible, since on-farm storage capacity is usually limited.

Conclusions

Manure and biowaste are resource for agriculture. However, the potential health risks associated with plant nutrient recycling in the food chain must not be ignored. Recycling of manure and biowaste to agricultural land can inadvertently spread infectious diseases, although opinion differs concerning the risk levels. The biosecurity risk for animals and humans may be sufficiently reduced if the material is properly sanitised before being spread on agricultural land. In order to be sustainable, suitable treatment methods must combine biosecurity aspects with environmental, economic and nutrient recycling aspects. Examples of treatments are composting, anaerobic digestion or treatment with ammonia, formic acid or lime. To obtain general acceptance for the use of biowaste as a fertiliser, a hygienically safe end-product is needed.

Environmental Effects of Cattle Rearing and Milk Production

18

Vladimir Surovtsev and Julia Nikulina

North-West Research Institute of Economics and Organization of Agriculture
St Petersburg – Pushkin, Russia

The changes in milk production to new labour- and re-source-saving capital-intensive technologies raise questions regarding determination of the economically and environmentally optimal animal concentration level in agriculture as a whole and on individual farms. Non-critical transfer of experiences from large farms (mega-farms) without taking into account regional aspects can create additional problems, which could considerably impair aspects of milk production, including its environmental safety.

Concentration of animals on large complexes with loose-housing systems (untied housing systems) and milking in milking parlours has a number of advantages in comparison with geographically dispersed cattle farms, in particular:

- Increased management efficiency.
- Reduced production costs (labour costs reduced 2.5-3-fold).
- Improved feed conversion efficiency, due to group feeding with the help of mixer-feed distributors, to 80 kg feed units per 100 kg of milk.
- Improved milk quality.

The competitiveness of production is increasing in terms of lower costs and better product safety. However, copying experiences from the most developed farms situated near big cities and concentrating the entire livestock on super-large complexes – mega-farms (1,200 milking cows and more) through farms having their livestock distributed between several dairy farms can lead to increased pollution load and environmental risks.

The increase in the dairy stocks in the Leningrad Oblast is mainly occurring in the form of agro-holdings at the present time. These commercial companies become larger, purchase new farms and usually concentrate their entire livestock in one mega-farm. Such tactics are most viable under the conditions of financial crisis, since they lead to minimum costs and since there are possibilities to buy farms with financial problems and incorporate these. However an organisational-economic concentration of agro-holdings is not always possible due to geographical distance.

The increase in environmental problems on farms (first of all water pollution by manure and slurry) becomes the determining factor of further livestock concentration. A high concentration of dairy cattle on the land leads to a sharp increase in manure output from the farm in connection with the change to new technologies. International studies of the agricultural load on the environment have revealed that a farm with 3,000 livestock units produces the same amount of waste as a city with 30,000 people (FGNU "Rosinformagrotech", 2005).

In a national survey, no serious problems existed with storage of manure in an agricultural company with 1,000 cows kept on five different farms remote from each other,

Figure 18.1. Round milking parlor in CJSC "Predportovyi", Leningrad Oblast. Photo: M.A. Ponomarev.

Figure 18.2. Modern milking parlor in CJSC "Rapri", Leningrad Oblast. Photo: M.A. Ponomarev.

using much bedding material. One farm with 200 cows kept on litter produced 4,000 tons of manure annually and 100 ha of nearby land was enough for efficient utilisation of manure and its consistency made it possible to transport and store the manure during the winter on nearby fields and then spread it before ploughing in spring time without harm to the environment. Construction of cattle houses (with mats) with local high concentrations of livestock, loose-housing, bedding-free systems of animal rearing and milking in milking parlours can produce a higher risk of pollution of groundwater and surface water due to mixing of rinsing water with manure, which increases the water content and the volume of manure 2-6-fold.

An area of 1,000 ha arable land is a necessary minimum amount to be able to spread 30,000 tons of manure. This increases the costs of transport and the number of work hours to spread the manure on the small-sized fields in the Leningrad Oblast. At the same time, the decrease in the dry matter content of the manure makes it impossible to store slurry in the field during winter.

An increased concentration of livestock is economically effective only when milk production is intensified. This is also connected to intensified feeding, which leads to an increase in environmental pollution for two reasons:

a) Animals with a high genetic productive potential produce more milk and consume more fodder and water, increasing the output of manure.

b) The composition of manure changes substantially with an increase in milk yield. The nitrogen concentration in manure increases from 0.35 to 0.50% with an increase in the protein content of the feed to allow the cow to increase its milk yield from 4,000 to 7,000 kg per year. A high protein content of milk leads to an increased need for calcium, nitrogen and phosphorus for the cow. A rise in the proportion of concentrate in the ration means that the overall nutrient content of the manure will increase. This will increase the problem of eutrophication of the Baltic Sea.

An increase in the volume of manure and changes in its composition lead to difficulties in storage and spreading. It is necessary to construct manure storage facilities with 6-10 months storage capacity considering the long winter period when spreading of manure is not possible. There is a problem of nitrogen losses in the form of ammonia from storage (especially open types). Such volatilisation pollutes not only the atmosphere but increases the environmental load to the drainage area of the Baltic Sea as precipitation and effluents.

Technologies aiming at decreasing production costs by concentration of livestock require appropriate capital-intensive technologies for storage and spreading of manure, i.e. significant investments are necessary which do not directly lead to a financial gain. The risks of equipment failures and leaking manure storage facilities increase

Table 18.1. Time required for manure spreading by a tank with a spreading aggregate with trailing hoses.

Type of work	Time, minutes					
	3 km	5 km	7 km	9 km	11 km	13 km
Transport, minutes	33	55	77	99	121	143
Other work	13.1	13.1	13.1	13.1	13.1	13.1
Total	46.1	68.1	90.1	112.1	134.1	156.1
Transport time, %	71.6	80.8	85.8	88.3	90.3	91.6
Productivity, ha/hour	0.36	0.24	0.18	0.15	0.12	0.11
Working days	28	41	55	68	81	95

Figure 18.3. 11 tonnes manure spreader in JSC "Udarnik", Leningrad Oblast. Photo: M.A. Ponomarev.

with a high concentration of livestock at one place. The consequences will be dire on farms in the event of a major event. The widespread river network in the Leningrad Oblast and the closeness of the Gulf of Finland aggravate this problem.

More than 70% of the arable land of the Leningrad Oblast is covered by perennial grasses to provide milk production with cheap forage. This index exceeds 90% on some farms. This grassland is only re-seeded once every 5-7 years, which decreases the possibilities of applying slurry unless special equipment is obtained so this operation can be performed in growing perennial grass crops. Thus, the area of nearby fields suitable for spreading slurry with existing equipment and technologies (surface application) is very limited, which increases the time needed for spreading (exceeded agronomic time limits) and the transport costs. A sample calculation is given in Table 18.1. The time is calculated for one machine surface-spreading a tank of 11 tonnes on 100 ha arable land. The time needed for the preparation, loading and spreading does not depend on the distance and is taken as a constant (4, 2.1 and 7 minutes respectively).

In the Leningrad Oblast more land is needed for spreading of manure/slurry in connection with high livestock densities. This makes the transport distance longer in combination with the small-sized fields of the Leningrad Oblast, which increases the total spreading time and requires more machines with higher tractive power. Super-large tankers lead to unacceptable compaction of soil and destruction of soil structure in non-chernozem soils with a high soil water content.

Spreaders for organic fertilisers can only be used during a limited time period of the year, but significant investments are required with a long payback time period. The possibilities of getting credit are limited for many farms due to deterioration of their financial conditions against the background of the economic crisis. The diversion of cash resources from turnover is not possible, which leads to the fact that many farms ignore the environmental aspects of production and increase pollution of the environment.

Conclusions

The pollution load to the environment of the Baltic Sea catchment area may be substantially increased as a result of increasing local concentration of livestock during the change to loose-housing systems of stock-keeping with milking in milking parlours, an increase in animal productivity and an intensification of feeding. It is necessary to take into account environmental problems connected with high livestock density when making a decision on this level in the individual agricultural company and on separate farms of this company.

It is necessary to take into consideration experience from the Scandinavian countries while developing a scientific approach to the correlation of savings from the economy of scale and alternative costs connected with livestock density. This experience shows the possibility of decreasing the costs of milk production on farms with

100-200 cows including the use of modern computer technologies (milking robots, automated control systems with telecommunication) without harmful effects on the environment.

Economic Analysis of Environmentally Safe Technologies in Agriculture

19

CASE STUI
Rus

Vladimir Surovtsev, Tujana Burkhieva and Mikhail Ponomarev

North-West Research Institute of Economics and Organization of Agriculture
St. Petersburg – Pushkin, Russia

In cattle and milk production in the Leningrad Oblast, there is an ongoing change to new loose-housing (untied animal keeping) technologies with cows milked in milking parlours. These technologies usually lead to production of higher amounts of slurry due to a lower dry matter content and higher production levels. This manure type requires the implementation and optimisation of new resource-saving technologies for storing, transporting and spreading of slurry in the fields. Otherwise, incorrect storage or lack of storage capacity and inefficient spreading (usually application of liquid organic fertilisers to fields during the whole year) can result in losses of nutrients (nitrogen, phosphorus and potassium), pollution of water bodies and ultimately eutrophication of the Baltic Sea.

The introduction of resource-saving technologies has a number of advantages. First of all, in contrast to the traditional technology of manure application before tillage, they allow the liquid organic fertilisers to be applied during the plant vegetation period (for example, after the first cut for perennial grasses), ensuring savings on expensive mineral fertilisers. Perennial grasses cover 77% of arable land in the Leningrad Oblast, as the farms are decreasing their potato and vegetable production area. Secondly, these technologies ensure maximum nutrient savings, of nitrogen in particular, and decrease the radius of odour distribution. Thirdly, they meet international requirements on the environmental safety of agricultural production.

Figure 19.1. One of the largest milking parlors in Leningrad Oblast, CJSC "Ruchi". Photo: I.K. Dubovik.

Investments in building manure storage facilities and purchasing special machines for transporting and spreading the slurry are required because of the current lack of high-quality manure storage capacity on some farms. It is usually not possible to store large volumes of slurry on many farms in the Leningrad Oblast. It has also been almost impossible in the past to spread the slurry during limited time periods as the fields are highly fragmented and remote.

These technologies of manure utilisation can solve environmental problems to a greater extent under the current price conditions and forms of state support, but do not lead to rising effectiveness of production in contrast to the technologies aimed at increasing production levels and quality of products. However in many cases, increases in production levels have been noted due to improved water quality as a result of these investments. In practice, the main criterion for the selection of manure utilisation technology in many cases has been the minimum investment possible giving a satisfactory solution of environmental problems without taking into account their cost-effectiveness.

Due to the fact that the price of mineral fertilisers is increasing at a faster pace than that of other resources, consideration of the resource-saving effects of manure storage and spreading technology is highly relevant. Calculations of the effectiveness of resource-saving manure storage and spreading technologies are based on an account of alternative costs and on savings on mineral fertilisers, which are determined as the cost of nitrogen, phosphorus and potassium from manure, saved and 'delivered' to the plants (on the basis of a farm nutrient balance calculation).

A farm nutrient balance calculation shows the efficiency level of agricultural production from a resource-saving point of view. It allows the analyst to:

- Estimate the environmental load from the agricultural production.
- Estimate the results and increase the efficiency of nutrient utilisation.
- Define and eliminate the sources of undesirable nutrient losses in the *manure removal, storing, transporting and spreading* chain.
- Increase nutrient savings and decrease the purchase of mineral fertilisers, which makes it possible to compensate for part of the investment costs of the resource-saving technologies.

The majority of nutrients entering the farm do not come from mineral fertilisers, but from purchased feeds. Thus, to increase the efficiency of nutrient utilisation, it is necessary to increase the savings on nutrients in the production cycle of livestock products and manure handling.

Figure 19.2. Cow-shed for 400 cows in CJSC "Ruchi", Leningrad Oblast. Photo: I.K. Dubovik.

Manure Storage

The investment costs for manure storage facilities depend on the desired volume, type of materials, equipment used, cost of construction and installation works, etc.

In practice, the majority of manure storage facilities take into account only the indicator that characterises the level of investment costs per m^3. As a rule, the higher the manure storage volume, the lower the investment costs per m^3 of manure storage. The volume of manure storage must be sufficient to store the manure within the period when it is not suitable to spread manure (the time period when the plants cannot use the nutrients and to avoid polluting the environment), stated by the normative documents (min. 6 months). In addition, calculation of the volume of open-type storage facilities must take into account the precipitation norm. To make an economic justification for choosing this or that type of manure storage, it is necessary to assess both the investment costs per m^3 and indicators such as: operational life, current costs for operation, including additional costs for cleaning of the storage facility and preservation of its net capacity during operational periods, conservation of nutrients, air pollution.

Furthermore, it has to be noted that open manure storage will allow precipitation to enter, leading to a higher manure moisture content and an increased manure volume. This increases the cost for application of organic fertilisers by up to 15%.

Table 19.1. Estimation of different manure storing and spreading technologies according to the level of marginal profits I and II.

Indicators	Alternatives		
	Inter-row surface applicator	Sub-soil injector	Splash plate spreader
Area of land, ha	500	500	500
Application rate, tons per ha	40	40	40
Total direct variable costs (fuel, spare parts, labour payments, etc.), k rub per year	1,088	1,355	1,496
Manure storage 10,000 m³, k rub	7,428	7,428	7,428
Manure spreaders, k rub	3,300	4,130	1,800
Total investments, k rub	10,728	11,558	9,228
Repayment of primary debt and interest on credit, k rub per year	1,964	2,159	1,564
Savings on mineral fertilisers, k rub per year	2,386	2,419	2,053
Marginal profit I, k rub per year	1,298	1,065	557
Marginal profit II, k rub per year	- 666	-1,095	-1,007

Manure Transporting and Application

The capacity of spreading machinery depends on the technology used (spreader; sub-soil injection; surface inter-row application), manure application rate, type of soil and distance between the manure storage facility and the fields. A factor such as the distance has a decisive impact on the efficiency of fertilisation. Comparing the efficiency of surface spreading by slurry spreaders and application by sub-soil injectors, the larger the transportation distance, the less difference in efficiency between these two technologies. Sub-soil injectors usually also have a smaller working width and higher need of tractive power compared to booms with trailing hoses.

Calculations show that application of the whole amount of liquid organic fertilisers produced by 1,000 dairy cows by one spreader (tractor with 11 tonne tanker) in the given conditions will take 140 days, which exceeds the standard application time. In the case when a slurry spreader is used both for transportation and spreading of slurry, the transportation only takes approximately 70% of the total 140 day period. To increase labour productivity, inclusion of transportation tankers is recommended in order to reduce the manure spreading period by 1.5-2-fold. This avoids the necessity of buying additional expensive equipment for manure application. It is also possible to use movable intermediate tanks with a high storage capacity to avoid idle time of transportation for the slurry spreader and to cut down on fuel and labour costs.

To conduct a comparative economic analysis of modern technological solutions of slurry storage and spreading, the machinery capacity and also the capital, current costs and resource-saving effects must be included. According to our calculations, a farm building a modern manure storage for slurry equipped with a pipeline system and buying a slurry spreader with a spreading boom with trailing hoses for application of liquid fertilisers on grasses is able to decrease nitrogen losses from 78 to 24%. Thus the farm can decrease the cost of buying ammonium nitrate 3-fold.

To support the choice of capital-intensive technologies, a comparative estimation of their cost-efficiency should be conducted on the basis of a calculation of marginal profit by using one spreading tank a year. The choice of this method is justified by the fact that a marginal profit allows an assessment of the effectiveness of technologies at different rates of change in prices of mineral fertilisers without taking into account the investment costs (marginal profit I) and with the investment costs (marginal profit II).

Marginal profit I is defined as the difference between the value of savings on costs for purchase of mineral fertilisers due to an increase in manure nutrient savings and the amount of direct variable costs. This indicator shows the potential increase in annual cash flow. Marginal profit II apart from the direct variable costs includes costs for primary debt repayment and the interest on the bank credit.

Table 19.1 gives the results of calculating the level of marginal profit I and II for three alternative manure

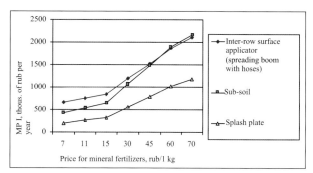

Figure 19.4. Increase in marginal profit I (MP I) from using different manure handling technologies in context of changes in the price of mineral fertilisers.

Figure 19.3. Slurry injector tank in CJSC "Predportovyi", Leningrad Oblast. Photo: M.A. Ponomarev.

spreading technologies to perennial grasses with an average transportation distance of 3 km.

The use of resource-saving manure storage and spreading technologies ensures considerable savings on the costs of mineral fertilisers. These have already increased and are going to continue to grow due to the rise in prices of mineral resources. Thus, the amount of marginal profit I from using resource-saving technologies is going to increase (Figure 19.4).

Conclusions

These studies allow us to draw the conclusion that in the current economic situation (prices for resources, cost of machinery and equipment) and with the existing state support system (subsidies for mineral fertilisers), the amount of cost savings on purchased mineral fertilisers resulting from increased nutrients savings does not recover the full costs of implementing the new high-performance and environmentally safe technologies for manure storage and spreading. Thus, additional state support is needed for those agricultural enterprises that are in the process of adopting these high-performance technologies within the framework of the priority national project 'State program of agricultural development and regulation of the markets of agricultural products, raw materials and foodstuff for 2008-2012'.

One more driver for development of the support mechanism for environmentally safe technologies is the fact that after entering WTO, the state will be able to subsidise agricultural producers by reimbursing part of the capital costs related to the adoption of these technologies. This is not included in the direct, limited support to agriculture.

Another conclusion must be that to be able to make agriculture sustainable in the long run it is always important to protect the water and ensure drinking water of high quality. This will also increase the production result on the farm as well as protect the Baltic Sea from eutrophication.

Sewage Sludge Management in Relation to EU-requirements

20

Ola Palm
Swedish Institute for Agricultural and Environmental Engineering, JTI,
Uppsala, Sweden

Christine Jakobsson
Uppsala University, Uppsala, Sweden

Summary

When Latvia implemented the EU directive on sewage sludge (Directive 86/278/EEC) it was done in a very complicated way. In practice, it meant that several permits were needed for sludge use in agriculture and for forest plantation purposes. Apart from being a costly process, it was very bureaucratic, time-consuming and an obstacle for sludge use. This was obvious to wastewater treatment plant operators, farmers, administrators and others. When planning for this project (year 2002) a revision of the EU sludge directive was under way, although the timetable was unclear. Drafts were available making it possible to see which directions the proposed new sludge directive would take. Apart from tightening limit values, the hygiene question would most probably be regulated in one way or the other in a new directive. The project 'Sewage sludge management in Latvia in relation to EU-requirements' was performed between the years 2004 and 2005. The project has given the following outputs:

- **Suggestion for revised Latvian legislation on the use of sludge**. A number of discussions took place with the Environmental Ministry to improve and simplify the legislation in order to promote the use of sludge.

Suggestions for changes were made and a completely new regulation for sludge was elaborated and enforced in 2006.

- **National recommendations for different treatments and outlets for sludge suitable for Latvia**. Fourteen information leaflets were produced and distributed on recommendations related to different sludge outlets and treatment methods.

- **Overview of sludge hygienisation methods for different sizes of wastewater treatment plants – technically and economically**. The knowledge about hygiene questions related to sewage sludge management was weak in Latvia. A baseline study of prevalence of microorganisms in sludge was performed with a total of 40 samples analysed (untreated, digested, composted and long-term stored sludge). The results from the study are in line with similar studies in other countries: mesophilic digestion is not enough for proper hygienisation; long-term storage is difficult to control, thus long-term stored sludge has to be managed and used with caution; composting can be an efficient treatment method if managed properly.

- **Knowledge among key-actors in Latvia about sludge management**. Eleven demonstrations and seminars were held all over the country. Establishment of practical demonstrations allowed sludge management processes to be experienced under Latvian conditions. This clearly showed opportunities and possible drawbacks with different methods, which are described in the recommendation and outlet leaflets.

- **A Latvian internet website, devoted to sludge production issues and utilisation possibilities**. The target of the website was to propose technical solutions and suitable information for sludge.

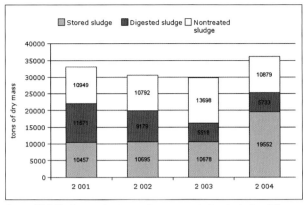

Figure 20.1: Sludge production and treatment in Latvia during different years.

Background and Use of Sewage Sludge in Latvia

There are more than 1,000 biological wastewater treatment plants in Latvia producing wastewater sludge. Accounting for the amount of produced wastewater sludge started in late 1990s, as part of the water consumption and wastewater treatment report. Starting from 2001, the Latvian environment agency started to enter these data into a separate database about sludge. Since there is no specific method for accounting for the amount of sludge, each analyst decides on the method independently and hence the results are very different and could quite often be questioned. Only some of the wastewater treatment plants of the municipal sector are reporting about sludge management; on average only about 30% of treatment plants. The largest producer of sludge is Riga city, which produces about 30% of all sludge in Latvia. Riga is also the only place in Latvia where the amount of sludge is weighed and hence not calculated.

Information published by the Latvian Environmental Agency shows that in 2003, about 223 million m³ of wastewater were produced in Latvia, including 136 million m³ that were treated in wastewater treatment plants. In total, 1,421 sewage treatment plants operated in Latvia at that time, including 964 biological treatment plants. On average for 2003, treatment of 1 m³ of wastewater in a treatment plant produced about 100-120 g of dry sludge. Calculated per person equivalent (p.e.) this means about

80 g of dry sludge per day, which is about the same as in Sweden.

In 2004 the production of sewage sludge increased to 36,000 tonnes (d.m.) from 29,000 tonnes d.m. in 2003, including 5,800 tons of digested sludge from Riga. About 12,000 tonnes (d.m.) of the sewage sludge produced in 2004 were utilised in agriculture, as compost material or in other ways. About 11,000 tonnes (d.m.) were stored in temporary storage. The production and utilisation of sludge during recent years are shown in Figure 20.1.

Most of the sludge is produced in treatment plants producing between 1,000 and 5,000 tonnes per year (Table 20.1). In second place are plants producing between 5,000 and 10,000 tonnes per year. Smaller treatment plants also have the most serious problems with sludge management. Very few investments in sludge treatment and utilisation have been made. Some of these treatment plants do not even have temporary storage facilities for sludge, in spite of this being required by legislation.

There are differences in sludge properties between different wastewater treatment facilities. For example, smaller facilities with a treatment capacity of about 2,500 p.e. and an annual sludge production of about 100 tons d.m. (296 facilities reported in 2004) produce about 4% of the total amount of sludge (Table 20.1). This sludge usually has a low dry matter content, is not treated and is non-polluted. The second group of treatment plants (up to 25,000 p.e. and annual sludge production between 100-1,000 tonnes d.m.) represents centres of districts. The sludge from these

Table 20.1. Production of sludge (size classes) in Latvia, 2004.

Sludge production capacity	Number of plants	Total amount of sludge produced, tonne d.m.
< 100 tonnes per year	299	2,625
100 - 1,000 tonnes per year	26	10,030
1,000 - 5,000 tonnes per year	6	12,532
5,000 - 10,000 tonnes per year	2	10,977
Total	333	36,164

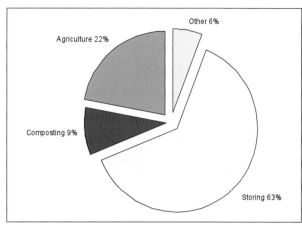

Figure 20.2. Sludge outlets in Latvia, average from the period 2001-2004.

plants is often not treated and could be dewatered or a liquid sludge with low concentrations of pollutants.

There were only 8 wastewater treatment plants producing more than 1,000 tons d.m. of sludge in 2004 (accounting for about 2/3 of the sludge produced in Latvia). The sludge from this group of treatment plants is usually dewatered, using filter presses or centrifuges (Riga city). These treatment plants also treat industrial wastewater, thus the sludge can have higher amounts of heavy metals and other pollutants compared with other sludges in Latvia. The most common sludge treatment method for this group of plants is long-term storage.

Two outlets of sludge are commonly used in Latvia – agriculture and composting with further utilisation in agriculture or for greening (Figure 20.2). About 22% of the sludge was utilised in agriculture and about 9% was composted, as an average for the period between 2001-2004. About 6% of the sludge was utilised in other ways (i.e. in forestry, land reclamation, greening). Data collected in the Environmental Agency show a slight increase in agricultural use of sludge. Most of the sewage sludge in Latvia (63% from the period 2001-2004) is stored at temporary storage sites, usually close to the treatment plants. Each year the amount of stored sludge increases by 10,000-20,000 tonnes (d.m.), corresponding to about 60,000-120,000 m³ sludge (wet volume). According to Latvian legislation, storage of sludge can continue without any time limit. Thus, there is no incentive for treatment plants to change the situation if they have enough storage capacity.

The information about sludge production and utilisation is not correct from all treatment plants, as essential equipment for measurement is lacking. Sludge has a high concentration of plant nutrients (nitrogen, phosphorus, calcium, microelements and organic substances) and the

interest in returning these nutrients to biological cycles and thus replacing mineral fertilisers is increasing in Latvia.

The Latvian sludge outlet (Figure 20.2) can be compared with the Swedish (Figure 20.3). The major difference between sludge management in Latvia and Sweden is that storage of sludge is less common in Sweden than in Latvia. Another difference is that sludge use for soil production and for coverage of landfills is an increasing outlet in Sweden and still very small in Latvia (compost will probably be used for these purposes in Latvia).

Recommendations for Different Sludge Outlets and Treatment Methods, Including Economical and Organisational Aspects

The recommendations relating to different sludge outlets and treatment methods are found in the information leaflets produced within the project. However, the leaflets are in Latvian.

There have been several studies in the EU about sludge management practices in so-called 'new' and 'old' European countries, including cost estimation and feasibility studies. Within the scope of the project these results were summarised to give some advice about the theoretical costs of sludge management and practically implementable technologies, taking into account Latvian conditions. The EU report 'Disposal and recycling routes for sewage sludge, Part 4 - Economic report' (2002) was used as the main information source for the calculations.

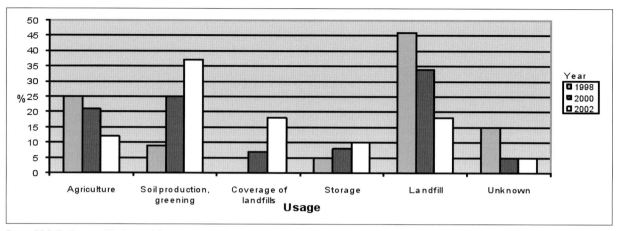

Figure 20.3. Sludge use (%) during different years in Sweden.

At the end of this section, a comparison is also made with estimations for Swedish conditions (from the VA-Forsk report 'Regional or Local Sludge Handling in Thirteen Municipalities in South Western Sweden – Technologies, Environmental Impact and Costs 2005'– in Swedish).

Costs of different methods of sludge treatment and utilisation consist of direct and indirect outcomes and incomes. Costs of sludge management consist of investments and maintenance costs. Maintenance costs consists of salaries, different resources, other applicable costs of different stages of technology, transportation, spreading, depositing and other costs.

The average costs of different wastewater treatment and utilisation in 'old' European countries are shown in Table 20.2. The average cost for utilisation of non-treated sludge is 160-210 EUR/tonnes d.m. Utilisation of dewatered sludge in agriculture or forestry, incineration with household waste or reclamation of degraded areas costs about 210-300 EUR/tonnes d.m., but utilisation of composted sludge for the same purposes, including composting, costs about 300-330 EUR/tonne d.m. This calculation does not include potential incomes. The depreciation period for the investment part is assumed to be 10 years.

Sludge management costs vary significantly among different counties, with the difference between minimum and maximum being at least 25%, but landfilling costs differ by up to 80%. When 'new' countries are taken into account the variation will increase further. For instance, in Latvia it is very common for wastewater treatment companies to

not include sludge management in their cost calculations. This means that these companies are not assumed to spend money on sludge treatment and utilisation.

During recent years composting technologies and production of different soil materials have been growing very rapidly in European countries. The common trend is for landfilling and agricultural use of sludge to radically decrease, and for production of soil material to increase by the same level. Compost is sold both as a commercial product (sometimes also mixed with other materials to make a soil product) or is freely distributed to farmers or landfills as soil amendment and covering material. Usually all costs for production of the compost and mixing with other material to a soil product are covered by the wastewater treatment plant.

One of the most significant sludge management costs is transportation, which in most cases comprises at least 30% of total sludge management costs. It is therefore very important to reduce transportation distances in all management steps, but especially in early steps where sludge contains a lot of water

The estimated costs in Sweden (Table 20.3) are generally lower than the costs for other European countries given in the EU report. The reasons for this are not clear. However, a feasibility study for a given treatment plant has to be carried out when deciding possible outlets or treatments. Such a study will give more correct figures and will also take into account the actual conditions for a plant, including transport distance, energy price, labour costs, etc.

Table 20.2. Costs of different treatment and utilisation methods.

Outlet	Costs, EUR/tonnes d.m.	Remarks and descriptions
Raw sludge in agriculture	160	It is forbidden to use raw sludge in agriculture in Latvia
Partly dewatered sludge to agriculture, (15-25% of d.m.)	160	This is the most common way of sludge utilisation
Dry sludge to agriculture	210	No drying equipment available in Latvia
Forestry	240	Utilisation of raw or partly dewatered sludge in forest cultivation
Composting	310	Composting with further utilisation of compost in agriculture and for greening
Incineration	315	Sludge drying and incineration
Combined incineration	250	Incineration of dewatered or dry sludge with organic waste or biomass fuel, for instance, using fluidised bed technology
Gasification	-	This method is not commonly used, so it's hard to predict costs when it comes conventional. Now it seems that costs of gasification can be at the same level as for incineration
Glasification or incineration at very high temperature	-	This method is not used in EC-countries and is applicable for polluted sludge, where there is a high risk of heavy metal leaching
Wet oxidation	-	This is an experimental method not used in conventional practice and it causes several other problems, for instance utilisation of nitrogen-rich by-products from the treatment process
Reclamation of landfills and degraded areas	255	Utilisation of sludge for landfill covers is becoming more and more common in European countries. It is recommended to use composted sludge, thus costs for composting should be added
Landfill	255	Landfill of sludge is decreasing due to restrictions on landfilling of organic waste in EC. It is also restricted in Latvia

Table 20.3. Costs for sludge outlets in Sweden, 2000 (from VA-Forsk report 2004-05).

Outlet	Cost, EUR/d.m.	Remarks and descriptions
Agriculture	100	Very dependent on transport distance
Landfill	215	Tax not included
Soil production	200	Sludge mixed with sand and other structural materials
Drying and incineration	240	Small unit for 1,000 d.m. sludge/year

Utilisation of sludge and compost in agriculture, energy crops and for greening replaces mineral fertilisers, which is especially important in case of phosphorus, as this is a limited resource.

Sludge Management Feasibility Study in a Latvian City

Within the scope of the project a separate feasibility study was carried out for reconstruction of a wastewater treatment plant and the sludge treatment system in one of the Latvian district centres, Valka city.

The sewerage system in the city has 4,000 customers in the household sector. Water production is 333,000 m³ per year. Electricity consumption for water production and distribution is 0.24 MWh/year (0.71 kWh/m³). The sewerage system manages 447,000 m³ of wastewater per year, including about 200,000 m³ of stormwater. Electricity consumption is 1.17 MWh/year (2.61 kWh/m³), including the wastewater treatment plant (0.5 MWh/year). Wastewater sludge comes from: primary settlers (10-20 tonnes/year) and secondary settlers (70-100 tonnes/year).

A nearby district heating facility produces about 170-200 tons of wood ash per year, which could be used together with the sludge. Sludge from primary settlers is landfilled, but sludge from secondary settlers is dewatered in filtration fields and then composted together with organic wastes from parks and gardens.

Sewage sludge properties:
• After treatment in filtration beds:
  - dry matter: 10-15%,
  - organic substances: 57%,
  - N: 3%,
  - P – 0.8%,
  - heavy metals (mg/kg): Cd 1.36; Cr 27; Cu 144; Hg 3.5; Ni 13; Pb 57; Zn 1 090.
• After composting:
  - concentration of heavy metals increases by 10-40%,
  - N decreases, P increases.

Sludge confirmed to quality class II by Latvian legislation. Annual production costs and tariff in sewerage sector in 2004:
  - electricity Ls 23,325,
  - salaries Ls 19,489,
  - other costs Ls 17,488,
  - sewerage tariff to households Ls 0.30 per 1 m³.

It is planned to reconstruct the existing wastewater treatment plant by installing new grids, sand catcher, new aeration tank with anaerobic, anox, aerobic zones (Celpox technology, developed in Sweden) and secondary settlers. Biological N and P removal will occur. A separate pumping station will be installed to pump filtrate from filtration beds to the wastewater treatment plant. Sludge treatment will start with thickening in a settling tank and dewatering in a centrifuge.

Reconstruction costs:
- pre-treatment plant Ls 70,000,
- biological treatment step Ls 250,000,
- pump stationing and pipeline Ls 20,000,
- dewatering equipment Ls 220,000.

Three methods are proposed for sludge treatment and utilisation (Table 20.4):
- raw sludge with reed beds or filtration beds – no need for dewatering, small energy consumption, insignificant maintenance costs,

Table 20.4. Cost comparison.

Treatment method	Investment cost (Ls/p.e.)	Maintenance costs (Ls/p.e.)
Reed beds	35	5.6
Dewatering	110	7.5
Liming	46	7.1
Composting	35	5.6

- dewatering and treatment with lime – larger dry mass outcome, hygienic effect, simple technology,
- dewatering and composting – sanitising effect, wider utilisation possibilities, simple technology.

Proposal for utilisation of treated sludge:
- agriculture – stable market, simple agricultural machinery,
- gardening (city parks) – small transportation distance, smaller costs for soil material for greening,
- plantation of forests and willow plantations – smaller hygienic risks,
- reclamation of landfills – stable market in near future, less quality requirements and control.

Cost comparison of different treatment methods and outlets:
- agriculture – Ls 100-120 /tonnes,
- gardening – Ls 150-180 /tonnes,
- plantation of forests and willow plantations – Ls 80-100 /tonnes,
- reclamation of landfills – Ls 150-170 /tonnes.

It was decided that composting could be the best alternative to treat sludge, despite reed beds seeming to be more feasible. Reed bed technology is not approved in Latvia and it is hard to predict whether this method would be considered sufficient and approved by funding sources financing reconstruction of wastewater treatment plants.

Further calculations were made for the compost utilisation.
Total sludge management costs:
- Utilisation of composted sludge in:
- agriculture – Ls 280-300 /tonnes,
- gardening – Ls 320-350 /tonnes,

- plantation of forests and willow plantations – Ls 250-290 /tonnes,
– reclamation of landfills – Ls 320-350 /tonnes.

Average sludge treatment and utilisation costs will reach about Ls 25,000 per year and per 2,000 p.e. Reconstruction of the wastewater treatment plant and introduction of sludge treatment will also influence production costs according to Table 20.5.

Most of the additional costs for sludge management come from the dewatering system and not from the composting part of the reconstruction.

It is recommended to compost dewatered sludge directly after dewatering. The amount of compostable material was calculated to about 400 m^3 of sludge + 300 m^3 of wood ash and incineration residues + 300 m^3 of sawdust = 1,000 m^3 per year. The predicted amount of compost is 400-600 m^3 per year (200-300 tonnes). Potential income from selling compost or replacing it with peat and soil substrates in city parks and gardens is about Ls 1,200-1,800 per year. An additional cost reduction (Ls 800-1,000 per year) comes from ash management, since the ash no longer has to be landfilled.

Overview of Suitable Sludge Hygienisation Methods and a Hygienic Investigation of Sludge

Use of sewage sludge in agriculture or on other land may be a resource-efficient method for returning plant nutrients to soils. It is important that it is not seen as a way to get rid of sludge, but rather used in a careful way, applying to guidelines for contaminants and according to 'best practice'. Regarding pathogens, the view should be to break the possible chain of environmental transmission and not to introduce new routes for disease transmission in the society. Since pathogens will be present in wastewater, they will also occur in the sludge, often in higher concentrations since they may be particle-bound and accumulate in the sludge. In Latvia the only pathogen that has been analysed for, and found, in sludge is *Salmonella*, but other pathogens have been detected in e.g. Swedish studies. For further information on the presence of pathogens, statistics on enteric infections in Latvia could be scrutinised.

Evaluating whether there is a risk regarding sludge use has proven difficult. The NRC (National Research

Table 20.5. Influence on production cost.

	Today	After reconstruction
Without sludge management	Ls 69,000 (0,30/m^3)	Ls 77,000 (0,45/m^3)
With sludge management		Ls 86,000 (0,51/m^3)

Council, USA, 2002) evaluated 23 studies of exposure to wastewater and sludge and concluded that there is no evidence to say that there is a risk, but on the other hand, there is no evidence to say that there is not a risk. The NRC suggested that further epidemiological studies and sophisticated risk assessments are necessary. How risks related to sludge are conceived is often discussed in a subjective manner, but in recent years hygiene risks have been acknowledged within Europe, including Sweden, and proposals for stricter regulations have been put forward within the EU and in Sweden. These proposals include demands on treatment in combination with restrictions on use and quality controls to various extents.

Treatment before use is considered the most efficient barrier towards disease transmission. By applying different treatment methods it is possible to inactivate (kill) the majority of pathogens present. These treatments need to be defined according to available experience on their efficiency, but the need for further evaluations has also been acknowledged and research is ongoing. Only relying on microbial analysis in order to state whether a treatment is acceptably efficient is not sufficient, since with current knowledge it is still uncertain how different indicators that are more easily analysed correspond to the behaviour of true pathogens. In most circumstances it is not possible to analyse for a range of relevant pathogens to get a proper picture of the quality of the sludge. Along with microbial analyses, there are always crucial parts regarding sampling procedures and choice of methods, and these are issues that need to be dealt with in Latvia as well, if regulations including quality control are to be introduced. In the drafts from the EU for a new sludge regulation, the organisms to analyse for and the severity of the reductions and limits required have been debated. In the Swedish proposal for new regulations some quality parameters are included, mainly to indicate possible regrowth, whereas requirements for reductions are not included. A demand on absence of *Salmonella* has been included since it is a zoonotic disease and considered to be of great health significance.

In the evaluation of Latvian biological treatment plants (BTPs) for sludge, efforts have been devoted to analysing indicator bacteria. As mentioned, how the results relate to inactivation of actual pathogens, especially those from other groups of microorganisms, e.g. viruses and protozoa, is still unclear. According to published literature it is difficult to find correlations between indicator bacteria and pathogens.

Even if uncertainties are connected to the indicator bacteria in how they represent pathogens, they are not considered to belong to the most persistent organisms. Therefore a significant reduction is expected in sludge treatment. The results from sludge sampling and analysis during this project in Latvia indicate that mesophilic treatment is not efficient, in accordance with other studies. Storage may be the only viable treatment before a plant has the possibility to invest in more a efficient treatment process, and a 12-month period is one of the methods included in both Latvian and Swedish (proposed) regulations. Even if inactivation occurs over time, it is important to remember that storage is an uncertain process, with the outcome being dependent on climate and season, which have little possibility of being controlled. This sludge should therefore be handled with care, and perhaps be subjected to further restrictions than sludge treated by other processes. Composting can be an efficient treatment, mainly due to the achievement of high temperatures, but it needs to be well managed. Results from the present study were variable and similar results have been seen in e.g. Nordic studies of composting of organic waste, where numbers of indicator bacteria increased during subsequent handling of the product.

Comparisons to suggested guideline values are at this stage not so relevant, but can of course be made. The reduction during 12 months of storage corresponded to demands for conventional treatment, but increasing numbers were also reported. Composting could have resulted in >2 $\log_{10}$-reduction but since starting concentrations are not specifically available, it is not possible to define actual reductions. The guideline value for *E. coli* of 500-1,000 cfu/g DM was reached for some of the storage and composting processes (1/3, respectively), but not after mesophilic digestion. Clostridia are considered too persistent

to be valuable as an indicator, and these results should therefore not be in focus. *Salmonella* was not detected in 50 g of sludge after storage, which is in compliance with proposed legislation.

Introduction of various treatment methods defined during the project is considered valuable in order to decrease the risks of disease transmission. Whether these treatments are to be divided into different classes depending on their efficiency and the possibility to control the material could be further discussed. As well as having proper parameters to monitor (e.g. temperature), it is necessary to oversee the full management of the treatment plants. For example, it was mentioned (during seminars in Latvia) that the same transport vehicle was used for untreated sludge and treated sludge, which could then be reinfected. Storage of sludge as a treatment method and after another treatment process should also be conducted as safe as possible so that exposure to humans and animals is limited. With different classes it is possible for the treatment plants to adapt to their own specific conditions.

With careful management of sludge, acceptance for sludge use could hopefully be obtained from all parties involved in Latvia. The views on sludge use differ between European countries, depending e.g. on how risks are perceived and the availability of other fertiliser products. In Sweden, the debate has in periods been intense, and due to 'unknown risks' and the food industry's concerns regarding consumer acceptance, other types of use than in agriculture are common, e.g. in land construction and for covering landfills. However, any application of sludge in the environment could lead to spread of pathogens. Partly removing the route of transmission to edible crops by not allowing sludge on vegetables (within a 10-month period), as now decided in Latvia, is considered a proper barrier and risk management measure.

Conclusions from the Project

In Latvia the need for careful management of sludge has been acknowledged and regulations that aim at reducing the risks of disease transmission are being adopted. A zero risk is not possible to achieve but the combination of rules for defined treatments and restrictions for use will together function as barriers and reduce the risks to what can be considered an acceptable level.

Three different biological treatment processes, partly differing from the new legislation, were evaluated regarding the reduction of indicator bacteria and *Salmonella*. Specific conclusions from these analyses and general statements based also on existing knowledge include:

- The quality indicators *E. coli* and Enterococci should be re-evaluated since it is unclear how well they represent pathogens.
- These indicator bacteria should not be used as the only means of controlling a sludge treatment process.
- Clostridia may not be a suitable indicator for determining sludge quality since the clostridia spores that are analysed are very persistent, and a reduction during treatment cannot always be expected.
- *Salmonella* was present occasionally both before and after treatment, as previously recorded in other studies.
- Aiming at absence of *Salmonella* is relevant, since it has implications for risks both to animals and humans and to the management of the treatment plant.
- Mesophilic digestion only reduces microorganisms slightly and is not considered a treatment that gives a safe fertiliser product.
- Mesophilic digestion is preferably used in combination with a treatment process that is specifically aimed at reducing pathogens.
- Storage of sludge gives varying results in reduction of indicator organisms and pathogens.
- Storage of sludge is a treatment method that is not possible to control and sludge that has only been treated by means of storage needs to be handled and used with caution.
- To further reduce hygiene risks from sludge, more efficient treatment methods than mesophilic digestion and long-term storage need to be applied.
- Composting can be an efficient treatment method but it is important to manage the process and ensure that basically all material is subjected to thermophilic temperatures.
- The Latvian regulations for sludge need to be further evaluated, not only in relation to process parameters

but also to the overall management of the treatment plants.

- To evaluate the efficiency of various treatment methods, it would be valuable also to include groups of microorganisms other than bacteria.
- The introduction of improved treatment of sludge will be costly, but other benefits such as more use of sludge/higher acceptance and further reduction of organic contaminants may be achieved.

Land Application of Biosolids by the Metropolitan Water Reclamation District of Greater Chicago

21

Albert E. Cox, Thomas C. Granato and Louis Kollias

Metropolitan Water Reclamation District of Greater Chicago, Illinois, U.S.A.

Introduction

Biosolids are derived from municipal wastewater treatment plant sludge that has been processed to meet federal and state regulations so that they can be safely applied to land. In the United States (U.S.) approximately 7.9 million dry metric tonnes of biosolids are produced annually and over 55% of this amount is beneficially utilized through land application (NEBRA, 2007). Land application is one of the most attractive and environmentally benign methods of managing biosolids because:

- they are a good source of nutrients for crop production and are high in organic matter
- the practice is environmentally sound when done in compliance with regulations
- nutrients from biosolids have lower leaching potential than the commercial fertilizers
- biosolids application improves long-term fertility and the physical characteristics of soils

This chapter presents a summary of regulations governing land application of biosolids in the U.S., and the experience of the Metropolitan Water Reclamation District of Greater Chicago (MWRDGC) in producing biosolids in compliance with federal and state regulations and utilizing them beneficially for crop production.

Regulations Governing Land Application of Biosolids

Federal Regulations

Land application of biosolids in the U.S. is regulated by the U.S. Environmental Protection Agency (USEPA) under Title 40 of the Code of Federal Regulations (CFR), Part 503, which was promulgated in 1993 (USEPA, 1993). The Part 503 rule was developed based on a comprehensive risk assessment conducted with the goal of protection of human health and the environment from contaminants that might be present in biosolids. The methods used in conducting the risk assessment were approved by a Science Advisory Board.

The Part 503 risk assessment addressed 25 potential pollutants through 14 exposure pathways (Table 21.1). In the final Part 503 rule, nine trace elements (arsenic, cadmium, copper, lead, mercury, molybdenum, nickel, selenium, and zinc) were regulated. The other pollutants were not regulated, primarily because they are not present in biosolids at significantly high concentrations, are banned from production and use, or there was no reasonably anticipated risk to human health and the environment. The most limiting pathway for each of the nine regulated trace elements was used to establish pollutant concentration limits and lifetime loading rate standards for land appli-

Table 21.1. Exposure pathways used in the Part 503 Risk Assessment.

Pathway	Description of Highly Exposed Individual
1. Biosolids→Soil→Plant→Human	Human (except home gardener) lifetime ingestion of plants grown in biosolids-amended soil
2. Biosolids→Soil→Plant→Human	Human (home gardener) lifetime ingestion of plants grown in biosolids-amended soil
3. Biosolids→Human	Human (child) ingesting biosolids
4. Biosolids→Soil→Plant→Animal→Human	Human lifetime ingestion of animal products (animals raised on forage grown on biosolids-amended soil)
5. Biosolids→Soil→Animal→Human	Human lifetime ingestion of animal products (animals ingest biosolids directly)
6. Biosolids→Soil→Plant→Animal	Animal lifetime ingestion of plants grown on biosolids-amended soil
7. Biosolids→Soil→Animal	Animal lifetime ingestion of biosolids
8. Biosolids→Soil→Plant	Plant toxicity due to taking up biosolids pollutants when grown in biosolids-amended soils
9. Biosolids→Soil→Organism	Soil organism ingesting biosolids-soil mixture
10. Biosolids→Soil→Organism→Predator	Predator of soil organisms that have been exposed to biosolids-amended soils
11. Biosolids→Soil→Air-borne dust→Human	Adult human lifetime inhalation of particles (dust) [e.g. tractor driver tilling a field]
12. Biosolids→Soil→Surface water→Human	Human lifetime drinking surface water and ingesting fish containing pollutants in biosolids
13. Biosolids→Soil→Air→Human	Human lifetime inhalation of pollutants in biosolids that volatilize to air
14. Biosolids→Soil→Groundwater→Human	Human lifetime drinking well water containing pollutants from biosolids that leach from soil to groundwater

cation of biosolids. Two pollutant concentration limits in biosolids were established: ceiling concentration limits for all biosolids that can be land applied, and lower pollutant concentration limits that define high quality biosolids that can be land applied with fewer restrictions.

The Part 503 rule also includes requirements for controlling pathogens, and ensuring stability to minimize odors and the attraction of vectors (such as flies and mosquitoes) to biosolids. These pathogen and vector attraction reduction (VAR) standards were based on 'best available technology,' and are met either by direct measurements or by using various well-defined processes approved under the Part 503 rule. The pathogen and VAR standards which can be established through direct measurement are shown in Table 21.2. Two pathogen content criteria are established in the rule. The Class A criteria define the highest quality biosolids, which have undetectable levels of pathogens, and can be land applied without restrictions. The Class A pathogen criteria can be met by one of six treatment methods. One of these six methods is called processes to further reduce pathogens (PFRP), which consists of seven well-defined processes. In addition, the Class A pathogen criteria can be met by using a process equivalent to PFRP, for which approval is obtained through application to a USEPA appointed pathogen equivalency committee.

Biosolids meeting lower pollutant concentration limits and the Class A pathogen status are termed exceptional quality (EQ). In most circumstances, EQ biosolids can be land applied with no restrictions.

The Class B criteria define biosolids in which pathogens are significantly reduced but are still at detectable levels. In Class B biosolids, about 99% of the bacteria, 90% of the viruses, and a lower percentage of the more resistant parasites are killed. The rule defined processes to significantly reduce pathogens (PSRP), which produce biosolids meeting the Class B criteria, without requirement for testing. The standards for land application of Class B biosolids provide additional protection through a number of site restrictions that allow for sufficient time for pathogen die-off before humans and animals can come in contact with the land application site or before crops can be harvested. Pathogen die-off on land amended with Class B biosolids occurs through exposure to sunlight and temperature and moisture fluctuations.

The VAR standard is achieved through one of 12 options that either reduce the attractiveness of the biosolids to vectors, or prevent vectors from coming in contact with biosolids. Some of the VAR methods include achieving a minimum of 38% reduction in volatile solids content beginning from the digestion step to the time the biosolids

Table 21.2. Part 503 rule pathogen requirement and vector attraction reduction for Class A and Class B biosolids.

Parameter	Measurement	Class A Biosolids	Class B Biosolids
Bacteria	Fecal coliform, or		
Salmonella	<1,000 MPN/g		
<3 MPN/4g	<2,000,000 MPN/g		
<2,000,000 MPN/4g			
Enteric viruses	Live viruses	<1 PFU/4g	NA
Parasites	Viable helminth ova	<1 ovum/4g	NA
Vector Attraction Reduction	Volatile solids reduction	>38%	>38%

MPN = most probable number, PFU = plaque forming unit, NA = not applicable

are utilized and incorporation of the biosolids into soil within six hours after it is land applied.

State Regulations

In the state of Illinois, biosolids land application is also governed by the Illinois Environmental Protection Agency (IEPA) regulation, 35 Illinois Administrative Code 391 'Design Criteria for Sludge Application on Land.' This regulation imposes more stringent and more site-specific management practices on the land application of biosolids than the Part 503 rule. The regulation also requires that each land application program be operated under a separate IEPA permit.

Application rates of biosolids to farmland in Illinois and most of the U.S. are based on agronomic nitrogen (N) rate, which is governed by biosolids plant available N (PAN) content and crop N requirement. This information is fundamental to estimating the amount of land required for managing the amount of biosolids produced at a WRP through land application. The biosolids analyses required for calculating biosolids land application rates include total Kjeldahl N and ammonia N. The calculation procedure assumes that nitrate N content is negligible and most of the inorganic N is in the form of ammonia N. An example of the procedure used in Illinois for calculating biosolids land application rate is as follows:

Assumptions:
Total Kjeldahl N = 30,000 mg N/kg
Ammonia N = 10,000 mg N/kg
Estimated Corn Yield = 9.4 tonnes/ha
Corn PAN Requirement = 23 kg PAN/tonnes

Procedure:
A. Determine the availability of nitrogen forms.
  i. Ammonia N plant availability is 80%. This assumes that the soil is non-sandy and biosolids are incorporated into the soil after application. Availability is adjusted based on application method and soil type. When surface applied, ammonia N availability is 25% and 50% for sandy soils and for other soils, respectively. When biosolids are incorporated, applied ammonia N availability is 50% and 80% for sandy soils and for other soils, respectively.
  ii. For anaerobically digested biosolids, organic N plant availability is 20% for the first year and decreases to 10%, 5%, and 2.5% for years 2, 3, and 4, respectively.
B. First year application rate.
  i. Organic N value is calculated as:
  Organic N = Total Kjeldahl N - Ammonia N
  Organic N = 30,000-10,000 = 20,000 mg N/kg
  ii. Calculate the PAN in the biosolids as follows:
  Ammonia N: 10,000 x 0.8 = 8,000 mg N/kg
  Organic N: 20,000 x 0.2 = 4,000 mg N/kg
  PAN = 8,000 + 4,000 = 12,000 mg N/kg
  (12,000 mg PAN/kg) x (1g/1,000 mg) x (1,000 kg/Mg) = 12 kg PAN/tonne dry biosolids.

This means that each metric ton of dry biosolids will have 12 kg of N available for utilization by plants when the biosolids have been incorporated into the soil.

iii. Calculate the agronomic N requirement for the corn grain crop:

9.4 tonnes/ha x 23 kg PAN/tonne = 216 kg PAN/ha

This means that each hectare of corn with the stated yield requires 216 kg of PAN for proper growth.

iv. Calculate the biosolids application rate needed to provide the required PAN:

(216 kg PAN/ha)/(12 kg PAN/tonne dry biosolids) = 18 tonnes dry biosolids/ha

Each subsequent year that biosolids are applied would need to account for residual organic N mineralization as noted in A.ii above.

Land Application of Biosolids
The Chicago Experience

The MWRDGC covers a service area of 870 square miles, which includes Chicago and 124 suburban communities in Cook County, Illinois. The MWRDGC serves a population of about 5.5 million people and together with industrial wastewater, treats wastewater from a population equivalent to 11 million people. The MWRDGC generates approximately 180,000 dry tonnes of biosolids annually at four of the seven water reclamation plants it operates. The sludge generated at the other three WRPs is sent to these other four plants for treatment. The MWRDGC is committed to managing biosolids beneficially, economically, and in full compliance with all federal and state regulations.

Biosolids Processing at the MWRDGC
A schematic of biosolids processing at the MWRDGC is shown in Figure 21.1. Wastewater entering the WRPs goes through a screen to remove debris, and then receives primary and secondary (activated sludge) treatment. The sludge from the secondary clarifiers is then sent to digesters, where it begins stabilization by anaerobic digestion for an average of 20 days at 95 ± 3.6°F. This digestion is carried out by *mesophilic* microorganisms and the methane gas produced during the process is a sustainable

energy source that is used to fuel other processes at the treatment plant. This process is a PSRP under the Part 503 rule and the resulting biosolids meet the Class B pathogen standard.

After digestion, the solids are classified as biosolids and contain about 3-5% solids. The anaerobically digested biosolids are then dewatered to concentrate the solids and reduce the amount of water that will be transported to utilization sites. Two separate process trains are utilized by the MWRDGC for dewatering biosolids. In the low solids process train, biosolids are dewatered through gravity settling during storage in lagoons for at least 18 months. In the high solids process train, the digested biosolids are thickened by centrifugation, aided by the addition of polymers. The resulting centrifuge cake biosolids are mostly utilized directly as Class B cake on farmland or further processed by storage in lagoons followed by air-drying. The process of lagoon aging of the biosolids followed by air-drying on paved drying beds to at least 60% solids content is a low-cost process that helps in stabilization and destruction of pathogens. The MWRDGC has received a site-specific award from the USEPA which qualifies the operation of these biosolids process trains as a PFRP for production of Class A biosolids (Tata et al., 1997; 2000). The Class A biosolids generated at MWRDGC are utilized primarily as fertilizer for turfgrass and as soil amendment on golf courses, recreational fields and parks.

Meeting Biosolids Quality for Use in Farmland Application
One of the first steps the MWRDGC took toward promoting land application of its biosolids was to improve biosolids quality. In 1969, the MWRDGC first adopted an ordinance that set specific concentration limits on the industrial discharge of critical pollutants that had the potential to impact its WRPs. In 1985 the MWRDGC submitted its final pretreatment program proposal to the USEPA as required by USEPA General Pretreatment Regulations, which were promulgated in 1978. Significant reductions in the concentration of trace elements in the MWRDGC biosolids resulted from implementation of the 1985 pretreatment program (Pietz et al., 1999; 2002).

In anticipation of the promulgation of the Part 503 regulation, in 1992 the MWRDGC conducted an assess-

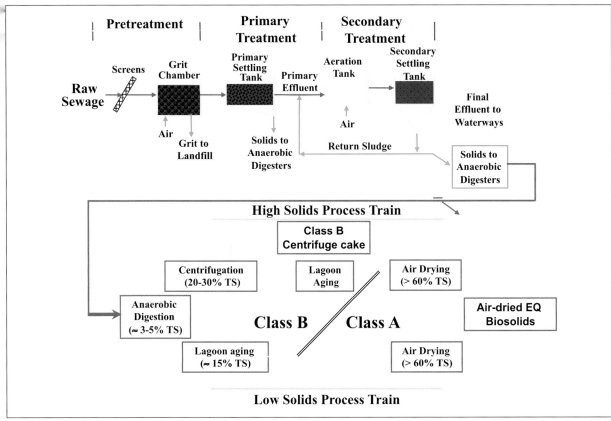

Figure 21.1. Schematic of the wastewater treatment process and the production of biosolids at MWRDGC.

ment of its biosolids quality with respect to the proposed high quality biosolids pollutant concentration limits. The MWRDGC determined that biosolids produced at some of its WRPs would not consistently meet the Part 503 pollutant concentration limits and thus would not qualify as EQ biosolids. There were occurrences where concentrations of cadmium, chromium, or lead in biosolids from some of the WRPs were above the Part 503 EQ limit. Therefore, the MWRDGC initiated a program referred to as the Part 503 Enforcement Initiative. The details of this program are discussed by Sustich et al. (1997). The Part 503 Enforcement Initiative was designed to optimize the MWRDGC's existing pretreatment program, increase the monitoring of industrial point source discharges in the MWRDGC's sewerage system, and to provide innovative pollution prevention assistance to the industrial community. The impact of the pretreatment program on reducing the concentrations of trace metals in the MWRDGC biosolids are shown in Table 21.3. The trace metal concentrations in all MWRDGC biosolids are well below the Part 503 EQ concentration limits.

The concentrations of constituents in Class B centrifuge cake biosolids from the MWRDGC Stickney WRP applied to farmland in 2006 are shown in Table 21.4. The biosolids contain relatively high concentrations of N and phosphorus (P), and lesser amounts of potassium and micro-nutrients. When applied at rates that are typically used in the MWRDGC farmland application program (about 22.4 tonnes dry biosolids/ha), the applied P usually exceeds the agronomic requirement, and adequate K is supplied, for crops grown on most soils in Illinois.

Farmland Application of Biosolids at MWRDGC

The MWRDGC has operated a diverse biosolids management program of land application of biosolids for almost 40 years which has consisted of the following:
1. Land reclamation at Fulton County
2. Farmland application in Cook and nearby counties
3. Hanover Park WRP Fischer Farm land application

Land Reclamation at Fulton County

The MWRDGC purchased a 15,006 acre site consisting of mostly strip-mined land about 200 miles southwest of Chicago in Fulton County, Illinois. In 1972, the MWRDGC began land application of Class B biosolids to reclaim the site for the production of grain crops. During the period of land application, which continued until 2004, biosolids were utilized in the forms of liquid biosolids, supernatant from holding lagoons and lagoon-aged air-dried. Biosolids were applied under a permit issued by the IEPA, which allowed high rates of biosolids application of up to 128 tonnes per hectare for soil reclamation. The biosolids application fields at the site were bermed such that runoff from the fields was collected in retention basins and monitored for chemical constituents before being discharged into local waterways. The permit requirements for operation of the site included monitoring of soil, crops, and ground and surface water at the site.

The information obtained from operation and monitoring of this site was valuable in developing the practice of land applying biosolids for crop production and reclamation, and assuring the long-term safety of the practice in the U.S. It has been hypothesized that with time following termination of long-term application of biosolids, the bioavailability and plant uptake of biosolids-borne metals will tend to increase, due to metal release as organic matter is decomposed (McBride, 1995). Granato et al. (2004) showed that compared with levels at the time of termination of long-term biosolids application on fields at the Fulton County site, concentrations of corn grain Cu and Zn were unchanged, while corn grain Cd and corn leaf Cd and Zn decreased at 12 years following termination of biosolids application. Evaluation of the environmental monitoring data collected at the Fulton County site indicated that the land application practice improved the crop productivity of the site with minimal impact on the

Table 21.3. Reduction of trace metal concentrations in MWRDGC biosolids resulting from implementation of the pretreatment program.

Trace Metal	1980	1990	2000	2007	503 EQ Limit
	--------- mg/kg dry weight ----------------------				
As	ND	ND	8	6	41
Cd	308	92	4	5	39
Cu	1,888	425.5	358.5	465	1,500
Hg	7.66	2	0.7	1.0	17
Ni	449	202	42	50	420
Pb	1,159	374	125	104	300
Zn	4,318	1,820	998	909	2,800

ND = no data

groundwater and surface water quality (Tian et al., 2006). Other studies conducted on the site include a corn fertility study, which begun in 1973 and is the longest running study in the U.S. evaluating the impact of biosolids application on corn production and soil quality. Data from this study were used in the Part 503 risk assessment.

The application of biosolids at the site was discontinued in 2004 as more opportunities became available for use of biosolids in the Chicago area. Based on the termination of land application at the site and on an evaluation of the environmental monitoring data collected for over 30 years, the IEPA revised the site permit to remove monitoring requirements.

Farmland Application in Cook and Nearby Counties

In the late 1990s, the MWRDGC began to develop its current farmland application program, which is now a predominant outlet for its biosolids. In the farmland application program, Class B centrifuge cake biosolids are used as a nutrient source for row crops such as corn, wheat and soybean in Cook and other nearby counties. In 2007, 82 000 dry tons of biosolids were utilized under this program. In this program, a land application contractor hauls the biosolids either directly from the centrifuge hopper or from lagoons or paved beds where the centrifuge cake (approximately 25% solids content) is temporarily stored. The MWRDGC pays the contractor on a cost per wet ton basis for hauling the biosolids to farmland. The contractor is responsible for enlisting farmers in the program. The farmers receive the biosolids at no cost, and the terms of biosolids use are between the contractor and the

Table 21.4: Chemical composition of centrifuge cake biosolids generated at the MWRDGC Stickney WRP and applied to farmland during 2006.

Constituent*	Unit	Concentration			Part 503 EQ Limit
		Mean	Minimum	Maximum	
pH		7.9	6.7	8.7	
TS	%	25.1	17.9	43.9	
TVS	"	48.5	37.3	63.5	
Volatile acids	"	1,344	462	3,414	
TKN	mg/kg	40,543	1,468	56,460	
NH_3-N	"	8,339	169	16,989	
Total P	"	21,967	16,693	30,979	
Ag	"	16	12	19	
Al	"	22,140	11,904	25,905	
As	"	<5	<5	7	41
B	"	62	7	104	
Ba	"	339	297	410	
Ca	"	37,170	31,646	57,469	
Cd	"	4	2	5	39
Co		7	5	11	
Cr	"	197	155	329	
Cu	"	331	159	782	1,500
Fe	"	18,359	13,723	33,247	
Hg	"	1.0	0.26	2.1	17
K	"	4,176	1,956	5,971	
Mg	"	16,472	9,930	29,665	
Mn	"	495	400	689	
Mo	"	18	13	25	75
Na	"	1,009	658	2,126	
Ni	"	56	43	104	420
Pb	"	129	57	211	300
Se	"	<4	<4	7	100
V	"	28	16	40	
Zn	"	905	691	1,157	2,800

* TS = total solids; TVS = total volatile solids.

farmer. The land application program is conducted under separate IEPA permits issued to the MWRDGC (biosolids generator) and to the contractor (biosolids land applier).

The MWRDGC provides oversight of the program to ensure that the land application of biosolids is conducted in accordance with all federal and state regulations and conditions under the IEPA permits issued to both MWRDGC and the contractor. The MWRDGC oversight activities are also conducted to ensure that the contractor is performing the land application of biosolids in a manner that will improve public perception and long-term sustainability of the farmland application program.

All farm fields the contractor identifies for land application of biosolids are pre-approved by the MWRDGC before use. For each field the contractor wishes to enlist in the land application program, information is submitted to MWRDGC to evaluate suitability of the field for land application before approval. The information submitted includes a biosolids land application information (BLAFI) form; soil survey and aerial photograph maps showing the exact location of fields and soil type; crop type and expected yield; planned biosolids application rate; and record of public outreach activities. An example BLAFI form, which indicates other requirements such as soil pH, and application buffer zones, is shown in Figure 21.2. For fields where the soil pH is below the required value of 6.5 (minimum pH limit is being reduced to 6.0 in pending revision of the Illinois biosolids rule), the contractor submits a form to show how lime requirement to increase soil pH is determined. The public outreach program includes notification to neighbors and community officials such as road commissioners and health departments. In addition, the con-

Figure 21.2: Example of Biosolids Land Application Field Information form used in. farmland application program.

tractor is required to include a full-time agronomist/public relations officer on staff, who will visit and distribute information to the neighbors in the vicinity of the land application fields to ensure that they are aware of and are comfortable with the land application activities.

To further help to educate the farming community on the benefits and safety of the biosolids farmland application practice, the MWRDGC established research plots on two farmers' fields in 2004. These plots are used to compare the biosolids with commercial fertilizers with respect to crop yields and impact on groundwater. The data obtained from these plots so far have been used to show the farming community the increased profits attainable through the use of biosolids. The MWRDGC and the biosolids farmland application contractor hosts field days on research plots annually.

Hanover Park WRP Fischer Farm Land Application

All of the approximately 900 dry tons of biosolids produced at the MWRDGC Hanover Park WRP are utilized on the Fischer Farm, which is a 130-acre site located on the grounds of the WRP. The liquid biosolids are held in storage lagoons and a contractor applies the material by subsurface injection approximately twice a year; in spring and fall. Corn is grown on the farm annually and the harvested crop is used either as animal feed or for ethanol production. This land application program is conducted under a permit issued by the IEPA.

Summary

Most of the biosolids generated from municipal wastewater treatment in the U.S. are beneficially utilised through land application. The processing and management of biosolids for land application are governed under both federal and state regulations aimed at protection of public health and the environment. The federal regulations governing land application of biosolids, commonly referred to as the Part 503 rule, are based on a comprehensive risk assessment. The Part 503 rule establishes limits and management practices with respect to pathogens, vector attraction and the concentrations of trace metals in biosolids intended for land application. In most states, the permitted rates of biosolids application on farmland are based on agronomic N requirements of crops. The state regulations are more stringent than the Part 503 rule.

The MWRDGC has vigorously enforced its Industrial Waste Pretreatment Ordinance, and as a result, the concentrations of trace metals in all biosolids produced by the MWRDGC are much lower than the limits established in the Part 503 rule for the highest quality biosolids that can be applied to land. This has helped in the development of successful land application programmes. The MWRDGC has been utilising most of its biosolids through application on farmland for nearly 40 years. The biosolids have been used during these years on a project in which strip-mined land was reclaimed into productive agricultural land, on a farm owned and operated by MWRDGC, and as a substitute for chemical fertilisers in farming communities located near Chicago. The MWRDGC's effort to continuously improve its biosolids land application programme is focused on decreasing the cost of production and transportation to farmland and on increasing public acceptance of the land application practice.

The MWRDGC also has maintained a programme of further processing its biosolids to a more soil-like product, which is applied to land as a fertiliser or soil amendment on recreational areas and for urban reclamation projects within the MWRDGC service area (Chicago and suburban communities). While this programme is not discussed in this chapter, it should be noted that the practice of applying biosolids to land in the metropolitan Chicago area through this programme has enhanced acceptance of biosolids application on agricultural land in outlying rural counties.

Phosphorus Recycling Using Residues from Bioenergy Production

22

Bettina Eichler Löbermann
University of Rostock, Germany

Bioenergy and Phosphorus Recycling

Bioenergy can be produced from agricultural and forest residues, industrial or residential organic wastes as well as from energy crops. Currently all countries significantly underuse their domestic potential of sustainable bioenergy (Fritsche et al., 2009). However, the use of biomass as a source of energy has strongly increased in the past decade and it is estimated to continue increasing in the European Union during coming decades (see Table 22.1 and Figure 22.1).

These developments in the bioenergy sector raise the question of how to use the residues from bioenergy processes. The reutilisation of these residues in agricultural and forestry systems can be an important factor in reduc-

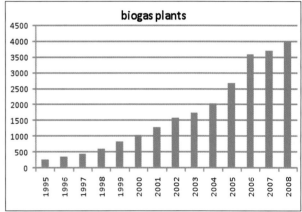

Figure 22.1. Changes in the number of biogas plants in Germany, 1995-2008.

Table 22.1. Predicted EU biomass production potential for bioenergy without harming the environment (Eurostat, 2003).

Mtoe*	Biomass consumption 2003	Potential 2010	Potential 2020	Potential 2030
Wood direct from forest (increment and residues)		43	39 - 45	39 – 72
Organic wastes, residues from wood industry, agriculture and food processing,	67	100	100	102
Energy crops from agriculture	2	43 - 46	76 - 94	102 - 142
Total	69	186 - 189	215 - 239	243 - 316

*Mtoe = Million tonnes oil equivalent

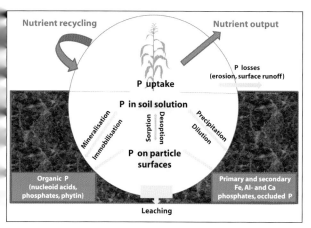

Figure 22.2. Soil P cycle and P fractions.

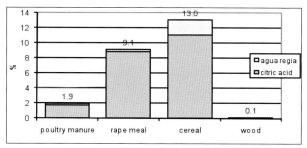

Figure 22.3. Percentage P content in different types of biomass ash. Total P content (extractable in aqua regia) and bio-available P content (extractable in citric acid).

ing the use of artificial fertilisers and in achieving nutrient recycling in agriculture. This has special importance for phosphorus (P), since the P resources world-wide are limited and the price of commercial P fertilisers will increase in the long run.

The application of the by-products of bioenergy production to soil affects the complex soil P cycle (Figure 22.2), not only due to P supply but also due to its influence on chemical, physical and biological soil parameters.

Since combustion of solid biomass and anaerobic biogas production are the most important bioenergy conversion processes in the Baltic Sea region, this chapter focuses on the fertiliser effects of biomass ash and biogas slurry.

Phosphorus Fertilisation Effect of Biomass Ashes

The residues of biomass combustion are the oldest mineral fertilisers in the world and they contain nearly all the nutrients plants require except nitrogen (N). Depending on the original biomass, the P content in ash varies widely (Figure 22.3). The P content in woody biomass ash is usually low, whereas the P content in ash based on cereals and oilseed crops or animal manure is higher.

In general, biomass ash has been shown to have positive effects on the dry matter yield of crop plants (Van

Reuler and Janssen, 1996; Krejsl and Scanlon, 1996; Patterson et al., 2004). Besides being a source of nutrients, the application of biomass ash may also influence the form and availability of nutrients, for example by increasing the pH of the soil (Ohno and Erich, 1990; Muse and Mitchel, 1995; Odlare, 2005).

The experimental results concerning the specific effects of biomass ash on plant P nutrition and plant-available P in soil are inconsistent. Little or no effect of ash application on P uptake and plant-available P has been reported by Mozaffari et al. (2002). On the other hand, Codling et al. (2002) found a positive effect of poultry litter ash on plant P uptake and high available P contents in the soil.

In pot experiments with different crops (Eichler-Löbermann et al., 2008), the effect of ash on crop yield and P uptake was comparable or even higher than the effect of highly soluble P compounds (KH_2PO_4 or triple-super-P) (see Table 22.2 and Figure 22.4).

The total P content of the soil increases when P is supplied, but depending on the P source provided, increasing the P supply does not necessarily result in an increase in the bio-available P content in soil. For biomass ash, positive effects with high available P contents in soil are usually found. For example in a pot experiment (Eichler-Löbermann et al., 2008), poultry litter ash increased the bio-available P content (Pdl) in soil even more than highly soluble P (KH_2PO_4) (see Table 22.3).

The biomass ash effects on soil P content also depend on the crop grown (Table 22.2). In another study of Schiemenz and Eichler-Löbermann (2010) eight different crops were investigated in combination with supply of

Table 22.2. Yield (g DM pot-1) and P uptake (mg pot-1) (shoot) of different crops with different fertiliser treatments in a pot experiment (6 kg of P poor loamy sand, 5 weeks vegetation time) (Eichler-Löbermann et al., 2008).

	Treatment	Phacelia	Buckwheat	Ryegrass	Oil radish
Yield	Without P	13.8	16.5	11.4 a	18.8 a
	KH$_2$PO$_4$	14.9	16.2	13.0 b	23.1 b
	PL ash[1]	16.3	16.1	13.3 b	23.8 b
	p	0.540	0.800	0.001***	0.001***
P uptake	Without P	56.0 a	51.6 a	42.0 a	86.1 a
	KH$_2$PO$_4$	68.7 ab	64.7 b	63.7 b	129.4 b
	PL ash[1]	87.1 b	68.7 b	60.8 b	149.1 c
	p	0.035*	0.002***	0.001***	0.001***

[1] Poultry litter ash. Different letters indicate significant differences between means for fertiliser treatments, p<0.05

Table 22.3. Soil pH, Pdl content in soil (mg kg-1) and Pw content in soil (mg kg-1) with different fertiliser treatments applied to four different crops in a pot experiment (6 kg of P poor loamy sand, 5 weeks vegetation time) (Eichler-Löbermann et al., 2008).

	Treatment	Phacelia	Buckwheat	Ryegrass	Oil radish
pH	Without P	5.1 a	5.7 a	5.8 a	5.7 a
	KH$_2$PO$_4$	5.2 a	5.7 a	5.7 a	5.8 a
	PL ash[1]	6.3 b	6.5 b	6.5 b	6.6 b
	p	0.001***	0.001***	0.001***	0.001***
Pdl	Without P	35 a	36 a	38 a	33 a
	KH$_2$PO$_4$	44 b	50 b	53 b	46 b
	PL ash[1]	64 c	74 c	74 c	56 c
	p	0.001***	0.001***	0.001***	0.001***
Pw	Without P	3.2 a	2.8 a	2.9 a	2.4 a
	KH$_2$PO$_4$	5.1 b	5.4 c	5.2 b	5.1 c
	PL ash[1]	4.9 b	4.8 b	4.9 b	3.8 b
	p	0.005***	0.001***	0.002***	0.001***

[1]PL = poultry litter. Different letters indicate significant differences between means, p<0.05, Pw = water soluble P, Pdl = double lactate soluble P

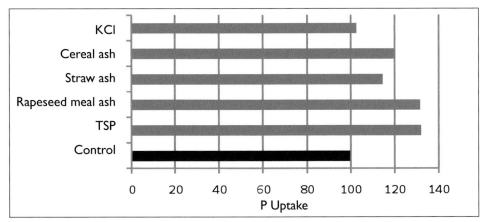

Figure 22.4. Mean crop P uptake with different fertiliser treatments (different types pf biomass ash, triple-super-P, potassium chloride) in a pot experiment (6 kg of P poor loamy sand, 8 weeks vegetation time), relative values, control = 100%.

Table 22.4. Nutrient content in non-digested dairy slurry and in different types of biogas slurry (% of fresh matter) (Bachmann and Eichler-Löbermann, 2009).

Substate	DM	OM	N	NH$_4$-N	P	K	Mg
Dairy slurry	9.3	7.5	0.46	0.23	0.08	0.32	0.07
Biogas dairy slurry	8.1	6.3	0.50	0.25	0.08	0.33	0.07
Biogas pig slurry	4.2	3.1	0.46	0.35	0.07	0.20	0.05
Biogas maize slurry	11.3	8.5	0.64	0.30	0.16	0.47	0.09

DM = dry matter, OM = organic matter

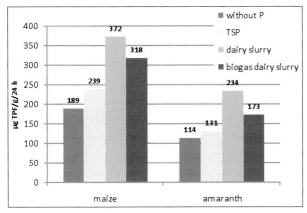

Figure 22.5. Microbial activity in soil (measured as activity of dehydrogenase (DHA, μg TPF g-1 24 h) with different cultivated crops and fertiliser treatments in an 8-week pot experiment.

Table 22.5. Crop P uptake (mg pot-1) and pH, Pdl and Kdl content in soil (mg kg-1) with different cultivated crops and fertiliser treatments in an 8-week pot experiment.

Parameter	Fertiliser	Maize	Amaranth
P uptake	Without P	90.3 a	103 a
	TSP	97.7 a	161 b
	Dairy slurry	108 a	137 ab
	Biogas dairy slurry	109 a	167 b
Pdl	Without P	26.6 a	25.6 a
	TSP	36.4 c	30.3 b
	Dairy slurry	33.0 b	31.0 b
	Biogas dairy slurry	34.0 b	28.9 b
Kdl	Without P	49.7 a	55.2 ab
	TSP	52.0 a	52.0 a
	Dairy slurry	50.7 a	66.5 c
	Biogas dairy slurry	49.6 a	58.4 b
pH	Without P	5.63 a	5.43 a
	TSP	5.72 a	5.44 a
	Dairy slurry	5.87 b	6.03 b
	Biogas dairy slurry	6.01 b	6.01 b

Mean values followed by different letters in the same column indicate significant differences between the fertiliser treatments (Duncan, $p < 0.05$). TSP = Triple-Super-P.

three different ashes. These investigations also confirmed the different potential of crops to utilize P from ashes. The exudation of ions, organic acids or enzymes into the rhizosphere enables crops to acquire P from less available fractions. These interactions between ash and crop cultivation may have an additional effect on utilisation of P from ashes. In particular, P-efficient catch crops, which are used as green manures, can be important in this regard. High uptake of P from biomass ash by green manure crops ensures high P release after decomposition of the green manure. Furthermore, the incorporation of plant material into the soil increases the soil organic matter content. Therefore, a combination of ash fertilisation with a P mobilising catch crop seems to be very promising.

Due to the varying nutrient content of biomass ash, general recommendations regarding the fertilisation ef-

ficiency cannot be given. However, a positive effect on plant P nutrition can usually be expected.

Phosphorus Fertiliser Effect of Biogas Slurry

Biogas slurry is usually applied on agricultural land. While there are data available regarding the effect of biogas slurries on nitrogen (N) and organic matter cycles in soil, the effect of biogas slurries on the soil P cycle has been much less well investigated.

To evaluate the benefits of biogas slurry, more knowledge is required about its effect on nutrient availability. This is complicated, since the transformation of organic compounds and nutrient release is a complex process and depends on many factors, such as the stability of organic substances (Gutser et al., 2005), climatic conditions (Dorado et al., 2003), soil properties (Huffman et al., 1996), type of cropping system (Van den Bossche et al., 2005) and interaction with mineral fertilisers (Kaur et al., 2005).

Biogas slurry contains P at concentrations between 0.4 and 0.8 kg/m^3. Regarding the solubility of the P in biogas slurry, different investigations have produced different results. High availability of such P was reported by Roschke (2003), whereas Umetsu et al. (2001) and Loria and Sawyer (2005) showed only delayed P release from biogas slurry.

Furthermore, biogas slurry contains N and C compounds, which have a decisive effect on the soil microflora. During the biodigestion process, the readily decomposable organic compounds become degraded and compounds such as lignin remain. However, lignin is not an adequate carbon and energy source for micro-organisms (Mokry and Bockholt, 2008). Therefore, a general effect of biogas slurry on the microbial soil P cycle can be expected.

A direct comparison between digested (biogas) slurry and non-digested (animal manure) slurry can help to evaluate the P fertiliser effect of the former. Chemical analysis of non-digested dairy slurry and biogas dairy slurry showed that these products had almost the same nutrient composition (Table 22.4).

As can be seen in Table 22.4, only the organic matter content decreased during the digestion process. In pot experiments with different crops, the effect of biogas dairy slurry on plant and soil parameters was similar to that of non-digested slurry (see Table 22.5 and Figure 22.5). However, investigation of the microbial activity showed a lower activity after biogas dairy slurry application. Since the nutrients supplied with the two types of slurry were similar, the different results can only be explained by the different quality of organic compounds in these two substrates.

Using biogas slurry as a fertiliser is an important way to close nutrient cycles in agriculture and to conserve nutrient resources. Based on preliminary results, good effects of biogas slurry can be expected regarding the P supply of crops. Some negative influences regarding the organic matter content in soil and the microbial activity may occur if biogas residues are the sole fertiliser used.

Part D

Reducing the Risks Associated with the Use of Plant Protection Products

Authors: Uladzimir Kapitsa, Jenny Kreuger, Eskil Nilsson, Roland Sigvald,
Lennart Torstensson and Peter Tóth

Coordinating Editor: Christine Jakobsson

Pesticides in the Environment and Risk Assessment

23

Lennart Torstensson
Swedish University of Agricultural Sciences
Uppsala, Sweden

Pesticides are found in the environment in all parts of the World, both in areas where pesticides are used and in areas where they never have been used, e.g. in the Arctic areas. Use of pesticides on a large scale started during the 1950s and 1960s and the use was rather careless during that time. The authorities and the users were then not aware of the dangers of using pesticides as regards to dispersal and side-effects in the environment. Since then, we have learned much about the mechanisms influencing the appearance of pesticides. Many countries have begun educational programmes for farmers to teach them about safe handling of pesticides.

Occurrence of Pesticides

Pesticides can of course be found within the areas where they are used and a minor part also in the harvested crops. A great problem is the undesired distribution of pesticides in nature causing pollution of the air, surrounding land and water areas as well as the groundwater (see also Figure 23.1).

Dispersal of Pesticides

The dispersal of pesticides in the environment depends to a large extent on the chemical and physical properties of the compounds, such as molecular structure, water pressure, solubility in water, stability and adsorption properties. A second important factor for dispersal of pesticides is the properties of the environment in which they are appearing, for example:

- Air – wind, UV-radiation, moisture, particles.
- Soil, surface – UV-radiation, adsorption capacity, precipitation, wind and water erosion.
- Soil, ground – texture and structure, pH, adsorption capacity, biological activity, oxygen content, temperature, moisture.
- Water – pH, biological activity, oxygen content.
- Sediment – pH, adsorption capacity, biological activity, oxygen content.

A third factor is how the pesticides are handled, for example:

- Normal use for crop protection recommended by advisors and safe handling of the pesticides.
- Normal use for crop protection recommended by advisors but without safe handling of the pesticides, e.g. at filling up and cleaning of the spraying equipment.
- Misuse of pesticides, e.g. mixing of pesticides where there may be a risk of contamination of the farm well or other waters, use of overdoses, use of inappropriate spraying equipment, dumping of remaining pesticides (concentrated or mixed) on unsuitable places, washing of used spraying equipment in open waters (creeks, rivers or lakes).
- Accidents may occur during transport and storage of pesticides, spills into surface and groundwater bodies.

Information on Pesticides

For about 30 years, the Pesticide Manual published by the British Crop Protection Council (BCPC) has served as a standard reference work on the active ingredients in products for the control of crop pests and diseases, weeds, animal coverage to include plant growth regulators, repellents, synergists, herbicide safeners and, latterly, beneficial microbial and invertebrate agents and pheromones. The manual contains information on pesticide nomenclature, e.g. its commercialisation, applications, physical chemistry, mammalian toxicology, ecotoxicology and environmental fate.

The 13th edition of the Manual, edited by C.D.S. Tomlin, was published in 2005 and a CD version also appeared.

Degradation of Pesticides

The rate and route of pesticide degradation depends on a number of factors (see Figure 23.2). There are three main mechanisms for degradation of pesticides:

- UV-radiation (occurrence in rays of sunshine). The energy in UV-radiation can break the bonds in many chemical molecules if they are directly hit:
  - in the atmosphere
  - on surfaces of leaves and soil.
- Chemical reactions
  - mainly pH-dependent reactions in water.
- Biological reactions in:
  - animals
  - plants
  - micro-organisms, bacteria or fungi (most important mechanism for degradation of chemicals in the environment), microbial reactions in water, soil and sediment.
    + Metabolic degradation: The pesticides serve as an energy source to supply growth of the decomposers (see Figure 23.3a and b). e.g. the phenoxyacetic acids.
    + Cometabolic degradation: The rate of decomposition is largely governed by the size and general activity of the soil microbial biomass (includes the capability of free soil enzymes to catalyse decomposition of pesticides) (see Figure 23.4a and b). All pesticides can be degraded by this mechanism.

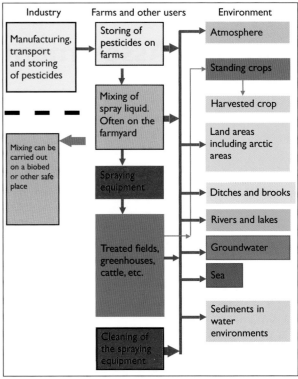

Figure 23.1. Occurrence, sources and dispersal of pesticides in the environment.

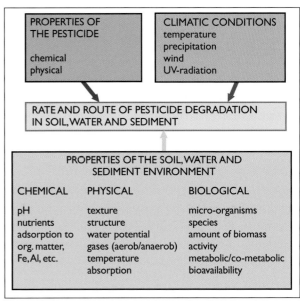

Figure 23.2. Factors influencing rate and route of pesticide degradation.

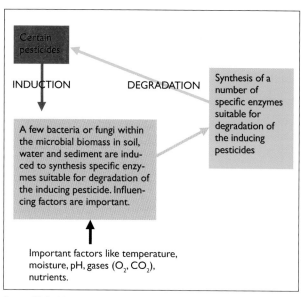

Figure 23.3a. Metabolic microbial degradation of pesticides.

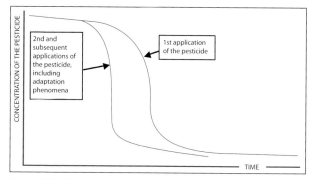

Figure 23.3b. Metabolic microbial degradation of pesticides.

Properties of the environment in which the pesticides are appearing that affect degradation of the chemicals include:

- Air – wind, UV-radiation, moisture, particles
- Soil, surfaces – UV-radiation, adsorption capacity, precipitation, wind and water erosion
- Soil, ground – texture and structure, pH, adsorption capacity, biological activity, oxygen content, temperature, moisture
- Water – pH, biological activity, oxygen content
- Sediment – pH, adsorption capacity, biological activity, oxygen content

Important factors regulating microbial degradation of pesticides are:

- Microbial biomass and activity
- Bioavailability of the pesticide
- Aerobic or anaerobic conditions.

Accelerated degradation of pesticides has been observed for herbicides known to be metabolically degraded, e.g. 2,4-D, MCPA, TCA, dalapon and chloridazon. The mech-

anism behind this is utilisation of the substances as energy substrates for growth of the degrading microorganisms and, because of this, an increase in their number.

The number of actively pesticide-degrading micro-organisms increases between the first and subsequent applications, since the pesticide is a source of carbon and energy for their growth. This is the main rate-regulating factor for degradation of the pesticide (see Figure 23.3b). The increased capability to degrade the above-mentioned herbicides can persist for several years.

Accelerated degradation of the soil-applied herbicides TCA and dalapon results in unsatisfactory weed control. Accelerated degradation in general means shorter persistence time which, from an environmental point of view, is desirable. The time for transport in the soil of the pesticides becomes shorter, which reduces the risk of groundwater contamination.

There is no increase in number of co-metabolic pesticide-degrading micro-organisms. The rate of degradation depends then on the size and activity of the normal microbial biomass and the strength of the influencing factors (see also Figure 23.4b).

Environmental Risk Assessment

Pesticide residues may have an impact on the ecosystem depending on the properties of the active substance but also directly on humans through contamination of drinking water or indirectly by transport through crops and animals upwards in the food chain. Risk assessments should be carried out for (see Figure 23.5):

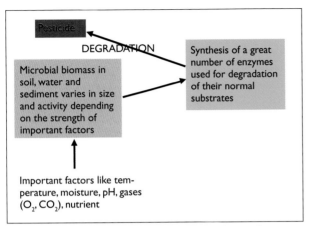

Figure 23.4a. Co-metabolic microbial degradation of pesticides.

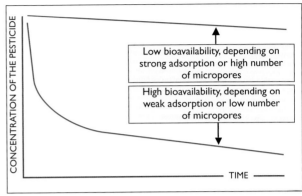

Figure 23.4b. Co-metabolic microbial degradation of pesticides.

- Landbased ecosystems – microorganisms, insects, animals (e.g. birds and mammals).
- Water and sediment ecosystems – microorganisms, algae, insects, plants, animals (lower forms e.g. earthworms and higher forms e.g. fish and mammals).
- Human beings – acute and long-term effects.

In work with pesticides it is often useful to make predictions of the risk of a certain pesticide polluting the environment. On comparing different pesticides with the same or similar fungicide/herbicide/insecticide effect, it may emerge that the risk of environmental pollution is different.

Information is needed on the chemical and physical properties of the pesticide and the chemical, physical and biological properties of the environment where the pesticide is expected to end up.

There are several possible ways to make predictions:

- With information on the chemical and physical properties of the pesticide, it is possible to predict its potential risk of polluting the environment compared with other pesticides. *However, this is a method that can give many misguiding predictions.*
- With information on the properties of both the pesticide and the environment where it is expected to end up, it is possible to predict the risk of a certain pesticide polluting a certain environment compared with

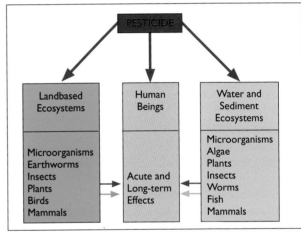

Figure 23.5. Risk assessments of pesticides should be carried out for human beings and for different ecosystems.

other pesticides. *However, it must be borne in mind that most data available on a specific pesticide and an environment are themselves predictions, meaning that the prediction to be made is not highly probable to be exactly true, but is just a guess depending on the quality of the data available.*

- In certain cases there are simulation methods that can help predict the risk of pesticide pollution. *However, here too, high quality data on the pesticide and the environment are needed for use in the simulation model. It must always be borne in mind that simulation models only give guideline values with plenty of pluses and minuses.*

Safe Handling of Pesticides

Pesticides can of course be found within the areas where they are used. A great problem is the undesired further distribution of pesticides in nature, causing pollution of water areas and the groundwater. It is now known that unsatisfactory management of pesticides at filling and cleaning of spraying equipment causes point sources of pollution of surface water and groundwater, as well as large areas of soils. Experiences from many countries have shown that point sources of pesticides are one of the most dominant reasons behind pesticide pollution of rivers, streams, lakes, groundwater and local water supplies.

However, the use of simple units (e.g. biobeds) can minimise the risks of pollution when filling spraying equipment. Many countries have started training programmes for farmers to teach them about safe handling of pesticides.

A biobed is a simple and cheap construction on the farm intended to collect and degrade spills of pesticides. Biobeds are facilities composed of a mixture of straw or other lignin-containing grass, mineral topsoil and peat or compost. They are covered with growing grass and, if the farm uses a sprayer carried or towed by a tractor, equipped with a ramp making it possible to drive the tractor and sprayer over the bed. The task of the grass layer is to regulate the moisture in the biobed as well as to serve as an indicator of pesticide spillage (See also Figure 23.6 and 22.7).

The composition of the biobeds is intended to absorb pesticides but sustain their bioavailability and support microbial activity, and thus degradation. Degradation of most pesticides is correlated with the amounts of straw present in the system, which indicates that straw supports an active microflora that provides a high degradation potential. Straw and its high lignin content favour the presence of microorganisms able to degrade this polymer. Fungi are important lignin degraders and it has been shown that the lignin-degrading system of these microorganisms is responsible for the degradation of a broad range of pesticides.

During recent years there has been increased interest in the use of biobeds for protection of the environment. Countries in Europe, Africa, South America and North America have started introducing the biobeds as a

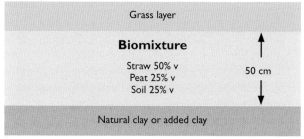

Figure 23.6. A biobed is a construction intended to retain and degrade spillage of pesticides. Typical construction of a biobed.

Figure 23.7. A simple biobed for a small sprayer with a wooden driving ramp. Notice the yellowspot in the grass under the sprayer pump indicating spillage of pesticides. Photo: L. Torstensson.

Remember: The simplest and safest way to avoid pesticide pollution of the environment is that all advisors working within advisory services and all users of pesticides are educated in safe handling of pesticides.

means of protection of surface waters and groundwater. The introduction of these systems requires prior studies about the type of material available and possible to use, the climatic conditions at which the biobeds are to be operated, the type of pesticides to be treated, the frequency of application, etc. Swedish experiences show that thorough knowledge of pesticide microbiology is of the greatest importance for a successful biobed.

Some points to bear in mind to get safe handling of pesticides are:

- It is important to know the chemical, physical and toxicological properties of a pesticide in order to predict its environmental behaviour and toxicological effects.
- It is important that the pesticide is tested in the environment where it is expected to turn up after usage and under the conditions prevailing there.
- Environmental risks when filling and cleaning spraying equipments can be minimised if the filling is done on a biobed or other safe place.
- All handling of pesticides must be carried out by persons educated in 'safe handling' of pesticides.

Key Issues for Reducing Pesticide Transport to Surface Waters

24

CASE STUDY
Sweden

Jenny Kreuger
Swedish University of Agriultural Sciences, Uppsala, Sweden

Eskil Nilsson
VISAVI AB/SYDEK, Lund, Sweden

Introduction

The occurrence of pesticides in Swedish aquatic environments was initially observed during the mid-1980s, when monitoring studies first revealed frequent findings of agricultural pesticides in streams and rivers (Kreuger and Brink, 1988). The findings were more frequent and the concentrations higher than had been anticipated based on earlier laboratory and field studies. As a result, a great deal of attention during the late 1980s focused on diffuse pollution of pesticides from agricultural fields to groundwater and surface waters.

To explore the reasons for pesticide contamination in stream water it was decided to initiate a monitoring programme, working beyond the well-controlled conditions (e.g. laboratory, lysimeters, field plots) under which, for good reasons, many environmental fate studies are made. The intention was to investigate pesticide sources, pathways and occurrence in stream water within a small agricultural catchment. The work was carried out in close cooperation with the farmers operating in the selected area. The programme was started in 1990 and continued during the entire 1990s. Here we describe risk mitigation efforts implemented in the catchment since 1995 and present the levels of pesticides occurring in stream water leaving the catchment during a 10-year period.

The Monitoring Programme at Vemmenhög

The Vemmenhög catchment is located in the extreme south of Sweden, in an area with undulating topography and glacial till soils. The total catchment area is 9 km^2 (900 ha) consisting of 95% arable land, with four major crops constituting ~95% of the cropped area (winter cereals, spring cereals, winter oilseed rape, sugar beet). None of the crops are irrigated. Sandy loam and loamy soils dominate the catchment. The climate in the region is maritime, with mean annual temperature 7.2°C and mean annual precipitation 662 mm. Extensive drainage systems have been installed in the catchment collecting tile drainage and also runoff water from surface runoff inlets, which are often used as inspection wells and located in the lowest-lying positions in the landscape along the tile drains in the field. Surface runoff inlets can also be found along roads and in some farmyards.

Information on crops and pesticide handling and usage within this area was collected annually through interviews with the farmers. The total amount of pesticides applied in each crop rotation was, on average, 1,300 kg of active

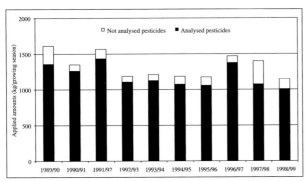

Figure 24.1. Total amount of pesticides applied in the catchment area during the growing seasons 1989/90-1998/1999. The columns are divided to show the distribution between pesticides included and not included in the analytical procedures.

ingredient (AI) and has been quite constant for the past seven years (Figure 24.1). About 35 different substances were used each year and ~90% (by weight) of these were included in the analyses (Figure 24.1). From 1990, an automatic water sampler collected time-integrated water samples during May-September/November at the outlet of the catchment. In addition, at different sites within the catchment, samples were collected to assess point sources. The analyses included up to 50 different pesticides. A more detailed description of the catchment, pesticide usage, data collection and analytical methods is given elsewhere (Kreuger, 1998).

Mitigation Efforts – Implementation of best Management Practices for Pesticides

General Measures
In 1997, new legislation was introduced with stricter demands regarding pesticide use and application. The legislation included requirements for spray-free buffer zones, regulations concerning the use of pesticides in water protection areas and compulsory book-keeping of pesticide applications. Also in 1997, an information campaign called 'Safe Pesticide Use' was launched on the initiative of farmers' organisations in a joint collaboration with five other organisations and authorities. The focus was to raise the awareness amongst farmers of the environmental and health risks when filling and emptying spraying equipment and the risks of wind and soil losses.

During 1998-1999, a programme entitled 'Sustainable conventional agriculture' was launched with EU and national money to give (mainly small and medium-sized) farmers financial compensation during a 5-year period on agreeing to comply with risk reduction measures within agriculture. This included, for example, demands for the farmers to have spray-free buffer zones, a safe place for filling and cleaning the sprayer (i.e. on a biobed, on a concrete area with collection of the liquid or in the field on active arable soil, see Figures 23.6 and 23.7), inspection of the sprayer and training courses.

In 1999, Swedish sugar beet growers and the sugar industry agreed to introduce an Environmental Management System as an integrated part of the contract for growing sugar beet in order to improve all environmental aspects of sugar beet growing, including the safe use of pesticides. These two last programmes involved giving growers an economic incentive to minimise risks when using pesticides

Site-specific Measures
In late 1994, a meeting was held with farmers operating in the catchment to give practical advice on the safe use of pesticides and risk reduction strategies. The advice primarily consisted of explaining to farmers possible sources of contamination and giving positive formulated examples of how to decrease these. Farmers attending the meeting were offered, free of charge, a personal visit on the farm.

Shortly following the meeting, about one-third of the farmers were visited. The farmers were guaranteed secrecy to make it easier to discuss problems. The advice were adjusted to local conditions on the specific farm, directed to safe storage of pesticides, how to avoid point sources when filling and cleaning sprayers and appropriate parking ground for the sprayer. Moreover, information was given about buffer zones to wells, drainage wells and open ditches when filling and spraying and about spraying herbicides on farmyards and other areas with low organic matter content. Voluntary inspection of sprayers in use was also encouraged to reduce the risks of point sources caused by leaking hoses and dripping nozzles.

Moreover, in early 1995, staff involved in this work met with sales agents selling plant protection products to farmers in the region, providing them with information and practical training on the safe use of pesticides. Since these people often meet with the farmers out on the farm, it was equally important to give them the same kind of information as the farmers.

Meetings with the farmers in the area have continued, providing them with feedback on the results of the monitoring program, as well as new knowledge and recommendations regarding sources of contamination and practical solutions. Other farmers operating in the area were also visited during the following years. All visits by the staff were made only at the request of the farmer.

Results

A total of 39 pesticides (31 herbicides, 4 fungicides and 4 insecticides) and 3 herbicide metabolites have been detected in stream water samples collected during the 10-year period, with approx. 10 pesticides having a detection frequency of >50% during individual years. Monitoring results obtained during the first years revealed elevated concentrations (up to 200 µg/l for single pesticides) and also pesticide residues entering the stream without preceding rainfall, clearly a result of accidental spillage when filling or cleaning the spraying equipment on surfaces with drainage in direct connection to the stream. Investigations also demonstrated very high concentrations (up to 2000 µg/l) in run-off water entering surface water inlet wells on farmyards close to areas where filling of sprayers had taken place and also where the farmyard had been treated with herbicides to keep it free of weeds. Calculations showed that pesticide application for weed control on farmyards alone contributed ~20% of the overall pesticide load in stream water. A more detailed presentation of the results is given elsewhere (Kreuger, 1998).

During recent years there has been a decrease in pesticide concentrations in stream water. The results demonstrate a considerable reduction in overall pesticide findings in the stream, with concentrations down by more than 90% (Figure 24.2). Transported amounts have also declined significantly during the time period 1990-2000 (Figure 24.3). The most notable decrease in concentration levels and transported amount occurred in 1995, coinciding with the onset of the information efforts that first took place in the area before the 1995 application season.

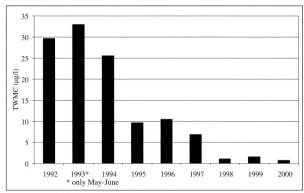

Figure 24.2. Time-weighted mean concentration (TWMC) for the sum of pesticides in stream water during May-September 1992-2000.

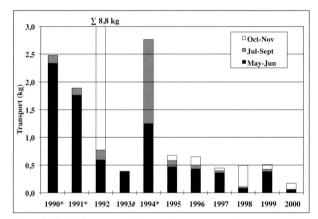

Figure 24.3. Total amount of pesticides transported in stream water during 1990-2000. The columns are divided to show different time periods.
* Sampled only during May-September.
# Sampled only during May-June.

The decreasing levels of pesticides in stream water from the catchment area can primarily be attributed to an increased awareness amongst the farmers of better routines for the correct handling of spraying equipment and application procedures (including the practice of total weed killing on farmyards). During late 1998, the first biobed (Torstensson and Castillo, 1997) was constructed in the catchment and since 2000 all farmers use either a biobed, a concrete area with collection of liquid or active arable soil when filling and cleaning the sprayer. The use of all kinds of herbicides on farmyards, including those registered for application on yards and hard surfaces, has discontinued and today only mechanical methods and glyphosate (which is registered for those purposes) is used on these areas.

However, there has also been a slight change in the usage of pesticides active at lower doses, although, as can been seen in Figure 24.1, the total amount used in the area has been quite constant for the past seven years. Moreover, the number of farmers applying pesticides in the area has gradually decreased (~50% since 1990), resulting in fewer possible point sources.

Another factor is the increased use of glyphosate, both in the field and as a total weed killer on farmyards, which has more than doubled and is not reflected by the monitoring results since glyphosate has not yet been included in the analytical procedures.

Conclusions

Based on the results obtained, it can be concluded that the occurrence of pesticides in surface water is the result of (i) natural processes influenced by soil and weather conditions, together with the intrinsic properties of the compound, as well as (ii) point sources such as spills and non-agricultural application (e.g. in farmyards).

In order to reduce the level of pesticides in streams and rivers, more efforts should be directed towards education and information to those using pesticides with the aim of minimising the quantities applied (e.g. by better calibrated spraying equipment and dose adjustment) and to avoid unintentional misuse and spillage.

The farmers were more willing to 'accept' information when given personally and adjusted to site-specific conditions than when received through general letters and pamphlets. It is essential to involve the farmers in the work and give them regular positive feed-back on the progress.

The implementation of agricultural best management practices appears to have had a positive effect on water quality in this area. However, both stream water and groundwater monitoring will be continued for several years to assess more definitively the changes in water quality.

Risk Assessments for Pests and Diseases of Field Crops, especially Forecasting and Warning Systems

25

Roland Sigvald
Swedish University of Agricultural Sciences
Uppsala, Sweden,

Introduction

The economic importance of pests and diseases of agricultural crops, the availability of new, highly effective pesticides, and the negative effects of insecticides, fungicides and herbicides have focused attention on forecasting pest outbreaks. To avoid great yield reductions, there has been an increased use of pesticides during recent decades in most European countries. However, the negative effects of insecticides, fungicides and herbicides have also been more obvious during this period. Minimising the use of pesticides will require better knowledge of insect population dynamics and the epidemiology of virus and fungal diseases, as well as economic threshold values. Such information is essential when developing pest management strategies and in decision-making related to pesticide treatments, etc. It has also become increasingly obvious during the past decade that it is not possible to minimise the use of chemicals in agriculture without an effective warning system based on the ability to forecast damage by pests and diseases. Such information is necessary in order to evaluate the costs and benefits associated with a particular chemical treatment. Forecasting pest outbreaks is very important in increasing profitability and at the same time minimising the negative effects on flora, fauna and drinking water.

In order to minimise the impact by pests and diseases on field crops it is important to use several methods that are favourable to the crop, but unfavourable to the pest or disease. A combination of control techniques in a particular cropping system includes cultural practices, crop rotation, use of resistant varieties and chemical treatment only when there is a real need. Crops must be protected to prevent unacceptably large yield losses and reduction in product quality. However, pesticides have to have a minimal impact on non-target organisms and be accepted by society. In several European countries including Sweden there is great interest in reducing the use of chemicals in agriculture and developing a more environmentally sound agricultural system. Forecasting and warning systems for pests and diseases have an important role in Integrated Pest Management (IPM) and also for advisory services. Since 1980 there has been increased interest in developing forecasting methods as well as in developing an effective warning system for pests and diseases in Sweden and many other countries in northern Europe. This chap-

Table 25.1. Estimated yield increase by treatment against pests and diseases in barley. Average of 10-year period. Proportion of area in different classes.

Yield increase, Dt/ha	Diseases % area	Aphids % area
0-2	30	30
2-4	30	25
4-6	20	20
6-8	10	10
8-10	5	5
10-12	3	5
12-14	2	2
14-16	0	1
16-18	0	1
18-20	0	1

Table 25.2. Estimated yield increase by treatment against pests and diseases in barley. Year with high incidence or attack by aphids. Proportion of area in different classes.

Yield increase, Dt/ha	Diseases % area	Aphids % area
0-2	20	5
2-4	30	10
4-6	20	15
6-8	15	20
8-10	10	25
10-12	3	10
12-14	2	5
14-16	0	5
16-18	0	3
18-20	0	2

ter describes forecasting systems for pests and diseases mainly in Sweden and the warning system.

Economic Importance of Pests and Diseases

Several pests and diseases cause great yield losses in Sweden. Some of the major agricultural crops affected are cereals, oilseed rape, potatoes, sugar beet and peas. Yield losses can vary greatly between years as well as between regions of the country – both within and between years.

Aphids are the most important insects on cereals. They not only cause direct damage but also transmit virus diseases. Aphicide treatments are profitable on about 70% of national barley and oat crops during years with heavy outbreaks of cereal aphids, especially *Rhopalosiphum padi*. In years with low attacks, spraying is only profitable on 10% or less of the cereal crop. Other insects of great economic importance include wheat blossom midge on wheat, frit fly on oats, blossom beetle on rapeseed and various aphid species on potatoes, sugar beet, oilseed rape and peas.

Economically important fungal diseases include powdery mildew and leaf spot diseases (*Stagonospora nodorum, S. tritici, Rhynchosporium secalis, Drechslera teres*) on cereals, especially on winter wheat and barley, *Sclerotinia sclerotiorum* and *Alternaria brassicae* on oilseed rape, late blight on potatoes, barley yellow dwarf virus (BYDV) on cereals and potato virus Y (PVY) on potatoes. Forecasting methods have been developed for some of these pests and diseases in Sweden.

The economic importance of different pests and diseases has been estimated in different crops in Sweden partly based upon surveys carried out every year and field experiments with treatment against pests and diseases. Based upon such results, economic threshold values have been estimated for the most important pests and diseases in cereals, sugar beet, potatoes and oilseed rape.

Estimates of the proportion of area that can be profitable to treat against pests or diseases are based on the cost of treatment (chemical, tramlines and driving) and the value of the yield increase. Tables 25.1 and 25.2 show some examples.

Forecasting Methods

Aphids on Cereals

In Sweden *Rhopalosiphum padi* is the most important aphid species on cereals, especially on oats and spring barley, but *Sitobion avenae* is also of some importance in southern Sweden. Because of the great variation in attack intensities between years and regions of Sweden, accurate forecasting methods are needed. For example, it is important to estimate the general need for aphicides long (several months) before the actual spraying, to allow time for delivery. However, specific forecasts can only be made a few weeks in advance. Thus both long-term and short-term forecasting methods are needed.

For more than 25 years suction traps have been used in Sweden to relate numbers of autumn and spring migrating aphids to the intensity of attacks on cereals and other crops, partly to develop the capability for making long-term forecasts. Aphid migration has been studied for about 25 years in Sweden, especially with regard to *R. padi* (Wiktelius, 1981).

There are now nine suction traps in Sweden, ranging from the extreme south to the north of the country. The distance between the most southerly and most northerly traps is approximately 1,600 km. In Sweden *R. padi* overwinters as an egg on *Prunus padus*. The migration during autumn has a great influence on the number of eggs laid on the winter host and on the number of spring migrators.

The number of autumn migrators gives rather good information on the risk of attack in the following year, but the relationship between number of overwintering eggs and proportion of fields above the damage threshold is stronger (r^2=0.4), and that between spring migration and proportion of fields above the damage threshold even stronger (r^2=0.7). In some years unfavourable weather (i.e. low temperatures and rainfall) makes it difficult for the aphids to migrate to spring cereals and during such years the severity of attack is much lower than predicted based on the winter egg counts. Under such conditions, suction traps give good information about the risk of attack by *R. padi* on spring barley and oats. The forecasts together with a good warning system and observations in the specific field give the farmer a good basis for decision-making.

Forecasting Aphids in Europe

For several years there has been collaboration between European countries concerning suction trap catches and aphid migration. About 20 countries participate, including data from 80 suction traps in Europe (EXAMINE: http://www.rothamsted.ac.uk/examine/). The map below shows the location of suction traps in Europe (Figure 25.1).

Results from suction trap catches in Sweden are used in forecasting aphids, e.g. *Rhopalosiphum padi*. The migration in autumn gives an indication of the risk of attack in the following year. In 1987 there were very few

Figure 25.1. Location of suction traps in Europe operating 2010. Source: http://www.rothamsted.bbsrc.ac.uk/examine/network.html

aphids in cereal fields and no need for chemical treatment against aphids in cereals. However, in the autumn 1987 there was a great migration, indicating that 1988 could be a problematic year if there were good conditions for spring migration in 1988. The results from suction trap catches showed that there was a great risk of severe attack by *R. padi* in 1988 and the results from field surveys later showed that about 70% of spring cereal fields in central Sweden had to be treated against aphids.

Forecasting Leaf Spot Diseases on Cereals
It is important to study relationships between weather and plant diseases in supervised controls. In Sweden the influence of rainfall before and during heading in winter wheat has been studied. A strong correlation was found between rainfall and attack by *Septoria spp*. Such information can be helpful when assessing the need for chemical treatments against leaf diseases (Wiik, 1993, 2009a,b).

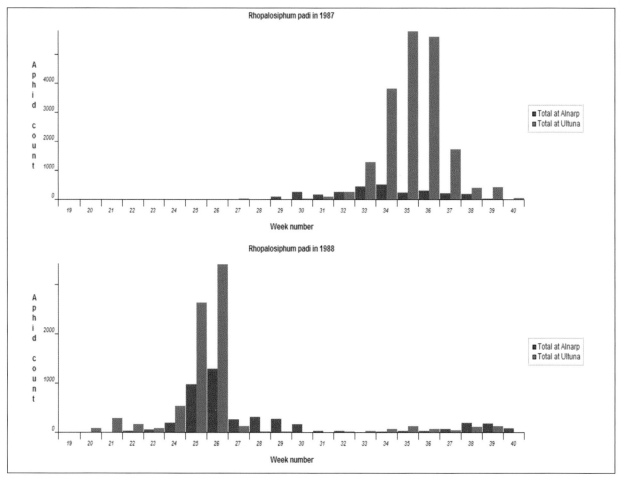

Figure 25.2. Suction trap catches of aphids in 1987 and 1988 in central Sweden

Besides *Septoria* spp., risk assessments for *Rhynchosporium secalis* and *Drechslera teres* have also been developed, partly based on weather data. These risk assessments also take cultivar, nitrogen level and crop rotation into account and include field inspection.

Forecasting the Incidence of Eyespot

The economic importance of eyespot (*Pseudocercosporella herpothricoides*) on winter wheat and rye has been studied in field experiments for several years. The disease seems to be of less importance in central Sweden than in southern and western parts of the country (Olvång, 1991). This is partly because of differences in weather conditions. During the past decade weather data have been used to assess the risk of eyespot on winter wheat and rye by using data from 50 meteorological stations in Sweden belonging to the Swedish Meteorological and Hydrological Institute. The data were transferred daily to a database at the Swedish University of Agricultural Sciences at Uppsala. From there the information is made directly available to plant protection officers.

Wheat Blossom Midge

During some years wheat blossom midge (*Contarinia tritici* and *Sitodiplosis mosellana*) are of great economic importance in winter and spring wheat. Severe attacks by the larvae cause considerable yield losses amounting to 20-30% in some fields. However, severe attacks are infrequent, which is an important fact to consider when making a decision on spraying. For more than 20 years, annual surveys have been carried out every year in wheat fields in central and southern Sweden. In each field, kernel sampling has been carried out to obtain information on wheat midge populations. This information together with weather data during the growing season allows the risk of attack by the midges to be estimated.

Frit fly on Oats

Frit fly (*Oscinella frit L.*) is a stem-boring fly which causes damage to cereals and grasses in many countries. In Sweden it is an important pest especially on oats, and can cause losses of up to 50%. Chemical control is based on the prevention of egg-laying by application of a pyrethroid before two-leaf stage. Therefore, the farmer has to decide the need for spraying early in the cropping season. To avoid routine spraying and at the same time apply insecticides when it is profitable, a reliable forecasting method is needed.

Since 1985 a method has been developed in Sweden which is now used in practice by advisory services and farmers. An important factor to consider is timing between insect and plant development, but also population level and weather during the egg-laying period. The method is partly based on meteorological data, biological observations and sampling. Sunshine hours in the previous year and suction trap catches give a good estimate of the present population level. During spring and early summer the temperature sum is calculated (base temperature +8°C), which gives an accurate prediction of when migration of frit fly will take place. Weather data such as temperature are also considered, because this has a great influence on frit fly activity and egg laying (Lindblad, 1993; Lindblad and Solbreck, 1998).

Based upon the research, a number of risk factors are considered when estimating the risk of attack in a specific field. The method has been validated in more than 800 oat fields. There is a very good agreement between risk assessment (risk points in the specific field) and the proportion of main stems infested by the larvae. The method is now widely used by farmers. They get necessary information via leaflets, but also interactively via the internet from the Swedish University of Agricultural Sciences.

Potato Virus Y

Aphids play an important role in the epidemics of both persistently and non persistently transmitted plant viruses. Many of the non persistently transmitted viruses are known to be vectored by aphids, and a number of species have been confirmed as vectors during the past few decades. However, only a small proportion of the world's aphid species have been tested to determine whether or not they can act as vectors. Interactions between host plants, viruses, vectors and the environment are very complicated. Environment influences the crop as well as vectors and the virus, and consequently there are many factors to consider in seed potato production.

Many aphid species are important vectors of non persistently transmitted viruses. Most viruses transmitted by aphids in a non persistent manner are believed to be acquired and transmitted within fields by the probing of aphids flying from plant to plant. Potato virus Y is transmitted mainly by aphid species that do not feed on the crop that they inadvertently infect (Sigvald, 1986). After probing for 5-10 seconds the aphids acquire the virus and are immediately able to transmit it to other plants, However, most aphids only remain infective for about 30 minutes. Starvation prior to probing source plants greatly increases the proportion of aphids transmitting non-persistently transmitted viruses.

Suction Traps

Although PVY can be transmitted by aphid species that feed preferentially on potatoes, other species that do not colonise potatoes seem to be far more important, e.g. *Rhopalosiphum. padi, Brachycaudus helichrysi, Acythosiphon pisum* and *Phorodon humili* (Sigvald, 1984). In Sweden and in many other countries where PVY is a serious problem for seed potato producers, the relationship between aphid migration and the spread of PVY has been studied by exposing bait plants to vectors in the field (Sigvald, 1989). Winged aphids (alates) have also been collected and placed on test plants to determine whether or not they are viruliferous.

Insecticide treatment against non-persistently transmitted viruses such as PVY is not very effective. However,

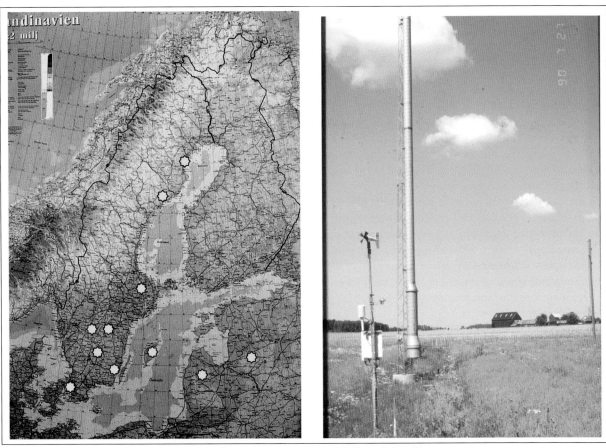

Figure 25.3. The location of suction traps in Sweden (left) and a suction trap (right). Photo: R. Sigvald.

PLRV (Potato leaf roll virus), which is transmitted in a persistent manner, can be reduced in seed potato fields by insecticide treatment. The main vectors of PLRV are those aphid species which feed on the potato plant, such as *Myzus persicae, Macrosiphum euphorbiae, Aphis nasturtii, Aphis frangulae* and *Aulacorthum solani*. To minimise the spread of PLRV, treatment with insecticide is effective.

In Sweden and many other countries in northern Europe, PVY is one of the most important virus diseases on potatoes (Sigvald, 1990). During the past decade there has been increasing interest in developing methods for PVY forecasting. The main variables used when forecasting the incidence of PVY include the number of winged aphids and their vector efficiency, the time of aphid mi-

gration in relation to plant age, and the availability of virus sources (Sigvald, 1985, 1986). Simulation models have also been used to describe the epidemiology of non-persistently transmitted viruses (Ruesink and Irwin, 1986; Sigvald 1986).

In most countries there are programmes for seed potato production to minimise re-infection of different diseases and thus produce healthy seed potatoes. In Scandinavia, aphid borne potato virus Y (PVY) is more frequent on potatoes than potato leaf roll virus (PLRV), which is also spread by aphids. This can probably be explained by the fact that the abundance of *Myzus persicae* (the main vector of PLRV) in potato fields is lower compared with that of the aphid species vectoring PVY. In central Europe and tropical countries PLRV is more important.

However, the degree of spread of PVY varies greatly between regions and years. In the northern regions of Scandinavia the spread of PVY is minimal because vectors are uncommon. By contrast, in southern regions the spread of PVY has led to serious problems for seed potato growers during some years. Nevertheless, few fields are infected so severely as to warrant rejection of the seed potatoes produced.

There are many different factors involved in the epidemiology of potato virus Y and several factors to consider to minimise spread of aphid-borne viruses. After meristem culture and production of pre-basic seed potatoes, some important factors to consider are:

- Virus-free seed potatoes.
- Isolated seed potato fields and special regions for seed potato production.
- Early planting and sprouted seed potatoes.
- Growing period of seed potatoes during periods with few vectors.
- Mineral oil to reduce virus infection.
- Minimise virus sources outside the seed potato field (potatoes, peppers, etc.).
- Field inspection and removal of virus-infected potato plants.
- Early haulm killing before viral infection of progeny tubers.
- Forecasting potato viruses to act before progeny tubers are infected.

The epidemiology of potato virus Y^o (PVY^o) in a given field has been studied in Sweden and described in a relational diagram. The model output predicts the extent to which the proportion of progeny tubers infected with PVY^o will increase during late summer. Some of the following parameters and variables are included in the simulation model for potato virus Y: Healthy potato plants, Newly PVY^o-infected potato plants, Potato plants with PVY^o-infected progeny tubers, Total PVY^o-infected potato plants acting as virus sources, Length of latent period, Level of mature plant resistance, Vector efficiency, Cultivar susceptibility, Mineral oil application rate, Date of haulm destruction, Removal of PVY-diseased potato plants and Proportion of progeny tubers infected with PVY^o.

There is a close correlation between forecasted and observed values. The study shows that the PVY^o simulation model can be used in forecasting the risk of virus spread. In Sweden during years when the incidence of PVY is low, there is no need to test progeny tubers after harvest. Thus by using the simulation model to forecast PVY incidence, farmers would be able to skip post-harvest testing during low-disease years, thereby reducing their operational costs. Similarly, disease incidence can be reduced by taking prophylactic measures at an early stage.

The seed potato grower would also benefit from being able to predict the proportion of progeny tubers infected in late summer. If there is a great risk that the level of infection of the tuber yield will exceed the threshold set for seed potatoes, it may be more profitable to delay haulm destruction and market the potatoes for consumption or industrial use (starch or ethanol). During the past five years the forecasting method presented here has shown great promise when applied under practical conditions.

In Sweden and several other countries suction traps have been used in aphid forecasting. There are often great differences in trap catches between years and regions. In Sweden, *R. padi* is the most common aphid species caught in the traps in southern, central and northern parts of the country in most years. In 1989 there was a great difference in suction trap catches between southern and northern Sweden (Table 25.3).

Several aphid species were more commonly trapped in southern Sweden than in northern, especially *Acyrthosiphon pisum*, *Aphis fabae*, *Brachycaudus heli-*

Table 25.3. Number of alatae caught in suction traps in southern and northern Sweden, 1989.

Aphid species	Southern (M)			Northern (AC)		
	May	June	July	May	June	July
Acyrthosiphon pisum	18	77	263	0	0	0
Aphis sp.	7	67	558	0	0	0
Brachycaudus helichrysi	104	400	983	0	0	0
Metopolophium dirhodum	10	158	664	0	0	0
Myzus persicae	0	0	0	0	0	0
Phorodon humuli	2	37	83	0	0	0
Rhopalosiphum padi	45	2,405	6,482	0	165	136
Other aphid species	234	2,161	3,646	2	88	136

Table 25.4. Number of alatae caught in suction traps in northern Sweden 1987 and 1990.

Aphid species	1987			1990		
	May	June	July	May	June	July
Acyrthosiphon pisum	0	0	0	0	0	3
Aphis sp.	0	1	11	0	3	1
Brachycaudus helichrysi	0	0	0	0	0	1
Metopolophium dirhodum	0	0	0	0	0	0
Myzus persicae	0	0	2	0	0	0
Rhopalosiphum padi	0	3	40	3	298	2,226
Other aphid species	0	2	228	2	137	286

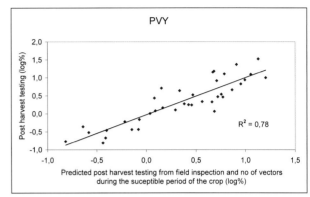

Figure 25.4. Relationship between total number of aphids in suction traps in different regions and years and post harvest testing of progeny tubers.

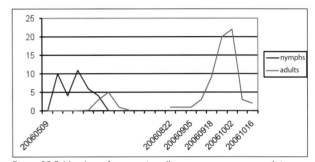

Figure 25.5. Number of vectors in yellow water traps per week in central Sweden (nymphs and adults).

chrysi, *Metopolophium dirhodum* and *R. padi*, which resulted in a great spread of PVY in the southern regions that year. However, in some years there is also a large migration of aphids in northern Sweden during the growing season of potatoes. In 1990 there were many aphids in the suction trap in northern Sweden in comparison to 1987 (Table 25.4) and this resulted in great differences in spread of PVY between those years.

There are also examples from other countries of Europe, where *R. padi* plays an important role in the spread of PVY. In 1976, there were large migrations of *R. padi* in both western and northern parts of Europe and this was probably the main reason for the great spread of potato virus Y during that year. Differences between years and regions in aphid migration have a great influence on the spread of several aphid-borne plant viruses, e.g. PVY, and this is very important to consider in seed potato production.

Results from suction trap catches in Sweden show that there is a rather weak relationship between the total number of winged aphids and proportion of PVY-infected progeny tubers ($r^2 \approx 0.5$), but this is increased by taking into account only the main vectors of PVY (Figure 25.4). The relationship is very good when also taking into account the effect of mature plant resistance and proportion of virus sources (Sigvald, 1985).

Wheat Dwarf Virus
Wheat dwarf virus (WDV) is a severe disease of winter wheat, with the causal agent being a geminivirus trans-

mitted by the leafhopper *Psammotettix alienus*. Field surveys of WDV incidence and vector occurrence have been conducted for the past 10 years in wheat fields in central Sweden. The objective was to estimate the extent of primary spread of WDV in the autumn by adult leafhoppers migrating into the fields, and the secondary spread in the following early summer by the progeny of the immigrants.

The aim of these studies is to estimate the risk of spread of WDV and make a risk assessment based upon number of vectors, developmental stage of the crop when infected with WDV, occurrence of virus sources and also weather data. The results so far indicate that occurrence of vectors at an early stage in the autumn will increase the risk of spread in areas with many virus sources.

Figures 25.5 and 25.6 show some results from the investigations. In the autumn 2006, many *P. alienus* were

Figure 25.6. Wheat Dwarf Virus in a wheat field in 2006 in the province of Uppland, Sweden. Photo: R. Sigvald.

caught in the yellow water traps in central Sweden. This indicated a high risk for 2007.

The number of wheat fields with WDV in 2006 was relatively low. Samples taken in winter wheat fields in autumn and winter 2006/2007 showed primary infection with WDV to be rather high. Early occurrence of the vector when the crop is still very susceptible will increase the risk of secondary spread. To prevent great yield losses, it is possible to use insecticides.

Forecasting Late Blight on Potatoes

Interest in reducing fungicides in potatoes has led to increased efforts to develop methods for forecasting the risk of late blight in potatoes. Attacks by late blight on potatoes in Sweden differ very much between regions and years. During 1992 the dry weather in most parts of the country was unfavourable to late blight, but in 1993 the weather was very favourable.

During the past decades we have evaluated a few models for late blight in Sweden (Andersson, 1994). The daily weather data needed are automatically transferred from the Swedish Meteorological and Hydrological Institute to the Swedish University of Agricultural Sciences. The results so far are promising. The forecasting method indicates that treatments recommended by the model are close to actual requirements and less than routine spraying, but further studies will have to be carried out to make the forecasts more reliable. During 1994 the model was tested with weather data from different sources, including synoptic weather stations, automatic weather stations in the potato field, interpolated weather data and weather data from 5-day forecasts. The results were very interesting and will be very valuable when validating the model for late blight.

About 15 years ago the mating type A2 was discovered in Europe and in 1986 in Sweden. During the past decade there has been increased interest in investigating the occurrence of A2 in several countries in Europe as well as in Sweden. Since 1995 observations in Sweden and in other countries in Europe have indicated the presence of soil-borne inoculum of late blight, *Phytophthora infestans* (Andersson et al., 1998, 2007). In potato fields in Sweden, both mating types A1 and A2 were isolated in 1996 and 1997 and oospores were found on leaves and stems as well as in stolons. The importance of soil-borne inoculum of late blight for early infections is of great interest.

Sclerotinia Stem Rot

Sclerotinia stem rot (*Sclerotinia sclerotiorum*) is one of the most important diseases on spring-sown oilseed rape. During years with high humidity, yield reduction can reach 60% in heavily infested fields and in such years chemical treatment is profitable in 40-60% of the fields. Sclerotinia stem rot can be effectively controlled by fungicide treatment during full flowering. Routine spraying is not profitable, since the cost of chemical treatment is high and disease incidence varies greatly between years and regions and also between fields within a region, thus justifying a forecasting system.

A method for forecasting the incidence of Sclerotinia stem rot has been developed in Sweden (Twengström and Sigvald, 1993). Besides field experiments and laboratory studies, data from more than 800 fields have been collected to improve the method as well as for validation of the risk assessment. The method is mainly based upon a number of risk factors, such as crop density, crop rotation, level of previous Sclerotinia infestation (estimation of inoculum in soil), time for apothecia formation from sclerotia, rainfall during early summer and during flowering and weather forecast. An initial risk assessment showed very good agreement between risk points and Sclerotinia stem rot incidence. To further improve the model, specific field data were analysed by logistic regression. The results showed that the model could be simplified and still give very good or even better predictions (Yuen et al., 1996; Twengström et al., 1998).

The method has been used by farmers during the past decade. It has been available in the form of risk points, but during recent years also interactively via the internet. Since the method was introduced about 20 years ago, the proportion of fields profitable to spray has increased, and today there is very good agreement between the need for spraying and actual treatments. This has been investigated e.g. in the province of Uppland from surveys in farmers' fields (unsprayed plots) and data from the statistical departments (Figure 25.7). The great success of the forecasting method for Sclerotinia stem rot is probably to a great extent due to the fact that advisory services and farmers have participated in validation and implementation.

Cabbage Stem Flea Beetle on Winter Rape Seed

A method for forecasting the intensity of attacks by cabbage stem flea beetle (*Psylliodes chrysocephala*) has been used in Sweden (Rufelt, 1993). Experience has shown that the method works very well and, furthermore, it is a very good example of a case where the use of chemicals could be reduced sharply with only a minor reduction in yield. Chemical treatment of winter rapeseed is recommended when the population exceeds the control threshold of 0.5 larvae per plant during the winter proceeding the growing season. During about half the years studied, seed treatment against cabbage stem flea beetles has been needed and thus a considerable reduction in the use of chemicals against this insect has been achieved.

Beetle populations fluctuate greatly between years. During the past 30 years there have been three peaks. These fluctuations seem to be strongly related to climatic conditions. Apparently, several successive mild winters allow the population to increase enormously. However, there are undoubtedly other factors involved in regulating populations of the cabbage stem flea beetle.

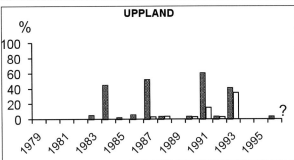

Figure 25.7a (above) Sclerotinia stem rot on oil seed rape. Photo: R. Sigvald. b (below). The figure shows the proportion of fields, which are profitable to treat (black) against Sclerotinia stem rot and the proportion of fields which have been treated (white) in central Sweden.

research and development of currant forecasting methods included validation using field-specific data from more than 3,000 fields of different crops. In addition, weather data have been included in the models to improve them. In the near future the availability of forecasting methods via the internet will increase and thereby improve the possibility for farmers to have direct access to new models for specific fields.

Future Aspects on Forecasting Pests and Diseases

Further improvements of forecasting systems for pests and diseases on field crops rely on close collaboration between researchers, advisory services and farmers, especially for validation and implementation of methods. The

Warning Systems for Pests and Diseases in Sweden and Northwest Russia

There is a great need for effective warning systems for pests and diseases. Growers need information about the risk of attack by different pests and diseases long before spraying. Warnings are especially critical when high levels of attack are expected, which would lead to severe losses if farmers were unprepared.

For more than 15 years a warning system has been under development in Sweden in a partnership between the Unit for Applied Plant Protection at the Swedish University of Agricultural Sciences and the Swedish Board of Agriculture. In each of five regions there is a Regional Plant Protection Centre to organise the work and handle the local information about the actual situation, which is then presented via the internet for different pests and diseases. Such information and availability of forecasting methods for different pests and diseases is very important in integrated pest management.

In southern and central Sweden, more than 1,200 fields representing a variety of crops are inspected weekly. The number of insects per plant or the disease incidence is recorded using special protocols. Surveys are made on Monday every week. The data are analysed and stored in computers. When the weekly analysis is ready, a summary is faxed to the extension service in the region. The day after the field evaluations are received, each Plant Protection Centre holds a telephone conference with advisors in the region concerned. The actual information is then mailed or faxed to farmers and advisory service personal.

Information Systems

During the past decade information systems have developed very rapidly in many different areas. In the agricultural sector there are many new ways of informing farmers and advisory services on new results from research and development. Besides the more conventional ways via reports, leaflets, conferences, field days and courses, there are also good possibilities via the internet.

Different organisations working in this area of information systems to agriculture have also changed greatly during the past decade. Traditionally there were a number of steps before the results reached the farmers. At the Swedish University of Agricultural Sciences about 20 years ago there were departments working on more basic research and applied departments. Then the results were rewritten in a more suitable way for advisory services by the Research Information Centre at SLU. Different reports and results from projects were then made available to farmers via regional plant production officers or the local branch of the Swedish Board of Agriculture.

That system of information channels has now changed. For more than 20 years, a number of individual advisors have been serving a number of farmers (each advisor about 40 farmers) and the farmers pay for this service. These advisors are sometime private consultants and sometime connected to a local or regional organisation. Besides these advisors, the farmers' organisations have many in-house advisors and the farmers pay for the service to some extent. Different companies also have advisors, who inform farmers about chemicals, fertilisers, etc.

In 1995 the Research Information Centre was reorganised at our university and now the different departments are responsible for the information from research activities. Besides the more conventional ways, we also use the internet. This makes it possible for advisory services and farmers to directly get new results from the university and this will probably be important in the future.

Forecasts for different pests and diseases are given via the internet. This information is available for advisory services and farmers.

Use of Meteorological Data in Forecasting Pests and Diseases

In Sweden weather data have been used as a complement to other data in forecasting pests and diseases for more than 30 years. From about 50 meteorological stations belonging to the Swedish Meteorological and Hydrological Institute, weather data are automatically transferred to a database at the Swedish University of Agricultural Sciences at Uppsala. Besides weather data, such as temperature, humidity, rainfall and radiation, various calculated values are also transferred automatically, e.g. the temperature sum for frit fly and carrot fly, risk values for *P. herpothrichoides*, output from different models predicting the risk of late blight on potatoes and the risk of Sclerotinia stem rot on spring rapeseed crops.

Such data together with other biological information on pests and diseases are directly available to plant protection officers at the Swedish Board of Agriculture and researchers in plant protection. These data are intended to complement other information, such as warning letters, articles in different magazines, telephone conferences, and meetings during the growing season.

Close Collaboration between Researchers and Persons Working with Applied Plant Protection

For several years there has been close collaboration between researchers at the Swedish University of Agricultural Sciences and plant protection officers at the Swedish Board of Agriculture as well as other plant protection specialists. The Unit for Applied Plant Protection at the Swedish University of Agricultural Sciences has two main objectives in the above-mentioned area: 1) To develop forecasting methods for important pests and diseases together with specialists at the university; and 2) to keep the general public informed about any developments in the area of plant protection.

Data from the warning system can be used to evaluate different models. From each of the 1,200 fields subjected to weekly inspections, field data as crop rotation, cultivar, soil preparation, sowing date, etc. are also collected. Such data are valuable when assessing the reliability of different forecasting methods. The data can also be used when calculating the economic impacts of pests and diseases. Data on disease incidence and pest attack intensity are also valuable when trying to establish relationships between climatic factors and various plant protection problems.

Impact of Climate Change on Pests and Diseases of Field Crops

Climate has a great influence on the occurrence of pests and diseases of field crops. Dry conditions are often favourable to insect pests and wet conditions to fungal diseases, but there are several other factors which have a great influence on pest and disease development. Calculations of the damage to crops as a function of climate are complicated and research within this area is working to develop methods for both understanding and predicting the effects of climate change on the dynamics of insects and diseases (fungal, viral, bacterial) and on the damage they cause to crops.

Insect attacks on crops will probably increase in the future. There are several reasons for this. Higher temperature will increase the number of generations during the growing season and warmer climate during the winter will be favourable to insects and they will prob-

ably survive and therefore be more numerous in the spring. Aphids are very important in many countries of the world not only because of direct damage since they feed on the crop, but also indirect damage through the ability to transmit various viruses of different crops. In Sweden there are more than 50 aphid species of great importance for various crops. Some of these species will probably survive during mild winters and most regions of Sweden will probably experience increased problems with damage caused by insects and virus diseases, but the increase will be greatest in southern Sweden and in dry areas. Insects will be active considerably earlier in the spring than at present since the growing period will be extended. However, in some regions more rain is expected in late winter and early spring and therefore sowing time can be delayed and earlier attack by insects can be expected in comparison to the developmental stage of the crop.

The greater numbers of aphids at spring sowing and the fact that spring crops will be exposed to virus diseases at an earlier stage of development will increase the need for pesticides unless there is an increase in other methods such as use of resistant varieties. Insects are also favoured by high temperatures in summers and the need for insecticides will probably increase in most crops.

Aphids and virus attacks in autumn are currently limited, but the future climate will make great changes. The number of aphids (vectors of virus diseases) is relatively low at present, but milder autumns and higher winter temperature by 3-4°C will have a great influence. Some aphid species such as *Rhopalosiphum padi* will probably survive during the winter on grasses and winter cereals. Winter wheat and winter barley can be infected with barley yellow dwarf virus (BYDV) by *R. padi*, which is an important vector of BYDV. *Sitobion avenae* will also contribute to transmission of BYDV on winter cereals. This will increase damage by aphids and viruses and increase the need for insecticides to winter cereals. Aphids can also transmit viruses of winter oilseed rape and the future warmer climate will probably increase numbers of such vectors and increase problems with viruses in this crop.

In autumn 2006 the weather in southern Sweden was very mild and this was very favourable to aphids. Winged aphids, mainly *R. padi*, were trapped in the suction trap in southern Sweden until late November (Figure 25.8).

This indicates that *R. padi* could be a problem in winter wheat in the following year because of its ability to transmit BYDV. In early spring 2007 many winter wheat fields showed symptoms of BYDV. Analyses from samples in southern Sweden showed that fields were infected with BYDV, mainly PAV strain. There were great differences in virus incidence in wheat fields in southern Sweden, from very low to high. In some fields the yield reduction was probably more than 25%.

In a future warmer climate, there will probably be more aphids in the autumn, while newly introduced spring-sown crops such as maize that grow long into the autumn can act as a green bridge for viruses from spring-sown to winter-sown crops and thereby virus attacks will increase on winter wheat and winter barley. New insect pests will probably become established in Sweden, depending on the crops grown and winter conditions, but it is difficult to predict the insect species involved and a monitoring system is needed to follow developments in this area. Colorado beetle is one example of an insect pest

that will probably be introduced in the coming 20 years. This will cause greater problems for potato growers. In addition, insects can be transmitted long distances by the wind, thereby increasing the risk of new insect pests.

In most crops moisture and higher temperature are favourable to fungal diseases. In some regions of Sweden with more rain during the growing season we can expect greater attacks of late blight in potatoes. On the other hand, there may be drier conditions in south-east Sweden and thereby less problems than today. Winter cereals will be particularly vulnerable since they will have a long infection period in the autumn and thus diseases such as brown rust will increase. For spring cereals the effect can be less than at present in areas with a predicted relatively dry early summer period, such as southern areas of the country. In northern Sweden fungal diseases of cereals will probably increase due to the generally wetter and warmer climate.

In the future warmer climate with more aphid species also in northern parts of Sweden, seed potatoes will run

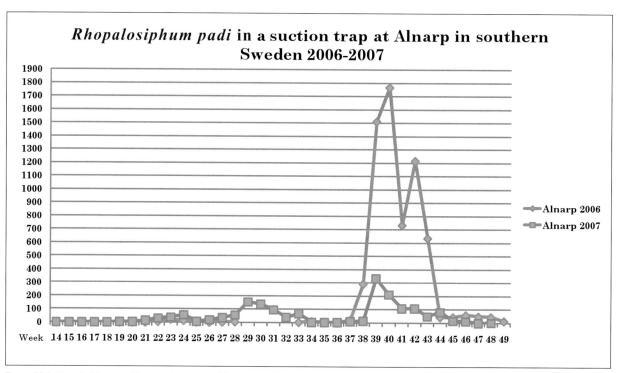

Figure 25.8. *Rhopalosiphum padi* in a suction trap at Alnarp in southern Sweden 2006-2007.

a greater risk of virus attacks than at present. The need may then arise to establish special areas for seed potato production in which cultivation of ordinary commercial potato crops with a high proportion of virus-infected potato plants are restricted. Increased incidence of different insect pests on most crops will increase the use of pesticides, an undesirable development from a number of perspectives. Improved cropping systems, increased use of resistant varieties and a good crop rotation to decrease the occurrence of pests and diseases will therefore be of increasing importance.

Forecasting System for Pests and Diseases of Field Crops in North-west Russia

The first regional plant protection stations in Russia were organised in 1870-1880. The Entomological Bureau was created in 1894 and the Phytopathological Bureau in 1907, both functioning under the State Department of Agriculture in St. Petersburg (since 1929 to present as laboratories of the All-Russian Institute of Plant Protection).

The single centralised Forecasting and Warning Service in the former USSR was finally established in 1957 to work with large collective and state farms. Each collective farm had a position for a plant protection agronomist responsible for phytosanitary conditions and information from the collective farm fields.

Regional observation posts had plant protection agronomists, who helped collective farms with the monitoring of pests and diseases in one or two small districts. The posts were managed by the Forecasting Departments in the Plant Protection Station in oblast, territory or republic. They had entomologists and phytopathologists, responsible for information from several regions. The Plant Protection Stations received information from all regions belonging to the oblast, territory or republic and, when necessary, entomologists and phytopathologists inspected fields in the regions and helped with pest and disease monitoring. The All-Russian Institute of Plant Protection (which used to be the All-Union Institute), gathered phytosanitary information from the territory of the whole Soviet Union.

This phytosanitary information was used for the creation of forecasts for major crop pests and diseases in the country. The forecasts were sent to the Ministry of Agriculture (located in Moscow), which planned the amount of pesticides needed for the country. Now the agricultural system is less centralised and the Ministry of Agriculture cannot plan the amount of pesticides needed nationally. The All-Russian Plant Protection Institute (VIZR) is responsible only for research in pest monitoring.

The present phytosanitary situation in Russia could be considered an emergency. The total number of plant protection activities has decreased dramatically, and consequently the losses to grain crops due to various insects and other harmful organisms have increased significantly. The plant protection services that were developed in the former Soviet Union cannot adequately function in the current situation. It is desirable, however, to develop sustainable agricultural systems based on the existing infrastructure. The current land use pattern in Russia includes large-scale farms created from the collective farms, small-scale farms and individual land ownership. All this land is affected by fluctuations in pests and diseases, and the farmers need information on the dynamics of pests and diseases in the different regions of NW Russia.

Forecasting Systems in Leningrad Oblast, Russia

All Regional Plant Protection Stations were re-organised in 2007 as Phytosanitary Departments of regional branches of the Russian Agricultural Centre of the Russian Ministry of Agriculture. The Regional Phytosanitary Department at Saint Petersburg contains about 10 small forecasting and diagnostic stations (sometime called local stations or observation posts), evenly distributed in the Leningrad region. Forecasting specialists, each using identical methods, inspect fields of all the main crops. They carry out observations noting phenological development and search for early symptoms of diseases and signs of impending pest outbreaks. Specialists from the Forecasting and Diagnostic Laboratory transfer information to plant protection agronomists in the districts.

At the moment this service mainly provides diagnostic and warning information, but there is a great need for additional information and implementation of methods in plant protection. Consequently, it is essential to develop new forecasting methods and effective warning and information systems. New agricultural producers and farmers, some of whom have no agricultural education, need good advice so that they can implement effective pest management practices in a timely fashion and, when possible, avoid the unnecessary use of chemicals.

Advisory Service and Information Systems in Crop Protection in NW Russia

Information on crop protection obtained through research at universities and at the All-Russian Institute is passed on to the advisory service at <u>Phytosanitary Departments</u> and farmers in different ways. There have been changes during the past 10 years, but in many ways contacts still work and new ways are being established. From the All-Russian Institute of Plant Protection, there are contacts between central (in Moscow) and regional advisory services (formerly Plant Protection Stations) in the following ways:

1. Exchange of written information by mail and e-mail.
    1.1. The All-Russian Institute of Plant Protection receives seasonal and annual reports from advisory services. Now all 76 <u>regional branches of the Russian Agricultural Centre</u> have active e-mail connections through the e-mail network in NW Russia (including Leningrad, Pskov, Novgorod and Karelia) established in 2007-2008.
    1.2. The All-Russian Institute of Plant Protection sends its reports and published information to central (the <u>Russian Agricultural Centre</u> at the Ministry of Agriculture of the Russian Federation in Moscow) and regional advisory services at the <u>regional branches of this Centre</u>. Now the Institute publishes dozens of recommendation books and collections of papers every year (in Russian). The Laboratory of Phytosanitary Diagnostics and Forecasts places some reports and information (in Russian mainly, with English abstracts) on the Institute website: http://www.vizrspb.narod.ru/index-en.htm/ (which is managed by the All-Russian Institute of Plant Protection).
2. The All-Russian Institute of Plant Protection organises meetings and training courses for advisory service workers in all of Russia and NW Russia every year. Many of the researchers at the All-Russian Institute also participate in regional meetings on Plant Protection in various parts of Russia, where they give lectures and reports. There was a long gap in this work, but now the number of participants is progressively increasing every year.

3. The Institute researchers work closely with Leningrad, Pskov Regional and with some district <u>branches of the Russian Agricultural Centre</u>, and with several collective farms in Leningrad oblast. They carry out demonstration trials on the Institute experimental plots and on fields of some collective farms. The Leningrad <u>branch of the Russian Agricultural Centre</u> supplies and receives written and oral information every week during the season, and the All-Russian Institute of Plant Protection helps them prepare recommendations and reports, e.g. in mapping of weeds, pests and diseases.

Therefore the combined work of this project between Sweden and Russia (in the form of published recommendations) can be quickly disseminated among farmers through regional and district <u>branches of the Russian Agricultural Centre</u>. In different ways, we plan to get comments from advisory service workers and farmers on the recommendations. This will help in future work to develop effective information systems on crop protection for advisory service workers and farmers.

Information Systems

Traditional problems in gathering, transferring and processing phytosanitary information with a view to forecasting yield losses from harmful organisms and the cost of protective actions are solved today using new methods of phytosanitary diagnostics and monitoring.

The development of modern systems of phytosanitary monitoring is impossible without the use of computer-based spatial modelling involving geoinformation systems and methods of molecular genetic diagnostics. A practical output of this long and labour-consuming scientific work is the computer handbooks supplied with the text information, together with high-quality colour photos and maps of the distribution and harmfulness of species and intraspecific forms of harmful organisms. The Agricultural Atlas of Russia and adjacent countries (2003-2008) is one example of the work completed in this area.

The Agricultural Atlas is accessible through the internet collection of agrobiocenotic and phytosanitary information, which makes up the information-diagnostic database for phytosanitary monitoring, as it contains references to huge amounts of printed materials, and also links to many biological and phytosanitary internet resources.

Active application of research findings in plant protection science is impossible without regular updating of internet resources, including updating by users. This requires electronic forecasting systems with which users can work in automatic mode, entering agroecological and phytosanitary data of a region. It is anticipated that this will become possible in the near future.

Since 2002, VIZR has created a system of exchange of new phytosanitary information between the central and regional laboratories and some industrial organisations. The Russian-Swedish cooperation within the Baltic Sea Regional Project allowed a similar system to be created in the conditions of NW Russia. The availability of modern techniques (portable laptops with wireless internet connection) facilitates and accelerates information interchange between experts of the agrarian and industrial complex, consulting services, administrative workers at all levels and experts at research organisations. Using microscopes equipped with digital cameras, practical workers can provide qualitative images of harmful objects or damaged plants from a site near the field, for example in a car. Using GPS-navigators, they can register the exact coordinates of a sample, while laptops with a 3G or Wi-Fi adapter allow the images and other information to be sent for identification to an expert in the area of pests, plant diseases or weeds. The image can also be placed on one of specialist biological internet forums, where preliminary identification of the material is frequently made within an hour.

A database (DB) was developed in 2009-2010 for accumulation of data on phytophages, plant pathogens and weeds populating agroecosystems in NW Russia. The main task is to simplify the problem of data storage, search and delivery experienced by the Plant Protection Service in forecasting and prevention of dangerous phytosanitary situations. The DB interface developed by means of SQL technology includes 22 connected tables. The DB scheme includes the components: "Province", where names of north-west regions (oblasts) are entered;

"Region", for names of administrative territories in oblasts and republics; and "Farm" for names of farms. The component "Field" is used to identify certain fields in which inspections will be made, their area and the geographical co-ordinates of their south-west corners. Co-ordinates can be defined by means of portable navigating equipment or maps on Google Earth. Latin, English and Russian names of agricultural crops are registered in the "Crop" component, while varieties of crops found in NW Russia (English and Russian names) are collected in the component "Variety". The component "Pest, Disease, Weed" contains English, Russian and Latin names of all pest animals, plant pathogens and weeds recorded in NW Russia. The Table "Unit" is for physical units used in the DB, i.e. hectares, kg, litres etc. "Indicator type" shows the types of indicators used at inspection of fields to define the population of harmful organisms, an estimation of their numbers, distribution and pathogenicity. Types of parameters (data on soil structure, crop, nitrogen status) are registered in the component "Param type"; while "Param" contains parameters measured in the field regularly every year; and "Year" a record of the calendar year. Names of types of actions performed in the field (application of pesticides, fertilizers, etc.) are entered in the component "Action type". The actions carried out during a vegetation season in the field are recorded in the "Action" component. The DB manager is responsible for entering and checking the information in the components listed above. Users cannot change these data, but should inform the manager about any discrepancies observed in the basic information. DB users fill and check the following DB components: "Field year", for data about the fields chosen for observation during a vegetation season (field year). "Indicator", the largest table where various information on the characteristics of indicators is recorded: phytophage, pathogen or weed species, crop name, type and indicator name, unit of measurement, minimum and maximum phases of crop development when a harmful species is observed, and dates of its occurrence on crops or plantings. Minimum and maximum values of an indicator (number, abundance, harmfulness etc.) are also recorded. "Field param" includes data on parameters by which a field is surveyed. The "Reading" component contains information on dates when a field is visited for recording, scoring and verbal estimation of crop developmental phase and other characteristics of field conditions. Data about parameters on which a field is surveyed on the current year are stored in the component "Field year param". Data about pests, diseases and weeds in a given field are stored in the component "Indicator reading". The component "Field year action" is for information accumulated about the actions performed directly in fields. Four shell components are preliminarily allocated: "Field history" for information on all actions in the field, results of inspections and measurement of parameters for all years of survey; "Distribution map", a cartographical block for creating on demand dot maps for phytophage, pathogen and weed distribution on the basis of data accumulated in the DB; "Statistics" a block of statistical operations necessary to calculate average indexes for farms, regions, oblasts and republics; and "Reports", summary forms for printing and electronic reports. The basic objective of such database "shells" is accumulation of data about numbers of pests and diseases, abundance of weeds, etc.

An offline version of the database has been established using SQL technology on two computers in St. Petersburg. It is already possible to work there on entering information and correction of the DB interface. A demonstration version (in English and Russian) of the basic components contained in the database is now available at the website www.plantprotection.narod.ru/Fitosan/Phytosanitary_ Eng.htm.

The information system developed after successful appraisal in NW Russia may be offered to other federal districts and republics for the organisation of information support systems. It will allow automated storage, search and delivery of the data needed by the Phytosanitary Service for forecasting and prevention of dangerous phytosanitary situations. The economic efficiency of such systems is not in question, as they will allow the information stream in plant protection to be accelerated compared with the old archaic system of information interchange.

The information system created has no counterpart in the plant protection service of the Russian Federation.

Reducing the Impact of Agriculture and Horticulture on the Environment

26

CASE STUI
Bela

Uladzimir Kapitsa

International Sakharov Environmental University
Minsk, Belarus

The modern situation in plant growing is such that to have high quality yields, effective plant protection is needed in most cases. Statistically, 30% of all yield is achieved due to plant protection. When there is no plant protection, in some cases the entire harvest may be lost or may be of very low quality with hardly any market value. There are many examples of this. For example, the history of official plant protection began in the 1840s, when the yield of potatoes in Europe was destroyed during some years by late blight (*Phytophthora infestans*). This was the cause of famine and many people emigrated to America as a result. The Academy of Sciences in Paris founded a prize that was awarded to the inventor of some means of controlling this disease. As a result, the famous Bordeaux mixture was invented. Nowadays there are a great number of different pesticides for disease agents, pests and weeds. They are used for effective plant protection.

On the other hand, people need ecologically clean or ecologically safe production. How can we speak about food quality when fruits in orchards are treated up to 30 times a season with different pesticides in some highly developed countries with modern intensive agriculture? Such apples appear very attractive, without any spots and damage. Agricultural products grown by means of ecologically clean technologies may have a less perfect appearance but are reported to have high nutritional quality and always have customers even if the price is higher.

An effective system of plant protection has been developed and successfully used in most developed state and agricultural enterprises in Belarus ('Snov' in the Nesvizh region, 'Progress', 'Vertilishki' and 'Ozery' in the Grodno region, 'Ostromechivo' and 'Rassvet' in the Brest region). This system permits high yields of ecologically safe products to be obtained. Similar systems of ecologically safe plant protection have been developed in other countries too and are called Integrated Pest Management (IPM). This is characterised by:

1. In order to consider the ecological characteristics of crops and pests affecting them, it is necessary to decrease the anthropogenic pressure on agrocenoses and the environment. It could be that in one case it is possible to reduce the number of pesticide treatments, and in another case not to use pesticides at all, by instead using optimal biological means and agrotechnical measures, such as:
   - Scientifically proven crop rotations that consider other factors as well as the biological characteristics of crops. For example, it is not recommended to sow related plants on neighbouring fields to

Figure 26.1. The codling moth, *Laspeyresia pomonella* (Photo: O. Leillinger. Source: http://en.wikipedia.org/wiki/Cydia_pomonella).

Figure 26.2. Damage caused by the larvae of the codling moth to apples (http://www.etc.usf.edu/).

avoid the spread of diseases, insects and weed infestation, as well as exhaustion of soil if the same crop is grown year after year on the same field.

- Agrotechnical methods and topography should be considered. Potatoes should not be grown on sloping land as potato planting requires making beds. Rainwater flows down along the beds and causes soil erosion.
- The biological specifics of plants, pests and useful organisms should be considered. As most fruit crops are pollinated by bees, spraying with insecticides is forbidden during flowering to protect the bees. Another example: Apple worm is the larvae of a moth called the codling moth (*Laspeyresia pomonella*). Like all moths, the codling moth is attracted by light and therefore it is much better to spray them at night when they are active and attracted by tractor headlights. They can then be controlled not only with insecticides, but also with the tractor movement and the streams from the sprayer. Only one single night treatment is needed, instead of three daytime treatments. This not only has a money-saving effect, but also protects the environment by reducing the number of pesticide treatments – reducing environmental pollution and protecting useful insects that are active in the daytime.

2. Forecasting of disease, pest and weed development. There are long-term (for a year) and short-term (under 10 days) forecasts. Precise information on the phytosanitary situation on agrocenoses is the main basis for Integrated Pest Management. Therefore it is very important to be able to forecast pest development. The basis of all forecasting is monitoring the pest and studying its ecological characteristics.

There are basic kinds of forecasting:

- Several-year forecasting. This is needed for determination of an average level of pest numbers and their dynamics. The most harmful species for different crops are determined using this forecasting.
- Long-term forecasting. This is usually prepared for the next season based on the previous year's pest monitoring of numbers, harmfulness and winter stock data. It is necessary to predict the most harmful pest for the coming season and to prepare for it.
- Short-term forecasting. This is needed to predict the most exact occurrence of pests or diseases in order to implement control measures at the most sensitive stage for pests and crops. Different traps

(pheromone, light, colours, glue, suction) are generally used. The treatments are conducted using an economic threshold of harmfulness. Such forecasting protects the environment from excessive pesticide treatments.

3. Considering the economic threshold of harmfulness (ETH) of pest organisms (agents, pests and weeds). ETH means the number of pest organisms per unit area that causes an economically notable harmful effect for the crop. Nowadays control is not a question of complete annihilation of the pests on cultured plants, but only controlling their numbers to a safe level for the crops. The insects feeding on cultured plants become pests. They have always existed in nature and played a relevant ecological role for stabilisation of the biosphere previously. Usage of an economic threshold of harmfulness allows optimal and ecologically safe measures for plant protection to be selected. Regular monitoring of pest organism populations is carried out for this purpose. If the number is low, chemical treatment is not necessary and the environment will not be polluted. If the number only slightly exceeds the ETH, the farmer can apply biological means that are safe for the environment, or wait and observe the development in the crop. Pesticides are applied only if the number of pests exceeds the ETH. Nowadays, the ETH is developed for most pests, insects, some weeds and diseases. For example, two butterflies per trap (ten per row) in a week is the threshold for codling moth in an apple orchard.

4. To choose means and ways of plant protection it is possible to use not only chemical spraying of plants but also agrotechnical, mechanical and biological control methods or seed treatments.

   Agrotechnical pest control means strictly observing a crop rotation to avoid accumulation of pests, disease agents and weeds or soil exhaustion. It is not recommended to sow related plants on neighbouring fields, or on the same field several years in a row. It is also necessary to be timely in all agrotechnical measures. The regulation of sowing terms can also be an agrotechnical pest control measures. Thus the numbers of pesticide treatments can be reduced by using agricul-

tural measures. Sometime it is possible to refrain from all chemical treatments.

For example: When peas are grown as green fodder, the use of pesticides is forbidden to escape the problem of pesticide residues accumulating in fast ripening production. However, green peas are popular with different insects, such as the pea moth (*Laspereysia nigrum*), the caterpillars of which eat peas. After studying the biological characteristics of the pest and the pea plant, scientists recommended a strategy for growing a high quality yield of peas without any chemical means of plant protection. This is possible because the occurrence of the pea moth and the biological characteristics of the pea plant are known. Peas can grow in rather cold conditions and are even resistant to weak frost (-4°C). Therefore they can be sown in early spring and can be harvested before the pests occur in harmful numbers. The peas can also be sown later, in the summer, and then harvest can take place after the pea moth has hibernated. Pesticides are not needed in either case.

Seed treatment

Seeds, bulbs, corms and tubers are frequently treated with chemicals to eradicate pathogenic bacteria, fungi and nematodes and to protect the seeds against organisms in the soil (mainly fungi) that cause decay and damping-off. Seeds are often treated with systemic fungicides, which are absorbed and provide protection for the growing seedlings. For example, ergot (*Claviceps purpurea*) which affects rye, can only be controlled by seed treatment because the agent is protected by the rye plant tissues when plants grow. The onion bulb fly (*Eumerus stringatus*) is a very serious pest because its live larvae damage onion bulbs from the inside and are protected by plant tissues. Therefore the treatment of seed bulbs with a long-acting insecticide (until two months after treatment) proved to be the best solution that excluded insecticide sprayings. Seed treatment has one more ecological advantage over spraying. Seed treatments are conducted in specialist machinery mounted on a concrete floor under a protective awning and therefore there is no environmental pollution as when spraying.

Biological control of plant diseases involves the use of organisms other than humans to reduce or prevent infection by a pathogen. These organisms are called antagonists; they may occur naturally within the host's environment, or they may be deliberately applied to those parts of the potential host plant where they can act directly or indirectly on the pathogen.

Although the effects of biological control have long been observed, the mechanisms by which antagonists achieve control are not completely understood. Several methods have been observed: some antagonists produce antibiotics that kill or reduce the number of closely related pathogens, some are parasites on pathogens, and some simply compete with pathogens for available food.

In Belarus some biological means for controlling insects and diseases have been applied and tested. One of them, Trichodermin, is a preparation based on the fungus *Trichoderma horceanum* or *T. lignorum*. These fungi are hyperparasites of several root fungal pathogens and can be used against root rots and other diseases of grain crops. Trichodermin not only suppresses pathogen activity but also stimulates plant growth. Therefore the results of applying such biopreparations are sometimes better than using pesticides.

Cultural practices that favour a naturally occurring antagonist and exploit its beneficial action are often effective in reducing disease. One technique is to incorporate green manure, such as alfalfa, into the soil. Saprophytic microorganisms feed on the green manure, depriving potential pathogens of available nitrogen. Another practice is to make use of suppressive soils, in which a pathogen that causes little damage to the crop is known to persist. Alternatively, suppressive soils may harbour antagonists that compete with the pathogen for food and thereby limit the growth of the pathogen population.

Other antagonists produce substances that inhibit or kill potential pathogens occurring in close proximity. An example of this process, called antibiosis, is provided by marigold (*Tagetes* species) roots, which release terthienyls, chemicals that are toxic to several species of nematodes and fungi.

A mechanical method of pest control can be to use different traps for pest insects. For decreasing the number of pest insects, it is recommended to use glue colour traps (blue or yellow, plated by a layer of a non-drying glue) (Figure 26.3). This is associated with the fact that some insects are attracted by a certain colour, allowing their

Figure 26.3. Yellow glue trap to monitor pest occurance. Photo: A. Wuoro, Växtskyddscentralerna.

capture. For example, the colour yellow is attractive to greenhouse whitefly, the most widespread pest of cucumbers, tomatoes, flowers and other greenhouse plants. The onion bulb fly is also attracted by the colour yellow. Blue coloured traps attract cabbage fly. Such coloured glue traps are applied in greenhouses and on small vegetable fields.

Biological Control

27

Peter Tóth

Slovak University of Agriculture, Nitra, Slovak Republic

Introduction to Biological Control

There are many different means for controlling pests but this chapter is concerned only with methods using living organisms to control pests, a strategy called biological control. Biological control is a rapidly growing area which brings together ecologists, entomologists, weed scientists, plant pathologists, insect pathologists and microbiologists. The modern concept of biological pest control has been developed primarily by entomologists and in practice is normally taken to mean the use of living natural enemies to control pest species. Biological control has been defined many times but a commonly accepted definition was provided by Eilenberg et al. (2001):

> *'The use of living organisms to suppress the population density or impact of a specific pest organism, making it less abundant or less damaging than it would otherwise be'.*

In this way, biological control is, generally, human use of a specially chosen living organism (including viruses) to control a particular pest. This chosen organism might be a predator, parasite, or pathogen which will attack the harmful species.

The predators, parasites and pathogens of pests that are used in biological control are a large component of world biodiversity. These natural enemies are of enormous value to sustainable agriculture, where they can often eliminate the need for pesticide input. They are also of value to the control of invasive alien species, which threaten natural ecosystems.

Biological control is a form of manipulating nature to increase a desired effect. Certain biological control approaches definitely have the potential to conform to the sustainable agricultural philosophy and can be effective in all types of agricultural systems, including organic, sustainable and conventional. The method represents an alternative to continued reliance on pesticides.

Use of biological control requires much more background information about the biology and ecology of pests than for the use of chemical pesticides. For all types of biological control, it is necessary to demonstrate that natural enemies are effective at controlling pests. Life tables are used to document the effects of natural enemies on pest populations of different ages.

Biological control has several advantages over other types of control. These advantages include:

- Long-term management of the target pest (valid for conservation and introduction).
- Limited side-effects.
- Attack of only one or a few related pests.
- Self-perpetuating agents.
- Non-recurring costs (valid for conservation and introduction).
- Known levels of risks identified and evaluated before agent introduction.

The most important disadvantage of biological control is that it takes more intensive management and planning. It can take more time, require more record keeping, more patience, and sometimes more education or training. Other disadvantages are:

- It often takes many years for the populations of the introduced biological control agents to increase to levels that permanently decrease the pest population (valid for conservation and introduction).
- Agents may be subject to natural enemies.
- Environmental conditions often exclude some agents from certain locations.
- Agents usually do not eradicate the pest population.

There are three overlapping strategies of biological control, each clearly separated from the other, and they are: **Classical biological control**, **Augmentation** and **Conservation**. Historically, most emphasis has been placed on classical biological control although more recently a great deal more effort has been directed at augmentative control.

Biological Control Agents

The types of natural enemy used in biological control of insects include parasitoids, predators and pathogens.

The major uses of biological control agents are: (1) biological control of invertebrate pests using predators, parasitoids and pathogens, (2) biological control of weeds using herbivores and pathogens, and (3) biological control of plant pathogens using antagonistic micro-organisms and induced plant resistance.

Parasitoids

Parasitoid is a term derived from the more general term parasite. Parasites are organisms living in (endoparasites) or on (ectoparasites) other organisms. The term parasitoid specifically refers to insects that parasitise on other insects when they are immature (larval stage) but free-living when adult. Parasitoids are taxonomically restricted to Hymenoptera and Diptera. Parasitoids are 'parasitic' as larvae only (but some parasitoids may also kill many pests by direct host feeding on the pest eggs or larvae). Parasitoids are usually smaller than the hosts upon which they develop and typically only attack one stage of host (egg/larva/ nymph/pupa/adult). Different species of parasitoids attack different life stages of the pest. Thus, *Trichogramma* spp. which attack the egg stage of insects are known as egg

parasitoids, Braconidae such as *Cotesia glomerata* which attack larvae are larval parasitoids and so on for adult or nymphal parasitoids. Parasitoid larvae kill their hosts near the end of the parasitoid's larval development. Adult parasitoids are free-living and usually feed on pollen, nectar, honeydew or even the body fluids of their host. Parasitoids exhibit a number of different life habits and are themselves parasitised by secondary hyperparasites.

Parasitised immature stages of pests are usually differently coloured. For example stages of immature whiteflies parasitised with parasitic wasp, *Encarsia formosa* (Encyrtidae) are darker or black when late in the parasite development compared with yellowish to creamy healthy ones. Aphids are hosts for species in the subfamily *Aphidiinae* (Braconidae) such as *Aphidius* spp. and others in the family *Aphelinidae* (Chalcidoidea). Parasitised aphids, called 'aphid mummies', appear puffed up, brown and hardened (Figure 27.1). The adults chew a round hole in the abdomen to emerge. Hymenoptera parasitoids are generally known as parasitic wasps.

Host-specific parasitoids are considered the most suitable for biological control. Many are commercially available with detailed guides on how 'to use' them.

Predators

A predator is an animal (invertebrates or vertebrates) that overpowers, kills and consumes other animals (the prey).

Figure 27.1. Mummies – aphids in the advanced stages of parasitism by internal parasitoids. Photo: P. Toth.

Figure 27.2. Spiders are predaceous primarily upon insect. Photo: P. Toth.

Figure 27.3. Many wasps are predatory, using other insects as food for their larvae. Photo: P. Toth.

Invertebrate predators are found among Coleoptera, Neuroptera, Hymenoptera, Diptera, Hemiptera and Odonata, but more than half of all predators are coleopterans. The most important families within Coleoptera for biological control are Coccinelidae and Carabidae. Other arthropod natural enemies include predatory mites and spiders (Figure 27.2). Adults and immatures are often generalists rather than specialists. They consume large numbers of prey (adult or immature) during their lifetime and are generally larger than their prey. Some of the adults feed on pollen if prey is not available. Invertebrate predators actively capture prey using several very different methods (Figure 27.3). Some mobile predators have good vision, such as ground beetles (Carabidae) and jumping spiders (Salticidae), and they chase their prey. Others with poor vision use a combination of vision and chemical cues to find their prey.

Vertebrate predators (especially birds, e.g. Ring-necked Pheasant, *Phasianus colchicus*) are better known to the general public than most invertebrate predators. However, the days for use of vertebrates for biological control are largely over, as the prey of vertebrate predators is too unpredictable.

Most beneficial invertebrate predators will consume many pest insects during their development, but some predators are more effective at controlling pests than others. Some species may play an important role in the suppression of some pests. Others may provide good late season control, but appear too late to suppress the early season pest population. Many beneficial species may have only a minor impact by themselves but contribute to overall pest mortality.

The predators specifically used for biological control include:

a) Predatory mites (Order Acari), which play an important role in biological control both in orchards (mainly *Typhlodromus pyri*) and glasshouses (e.g. *Phytoseiulus persimilis*) by feeding on phytophagous mites and thrips.

b) True bugs (Order Hemiptera), which are often general feeders (e.g. *Orius* spp.), both immatures and adults eating eggs, immatures and adults of a diversity of insects and mites.

c) Lady beetles (Order Coleoptera, family Coccinelidae), adults and larvae feed on soft-bodied prey, mainly aphids but also whiteflies, mites, mealybugs and scale insects. For example *Stethorus punctillum* feeds on mites in glasshouses.

d) Lacewings (Order Neuroptera), e.g. Green Lacewing, *Chrysoperla carnea*, adult lacewings can be predaceous; some feed on pollen or do not feed. Larvae

Figure 27.4. Larvae of lacewings (Neuroptera) inhabit foliage where they attack aphids, mites, soft-bodied insects and eggs. Photo: P. Toth.

Figure 27.5. Hover fly (Syrphidae) feeding on flower nectar and pollen. Females lay white, oval eggs near colonies of aphids. Photo: P. Toth.

prefer to feed on aphids but also eat other small insects as well as mites (Figure 27.4).

e) Predatory flies (Order Diptera), mostly hover flies (family Syrphidae), aphid flies (family Chamaemyiidae) and predaceous midges (Cecidomyiidae). While adults feed on pollen (Figure 27.5), nectar or do not feed, the larvae are predatory (Figure 27.6). Many of the species mentioned above are commercially available with a detailed guide on how 'to use' them.

Among the invertebrate predators that provide a naturally occurring biological control are praying mantises (Order Mantodea), ground beetles (Order Coleoptera, family Carabidae), ants (Order Hymenoptera, family Formicidae), and spiders (Order Araneae).

Figure 27.6. Magot like larvae of hover flies (Syrphidae) are active predators on aphids. Photo: P. Toth.

Pathogens

A pathogen is any disease-producing microorganism. In principle, pathogens include bacteria, viruses, fungi and nematodes. Pathogens represent one of three principal categories of natural enemies used in applied biological control. Most insect pathogens are relatively specific to certain groups of insects and certain life stages. Unlike chemical insecticides, microbial insecticides can take longer (several days) to kill or debilitate the target pest. Although they kill, reduce reproduction, slow growth, or shorten the life of pests, their effectiveness may depend on environmental conditions or host abundance. The degree of control by naturally occurring pathogens may be unpredictable. Microbial insecticides are compatible with the use of predators and parasitoids, which may help to spread some pathogens through the pest population.

The most important pathogen used in biological control as a biopesticide is the rod-shaped soil bacterium *Bacillus thuringiensis* (Bt). Bt can be found worldwide on plants, in insects and in soil, surviving in the environment as resistant spores. It is only rarely found to cause epizootics in insect populations under natural conditions. Yet, Bt has the power to control numerous chewing-insect pests, particularly Lepidoptera larvae with alkaline pH in the gut (Figure 27.7). It has been developed extensively for pest control in a variety of habitats, and it is applied to virtually all tree, field and vegetable crops. Bt is photosensitive, with its life limited to a few days at most and only effective when ingested by insects, where it acts as a stomach poison. Insects that eat leaves treated with Bt die from hunger or infections. Insects are most sensitive to Bt during early larval instars (stages).

There are different strains (subspecies) of Bt, each with specific toxicity to particular types of insects: Bt *kurstaki* and Bt *azaiwai* are used against lepidopteran larvae; Bt *israelensis* is effective against dipteran larvae and Bt *tenebrionis* is active against coleopteran larvae.

Another species of *Bacillus*, *B. popilliae*, infects coleopteran larvae causing 'milky disease' of larvae and *B. sphaericus* is active against mosquito larvae.

There are six main groups of insect viruses but only three are sufficiently different from human viruses to be considered safe and these are: the nuclear polyhedrosis virus (NPV), the granulosis virus (GV) and the cytoplasmic polyhedrosis virus (CPV). These viruses produce an occlusion body, a structure that protects virus particles or virions.

The occlusion body is resistant to environmental insults and could be considered analogous to a bacterial spore.

Viruses can be highly effective natural regulators of several lepidopteran larvae especially. Different strains of naturally occurring NPV and GV are present at low levels in many insect populations. Epizootics can occasionally devastate populations of some pests, especially when insect numbers are high.

Insect viruses need to be eaten by an insect to cause infection. They invade an insect's body via the gut and replicate in many tissues where they can disrupt components of the insect's physiology, interfering with feeding, egg laying and movement. On the other hand viruses may also spread from insect to insect during mating or egg laying.

Different viruses cause different symptoms. In general, infested larvae stop feeding, turn white (NPV) or very dark (GV), climb to the top of the crop canopy, the body contents are liquefied and within three to eight days they die. However, especially with NPV strains that are commercially produced, the number of commercially successful products is limited.

Some insect species, including many pests, are particularly susceptible to infection by naturally occurring, entomopathogenic fungi. Those with the most potential as biopesticides are fungi from the Deuteromycetes (imperfect fungi), namely species of *Beauveria*, *Metarhizium*, *Verticilium*, *Nomuraea* and *Hirsutella*. These fungi are often very specific to insects. Fungal growth is favoured by moist conditions but fungi also have resistant stages that maintain an infection potential under dry conditions. Fungi have a considerable epizootic potential and can spread quickly through an insect population and cause its collapse. Entomopathogenic fungi do not need to be consumed by insects, because they penetrate the insect body through the cuticle and can infect in this way, also infesting insects such as aphids and whiteflies that are not susceptible to bacteria and viruses. The fungus proliferates in the host's blood and invades the host's organs shortly before the host dies, or kills the insect more quickly, possibly through use of fungal toxins. It generally takes several days for a fungus-infested host to die.

The only insect-parasitic nematodes that kill their hosts in a relatively short time are entomopathogenic nematodes from the families Steinernematidae and Heterorhabditidae. These two families have very similar

Figure 27.7. Impact of the most important biopesticide, *Bacillus thuringiensis* (Bt), on larvae of *Helicoverpa armigera*. Photo: P. Toth.

life histories. The nematodes have searching ability. The infective stage of the nematode (third stage larva) can detect its host by responding to chemical and physical cues. When a host has been located, the nematodes penetrate into the insect body cavity, usually via natural body openings (mouth, anus, spiracles) or areas of thin cuticle. The third-stage infective larva carry symbiotic bacteria in their guts and, after invading a host, release the bacteria (*Xenorhabdus* for steinernematids, *Photorhabdus* for heterorhabditids). The bacteria are responsible for killing hosts very rapidly, within 2-3 days. The nematodes feed upon the bacteria and liquefy the host, and mature into adults. Nematode generations continue to develop within the same cadaver and infective larvae exit when density of nematodes is high and nutrients are low.

The most important species are *Steinernema carpocapsae* against Lepidoptera and Coleoptera (Curculionidae and Chrysomelidae), *S. feltiae* against dipteran pests, *Heterorhabditis bacteriophora* against Lepidoptera and Coleoptera and *Phasmorhabditis hermaphrodita* against slugs and snails.

Classical Biological Control

'The intentional introduction of an exotic, usually co-evolved, biological control agent for permanent establishment and long-term pest control' (Eilenberg et al. 2001)

Biological control through introduction is most frequently used against introduced pests which arrive in a new area and become permanently established without an associated natural enemy complex. Thus, classical biological control involves travelling to the country or area from which a newly introduced pest originated and returning with some of the natural enemies that attacked it and kept it from being a pest there. New pests are constantly arriving accidentally or intentionally. Sometimes they survive. When they come, their enemies are left behind. If they become a pest, introducing some of their natural enemies can be an important way to reduce the amount of harm they can do. The search for suitable natural enemies (parasitoids, predators, pathogens) should in principle include all organisms closely related to the target pest, with special consideration to those organisms that affect pest density and distribution.

The first example of classical biological control dates back to the end of nineteenth century, when Californian citrus orchards had suffered attacks from the Australian scale, *Icerya purchasi*. This scale was successfully controlled with the introduction of its natural enemy, the coccinellid cardinal ladybird, *Rodolia cardinalis*. The most famous example of this technique within Europe is control of woolly apple aphid, *Eriosoma lanigerum*, through the introduction of its specific parasitoid *Aphelinus mali* and that of San José scale, *Quadraspidiotus perniciosus*, through the introduction of the parasitoid *Prospaltella perniciosi*.

When a natural enemy is introduced, it should (if established) reduce the pest's abundance to a level below the pre-introduction population size. After an initial phase of rapid reduction of the pest population and equally rapid growth of the natural enemy population, a long period of equilibrium generally follows. In successful introduction, the new population level will be well below the economic damage threshold. When successful, this traditional use of biological control offers permanent levels of control with few risks and leads to a very cost-effective solution.

Classic biological control is most successful with environmental pests and pests in orchards and forests, where the perennial nature of the crop permits continuous interaction between its natural enemy and host without the agroecosystem disturbance associated with annual crops.

Augmentation

Augmentation is a method of increasing the population of a natural enemy which attacks a pest. This can be done by mass-producing a pest in a laboratory and releasing it into the field at the proper time. Another method of augmentation is breeding a better natural enemy that can attack or find its prey more effectively. Mass rearings can be released at special times when the pest is most susceptible and natural enemies are not yet present, or they can be released in such large numbers that few pests go untouched by their enemies. The augmentation method relies upon continual human management and does not provide a permanent solution, unlike the introduction or conservation approaches. There are two basic approaches of augmentation: Inoculation and Inundation.

Inoculation biological control

> *'The intentional release of a living organism as a biological control agent with the expectation that it will multiply and control the pest for an extended period, but not permanently'(Eilenberg et al., 2001)*

Inoculation is used in cases where a native natural enemy is absent from a particular area, or an introduced species is unable to survive permanently. Inoculative releases are made at the beginning of the season to achieve seasonal control, i.e. to colonise the area for the duration of the season or crop and thus prevent pest build-up.

Inundation biological control

> *'The use of living organisms to control pests when control is achieved exclusively by the released organisms themselves' (Eilenberg et al., 2001)*

Releases made with biological control through inundation involve very large numbers of native or introduced natural enemies, in a way similar to the application of chemical pesticides. The natural enemy is usually a pathogen and is often formulated so that it can be applied using conventional pesticide spraying equipment. Sometimes used as substitutes for chemical pesticides, inundative control agents are applied for short-term control when pest populations reach damaging levels.

This technique is specifically used in greenhouses because of its relatively elevated costs. In addition, greenhouses are circumscribed places in which control of exogenous factors determining the success of the intervention is easier. The most successful agent in this category is the bacterium *Bacillus thuringiensis* used to control pests such as lepidopterans, dipterans and coleoptera, although other entomopathogens based on fungi and viruses have also found niches.

Conservation

> *'Modification of the environment or existing practices to protect and enhance specific natural enemies or other organisms to reduce the effect of pests' (Eilenberg et al., 2001)*

Conservation is an important part of any biological control effort. This involves identifying any factors that limit the effectiveness of a particular natural enemy and changing them through environmental modifications to help the beneficial species. Conservation of natural enemies involves either reducing factors which interfere with the natural enemies or providing needed resources that help natural enemies.

Many environmental modifications are designed to both preserve and enhance natural enemies and thus lie at an intermediate point on this continuum. In certain situations biological control of insect pests through environmental modification has inherent advantages over either classical biological control or augmentative releases. Conservation relies on naturally occurring enemies that are well adapted to the target area. Natural enemies occur from the backyard garden to the commercial field. Therefore, conservation is probably the most important and readily available biological control practice available to growers. The method is generally simple and cost-effective. With relatively little effort the activity of these natural enemies can be observed. For example lacewings, lady beetles, hover fly larvae, and parasitised aphid mummies are almost always present in aphid colonies. Fungus-infected adult flies are often common following periods of high humidity.

The usage of pesticides has a side-effect on natural enemies. When a pesticide kills the pest, the natural enemies disappear too. They migrate from the agroecosystem or die. Certain cultural practices can also damage the natural enemies or their habitats, e.g. removal of uncultivated areas, field margins, weedy areas, roadsides, etc.; soil cultivation; crop establishment; fertilisation, growth regulators, or harvesting especially at the critical periods of beneficial organism's life cycle.

To conserve natural enemies, pest management decisions must be carefully planned. Conservation involves planning a programme for the whole farm, including the non-farmed land, to enhance biodiversity and landscape features. This may include developing and maintaining a network of hedges, ditches, field margins, beetle banks and conservation headlands, which enable wild species to establish and migrate. A greater diversity of broad-leaved weed species may be left within crops to provide food sources for birds and insects, so long as the numbers of aggressive, crop-damaging weeds are contained.

Conservation, creation and improvement of habitats for parasitoids and predators of crop pests may regulate pest populations by increasing the natural level of biocontrol, thereby reducing the need for insecticidal intervention. Often the best we can do is to recognise that beneficial organisms are present and minimise negative impacts on them. If an insecticide is needed, every effort should be made to use a selective material in a selective manner.

One of the best examples of conservation biological control is the practice of strip-harvesting hay alfalfa in California. When an entire field of alfalfa is moved during hot weather, the native Western tarnished plant bug, *Lygus hesperus*, migrates within 24 hours, often to cotton where it is a key pest. However, when fields are harvested in alternating strips up to 120 m wide (=strip cut), lygus bugs move from the cut strips to the remaining strips rather than migrating to cotton. This cultural practice can conserve natural enemies in cotton (due to reduced chemical control of *Lygus*) and in hay alfalfa, where mobile natural enemies can disperse from cut strips to half-grown strips. Another method for conserving natural enemies in cotton is to interplant alfalfa (a preferred host of *Lygus*) at regular intervals to hold *Lygus* bugs and prevent them from dispersing into the adjacent cotton.

Other Non-chemical Control Strategies

In addition to the above-mentioned examples, there are nowadays many other non-chemical control strategies of pests, such as semiochemicals for mass trapping, mating disruption, etc.; insect hormones to manipulate development and sterile insect technique for 'birth control of insects'.

Conclusion

Biological control offers an environmentally friendly, safe and cost-effective pest management option. The above examples highlight important bio-tools. Successful biological control requires not only a better understanding of biological control agents but also a more comprehensive picture of the whole agro-environment. The key has to be an area-wide pest management, which differs from traditional pest management in that the primary focus is on creating an environment unfavorable for pest establishment, growth and reproduction. This management is supported with pest-to-pest specific control tactics. The best approach may be to integrate plant growing and knowledge of ecology with all available biological control strategies into comprehensive pest management system. Enhanced research acting in this area in recent years has greatly augmented our knowledge. This progress could be translated into new and innovative concepts for biological pest control.

Part E

Combatting
Soil Degradation

Authors: Laura Alakukku, Johan Arvidsson, Marina Efremova, Marija Eidukevičiene,
Ararso Etana, Folke Günther, Lars D. Hylander, Alexandra Izosimova,
Benediktas Jankauskas, Åsa Myrbeck, Tomas Rydberg and Liudmila Tripolskaja

Coordinating Editor: Christine Jakobsson

Soil Compaction

28

Laura Alakukku
University of Helsinki, Finland

Introduction

More than one hundred years ago, Wollny (1898) described the importance of a favourable soil structure for crop growth and yield. Compaction of the soil is one of the major ways in which treatments affect soil structure, and soil compaction problems plague agricultural, horticultural and forest crop production everywhere in the world. For this reason, soil compaction has been defined as one of the five threats to sustained soil quality by the EU Soil Framework Directive (Commission of the European Communities, 2006). Globally, soil compaction accounts for 4% (68.3 million hectares) of anthropogenic soil degradation (Oldeman et al., 1991). In Europe, compaction accounts for about 17% of the total degraded area. Soil compaction is a complex problem in which machine/soil/crop/weather interactions play an important role and may have economic and environmental consequences for world agriculture (Soane and Ouwerkerk, 1995).

The focus of this chapter is on soil compaction due to field traffic. The harmful compaction of arable and forestry soils is mainly attributable to wheel or track traffic with heavy machines under unfavourable soil conditions. Intensification of cropping practices is also accompanied by diminished soil structure stability and the expansion of intensive cultivation to new land areas leads to soil compaction. This chapter reviews reasons for arable soil compaction and the effects of compaction on crop production and the environment.

Definition of Soil Compaction Processes

Soil compression refers to the decrease in porosity or increase in bulk density of soil when it is subjected to externally or internally applied loads. External static and dynamic loads may be caused by rolling, trampling or vibration, while the internal loads are associated with water suction or water pressure due to a hydraulic gradient (Horn and Lebert, 1994). Soil consolidation is a process by which a saturated soil is compressed under a long-term load accompanied by a reduction in porosity with expulsion of water. In contrast, soil compaction is a process in which an unsaturated soil is compressed by a load applied for a short time with no expulsion of water. Short-time loads are applied by field traffic, tillage implements and trampling by livestock. Soil may also become compressed naturally under its own weight and by rain, or by shrinking due to drying of clayey soil

In agriculture, soil compaction is usually accompanied by deformation since besides compression, lateral movement occurs during field operations and animal trampling (Koolen and Kuipers, 1983). Thus, soil compaction results in a decrease in porosity but also causes non-volumetric changes in soil structure.

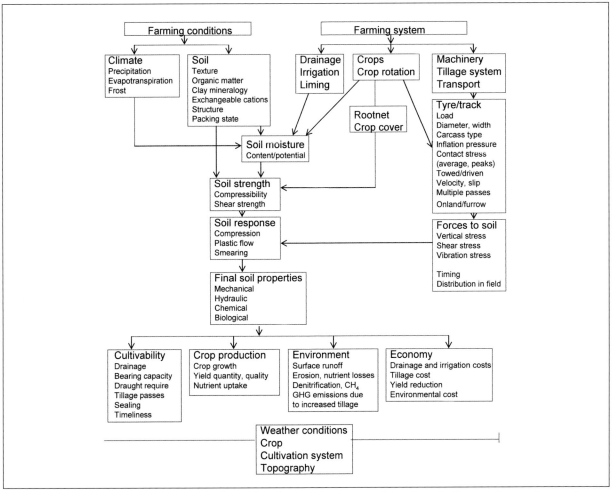

Figure 28.1. Field traffic factors and soil properties affecting the soil compaction process and the effects of soil compaction on soil properties, crop production, environment, economy and soil workability.

Effects of Soil Compaction on Soil, Crop Growth and Environment

Virtually all physical, chemical and biological soil properties and processes are affected to varying degrees by soil compaction (Figure 28.1). Many studies have found that compaction modifies the pore size distribution of mineral soils, mainly by reducing the porosity and especially the macroporosity (diameter > 30 μm, e.g. Eriksson, 1982; Ehlers, 1982). Besides the volume and number of macro-pores, compaction also modifies the pore geometry, continuity and morphology, which is very important since in wet soil rapid water and air movement occurs in continuous macropores.

Soil compaction can have positive impacts, for instance by increasing the plant-available water capacity of sandy soils (Rasmussen, 1985) or by reducing nitrate leaching (Kirkham and Horton, 1990). However, soil compaction has often been found to have harmful effects on many soil properties relevant to soil workability,

Figure 28.2. Autumn-ploughed heavy clay soil in the following spring. The soil was compacted with a 21 tonne tandem axle load (tyre inflation pressure 700 kPa) four months before autumn ploughing (left) or kept uncompacted (right). Photo: L. Alakukku.

drainage, crop growth and the environment (Figure 28.1). Compaction due to field traffic increases the dry bulk density (Arvidsson, 1998), shear strength and penetrometer resistance (e.g. Blackwell et al., 1986) of different soils, limiting root growth and increasing the draft requirement in tillage (Figure 28.2). Soil compaction has been found to reduce water infiltration (Pietola et al., 2005) and saturated hydraulic conductivity (Alakukku et al., 2003). Simojoki et al. (1991) found that soil compaction reduces CO_2 and O_2 exchange. The likelihood of drainage problems increases when compaction reduces the permeability of soil, especially subsoil, and may lead to waterlogging problems in rainy years. Poorly drained soil may also dry slowly, reducing the number of days available for field operations and hampering crop growth due to soil wetness. The reduction in drainage rate attributed to soil compaction can be expected to increase the emissions of greenhouse gases from soil (Ball et al., 1999), for instance by increasing denitrification. Furthermore, compaction may increase surface runoff and topsoil erosion by impeding water infiltration (Fullen, 1985). The effects of compaction on soil properties are reviewed by Soane et al. (1982), Lipiec and Stępniewski (1995) and Alakukku (1999). Environmental and soil workability responses have been reviewed by, among others, Soane and Ourwerkerk (1995) and Chamen et al. (1990), respectively.

By affecting soil properties and processes, soil compaction influences crop growth, yield and the use efficiency of fertilisers (Figure 28.1). After tillage the tilled layer is often too loose and moderate recompaction of topsoil improves crop growth. Harmful soil compaction has been reported to reduce yield (e.g. Schjønning and Rasmussen, 1994; Arvidsson and Håkansson, 1996; Hanssen, 1996), crop water use efficiency (Radford et al., 2001) and nutrient uptake (Arvidsson, 1999; Alakukku, 2000). Crop responses and the reasons for the effects of soil compaction on crop growth, yield and nutrient uptake have been widely discussed by Lipiec and Stępniewski (1995) and Håkansson (2005).

Persistence of Soil Compaction

Compaction induced by field traffic has both short- and long-term effects on soil and crop production. Short-term (1–5 years) effects are mainly associated with topsoil (0–30 cm) compaction, which is largely controlled by tillage operations, field traffic and the way in which these operations are adapted to soil conditions. Topsoil compaction is alleviated by tillage and natural processes of freezing/thawing, wetting/drying and bioactivity.

Normal tillage does not loosen the subsoil (below about 30 cm). The effects of subsoil compaction may persist for a very long time. In spite of cropping and deep frost, the effects of heavy machine traffic have been detected in mineral soils more than 10 years after application of the load (Blake et al., 1976; Etana and Håkansson, 1994; Wu et al., 1997). In all these investigations, the effects of compaction persisted for the duration of the experiment.

Subsoil compaction has also been found to decrease grain yield (Håkansson and Reeder, 1994) and nitrogen uptake (Alakukku, 2000) several years after subsoil compaction. The long-term effect on crop growth and yield has been found to depend on the climatic conditions and is most evident in rainy growing seasons (e.g. Alakukku, 2000). Håkansson and Petelkau (1994) suggested that subsoil compaction tends to be highly persistent, and in non-swelling sandy soils and tropical areas it may be permanent immediately below tillage depth. Thus, subsoil compaction is a severe invisible and cumulative problem which is difficult to correct by, for instance, deep loosening (Kooistra and Boersma, 1994; Olesen and Munkholm, 2007).

Prevention of Field Traffic-induced Soil Compaction

Factors influencing the compaction capability of machinery traffic can be divided into two main variables: soil bearing capacity and soil stress caused by field traffic (Figure 28.1). Soil bearing capacity or strength means the capability of a soil structure to withstand stresses induced by field traffic without changes in the soil structure. Soil strength varies temporally, spatially and vertically owing to differences in soil properties (Figure 28.1). In this section the major soil properties and traffic factors relevant to avoiding soil compaction are discussed. The causes and prevention of soil compaction have been reviewed in more detail by Alakukku et al. (2003), Chamen et al. (2003), Håkansson (2005) and Hamza and Anderson (2005).

Influence of Soil Moisture Content on Soil Compaction

Working the soil at the wrong moisture content increases the probability of soil compaction. Soil moisture content/or potential is the dominant property affecting soil strength during field traffic (Hamza and Anderson, 2005). As the moisture content increases, the strength of an unsaturated soil drops. Thus, the same stress compacts a soil more when it is moist than when it is dry (e.g. Arvidsson, 2001). Saturated soil does not technically compact without the water draining out from the soil. However, wet soil is in a very weak state and may smear, with resultant

puddling disturbing pore continuity and causing soil compaction when the homogenised soil dries (Guèrif, 1990). In the climate of the Nordic countries soils are often wet in spring after snow melt and in autumn. This creates critical conditions for traffic in manure/slurry/sewage sludge application, tillage and crop harvesting. A good drainage system is of critical importance to limit the periods during which the soil is wet and therefore reduces the risk of soil compaction damage. Likewise, adapting practices and cropping to avoid field traffic during moist soil conditions reduces or avoids soil compaction.

Stresses Applied to Soil by Machines

Stresses on soil can be limited by controlling surface contact stress and wheel loads (Figure 28.1). The average ground contact stress (wheel load divided by contact area between tyre and soil surface) estimates the average value of the vertical stress in the contact area. The contact stress is often evaluated from the tyre inflation pressure. Tijink (1994) offers a detailed examination of the determination of ground contact pressure. Stress on the soil can be reduced by lowering the ground contact stress by decreasing the tyre inflation pressure, through larger tyres with the same load, lower wheel load or lower inflation pressure or a combination of these. With the aim of avoiding soil compaction, recommendations have been given for maximum values of average ground contact stress, inflation pressure and stress at 50 cm depth (subsoil compaction). For wet and loose soils (extremely vulnerable) Spoor et al. (2003) recommend a maximum ground contact stress of 65 kPa (tyre inflation pressure 40 kPa), while for hard (not particularly vulnerable) soils the recommended maximum is 200 kPa (160 kPa). Technical solutions to reduce ground contact stress (e.g. number of wheels, tyre construction, tracks) and inflation pressure are discussed by Chamen et al. (2003), Hamza and Anderson (2005) and Ansorge and Godwin (2007).

In unsaturated soils, external stresses are transmitted three-dimensionally via solid, liquid and gaseous phases. As far as the extent of stress in the soil and the probability of subsoil compaction are concerned, surface contact stress and wheel load are the dominant influences. Contact stress determines the initial level of stress at the surface, but wheel load decides the rate at which the stress decreases with depth (e.g. Chamen et al., 2003). From analyses and experimental results, the following conclusions can be drawn: for a particular surface contact stress, larger tyres or tracks (with larger wheel/track load) transmit stress deeper than smaller tyres or tracks with lower load (e.g. Lebert et al., 1989), while a higher moisture content decreases the strength of the soil and increases the stress transmitted deeper into the soil (Arvidsson et al., 2001). In summary, it can be stated that the risk of subsoil compaction exists whenever a moist or weak soil is loaded by a moderate to high surface contact pressure on a large contact area, i.e. with a high wheel load.

Number of wheel/track passes

The number of passes affects the number of loading events and the coverage, intensity and distribution of wheel traffic. When a vehicle has been converted to low wheel load and ground pressure by increasing the number of wheels that follow in the same track (tandem axle-concept), average ground contact pressure is lower, but the number of wheel passes in the same track is higher. Because of the multi-pass effect, tandem axle construction is less efficient in avoiding high levels of compactness in the topsoil than wide tyres and dual wheel arrangements. The first pass of a wheel/track causes most compaction, but repeated wheeling can still increase the compactness of soil. The repeated number of wheel passes may also increase the risk of subsoil compaction. Annually repeated traffic may cause cumulative effects if the effects of earlier subsoil compaction have not disappeared before new loading. Unnecessary field traffic can be avoided e.g. by adapting the size of implements well to the size of the tractor used and by combining field operations. In a controlled traffic system, all field traffic is concentrated to temporary or even permanent wheel tracks (tramlines) (Chamen et al., 2003; Hamza and Anderson, 2005). Håkansson (2005) discusses the planning of traffic pattern to minimise the area covered by wheels/tracks.

compaction is high when the stresses exerted are higher than the strength of the soil. Soil wetness decreases the soil strength. To prevent soil compaction the machines and equipment used on fields in critical conditions should be adjusted to the actual strength of the soil by controlling wheel/track loads and using low tyre inflation pressure. Traffic management should also be planned to minimise the amount of unnecessary field traffic.

Conclusions

Compaction is one of the major ways in which agricultural treatments affect soil structure, threatening soil quality and productivity everywhere in the world. The risk of soil

Ploughless Tillage in Long- and Short-term Experiments

29

Johan Arvidsson, Ararso Etana, Åsa Myrbeck and Tomas Rydberg
Swedish University of Agricultural Sciences
Uppsala, Sweden

Introduction

The Swedish University of Agriculture (SLU) finances a total of 13 long-term soil tillage experiments, which are run by the Division of Soil Management at the Department of Soil & Environment. The experiments are used to study the effects of different soil tillage and soil management systems on environmental and agronomic aspects. They are situated all over Sweden, although the majority are located in Uppsala.

Most of the experiments deal with various effects of reduced or non-inversion tillage to a depth of 7-15 cm compared with conventional tillage including mouldboard ploughing to a depth of 22-24 cm (Figure 29.1).

During the past 30 years the Division has also carried out a large number of short-term (1-6 year) field trials where different reduced tillage systems have been tested.

Results from long- and short-term experiments are published every year in the Annual Report from the Division of Soil Management. The results can also be found on http://www.mv.slu.se/JB/jb.htm and www.ffe.slu.se

Figure 29.1. Frequently used implements replacing the mouldboard plough in Sweden. Tine cultivator (left) and disc cultivator (right). Photo: Väderstad-Verken AB.

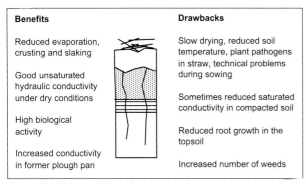

Benefits	Drawbacks
Reduced evaporation, crusting and slaking	Slow drying, reduced soil temperature, plant pathogens in straw, technical problems during sowing
Good unsaturated hydraulic conductivity under dry conditions	Sometimes reduced saturated conductivity in compacted soil
High biological activity	Reduced root growth in the topsoil
Increased conductivity in former plough pan	Increased number of weeds

Figure 29.2. General view of benefits and drawbacks of non-inversion tillage compared with mouldboard ploughing.

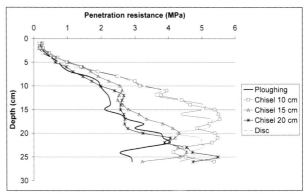

Figure 29.3. Penetration resistance in one experiment on Ultuna clay loam, measured in June 2006, 15 years after the start of the experiment.

In the following, we discuss some of the questions to which answers can hopefully be found mainly in the long-term tillage experiments, but including some results from the short-term trials. Figure 29.2 presents the benefits and drawbacks of non-inversion tillage.

Which Tillage Depth Should be Used in Ploughless Tillage?

Five of the long-term experiments include different tillage depths in the ploughless tillage treatments. Figure 29.3 shows the penetration resistance in one of these experiments, and clearly demonstrates a better loosening effect for a greater tillage depth. Crop yields in all experiments are shown in Table 29.1. On average, yield effects are small. In general, on heavier soil and where ploughless tillage gives good yield relative to mouldboard ploughing, there seems to be little benefit to increasing tillage depth. Table 29.2 presents measurements of fuel consumption in two experiments at Ultuna, Uppsala, during 2005. Increasing tillage depth from 10 to 20 cm increased fuel consumption from 13 to 37 l/ha, and the deep chisel plough tillage required almost twice as much fuel as mouldboard ploughing.

Should Ploughing or Ploughless Tillage be Continuous or Can the Systems be Mixed?

Ploughless tillage increases organic matter content in the surface layer, which may improve seedbed properties and reduce the risk of slaking and crusting. Occasional ploughing will level out these differences in organic matter content within the topsoil, and may therefore be detrimental to soil structure. On the other hand, autumn ploughing increases the potential for wind and weather to have a positive effect on the structure. An autumn ploughed area of a heavy clay has a finer surface structure in spring than an area that was only stubble cultivated. This is because the ploughing exposes a greater surface area of soil to the effects of freezing-thawing and wetting- drying cycles.

One question often asked by farmers is whether ploughless tillage should be continuous or whether it

Table 29.1. Relative crop yields in experiments with different tillage depths in ploughless tillage. From Arvidsson et al. (2003).

Place	Ultuna	Ultuna	Ultuna	Ultuna	Lönnstorp	Average
Soil type	clay loam	heavy clay	clay loam	heavy clay	clayey till	
Exp. years	12	12	8	32	11	
Ploughing	100	100	100	100	100	100
Shallow chiselling (10 cm)	86	97	104	105	98	98
Deep chiselling (20 cm)	92	99	100	105	101	99

Table 29.2. Diesel consumption and calculated cost of primary tillage in 2005. Average for the two experiments. with clay loam at Ultuna.

Treatment	Diesel, l/ha	Calculated cost, SEK/ha
A=Mouldboard ploughing	21	729
B=Chisel to 10 cm, 2 passes	13	362
C=Chisel to 15 cm, 2 passes	21	459
D=Chisel to 20 cm, 2 passes	37	714
E=Disc 2 passes	11	370

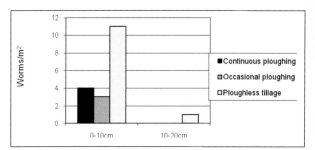

Figure 29.4. Number of earthworms (*Lumbricus terrestris*) on a heavy clay soil at Ultuna. Measurements in 2005, 31 years after the start of the experiment.

can sometimes be interspersed with mouldboard ploughing. A series of experiments included these systems as treatments, where occasional ploughing meant ploughing every third to fourth year (Table 29.3). On average, the system with occasional ploughing gave the highest crop yield. The system with continuous ploughless tillage was clearly beneficial only in one experiment, which was situated on a silty soil, sensitive to crusting.

Figure 29.4 shows the number of earthworms (*Lumbricus terrestris*) in 2005 for one experiment at Ultuna. The number was highest for continuous ploughless tillage and approximately the same for continuous and occasional mouldboard ploughing.

Effects of Low Tyre Inflation Pressures in Conventional and Ploughless Tillage
In 1997, three long-term experiments were started to study the effect of low inflation pressure, primarily on soil structure and crop yield. The experiments are situated at Ultuna, on soils with clay contents ranging from

18 to 36%. There are two tyre treatments, one with single wheels at 0.9 bar inflation pressure and one with dual wheels at 0.4 bar inflation pressure, both tested in conventional (mouldboard ploughing) and ploughless tillage. The hypothesis was that improved tyre equipment would be more beneficial in ploughless compared with conventional tillage, due to a smaller depth of soil loosening in the former.

Crop yield for low inflation pressure compared with normal (average for both tillage systems) is shown in Figure 29.5. The low ground pressure was most beneficial on the heaviest soil. There also seems to be a trend for the effect of low ground pressure to increase with time, at least on the lighter soils. In contrast to the original hypothesis, no interaction has so far been found between the effect of tyre inflation pressure and tillage system on crop yield.

Table 29.3. Relative yield in experiments with continuous and occasional (every third to fourth year) mouldboard ploughing and continuous ploughless tillage.

Place	Ultuna	Lönnstorp	Källunda	Röbäcksdalen	Rudsberg	Knistad	Vreta Kloster	Lanna	Average
Exp. series	4,007	4,008	4,009	4,009	4,010	4,010	4,010	4,010	
Soil type	heavy clay	clayey till	sandy loam	sandy loam	silt clay loam	silt clay loam	clayey till	heavy clay	
Exp. years	27	11	9	18	11	7	8	26	
Cont. ploughing	100	100	100	100	100	100	100	100	100
Occ. ploughing	105	104	97	99	105	105	99	98	102
Cont. ploughless	105	98	95	94	109	107	92	95	99

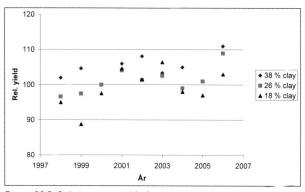

Figure 29.5. Relative crop yields for low tyre inflation pressure (normal inflation pressure=100) in three experiments at Ultuna. Average for treatments with and without mouldboard ploughing.

Is Ploughless Tillage Recommended on Certain Soil Types?

Figure 29.6 shows the relative yields of barley and winter wheat depending on soil type (Rydberg, 1992). The results of ploughless tillage were generally better with increasing clay content with the exception of results from the silty clay loam. Well structured clay soils seem to manage without yearly loosening by mouldboard ploughing. Normally a silty clay loam is very prone to soil compaction because it is rather weak-structured. The main reason for the good results on the compaction-prone silty soils is probably that the positive effects of improved self-mulching outweigh the negative effects of soil compaction. The better self-mulching ability is created by more crop residues and increasing humus content in the upper part of the topsoil, thereby reducing the risk of slaking and thus the rate of evaporation. The need for better water retention is especially great on silty soils in areas with a water deficit during the growing season.

Which Crops and Preceding Crops should be Grown?

In Table 29.4, all yield results with ploughless tillage for different crops during 1986-2002 are presented. On average, no large difference can be seen between ploughed and non-ploughed treatments. Some reduction in yield with ploughless tillage can be observed for peas, potatoes and sugar beet, all of which are prone to soil compaction.

Table 29.5 shows the importance of choosing a good preceding crop for winter wheat. Positive effects on yield, overall and with ploughless tillage, were obtained when

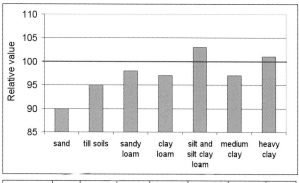

Clay content:	0-5	5-15	5-15	15-30	15-30	30-40	>40
Years of harvest:	5	60	14	14	15	14	30

Figure 29.6. Relative yield for ploughless tillage on different soils. Mean values for spring barley and winter wheat. Relative yield for conventional tillage = 100.

the preceding crop was peas or an oilseed crop. The importance of a good crop rotation cannot be overestimated, especially in tillage systems with ploughless tillage. This is probably related to ploughless tillage leaving more straw residues on the surface, thus increasing the risk of fungal spread.

Will the Use of Fungicides, Herbicides and Insecticides Increase in Reduced Tillage?

Fungicides

In our trials in Sweden with reduced tillage using a tine cultivator or disc cultivator to approx. 7-15 cm instead of ploughing to approx. 22-24 cm, we have observed an increase in the incidence of leaf blotch (*Rhynchsporium secalis*) in barley in the ploughless plots. This is probably related to the ploughless tillage leaving considerably more straw on the surface, thus increasing the risk of fungal spread (Figure 29.7). Likewise, in trials with winter wheat we have found a sparser and weaker crop stand in the unploughed plots. The reason is presumably an increase in the incidence of overwintering fungi, primarily *Fusarium* species, which are found on straw residues at the surface. It could also be due to poorer covering of the seed due to the seed coulters being hampered by abundant straw masses on the surface. We also know that both eyespot (*Cercosporella herpotrichoides*) and take-all

225

Table 29.4. Crop yields from field experiments with conventional tillage and ploughless tillage, 1986-2002.

Crop	Years of harvest	Conventional (kg/ha)	Ploughless (relative value)
Spring barley	167	4,530	98
Winter wheat	142	6,160	98
Spring wheat	27	4,830	103
Oats	94	4,660	97
Oilseeds	37	2,080	98
Peas	11	2,840	83
Potato	11	36,700	96
Sugarbeets	8	52300	96

Table 29.5. Yields of winter wheat after different preceding crops in conventional and ploughless systems, 1986-2002.

Preceding crop	Years of harvest	Conventional (kg/ha)	Ploughless (relative value)
Total	142	6,160	98
Spring barley	14	5,710	98
Winter wheat	49	5,560	96
Spring wheat	3	5,900	95
Oats	14	6,050	95
Oilseeds	38	6,790	102
Peas	16	6,410	99

A

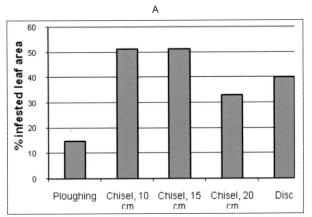

B

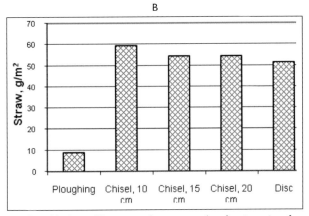

Figure 29.7. Field experiment with different cultivation depths. a) Percentage infested leaf area, b) amount of straw on soil surface in spring after autumn tillage. From Arvidsson et al. (1997).

(*Gaeumannomces graminis*) fungi are favoured by straw being left on the soil surface. However, the international literature does not show any consistent results regarding the risk of attack from these fungi in ploughless tillage. The take-all fungus can also overwinter in couchgrass. It is generally accepted that it is more difficult to combat couchgrass in ploughless tillage than in conventional.

Herbicides
In our long-term trials on ploughless tillage, we have only occasionally increased the amount of herbicide used. In all cases, this involved an extra treatment against couch-grass. Weed counts indicate that the number of seed weeds has increased by around 25% but this has never posed a major problem. In general terms, however, the

quantity of weed seeds and rhizomes decreases with increasing ploughing depth. Our ploughing trials show that ploughing to 27 cm is more effective against weeds than ploughing to 15 or 23 cm. On the other hand, energy consumption in ploughing is generally in direct proportion to ploughing depth. Advantages and disadvantages have to be weighed up. A greater ploughing depth also means a dilution of the organic matter content of the surface layer, with many negative effects as a result, see below. In tillage trials, we have found that living couchgrass is not found below the maximum ploughing depth. If a soil is ploughed to 12 cm only, couchgrass roots will not be found below this depth after a few years. It should be possible to exploit this in subsequent mechanical control strategies for couchgrass.

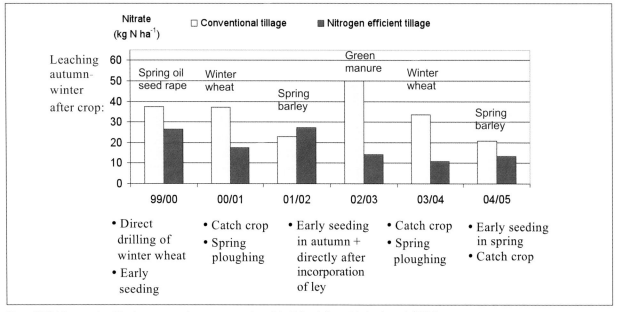

Figure 29.8. Nitrogen leaching in one experiment on a sandy soil in Halland. From Myrbeck et al. (2006).

Insecticides

In Sweden, researchers working with reduced tillage for more than 40 years have not been able to see any major differences in the incidence of insects between ploughed and only stubble cultivated plots. In direct drilling, severe slug attacks on winter oilseed crops have sometimes been observed.

Environmental Effects of Tillage Systems

What are the environmental effects of different tillage systems? Important processes that might be affected are leaching of nitrogen, phosphorus and pesticides. All these issues have been addressed in the long-term experiments, but further research in this area is needed.

Nitrogen Leaching

The effect of tillage on nitrogen mineralisation and leaching has been studied in a large number of experiments. It has generally been found that delaying the time of tillage reduces nitrogen mineralisation. One of these experiments, on a sandy soil (Mellby) in southern Sweden, is within the long-term experiments funded by SLU. In this experiment, nitrogen leaching is studied in drained plots with three replicates in a whole crop rotation. Two treatments are included: one 'conventional' system and one 'nitrogen-efficient' system. The nitrogen-efficient system includes delayed or reduced tillage and catch crops when this is possible within the crop rotation. During the first 6 years, the measured nitrogen leaching was in total 92 kg/ha lower in the nitrogen efficient system (Figure 29.8).

Phosphorus

Tillage systems may have an impact on transport of phosphorus to surface waters, by runoff and by transport processes in the soil. In general, reduced tillage increases aggregate stability and may thereby reduce particle transport of phosphorus. In an experiment on a clay soil at Lanna, Västergötland, lysimeters were collected from treatments with mouldboard ploughing and treatments which had been direct-drilled for 22 years. The concentration of phosphorus in the drainage water from the lysimeters was significantly lower for the direct-drilled soil (Figure 29.9).

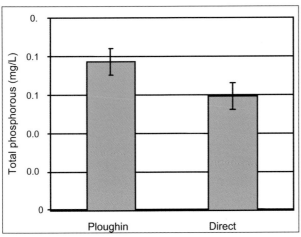

Figure 29.9. Total P in drainage water from lysimeters from a clay soil at Lanna in Västergötland. From Etana & Rydberg (2006).

Another form of reduced tillage is shallow (10-15 cm) mouldboard ploughing. Our results from the last five years are very promising. We think that this form of 'reduced' tillage has many advantages both in relation to conventional and ploughless tillage.

The long-term experiments are a very valuable resource. The effects of tillage on soil structure and crop growth are very often truly long-term and cannot only be studied in short-term experiments. When new questions arise, for example new environmental issues, the long-term experiments form our natural laboratory that we use for finding answers.

Pesticides

At present, one research project is studying pesticide transport in two long-term experiments at Ultuna. The results are not yet published, but indicate more rapid transport of pesticides in ploughless compared with conventional tillage.

Conclusions

One main question concerning primary tillage is whether to plough or not. Nature strives for biological diversity but farmers wish to have uniform crop stands and high yielding crops and there is a constant struggle between those two forces. Crops can be kept uniform and high yielding by different kind of energy inputs, e.g. mechanical inputs (tillage) and chemical inputs (pesticides). The best and cheapest way for farmers to save energy and money is to use knowledge and/or experience to reduce input costs by adjusting tillage operations to current circumstances, while still obtaining a uniform and high yielding crop. So the answer to whether to plough or not is simply: *It depends*. In some cases continuous ploughing might be the best alternative. In other cases continuous ploughless tillage might be the best system. Sometimes a combination of mouldboard ploughing and ploughless tillage might be preferable.

Effects of Lime and Fertilisers on Soil Phosphate Contents

30

CASE STUDY
Lithuania

Liudmila Tripolskaja
Lithuanian Institute of Agriculture, Voke, Lithuania

About 66% of soils in Eastern Lithuania are very low or low in plant-available phosphorus (Mazvila, 1998). Many of them are also acid and light-textured. One long-term experiment with the objective of evaluating the impact of liming practices on P fertiliser efficiency and forms of phosphates was conducted on *Haplic Luvisols* in Voke, Eastern Lithuania. The soil was characterised by low humus content (about 2%), acid reaction (pH_{KCl} 4.4-4.5), low content of available P, and low fixation capacity. Solubility of phosphates was determined according to the method of Chang and Jackson (1957), modified by Askinazi et al. (1963). Plant-available P was determined by the A-L method. After all the extractions, the remaining part was soil insoluble phosphorus. The results showed that the liming of acid soils increased the mobility of phosphoric forms (Tripolskaja and Marcinkonis, 2003) (Table 30.1).

The extent of changes was dependent on the amount of lime and the time since the last liming. More frequent liming enabled phosphoric compounds to be preserved in a more mobile form and was more rational from the point of view of mineral fertiliser efficiency. Determination of the mobile forms of phosphorus in hot water most precisely reflected the effect of liming. This method showed that liming almost doubled the amount of phosphates available to plants. Determination of phosphates in hot water was correlated to the data obtained by the A-L method, i.e. with regular liming the mobility of phosphoric compounds increased.

Table 30.1. Impact of liming on labile forms of phosphates.

Treatment	pH_{KCl} after liming cycles	Extraction			% from P total		
		A L method	In hot water	In NH_4Cl	A L method	In hot water	In NH_4Cl
		P_2O_5 mg kg-1 of soil					
Without NPK and $CaCO_3$	4.2	112	5.1	10.2	8.4	0.4	0.8
NPK	4.2	195	8.5	10.8	13.7	0.6	0.8
NPK + 7.2 t/ha $CaCO_3$*	4.4	200	20.2	9.0	12.4	1.2	0.6
NPK + 14,4 t/ha $CaCO_3$	5.4	202	25.3	7.2	10.3	1.3	0.4
NPK + 24.6 t/ha $CaCO_3$	6.4	241	24.1	10.5	12.9	1.3	0.6
LSD_{05}		13.1	13.4	3.3			

*amount of limestone (t ha-1 $CaCO_3$) per 20 years of liming cycle

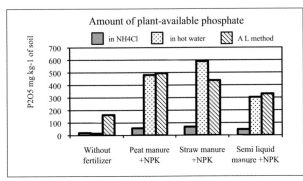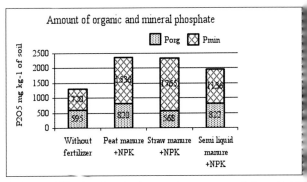

Figure 30.1. Influence of fertilisation on the amount of organic, mineral and plant-available phosphate in the experiment on a sandy loam *Haplic Luvisol* in Lithuania (Place and time of experiments: Lithuanian Institute of Agriculture, Voke, 1986-1998.). Source: Tripolskaja & Marcinkonis, 2003.

Another experiment with different types of manure in relatively high amounts (46 t ha^{-1} peat-based farmyard manure FYM, 60 t ha^{-1} straw-based FYM, 75 t ha^{-1} semi-liquid manure) together or without mineral $N_{150}P_{50}K_{150}$ fertilisers, was conducted on the same soil type to study the mobility of phosphorus and fractional composition of phosphates (Tripolskaja, 2002). One rate of manure was calculated according to the amount of nitrogen it contained, which corresponded to 300 kg N ha^{-1}. It was established that application of peat FYM increased the content of total and mobile phosphorus (Figure 30.1). The application of semi-liquid manure had a less marked effect on the accumulation of soil phosphates. Regular application of both FYM and mineral fertilisers changed the fractional composition of phosphates: the amount of water-soluble phosphates increased 1.99-4.20-fold, and that of phosphates determined in hot water 22.5-54.8-fold compared with unfertilised soil. The amount of organic phosphates in the soil increased only while manuring with peat and straw FYM, and accounted for 57.1-65.1% of the total P (in the unfertilised soil -47.3%). Application of FYM and NPK mineral fertilisers increased the amount of Ca-phosphates and insoluble residues of phosphorus. Experiments with lysimeters showed that 12 years of periodic application of FYM and mineral fertilisers resulted in more intensive leaching of phosphates bound to organic compounds (Tripolskaja, 2004). Regarding this fact – the impact of organic fertilisers on higher migration of phosphates within a soil profile – more research results have been obtained on light-textured soils in Russia (Titova

et al., 1998; Lukin et al., 1999). Titova et al. (1998) argue that the migration of organic phosphorus compounds bound to fulvic acids is increased by manuring with pig or poultry manure.

Conclusions

1. Regular liming (every 5 years) of acid soils increased the mobility of phosphoric forms. The amount of most plant-available hydro- and dihydro-phosphates increased to 34.6-40.9% of total P (compared with 32.8% in unlimed soil). The amounts of insoluble phosphoric forms were dependent on soil pH_{KCl}. Changing the soil reaction from pH_{KCl} 4.4-5.4 to pH_{KCl} 6.4-6.7 significantly increased the insoluble P amount (from 23-25 mg kg^{-1} P_2O_5 to 43-50 mg kg^{-1}).

2. With relatively high regular applications of manure (peat-based farmyard manure FYM, straw-based FYM, semi-liquid manure), the content of mobile phosphorus in a sandy loam *Haplic Luvisol* increased considerably from 161-182 mg kg^{-1} to 322-495 mg kg^{-1}. The migration of phosphorus in the subsoil horizon also increased. When fertilising with straw and peat manure, the amount of organic phosphorus decreased by 9-18%, and when fertilising with semi-liquid manure it increased by 6%. The accumulation of organic phosphate is basically dependent on the amount of readily soluble organic phosphate.

Soil Erosion

CASE STUDY
Lithuania

Benediktas Jankauskas
Kaltinenai Research Station
Lithuanian Institute of Agriculture
Kaltinenai, Lithuania

Everywhere in the world where people change a natural ecosystem into agriculture, the land degrades. The visible effect is erosion, when soil particles leave their primary position on the land, transported by soil tillage or other implements, gravity, water or wind. Highly eroded soils tend to have reduced productivity, degraded soil structure, lower soil organic matter and a poor environment for root growth. Soil erosion on the hilly undulating agricultural landscape is a complex phenomenon involving the detachment and transport of soil particles by tillage, water (Figures 31.1 and 31.2) and wind , storage and runoff of rainwater and infiltration. Some erosion is natural but current rates of accelerated erosion are more than worrying. Fortunately, there are many ways to reduce soil erosion (Boile, 2002).

Soil Erosion in the Nordic countries.

Conditions for soil erosion in different Nordic and Baltic countries are very different, and therefore the risk of erosion as well as erosion prevention measures are different too. In Norway, Sweden, Finland and Denmark, water erosion is considered to be the main problem, not only because of the negative impact it may have on soils and agriculture, but also because of its significant contribution to the phosphorus loading of freshwater bodies.

Mountains and lakes cover 75% of Norway, farmland only 3%. The agricultural areas are concentrated in southern and south-eastern parts, as well as in some areas of central Norway. The highest soil erosion risk to agricultural land in Norway mainly occurs in autumn through heavy rainfall, and in spring through heavy snowmelt (Oygarden et al., 2006). Therefore, extremely different measures have been used: from artificial land levelling as a form of mechanical soil erosion (1970-85), leading to increased rates of water erosion, to increasing areas under perennial grasses, avoiding autumn ploughing, establishment of vegetative buffer zones and sedimentation ponds as erosion resisting measures (Njos, 1991; Oygarden et al., 2006) leading to decreasing soil erosion rates.

There have been very few studies of soil erosion in Sweden. Various amounts of eroded material, between 0.5 and 300 Mg ha^{-1}, are lost from the fields. High relative erosion risk areas, calculated using the USLE (Universal Soil Loss Equation) equation and large-scale topographical data, indicate the erosion risk areas to be situated in the east and west of Sweden (Ulen, 2006).

In Finland, the loss of eroded material and nutrients is highly dependent on the hydrological cycle. The actual effects of snowmelt and rain-induced erosion on annual sediment loss and the efficiency of different management methods for reducing erosion and nutrient losses are currently being studied in long-term field experiments. Erosion rates vary between 0.03 and 3.3 Mg ha^{-1} yr^{-1} in agricultural areas, while the corresponding figures in forested catchments are considerably lower, namely 0.02-0.2 (Tattari and Rekolainen, 2006).

Figure 31.1. Gully erosion (Kaltinenai municipality, Silale district, Lithuania): gully formatted after the Glacial Period (left) and early stage of gully formation on the road-side slope. (right). Photo: B. Jankauskas.

Figure 31.2. The samples of water erosion on the arable land of the hilly-rolling relief (Kaltinenai municipality, Silale district, Lithuania): rill's formatted after snow melting and after runoff on the slope under early stage of rye crop (top); rill erosion on the slope and buried crop of the barley on the foot-slope after runoff (below). Photo: B. Jankauskas.

The Climate of Lithuania

The climate of Lithuania is transitional between maritime and continental. Weather conditions are unstable, with frequent thawing in winter, and cloudy skies, damp and cool weather in summer. There is a characteristic abundance of moisture and lack of warm temperatures. The average annual temperature is +6°C: the average for January is -4.8°C, and that for July +17.2°C. Average annual precipitation is 675 mm, with precipitation being highest (920 mm) in the south-western part of the Zemaiciai Upland and lowest (520 mm) in the northern part of the Central Lithuanian Lowland. The Lithuanian climate is favourable for the occurrence of water erosion. Heavy showers cause most danger. The average wind speed on the Baltic Sea coast is 5.5-6.0 m s^{-1}, and on dry land it decreases to 2.9-3.5 m s^{-1}. In the cold season, due

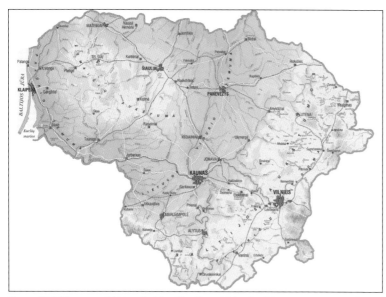

Figure 31.3. The map of Lithuania: islandlike Zemaiciai upland in western part; prolonged Baltic uplands in eastern part.

to active cyclonic activity, the wind speed is 1-2 m s^{-1} greater than in summer (Jankauskas and Fullen, 2002).

Soil Erosion in Lithuania

Lithuania is mainly a lowland country, but has two upland regions, the 'island-like' Zemaiciai Upland in the west and the western edge of the Baltic Uplands in the east and south (Figure 31.3). About 52% of Lithuania's relief consists of undulating hills, where the soil is erodible (Kudaba, 1983). About 17% of Lithuania's agricultural land is eroded, increasing to 43-58% in hilly regions (Jankauskas, 1996; Jankauskas and Fullen, 2002). Erosion processes affect the majority of the overall rolling terrain of Lithuania by over 20-30% and by more than 30%. Different soil types are affected by soil erosion: Albeluvisols, Cambisols, Luvisols and Regosols are affected mostly by tillage and water erosion, while Arenosols and Histosols are affected by wind erosion, when they are under tillage and dried.

Tillage Erosion

Soil erosion intensity in Lithuania depends mainly on tillage erosion, which has been identified as the main cause of accelerated soil erosion on arable slopes (Kiburys, 1989; Jankauskas, 1996). The rate of soil translocation under tillage erosion depends on slope steepness, tillage equipment and the direction of tillage operations. For example, the mass of soil moved downslope was 17.6 Mg ha^{-1} after a single mouldboard ploughing across the slope (along the contour) on a 100 m length and 10° (17.7%) slope and the mass of soil moved upslope was 1.9 Mg ha^{-1}. Therefore, the net rate of tillage erosion (difference between downslope and upslope movement) was 15.7 Mg ha^{-1}. Tillage erosion was 11.4 Mg ha^{-1} when ploughing slantwise across the slope to the left and 8 Mg ha^{-1} when ploughing slantwise to the right. Tillage erosion was only 5.2 Mg ha^{-1}, when ploughing up and down the slope (Kiburys, 1989). Tillage erosion rates due to a single sequence of mouldboard ploughing on slopes from 3-15° (5-26.3%) were from 1.0-7.2 Mg ha^{-1} when ploughing up and down the slope, or from 11.2 to 16.8 Mg ha^{-1} when ploughing across the slope (Figure 31.4).

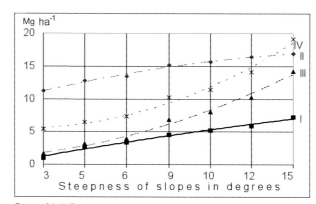

Figure 31.4. Dependence of tillage soil erosion (Mg ha^{-1}) on slope steepness after single mouldboard ploughing in different directions (Jankauskas and Kiburys, 2000). I: up and down the slope, II: along the contour III: slantwise across the slope to the right, IV: slantwise across the slope to the left.

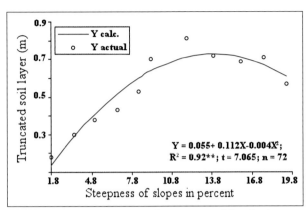

Figure 31.5. Relationship between slope steepness (X) and soil truncation (Y).

According to the data presented in Figure 31.4, the relationship between slope steepness and tillage erosion can be expressed by the equations:

$y_I = -0.09x^2 + 1.67x + 9.63$, $R^2 = 0.987$, $P < 0.05$;
$y_{II} = -0.03x^2 + 1.22x + 0.04$, $R^2 = 0.987$, $P < 0.05$;
$y_{III} = 0.18x^2 + 0.53x + 1.1$, $R^2 = 0.987$, $P < 0.01$;
$y_{IV} = 0.3x^2 - 0.28x + 5.6$, $R^2 = 0.986$, $P < 0.01$.

where y is soil losses (Mg ha^{-1}) and x is slope inclination (degrees).

Tillage erosion is a direct consequence of soil profile truncation on arable sloping land. Soil profile truncation increased with increasing slope steepness up to 100

(17.7%) (Figure 31.5). A plausible explanation for the stabilisation by soil profile truncation on the steeper slopes is the tendency to avoid use of slopes >18% for crop rotations in Lithuania. These slopes are usually pastures with perennial grasses (Jankauskas and Fullen, 2002).

Tillage erosion only moves soil over a short distance (75-85 cm), whereas water and wind erosion transports soil over much greater distances (Kiburys and Jankauskas, 1997). Therefore, formation of natural agro-terraces near natural or artificial boundaries is characteristic for arable hillslopes (Jankauskas and Kiburys, 2000).

Water erosion

Investigations of water erosion on 5-7° slopes of the Baltic uplands (Eastern Lithuania) show that runoff and losses of clay loam soil due to water erosion range markedly: from 6.6 mm of runoff water under wasteland to 151 mm under bare fallow, or from 4.5 Mg ha^{-1} yr^{-1} of soil under cereal crops to 46.6 Mg ha^{-1} yr^{-1} on bare fallow (Bundinienė and Paukštė, 2002).

Heavy losses of Eutric Albeluvisols occur due to water erosion on the Zemaiciai Uplands (Western Lithuania). At the long-term monitoring sites, soil losses were 3.2-8.6 Mg ha^{-1} under winter rye, 9.0-27.1 Mg ha^{-1} under spring barley and 24.2-87.1 Mg ha^{-1} under potatoes, on slopes of 2-5° (3.5-8.3%), 5-10° (8.3-17.7%) and 10-14° (17.7-24.5%), respectively, increasing with slope steepness. Perennial grasses completely stabilised soil erosion (Jankauskas et al., 2004). The extent of water ero-

Figure 31.6. The long-term (24 year) soil erosion sites of Kaltinenai Research Station of Lithuanian Institute of Agriculture (Silale district, Lithuania). Photo: B. Jankauskas.

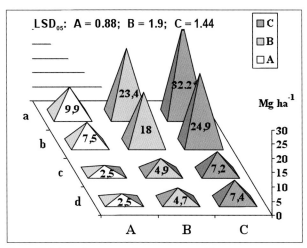

Figure 31.7. Annual water erosion rates under different crop rotations.

sion rates depends on the erosion prevention capabilities of different crop rotations, on land use systems and on slope gradient (Figure 31.6). According to the mean data of 36 experiments (duration 18 years), the mean annual erosion rates under the grass-grain rotation decreased by 75-80% compared with the field crop rotation, while under the grain-grass crop rotation it decreased by 23-24%. However, even the grass-grain crop rotation could not completely prevent water erosion, with mean annual rates of 7.2-7.4 Mg ha^{-1} on the 10-14° slopes.

The heights of the pyramids in Figure 31.7 represent the mean of 18 years of data on the slopes: A. 2-5° (3.5-8.3%), B. 5-10° (8.3-17.7%), C. 10-14° (17.7-26.3%). Crop rotations: a) field, b) grain-grass, c) grass-grain I,

d) grass-grain II. *On the 10-14° slope (17.7-26.3%) potatoes were not grown. The data were calculated by the method of group comparison.

Soil erosion has led to significant deterioration in the physical and chemical properties of loamy sand and clay loam Albeluvisols. Dry bulk density and percentage of clay-silt and clay fractions have increased and the percentage total porosity and water field capacity decreased. Strong acidity of E, EB and B1 soil horizons, exhumed due to soil erosion, is a characteristic feature of eroded Albeluvisols. Deterioration of soil attributes leads to decreased soil fertility (Jankauskas and Fullen, 2002). The natural fertility (using barley yield as a surrogate measure) is lower on eroded soils. On slopes of 2-5° (3.5-8.3%), 5-10° (8.3-17.7%) and 10-14° (11.7–24.5%), barley yield decreased by 21.7-22.1, 38.9-39.7 and 62.4%, respectively (Table 31.1). These results demonstrate the need for soil conservation measures on arable undulating environments in Lithuania.

Erosion-resisting Measures

Erosion-resisting land use systems have been suggested for the vulnerable hilly-undulating terrains of Lithuania to combat soil degradation due to soil erosion. Analysis of the complex rolling relief of Lithuanian Uplands has revealed different conditions for water erosion on the arable slopes with different inclination and containing different soil textures. The most vulnerable to water erosion are terrains having light soil texture on steep slopes.

Table 31.1. Dependence of barley yield on slope steepness and soil erosion severity.

Landscape segment	Severity of soil erosion	Yield* from 48 study plots		
		in Mg ha^{-1}	in relative numbers	decrease Mg ha^{-1}
Flat land	Non-eroded	18.9	100	-
Slopes of 2-5° (3.5-8.3%)	Slightly eroded	14.8	78.3	4.1
Slopes of 5-10° (8.3-17.7%)	Moderately eroded	11.4	60.3	7.5
Slopes of 10-14° (17.7-26.3%)	Severely eroded	7.1	37.6	11.8
Footslopes	Deposited soil	19.5	103.2	-
LSD$_{05}$		1.1		

* Mean of 3-year grain and straw gross yield.

Table 31.2. Grouping erodible terrain for better erosion control and erosion-resisting measures.

Groups	Soil texture†		Type of land use	Requirements for group formation	Recommended erosion-resisting measures
	S, LS, G	L, C			
I	< 10°	< 15°	Woodland	Pick out slopes over 10° and 15°. Slopes over 10° of heavy texture and over 5° of light texture are unsuitable for land reclamation	Plant trees or shrubs, carefully maintain perennial grasses
II	7-10°	10-15°	Grassland	Along with the indicated slopes, land inconvenient for tillage, more plain arable plots and establishment of pasture or grassland	Plant perennial grasses for long-term use. Renovate by using a mixture of another composition. Cover crop must be annual grasses
III	5-7°	7-10°	Arable land or grassland	Similar to Group II, only indicated plots must be in a suitable form for tillage	Introduce the erosion-preventing grass-grain crop rotation. Apply erosion-preventing tillage means
IV	2-5°	3-7°	Arable land	Similar to Group III, only 10% of light soil slopes up to 7° can be annexed	Introduce the erosion-preventing grain-grass crop rotation. Apply erosion-preventing tillage means. Avoid growing tillage crops and flax
V	Up to 2°	Up to 3°	Arable land	Plains, suitable for tillage practice, that remain after forming groups I-V	Use intensive field crop rotations. On the slopes of 2-3°, apply soil conserving tillage practices

†S – sand, LS – loamy sand, G – gravel, L – loam, C – clay.

Table 31.3. Erosion-resisting crop rotations for the fields of Group II (see Table 31.2).

I. Minimum grass 80%	II. Minimum grass 74%	III. Minimum grass 67%
1. Winter grain or spring barley.	1. Winter grain	1. Winter grain
2. Perennial grasses	2. Spring barley	2. Spring barley
3. Perennial grasses	3. Perennial grasses	3. Perennial grasses
4. Perennial grasses	4. Perennial grasses	4. Perennial grasses
5. Perennial grasses	5. Perennial grasses	5. Perennial
	6. Perennial grasses	6. Perennial grasses
	7. Perennial grasses	
IV. Minimum grass 63%	**V. Minimum grass 63%**	**VI. Minimum grass 60%**
1. Winter grain	1. Winter grain	1. Winter grain
2. Winter grain	2. Spring barley	2. Spring barley
3. Spring barley	3. Spring barley	3. Perennial grasses
4. Perennial grasses	4. Perennial grasses	4. Perennial grasses
5. Perennial grasses	5. Perennial grasses	5. Perennial grasses
6. Perennial grasses	6. Perennial grasses	
7. Perennial grasses	7. Perennial grasses	
8. Perennial grasses	8. Perennial grasses	

However, cover crops determine water erosion rates on the different soil and relief conditions. Therefore, the main attributes of the proposed land conservation and sustainable land use system are the careful selection of optimum erosion-preventing agri-phytocenoses (sod-forming perennial grasses or erosion-preventing crop rotations) with high erosion-resisting capabilities. These systems would vary in response to slope and soil conditions. Such ecosystems assist erosion control and thus the ecological stability of undulating topography, the main component in a soil protection strategy for the undulating relief of the Temperate Climate zone of Lithuania.

The erosion-resisting grouping of the erodible undulating terrain contains 5 groups of reliefs depending on

Table 31.4. Erosion-resisting crop rotations for the fields of Group III (see Table 31.2).

I. Minimum grass 57%	II. Minimum grass 57%	III. Minimum grass 50%
1. Winter grain	1. Winter grain	1. Winter grain
2. Winter grain	2. Spring barley	2. Spring barley
3. Spring barley	3. Spring barley	3. Spring barley
4. Perennial grasses	4. Perennial grasses	4. Perennial grasses
5. Perennial grasses	5. Perennial grasses	5. Perennial grasses
6. Perennial grasses	6. Perennial grasses	6. Perennial grasses
7. Perennial grasses	7. Perennial grasses	
IV. Minimum grass 50%	**V. Minimum grass 43%**	**VI. Minimum grass 40%**
1. Winter grain	1. Winter grain	1. Winter grain
2. Cereal grains with legumes	2. Cereal grains with legumes	2. Cereal grains with legumes
3. Spring barley	3. Cereal grains	3. Spring barley
4. Perennial grasses	4. Spring barley	5. Perennial grasses
5. Perennial grasses	5. Perennial grasses	6. Perennial grasses
6. Perennial grasses	6. Perennial grasses	
	7. Perennial grasses	

slope gradient and soil texture (Table 31.2). The requirements for identifying groups and recommending soil conservation measures were decided using research data from field experiments. Group I includes the highly erodible soils that are on slopes <10° having sandy, loamy sand or gravel texture (light soils) or on slopes <15° with loamy or clay texture (heavy soils). We suggest planting trees on such slopes, increasing woodland and biodiversity, enabling accumulation CO_2 and decreasing the greenhouse effect (Jankauskas et al., 2006; Jankauskas et al., 2007).

Growing long-term perennial grasses is recommended (Table 31.3) on light soils with prevailing 7-10° slopes and heavy soils with 10-15° slopes, and on surrounding soil that is unsuitable for any other land use (Group II). Because perennial grasses provide full protection from soil erosion, even on the 10-15° slopes, the grass mixtures with a high percentage (90%) of common alfalfa are recommended for hilly pastures, if soils are suitable for growing alfalfa. The annual average yield has been found to be 6.12 Mg ha^{-1} dry matter or 0.92 Mg ha^{-1} digestible protein. However, the majority of soils on the Zemaiciai Upland are not suitable for growing alfalfa due to excess soil acidity and a high percentage of waterlogged subsoil. Therefore, grass mixtures of high fertility for early, medium and late hay making or grazing should

be established. The annual average productivity of the most fertile hay meadow mixture during a 6-year study period was 7.9-9.2 Mg ha^{-1} dry matter. The productivity of the pasture land was 5.6-7.1 Mg ha^{-1}. The productivity of these grass mixtures did not decrease during the 6-year period, indicating that the duration of these grass mixtures might be longer (Norgailiene and Zableckiene, 1994). These long-term perennial grass mixtures can be used for grasslands on the areas in Group II with erodible terrain.

Soil conserving grass-grain crop rotations, including 50-80% of perennial grasses (Table 31.4), are suggested for soils in Group III on 5-7° slopes with light soils and on 7-10° slopes with heavy soils. These slopes should be arranged into fields suitable for tillage.

Group IV includes 2-5° slopes with light soils and 3-7° slopes with heavy soils, and utilises the soil conserving grain-grass crop rotation, including 33-50% perennial grasses (Table 31.5). When growing grain crops, it is important to use soil conservation tillage and fertilisers on the undulating and rolling relief.

Group V includes the remaining fields with flat to gently undulating relief. Common field crop rotations, containing tillage crops, can be used on these soils. However, using conservation tillage on 2-3°slopes is useful.

Table 31.5. Erosion-resisting crop rotations for the fields of Group IV (see Table 31.2).

I. Minimum grass 38%	II. Minimum grass 33%	III. Minimum grass 33%
1. Winter grain	1. Winter grain	1. Winter grain
2. Cereal grains with legumes	2. Spring grains	2. Winter grain
3. Spring barley	3. Cereal grains with legumes	3. Cereal grains with legumes
4. Winter or spring grain	4. Spring barley	4. Spring barley
5. Spring barley	5. Perennial grasses	5. Perennial grasses
6. Perennial grasses	6. Perennial grasses	6. Perennial grasses
7. Perennial grasses		
8. Perennial grasses		

Deep soil chisel tillage can be used instead of deep mouldboard ploughing, and stubble can be sprayed with the herbicide glyphosate ($C_3H_8O_5NP$) instead of the stubble tillage and deep ploughing common in autumn soil tillage systems. Soil erosion rates can be reduced 2-9 fold by using these measures while productivity is maintained at the same level (Feiza et al., 2004). Differentiation of nitrogen fertiliser rates on various parts of hilly-undulating landscapes (Feiziene, 1996) and matching fertiliser and liming rates to the sensitivity of the crops to soil acidity and erodibility (Jankauskas, 1996) are also important parts of this erosion control system.

off and erosion and to combat physical soil degradation in the temperate climate zone.

Conclusions

Soil erosion in Lithuania becomes a risk when the plant cover has been disturbed. This can be caused by fire, overgrazing of pastures and by tillage equipment on arable soils. Therefore, tillage erosion is a primary cause of water and wind erosion on arable soils.

The mean annual erosion rates under a field crop rotation were 9.9, 23.4 and 32.2 Mg ha^{-1} yr^{-1} from 2-5°, 5-10° and 10-14° slopes, respectively. A grass-grain crop rotation decreased the mean annual erosion rates by 75-80% compared with a field crop rotation, while a grain-grass crop rotation decreased erosion by 23-24%.

The need for soil conservation measures on the rolling landscape increases with increasing slope gradient and with increasing human activities. The erosion control system presented above is able to minimise surface run-

Soil Acidification

32

Marija Eidukevičiene
Klaipeda University, Klaipeda, Lithuania

Concept

Soil acidification is described as a process whereby soil becomes acid (pH <7) because acid parent material is present or in regions with high rainfall, where soil leaching occurs (Soil Atlas of Europe, 2005). Soil acidification takes place in both natural and anthropogenic environments. That is precisely why in practice soil acidification is usually also perceived as acidification of limed soils (renewal of acid soil reaction after liming). The evidence for soil acidification is a change in soil acidity expressed as a pH value or by terms ranging from slightly acid for pH values <6.5 to extremely acid for pH values <4.5. Acidification is a slow process. For example, moraine loam Albeluvisols (initial pH in KCl suspension 4.6) in Lithuania after initial liming at 1.0 rate with rapid and slow activity liming materials, acidified to the initial level after 13 and 40 years, respectively. The intensity of soil acidification in the case of rapid activity liming materials is about 0.8 pH units (in KCl suspension) per 10-13 years (Eidukevičiene, 2001; Eidukevičiene et al., 2007). At present, the acidification of cultured (anthropogenic) soils is understood as cation leaching and removal with plant production in a theoretical sense, while practically it is regarded as soil degradation, i.e. the process of deterioration of its chemical, physical and biological properties (Eidukevichiene et al., 2001; Chwil, 2002). Acidification can be accelerated by human activities, e.g.

use of fertilisers or deposition of industrial and vehicular pollutants (Soil Atlas of Europe, 2005).

Soil acidification (pH value moves down towards 4) is the opposite process to acidity neutralisation (pH value moves up towards 7). However, soil acidification and acidity neutralisation are different processes that proceed simultaneously, and the degree of intensity of both depends on the buffering capacity of the soil (Eidukevičiene, 1993; Eresko, 2005). This is the explanation for the dependence of both processes on the carbonate content of parent rocks or bedrocks (Eidukevičiene, 1993).

Problem Research and Results

Soil acidification as a process has been studied far less comprehensively than acidity neutralisation because since the mid-1960s it has been not analysed per se but most often only in the context of liming as a result of the chemical activity of liming materials (chemical ameliorator, lime fertilisers that are referred to as agricultural limes). In Europe over the last 150 years, studies of liming as the most efficient and irreplaceable preventive means of soil degradation have been exhaustive and have encompassed the object of liming (soil genesis), the duration of the effect of liming materials and their impact on soil and yield. In the sense of knowledge, the core problem has always been, and still remains, the lack of systemic analysis. Experimental results have revealed the various effects of liming – agrochemical, agrophysical, biological, agronomic, environmental (Eidukevičienė, 1993; Eidukevichiene et al., 2001), both the widely known positive effects and potentially negative effects (Eidukevichiene et al., 2001). There is evidence to suggest that potentially negative effects of intensive periodical liming lead to soil acidification (Eidukevichiene et al., 2001).

With the conception of the nature-friendly anthropogenic environment gaining in increasing importance since the 1990s and with the present day concepts of the profitable market economy, elucidation of soil acidification processes has become of particular significance.

The concept of a correlation between soil as the object of liming and soil acidification as a process in the 20th century underwent changes because of different approaches to the soil and to the need for liming:

- The scientific approach to an individual soil profile and the resulting concept of differentiated liming depending on the depth to carbonate layer in the soil (Lithuania, 1960s) was formulated.
- Overestimation of the upper soil horizon and the concept of liming depending on the upper horizon properties (Eastern Europe, 1970-1980s) became a feature.
- The scientific spatial approach to soil, the dependence of activity of natural and anthropogenic factors of soil acidification on the carbonate content of parent rocks, the depth of parent rock and bedrock and recognition of the significance of the geological and hydrological state of the soil cover for the profile pH were included (Bulgaria, Denmark, the United Kingdom, Poland, Lithuania, the Netherlands, Russia, Hungary, Germany – 1990s).
- Finally, the revival of the concept of differentiated liming on the properties of soil profile horizons or parent rock (Poland, Lithuania, Russia – 1990s) was validated (Eidukevičienė, 1993; Eidukevičienė et al., 2007).

In Eastern European countries, nowadays the problem of soil acidification is especially urgent. In Lithuania, both for economic reasons and because of the underestimation of scientific knowledge, 15 years ago the soil liming intensity was reduced, and the cessation of liming in 1997 due to lack of financing is already showing its first results in soil acidification (Mažvila et al., 2006). This applies to both heavy and light-textured soils. In Belarus, even a temporary (three-year) reduction of liming by 50-60% evoked soil acidification (Bogdevitch et al., 2005). In Russia, where the volume of liming was drastically reduced after 1990, soil acidification is expected to increase (Ivanov, 2000).

The turn of the century did not manifest any leap of the scientific thoughts; on the contrary, a strengthening of the former ideas was evident (Ivanov, 2000; Eresko, 2005; Mažvila et al., 2006). When interpreting the results of the most recent investigations in terms of present day reality, it has been recognised that under real conditions of farming on light loam moraine soils, only intensive liming gives fast results as it allows rapid optimisation of the acidity/basicity indices (Ivanov, 2000; Eidukevichiene al., 2001).

The state of soil acidity/basicity is related to the chemical composition of parent rocks and therefore even in well managed soils the influence of genetic differences remains preserved (Ivanov, 2000; Mažvila et al., 2006). It has been acknowledged that soil acidification differences in the territory of Lithuania, in the absence of liming, are essentially dependent on the genetic diversity of soil acidity in the profile. Therefore, when considering the renewal of soil liming, the concept of differentiated liming is proposed. The concept prioritises so-called originally acid soil areas that were present before intensive liming (Mažvila et al., 2006). The search for a correlation between the above-mentioned concepts and a practical solution for the problem gave the following results in Lithuania: Spatial differences in soil acidity neutralisation were elucidated and substantiated; the solution of differentiated liming depending on the depth to carbonate was proposed (Eidukevičienė, 1993); spatial differences in soil acidification in the territory of Lithuania were established (Mažvila et al., 2006), and the methods of investigation – GIS statistical analysis (Eidukevičienė et al., 2006; Volungevičius et al., 2006) – were improved and provided a scientific background for developing the theory of soil acidification prognosis. Finally, retrospective systems analysis was performed on acid soil gradation on the national level as well as on soil acidification rates at a local level, i.e. field trials (Eidukevičienė et al.,

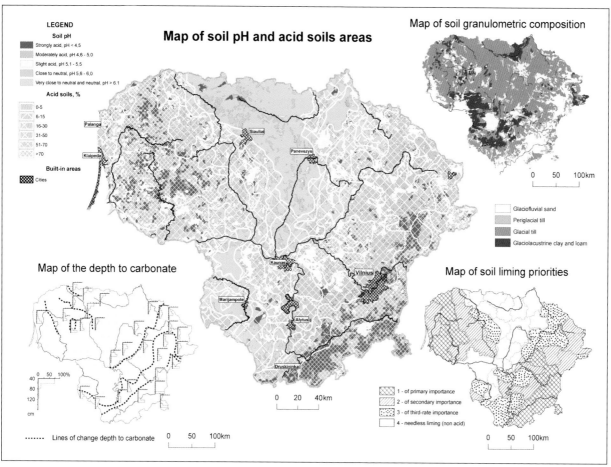

Figure 32.1. National map of acid pH of Lithuania (Eidukevičiene et al., 2010).

2007). This revealed that in moraine loam Albeluvisols, the rate of both neutralisation and acidification processes depends on the initial soil acidity level and on the type of lime materials applied. In both cases, pH changes in the upper soil horizon modify the properties of the whole soil profile as an indivisible natural body resulting from the genesis of the parent rock. The correlation between the spatial structure of pH in the upper soil horizon (0-20 cm) of agricultural lands limed one or two times and the regularities of an increase or decrease in acid soil plots over a period of 40 years is positive proof of the spatial localisation of acid soils and indicative of potentially acid territories. Soil acidification in the whole territory of Lithuania, if no liming is applied, confirms the necessity

for regular uninterrupted liming. The case study results of system analysis are presented below for the well-known Baltijos Highlands (Figure 32.1).

Carbon Flows and Sustainable Agriculture

33

Thomas Kätterer

Swedish University of Agricultural Sciences, Uppsala, Sweden

The way we treat ecosystems influences the global flows of carbon. This is already well discussed when it comes to phosphorus and nitrogen. But also the flows of carbon, the major constituent of life on earth, are critically affected by land use and our way to conduct agriculture and forestry in particular. Besides the emissions caused by burning fossil fuels, land use and management has come up as a major concern in connection with climate change since global warming is caused by large-scale changes in the global carbon flows.

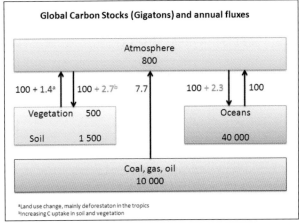

Figure 33.1. Global carbon stocks (Gigatonnes) and annual fluxes. (Based on Le Quéré et al., 2009).

Global Carbon Stocks and Flows

Figure 33.1 presents a simplified version of the global carbon cycle. Boxes represent carbon stocks as fossil fuels, in the oceans, terrestrial ecosystems and atomosphere. Arrows represent annual carbon exchange between these compartments.Stocks measured in billions of metric tons (Gigatonnes). Numbers are based on Le Quéré et al. (2009).

Large amounts of carbon are cycling between the atmosphere and ecosystems (about 200 Gigatonnes per year). Thus, natural carbon fluxes due to photosynthesis are about 25 times higher than those caused by the burn-ing of fossil fuels and cement production (7.7 Gigatonnes per year). Clearing of mainly tropical forests for pastures, croplands and infrastructure, are also contributing to human induced carbon emissions (about 1.4 Gigatonnes per year) since carbon in the vegetation is released as carbon dioxide and often also soil carbon stocks are declining after this conversion. About 45% of total human induced carbon emissions (7.7 + 1.4 = 9.1 Gigatonnes) are accumulating in the atmosphere (4.1 Gigatonnes), whereas the remaing parts are adsorbed in the oceans (2.3 Gigatonnes) and terrestrial ecosystems, mainly temperate and boreal forests (2.7 Gigatonnes). All figures presented here are based on compilation from different data sources and modelling and are highly uncertain (Le Quéré et al., 2009). Between years, fluxes also vary due to natural climatic variation and disturbances such as forest fires and storms. However, relative magnitudes of the different carbon stocks and fluxes are much more certain. For examples, total amounts of carbon stored in soils down to 1 m depth are about three times higher than those in vegetation and about twice as high as those in the atmosphere. Thus, a change in land use and management that will change soil carbon stocks with 1% will result in a 2% change of atmospheric carbon dioxide. The soil carbon balance has therefore significant impact on our climate.

Carbon and Soil Fertility

In a typical soil profile, organic carbon concentrations are decreasing exponentially with depth. About the same amount of carbon is usually found in the upper 25 cm as in the subsoil between 25 and 100 cm depth. This can be visually observed when digging a soil pit where the darker upper horizon indicate a high carbon content compared to deeper horizons which are more greyish or reddish due to less amounts of minerals and oxides with organic material. Soil organic carbon content is a key-indicator for soil fertility since it affects soil structure and is positively correlated with aggregate stability, water infiltration, water holding capacity, nutrient delivery, nutrient use efficiency and soil erosion control. Therefore, keeping reasonable high levels of soil organic carbon is fundamental for sustainable management practices.

Soil Organic Matter

A typical mineral soil used for agriculture consists of about 45% minerals, 5% organic matter and 50% pores of different sizes, which partly are filled with water. Carbon concentration in soil organic matter is about 50%.

Excluding plant roots, only about 2% of this carbon is in living soil organisms (about 90% thereof in archaea, bacteria and fungi and about 10% in eukaryotic organisms such as amoebas, nematodes and earthworms). The rest, about 98%, is a heterogeneous mixture of soil organic material deriving from vegetation and soil organisms at different stages of decomposition.

Soil Carbon Balance

The amount of carbon stored in the soil profile is determined by the balance between carbon inputs (crop residues, roots, root exudates and exogenous organic materials applied in fields such as farmyard manure, sewage sludge or other organic soil amendments) and outputs from decomposition (main part as carbon dioxide). Carbon input is controlled by the plant species and management. Since both choice of plant species and management such as crop residue treatments and manure addition are controlled in agricultural systems, the soil carbon balance is also under human control. All options like fertilization or irrigation that stimulate photosynthesis are likely to increase carbon inputs. Crop residue removal (e.g. for bioenergy) will result in less input, although this option may be favourable for reducing greenhouse gas emissions in a global perspective due to mitigation of emissions from fossil fuels. However, it is not only the quantity of organic inputs that matter for the soil carbon balance but also the quality of its organic constituents. Different organic substances are decomposed through different metabolic pathways and contribute differently to the built-up of soil organic matter. Whereas simple organic substances like sugars are almost instantly assimilated by the soil organism community, more complex molecules like cellulose or lignin are decomposing at a much lower rate. Thus, depending on its composition, the same amount of carbon input will contribute differently to the soil organic matter. It has been shown that for example the same amount of roots from agricultural crops or farmyard manure contribute more than twice as much to soil organic matter compared with above-ground crop residues (Kätterer et al., 2011).

Both input and decomposition are under climatic control. Due to long winters, the length of the vegetation period is decreasing with latitude. This is constraining photosynthesis and decomposition. The activity of decomposers in soil is very low during winter but they are responding fast when temperatures rise in spring. In general, decomposer activity increases exponentially with temperature. Heterotrophic organisms which are adapted to aerobic conditions need both water and oxygen. Decomposer activity is generally highest when 50-80% of the soil pore system is filled with water. Due to the interaction between temperature and soil moisture, decomposition rates are highest under relatively moist and warm conditions and are lowest under either cold or dry conditions. Therefore, the same organic material will decompose almost 5 times as fast in the same soil type at Brazzaville (Congo) compared to Uppsala (Sweden) but at about the same rate as in Uppsala at a hot and dry site in Chad (Andrén et al., 2007). Apart from temperature and moisture, also the soil chemical conditions like salinity and acidity are affecting soil microbes. Low salinity and acidity are generally favourable for decomposition.

Depending on soil type, a large proportion of soil pores are at the sub-micron scale and thus too small for any organism to enter. Soil organic molecules in these tiny pores are therefore more protected from decomposition than those in larger pores. Moreover, organic molecules interact with mineral surfaces through chemical binding to form organo-mineral complexes, which are not easily accessible to soil microorganisms. These interactions differ between soil types and are more pronounced in fine textured soils (clay) than in course textured soils (sand). Soil aggregation is favoured in fine textured soils where soil organic matter is gluing together mineral particles. Both the affinity of clay particles binding to organic substances and the large amount of narrow pores leads to stabilization of soil organic matter in clay soils. According to a Swedish inventory of agricultural soils, soils classified as clay contain about twice as much carbon as those classified as sand (Kätterer et al., 2006). Thus, carbon in soil is stabilized due to physical, chemical and biological reasons and is therefore not readily decomposed. This also implies that all management options affecting carbon input to soil have long-lasting consequences.

Figure 33.2. shows the remaining mass of decomposing crop residues during 10 years in the field. Decomposition is fast during the first year whereafter it slows down.

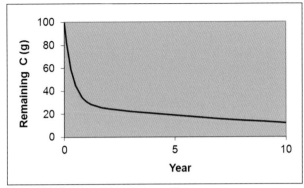

Figure 33.2. Decomposition of crop residues.

After 10 years there is still more than 10% of the original added carbon present in the soil.

Inputs of fresh organic materials (crop residues, roots, manure etc.) are stimulating the decomposer community to breathe and to grow. Organic carbon is transformed into microbial biomass and carbon dioxide. Decomposition rates are high in the beginning but are decreasing with time when sugars, proteins and other easily decomposable substances are depleted. A part of the decomposition products (mostly dead microbial cells en exudates) are entering small pores or are chemically interacting with mineral surfaces. Their further decomposition is very slow, governed by different processes and limited by diffusion and their solubility in water.

Carbon inputs in agricultural systems occur mainly through roots and also a higher proportion of root input compared to above-ground crop residues contributes to the build-up of soil carbon stocks. Cereals like wheat and barley have been bred for thousands of years for optimizing grain yields. Therefore, a lower proportion of assimilated carbon ends in roots and straw and a higher proportion is exported compared with many grassland species. This is the main reasons at many sites for higher carbon stocks under grassland or forests compared to cultivated soils. Intensive tillage methods like mouldboard ploughing may also stimulate decomposition since parts of organic material that not were accessible to microbes maybe exposed through breaking up of soil aggregates. In some regions, soil tillage has been shown to result in decreasing soil carbon stocks although earlier studies

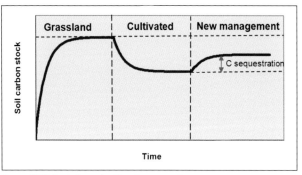

Figure 33.3. Evolution of soil carbon over time.

were overestimating this effect. This effect seems to be more pronounced in semi-arid areas like the prairies in the US and Canada. Under more humid conditions, in the eastern part of Canada or in the Baltic region, this effect is probably much smaller or even negligible. However, reduced tillage has many other positive effects. Generally it decreases risks for water and wind erosion and it also reduces cost for labour and diesel and thus, emissions of carbon dioxide. On the other hand, no-till systems favour weeds and the survival of plant pathogenic fungi under certain conditions. Therefore, the need for both herbicides and fungicides increases when reducing tillage intensity.

Figure 33.3. shows a hypothetical evoluton of soil carbon over time, from mineral sediments almost free from organic matter to natural grassland or forest vegetation. At a certain time, land use is changed to agricultural usage which results in lower carbon stocks. Thereafter, agricultural management is changed in order to sequester carbon in soil. The time scale in this example maybe more than 1000 years since it takes hundreds of years until the soil system has adjusted to new conditions, i.e., carbon stocks have reached a dynamic equilibrium (carbon input = carbon output), after the change of land use or management.

Organic Soils

Soils with high content of soil organic matter have been formed under water-logged conditions. Under low oxy-

gen conditions, organic material is accumulating as peat since decomposition is strongly limited. A typical organic soil used for agriculture in the Baltic area is derived from drained wetlands around lakes that were reclaimed for agriculture by lowering water tables, thus allowing oxygen to enter the soil profile. This lowering of the water table is resulting in soil subsidence, i.e., the sinking of the soil surface, due to physical compaction caused by gravimetric forces and increased decomposition. During the years, water tables have to be lowered from time to time due to this subsidence and the organic layer, up to several meter thick from the beginning, is decreasing. Finally, the remains from this organic layer are mixed with the mineral sediment below and what is left is a mineral soil with a high soil organic carbon content. Around the Baltic sea around 5-10% (depending on classification criteria) of the agricultural soils share this history and are today at different stages along the way from organic to mineral soils. The oxidation of organic material caused huge emissions of carbon dioxide. Moreover, decomposition of organic material is also resulting in nitrogen mineralization and nitrification. Since nitrate can be transformed to nitrous oxide, these soils also contribute to significant emissions of this greenhouse gas, which is about 300 times as effective as a greenhouse gas as carbon dioxide. Organic soils are therefore a major source for greenhouse gas emission and management options for mitigation of emissions are presently under discussion. Raising the water table and reconverting them into wetlands may be only an effective mitigation strategy for some of these soils since emissions of methane, another potent greenhouse gas, will probably not be totally compensated for by decreased emissions of the other gases. Research is presently conducted for optimal management strategies for minimizing climate impact from different kinds of organic soils.

Climate Negotiations

Soil carbon dynamics have received much attention in recent years due to the demand for national reporting of changes of soil C stocks in national Greenhouse Gas Inventories according to IPCC guidelines (IPCC, 1997). Further, Article 3.4 of the Kyoto Protocol of the United

Nations Framework Convention on Climate Change (UNFCCC) indicates that C sequestration in agricultural soils can be accountable for national budgets, and thus of value for balancing out emissions from fossil fuels.

Ways to Increase Soil Carbon

Carbon Sequestration in Agricultural Soils.
Since grasslands and forests generally lose carbon upon conversion to agriculture, prevention of land use change in this direction is an effective measure for reducing greenhouse gas emissions. Increasing demand for food, fibres and bioenergy are setting natural ecosystems under pressure and will probably result in changes in land use towards more agriculture in the future. More intensive (higher production per unit area), more efficient and sustainable agricultural and aquacultural production systems have to be developed for minimizing the impact on natural ecosystems. Carbon sequestration as a mitigation strategy for reducing greenhouse gas emissions can be a win-win strategy, since increased soil carbon is also crucial for soil fertility. Many agricultural practices have the potential to mitigate greenhouse gas emissions. At global level, this potential was estimated to about 1.5 Gigatonnes per year (Smith et al., 2008) excluding potential fossil fuel offsets due to bio-energy production in agricultural systems. If all these potential changes in agronomic practices were included in the carbon trading market, a certain portion of these potentials could be realised depending on the price of carbon dioxide equivalents. Carbon sequestration in soil is one of these options. Carbon inputs are the more controllable part of the soil carbon balance since decomposition is mainly governed by climatic conditions. The most prominent carbon sequestration strategies are therefore practices that result in higher carbon inputs to soil. However, optimizing a system only in one dimension (e.g. carbon sequestration) may under certain circumstances lead to unwanted consequences like higher nitrous oxide emissions or higher nitrate leaching. Therefore, agricultural systems have to be optimized in many dimensions at the same time for providing enough food, fibers and other ecosystem services for a growing population with less negative impact on climate and nature.

Sustainable Agriculture and Climate

Saving Soils with Biochar

34

Lars D. Hylander
Uppsala University, Uppsala, Sweden
Folke Günther
Lund University, Lund, Sweden

Biochar and Terra Preta

Soil organic matter is of fundamental importance for soil fertility. Increased mineralisation due to global warming and increased harvesting of crop residues such as straw and branches for energy recovery will reduce soil organic matter in farm fields and in forest soils. Thereby the growth and future harvests may decrease. Biochar may mitigate soil degradation and has in tropical soils demonstrated drastically increased soil fertility, lasting for thousands of years in the form of Terra Preta (Lehmann, 2007). This extremely fertile, black soil was produced by Indians in the Amazon before their contacts with the Western culture. The Western scientific community was until recently not aware about biochar, although practitioners in historic times sporadically employed biochar as a soil conditioner to fields with poor soils in forested regions of Sweden, adjacent to char production.

Biochar is a term used for charcoal, when the intention of the production and use of the charcoal is as a soil conditioner rather than traditional applications such as for heating, BBQ grilling or processing steel. Although bio-char and charcoal are identical materials until put into the soil, the term biochar will be used also in the production perspective in this chapter in order to consequently use just one term.

Production and Usage of Biochar

Biochar is produced by heating organic materials to several hundred degrees (typically 500-700 °C; Lehmann and Joseph, 2009) at limited oxygen supply, so called pyrolysis. It has a large specific surface, ranging from a few to several hundred square meters per gram char, depending of raw material, temperature, time and water content (Figure 34.1). Its large porosity makes it capable of holding large volumes of plant available water, nutrients and soil microbes. Mixed into soil, biochar is persistent to further degradation with a half life typically around 5000 years (Preston and Schmidt, 2006). This is in contrast to organic matter, having a half-life ranging from less than a year to a few decades.

Figure 34.1. Biochar is highly porous and has thereby a large specific surface. The pores and surfaces attract micro-organisms, water and nutrients. Photo: Folke Günther.

Figure 34.2. Golden water is gold worth to the plants! But a piss in the Baltic is not water worth! Biochar reduces leakage of nutrients and thereby facilitates recycling of nutrients. Photo: Lars Hylander.

The potential of adding biochar to soil is threefold: I.) it mitigates high air CO_2 levels by being a reliable carbon sink; II.) it improves soil fertility by increasing plant available water, nutrients, and soil microbes as well as improving soil structure; III.) it reduces nutrient leakage and losses to ground and surface waters. In addition, production of biochar delivers energy at the processing unit and other raw materials possible to use in the synthetic industry. Biochar itself is inert and will not deliver nutrients until it has been charged with nutrients via direct application of urine or other fertilizer or by sorbing nutrients dissolved in soil water (Figure 34.2).

Burning bioenergy for heating purposes can maintain the present CO_2 level, but it cannot reduce air CO_2 levels, as biochar production can. One kg biochar buried in the soil corresponds to 3.67 kg CO_2 removed from the atmosphere. The present taxation system in Sweden for CO_2 emissions could contribute to sequester carbon if paid CO_2 taxes were refunded to farmers for sequestring elementary carbon in the form of biochar. This would create cash revenues in parity with the ones created from grain with the present level of CO_2 taxes. It should be observed that biochar, once spread into soil, cannot be recovered and its content of CO_2 cannot intentionally be released as is the case if logging forests, initially intended to be a carbon sink. Similarly, Carbon dioxide Cap and Storage (CCS), presently being developed at certain fossil fuel fired power and heat generation plants, cannot reduce the actual CO_2 content in the atmosphere. In addition, these techniques are costly and demand technically advanced units at large scale.

Conclusions

To sum up, biochar production and application to agricultural soils may create a triple wins scenario, where farmers get higher yields and compensation for environmental services; society gets reduced eutrophication and less negative environmental impacts from intense farming practices; and humanity gets sustainable food production at the same time as climate change effects and the connected risk of reaching climate tipping points are reduced. Biochar contributes to a sustainable society in its true meaning for future generations by closing the cycles between arable land and human habitations. The technique is democratic, since it can be applied anywhere around the globe where plants are growing and it is not dependent of economic, technical or infrastructural development. It is independent of scale, too, so also home gardeners may transform garden waste into a soil improver to use in their own garden.

Contamination of Agricultural Soils with Heavy Metals

35

Marina Efremova
St Petersburg State Agrarian University, St Petersburg, Russia
Alexandra Izosimova
Agro-Physical Research Institute, Pushkin, Russia

Trace elements are introduced into soils from various sources, including atmospheric deposition of metal/metalloid-bearing particles, application of sewage sludge, phosphate fertiliser, pig slurry and pesticides, where they exist in several chemical forms. Their fate in soil depends on the chemical state of the element in the contaminating material.

Risks associated with polluted soils are contamination of the food chain. They are closely related to the bioavailability of toxic elements (i.e. ability to enter the different compartments of the food chain) and primarily to the phytoavailability (i.e. availability to plants). Plants are essential components of natural ecosystems and agroecosystems, and are the first compartment of the terrestrial food chain. When grown on polluted soils they become a potential threat to human and animal health, as they may accumulate toxic elements (e.g. metals) in their tissues, as dramatically illustrated by the Itai-Itai disease that affected farmers on a long-term diet of cadmium-contaminated rice. Plants may also have their growth sharply reduced by high levels of toxic elements in their tissues, causing a decrease in crop yields and further economic damage to farmers, as can be observed near metal smelters or mine spoils. On the other hand, some elements, toxic when present at high concentration in tissues, are also essential to plants, and their deficiency induces loss in biomass production and physiological disorders in plants.

It is necessary to determine the pathways of transfer of trace elements from soil to plants in order to properly manage polluted soils:

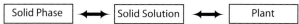

Plants take up trace elements from the soil solution, where ions are in equilibrium with those located in the solid phase through various reactions, including adsorption, exchange, complexation with organic and inorganic ligands, redox reactions, and precipitation-dissolution (Zyrin et al., 1985; Morel, 1997). The extent of the reactions, and hence the solubility of trace elements, is a function of soil mineral content (e.g. silicate layers, carbonates, oxides and hydroxides), soil organic matter (e.g. humic and fulvic acids, polysaccharides and organic acids), soil pH, redox potential and soil temperature and humidity.

The risks of heavy metal transfer into the food chain are dependent on the mobility of the heavy metal species and their availability in the soil (Richards et al., 2000). Different kinds of extractants are used for the extraction of the mobile forms of heavy metals. 1.0 M mineral acids extract most heavy metals and the species extracted are considered to represent a pool closely related to the total concentration, which can be mobilised potentially. Heavy metals extracted by an acetate-ammonium buffer solution characterise these mobile pools. Even more mobile is the exchangeable form of the elements extracted by neutral salts, which is also considered the most available fraction for plants (Gorbatov and Zyrin, 1987). The other forms of elements are more or less immobile. Mobilisation of metals from these forms or transformation from mobile fractions into immobile are very slow processes, which are controlled mainly by kinetic factors.

Haq et al. (1980) evaluated the effectiveness of strong and weak acids, as well as chelates, in extracting Ni and revealed the following order of effectiveness:

DTPA (Diethylenetriaminepentaacetic acid) > EDTA (Ethylenediaminetetraacetic acid) > NTA (Nitrilotriacetic acid) > CH_3COOH (acetic acid) > H_2O.

Obviously chemical forms do not show the real metal distribution in agrocoenosis and allow the contribution of one certain compartment to be deduced. They only reflect the combined contribution of several compartments in forming one or another metal fraction in soil. In measuring the metal availability for plants, it is necessary to take into account a wider range of soil properties.

Uptake and accumulation of trace elements by plants are affected by several soil factors, including pH, Eh, clay content, organic matter content, cation exchange capacity, nutrient balance, concentration of other trace elements in soil, and soil moisture and temperature.

Liming is considered to be an economically acceptable measure that generally helps to reduce the transport of heavy metals into the food chain. Liming has two effects. First it induces an increase in soil pH and supplies Ca^{2+}. The solubility and availability/toxicity to organisms of heavy metals Cd^{2+}, Cr^{3+}, Fe^{n+}, Pb^{2+}, Mn^{n+}, Hg^{2+}, Ni^{2+}, and Zn^{2+} decreases as soil pH increases (McLaughlin, 2002). This is due to the increase in the negative charge on variable charge surfaces in soil (Bolan et al., 2003). Nebolsin and Sychev (2000) and Cho and Han (1996) reported a general decrease in Ni uptake with increasing lime doses from experiments with *Vicia*, barley and radish plants.

Increasing pH, induced by lime, activates microbiological processes in the soil. Weyman-Kaczmarkowa and Pedzivilk (2000) reported that alkalinisation has a very strong stimulatory effect on bacterial growth, especially in loose sandy and sandy loam soils. The microbial biomass increases and can accumulate considerably high amounts of certain heavy metals. On the other hand microbiological increases in the heavy metal availability are caused by microorganisms capable of reducing certain compounds (generally Mn and Fe) and also by their variable bioaccumulation of heavy metals (Kovalskiy and Letunova, 1974).

In the pH range 7.1-8.5, carbonate acts as a pH buffer. The surfaces of calcite are reactive and various ions may adsorb or interact at the crystal's surface. For example Mg^{2+}, Zn^{2+}, Cu^{2+}, Fe^{2+} and Al^{3+} may replace Ca^{2+} on exposed surface lattice sites. The reactive surfaces of carbonates may adsorb soil contaminants such as Ba^{2+}, Cd^{2+} and Pb^{2+} (Ming, 2002).

In some cases, however, an increase in soil pH may not necessarily result in a decrease in metal availability. Molybdenum in soil, which is in the form MoO_4, is more soluble when the pH increases (Kabata-Pendias and Pendias, 1992). A surprisingly higher Cd uptake or even toxicity has been observed in high pH soils compared with low pH soils (Eriksson, 1989), but the mechanisms are not clearly elucidated.

Many findings confirm that the solubility of heavy metals in soil is directly correlated with the redox potential (Patrick et al., 1990; Masscheleyn et al., 1991). Yaron et al. (1996) showed that under same pH values, metal solubility increases as redox potential decreases. As redox potential decreases, trace elements become less available. The uptake of Cd by rice seedlings is at a minimum at low Eh values, where metals may have precipitated as sulphides (Reddy and Patrick, 1977). Availability of the metalloid As increases with increasing concentration in solution (lower soil pH) and with increasing amounts of soluble As (IV) (lower soil redox) compared with As (V) (Marin et al., 1993). Fe and Mn are particularly soluble under water-logged conditions, and precipitates may appear on the root surface through the oxidation of metals supplied by the mass flow. Large amounts of metals (e.g. Zn and Cu) can be adsorbed to those iron oxides, leading to an increase in metal uptake by roots (Morel, 1997).

Metals are more available in sandy soils than in clayey soils, where they are firmly retained on the surface of clay minerals. They may form types of complexes on clay surfaces: outer-sphere ion-exchange complexes on the basal plane, and coordination complexes with SiOH or AlOH groups exposed at the edge of the silicate layers (Zachara et al., 1993). Other minerals, including amorphous hydroxides and oxides, gibbsite and allophane clay, adsorb metals and reduce their mobility in soil. For example, uptake of Cd by soybean is lower from soil low in organic matter and high in oxides of Fe and Mn compared with soil low in oxides and high in organic matter (White and Chaney, 1980).

Organic matter in soil, e.g. humic compounds, bears negatively charged sites on carboxyl and phenol groups, allowing for metal complexation (Stevenson, 1982). Metals can be precipitated or adsorbed organic matter, or can be in the soil solution as soluble organic complexes with low molecular weight compounds (e.g. organic and fulvic acids). The presence of high amounts of insoluble organic matter in soil is negatively correlated with plant uptake, as often observed on peat soils with Cu.

Cation exchange capacity (CEC), a function of clay and organic matter content in soil, controls the availability of trace elements. In general, an increase in CEC decreases uptake of metals by plants (Haghiri, 1974; Miller et al., 1976; Hinesly et al., 1982, Tyler and McBride, 1982).

Absorption of trace elements by roots is controlled by the concentration of other elements and interactions have often been observed. They may be positive or negative, the uptake of a given element being improved or depressed by others present at high concentrations in the soil. Macronutrients interfere antagonistically with uptake of trace elements. Phosphate ions reduce the uptake of Cd and Zn in plants (Haghiri, 1974; Smilde et al., 1992), and diminish the toxic effects of As, as observed on soils treated with arsenic pesticides (Benson, 1953). Calcium controls the absorption of metals, e.g. Cd, as a result of competition for available absorption sites at the root surface (Cataldo et al., 1983). Antagonism between micronutrients is quite frequent. Leaf chlorosis, a symptom due to Fe deficiency, can be induced by an excess of other metals such as Zn, Ni, and Cu, which depresses Fe uptake by plant roots. Conversely, Fe affects Cd absorption, acting as a strong antagonist against the toxic metal. Cd and Zn, two metals chemically close similarity in electronic configuration and reactivity with organic ligands, interact in the soil-plant system, causing the well-known Cd/Zn antagonism (Smilde et al., 1992). Zn depresses Cd uptake (Cataldo et al., 1983). On the other hand, at low concentrations the interaction is synergistic and the input of Zn increases Cd uptake (Haghiri, 1974). Application of K fertilisers to the soil leads to increasing uptake of Cd, Zn, Cu and Ni by oats. This is assumed to be the result of competition between K and microelements for exchange sites on the solid phase of the soil.

It is necessary to remember that fertilisers can contain considerable amounts of trace elements. Two major sources of soil contamination are sludges and phosphate fertilisers. During the period of sludge decomposition, after application to soils trace elements may remain highly available to plants as a result of the release of soluble organic carbon and the decrease in pH following mineralisation/nitrification, which increases the solubility of heavy metals (Dudley et al., 1986; Alekseev, 1987). Long-term use of phosphate fertilisers can elevate the content of many trace elements (e.g. Cd, Hg and As) in soils. It has been shown that the use of these fertilisers significantly increases Cd in soil and the subsequent uptake of the metal by plant roots (Mulla et al., 1980; Rothbaum et al., 1986; Mineev, 1990).

Manifold environmental pollution with different risk potential has been produced by unfavourable waste management and intensive mining activities. Detailed investigations of heavy metal mobility behaviour from waste dump material of typical smelting products (e.g. Mansfelder Land county, mining area of Eastern Thuringia) have been performed in Germany. From these investigations conclusions have been drawn on the long-term behaviour of components and estimates of the risks have been made. Based on different German studies, the transfer behaviour of heavy metals, including Ni, from soil to well-chosen food and forage plants has been analysed. On this basis, a concept for hazard assessment concerning the adverse effects of soil contamination to plants has been developed (Knoche et al., 1999; Schoenbuchner, 2005).

The availability to plants of trace elements from the soil is also controlled by plant micronutrient requirements and their ability to take up or exclude toxic elements. Some plants are well adapted for survival in stressful environmental conditions. They can hold in their tissues amounts higher than 1% of the metal and up to 25% on a dry matter basis. These plants are called 'hyperaccumulators'.

Grasses take up less trace elements than fast-growing plants, e.g. lettuce, spinach and carrots. When grown in the same soil, accumulation of Cd by different plant species decreases in the order: leafy vegetables > root vegetables > grain crops (Morel, 1997). Screening of cultivars that exclude toxic elements should be a priority to protect food quality.

Contamination of Agricultural Soils with Radionuclides

36

Marina Efremova
St Petersburg State Agrarian University, St Petersburg, Russia

Alexandra Izosimova
Agro-Physical Research Institute, Pushkin, Russia

All organisms on earth are permanently exposed to ionising radiation coming from natural and artificial sources. Natural radionuclides (NRN) come to the planet without anthropogenic activities. They are generated in the atmosphere under the influence of cosmic radiation (^{14}C, ^{3}H, ^{22}Na etc.) and are found in rocks (radioactive long-life isotopes ^{40}K, ^{87}Rb and members of two radioactive series originating from ^{238}U and ^{232}Th). It is mainly ^{238}U and ^{232}Th that form background radiation in ecosystems. The level of radiation is not the same in different places on the globe and depends on the concentration of radionuclides in the Earth's crust. Concentrations of natural radionuclides in soil usually correlate to the radionuclide concentration in bedrock. Concentrations of radionuclides (ultra microelement) in plants are linearly related to the radionuclide concentration of the soil.

The natural background levels of an agroecosystem can be increased if phosphorus fertilisers are applied. Concentrations of natural radionuclides (NRN) in phosphorus fertilisers can be similar to mean concentrations in soil (25 Bq kg^{-1}), or ten-fold higher (Tables 36.1 and 36.2) (Drichko et al., 2008).

Production, transportation, storage and application of such fertilisers cause an additional exposure dose for humans. Therefore it is necessary to set limit values for NRN concentrations in fertilisers.

The strictest normative value in Russia has been set for exposure to fertiliser dust and this still remains today.

However, during the past 20 years numerous regulations were revised and finally the normative rate of NRN in phosphorus fertilisers was set to:

$$C(U) + 1.5C(Th) \leq 4.0 \text{ kBq kg}^{-1}$$

where C(U) and C(Th) are the concentrations of ^{238}U (^{226}Ra) and ^{232}Th (^{228}Th) in radioactive equilibrium with the other isotopes of the U and Th series. This limit value has been included into the valid normative documents on radiological safety in Russia (Anon., 1999).

The content of artificial radionuclides in soil depends on the number of nuclear weapons tests and on the quality of work at atomic industries. With nuclear weapon testing the majority of radioactive substances go to the stratosphere (10-50 km from the Earth's surface). They stay there for a very long time, slowly descending and dispersing everywhere on the Earth's surface. Radioactive fallout contains hundreds of different radionuclides. The most significant in soil contamination are ^{14}C, ^{137}Cs, ^{95}Zr, ^{90}Sr.

The nuclear fuel cycle, part of which are nuclear power stations, is also accompanied by emissions of radioactive substances to the environment. The highest amounts of radionuclides reach the environment after accidents at nuclear power stations. In this case, most important from the agroecological point of view are ^{137}Cs and ^{90}Sr. These radionuclides are chemical analogies of the macro-elements K and Ca respectively and they actively migrate in

Table 36.1. NRN concentrations in raw phosphate materials in Russia.

Deposit, mine	Number of samples	$^{238}U(^{226}Ra)$ [Bq kg^{-1}]	$^{232}Th(^{228}T)$ [Bq kg^{-1}]
Apatite			
Kola	4	26	70
Seligdar	1	100	1,030
Belaya Zima	2	80	610
Phosphorite			
Kingisepp	9	190	40
Podmoskovnoe	1	410	17
Bryansk	4	140	11
Verhnekamskij	3	360	18
Gornaya Shoriya	2	440	35
Aktyubinsk	1	390	30
Sejbinskoe	1	410	6
Belkinskoe*	2	1,480	<1
Oshurkovskoe	1	19	20
Telekskoe*	1	430	22

*Concentrated product after flotation

Table 36.2. Average weighted NRN concentrations in selected Russian phosphorus fertilisers.

Fertiliser	$^{238}U(^{226}Ra)$ [Bq kg^{-1}]	$^{232}Th(^{228}Th)$ [Bq kg^{-1}]
Phosphorite concentrate	460	30
Superphospate	24	44
Triple superphosphate	130	48
Phosphate slag	30	11
Ammophos	4	40
Nitroammophos	4	33
Nitrophos	330	26
Nitroammophoska	4	19
Nitrophoska	9	19
Foreign fertilisers	400-4,000	15-440

the food chain. If soil is contaminated with ^{137}Cs and ^{90}Sr, the quality of agricultural products may be degraded for a long time, because the half-life of these radionuclides is 30 years. ^{137}Cs and ^{90}Sr transfer from soil to plants is dependent on the physical-chemical properties of the radionuclides and the soil, climate factors and genetic peculiarities of the plants.

Cs belongs to a group of alkaline elements and has the oxidation state I, which means that it does not form insoluble compounds naturally. Sr belongs to a group of alkaline-earth elements. It is a metal and has oxidation state II.

The mobility of radionuclides in the soil and their availability to plants depend on the following soil properties:

• Mineralogical composition and soil texture.
• pH.
• Organic matter content.
• Cation composition of soil solution.
• Ca and K concentrations.

The fate of artificial radionuclides in soil is determined by general sorption processes. Radionuclides take part in the processes of ion exchange, physical adsorption, co-precip-

itation, etc. However Klechkovsky (Cigna and Durante, 2005) indicated that sorption of radionuclides is specific, e.g. takes place under conditions of very low concentrations of sorbed substance. Due to extremely low concentrations, the behaviour of artificial radionuclides depends considerably on natural isotopic and non-isotopic carriers – stable nuclides of the element or its chemical analogues. Changes in concentration of a macroelement (K, Ca) in the soil can influence the distribution of a radionuclide (^{137}Cs, ^{90}Sr), while changes in concentration of a radionuclide do not influence the distribution of the macroelement in the soil. Indeed, even in very severe radiological situations, the mass concentration of radionuclides in soil is very low and equal to about 0.4-1.0 g km^{-2}.

Clay minerals with layered structures (such as montmorillonite and hydrous micas) considerably influence the stability of artificial radionuclides in soil. Minerals of this group determine exchangeable (on the surface) and non-exchangeable (in interlayer space) sorption of ^{137}Cs. Sorption of ^{90}Sr is mainly exchangeable and therefore this element is more mobile in the soil-plant system than ^{137}Cs.

Non-exchangeable fixation of ^{137}Cs in the interlayer space of clay minerals determines the long-term presence of this element in the root habitable zone, while its biological availability generally decreases. If there is K in the system, the sorption of ^{137}Cs may be decreased because macroelements displace radionuclides from exchange sites (Wauters et al., 1994; Nisbet et al., 2000). However rather high K concentrations are needed for the decreasing coefficient of ^{137}Cs distribution in the solid phase-soil solution system. The influence of K is not significant if its concentration in the soil solution is 0.4 g l^{-1}, but the effect is 2-3 times stronger if the K concentration is 4.0 g l^{-1}. Therefore, when K concentration in soil is very high, an increase in availability of Cs for plants may be observed. However K fertilisers (within the range of agronomically reasonable doses) decrease Cs uptake 3-5-fold more in comparison with the control, because K competes with Cs for the sorption sites on the root surface (Drichko and Tsvetkova, 1990).

Competition between the chemical analogues Ca and Sr is also rather distinct in the soil-plant system. Liming decreases Sr accumulation in agricultural products 3-20-fold depending on biological characteristics of the plants and soil properties. Increasing pH, induced by lime, decreases the mobility of radionuclides. Thus neutralisation of soil acidification decreases accumulation of ^{137}Cs in harvested crops 2-4-fold (Aleksakhin and Korneeva, 1992). Yudintseva et al. (1980) observed an antagonism between Ca^{2+} and Mg^{2+} in lime and pollutant cations in soil solution. The application of lime decreased plant uptake of radionuclides belonging to the Periodic Table groups I and II, although the solubility of their hydroxides is very high.

Organic fertilisers should be applied to decrease accumulation of ^{137}Cs in the food chain. Organic fertilisers increase the sorption capability of the soil and this measure is most effective on light soils. For example, application of organic fertilisers to soddy podsolic sandy loam soil decreased Cs uptake by peas 3-fold, while organic fertilisers applied to the soddy podsolic light loam soil decreased Cs uptake 1.5-fold. However, radionuclides are weakly sorbed by organic matter and therefore their transfer from peat soils is more intense than from mineral soils (Drichko et al., 1996).

Low quantities of Sr are very well co-precipitated with Ca phosphates, which is why application of phosphorus fertilisers on soils contaminated by ^{90}Sr decreases Sr uptake by plants 5-8-fold (Firsakova et al., 2002). Nitrogen fertilisers should be applied carefully, as higher doses give higher Cs and Sr concentrations in plants. The selection of crops that accumulate relatively low amounts of radionuclides is also a very important measure for the management of contaminated territories. Cereals in this case are more preferable for cultivation than vegetables and root crops. Cultivation of technical crops and seed breeding are the safest activities on contaminated lands.

Part F

Production of High Quality Products & Balanced Feeding

Authors: Allan Kaasik, Magdaléna Lacko-Bartošová, Ragnar Leming, Are Selge, Rein Viiralt and Michelle Wander

Coeditor and Coordinating Author: Allan Kaasik and Christine Jakobsson

Consumer Demands: Organic Agriculture

37

Magdaléna Lacko-Bartošová
Slovak University of Agriculture
Nitra, Slovak Republic

Origin and History

Organic agriculture movements in the major industrial countries, e.g. Germany, Britain, Japan, USA, emerged in the 1930s and 40s as an alternative to the increasing intensification of agriculture, particularly the use of synthetic nitrogen fertilisers. Synthetic nitrogen became available after World War I, when the infrastructure for the manufacture of explosives was converted to nitrogen fertiliser production. A consequence of this process was that organic carbon was decoupled from nitrogen and, along with the soil microbe community dependent on its energy, was essentially left out of the science of crop and soil fertility management for the next 50 years (Lotter, 2003).

In spite of that, the scientific basis for crop and soil management based on organic inputs as an alternative was developed quite early. In the 1920s, Rudolf Steiner outlined the principles of 'biodynamic farming'. This farming system was founded in June 1924, when Steiner met around 60 farmers in Koberwitz near Wroclaw (Poland) and gave eight lectures about modern agriculture based on spiritual science. The concepts underlying biodynamic agriculture relate to the spiritual radiance of all earthly phenomena, including that of the inorganic pedosphere and the cosmos. The physical-sensory reality is seen as an expression of the diversely structured spiritual world, the development of which takes place through the processes in the physical world. This idea of development regards human beings as active creators of future development, both in the positive and in the negative sense. These views are based on anthroposophy, inspired by Steiner, with the core opinion that any thing, any occurrence in the world has its cause in a spiritual world that is actually present and can fundamentally be an object of human awareness. Anthroposophy, as it concerns the perception of nature, understands itself as giving an additional dimension – the spiritual one – which in no case would replace or deny any basic natural law (Leiber et al., 2006). Central to biodynamics is the concept that a farm is healthy only as much as it becomes an organism in itself – an individualised, diverse ecosystem guided by the farmer, standing in living interaction with the larger ecological, social, economic and spiritual realities of which it is a part.

A farm becomes an 'individuality' in which the various factors, like organs, have specific functions and are interlinked through feedback relationships. The prime objective is to encourage healthy conditions for life. Soil fertility, plant and animal health, product quality are to be maintained and continuously improved in a largely closed system. For farms producing under the Demeter trademark, the following principles are compulsory:

- mixed holdings
- site-appropriate crop rotations
- intensive organic fertilisation
- biodynamic preparations
- animal welfare
- breeding locally adapted crop varieties
- maintaining plant health
- cosmic rhythms consideration
- low-impact soil management
- food quality
- including the landscape (Lieber et al., 2006).

In India, Robert McCarrison researched the vitality of soldiers and the reason why they lacked diseases common in the West, and promoted health as a positive concept of vitality rather than a negative form viewed as an absence of disease. Good health was based on a diet of wholesome food – mostly fresh plants and grains with modest amounts of meat, grown on land to which all manures were returned. McCarrison followed up his observations with dietary experiments on rats, feeding one group on the diet of the Indians and the other on the diet of the British poor. The rats on the Indian diet flourished, while the others suffered a range of diseases and negative sociological effects. This led McCarrison to expound the importance of a wholesome diet grown on soil fertilised with manures and other organic matter.

Sir Albert Howard also worked in India in the 1920s on an experimental research institute. He was a keen observer of the local peasant farmers and said that he learnt far more from them than from his scientific training. He undertook a wide range of activities including a highly successful plant breeding programme and observed the effects of how forage was grown on the health of farm animals. This led him to believe in links between the health of the soil and the health of the plants and animals fed by that soil. Howard adapted oriental methods of composting to Indian conditions, which resulted in the 'Indore process' of composting now linked inextricably to his name. These experiences were documented in his book *The Waste Products of Agriculture* (Howard,

1931), which spread his message across many continents (Kristiansen and Merfield, 2006).

The work and publications of Howard, McCarrison and Steiner influenced further development of organic movements. The first use of the term 'organic farming' was in 1940 by Lord Northbourne in his book *Look to the Land*. Northbourne used the term not only in reference to the use of organic materials for soil fertility, but also to the concept of designing and managing the farm as an organic or whole system, integrating soil, crops, animals and society. This systemic approach is still at the core of organic agriculture today.

The social and practical groundwork for the modern organic agriculture movement was laid in the 1940s in publications by Howard (1940) and Balfour (1943) in the UK, and Rodale (1945) in the USA, and centred on the importance of organic matter in agriculture. By the late 1940s, organisations such as the Soil Association in the UK, Rodale's publishing house in the USA and the Bioland organic label in Germany were established as the first OA organisations (Lotter, 2003).

In the UK, Lady Eve Balfour was setting up the 'Haughley experiment' which compared organic and non-organic production over the long term. She also wrote the highly influential book The Living Soil (Balfour, 1943), which was partly informed by the Haughley experiment. She was the first president and founding member of the Soil Association, in 1946 (Kristiansen and Merfield, 2006).

Sir Howard and Lady Balfour developed the 'organic farming' method with more or less closely prescribed guidelines based on the ideas of Sir Howard regarding composting, and Lady Balfour regarding the utilisation of the mineral reserve in the subsoil by means of deep-rooting clovers and herbs, and the important role that the symbiotic mycorrhizae play in the maintenance of crop health (Boeringa, 1980).

In France, the pioneering work of Lemaire and Boucher led to the development of the 'biological farming' method based upon the notion that mineral fertilisers, chemical pesticides and large amounts of uncomposted organic fertilisers disturb the 'balance' of the soil and thus induce diseases and pests. Through administration of composted organic fertilisers, leguminous plants and Calmagol (a product characterised as unique and consisting of coral algae, *Lithothamnium calcareum*), they claimed that balance is restored and maintained.

Calmagol was also claimed to be the catalyst of the so-called biological transmutations by which, under the influence of primarily microbiological processes, elements change into other elements, in ideal circumstances according to the requirements of the crop. Biological transmutation, a theory developed by C.L. Kervran, plays an essential role not only in Lemaite-Boucher agriculture, but also in the macrobiotic dietetics of Ohsawa. However, Kervran's research has not confirmed the existence of biological transmutation (Boeringa, 1980).

The Swiss biologist Dr. Hans Müller and his wife Maria, in cooperation with Hans-Peter Rusch, a medical doctor, first demonstrated the practical possibilities of organic-biological agriculture. What they did was in fact to carry out an agricultural experiment on an ever-increasing scale, the consequences of which are of world-wide significance. The task of this 'biological holistic experiment' can be briefly summarised in the following points:

• Only a closed cycle of completely biological materials, a system comprising soil, plants, animals and man, can be the object of research for the determination of the functional quality of the life processes.

• The only valid criterion is the health and fertility of every separate link in the cycle, and the only organism worthy of testing is one that is demonstrably in relation to all the other links in the cycle.

• The attempt must be made to observe simultaneously as many as possible of the objects (of research) so as to distinguish the generally valid conditions from the particular ones and thus to arrive at generally applicable statements.

• Disturbing environmental influences and the effects of mutagenic foreign substance ought to be excluded. Only in this way can a model of the intact spontaneous biological cycle be realised which can lead to valid conclusions.

• Sufficient time must be allowed for the study of each member of the biocoenose, which will be determined by the biological regenerative capacity of the individual, and will in general be at least three generations.

As a link in the food chain, in their nutrition crops need inorganic salts and cell particles containing nucleic acids. Organic fertilisation is an absolute necessity for this. Because plants are unable to split up the cells from animal or vegetable manure themselves, this must be done by soil organisms. The soil is thus not only a substrate for the plant to grow in and, if its structure is good, a regulator of water and air supply, but also the 'digestive' organ for the plants. The optimal conditions for the 'digestive' processes were established by Rusch on the basis of his observations and experiments. His guide was undisturbed nature.

The working hypothesis of Rusch, which lies at the basis of organic-biological agriculture, was a cycle of lactic-acid forming bacteria of the forms: soil → plant → animal →soil and soil → plant → man → soil; and the possibility of gene induction by lactic acid-forming bacteria in plants. In light of current knowledge, this working hypothesis is plausible to only a limited extent (Boeringa, 1980).

In the late 1930s in rural Pennsylvania, USA, J.I. Rodale was keen to learn about and practise organic agriculture. He quickly came to realise the importance of restoring and protecting the natural health of the soil to preserve and improve human health. In 1947 he founded the Soil and Health Foundation, which later became the Rodale Institute. He was also responsible for a wide range of publications on health and farming and gardening organically, with a central message and philosophy of 'healthy soil equals healthy food, equals healthy people'.

Independent developments were occurring in Japan. In 1936, Mokichi Okada began practising 'nature farming'. Nature farming includes spiritual as well as agronomic aspects, with a view to improving humanity. It therefore has strong similarities to the biodynamic agriculture and anthroposophy of Rudolph Steiner. The Sekai Kyusei Kyo organisation was formed and continues to promote 'Kyusei nature farming' with experimental farms and offices located throughout South-East Asia.

Masanobu Fukuoka initiated a different approach to natural farming in Japan. With a background in microbiology and soil science, Fukuoka aimed to practise a simple form of agriculture, sometimes known as 'do nothing farming'. Like Okada, Fukuoka's farming approach also had a spiritual underpinning. The continuation and spread of these movements highlights the importance of seeing organic agriculture as a global phenomenon, not simply a European one.

While many of the ideas of these organic pioneers are still relevant to modern organic agriculture, there were a considerable number of pioneers whose political and religious views would be anathema to today's environmentally minded, socially concerned, politically left-of-centre, organic supporters (Kristiansen and Merfield, 2006).

Modern Organic Movement

The ideas of some organic pioneers are now foreign to the modern organic movement, which underwent significant change and upheaval in the 1960s. While there is a continuum of thought and membership from the earliest days to the present, the modern organic movement is radically different from its original forms. The environmental sustainability is its core, in addition to the founders' concerns for healthy soil, healthy food and healthy people. The publication *Silent Spring* by Rachel Carson (1962) was a key turning point and the start of the modern organic and environmental movements. Its publication brought new arguments against industrial farming in addition to those that the organic movement had been pushing for many decades.

In the 1970s, organic agriculture re-emerged and there was a strengthening of existing organic organisations and the founding of new ones. Many of these focused on the process of certification of farmers and growers. In spite of growing interest in organic agriculture, it was still outside mainstream agriculture and national politics.

The formation of a formal global network is one of the landmarks by which social and political movements can say they have come of age. For the organic movement this was the founding of the International Federation of Organic Agriculture Movements (IFOAM) in 1972, which to this day remains the only global organic non-governmental organisation (NGO) (Kristiansen and Merfield, 2006).

IFOAM has grown from a body that national governments ignored or argued against to one that now is respected by governments and intergovernmental organisations. The IFOAM mission is 'leading, uniting and assisting the organic movement in its full diversity' (IFOAM, 2005).

The main aims of the organisation are to:

- Provide authoritative information about organic agriculture, promote its worldwide application and exchange knowledge.
- Represent the organic movement at international policy-making forums.
- Make an agreed international guarantee of organic quality a reality.
- Maintain the Organic Guarantee System, setting international organic standards and certification procedures and auditing member certification organisations to these standards.
- Build a common agenda for all stakeholders in the organic sector.

Trends that began in the 1970s and accelerated through the 1980s continued to grow during the 1990s and into the new millennium. Demand and production continued to grow exponentially around the world. Formal political and legislative recognition was achieved.

Definitions of Organic Farming

Definitions of organic agriculture are similar world-wide and focus on ecological principles as the basis for crop production and animal husbandry. In current definitions of organic farming, the connections between health of the soil, health of people and health of society are recognised. According to the National Organic Standards Board, organic agriculture is:

> 'An ecological production management system that promotes and enhances biodiversity, biological cycles and soil biological activity. It is based on minimal use of off-farm inputs and on management practices that restore, maintain and enhance ecological harmony' (ATTRA, 1995).

The IFOAM goes further in defining organic agriculture (IFOAM, 2004):

Organic agriculture (OA) 'is an agricultural production system that promotes environmentally, socially and economically sound production of food and fibres, and excludes the use of synthetically compounded fertilisers, pesticides, growth regulators, livestock feed, additives and genetically modified organisms. The purpose of organic agriculture is to optimise the health and productivity of interdependent communities of soil life, plants, animals and people'.

The international food standards, Codex Alimentarius (FAO 1999) state:

'Organic agriculture is a holistic production management system which promotes and enhances agro-ecosystem health, including biodiversity, biological cycles, and soil biological activity. It emphasises the use of management practices in preference to the use of off-farm inputs, taking into account that regional conditions require locally adapted systems. This is accomplished by using, where possible, agronomic, biological and mechanical methods, as opposed to using synthetic materials, to fulfil any specific function within the system'.

EU Council Regulation (EC) No 834/2007 on organic production and labelling of organic products, applied from January 1, 2009 states:

'Organic production is an overall system of farm management and food production that combines best environmental practices, a high level of biodiversity, the preservation of natural resources, the application of high animal welfare standards and a production method in line with the preference of certain consumers for products produced using natural substances and processes. The organic production method thus plays a dual societal role, where it on the one hand provides for a specific market responding to a consumer demand for organic products, and on the other hand delivers public goods contributing to the protection of the environment and animal welfare, as well as to rural development'.

The Principles of Organic Agriculture

The principles of organic agriculture have changed with the evolution and development of the movement. At the beginning, the principles were unwritten, because they were inherent in the philosophy and practice of the farmers. IFOAM has been the key organisation defining the principles of organic agriculture. The original principles defined in 1980 are as follows (Woodward and Vogtmann, 2004):

- To work as much as possible within a closed system, and draw upon local resources.
- To maintain the long-term fertility of soils.
- To avoid all forms of pollution that may result from agricultural techniques.
- To produce foodstuffs of high nutritional quality and sufficient quantity.
- To reduce the use of fossil energy in agricultural practices to a minimum.
- To give livestock conditions of life that conform to their physiological needs and to humanitarian principles.
- To make it possible for agricultural producers to earn a living through their work and develop their potentialities as human beings.

The principles have been published as an introduction to the IFOAM 'basic standards' of the organic guarantee system. They clarify the aims of organic agriculture. The original seven principles have frequently been amended and added in a process carried out at the biennial General Assembly, where the changes are debated and voted on by members.

This process has led to the formulation of 'principle aims of organic agriculture for production and processing' in 2002 (IFOAM).

- To produce sufficient quantities of high quality food, fibre and other products.
- To work compatibly with natural cycles and living systems through the soil, plants and animals in the entire production system.
- To recognise the wider social and ecological impact of and within the organic production and processing system.

- To maintain and increase long-term fertility and biological activity of soils using locally adapted cultural, biological and mechanical methods as opposed to reliance on inputs.
- To maintain and encourage agricultural and natural biodiversity on the farm and its surroundings through the use of sustainable production systems and the protection of plant and wildlife habitats.
- To maintain and conserve genetic diversity through attention to on-farm management of genetic resources.
- To promote the responsible use and conservation of water and all life therein.
- To use, as far as possible, renewable resources in production and processing systems and avoid pollution and waste.
- To foster local and regional production and distribution.
- To create a harmonious balance between crop production and animal husbandry.
- To provide living conditions that allow animals to express the basic aspects of their innate behaviour.
- To utilise biodegradable, recyclable and recycled packaging materials.
- To provide everyone involved in organic farming and processing with a quality of life that satisfies their basic needs, within a safe, secure and healthy working environment.
- To support the establishment of an entire production, processing and distribution chain which is both socially just and ecologically responsible.
- To recognise the importance of, and protect and learn from, indigenous knowledge and traditional farming systems.

In recent years there has been an increasing feeling that these principle aims lack consistency and have been weakened. Therefore in 2005, revised principles of organic agriculture were accepted. These revised principles differ notably from the principal aims and are closer in philosophy and structure to the original from 1980.

Principle of Health

Organic Agriculture should sustain and enhance the health of soil, plant, animal, human and planet as one and indivisible. This means that the health of individuals depends on the health of ecosystems – healthy soil produces healthy crops that foster the health of animals and people. Immunity, resilience and regeneration are key characteristics of health. Organic farming is intended to produce high quality, nutritious food that contributes to preventive health care and well-being. In view of this it should avoid the use of fertilisers, pesticides, animal drugs and food additives that may have adverse health effects. This principle is holistic in its outlook and applies to the whole agricultural sphere from ecosystems as a whole to the individual parts such as soil, plants, animals and people.

Principle of Ecology

Organic Agriculture should be based on living ecological systems and cycles, should work with them, sustain them and keep ecological balances in nature. Production must be based on ecological processes, and recycling. Nourishment and wellbeing are achieved through the ecology of the specific production environment. For example, in the case of crops this is the living soil; for animals it is the farm ecosystem; for fish and marine organisms, the aquatic environment.

Organic management must be adapted to local conditions, ecology, culture and scale and it should attain ecological balance through the design of farming systems, establishment of habitats and maintenance of genetic and agricultural diversity. Those who produce, process, trade, or consume organic products should protect and benefit the common environment including landscapes, climate, habitats, biodiversity, air and water. Inputs should be reduced by reuse, recycling and efficient management of materials and energy in order to maintain and improve environmental quality and conserve resources.

Principle of Fairness

Fairness is characterised by equity, respect, justice and stewardship of the shared world, both among people and in their relations to other living beings. There must be fairness at all levels and for all groups of people – farmers, workers, processors, distributors, traders and consumers. This principle insists that animals should be provided with the conditions and opportunities of life that accord with their physiology, natural behaviour and well-being.

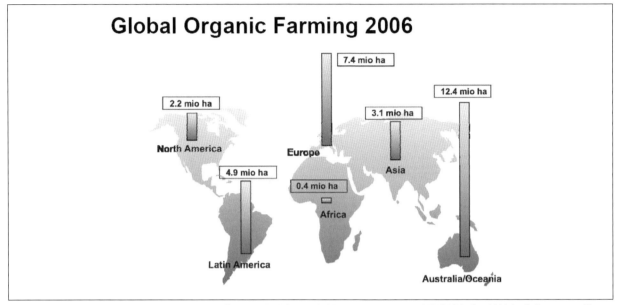

Figure 37.1. Global farming (Million hectares 2006). © SOEL, (FiBL Survey 2008. http://orgprints.org/13184/1/willer-2008-biofach-europe.pdf).

Principle of Care

This principle states that precaution and responsibility are the key concerns in management, development and technology choices in organic agriculture. Science is necessary to ensure that organic agriculture is healthy, safe and ecologically sound. However scientific knowledge alone is not sufficient. Practical experience, accumulated wisdom and traditional and indigenous knowledge offer valid solutions, tested by time. Organic agriculture should prevent significant risks by adopting appropriate technologies and rejecting unpredictable ones, such as genetic engineering. Decisions should reflect the values and needs of all who might be affected, through transparent and participatory processes (IFOAM 2005).

A key policy role for many governments is defining organic agriculture in law and creating enforcement mechanisms. In order to keep differing national organic regulations from becoming trade barriers, there is a need to adopt one set of internationally recognised organic guarantee tools, including production standards, certification procedures and accreditation requirements. One example of this is EU Council Regulation (EC) No 834/2007 on organic production and labelling of organic products.

Laws and Regulations are often as much for the protection of consumers as for the advancement of organic agriculture. Policy formulation based on local food needs, rural development imperatives and environmental conservation can greatly influence producers' decisions through accurately targeted subsidies, fiscal measures and other policy instruments for multiple societal goals such as employment, environmental services and health (El-Hage Scialabba, 2007).

In Europe, such incentives have been used for several years to encourage farmers to convert to organic agriculture. More recent government policies have actively assisted and promoted organic agriculture as a means of addressing the problems of agriculture (e.g. development of 'action plans' to ensure stable and strategic growth of organic food production). Organic agriculture is now widely recognised by the public and governments as a valid alternative to conventional agriculture and is a source of ideas and approaches that conventional agriculture can also adopt to make it more sustainable (Kristiansen and Merfield, 2006).

The Growth of Organic Farming

Recent years have seen very rapid growth in organic farming. In 1985, certified organic production accounted for 103,000 ha in Europe, approximately 0.1% of the total agricultural area. By the end of 2000, this area increased to 4.3 million ha, in 2006 representing 7.4 million ha in Europe (1.65% of European agricultural area) and 6.8 million ha in EU 27 (4.0% of agricultural area). World-wide, 30.4 million ha are certified according to organic standards (0.65% of global agricultural land). Australia, with its vast grazing lands, continues to account for the largest certified organic surface area, 12 million hectares, followed by Argentina (2.8 million ha) and Brazil (1.8 million ha). In terms of certified land as a share of national agricultural area, the Alpine countries, such as Austria (13.4%) and Switzerland (11%) top the statistics. The global market for organic products reached a value of over 46 billion US Dollars in 2007, with the vast majority of products being consumed in North America and Europe (IFOAM, 2009; Willer et al., 2008). Although difficult to quantity, non-certified organic systems of several million small farmers may represent at least an equivalent share in the subsistence agriculture of developing countries (El-Hage Scialabba, 2007).

Environmental Impacts of Organic Agriculture

Organic agriculture has become an important aspect of European environmental policy. Since the implementation of EC Reg. 2078/92, the EU promotes organic farming explicitly due to its positive effects on the environment. EU supports organic agriculture through agri-environment programmes. In most EU countries OA is growing in importance or plays a central role in national agri-environment policy.

The most advanced indicator concept in the area of environment and resource use has been presented by OECD. The OECD also provides a set of environmental indicators adapted for the agricultural sector (OECD, 1997). This concept is based on the Driving Force – State – Response framework (DSR). 'Driving forces' are those

elements that cause changes in the state of the environment. Driving force sub-categories are: Environment, Economic and social framework, Farm inputs and outputs. 'State', or condition, refers to changes in environmental conditions that may arise from various driving forces. State sub-categories are: Ecosystem, Natural resources, Health and welfare. 'Responses' refer to the reaction by groups in society or policy-makers to the actual and perceived changes in the state. Response sub-categories are: Consumer reaction, Agro-food chain responses, Farmer behaviour, Government policies.

In a study by Stolze et al. (2000), the environmental and resource use effects of organic farming relative to conventional farming in a European context were assessed. The original set of OECD indicators was adapted with the aim of evaluating and analysing the system effects rather than evaluating policies. The results of the comparison of organic and conventional farming systems are shown in Table 37.1 in the form of indicators according to the Stolze et al. (2000) assessment and absolute and relative environmental impacts according to Kasperczyk and Knickel (2006).

Ecosystem Indicators: Floral, Faunal, Habitat Diversity and Landscape Conservation

Organic farming performs better than conventional farming in respect to floral and faunal diversity due to the ban on synthetic pesticides and N fertilisers, with secondary beneficial effects on wildlife conservation and landscape. Diverse crop rotations in organic farming provide more habitats for wildlife due to the resulting diversity of housing, breeding and nutritional supply. However, direct measures for wildlife and biotope conservation depend on the individual activities of the farmers. With respect to habitat and landscape diversity, research deficits have been identified. As with any other form of agriculture, organic farming cannot contribute directly to wildlife conservation goals. Nevertheless, in productive areas, organic farming is currently the least detrimental farming system with respect to wildlife conservation and landscape (Stolze et al., 2000).

Genetic diversity of crops within conventional farms is very low, usually one variety per planting. Organic farms have a greater diversity due to mandatory crop rotation. One pillar of organic plant protection and animal health

Table 37.1. Assessment of the environmental impact of organic farming (Stolze et al., 2000; Kasperczyk and Knickel, 2006).

Indicators		Environmental impact A					Environmental impact B	
		++	+	O	–	– –	Absolute	Relative
Ecosystem			X					
	Floral diversity		X				+	++
	Faunal diversity		X				+	+++
	Habitat diversity			X			+?	+
	Landscape			X			+?	+
Soil			X					
	Soil organic matter		X				?	++
	Biological activity	X					+?	+++
	Soil structure			X			?	+
	Erosion		X				–	++/–
Ground and surface water			X					
	Nitrate leaching		X				–	++/–
	Pesticides	X					–	+++
Climate and air				X				
	CO_2		X				+?	+?
	N_2O			X			–	+/–?
	CH_4			X			–	?
	NH_3		X				–	+/–?
	Pesticides	X						
Farm input and output			X					
	Nutrient use		X					
	Water use			X				
	Energy use		X				na	+?
Animal health and welfare				X				
	Husbandry			X				
	Health			X				
Genetic diversity							+	+
Desertification							+	+
Nutrient use and balance							–	++
Pathogens							–	–?
Intensity of energy use							na	++/–

Legend A: Organic farming performs: ++ much better; +better; 0 the same; - worse; -- much worse, than conventional farming. When no data were available, the rating was '0'. X – subjective confidence interval of final assessment.

Legend B: 'Absolute' refers to the impact of organic farming on the environment, 'relative' refers to the relative impact in comparison with conventional system. + slightly better; ++ better; +++ substantially better; ++/- better with same aspects that are negative; +? better with some uncertainties; +/-? partly better and party worse with some uncertainties; ? unclear; - worse; 0 no impact or change; 'na' not applicable.

is the use of a more diverse range of diseases, pest and parasite tolerant or resistant varieties and breeding lines. The potential of genetic diversity on crop level for stabilisation of low-input farming systems and for adaptation to environmental changes is theoretically well understood in organic farming, but cultivar or race choice is still strongly based on immediate market needs (Niggli et al., 2007). Since 1995, organic agriculture has indirectly established a rescue process for species, varieties and breeds threatened by underuse or extinction. Organic agriculture is providing an important contribution to the in situ conservation, restoration and maintenance of agricultural biodiversity (El-Hage Scialabba et al., 2002). As resistance and robustness to environmental stress are multigenetic characteristics, *in situ* conservation and on-farm breeding are likely to be more successful than genetic engineering (Niggli et al., 2007).

Soil Indicators: SOM, Biological Activity, Structure and Erosion

Organic farming tends to conserve soil fertility better than conventional farming. This is mainly due to higher organic matter content and higher biological activity. Therefore, organic farming systems control erosion more effectively. The more continuous soil cover due to close crop rotations also assists in this. In contrast, no differences between the farming systems have been identified for soil structure (Stolze et al., 2000).

Groundwater and Surface Water Indicators: Nitrate Leaching and Pesticides

As a result of fertiliser or manure application and N fixation by leguminous crops, N accumulates in the soil. Nitrate leaching occurs when the amount of nitrate in the soil exceeds plant requirements and when water from rain, irrigation or snowmelt moves through the soil into the groundwater. Nitrate in water can lead to toxic contamination of drinking water for humans and animals, as well as surface water eutrophication with excessive algal growth.

Organic farming results in lower or similar nitrate leaching rates to other systems. Leaching rates per hectare are up to 57% lower. However, the leaching rates per tonne of output produced are similar or slightly higher. Ploughing legumes at the wrong time, unfavourable crop rotations and composting farmyard manure on unpaved surfaces increase the risk of nitrate leaching in organic farming. However, awareness of the problem and alternative measures have been developed and introduced in practice (Stolze et al., 2000).

The other nutrient that can occur as a major pollutant is phosphorus (P). However, for P the literature shows substantially and systematically less leaching from organically fertilised soils than from soils treated with synthetic fertiliser, probably due to formation of complexes with organic molecules that facilitate immobilisation by binding to soil particles (Hart et al., 2004). The risk of groundwater and surface water contamination with synthetic pesticides is zero.

Persistent pesticides (such as DDT) have damaged wildlife globally and are still being used in many developing countries. Organic agriculture has the potential to benefit the global situation if the proportion of land under organic management becomes large enough to reduce the total use. Recent data indicate that organically managed soil may be more efficient at denitrification, releasing most of the nitrate into the atmosphere as harmless N_2. If this is a general trend, the benefits of organic farming are much larger than previously estimated (Brandt, 2007).

Climate and Air Indicators: CO_2, N_2O, CH_4, NH_3, Pesticides

Research on CO_2 emissions shows varying results. On a per hectare scale, the CO_2 emissions are 40-60% lower in organic farming systems than in conventional, whereas on a per unit output scale CO_2 emissions tend to be higher in organic farming systems. Similar results are expected by experts for N_2O and CH_4 emissions, although to date no research results exist. Calculations of NH_3 emissions in organic and conventional farming systems have concluded that organic farming has a lower NH_3 emission potential than conventional farming. Nevertheless, housing systems and manure treatment in organic farming should be improved to reduce NH_3 emissions further (Stolze et al., 2000).

The carbon sequestration efficiency (tonnes CO_2-C per ha) of organic systems in temperate climates is almost double that of conventional systems, when the total of above- and below-ground biomass of cash and catch crops and weeds is calculated (Haas and Köpke, 1994, cit. Niggli et al., 2007). Air contamination with synthetic pesticides is significantly lower due to their ban under organic standards.

Farm Input and Output Indicators: Nutrient, Water, and Energy Use

Nutrient balances of organic farms are generally close to zero because organic farms rely heavily on internal nutrient cycling: N surpluses of organic farms are significantly lower than on conventional farms, but P and K deficits can arise. These deficits are related to the relatively infrequent use of P and K (potassium) fertilisers in organic farming, with some authors reporting a decline in the concentration of extractable P and K in soil after conversion to organic management (Nguyen et al., 1995). The energy efficiency of annual and permanent crops seems to be higher in organic farming than in conventional, mainly due to lower inputs of elements requiring a high energy input, i.e. N. Research results comparing water use in organic and conventional farming systems are not available (Stolze et al., 2000).

Animal Health and Welfare Indicators: Husbandry, Health

Husbandry, healthy housing conditions and health status depend highly on farm-specific conditions. Thus, housing conditions do not differ significantly between organic and conventional farms. Preventive use of synthetic, allophatic medicines is restricted by some national standards and recently also by EU rules. Although the application of homeopathic medicines is preferred, conventional veterinary measures are permitted and used in acute cases of disease. Health status seems to be closely related to the economic relevance of animal husbandry on the farm: significantly fewer incidences of metabolic disorders, udder diseases and injuries are found when dairy production is properly managed. Organic dairy cows tend to have a longer average productive life than conventional dairy cows (Stolze et al., 2000).

With a view to future developments, it seems to be important to keep in mind that the relative economic and environmental performance of organic farming compared with conventional might change. There might be changes in relative yields through technological progress. Technological development will also influence relative

environmental performance, e.g. by using precision farming methods more widely in conventional farming, but possibly also in organic systems. If legal restrictions on conventional agriculture lead to a 'greener' conventional system, it will be interesting to see whether the organic sector reacts by tightening its own standards in order to keep a clear distinction. The magnitude and the resulting net effect of these developments is an interesting area of speculation. For practical policy, two lessons emerge from such discussion: First, technological development within the organic sector is a key question for its future development. Second, policies geared at conventional agriculture might heavily influence the future development of organic farming (Dabbert, 2003).

Soil Fertility

Soil is one of the most important natural resources because it is the central basis for all agricultural activity. Soil quality can be defined as the capacity of a soil to function, whilst maintaining environmental quality and promoting plant and animal health. It also refers to the capability of soil to function at present and in the future for an indefinite period of time. Soil quality is a basic concept in the sustainable management of any agricultural system aimed at producing, avoiding or reducing negative effects on the environment, preserving resources and saving energy on a medium or long-term basis (Canali, 2003).

The effective management of soil fertility is based on understanding processes associated with its chemical, physical and biological components, with greater emphasis having traditionally been given to soil chemical fertility. Organic farming is based on the maintenance and enhancement of soil life and natural soil fertility, soil stability and soil biodiversity preventing and combating soil compaction and soil erosion, and the nourishment of plants primarily through the soil ecosystem.

Soil Organic Matter

The soil's supply of organic matter plays a central role in the maintenance of soil fertility. Ewel (1986) describes soil organic matter (SOM) as 'the warehouse of most of the nitrogen, phosphorus and sulphur potentially avail-

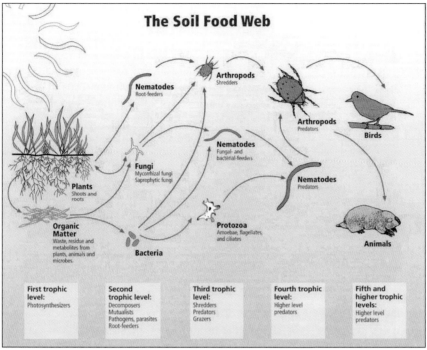

The Soil Food Web

First trophic level:
Photosynthesizers

Second trophic level:
Decomposers
Mutualists
Pathogens, parasites
Root-feeders

Third trophic level:
Shredders
Predators
Grazers

Fourth trophic level:
Higher level predators

Fifth and higher trophic levels:
Higher level predators

Figure 37.2. Relationships between soil food web, plants, organic matter and birds and mammal. (USDA Natural Resources Conservation Service, 2009. http://soils.usda.gov/sqi/soil_quality/soil_biology/soil_food_web.html).

able to plants, is the main energy source for microorganisms and is a key determinant of soil structure'.

Various comparison trials and on-farm investigations show that organically managed soils tend to have higher total soil organic carbon contents (% C_t) than conventionally farmed arable land. This is indicated by a higher ratio of soil microbial biomass to total soil organic carbon and lower metabolic quotient, characterising biomass specific soil respiration (Mäder et al., 1995).

In a long-term DOC (bio-Dynamic, bio-Organic, Conventional) experiment (Mäder et al., 2002), the organic system accumulated 12% more carbon in the soil and the bio-dynamic 15%. The carbon sequestration rate was 575-700 kg carbon per ha per year. Pimentel et al. (2005) in the Rodale experiment, USA, reported an annual soil carbon increase of 981 kg per ha in the manure-based organic system and an increase of 574 kg per ha in the legume-based organic system.

In a study by Marriott and Wander (2006), soil organic carbon concentrations were 14% higher in the organic system compared with the conventional. The labile fraction of the soil organic matter, a source of mineralisable C and N with important implications for plant nutrition, showed 30-40% higher values in organic soils.

Soil organic matter contributes significantly to soil quality and health. SOM enhances and drives numerous chemical, biological processes and soil physical properties. Higher levels of soil organic matter have been observed regularly in organically managed soils compared with conventional. Foereid and Hogh-Jensen (2004) estimated that conversion of Northern Europe from conventional arable crops to organic crops would result in an increase in SOM during the first 50 years of about 10 to 40 g C per m^2 per year. Steady state (stable level of SOM) would be reached after 100 years. The main factors for the increase in SOM were use of grass-clover leys for feed and cover crops in organic rotations.

Soil physical fertility contributes to the sustainability of organic farming systems by creating the framework in which biological and chemical processes supply nutrients to plants and protect soil from erosion. The environmental significance of favourable soil structure lies in an improved resistance to structural soil damage, such as compaction and erosion. Soil physical fertility can be measured by diverse parameters, such as the stability of aggregates, air capacity, water-holding capacity, bulk density.

A long-term Swiss field experiment on loess soil that began in 1978 found the aggregate and percolation stability of bio-dynamic and organic plots to be significantly higher (10-60%) than that of conventionally farmed plots. This also affected the water retention potential of these

Figure 37.3. Organic (B) and conventional (A) soils. Photo: M. Lacko-Bartošová (Amaranthus, Sipmson, 2009).

Figure 37.4. Spade diagnosis, sensory soil quality evaluation. Photo: M. Lacko-Bartošová.

soils in a positive way and reduced their susceptibility to erosion. Soil aggregate stability was strongly correlated to earthworm and microbial biomass, important indicators of soil fertility (Mäder et al., 2002). Compared with stockless conventional farming, values of aggregate stability on plots in livestock-based integrated production were 29.4% higher, while in organic and bio-dynamic plots they were 70% higher (Siegrist et al., 1998). The percentage of water-stable macro-aggregates on organically farmed sites was 72% higher than on conventional. The higher physical stability was linked to significantly increased soil organic matter content and to a larger volume of worm-worked soil (organic 28%, conventional 8%). The investigation was carried out on farms that had been under organic management for 70 years (Niggli et al., 2007). In many other experiments, a positive effect of organic farming on soil structure could not be confirmed or, if at all, only for topsoil. An improvement in soil structure can only be observed after decades of farming organically (Stolze et al., 2000).

Water is becoming increasingly scarce in certain regions of the world, so it will be important to increase water efficiency in both rain-fed and irrigated agriculture. The soil fertility building techniques of OA that lead to higher organic matter content, better aggregate stability and biologically more active soils in turn increase water retention in soils and improve water use efficiency. Soils retain significantly more rainwater thanks to the 'sponge properties' of organic matter. In heavy loess soils in a temperate climate, the water-holding capacity is 20 to 40% higher in organically managed soils (Mäder et al., 2002).

Organic management of soils leads to improved soil stability and resistance to water erosion compared with conventionally managed soils, due to higher soil C content and improved soil aggregation and permeability. Lotter et al. (2003) presented evidence that organic systems perform better than conventional during climate extremes, in this case for both drought and excessive rainfall. In the 21-year Rodale trial, in which two organic and a conventional crop rotation were compared, the organic crop systems performed significantly better in 4 of 5 years of moderate drought. In the severe drought year of 1999, three out of the four crop comparisons resulted in significantly better yields in the organic systems than the conventional. The evidence indicates that the better water-holding capacity of organically managed soils is a likely mechanism for better yields during water deficits. Water harvest, important for groundwater recharge, was significantly better in the organic systems in both the severe drought year and over a 5-year period. Organic crop management techniques will be a valuable resource in an era of climatic variability, providing soil and crop characteristics that can better buffer environmental extremes.

Soil chemical fertility reflects the capacity of soil to provide a suitable chemical and nutritional environment to the plants and support biological and physical processes. The maintenance of soil chemical fertility depends strongly on processes that govern transformations from fixed to soluble forms of nutrients, such as mineralisation of organic matter and dissolution of minerals.

- Nutrient sources in organic systems are predominantly organic or poorly soluble and therefore slow to become available.
- Nutrient availability is more dependent on dynamic soil biological processes.
- Release and uptake of nutrients occurs without demonstrable changes in soil chemistry, because nutrients are rapidly taken up by the plants or soil microorganisms without accumulating in the soil solution (Davis & Abbott, 2006).

Soil biological fertility can be quantified by measuring the size, activity, diversity and function of communities. Central to organic farming is the aim of optimising plant production by maintaining a rich biological diversity in the soil. High biological activity promotes metabolism between soil and plants, worms and other beneficial soil biota that help process nutrients from residues for plant uptake, while also creating stable organic matter. Earthworms, as a key species for soil macro-fauna, are an appropriate indicator of soil biological activities due to their sensitivity to any kind of disturbance. A high supply of organic matter and manure provides favourable living conditions for worms and other fauna in soils (Stolze et al., 2000).

Relevant scientific results as summarised by Pfiffner and Mäder (1997) resulted in these general conclusions:

- A significantly higher biomass and abundance of earthworms.
- A significantly higher diversity of earthworm species.
- Changes in population composition, indicated by the presence of more anecic and juvenile earthworms in organically farmed soils.

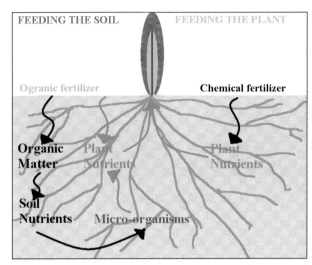

Figure 37.5. Differences in plant nutrition in organic and conventional farming (http://www.tigerblue.net/images/soil%20life.jpg).

Organic farming may alter the function of the soil microbial community, increasing its ability to release nutrients from organic and poorly soluble sources, thereby compensating for the absence of soluble nutrients inputs (Ryan, 1999).

A synthesis of comparative studies conducted to observe soil microbial activity found:

- Improvement of soil microbial activity, 20-30% higher microbial biomass in organic systems.
- Higher microbial diversity, higher efficiency in organic carbon turnover.
- More efficient use of available resources by soil organisms, indicated by a lower metabolic quotient for CO_2.
- Higher mycorrhization in soil under organic winter wheat, cover crops and clover-grass.
- Higher numbers and abundance of saprophytic soil fungi with higher potential to decompose organic material (Stolze et al., 2000).

In parallel to the changes in organic matter in soils, soil microbial biomass and the physiological functions of soils are enhanced by organic agriculture. Important soil enzyme activities such as dehydrogenase, protease and phosphatase are higher in organic field plots, leading e.g.

Figure 37.6. Organic potatoe field. Photo: M. Lacko-Bartošová.

Figure 37.7. Organic wheat field. Photo: M. Lacko-Bartošová.

to faster phosphorus flux through the microbial biomass and contributing to plant phosphorus supply (Mäder et al., 2002). Some of the changes in soil biological and chemical fertility upon conversion to OA can take many years, such as increases in SOM and microbial community structure, while others can change almost immediately, as with aggregate microbial biomass and activity (Gunapala et al., 1998, cit. Lotter, 2003).

Productivity and Yields

There have been several reviews of comparative studies of organic agriculture (OA) and conventional agriculture (CA) crop yields. The productivity of OA compared with CA depends strongly on environmental factors such as soil, water resources and climate conditions, as well as on the crops being compared. Padel and Lampkin (1994) reviewed comparative studies of crop yields in OA versus CA. Organic yields in the UK were on average 11% lower, while in the US differences were highly variable, ranging from 50% higher in the Midwest (oats) to 60% lower in California (rice). In intensive production areas of Europe, OA yields are on average 30-40% lower than CA yields.

Organic crop systems in North America have been shown to produce on average approximately 90-95% of the yields in conventional crop systems. Where organic crop systems excel, however, is in water and climate stress situations. A number of studies have shown that under drought conditions, crops in organically managed systems produce higher yields than comparable conventional crops (Lotter, 2003). Mechanisms that may increase the drought tolerance of organic cropping systems are discussed within soil physics.

Discussions of yield comparisons need to take into consideration the type of crops being compared. For maize and soybeans, Pimentel et al. (2005) reported equal yields for OA and CA under less favourable soil conditions. The importance of fertility-building crops in rotations and crop sequences on grain yields is stressed by Younie et al. (2000) and Olesen et al. (2000). Grain yield of spring barley decreased in rotations without manure or catch crops. Differences in oat grain yield were caused by its place in the crop rotation. In long-term trials established on fertile soil in Central Europe, organic winter wheat yield was 82% of that in an integrated system and organic pea yield 92%, but organic maize outyielded integrated maize by 19.6% and spring barley yields were equal in both farming systems (L.-Bartošová, 2006).

Extensive and rigorous research with regard to the productivity of the organic agriculture system has been carried out in developed countries, but scientific evidence from developing countries is still rare. In developing tropical countries in which organic practices were introduced, a survey of more than 200 projects showed an average yield increase of 5-10% for irrigated crops and 50-100% for rain-fed crops (Pretty and Hine, 2001).

A report by Zundel and Kilcher (2007) summarised the information available on the productivity of OA by considering four different agro-ecological zones in terms of their productivity when converting from conventional to organic management. In all four, yield reductions were usually low (or sometimes nonexistent) in the first two to three years if conversion was from a low-input system but after the conversion period, organic yields could reach levels even higher than conventional yields. Yield reductions were generally higher if the system had been run on a high-input level. Yields recovered after the conversion period, but usually not to the level of the previous conventional yields.

Agriculture *in temperate and irrigated areas* is generally characterised by favourable soils, high levels of mechanisation and functioning markets for farm supplies. In these areas, high external inputs make it possible to obtain high production levels but productivity may be pushed beyond the actual ecosystem capacity. Soils receive a high level of inputs and the crop varieties and hybrids used are often designed to perform well under intensive conditions. Conversion to organic management from these conditions usually means a considerable drop in yields, during two to three years of conversion. The estimated yield reductions during conversion are 20-30% for cereals, 10-20% for maize, 30-40% for potatoes, 10-40% for vegetables and around 30% for fruits. In the medium and long term, when soil fertility recovers, yields are slightly lower or comparable to the pre-conversion yields. Studies in several short and long-term field trials with field crops found no difference between organic and conventional crop yields. Other field trials reported crop yields to be 5 to 35% lower than conventional. Lower yields are often a result of lower availability of nitrogen and higher weed pressure, generally due to inexperienced management of the system. If conventional farm management was on a low-input level prior to conversion, organic farmers can expect to maintain similar yields. If the farm was previously managed at a high-input level, yields will drop initially, recover as soil fertility recovers and then stabilise at a level corresponding to the carrying capacity of the ecosystem.

In *semi-arid environments*, the main challenge in converting to organic agriculture is dealing with water scarcity and the disrupted dynamics of biomass decom-position during the long dry season. In Ethiopia, a case study reported double yields as the result of organic soil management. In tropical humid and peri-humid areas the main challenges are increased crop rotations, diversification, agroforestry and integration of livestock.

Considering the complexity and diversity of organic farms, participatory development of site-specific technologies is of immense importance for later adoption and positive impact on productivity. Many studies have shown that a technology can be successful at one site but not another, even with only slightly different agro-ecological conditions.

Going head-to-head in yield comparisons may be unfair until research and extension investment in OA catches up and allows OA systems to reach a mature stage comparable to CA systems (Lotter, 2003). The common claim that large-scale conversion to OA would result in drastic reductions in world food supplies or large-scale conversion of virgin land to agriculture has not been proven in modelling studies. Conversion of existing global agriculture to organic management, without converting virgin land to agriculture and or using artificial N fertilisers, would result in a global agricultural supply of 2640-4380 kcal/person/day. Sustainable intensification in developing countries through organic practices would increase production by 56%. Organic farms use 33-56% less energy per ha than conventional. Nutrient use is enhanced through recycling and minimising losses, but the availability of phosphorus can be a challenge (FAO, 2007).

Food Quality

In organic agriculture the term 'quality' has a larger scope and wider content than in conventional agriculture and aims at the holistic and not only the analytical perspective. Internal nutritional attributes of quality are highly valued. The technological quality is considered to be of less importance, with quality given priority over quantity. Among the factors determining quality there are also those that are more difficult to define, such as vitality, fertility, health, resistance, etc. The quality of the product is thus a result of the quality of the entire production system. The OA interpretation of quality leads to a wider definition, where new dimensions and aspects are involved (Dlouhý, 1990; L.-Bartošová, 1995):

- Sensory quality – e.g. size, shape, taste, colour, appearance
- Technological quality – suitability for various food processing technologies, storage, transport
- Nutritional quality – e.g. desirable compounds, proteins, vitamins, essential amino acids
- Hygiene quality – contamination of food by non-natural substances, pesticide residues
- Social-psychological dimension – e.g. working conditions, trust of consumers, welfare of animals,
- Environmental dimension – e.g. effects on the environment, energy input, processing technologies
- Political dimension – e.g. import from developing countries, world prices, hunger

In OA, emphasis is placed not only on food quality in a narrow sense (directly measured by scientific methods), but also on aspects such as the links between the agricultural system and environment, agricultural system and product, and its influence on consumer health and welfare.

So far, only conventional chemical analyses of food quality have been reviewed. The potential deficiency of analyses that only consider food composition in describing food quality has been recognised by various scientists. The development of holistic methods can lead to better characterisation of product quality, while its dynamic aspects can be revealed in the behaviour and the effect of the product on other organisms. Several holistic/alternative methods of assessing food quality have been proposed, such as:

- Picture-developing methods, e.g. cupric crystallisation method according to Pfeiffer; capillary dynamolysis method according to Wala; circular chromatographic method according to Pfeiffer (Balzer-Graf, 1987; Pfeiffer, 1984; Balzer-Graf and Balzer, 1991).
- Food preference tests (Phochberger & Velimirov, 1992).
- Feeding experiments (Plochberger, 1989).
- Low level illuminescence (Popp, 1988).
- Self-decomposition tests, storage quality and others.

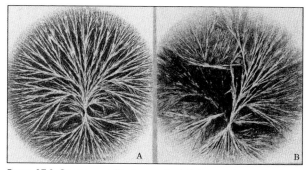

Figure 37.8. Cupric crystallization method; A: Extract from spinach, applied compost, 100 kgN/ha, B: Extract from spinach, applied chemical fertilizer, 300 kgN/ha (Vogtmann, 1992).

Promising results have been obtained with food preference tests that differentiate product quality on the basis of the instinctive feeding behaviour of the test animals. Animals were able to distinguish between the two foodstuffs and preferred the biologically cultivated option. Feeding experiments with animals have revealed positive effects on parameters such as fertility, susceptibility to infections, feed conversion, perinatal mortality, liveweight gain, egg weight, yolk fraction, litter weight and others.

With picture-developing methods attempts are made to visualise the vitality of foodstuffs and assess the physiological state of plant substances according to the pattern of crystallisation. Mäder et al. (1993) suggested that picture-developing methods should be standardised for a large number of crops and varieties in order to identify products from various cultivation systems.

In response to the greatly increased market share of organic food, there is an increasing interest in investigating whether there are any differences in the effects of organic and conventional food on health. There are ample examples that the methods used for food production make a difference for food composition or other quality aspects, and that these differences are large enough to make a difference to consumer health (Brandt and Molgaard, 2006).

Rembialkowska (2004) summarised the studies conducted in several countries regarding organic food quality. Positive attributes of organic plant and animal products compared with conventional include:

- Organic crops contain fewer nitrates, nitrites, pesticide residues; lower total protein content.

- More dry matter, vitamin C content, B-group vitamins, essential amino-acids, total sugars, plant secondary metabolites (phytochemicals).
- Higher content of some minerals (iron, magnesium, phosphorus, selenium, calcium, zinc and others).
- Better sensory quality, e.g. smell and taste, fruits sweeter and more compact because of higher dry matter content.
- Vegetables, potatoes, fruits have better storage quality during winter, lower mass losses caused by transpiration, decay and decomposition processes.
- Farm animals have fewer metabolic diseases, e.g. ketosis, lipidosis, mastitis, milk fever.
- Milk and meat have different lipid composition, with more unsaturated and conjugated fatty acids, more vitamin E.
- Animals have better health and fertility parameters, e.g. lower incidence of prenatal mortality, higher birth weight, better immunity to disease.
- Environmental contamination (heavy metals, PCB, dioxins, aromatic hydrocarbons) can be similar, because the impact of industrial, transport and communal sources is equal for organic and conventional farms located in the same area.

The organic preference for outdoor rearing, using manure as fertiliser and on-farm slaughtering often raises concerns about the potential risks of contamination by a range of zoonotic bacteria, parasites and viruses. Surveys have not found consistently higher levels of zoonotic disease in organic animals, which means that there are other factors in OA that protect animals against disease as efficiently as the use of medication and biosecurity. Possible explanations are that:

- A diet containing a variety of fresh herbs can support the immune system of animals.
- Early exposure to a variety of micro-organisms may improve immunity.
- A diet containing roughage inhibits the proliferation of pathogens in the gut of ruminants.
- Selection of resistant breeds, intensive monitoring for early signs of disease, and others.

Mycotoxins are toxic compounds produced by the secondary metabolism of toxic fungi in the Aspergillus, Penicillium and Fusarium genera occurring in foodstuffs and food commodities. The impact on human health includes carcinogenic and immunosuppressive activity. It has been suggested that organic food may be more susceptible to contamination by mycotoxins than conventional, because no fungicides are permitted (Rembialkowska, 2004). However, recent studies and reviews report 50% lower frequency of toxic levels of mycotoxins in organic food across a large range of climates (Benbrook, 2005).

Greater availability of nitrogen in conventional systems reduces the plant's ability to fight against pathogens. If plants grow relatively slowly, they build up their chemical defences to a level that prevents most diseases and pests. However, if a plant is allowed to grow unusually fast by providing it with an abundance of nutrients, the accumulation of defence compounds (plant secondary metabolites) is reduced (Stamp, 2003, cit. Brandt and Molgaard, 2006).

There are many indications that secondary plant metabolites are responsible for beneficial effects of vegetables and fruits. Many scientists believe that the antioxidant effects of phenolics, carotenoids and related compounds are responsible for health benefits, but this hypothesis has not been proven. This indicates that the documented benefits of vegetables and fruits probably result from the properties of plant secondary metabolites other than their antioxidant capacity. The levels of plant secondary metabolites/plant toxicants are more strongly and systematically determined by the production system than the other factors on the list (Brandt and Molgaard, 2006).

Definitive benefits of organic foods on human health have not been confirmed, but several studies list important conclusions:

- It is possible to detect health impacts that are definitely due to the production methods.
- All of the five markers of health (accumulation of adipose tissue, content of IgA, protein oxidation, sleep, lymphocyte proliferative capacity) indicated as relevant for this purpose have not been tested in earlier studies (Brandt and Molgaard, 2006).

Consumer Demands: Sustainable and Organic Agriculture in the Great Lakes Region

38

Michelle Wander

University of Illinois, Urbana-Champaign, Illinois, USA

Agriculture in the Great Lakes Region

The Great Lakes region supports one of the largest agricultural economies ($40 Billion yr[1]) in the world (NASS, 1999). The Great Lakes basin encompasses 798,100 km², and the Great Lakes themselves cover 247,000 km² and contain about 20% of the world's supply of fresh, non frozen water. The basin encompasses the North American heartland which contains over 100 million acres (40,470,000 hectares) of agricultural land (Figure 38.1). Land use patterns reflect the region's soils and sediments, which are the result of glacial history (Larson and Schaetzl, 2001). Past glaciations began 2.4 million years ago and ended approximately 20,000 years ago. Ice finally left the region about 9,000 years ago. Together the states of Minnesota (MN), Wisconsin (WI), Michigan (MI), Ohio (OH), Indiana (IN), and Illinois (IL) contain over 380,000 farms, but this number has declined by nearly 20% during the past decade. The region has important production in rain-fed cash grains (corn, soybean, wheat) and livestock sectors and ranks high nationally in production of horticultural crops and fresh market fruits and vegetables. In general, livestock has been more important in the northern section of the region, with row crops dominating the south and horticultural crops being more important in the northeastern sector.

The conversion of large areas of land to agricultural production during the 19th century transformed the Midwest landscape. Lighter textured soils adjacent to waterways were cleared first, followed by cultivation of lowland prairies and wetlands that was brought about by large-scale drainage projects and the invention of the moldboard plough (Edwards, 1994). The US grain

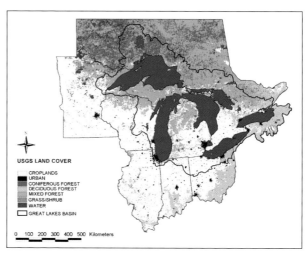

Figure 38.1. Land use in the Great Lakes region (Illinois State Water Survey).

industry was built up in this region where favourable climate and good soils supported rain-fed production of grains. Yields climbed steadily between the 1940s and 2000, with inputs of fertilisers and agrichemicals (Clay, 2003). Research spearheaded by the land grant universities brought dramatic increases in productivity (Runge and Stuart, 1998); this combined with industry consolidation, vertical integration of industry, and international trading of grains through the Chicago board of trade has made Chicago the epicenter of an agri-industrial empire (Anonymous, 2006). U.S. farm policies that have subsidized grain production have made it difficult for developing countries to compete effectively (Clay, 2003).

Production trends in the region have contributed notably to nutrient inputs to the Mississippi River during the last half decade (McIsaac et al., 2001; Donner, 2003). Off-site costs of dredging are estimated (adjusted to 2008 dollars) at $128 million for the lake states of Minnesota, Wisconsin, and Michigan and $283 million for the Corn Belt states of Illinois, Indiana, Ohio, Iowa, and Missouri. Concern over water quality and downstream costs to restore or maintain safe drinking water standards have increased scrutiny of present-day rates of fertiliser use on corn and the expansion of row crop cultivation. Erosion of soil and runoff of agricultural wastes will increase with flooding and intense rainfall events associated with climate change. Changes in precipitation patterns are making runoff pulses more frequent (Adams et al., 1999; Interlandi et al., 2003). Tile drainage in agricultural fields, draining of wetlands, water diversion, and floodplain development all increase the frequency of flash flooding. These alterations are likely to exacerbate climate change effects on stream flow, by increasing the frequency and height of flood events, and increasing drought potential through loss of groundwater recharge. Increases in precipitation intensity will also increase the erosive power of rainfall (Nearing et al., 2004). This will disproportionately impact wetlands, which are predominately small, isolated water bodies, and ephemeral wetlands. About 70% of the total number of wetlands has been lost from the lower Great Lakes and lower St. Lawrence River valley of Canada (Mitsch and Gooselink, 2000). The loss has been greatest in the southern portion of the region

where agriculture is most intense. Remaining wetlands are especially sensitive to hydrologic alterations due to climate change, geomorphic alterations (dredging and filling), water diversion, and degraded water quality (Wilcox, 1995; Singer et al., 1996). Eroded sediments and water runoff that degrade waterfowl habitats are ultimately expected to lower duck populations in the region (Root et al., 2003) Streams in agricultural areas are particularly vulnerable, where channelization has reduced nutrient and sediment retention (D'Angelo et al., 1991).

Factors shaping agriculture in the region include National farm programs that subsidize production agriculture, vertical integration of farming systems, changing domestic and international markets, shifting regulatory frameworks and new technologies. Fluctuating energy, land rent and input prices in the last few years have made the traditional row crop systems quite volatile. Record crop prices were followed closely by input prices, with both propelled by the price of oil (Rosen and Shapouri, 2008). Expansion of corn-grain production for ethanol is likely to increase the problems associated with row crop agriculture already cited. Removal of land from conservation reserve programs to satisfy demand for land is likely to add to historic declines in biodiversity and associated services including pest suppression and wildlife amenities. Development of cellulosic biofuels may suffer from many of the same sustainability issues if not developed with care (Robertson et al., 2008). Export of food dollars, hunger among the poor, and environmental degradation are cited as failings of conventional agriculture (French & Gardner, 2002). A range of voluntary and contractual instruments that could compensate farmers for the costs of maintaining environmental services and reimburse them for income foregone by adopting alternative management practices have been developed to counter traditional agricultural supports (Buller and Morris, 2004). Consumer driven initiatives may allow alternative approaches to agriculture to compete with present land uses (Vesterby and Krupa, 2001). Such strategies may provide a way to transition from a subsidy-based approach to policies compatible with international trade rules (Zinn, 2005).

Organic Agriculture and the Local Foods Movement

Interest in organic and alternative production practices has surged in recent years with these options being seen to be more sustainable than commodity crops. Organic agriculture has been the fastest growing sector in all of agriculture for the past decade. The EU and the U.S. together accounted for 95% of the $25 billion in world retail sales of organic food products in 2003. Sales of organic food and non food products in the US had reached $17.7 billion in 2006, up 21% from 2005, and $18.9 billion by 2007 and are estimated to exceed $24 billion in 2010 (Lin et al., 2008). Organic markets in the European Union have also grown rapidly; with 2006 sales growing by 10% alone. The European organic markets are more mature than the U.S. markets, and this is in large part due to differences in policies favouring organic practices and investment in associated research (Gibbon, 2008).

Both the EU and U.S. have organic food standards supported by certification methods intended to guarantee that standards are met. Organic plant and livestock products are governed by EU Regulations 2092/91 (enacted in 1993) and 1804/99 (enacted in 2000), respectively. The regulations set minimum rules for production, labelling, and marketing for the whole of Europe, with member states being responsible for implementation and enforcement of the rules. Organic product labelling is complex as rules vary among nations. In December 2005, the European Commission made the use of either the EU logo or the words 'E.U.-organic' compulsory on products that contain at least 95% organic ingredients. Organic labelling in the U.S. is governed by the 1990 Organic Foods Production Act (OFPA) and the national organic standards (NOS), which were implemented in 2002. To be certified, organic producers must not use prohibited substances and must use management practices that enhance soil quality while protecting the environment from degradation. Both EU and U.S. systems rely on certification by a third-party to assure that a product was raised, processed, and distributed according to the official organic standards (Dimitri and Oberholzer, 2006). In the U.S., penalties are clearly outlined for anyone using the organic label inappropriately. The EU leaves enforcement up to individual member states. Certified organic land in the EU rose from 2.1 million hectares (5.2 million acres; 0.405 hectares = 1 acre) in 1997 to 5.1 million hectares in 2003, and now accounts for about 4% of total agricultural area. In the U.S., organic land increased from 549,406 hectares in 1997 to 889,734 hectares in 2003. This acreage is just a tiny fraction (0.24%) of all agricultural land (Dimitri and Oberholzer, 2006). There is general agreement that standards-based regulation has played a major role in this mainstreaming of the organic sector (Gibbon, 2008).

Critics of the organic standards dislike the influence that regulation has had, citing industrialization and/or commercialization of the organic sector as counter productive from a social perspective (Guthman, 2004; Raynolds, 2004). Failure to include adequate requirements for labour protection or to address social issues including equity and community concerns has reduced the appeal of the organic brand to some of its traditional supporters. Dissatisfaction with a regulated organic sector seems to have propelled the local foods movement in both the U.S. and in Europe (De Linde, 2000). In recent years, concerns about food safety and health, environmental sustainability, and the decline of rural communities have contributed to a groundswell of consumer interest in fresh, locally produced foods. This has resulted in the rapid growth of direct-market outlets for local produce, including Farmer's Markets, Community-Supported Agriculture (CSAs), and local grocery stores, schools, restaurants, and other institutions. Most of these

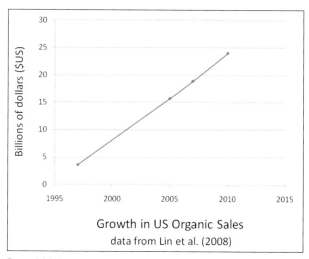

Growth in US Organic Sales

data from Lin et al. (2008)

Figure 38.2. Economic value of US organic sales (Lin et al., 2008).

direct marketing outlets have been around for a long time, with the exception of Community Supported Agriculture (CSA), which emerged in the 1980s. Community Supported Agriculture is a direct-to-consumer marketing arrangement where consumers purchase produce for the entire season ahead of time in order to receive weekly shares throughout the growing season. This allows the farmer to purchase inputs and to plan for production levels based on a guaranteed demand. CSA also frees the growers from marketing work during the growing season.

Estimates indicate that the number of CSA operations in all of the U.S. grew from about 60 in 2002 to 1,100 in 2006 (USDA-AMS, 2008a). Today, the local food directory Local Harvest lists 2,064 CSAs and shows a high concentration of CSAs in the north-eastern US, with clusters and around large urban areas of the western seaboard and the Midwest. In 2006, the Farmers' Market Directory listed 4,385 farmers' markets operating in the United States, representing an 18% increase from the number of farmers' markets in 2004. Total sales volumes for Farmers' Markets are estimated at about $1 billion for 2005 (USDA-AMS, 2008b). Farmers' markets are critical or sole outlets for many producers (USDA-AMS 2006). These kinds of farms may deserve special attention because they have the potential to contribute to the next generation of farmers. Small organic and specialty farms provide opportunities for new younger farmers to get involved in agriculture (Zander, 2008). For example, the age distribution of CSA farmers includes many more farmers in the age groups 25-34, 35-44, and 45-54 than are found on the average U.S. farm (Lass et al., 2003). Small farm operators, defined by the USDA Agricultural Marketing Service as 'those with less than $250,000 in annual receipts who work and manage their own operations' (USDA-AMS, 2008c), are the typical suppliers for direct-local markets. Direct marketing channels appeal to small and beginning farms because these vendors obtain better prices for their products marketing them directly to consumers than they would get from wholesalers.

The numbers of local producers and farmers' markets have grown rapidly in Illinois in recent years (Figure 38.3). Fruit and vegetable growers are currently clustered around larger urban markets (Chicago and Saint Louis) or in the central sands area where sandy soils are well suited for intensive production of vegetables for wholesale markets. These trends begin to recover from historical shifts in land use that dramatically reduced food production for local consumption. At present only 0.2% of Illinois farm sales are agricultural products sold directly for human consumption. Only 5% of food consumed is produced in Illinois and 95% of organic food sold in Illinois is grown and processed outside of the state (Curry, 2008). This is not because Illinois could not grow more food. As recently as 1950, Illinois had 6,520 farms reporting sales of vegetables with an inflation-adjusted value of $106 million in 2007 dollars, while an additional 136,431 farms harvested vegetables for home use (USDA, 2007). At that time, 84,593 farms had land in tree fruits, nuts and grapes – in the most recent census there were only 73,027 farms in Illinois. With an average travelling distance of 1,500 miles for food items consumed in Illinois, the dissonance between the growing demand for local and organic food and expansion of commodity crops is intensifying.

Sustainability Metrics
Marketing a Green Foot Print

The success of the organic and local food movements is credited to the public's desire to reconnect with the food system and promote heath for themselves and communities through food proxies (Bryant and Goodman, 2004). Small-scale farmers marketing through direct market channels frequently appeal to customers using branding strategies that tout green services (Lass et al., 2003). Conservation is emphasized because consumers and producers both support practices that will result in agricultural land preservation (Selfa et al., 2008). It is frequently assumed that by promoting a landscape level or whole-farm valuation of agricultural practices, green branding can enhance the contributions of agriculture. It is difficult for economic markets to properly assign value for social and economic services (Pascual and Perrings, 2007). Diversified farming systems are thought to supply biodiversity-based ecosystem services as a public good without adequate compensation in the marketplace. It is after all, the neighbouring communities that might benefit from ecologically responsible practices that pro-

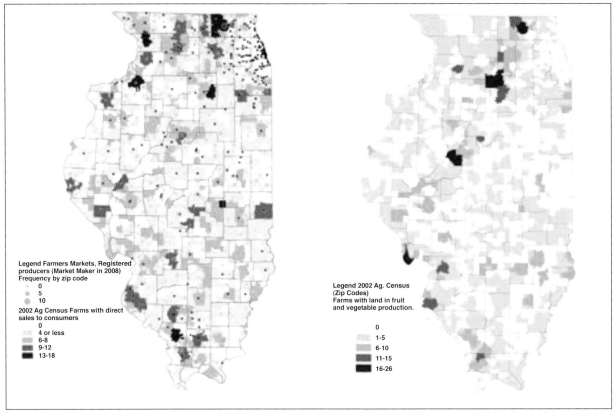

Figure 38.3. Registered producers and farmers markerts (left), location of speciality crops (right). 2002. Source: Data from the State Agricultural Statistics Service prepared by Pat Curry.

tect water and wildlife that are impacted by within-farm management (Robins et al., 2001). The value of green services might be rated more highly if contributions to local wellbeing were better documented. This could help reduce the scepticism about the efficacy of alternative food choice solutions that has arisen (Eden et al., 2008). Citizens' groups actively promote the use of market devices to support local and organic production while acknowledging the need for greater evidence to substantiate stewardship claims (see Lynch and Batie, 2006). There is mounting evidence that organic practices can deliver on claims that their use can enhance biodiversity (Bengtsson et al., 2005).

A variety of marketing and/or payment strategies that rely on green or community branding or certification are being explored. In addition to socially driven brands like local and organic, sustainability metrics are proliferating. The generalized relationships between farming practices and sustainability outcomes developed empirically through field experimentation are currently being converted into marketable goods using simple spreadsheets, models or summary tools like life cycle analysis (LCA) or environmental footprinting (Fiskel, 2007). Such tools may prove useful to environmentally minded growers who understand that as climate change progresses changes in agricultural management are needed to maintain soil quality with less dependence on fossil fuel-based inputs. Reductions in energy use can hold down costs and greenhouse gas emissions caused by fertiliser application, input production, heating and irrigation. Improved management options, such as precision agriculture, drip irrigation and increased nitrogen

281

and water use efficiency are all opportunities to reduce global warming impacts.

Currently, leading work in the area of energy analysis for agricultural systems includes two approaches: life cycle analysis (Hill et al., 2006; Kim and Dale, 2005) and carbon/ecological footprinting (Wachernagel and Rees, 1996; Burnham et al., 2006). Both approaches seek to evaluate all environmental impacts incurred during the whole life cycle of products. LCA quantifies environmental burdens associated with a product, process, or activity. The resources consumed and the emissions to the environment, both on-farm and associated with the production and delivery of the inputs used on the farm, are inventoried. The impacts of resources used and emissions generated are evaluated in terms of environmental impact. The ecological footprint is generally defined as the biologically productive land and water a population requires to produce the resources it consumes and to absorb part of the waste generated by fossil and nuclear fuel consumption (Wackernagel et al., 2002; Monfreda et al., 2004). Ecological footprints are anthropocentric in nature, focusing on the land and water resources needed for human support (Wackernagel et al., 2005). In the context of LCA, the ecological footprint of a product is defined as the sum of time-integrated direct land occupation and indirect land occupation, related to nuclear energy use and to CO_2 emissions from fossil energy use and cement burning (Huijbregts et al., 2008): Even though these techniques are well established in the research community, results can vary by wide margins, causing uncertainty or even conflict (Farrell et al., 2006). Errors in life cycle analysis associated with studies of dominant agricultural production systems can result from the use of inappropriate or outdated information being used as inputs to describe the production practices (Wang and Hag, 2008). Outcomes vary with tools and so care must be used when applying and interpreting results from these kinds of assessment tools (van der Werf et al., 2007). Application of such metrics to diversified systems will be a challenge as the data needed are limited. The alternative and organic communities have so far not been completely receptive to these tools, asserting that community standards and green brands like organic are sufficient (Lipson, 2009).

Development of green metrics for organic and alternative farmers growing and selling into local markets may be one of the most challenging, yet rewarding, efforts in terms of profitability and efficacy. Fruit and vegetable production claimed 15.6% of all agricultural energy costs in 2002; of course total production expenses, and the relative importance of energy costs vary greatly by region (Schnepf, 2004). Costs and price uncertainty are greatest for fertiliser inputs, which are higher per acre for fruit and vegetable crop production than for row crop systems (Schnepf, 2004). Energy prices, the need for heating and cooling, and risks associated with weather all influence the costs and risks of specialty crop growers. Growers who reduce input intensity save energy by increasing biodiversity. Smaller, frequently organic farmers, growing and supplying local outlets, often choose to manipulate plant species richness and evenness within the constraints of their commercial operation, to maintain supply while controlling pests, weeds, and reducing risks (Zehnder et al., 2007; Jackson et al., 2008). The local food movement is also propelled in part by the assumption that shorter food chains are more energy efficient and possibly provide greater food safety, or at least traceability. Consumers assume that the regional production and distribution of food requires less energy turnover compared with global transport of food, but there is a lack of empirical data to support this idea. Economies of scale for processed and fresh-direct market products are likely to differ. Energy costs fall per unit of product for highly processed goods because industries can afford energy saving technologies (Schlich and Fleissner, 2005). General summaries may not be as effective as crop-to-market analyses. A comparison of energy use by certified organic and conventional sectors carried out in England found an energy savings of 20% overall if food production converted to organic methods, but the balance of energy savings varied greatly for different crops (Azeez and Hewlett, 2008). Organic greenhouse production of tomatoes, for example, required three times more energy than conventional production. Another critical factor is food distance and refrigeration. The use of generic food miles as an indicator of the environmental and ethical impacts of food production has been questioned, with the suggestion that it is only through combining spatially explicit LCA with analysis of social issues that the benefits of local food can be assessed (Edwards-Jones et al., 2008). There is a need for investigation of 'partial systems' that describe the LCA of a crop, breed, or brand of food production that includes packaging, transport and distribution up to the point of sale.

Summary

Organic production and local-fresh and green-market outlets may provide an important opportunity for the Midwest U.S. Local markets are particularly attractive and accessible to younger farmers just starting out. Science based tools are developed to help farmers satisfy green production goals that have been articulated by certifying bodies, governmental agents, financial markets and not-for-profit groups. The needs for agriculture are similar in the Baltic States and Great Lakes regions, as populations rely on agriculture for food, fibre and energy supply. The ability to sustain agriculture's provisioning services in these places depends upon their natural resource endowment, history of use and emerging frameworks for management that influence production patterns and norms.

Consumer Demands: Feeding in Organic Farming

39

Ragnar Leming

Estonian University of Life Sciences, Tartu, Estonia

Organic farming is based on a set of principles that are related to nature, environment, food production, farming and society. These principles are to be implemented in practice by standards and regulations. European countries implemented EU Organic Farming Regulations (EC) No 834/2007 and (EC) No 889/2008 that provide common minimum standards for housing conditions, animal feeding, use of veterinary medicine and animal care, etc. However, to a certain degree these common EU regulations provide flexibility in some areas of livestock production. This flexibility in the rules allows organic principles to be implemented in different EU countries that have huge variation in local agro-ecological, cultural, social, economic and technical conditions. Differences in the regulations reflect differences in local conditions such as climate and culture, as well as the level of development of organic agriculture and the standards themselves. Size, structure, productivity, profitability and policy environment surrounding typical organic farms differ widely between countries. Some countries have more stringent organic standards than those specified under common EU regulations, which may lead to higher production costs and lower competitive ability. The principles and level of subsidies being paid to organic farmers in the EU also vary to a great extent (Stolze and Lampkin, 2006).

In organic farming, animal husbandry is often understood in terms of natural living (Lund, 2006). That includes the possibility for the animal to perform natural behaviour, getting feed adapted to its physiology and living in an environment similar to that to which the animal is evolutionarily adapted. One of the main and basic principles of organic farming is that animals are kept as part of the whole production system and their nutrition should be based on locally grown organic feedstuffs. Aiming for a high level of self sufficiency, the feed should preferably be obtained from the same holding where the animals are kept. In countries with well-established organic production, it is possible to purchase feed so that animals can be fed 100% organically, but the feed is not always locally grown.

General Livestock Production Standards Affecting Feeding Strategy

As a general rule, all natural (non-synthetic) feed substances are allowed in organic production and all synthetic substances are prohibited. Organic farming standards are to a large extent devised around the concept that animals should be able to live their lives as naturally as possible, meeting their biological and ethological needs. Feeding synthetic amino acids is forbidden not only because they are synthetic but also because the production of these feed additives involves the use of several chemicals and energy. For instance, synthetic production of DL-methionine involves a number of toxic source chemicals and intermediates (West Virginia University, 2009). Each of the several manufacturing processes used to produce DL-methionine creates an additional load to the environment. The methionine production process is listed by the U.S. Environmental Protection Agency as a hazardous air pollutant. The approach of natural living in organic farming is not just avoiding chemicals, it is also about respecting ecological principles and the integrity of living nature as a whole.

Feed is intended to ensure high quality of the products rather than maximising production, while meeting the nutritional requirements of the livestock at various stages of their development. The probability of feeding-, health- and welfare-related problems increases with higher levels of production. Fattening practices are authorised in so far as they are reversible at any stage of the rearing process. Force-feeding is forbidden. Positive measures such as minimisation of veterinary medicines, free-range outdoor systems, grazing, feeding natural and organic feed with no synthetic additives should be practised to secure high quality of animal products.

Organic animal health management should be based on prevention of diseases. Adequate diets and breeds, good housing conditions and sound management practices should provide the right environment for organic animals to maintain good health. Preference should be given to indigenous breeds and strains of animals. Basically all high-yielding and fast-growing modern animal breeds have certain health problems that are caused by selective breeding and therefore are not recommended for organic conditions. Animal breeds with very high productivity levels also have high nutrient requirements that are difficult to meet using 100% locally grown organic feed. Choice of animals for an organic farm should be based on their vitality, long productive life and resistance to disease (Pryce et al., 2004).

All animals must have access to pasture or an open-air exercise area (Figure 39.1) which may be partially covered, and they must be able to use this area whenever the

Figure 39.1. Animals must have access to outdoor areas (Photo: R. Leming).

physiological condition of the animal, the weather conditions and the state of the ground permit.

From an ethological point of view, regular access to outdoor areas is seen as an essential requirement for livestock. Another reason is that permanent outdoor access is considered better for animal health. Outdoor pasture must be of sufficiently low stocking density to prevent poaching and overgrazing. EU regulations restrict the maximum stocking rate to an equivalent of 170 kg N/ha. Minimum indoor and outdoor surface area and other characteristics of keeping in the different species and types of production are defined in EU regulations. Periodic changing or switching the outdoor area is recommended since it reduces the risks of parasite infections. The final fattening phase of animals for meat production may take place indoors, provided that this indoor period does not exceed one-fifth of their lifetime and in any case for a maximum period of three months.

All young animals (mammals) must be fed on natural milk, preferably maternal milk for a minimum period, depending on the species concerned:

- 3 months for cattle
- 45 days for sheep and goats
- 40 days for pigs

Roughage, fresh or dried fodder or silage must be added to the daily ration for pigs (Figure 39.2) and poultry. Pigs

Figure 39.2. Roughage must be added to the daily ration for organic pigs (Photo: R. Leming).

and poultry are omnivores, like human beings, and grass is a very natural part of their diet. Omnivorous animals have a single stomach and cannot digest cellulose well. Forages for pigs need to be young and leafy, with less stems and straws. Older pigs can eat and utilise all forages sufficiently, but young pigs need more of the high quality grain and protein.

Rotational grazing on high quality pasture, supplemented with local grains and legumes can be recommended on organic pig farms. Forage species, maturity, growing conditions and grazing habits of pigs all influence the nutritional value of the forage consumed. Animals on pasture may grow more slowly and require more feed per unit weight gain due to high fibre intake and increased exercise compared with conventional animals. Insufficient amino acid supply in feeding pigs and poultry with locally grown feed is one of the biggest challenges in organic farms where monogastric animals are raised.

Sources of Feedstuffs

EU regulations require that 50% of the feed for herbivores be obtained from the farm itself or, if that is not possible, produced in cooperation with other (local) organic farms. The meaning of this principle is to conserve energy resources by reducing feed transport and to encourage producers to design their organic holdings or groups of holdings as whole farm systems with relatively closed production cycles, minimising inputs and so conserving resources for sustainable best practice. Therefore, crop rotations must be well planned considering animal needs, soil quality, climatic conditions and technical requirements of the farm.

Up to 30% of the feed formula of rations on average may comprise 'in conversion' feedstuffs. When the 'in conversion' feedstuffs come from an on-farm unit, this percentage can be increased to 60%. Although all animals should be fed organic feed, this has not been possible for many years due to shortage of supplies. Therefore, a limited proportion of conventionally grown feed has been permitted. For a transitional period, the use of a limited proportion of conventional feedstuffs is authorised when the farmer is unable to obtain food exclusively of organic origin. The maximum percentage of conventional feedstuffs authorised per year for pigs and poultry is 5%, calculated annually as a percentage of the dry matter of feedstuffs of agricultural origin. In the near future this proportion will be gradually reduced until total removal. The maximum percentage of conventional feed in the daily ration must not be more than 25%, calculated as a percentage of the dry matter. Since 1 January 2008, all ruminants (cattle, sheep and goats) and herbivores in EU must be fed 100% organic feed as consumers expect that animals used for organic food production are fed 100% organic feed products.

Rearing systems for herbivores are to be based on maximum use of pasturage according to the availability of pastures in the different period of the year. At least 60% of the dry matter in daily rations is to consist of roughage, fresh or dried fodder, or silage. In dairy cows the risk of nutrient undersupply is higher during the 2-3 months of lactation, when energy intake is lower than is needed for daily milk production. As a result, body reserves are used to compensate for this energy deficiency and animals lose body weight. When the energy content of the feed is low then using body reserves will exceed physiological limits, resulting in an increased risk of metabolic and fertility problems (Zollitsch et al., 2004). To avoid or reduce these problems on organic farms, according to EU regulations the roughage proportion in the diets can be lowered to 50% during the first 3 months of the lactation, so the amount of energy-rich concentrates can be increased. However, problems related to the feeding in early lactation are still very common in organic dairy farms where high yielding animals are used. Ensuring high quality and nutritional value of roughage has extremely high importance in organic dairy farms. Diets based on early harvested, high quality roughage are primary inputs for high milk yield, limited use of concentrates and higher economic returns.

Limitations on Raw Materials

Feedstuffs, feed materials, compound feedstuffs, feed additives, processing aids for feedstuffs and certain products used in animal nutrition must not have been produced with the aid of genetically modified organisms or products derived therefrom. Genetically modified organisms are prohibited from use in organic farming because of the unpredictable nature of the technology and the risks to health and the environment. GMOs are incompatible with the concept of organic production, as well as consumers' perception of organic products.

Conventional feed materials of plant origin can be used only if listed in EU regulations and only if they are produced or prepared without the use of chemical solvents. For instance, soybean meal, the most popular protein feed in the world, is not listed in the regulations since during its production process chemical solvents are used. The list of permitted conventional feedstuffs in the regulations will be reviewed at certain intervals with the aim of removing, in particular, conventional feed materials of agricultural origin produced organically in sufficient quantities in the EU.

Feed materials of animal origin, whether conventionally or organically produced, can only be used if listed in the regulations and quantitative restrictions must be considered. There is a limited list of feeds of animal origin (dairy and fish products) permitted for feeding to livestock. Certain items on this list are permitted to be fed only to non-herbivores.

Feed materials of mineral origin, trace elements and vitamins can only be used if listed in the regulations. Organically grown feedstuffs may contain higher levels of some minerals and trace elements, but their variability is high and data are still relatively scarce. Monogastric animals like pigs and poultry at pasture can also consume significant amounts of soil, which provides minerals and trace elements. The use of synthetic vitamins is only permitted for monogastric animals. The use of synthetic vitamins of types A, D and E for ruminants is allowed under limited conditions.

Additives such as enzymes, micro-organisms, binders, processing aids can also be used if listed in EU regulations. In a case of essential need or for a particular nutritional purpose there is a list of feed additives and processing aids that are permitted for use in organic farming.

To ensure high quality of the products, additives such as antibiotics, coccidiostatics, medicinal substances, growth promoters or any substance intended to stimulate growth or production may not be used in organic animal feeding.

Conclusions

The way feed production and feeding takes place is a key element in organic livestock farming. The principle aim of organic production is that a harmonious balance between crop production and animal husbandry be established and that the biological cycles within the farming system be encouraged. Many organic farmers still rely on external sources of feed for their animals, particularly cereals and protein crops. Since the introduction of the 100% organic feeding rule for ruminants in EU and the rise in fuel and feed prices seen in recent years, the need and costs of purchasing organic feed have risen significantly, requiring farmers to reassess their feeding systems.

Producing High Quality Feed
Grassland Management

40

Rein Viiralt and Are Selge
Estonian University of Life Sciences, Tartu, Estonia

Planning of Sown Grasslands

Pastures

A prerequisite for establishing sown pastures is the presence of suitable land around a farm. Efficiency of the use of pastures is significantly influenced by the area of conjoined pasture plots and their location on the farm(s). Large pasture plots close to the farm make it easier to arrange grazing and reduce the expenditure on cow lanes, fences, watering points etc (Figure 40.1). The distance between the farthest part of the pasture and the farm should generally not exceed 2 km. Too long a distance from the barn to the pasture and back causes a decline in milk production. The area of sown pasture is planned according to the type of enterprise and the number of animals. The main factor affecting animal productivity and weight gain is the amount of grass eaten by an animal – intake. It depends on the palatability of grass, which in turn is mainly affected by the botanical composition of the pasture, developmental stage of plants and the amount of fertiliser applied. In addition, intake is strongly affected by grass supply, animal weight and appetite, health condition, age, milk yield and several other factors. As a rule of thumb, the daily intake of grass dry matter by a dairy cow comprises about 2.5-3% of its live weight. Consequently, a highly productive dairy cow needs about 80 kg high quality pasture grass per day. Daily feed requirement should be partly covered by roughage with high dry matter content. The grazing area per animal should be about 0.6 ha, provided that the average duration of the grazing period is 160 days and the dry matter yield of legume-rich sown pasture in the vegetation period is 5-6 tonnes per hectare (30-35 tonnes as green fodder). It should also be taken into account that the distribution of grass yield during the vegetation period is uneven and that 20-25% of high quality grass remains unused due to dung patches and treading. It is inevitable that in spring, during periods of most intensive grass growth, there is a lot of excess grass which should be ensiled, especially on sites located far from the farm. Consequently, it is reasonable to plan for most of the pasture area to be used rotationally for both grazing and silage-making. When planning sown pasture for young cattle, it should be considered that the area required is 70-100 m^2 per calf and 1,500-2,500 m^2 per heifer.

For grazing young cattle, a uniform pasture area, which need not be located in the immediate neighbourhood of the barn, should be established. During the grazing period young cattle do not necessarily need supplemental feed or shelter. After having calculated the amount of summer feed needed by the cattle and the area of relevant pastures, it is necessary to check whether there is sufficient land stock for establishing the pastures. Specific features and soil types of the area in the immediate neighbourhood of the already existing barns are predetermined. The exception is establishment of a new farm. Planning of grasslands is based on knowledge of soil properties.

Figure 40.1. Sown and natural grasslands (Photo: A. Nõmmeots).

Data needed for planning the types of grasslands and rational use of land stock include:

- Relief of land surface.
- Type of soil.
- Soil acidity - pH_{KCl}.
- Water regime.
- Soil nutrient content – mainly that of phosphorus, potassium, calcium, organic matter.
- Previously applied rotation of crops.

In order to get a reliable overview of the nutrient content of soil, samples for chemical analysis should be taken from the top 20 cm soil layer. As establishment of sown grasslands is relatively expensive, it would be wrong to think that they can be located on unfertile lands which are unsuitable for cultivating other crops. It is reasonable to establish sown grasslands on flat or evenly sloping land plots where snow melt water cannot accumulate in early spring. The soil should be rich in nutrients and if necessary, also drained.

Meadows

Multi-cut sown grasslands are established mainly for supplying cattle with winter forage, but today also more and more for making year round forage – silage. In some cases it is necessary to make hay as well. In planning mown meadows, the (winter) feed requirement of the herd and feed quality should be considered. A rule of thumb says that:

- The planned amount of high quality silage should be 12-13 tonnes per cow.
- If dairy cattle nutrition is based on year-round silage diet, the amount of feed needed per cow should be increased to 15 tonnes.
- Feed requirement for young cattle should be considered as well.

To simplify the planning of areas needed for grasslands, average yields of the main types of sown meadows are given in Table 40.1.

Table 40.1. Average yields of forage crops.

Silage crop	Approximate yield, DM tonnes/ha	Area of sown grassland needed for making 1,000 tonnes of prewilted silage
Red clover + timothy	5...7	50
Lucerne	6...7	45
Italian ryegrass	6...8	40
Annual ryegrass	7...8	40

Table 40.2. Grass species according to usability and soil type of grassland.

Species	Usability		Soils				
	Grazing	Rotational use (grazing and mowing)	Dry, limestone and gravelly soils	Dry sandy soils	Moderately moist loam soils	Moist clay soils	Peat soil
Legumes							
White clover (*Trifolium repens*)	Very suitable	Suitable	Less suitable	Unsuitable	Very suitable	Very suitable	Less suitable
Red clover (*Trifolium pratense*)	Less suitable	Suitable	Less suitable	Less suitable	Very suitable	Suitable	Less suitable
Lucerne (*Medicago sativa*)	Suitable	Suitable	Very suitable	Suitable	Very suitable	Unsuitable	Unsuitable
Bird's-foot trefoil (*Lotus corniculatus*)	Suitable	Suitable	Very suitable	Suitable	Very suitable	Suitable	Unsuitable
Tall grasses							
Timothy (*Phleum pratense*)	Suitable	Very suitable	Suitable	Less suitable	Very suitable	Suitable	Very suitable
Meadow fescue (*Festuca pratensis*)	Suitable	Suitable	Less suitable	Unsuitable	Very suitable	Suitable	Suitable
Meadow foxtail (*Alopecurus pratensis*)	Suitable	Suitable	Unsuitable	Unsuitable	Suitable	Very suitable	Suitable
Cocksfoot (*Dactylis glomerata*)	Suitable	Very suitable	Suitable	Suitable	Very suitable	Less suitable	Less suitable
Tall fescue (*Festuca arundinacea*)	Suitable	Suitable	Suitable	Suitable	Very suitable	Suitable	Less suitable
Low grasses:							
Perennial ryegrass (*Lolium perenne*)	Well suitable	Suitable	Not suitable	Not suitable	Well suitable	Suitable	Less suitable
Smooth meadow-grass (*Poa pratensis*)	Well suitable	Less suitable	Less suitable	Less suitable	Well suitable	Suitable	Suitable
Red fescue (*Festuca rubra*)	Suitable	Less suitable	Well suitable	Well suitable	Suitable	Suitable	Not suitable

Choosing Seed Mixtures

A properly formulated grass seed mixture is essential for establishing permanent pasture herbage with high nutritive value and fast regrowth. In formulating pasture mixtures, the effect of grazed animals on herbage development and botanical composition, as well as competition between species, should be considered. Only grass species and varieties that are tolerant to grazing and competition between species should be used.

The next step in choosing species and varieties in the pasture grass mixture is to define the objective of the pasture establishment and the way of using the pasture – which animal species will be grazed and which other purposes the pasture will fulfil.

Pasture grass should be highly palatable for the grazing animal species – with high intake and nutritive value. Timothy among the tall grasses and perennial ryegrass among the low grasses have the highest palatability, nutritive value and resistance to grazing. Leguminous plants play an important role in increasing palatability and nutritive value of pasture grass. The most widespread forage legumes that tolerate grazing are white clover, bird's-foot trefoil and lucerne varieties for pasture. Pasture sward should be dense and resistant to treading. Therefore in pasture mixtures low grasses such as perennial ryegrass, smooth-stalked meadowgrass and red fescue play an important role. Low grasses create dense low herbage undergrowth and a sward resistant to grazing. Low grasses prevent the invasion of weeds and other unsown herbaceous plants to pasture sward. In order to get permanent sward in given growing conditions, grass and legume species should be selected according to the soil type and local growing conditions. Usually soil characteristics do not constitute obstacles to the establishment of grasslands, as there is a wide choice of grass species and varieties suitable for growing on different soil types (Table 40.2). The main soil characteristics are:

- Soil reaction: acidic pH_{KCl} <6.5, neutral pH_{KCl} 6.6-7.2 or alkaline pH_{KCl}>7.2;
- Soil texture (light, heavy, peaty etc.);
- Soil water regime (dry, moderately humid, temporarily waterlogged etc.)

Although seed companies offer ready-made seed mixtures, in many cases it is rational for the producers to formulate the mixtures themselves as the growth conditions and usage objectives of grasslands may vary greatly.

Multi-species mixtures have proven to be more efficient than pure swards. Although in Western Europe (England, the Netherlands) pasture mixtures for dairy cows and sheep mainly contain the seeds of different varieties of perennial ryegrass, pure perennial ryegrass swards are quite sensitive to winter damage. Therefore sowing seeds as monocultures to establish a pasture is rarely recommended. Properly chosen companion species in the mixtures increase the nutritive value and intake of herbage and lengthen the duration of the grassland. Winter damage and weed infestation have been found to be less severe in mixed grassland swards than in pure swards.

The use of forage legumes, mainly white clover and treading-resistant lucerne varieties, in seed mixtures has proven to be effective regarding aspects of economy and sustainable agricultural production. Air nitrogen bound by the root nodules of legumes helps save expenditure on nitrogen fertilisers. Leaching of nitrogen compounds into the groundwater is reduced as no nitrogen fertilisers are applied. Legume-rich pasture herbage (legumes comprise 30-35% of DM yield) which has not been treated with

nitrogen fertilisers gives the same yield as a grassland to which 200 kg nitrogen per hectare has been applied. Legumes increase the nutritive value (mainly protein), palatability and intake of pasture grass. Many field trials have shown that increasing the percentage of white clover in the herbage results in an increase in daily weight gain of cattle and in milk yield of dairy cows. Increasing the percentage of white clover in pasture herbage by 10% has been reported to increase daily milk yield by 0.30 to 0.45 kg per cow.

Use of forage legumes in pasture mixtures is mainly restricted by acidic soil (pH_{KCl} <6.0 for lucerne, especially) and either too wet or too dry soil regime. White clover has also a shallow root system, which makes it intolerant of long drought periods. Another disadvantage is the quite short duration of white clover grasslands – in Estonia the average duration of sown white clover is 5 years. If the content of legumes in dry matter yield of pasture grass drops below 20%, the grassland should be re-seeded. If the composition and density of grass are suitable, the pasture can be treated with nitrogen fertilisers and its utilisation may be continued. If the percentage of valuable forage plants in pasture herbage is low (below 30% in DM), direct seeding of legumes into the old sward should be considered as well.

Simultaneous growing of legumes and grasses reduces the risks arising from unfavourable weather conditions. Legume-rich pastures should constitute 50 to 80% of the total area of sown pastures.

As to pasture utilisation schedule, it is essential to establish pasture swards which have different rates of development. This allows spring grazing to be started earlier and prevents a situation where the entire herbage simultaneously reaches the stage of development suitable for grazing. The growth and development rate of pasture herbage can be regulated by growing different grass species or by using early, intermediate and late grass varieties.

Smaller areas in the immediate neighbourhood of farms should be seeded with grass mixtures which have rapid initial development and regrowth in spring. Suitable dominant grasses can be cocksfoot or meadow foxtail, as both compete strongly with other species and have a high development rate. Pastures dominated by cocksfoot can be established in dry habitats and those dominated by meadow foxtail in moist habitats. It must also be mentioned that the duration of swards rich in those grasses is very long – over 10 years.

Long duration of high-quality grasslands is usually profitable as it saves expenditure on reestablishment of grasslands. At the same time, breeding of grass varieties is being directed to maximally intensive yield consumption. Sowing early in spring enables up to two-thirds of the potential annual yield of herbage to be obtained. For that reason, the use of 'short- and long-duration sown pastures' has decreased.

Today the optimal duration of a sown pasture is 5 to 6 years. At the same time attempts should be made to maintain high-quality herbage and thus elongate its duration. Duration of legume-rich grasslands can be elongated by using long-lived legumes like treading-resistant lucerne varieties in pasture mixtures. For longer duration of pastures it is important to manage the grazing load and avoid intensive treading of the sward by animals or heavy machinery in rainy periods. It is difficult to recommend conventional seed mixtures suitable for establishment of pastures. Producers can choose from a very wide range of different grass and legume species and varieties in order to select a seed mixture proper for growing in specific habitats. Table 40.3 represents some of the recommended seed mixtures which are simple, contain only few species and have a low sowing rate. It was assumed that the germination rate of seeds is 100%.

Key factors which should be taken into account in the formulation of seed mixtures:

- Keep seed mixtures as simple as possible; use grass and legume species suitable for specific soils and habitats.
- Select grass species which are preferred by the grazed animal species.
- Under favourable growing conditions establish legume-rich pasture herbage (legumes comprise 30% of DM yield) covering at least half of the total pasture area.
- Consider the suitability of development rate of grasses for growing in mixtures.
- Do not establish sown pastures as undersown crops in grain.
- For establishing sown pastures, do not use short-lived grass species with high competitiveness such as Italian ryegrass.

Establishment of Grasslands

The objective of establishing grasslands is to get a sward producing quite cheap but high-quality grass feed. Re-establishment of older grasslands is necessary if the yield and its quality are low. The first indicators of sward ageing can be low yield of grassland and in pastures also poor intake of grass by animals. The grass quality generally declines due to changes in the botanical composition of the sward – loss of high quality grasses and legumes from the herbage, and invasion and spread of unsown herbaceous plants with low yield and nutritive value in the sward.

Frequently, the degradation of the botanical composition of the sward is the result of improper use and management of grasslands, alterations in soil nutrient content, pH and moisture regime. Application of insufficient amounts of fertilisers, delayed mowing or grazing, intensive grazing or using heavy machinery on waterlogged soils can all be reasons for shortening the duration of a high quality sward.

Table 40.3. Seed mixtures for sown pastures (seed germination rate 100%).

Grass species	Content in seed mixture, weight %	Seed kg/ha	Total seed mixture kg/ha
Dry gravelly soil			
Grazing-tolerant lucerne	66	12	18
Timothy	17	3	
Smooth meadow-grass	17	3	
Moderately moist mineral soil duration of legume-rich herbage is 5 years, afterwards it is rich in grasses			
White clover	20	3	15
Timothy	40	6	
Perennial ryegrass (diploid variety)	20	3	
Perennial ryegrass (tetraploid variety)	20	3	
Dry mineral soil with heavy texture			
Cocksfoot	65	15	23
Timothy	26	6	
Smooth meadow-grass	9	2	
Moderately moist peat soil			
Timothy	42	8	19
Meadow fescue	42	8	
Smooth meadow-grass	16	3	

Depending on a climatic zone, grasslands may be temporarily damaged by winter cold, especially snowless and frosty winters, lasting spring meltwater and its icing, and also abrupt fluctuations in air temperature in early spring. Grass cultivars imported from warmer climatic zones are especially susceptible to such weather conditions. Loss of short-live grass species from the herbage is unavoidable.

Ageing of grasslands is a natural process and the optimal duration of the herbage depends mainly on selected/ sown grass species and varieties as well as on usage regime and climatic conditions.

When to Re-establish Grassland?

Re-establishment of grassland is very expensive. It should be undertaken only if the botanical composition of the sward has degraded, the grassland needs to be levelled or the soil needs to be drained. Re-establishment of grasslands is justified if the costs involved are repaid by the subsequent higher yields of better quality.
Grassland renovation is needed if:

- The sward contains less than 50% high quality grasses.
- The sward contains more than 30% unsown forage herbs and weeds.
- The soil surface is very uneven.
- The sward has been severely damaged by cold or heavy tilling machines.
- Soil drainage is urgently needed.

The quality of the sward decreases rapidly due to the spread of dandelion, couch grass and other herbaceous weeds. Grasslands with medium quality botanical composition (50-70% quality species and less than 25% couch grass) can be improved by using an appropriate technology and usage regime. However, this kind of improvement may take several years.

Establishment of grasslands by reseeding is the most effective method for renewing old and weedy grasslands (meadows, pastures). As reseeding is preceded by sward destruction, it is possible to incorporate organic fertilisers into the soil, level the soil surface and select the botanical composition of herbage according to the growth conditions and producer's needs.

Re-establishment of grasslands allows the seeds of weeds and unwanted grasses to be ploughed into the low-er soil layers. The soil surface can also be further levelled by appropriate tillage.

Tillage Prior to Reseeding

Besides correctly formulated seed mixtures and selected seed material, it is very important to apply suitable tillage techniques

Soil cultivation in autumn

As regards tillage prior to sowing, to the first considerations are autumn ploughing in the previous year and determination of fertilisation rate on the basis of soil analysis. Autumn ploughing in September or October is inevitable for re-establishment of old and weedy herbage. On grasslands use of semidigger or breaker ploughs is recommended. The ploughing depth is usually 22 to 25 cm. Harrowing of the grassland prior to ploughing by disc harrow is not always necessary and can even be detrimental if the percentage of couch grass in the sward is high, as rhizomes of the couch grass are multiplied. After the sward has been turned over, it must have enough time for decomposition. Therefore ploughing in early autumn is more effective than ploughing in late autumn. On peat soils and on soils with heavy texture, it is recommended to plough at least by July as decomposition of the old sward takes place more rapidly in warm soil.

Use of herbicides

When the existing grassland contains couch grass, dandelion, stinging nettle or other forbs, these should be wiped out using herbicides before ploughing. The most widely used herbicide is Roundup or Roundup Bio – a systematic herbicide (active ingredient glyphosate) for long-lived weeds. In order to maximise the effect of glyphosate, couch grass should have at least 3 or 4 green leaves and be 10 to 15 cm high. Weeds should be sprayed in dry weather. The application rate of Roundup is 3-4 litres per hectare and the effect becomes apparent 10-14 days after spraying. Soil cultivation of fields treated with Roundup may be started after the weed mass has completely browned – 2 to 4 weeks after spraying, depending on the time of spraying.

Solid organic fertilisers (manure, compost) should be applied prior to autumn ploughing and liquid manure (slurry) during soil cultivation in spring. Application of organic fertilisers is particularly important for establishing grasslands on eroded soils and other soils poor in humus.

The recommended application rate for organic fertiliser is 40 to 60 tonnes per hectare. Organic fertiliser applied prior to sowing and by top-dressing at lower rates, e.g. 20-30 tonnes per ha in the following years stimulates microbial processes in the growth environment of the roots and supplies soil with essential nutrients. Soil samples must be analysed for nutrient content and acidity – an important indicator of the growing environment.

Application of agricultural lime to acidic soils (pH<6.0) prior to sowing is essential if legumes or legume-rich seed mixtures are used. Forage legumes are very susceptible to soil acidity. For growing legumes, agricultural lime should be applied if pH_{KCl} in the top layer of soil (up to 10 cm) is below 6.0. For growing grasses, lime should be applied if pH_{KCl} is below 5.5. Few peat soils need liming if the soil pH_{KCl} is below 5.0.

Agricultural lime should be applied in two portions: the first one prior to autumn ploughing and the other prior to soil cultivation in spring. This ensures that there is contact between lime and seeds in the germination environment. The recommended application rate of oil-shale ash (a liming agent used in Estonia) is 5 to 6 tonnes per hectare. Oil-shale ash gives a quick response after application. Besides calcium, it contains potassium, sulphur, sodium, phosphorus and trace elements such as B, Cu, Mn, Mo, Zn, Co (Turbas, 1996). Soils can be also limed with cement clinker dust (from cement industry), dolomite or limestone meal.

Soil cultivation in spring should be started early in order to create favourable development conditions for grass seeds. Sufficient soil moisture is one of the most important factors for initial development of small-sized grass seeds. Therefore soil cultivation should begin as early as possible – when the soil can bear tractors without being rutted.

The first operation should be cultivation, preferably with a cultivator with S-shaped tines, followed by smoothing the soil with a slight float. The first cultivation creates 'loose soil'. With a light float, micro-grooves on the soil surface are flattened and soil capillaries on the surface

layer are 'covered' in order to prevent evaporation of soil water from the top layer. This is followed by cultivation. It should be borne in mind that over-cultivation of soil dries out the top layer, which is the germination environment of seeds. The soil cultivation depth in spring is 10 to 15 cm. After ploughing the soil sinks so the depth of the loose layer should be only 5 cm.

If reseeding is planned immediately after cultivation, the soil must be rolled to ensure an even sowing depth of the seeds. An important operation prior to sowing after the last soil cultivation is clearing the field of stones.

Optimal Time for Sowing Grass Seed
For germination of seeds and fast development of plants, a certain temperature and degree of humidity are needed. Optimal sowing time depends mainly on climatic and soil characteristics of the region. In Estonia, early spring or late summer is the best time to sow grass seed.

Sowing in early spring provides favourable growth conditions for grasses due to the high moisture content of soil. Sufficient moisture content in the upper soil layer is one of the most important factors for successful establishment of grasslands. On grasslands established at the end of spring or beginning of summer (end of May to end of June), weed infestation can be severe, especially from wind-born dandelion seeds falling on bare soil. As a result, besides having moisture deficiency, these types of grasslands are often weedy.

Sowing in early spring has the advantage over late summer sowing that the grassland can be mown or grazed in the first year of use.

The main advantage of sowing in summer (July until early August) is systematic weakening and disturbance of weeds by soil cultivation (mainly rhizomes of couch grass). Simultaneously, the surface of soil is levelled and favourable preconditions for establishing a weed-free sward are created. In Estonian peat soils, sowing is suggested to take place in summer. However, the greater expenditure accompanying soil cultivation during the spring-summer season should be considered. However late summer sowing should not be delayed too long, as grasses and legumes must have enough time for storing reserve nutrients for winter months. Legumes are particularly sensitive to late sowing. In Estonian climatic conditions, forage legumes should not be sown later than August 5 in order to avoid out-wintering risks.

Reseeding Methods for Establishing Grasslands

Well-prepared soil for sowing should be level, sufficiently compacted and loosened to a depth of 20-30 mm. The well-compacted lower soil layer provides seeds with sufficient moisture and creates favourable conditions for the development of young plants. Constant sowing depth plays an important role for uniform germination of grass seeds. As grass seeds are relatively small, the optimum depth of sowing ranges between 10 and 20 mm. Such a sowing depth can be achieved by preparing smooth and shallowly loosened soil. Table 38.4 shows the effect of sowing depth on the germination of grass seed.

Compacted soil and a smooth soil surface create good conditions for sowing at even depth, guarantee good carrying capacity and result in the new sward being more resistant to animal treading and wheel traffic of agricultural machinery. The smooth soil surface also allows a low and even mowing height in the period the grassland is used.

For preparation of soils (particularly light and peat soils), the use of rollers after the last cultivation is recommended in order to compact the soil. On mineral soils, riffle land rollers have the advantage over flat rollers since they crumble chunks of the upper layer of soil and compact the soil more efficiently

Drilling. For sowing in drills, special grass drills are recommended. The distance between drill coulters should be up to 75 mm and sowing depth 2 to 3 mm for grasses, and up to 2 mm for grass/clover mixtures.

Broadcast sowing. Satisfactory results can also be achieved by using a grain seed drill after removing the coulters – seeds are broadcast on the soil surface where they are covered with soil by the following harrow. Irrespective of sowing method, the seed drill must be fitted with a light harrow. Rolling the soil after sowing plays an important role in creating favourable conditions for plant development. Rolling is not recommended after rainfall when soil is wet. It is also important to choose a suitable weight of roller – on peat soils heavier rollers are needed.

Resowing of Grasslands in Cover Crops

Reseeding in a cover crop is an opportunity to attain the maximum yield per area unit. It is recommended that leys (red clover+timothy) be established by undersowing in a cover crop. Early ripening barley varieties are usually used as cover crops. However, the seed rate of barley should be lowered by 25-30% and application of nitrogen fertilisers is not recommended. Grass seed may be sown simultaneously with the cover crop or later when the cover crop is at 2- or 3-leaf stage. Undersowing in a cover crop has several disadvantages: shading of grass seedlings by cereals, competition for soil nutrients and water, the cover crop may be prone to lodging, etc.

Pasture swards should not be established under a cover crop, as e.g. white clover, low grasses and lucerne are particularly sensitive to the effects of the cover crop. When establishing grassland, it is necessary to:

- Determine soil pH and nutrient content.
- Select seed mixture according the use of grassland and the type of soil.
- Use simple seed mixtures.
- Pay attention not only to the species but also to the VARIETY of the grass seed in the mixture.
- Avoid purchasing seeds of unknown origin.
- When establishing grassland for rotational usage, it is reasonable to choose a seed mixture suitable for grazing as well as for silage-making.
- Avoid red clover in pasture mixtures.
- Include Italian ryegrass in the mixture only if there is an "urgent need".
- When sowing perennial ryegrass choose moderately moist and fertile soil.
- Avoid delaying sowing.

Table 40.4. Effect of sowing depth on germination of white clover and perennial rye-grass (Frame *et al.*, 1998).

Sowing depth (mm)	Germination (%)	
	White clover	Perennial ryegrass
10	81	94
20	63	95
30	21	86
40	12	68

- The soil surface should be only shallow-loosened prior to sowing. Seeds should not be sown too deep.
- Sowing should be timed so that emerged young seedlings are not exposed to draught.

Grassland Management in the Year of Sowing

After creating favourable germination conditions for grass seeds, it is essential to ensure subsequent continuous fast development of young grass plants. The initial management technique for reseeded grasslands without a cover crop is topping to control weeds. Weeds compete with crops for nutrients, light and water. Infestation by annual weeds on reseeded grassland is rather frequent and therefore it is necessary to cut the herbage at a height of approximately 15 cm. Cutting at that height does not disturb crop plants but inhibits the development of weeds and prevents the maturing and spread of seeds.

Weed topping in the year of sowing must not be delayed as the mown biomass may cause 'suffocation' of crops and create gaps in the sward. However, if the spread of weeds is not a problem and crops are not shaded by them, it would be more reasonable to harvest the first cut together with weeds as green fodder. In some cases, e.g. with ephemeral dicotyledonous weeds, it may also be necessary to apply chemical herbicides on newly established grasslands (e.g. Basagran, application rate 2.5-3.0 litres per ha).

After one or sometimes two toppings, the grassland is ready to be grazed. Grazing of spring-sown pastures should start in the second half of summer by grazing young cattle under dry weather conditions. It is important to let the plants form a thick sward and give them enough time to develop a root system in order to create a sward resistant to treading by animals. Grazing of pastures on rainy days when soil is very wet is not recommended. The crop should be harvested for use as green forage or silage material.

Before wintering, the sward must not be too low or too high (min. height 7 cm). Late and intensive grazing or mowing is to be avoided.

Use of Mineral Fertilisers for Establishment of Grasslands and on Harvest Years

Application of mineral fertilisers to grasslands is mainly affected by nutrient content of the soil and grass species in the sward.

Regarding economic as well as ecological aspects, it is first necessary to take average soil samples in the field and draft a fertilisation plan on the basis of chemical analyses. If for some reason organic fertilisers were not applied prior to ploughing, it would be necessary to use mineral fertilisers for establishing grassland with high quality and stable yield.

For plants, the balance of the major nutrients in soil is essential. Deficiency of even a single nutrient in soil can result in a decrease in crop quality, yield and winter hardiness. When re-establishing old and unfertilised (semi-natural) grasslands, particular attention should be paid to the potassium content of soil, as grasses need high amounts of this element.

For forage legumes, especially pure stands of lucerne, it is important to pay attention to the content of calcium (Ca), phosphorus (P), sulphur (S), boron (B) and magnesium (Mg). Phosphorus (P) and potassium (K) or complex fertilisers should be applied prior to seeding during spring or summer tillage according to the soil nutrient supply. Mineral fertilisers should be applied in spring, after the soil has dried and before the last cultivation, as then the fertiliser is mixed into the top layer of soil. If necessary, agricultural lime should be applied during cultivation.

In harvest years, PK fertilisers are applied to grasslands by top-dressing in autumn after the last cut or grazing. Table 40.5 presents limit values of P and K content in mineral soil and recommended P and K application rates.

Higher rates of PK fertilisers (P 45-55 and K 125-150 kg per ha) are recommended on peat soils as they are usually much lower in phosphorus and potassium than mineral soils. Peat soils are also poor in copper (Cu) and need to be treated with fertilisers containing Cu if this is possible or required.

Application of nitrogen fertilisers – in the form of ammonium nitrate, ammonium sulphate, and urea – is necessary mainly for swards consisting of grasses. N fertilis-

Table 40.5. Limit values of K and P content (determined by using A-L method) in mineral soil and recommended P and K application rates for grasslands.

Content	P mg/kg	K mg/kg	Recommended nutrient application rates, kg/ha			
			leguminous-rich herbage		grass-rich herbage	
			P	K	P	K
Very low	<20	<50	26	75	35	100
Low	21...40	51...100	17	50	26	66
Medium	41...80	101...200	15	30	17	50
High	81...120	>200	10	25	11	38

ers are not recommended if the proportion of legumes in yield is more than 30%. Use of moderate N fertilisation rates is inevitable for managing grasslands rich in Italian ryegrass, perennial ryegrass, reed canarygrass, meadow fescue, cocksfoot, timothy and tall fescue. Application of N fertilisers can significantly improve the quality of grass feeds and increase the yield. N fertilisers can be applied in the year of sowing as a top-dressing of herbage and the suggested N application rate is 60-80 kg per ha. Fertilisation with N in late summer (from August) should be avoided – it can stimulate grass growth but reduce winter hardiness and in spring the sward may be damaged. The suggested application rate for top-dressings of N to grasslands rich in tall grasses is 150-210 kg per ha, applied in two or three equal portions during the whole vegetation period.

Application of Slurry to Grassland. Technologies

Manure spreading restrictions and establishment of liquid manure storage facilities at large-scale cattle farms have created a problem concerning agronomically effective and sustainable application of slurry as a fertiliser, particularly reducing of nutrient losses during application to land.

Nutrient Losses from Liquid Manure
Nitrogen in manure occurs in organic and inorganic forms. Inorganic forms of nitrogen are immediately plant-available but organic compounds can become plant-available through mineralisation in the soil. The largest nitrogen

emissions occur through intensive volatilisation of ammonia (NH_3) from field-applied (to crop or grassland) manure. The chemical process is quite simple – urea $CO(NH_2)_2$ excreted by an animal is hydrolysed into ammonium nitrogen (NH_4^+-N) by the activity of urease and release of ammonia (NH_3) follows. Emissions of ammonium nitrogen (NH_4^+-N) as volatilised NH_3 during spreading of liquid manure usually amount to 40-50% of the N content prior to spreading, i.e. nearly half of plant-available inorganic nitrogen (Mattila, 2006). It is known that the greatest losses of NH_3 occur in the first 3-4 hours after application. Emissions of NH_3 continue for at least 3 days, but at one-tenth of the intensity in the first hours after application (Viiralt, 2007).

Ammonia emissions are more intensive with high air temperature and strong winds. Losses of NH_3 are lower from slurry with lower dry matter content, as diluted slurry infiltrates into the soil more rapidly (if soil conditions allow this); ammonium nitrogen (NH_4^+) is bound by soil and volatilisation of NH_3 decreases. Measurements carried out in England revealed the following relationship: when the dry matter (DM) content of slurry was 3%, emissions of plant-available nitrogen from slurry amounted to 20%, while for slurry with a DM content of 6% and 9%, emissions comprised 35% and 50%, respectively. Organic nitrogen compounds which have leaked from slurry into soil are subjected to ammonification (NH_4^+) by the activity of specialist bacteria, and later to nitrification (NO_3^-). Plant material present in slurry partly remains on the soil surface and decomposes, releasing some ammonia. Lack of air in the soil – caused by excessive moisture, compacting with heavy machines, etc. – can lead to denitrification under anaerobic conditions. As a result, nitrogen oxides (N_2O; NO and NO_2) and molecular nitrogen (N_2) are volatilised.

During spreading of manure on grassland, nitrogen losses due to denitrification fluctuate within the range 0.1-30%, depending on climate and soil conditions.

Losses are higher in autumn than in spring. In spring, soil nitrates are rapidly assimilated by fast growing crops and smaller amounts of nitrate are subjected to denitrification. In spite of that, denitrification losses from liquid manure per kg total N are higher than those from mineral nitrogen fertiliser.

If liquid manure is applied in autumn (under winter crops or on grassland after the second or third cut) it is possible that nitrates (NO_3^-) formed during nitrification are leached from the topsoil. However, the risk of nitrate leaching is much lower on grasslands than on arable land due to the presence of permanent herbage. In any case, the forage crops (maize included) should not be over-fertilised with liquid manure – otherwise nitrates subjected to leaching are accumulated in the soil by autumn.

The amount of accumulating nitrates in soil is affected by the content of soluble ammonium (NH_4^+) in the applied manure. The percentage of soluble nitrogen in total nitrogen is 40-60% for liquid manure and approximately 10% for solid manure (Viiralt, 2007).

Phosphorus (P) present in animal manure can exist in inorganic (mostly) or organic compounds. The changes in phosphorus compounds are complex and mainly result from the activity of soil microbes. Phosphorus in the soil is relatively immobile and does not leach readily. However, if annual application rates of liquid manure are higher than the soil's ability to bind P, organic soluble phosphorus compounds can move in the water-saturated soil down into the groundwater or out into bodies of surface water and result in eutrophication. Phosphorus can also move into the environment with surface runoff.

Potassium (K) in the soil is mostly water-soluble and readily available to plants. Water-soluble potassium is absorbed well in heavier types of soil but in sandy soils there is a risk of leaching. Few data are available about negative effects of potassium on the quality of surface water or groundwater. However, there is a risk of over-fertilising grass pastures with excessive potassium applied with liquid manure. Excessive assimilation (twice the level required by cattle) of potassium by grasses at the expense of magnesium creates a risk of hypomagnesaemic pasture tetany of cows (Viiralt, 2007). Other nutrients present in liquid manure are sodium (Na), calcium (Ca), magnesium (Mg), manganese (Mn) and sulphur (S).

Technologies to Reduce Nutrient Losses During Liquid Manure Management

The application time and rate of liquid manure application should be determined by the crop nutrient requirements during the vegetation period. Applying liquid manure to grasslands in spring and spring-summer has proven to be more effective. The annual application rate of liquid manure (tonnes/ha) and the rate per application should be determined on the basis of nitrogen content, such that the annual dose of N supplied with liquid manure does not exceed 170 kg N per hectare (Estonian Water Act, § 26 and EU's Nitrate Directive).

The approximate content of N in liquid manure is 2-4 kg per m^3 and consequently the amount of manure per application can be 30-50 tonnes per ha depending on DM and N content in manure. The rather frequent problem is a very wide P:K ratio of 1:5-6 in liquid manure, as optimally it should be 1:2.5. If large amounts of liquid manure is applied to grassland, supplemental mineral P fertiliser should be applied (Viiralt, 2007).

In recent years there have been attempts to find ways of reducing high nitrogen losses from animal slurry during its application. In Finland, three application technologies for unprocessed slurry were studied (Mattila, 2006): (1) broadcast spreading evenly on the soil surface; (2) band spreading; and (3) injection with a spreading device equipped with high pressure pump and special injection nozzles. The application rate of cattle slurry was 44-45 tonnes/ha, containing 7.1% dry matter and 91-95 kg/ha ammonium nitrogen (NH_4^+-N). The pH of manure was 7.1.

Over a three-day period, the loss of NH_4^+-N from manure after broadcasting was 40% and after band spreading 31%. The loss of NH_4^+-N was only 0.4% when liquid manure was injected into closed slots. Losses of NH_4^+-N from slurry application were even higher if the slurry had been previously aerated (DM 6.5%) or separated (DM 4.5%) in the manure storage facility – 59% and 42%, respectively.

Consequently, these techniques are not effective and the only way for reducing nitrogen losses (volatilisation of NH_3) is application of slurry to grassland with a special injector and to arable land by cultivation.

Application technology also affected the use efficiency of the slurry: 32-37% of NH_4^+-N was recovered in grassland yield when injection was used, while for broadcasting and band spreading the corresponding value was 24-30% (for untreated and aerated liquid manure 24-25%; for separated or diluted manure 30%).

As devices for injection of slurry into grass sward are considerably more expensive than band spreaders, economic calculations must be made in order to find out if the increase in yield resulting from significant reduction of ammonia nitrogen (NH_3-N) volatilisation covers the price difference between the devices. Incorporation of slurry into topsoil is a much more environmentally friendly technique than broadcasting (Viiralt, 2007). After band spreading it is necessary to harrow the surface of grassland with an ecological harrow in order to prevent the formation of a thin film (consisting of undigested feed particles) on the soil surface, which may inhibit air exchange in the soil as well as the growth of young shoots.

Grazing Management and Hygiene

Herbage utilisation by grazing animals depends on forage acceptability and nutritive value. Animals have a preference for grasses in either tillering or leaf-tube formation stage. The feed value of white clover does not decrease before the full-bloom stage. Highly palatable forage grass for dairy cows is short, thick and weed-free. Cows spend more time and expend more energy consuming very short (<10 cm) and sparse vegetation, while if the grass has grown too tall and is too mature they choose only leaves and tillers and, despite abundant forage, do not consume enough feed. The optimum height of grass for grazing is 12-15 cm on pastures rich in low grasses and white clover, and 15-20 cm on pastures rich in tall grasses.

Pastures reach spring grazing readiness when the soil surface is dry enough and the forage is 10 cm high. Grazing is started on mineral soil pastures with early-maturing swards. Grazing time on the pastures with highly palatable grass of a suitable height can be prolonged by gradual transition from early-maturing

swards to medium-maturing and late-maturing swards. The first grazing cycle should be terminated as soon as the second cycle starts. Forage which is not used for grazing during spring (~20-40% of the whole pasture area) should be harvested and stored as silage or green forage to allow fast grass regrowth for grazing animals. In Estonia, a pasture can usually be grazed 4 to 6 times during summer, depending on onset of grazing, species composition of sward, and weather conditions.

Grazing Methods

Free grazing or continuous stocking is the oldest grazing method for keeping livestock on a single pasture unit not split up into small paddocks, for longer periods or throughout the grazing season. Due to high stocking the palatability declines as the most palatable plants suffer from continuous trampling and are grazed too short. As a result, the plants are not able to store reserve substances to survive winter and die out. Continuous grazing on sown pastures is unsuitable for cattle, and can only be applied for sheep grazing on natural pastures with low stocking rates.

Rotational grazing. Under this system the grazing area is divided into several small paddocks, where cows normally spend 0.5 to 3 days at a time on a scheduled rotational basis. Following the grazing period, animals are moved to another paddock for grazing, and the previously grazed paddock is allowed to rest and regrow. When forage has recovered, reached optimum height and is again suitable for grazing, livestock can move back into the paddock.

For larger herds (over 50 head of cattle) one-day paddock systems are recommended, while for smaller herds (less than 50 heads) 2-day or 3-day paddock systems are suitable. In the latter case, 23-24 or 15-16 paddocks are needed, respectively. The size of one paddock should be 0.2-0.3 ha per 10 cows or 1.0-1.5 ha per 50 cows.

Strip grazing. Grazing of livestock in narrow strips of land, generally behind a frequently moved electric fence, further reduces the grazing time of animals on a paddock, and ensures uniform and efficient utilisation of forage species. The one-day rotational pasture can be divided into more strips to apply a rationed grazing system. A new grazing area should be of sufficient size for at least a 2.5 to 3 hour grazing period. This is the length of the cattle grazing-resting cycle, during which they should not be disturbed by providing them with fresh pasture. On a basis of grazing time and length of grazing-resting cycle, the daily grazing area of cows should be divided into 3 strips.

To obtain a higher grass utilisation coefficient, cattle can be given a fresh strip of pasture before being moved to a cowshed. In subsequent grazing, hungry cows will return to the same pasture to ensure the most effective use of forage. Applying the daily rationed grazing system requires the routine to be established in spring and maintained throughout the summer.

Fencing of pastures. Fences can be used on a permanent or temporary basis. Permanent fences are used on pastures and roadways for livestock. Permanent fences can also be used in paddock fencing, but from the point of view of grazing management and pasture care, especially in the case of strip grazing, mobile electric fences are preferable. Width of the roadway for livestock depends on the livestock numbers, but even in the case of a small herd the roadway should enable a tractor with fertiliser spreader or grass mower to pass to a paddock. Thus, the livestock roadway track should be 4-6 m in width. The same width applies for gates to each paddock, in the nearest corner to a shed.

Pasture Care

The first task in spring pasture care is harrowing using a special grass harrow. This breaks up and scatters dung patches, molehills and suchlike to level the soil surface in a pasture. If needed, piles of animal manure and molehills can also be levelled in summer and at the end of the grazing season.

Good pasture management requires mowing of ungrazed herbage 2-3 days after grazing. Low value and noxious plant species, over-mature grasses, and herbage growing in dung and urine patches remain uneaten. Grass cutting helps to control the spread of unfavourable plant species via seeds, prevents overmaturation of valuable pasture plants, and contributes to the uniformity of grass growth, thus maintaining herbage acceptability. To be well maintained, the pasture should be mowed 3 times per summer.

Grazing of Different Livestock Species

Dairy cows are very selective grazers and only the best quality pasture herbage is eaten. The most preferable forages for cattle are sown pasture swards rich in low grasses and legumes, and swards rich in tall grasses. Grass on improved natural pastures is also an adequate forage for dairy cattle.

Dairy cattle pastures should be on moderately moist soil and be located in the immediate neighbourhood of farms. Long distances (> 2 km) to the pasture and back can cause a 20% decrease in daily milk yield. Taking into consideration the seasonality of herbage growth on mineral and peat soil, two-thirds of the pasture area should be on mineral soil and one-third on peat soil to minimise the negative effects of mid-summer drought periods and cool late-summer weather.

The grazing area requirement depends on forage yield and forage requirement of cows. Depending on milk yield and body weight, a dairy cow needs 60-80 kg pasture grass per day. The average grazing area per adult cow should be 0.5 ha. The optimum supply of mature forage grasses and legumes before each grazing is 6-8 tonnes/ha.

Paddocks for cows should be square or rectangular in shape. It should be borne in mind that depending on breed and forage yield, a dairy cow spends 6-12 h/d grazing, 6-9 h/d lying and ruminating, 1-3 h/d walking on pasture, 1-2 h/d standing and ruminating, and 0.2-0.4 h/d drinking water. Cattle do most of their grazing in early morning and late afternoon. At noon and after sunset, cows graze for only a short time. Besides grass forage, high-yielding dairy cows need 100-250 g concentrate supplement per kg milk yield.

During the grazing period, dairy cows also need roughage rich in dry matter. This is of particular importance during the 10-12 days of early spring transition from cowshed to pasture, and from grazing to cowshed in the autumn. Abrupt spring transition from fibre-rich winter feed to low-fibre pasture forage causes changes in digestive tract microflora, which induce diarrhoea and other symptoms in cows. As a rule, health disturbances have a negative impact on milk yield, milk fat content and body weight gain of animals.

During the grazing season, cows must have a freely available supply of clean, fresh water, which affects forage consumption as well as milk yield. If adequate fresh water is available, dairy cows will consume approximately 40 to 80 (maximum 100) litres a day.

Young cattle are not as selective as adult cows with regard to pasture herbage. Young cattle do not consume high-yielding sown pasture grass as effectively as dairy cows. They prefer swards rich in low grasses of sown pastures or swards growing on improved natural pastures. Grazing of young cattle contributes to more effective development of their performance traits, hardens the body and improves their overall health. Young cattle should be grazed in paddocks located some distance away from dairy cows in order to avoid disturbing the dairy herd and to prevent damage to paddock fences. Furthermore, grazing of cows and young cattle on separate pastures reduces the spread of animal diseases.

The land area required to provide adequate herbage for young cattle is 0.15-0.25 ha per animal. The pasture herbage requirement of an animal over one year of age is 30-40 kg per day, and for an animal less than one year of age 15-25 kg per day. Female and male young cattle should be grazed on separate pastures. Subdividing the pasture area into 8-10 paddocks is recommended provided that young cattle are moved from paddock to paddock every 3-4 days. Before the grazing period, young cattle are grouped according to their age as follows: less than one year, 1-1.5 years, over 1.5 years.

Grazing is essential for the normal growth of *calves*. Calves should be grazed in the neighbourhood of the cowsheds on dry or moderately moist fertile soils. On damp and cold loamy soil pastures, calves are often prone to illnesses. Various supplementary feeds should be provided during the grazing period. Calves should be kept in a cowshed when it is cold and rainy.

Calves prefer to graze swards rich in low grasses of sown pastures that are 10-15 cm tall. The grazing land requirement per calf is 0.08-0.1 ha. Pasture herbage may cover 30-60% of the calf's feed requirement, i.e. 10-15 kg of grass per calf per day. The pasture area should be subdivided into 8-12 paddocks, with calves moved from one paddock to another every 3 to 4 days. At the beginning of the grazing season calves are grouped according to their age: 1-2, 2-4, 4-6 and over 4 months.

Sheep have the lowest grazing selectivity in what they consume and tend to eat almost all grasses, clovers and herbs. They prefer swards rich in low grasses of sown pastures or swards growing on natural pastures. Pastures for sheep should be located on moderately moist or dry mineral soils. Sheep grazed on damp soil are prone to illness. The grazing area requirement per mature sheep is 0.1 ha. During the grazing season, pasture herbage can completely satisfy the nutritional requirements of sheep. Estimated daily pasture forage consumption of mature sheep is 15-20 kg and that of lambs 2-3 kg. The sheep pasture should be subdivided by use of permanent or temporary electric fences into 10-15 paddocks, with sheep grazing a paddock for 2-3 days. Sheep may spend 24 hours a day grazing. Where pastures are not in the immediate neighbourhood of sheep sheds, sheep shelters should be built. At the onset of the grazing season, sheep should be grouped as follows: (1) ewes with lambs; (2) barren ewes and yearling sheep; (3) rams.

Horses are grazed either in 5-8 paddocks located close to the stables, or post-grazed in cattle paddocks. Horses consume the pasture herbage left uneaten by dairy cows and other animals, thus minimising the need for post-grazing topping of pastures. Horses have a preference for more mature pasture herbage. Grazing is of particular importance for young horses, which, besides pasture forage, also need continuous movement to harden and toughen them up. Mares in early and late lactation are also good foragers on pastures. It should be noted, however, that horses have a grazing behaviour that leaves a relatively large quantity of herbage uneaten due to them avoiding manure-contaminated forage. Their manure tends to accumulate in certain places, which constitute on average 10-40% of the paddock area.

Horse paddocks should be located on mineral soils and have a smooth solid surface to avoid leg injuries. The latter occur more frequently when horses are grazed on peat soils and tufted swards. The estimated pasture area requirement of an adult horse is 0.4-0.5 ha, and that of young horse 0.2-0.3 ha. A horse pasture should be divided into 8-12 paddocks, where horses are grazed on the same area for 3-4 days. A young horse can eat 30-40 kg of pasture forage per day, while an adult horse and a mare with foals can consume 50-60 kg. Horses are divided into the following grazing groups: (1) mares with foals; (2) young horses; (3) barren mares.

Pig grazing is practised in outdoor production systems for young pigs and breeding swine. Wise use of pasture can significantly lower feed costs. Pigs prefer low-fibre herbage consisting of nearly 70% clovers, and 30% smooth meadow grass and meadow fescue. Young pigs can get 20-40% of their nutritional needs from pasture herbage and barren sows as much as 50%. The estimated herbage requirement is 5-15 kg per pig per day. Swine pastures should be located in the immediate neighbourhood of piggeries, on moderately moist fertile soils. An adequate space for a sow with piglets is 0.18-0.2 ha, and for a young pig 0.1 ha. Swine pasture should be divided into 8-10 paddocks. Pigs should be grazed in the same paddock for 3-4 days.

Chickens, turkeys and geese are excellent foragers, and it is reasonable to keep them on an open-air individual pasture near the poultry farm. When grazed in cattle paddocks, they reduce the herbage acceptability by leaving their dung across the pasture and impair the clovers by too short grazing. Pasture vegetation supplies approximately 60% of the nutritional needs of poultry during summer. Highly suitable forage crops for poultry are low-fibre swards rich in legumes and low grasses. An adequate stocking density is one goose or turkey per 10 m^2 and one chicken per 1.5-2 m^2. Poultry pasture should be divided into 15-20 paddocks, with fowls grazed in the same paddock for 1.5-2 days. The daily pasture vegetation requirement is 1-2 kg per chicken and 2-4 kg per goose and turkey. Net fencing (height 1-1.5 m) should be used for poultry.

Parasite Control in Grazing Ruminants

Ruminants pick up infective larvae of parasites by grazing contaminated pastures. Intestinal helminths affect intensive sheep production in damp soils, being even a more significant limiting factor than the poor productivity of grasslands (Frame, 1994). Ewes and lambs mostly suffer from gastrointestinal helminthiasis; typical symptoms are indigestion, weakness, anaemia and extenuation. Severe infection, followed by gastroenteritis, causes considerable productivity losses or even mortality in lambs. During

spring and summer grazing, animals become infected with larvae of helminths when grazing contaminated pasture herbage or drinking water from small water bodies. The control of gut worms from the genus *Nematodirus* is problematic since the eggs deposited in pastures with faecal matter stay inactive for extended periods, whereas in summer the hatched larvae become infectious within a couple of weeks (Frame, 1994; Mägi, 2006).

Productivity loss due to helminth infections can be substantially reduced through implementation of effective disease control strategies. An optimum grazing system along with effective environment-saving dosing of anthelminthics should be applied. Distribution of helminthoses is highly regional. It depends on the climatic conditions in various agro-ecological zones and the production system used. The helminth infection rate and disease outbreak risk can be substantially reduced by applying appropriate pasture management systems, e.g. by using pasture rotation – dividing pastures into parcels of land (three more or less equal parts) and moving the animals from one to another on a yearly basis: (1) sheep pasture; (2) cattle pasture; (3) grass cut for hay and silage (zero grazing), or a growing one-year crops. The objective is to avoid putting the animals back into the same field until the risk of infection has diminished. The role of growing grass for silage or a one-year crop in the rotation cycle on pastures is to prevent worm transmission from sheep to cattle and vice versa. Ewes and lambs should not be grazed on the same pastures where lambs or hoggets have been grazed the previous year.

Different control strategies can be implemented in different situations to prevent infections, however, success cannot always be guaranteed. For instance, eggs of gut worms of the genus *Nematodirus* have been shown to survive on pastures in England for several years and the hatched larvae can infect the calves. Therefore, *Nematodirus* from cattle can pose a risk also to sheep despite the use of the above-mentioned three-field or 'clean' grazing. Nevertheless, clean grazing reduces both helminth infection and the need for anthelminthics to control parasitism. Long-term data on clean grazing systems in England have demonstrated benefits of the system from several aspects (Frame, 1994): (1) stocking rate increases, i.e. more ewes kept on the same area; (2) higher lamb performance rate; (3) reduced need for chemicals to control parasitic diseases; (4) better pasture utilisation by cattle and sheep.

Recent studies have demonstrated that in Estonia, cattle are more susceptible to parasites than sheep. Besides intestinal parasites, sheep can also be infected by lungworms. Parasites are picked up more frequently on natural pastures than on sown pastures. All farm animals should be coprologically investigated before the onset of spring grazing period and before autumnal confinement in the barn. Anthelminthic treatment of infected herds, i.e. when eggs of parasites are found in faeces, should be performed (Mägi, 2006). Control measures against helminthoses involve better nutrition, better pasture and grazing management, hygienic natural water bodies or provision of safe well water supplies, and rotational grazing.

Relationship between Livestock Nutrition and Excreted Nitrogen and Phosphorus Content

41

Allan Kaasik
Estonian University of Life Sciences, Tartu, Estonia

The conflict between intensive animal rearing and the environment is revealed in manure management. Intensive and simultaneously environmentally friendly animal farming is primarily based on an appropriate feeding strategy by which it is possible to affect the amount of excreted manure and nutrient content.

Livestock and poultry do not use feed nutrients entirely for their maintenance and production synthesis, so wastes are discharged from the body with faeces and urine (Figure 41.1).

In intensive livestock management, which aims at achieving high production (profit), nutrients originating from manure frequently become a source of pollution. The main risk factor for pollution of the environment is excreted nitrogen – its emission to the atmosphere in the form of ammonia and nitrogen oxides, leaching as nitrates into groundwater and surface water – and also phosphorus and potassium leaching into surface water and groundwater. Reducing the nutrient content of the diet can decrease the content of excreted nutrients (N, P) and thus also the risk of nutrient emissions (odour emissions, leaching) to the environment. The nutrient content of diets can be reduced, simultaneously covering the animals' needs, by improving the digestibility of the feed and by balancing the concentration of essential nutrients in the diet, thus improving the efficiency of the body's protein synthesis.

For both pigs and poultry, a 1% reduction in the protein content of the diet leads to a 10% reduction in the nitrogen content of excreta.

In several EU Member States (Belgium, Denmark, France and Germany) where agriculture is responsible for high environmental pressure, the minimum and maximum limits for the nutrient content of pig and poultry feeds (concentrates) are legally regulated. Farmers in these four Member States are also obliged to keep a record of their nutrient (N, P) applications at farm level.

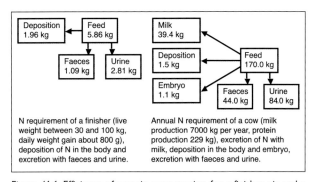

N requirement of a finisher (live weight between 30 and 100 kg, daily weight gain about 800 g), deposition of N in the body and excretion with faeces and urine.

Annual N requirement of a cow (milk production 7000 kg per year, protein production 229 kg), excretion of N with milk, deposition in the body and embryo, excretion with faeces and urine.

Figure 41.1. Efficiency of protein consumption for a finisher pig and a dairy cow.

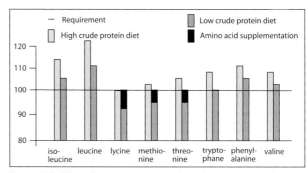

Figure 41.2. Effect of synthetic amino acid supplementation on diet protein content.

Multiphase Feeding Strategies

Multiphase feeding strategies aim to cover the needs of animals/poultry of all ages and production groups. Precision feeding at different stages of age and production enables the excreted nutrient content to be reduced significantly (EC, 2003).

a) Poultry farming. In the diet of layers, concentrates with different levels of Ca and P are used according to the stage of age and egg production. A uniform group of animals and a gradual transition from one feed to the next are required.

In broiler farming, multiphase feeding strategies aim at optimising the feed conversion ratio. Frequently, a three-phase feeding strategy is used, as broilers show a considerable change in their nutritional requirements with age. Applying a slightly restricted feeding regime in the first phase results in more efficient growth at a later stage. At the same time, proteins and amino acids must be fed at a high level and balanced. In the second phase the digestive tract of the birds is fully developed and they can convert maximum amounts of feeds. The proportion of energy-rich feeds in the diet is increased. In the third phase, the protein and amino acid content are increased, but the energy concentration remains at the level of the second phase. In all phases, Ca-P balance remains the same, but the concentration is reduced according to the age of the broilers.

b) Pig farming. Phase feeding for finishers consists of giving 2 to 4 concentrates with different contents of nutrients to pigs with weights 25 to 100 kg. In high-tech pig farms multiphase feeding strategies are used where the content of amino acids, energy and minerals in the diet is changed according to the growth of pigs. For sows, phase feeding consists of giving at least two different concentrates: one for lactation and one for gestation. In fewer cases, a specific feed might be given before farrowing.

Use of Amino Acids in Low-protein Diets

The aim of feeding synthetic amino acids is to reduce the use of expensive protein feeds in poultry and pig diets, but also to meet animal requirements (EC, 2003). It should be considered that natural feeds do not contain essential amino acids in the correct proportions. Due to that, compound feeds with excessive amino acids increase the excretion of nutrients, especially that of N (Figure 41.2).

Table 41.1. Relationship between dietary protein, nitrogen excretion and ammonia emissions for finisher pigs.

Parameters	Effect of 1 point reduction of dietary protein, %
Total nitrogen excreted	- 10
Ammonia content in slurry	- 10
Ammonia emission	- 10
Water consumption (ad libitum)	- 2…- 3
Slurry volume	- 3…- 5

Table 41.2. Content of total phosphorus and phytate-phosphorus in selected plant feedstuffs.

Feedstuff	Total P, %	Phytate-P, %
Maize	0.28	0.19
Wheat	0.33	0.22
Barley	0.37	0.22
Triticale	0.37	0.25
Rye	0.36	0.22
Sorghum	0.27	0.19
Wheat bran	1.16	0.97
Rice bran	1.71	1.10
Soybean meal	0.61	0.32
Peanut meal	0.68	0.32
Rapeseed meal	1.12	0.40
Sunflower meal	1.00	0.44
Peas	0.38	0.17

Some currently produced and supplemented amino acids are lysine (L-Lysine), methionine (DL-Methionine and analogues), threonine (L-Threonine) and tryptophan (L-Tryptophan).

The effects of using low-protein diets (supplemented with synthetic amino acids) in poultry farming are the following:

The excretion of N decreases by 10% per 1% reduction in dietary protein for finisher pigs (Table 41.1). It is possible to reduce the protein level in feed by up to 2% for all age and production categories. However, it is necessary to add four essential amino acids (lysine, methionine, threonine and tryptophan) to prevent growth reduction.

Use of Phytase in Pig and Poultry Diets

Phytate-phosphorus (compound of phytanic acid and phosphorus which is normally present in plant feed mate-rials) is not available to pigs and poultry as they lack the appropriate enzyme activity in their digestive tract (Table 41.2). This leads to large amounts of non-digestible phosphorus being excreted, posing a great risk to the environment. The digestibility of P can be improved (reducing its content in the diet and excreta) by the following methods (EC, 2003):

- Adding the enzyme phytase,
- Increasing the availability of P in plant feed materials,
- Reducing the use of inorganic phosphates in feeds.

Four phytase preparations are currently authorised as feed additives in the European Union (Directive 70/524/EEC).

Effects of using phytase in pig diets:

- Improvement of plant phosphorus digestibility by 20-30% in piglets and 15-20% in growers, finishers and sows
- A 0.1% reduction in phosphorus in the diet through using phytase results in a reduction in phosphorus excretion of 35-40% for piglets, 25-35% for growers and finishers, and 20-30% for sows.

Effects of using phytase in poultry diets:

FACT BOX 3

A reduction in dietary protein content of 1% results in a reduction in N excretion of 10% for layers and 5-10% for broilers.

Low protein diets contribute to a reduction in ammonia emissions from poultry houses. A 2% reduction in crude protein in the broiler ration results in a 24% reduction in ammonia emissions.

Water consumption of poultry decreases. When the protein level in broiler diet is decreased by 3%, there is an 8% reduction in water consumption.

Table 41.3. Comparison of feed phosphates used in poultry diets.

Feed phosphate	Digestibility, %	Inclusion rate, %	Inclusion rate of P, g	Absorbed P, g	Excreted P, g
Defluorinated phosphate	59	1.56	28.0	16.5	11.5
Monocalcium phosphate	84	0.87	19.6	16.5	3.1

- Improvement of plant phosphorus digestibility by 20-30% in broilers, layers and turkeys
- A 0.1% reduction in total P in the feed through using phytase results in a reduction in phosphorus excretion of more than 20% for layers and broilers.

Highly Digestible Inorganic Feed Phosphates

In pig and poultry diets several inorganic phosphates with different chemical composition (different P content and digestibility) are used (EU Directive 96/25/EC; (EC, 2003)). The inclusion of highly digestible feed phosphates in animal feed will result in lower phosphorus levels in the feed and thus a reduction in nutrient excretion into the environment. Table 41.3 presents some comparative results for different inorganic feed phosphates used in poultry rations.

Inclusion of highly digestible inorganic feed phosphates in pig diets is also efficient.

Other Feed Additives

Other feed additives that are added in small amounts to the feed of poultry and pigs are (EC, 2003):

- Enzymes,
- Micro-organism cultures

As a result of using enzymes, the feed conversion rate of the pigs and poultry improves (less feed is needed to achieve the same rate of growth) and the amount of excreted nutrients is reduced. A 3% reduction in total nutrients excreted by pigs (as a general approximation) can be obtained; for poultry the corresponding reduction is approximately 5%.

Cattle Diets with Reduced Protein and Cattle Diet Balancing

The peculiarities of bovine digestive organs require the protein content of the diet on a dry matter basis to be significantly lower than that of monogastric animals and poultry. Due to diverse microbe populations in the forestomach, ruminants are able to consume large amounts of grass feeds rich in fibre. Inclusion of amino acids in the diet of cattle is not effective, as ruminal microbes are able to synthesise from dietary nitrogen those amino acids which are present in low concentrations in the rumen or not present at all. Consequently, the content of excreted nitrogen can be regulated mainly by balancing the diet protein content, nitrogen compounds available to ruminal microbes in synthesis (ruminally soluble and degradable protein), and energy (carbohydrates). Reducing the dietary crude protein content from 19% to 13% on a dry matter basis can reduce ammonia emissions from excreta three-fold (Frank et al., 2002; Swensson, 2003). Besides adjusting dietary protein content, excreted nitrogen losses can also be reduced by regulating the amounts of ruminally soluble, degradable and undegradable protein. Ammonia emissions from cattle excreta can be mostly reduced by decreasing the content of rumen-degradable protein (van Duinkerken et al., 2005; Reynal et al., 2005).

Part G

Animal Welfare

Authors: Andres Aland, Bo Algers, Michael C. Appleby, David Arney, Charlotte Berg, Harry Blokhuis, Ruth C. Newberry, Jaak Panksepp, Oriol Ribó and Bernard Rollin

Coeditors and Coordinating Authors: Allan Kaasik and Borje Gustafsson

What is Animal Welfare and How is it Assessed?

42

David Arney
Estonian University of Life Sciences, Tartu, Estonia

Defined by Broom (1986): *The welfare of an animal is its state as regards to its attempts to cope with its environment.*

So, what does this mean? Animals have to cope with a complex environment, such as high temperature, hunger, fear of predation. Animals have a range of means of coping with these stressors, principally through the adrenal stress response. This is the same mechanism of response – the flight or fight response – irrespective of the type of stressor. Increased respiration rate, heart rate, increased blood supply to the muscles, erection of hair, pupil dilation. These physiological changes are linked to behavioural responses that ameliorate the stressors: move to a cooler shaded area, find a food source, escape from the predator.

Stress is therefore an entirely normal response to challenges from the environment, and animals are able to cope with small amounts of stress, and with stressors from which they can escape. Stress is therefore not necessarily a cause of poor welfare, but distress does have a negative effect on welfare.

However, the animal may be unable to cope. There may be no shaded area, no food available, and flight from the predator may not be possible. The animal's welfare, and wellbeing will then be compromised, and this leads

to a chronic stress response, related to raised levels of cortisol. In this case the animal's fitness may be reduced, it may not grow and it may fail to reproduce. We can rank the state of welfare from poor to good, using a range of measures, rather than all or nothing.

Measures that are commonly used include:

- Fertility; but some species, notably dogs, can reproduce prolifically in very poor conditions. Indeed, almost by definition domesticated animals will do so, as they have been selected to produce large numbers of offspring in captivity.
- Disease; but this, and the following two on the list, do not necessarily indicate poor conditions.
- Morbidity.
- Mortality.
- Levels of stress hormones.
- Behavioural indicators; but these may be learnt and not indicate current welfare conditions.

Individual parameters may be caused by incidental factors, unrelated to the welfare conditions prevailing on an animal unit. Measurements should be collected to produce a portfolio of evidence rather than reliance on a single measure. The first four of these are simply a matter of

Figure 42.1. On this farm several cows were observed standing in the drinking trough. This may have been a means of cooling inflamed hooves. These were treated and the behaviour ceased. Photo: M. Ots.

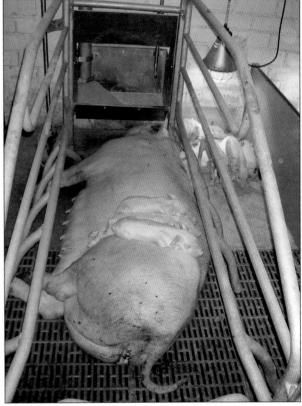

Figure 42.2. Piglets do not normally lie on the sow's belly. If they do so this indicates that the sow may have a medical problem. Photo: A. Pavlenko.

record. The capture of stress hormones is made difficult as the nature of collecting them can itself be stress-inducing. However, residues can be collected from faeces and saliva as well as directly from blood.

Preferred methods of assessing welfare are behavioural measures, as they are:

- Easy to use
- Non-invasive
- Non-intrusive
- Expressions of emotions
- Reflect first attempts to cope
- More sensitive than injury or disease

Behavioural measures include:

- Abnormal behaviour (Figure 42.1).
- Comparison with normal behaviour (such as time budgets). The researcher will need to know the normal behaviour profile in order to compare differences (Figure 42.2).
- Incidents of aggressive behaviour (Figure 42.3)
- Stereotypies: repetitive patterns of behaviour with no obvious function (Figures 42.4 and 42.5).
- Increased vocalisations
- Choice tests

Problems of behavioural measures of stress:

- Not always reliable: some of the abnormal behaviours may be learnt behaviours resulting from previous stress events that are no longer extant. Example: cribbiting by a horse may be a learnt behaviour from a previous stable.
- Human interpretation of the cause or purpose of some of these behaviours may be inaccurate. We can guess, but our perception is limited by our human experience.
- Individual animals will respond differently to the same source of stress. For example, individual animals have different temperature thresholds, as do individual humans.

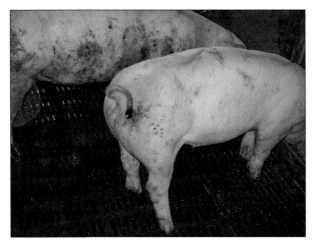

Figure 42.3. Tail biting, a common outcome of aggressive behaviour shown by pigs in confined, barren housing conditions. Photo: A. Pavlenko.

Figure 42.4. Sterotypic behaviour; tongue-rolling shown by a housed dairy cow. Photo: A. Pavlenko.

- Stereotypies may be a method of coping with stress: Wiepkema et al. (1987) showed that veal calves performing stereotypies more often had fewer abomasal ulcers than the other calves.

However, stereotypies are often observed in animals in poor housing conditions. Broom and Johnson (1993) proposed the following assessment tool (See fact box 1).

Choice tests involve giving animals a choice between two or more environments or resources, such as offering dairy cows the choice of entering a cubicle area or a straw yard. The assumption is that the animal will choose the option that is in its best interest. Problems with choice tests include:

- The choice may satisfy some transitory need or preference. An animal may make the choice in its short-term interest at the expense of its long-term interest.
- Individual animals may have individual preferences not indicative of the group as a whole.
- Choices may change over time: age of the animal, time of day, stage of reproductive cycle.
- A choice may be preferred, but actually be poor for welfare: e.g. the choice of a sugar-rich food by rats does not indicate that these should form the diet of the housed rat.

- The choices offered are relative. They do not indicate good or poor welfare, only that one of the options may be better than the other. Both options may be good or bad for the animal's welfare.

Choice tests can be refined to indicate the strength of preference for one option over another. This can help to determine whether a resource is a necessity or a luxury. The less favoured option can be baited with a desirable resource (often food). The favoured option can be encumbered with difficulty or unpleasantness (the length of a darkened walkway in the case of the dairy cow, or the length of a cat urine-soaked walkway in the case of the laboratory mouse). Animals can be trained to use an operant device that can be calibrated to altered levels of work required by the animal to choose one option over another.

The UK farm animal welfare council suggested five freedoms that should be satisfied for an animal to be regarded as being in a state of good welfare. These were first formulated in 1979, principally regarding farm animals, but there is a general consensus of agreement among animal welfare scientists that they are a useful guide to assessing the welfare of an animal. The five freedoms remain the basis on which the European Union frames its animal welfare policy. The five freedoms are:

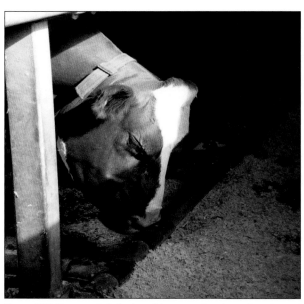

Figure 42.5. Stereotypic behaviour; Nose-pressing shown by a housed dairy cow. Photo: A. Pavlenko.

1. **Freedom from hunger and thirst**, access to fresh water and a diet for full health and vigour.
2. **Freedom from discomfort**, an appropriate environment with shelter, and comfortable rest areas.
3. **Freedom from pain**, injury and disease, prevention or rapid treatment.
4. **Freedom from fear and distress**, conditions and treatment which avoid mental suffering.
5. **Freedom to express normal behaviour**, adequate space and facilities, company of animal's own kind.
(European Commission, 2007)

More recently, Bartussek (2001) has proposed an animal needs index that uses a scoring system for a variety of factors, leading to a sum that is designed to represent a meaningful welfare assessment of housing conditions. There are five broad sections to this system of assessment:

1. Possibility of mobility
2. Social contact
3. Condition of flooring
4. Stable climate (including light and noise)
5. Quality of stockman's care

However, this system does not seem to have been adopted much outside its native Austria.

There is a method for determining the priorities of animals for resources through measuring their motivation for access to the resources. The concept is derived from human behaviour expressed by the economic theory of demand function (Dawkins, 1983; Hursh, 1984). In the context of animal behaviour, 'cost' is the amount of time spent on an activity or work the animal is prepared to do to achieve the resource. For example; rats pushing a lever or chickens or mink pushing through an increasingly weighted gate to access nesting material. This demand may be described as elastic if the animal adjusts the price it is prepared to pay for differing quantities of the resource, such as space. As the amount of work, or cost, increases, the animal becomes less prepared to pay the cost in order to achieve the resource. Plotting the outcomes on a logarithmic scale produces a straight line, the demand function. Resources producing this kind of response are typically described as luxury resources. In contrast, an inelastic demand is for an essential resource, such as food. Changing the amount of work the animal has to do to achieve an essential resource has little effect – the price will continue to be paid. In addition, the expenditure an animal is prepared to make, in amount of time or work, can be used to rank the importance of a range of resources. The steepness of the demand function gradient indicates the degree of motivation. The resource may be the opportunity to perform a behavioural activity, such as digging, swimming or even rest. Criticisms of this method include: the artificial nature of the test, the influence of prior deprivation, prior experience and external factors, including the time of day.

Conclusions

The welfare of animals concerns not simply stress, experienced by an animal, but its ability to manage stress, whether it be physical or mental stress. Animals in the wild and in captivity are exposed to many and varied stressors. If the stressor continues despite an animal's efforts to remove it, we can consider the animal to be in a poor state of welfare. Welfare can be ranked; there is not simply good or bad welfare, but many gradations of wellbeing. We can measure and record many factors that can indicate poor or good welfare, and the more measures we take the more likely we are to make an accurate assessment. Behavioural measures are particularly good as they are, among other things, relatively easy to use, are (or ought to be) non-intrusive, show an animal's first responses to cope and are sensitive. However, caution should be used with such measures as they can be misleading to a human observer. Stereotypies can also indicate poor welfare, and particularly a poor environment. Letting an animal choose from options, using a choice test, can give us clues as to the relative preference of the options offered, and this can be refined to include positive and negative outcomes to assess the strength of preference of one option over another. The five freedoms are an enduring guide to the assessment of welfare, but other systems are also in use. An index system of scoring welfare factors and deriving an overall index of welfare has been developed, though there is some doubt as to whether an animal's welfare can be adequately expressed by a single number.

Animal Minds
Do Animals have Emotional Lives?

Jaak Panksepp
Washington State University
Pullman, Washington, USA

Do animals have emotional lives? Most intelligent people, not involved in logical-philosophical nuances and the rules of scientific evidence, would respond 'obviously they do'. Most neuroscientists who study animal behaviour (i.e., behavioural neuroscientists) are considerably more sceptical; many would claim that anthropomorphic reasoning is not an appropriate starting point for any scientific question. In fact, many brain scientists believe that issues such as internal experiences in other animals are not questions that science can ever answer, since we have no direct empirical access to the experiences of other animals. Of course we have no such access to other human minds, unless we believe what they say. Thus one common critique is that, since animals cannot symbolically communicate their feelings, it is the responsibility of those who believe in the existence of emotional feelings in animals (like most reasonable people) to empirically validate their thesis in some scientifically credible way. Of course, without incontrovertible evidence either way, the assumption that animals have no emotional feelings has no greater intrinsic truth-value than the claim that

they do. That, of course, is the path of perpetual agnosticism, with different intellectual camps arguing for their beliefs.

Fortunately the situation is not that bleak. Many investigators recognise that if certain processes in nature (e.g. gravity and animal feelings) cannot be observed with direct objective measures, they must be tested using indirect measures, which is the time-tested scientific tool for evaluating many kinds of theoretical predictions. Since there are no absolute proofs in deep-science, what matters in such difficult situations is the weight of evidence for one position or another.

Because of advances in brain research, a credible scientific argument can finally be made for the thesis that animals do have emotional feelings. Abundant indirect scientific data currently supports that claim. Although the weight of scientific evidence may have been insufficient in the 19th century, and even most of the 20th century, we can now be confident that various affective feelings do exist in all mammals and birds. The most robust evidence comes from the discovery that all such species studied so far do have brain systems for generating various feeling of 'goodness' or 'badness' that can be monitored through their behavioural choices.

The most compelling and most informative evidence comes from the study of emotional responses to specific kinds of brain manipulations such as electrical or chemical stimulation of specific parts of the brain. When given control of the stimulation – to turn it on or off – animals clearly indicate that they either like or dislike such forms of brain stimulation. They typically also exhibit distinct types of instinctual emotional responses to such stimulation. This evidence is supplemented by the kinds of emotional vocalisations animals make in various arousing situations, which are not all that different from emotional sounds made by humans. For instance, the experience of pain can cause shrieking and crying, and the stronger the pain stimulus, the stronger the vocal response. It is the same in animals and certainly young humans. And when we artificially activate such brain circuits, including ones that generate spontaneous anger and fear responses, animals rapidly learn to turn off the stimulation. A similar phenomenon has been found in the experience of joy. When humans feel joy, they laugh, and many animals also make laughing-type sounds when they play, or when they are tickled. When allowed to self-stimulate brain systems that generate such happy sounds, rats readily do so. The same goes for brain circuits that generate foraging, sexual and maternal behaviours. Further, all other mammals learn to vigorously self-inject drugs that are addictive in humans, probably because they produce similar desirable feelings. Such findings would be very hard to explain if animals had no feelings. Of course similar types of feelings cannot be identical across species, since nature is adept at building diversities of form and function. Still, the weight of evidence currently indicates that many other animals do possess quite similar brain mechanisms that mediate a large number of emotions easily recognised in humans.

A more strictly behavioural analysis has long been consistent with this thesis. If animals had no internal feelings, it would be hard to put together a coherent story explaining why they make various choices when confronted by various environmental options. Animals select warm locations when their body temperature is below normal, and colder locations when their core temperature is above

normal. They exhibit behaviours very similar to those that humans exhibit in response to stimuli easily described as being pleasant or unpleasant. Of course, sceptical behavioural neuroscientists might respond that we already have concepts such as 'rewards' and 'punishments'– things we do to animals that can modify rates of learned behaviour. Some would say that claiming that these events feel good or bad adds nothing to our knowledge base. That is not correct. If the ancient brain mechanisms for affective feelings are evolutionarily related, and hence similar, in humans and other animals, we can finally begin to understand the deep neural nature of human feelings by studying the apparently homologous neuroanatomies and neurochemistries of these systems in animal models. This would be a great advance in our understanding of the human brain and mind. Thus, it should come as no surprise that most brain areas that mediate approach and avoidance behaviours in animals also generate positive and negative feelings in humans.

Although some doubt is bound to continue about such difficult scientific issues, we should remember that the goal of science is not to resolve philosophical-logical dilemmas, which are often created by the way we use language, but to describe nature as it really is. The existence of feelings in other animals is also rich with ethical implications. The ways in which we treat animals are based in part on their abilities to experience pain, hunger, and thirst. If we respect the existence of anger and fear, desire and joy in animals, these feelings would also be considered in our treatment of animals; we could not treat them as if they had no such feelings. Thus it is important for intelligent, scientifically-informed people to consider all the evidence in order to determine where they should stand on such important animal mind and well-being issues.

At present, the most compelling scientific evidence about the nature of animal emotions comes from behavioural brain research, where specific brain systems are manipulated. So how did scientists begin to empirically discover how emotional feelings are created within brains? The most important lines of research have used localised electrical and chemical stimulation of the brain. Walter Hess, who received the Nobel Prize in 1949, initiated his most influential work starting in the 1930s. He found that localised electrical stimulation of cats could transform them from friendly animals into intensely angry creatures. Eventually various distinct forms of attack were identified, the main two being an angry-emotional attack and a methodical stalking-predatory attack. When investigators finally inquired whether animals 'cared' about such stimulation, by asking whether they would turn the stimulation on or off, the answers were clear. Animals would turn off the stimulation that provoked angry 'affective attack' and activate sites that provoked predatory attack. Likewise, animals would terminate stimulation to brain areas that produced fearful behaviours, and would self-stimulate sites that generated exploratory and consummatory (e.g. feeding, drinking and sexual) behaviours.

Activation of many of these emotion-provoking brain sites also promoted conditioned place preferences (animals returning more frequently to places where they had those neurochemical experiences) or conditioned place avoidances. There have also been studies evaluating self-administration of various neurochemicals directly into these brain regions. Taken together, these studies confirm that affective states are organised within primitive regions of the brain that anatomically and neurochemically resemble each other very closely in all mammals.

Various general principles have emerged from this kind of work:

1. A diversity of brain networks for basic emotional instinctual behaviours are situated in ancient brain regions evolutionarily similar (homologous) in all mammals.
2. The lower regions of the brain are more important for generating emotional feelings than the higher regions of the brain.
3. There is a correspondence between brain systems that generate emotional instinctual behavioural responses and the feelings that accompany those states.
4. The basic chemistries for emotional feelings are similar in all mammals. Through a study of these brain systems in animals, we can generate a solid understanding of the basic emotional systems of human beings. This work is also important for the next generation of scientific development in biological psychiatry.

The Basic Affective Circuits of Mammalian Brains

Past work supports the existence of at least seven distinct types of emotional arousal – seven basic types of highly interactive emotional systems – in all mammalian brains (see Panksepp, 1998, for fuller anatomical, neurochemical and behavioural descriptions of these systems). The names of these emotional systems are capitalised to emphasise that specific neural networks (i.e. functionally dedicated emotional systems) exist in the brain. These systems are all situated subcortically, and consist of large transverse networks that interconnect midbrain circuits concentrated in midbrain regions such as the periaqueductal grey and ventral tegmental area, with various basal ganglia nuclei, such as amygdala and nucleus accumbens, as well as cingulate and medial frontal cortex, via pathways that run through the hypothalamus and thalamus. Each system has abundant descending and ascending components that work together in a coordinated fashion to generate various instinctual emotional behaviours as well as the raw feelings normally associated with those behaviours. These systems can be activated by higher brain mechanisms but they can also control how those higher brain mechanisms process information. There is much work left to do before we understand these systems in detail, but there is no longer any doubt that all mammals do have a variety of basic emotional systems that coordinate the autonomic, the behavioural and the raw feeling aspects of emotions. The seven systems that have the most abundant evidence are the following:

The SEEKING/Desire System
For literature overview, see Alcaro et al. (2007) and Panksepp and Moskal (2008). This is a general-purpose appetitive motivational system that may be essential for many other emotional systems to operate effectively. It seems to be a major source of the life-energy that has at times been called 'libido.' It induces animals to be intensely interested in exploring their world and in learning, leads them to become excited when they are about to get what they desire (a pictorial example of this system in action in a cat is depicted in Figure 43.1, and it should be emphasised that predatory behaviour is one manifestation of this system in action in predatory spe-

Figure 43.1. The SEEKING System in action (reprinted Fig 8.6 Panksepp, J. (1998) *Affective Neuroscience*, with the permission of Oxford University Press).

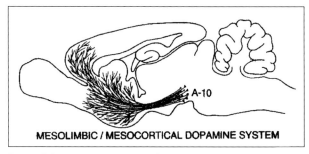

Figure 43.2. Schematic summary of the mesolimbic and mesocortical dopamine system, which energizes the SEEKING urge, on a lateral mid-saggital view of the rat brain. (reprinted Fig 3.6 from Panksepp, J. (1998) *Affective Neuroscience*, with the permission of Oxford University Press).

cies). It eventually allows animals to find and eagerly anticipate all kinds of resources they need for survival, including water, food, warmth or coolness depending on the status of thermoregulatory systems, and their ultimate evolutionary survival need, sex. When fully aroused, the SEEKING urge fills the mind with interest and motivates organisms to move their bodies seemingly effortlessly in search of the things they need, crave and desire. In humans, this system generates and sustains curiosity from the mundane to our highest intellectual pursuits. When this system becomes under-active for various reasons, such as drug withdrawal, chronic helplessness/stress or neural deficits of old age, a form of depression results. When the system becomes spontaneously overactive, which can happen as a result of various drugs, behaviour can become excessive and stereotypical, guided often by psychotic delusions and manic thoughts.

Neuroanatomically, the SEEKING system corresponds to the major self-stimulation system that runs from mid-brain up to the medial frontal cortex (Figure 43.2). Animals will activate this system readily, whether with drugs of abuse such as cocaine or direct electrical or chemical stimulation of the brain (after they have been surgically prepared with the necessary delivery devices, of course). This system has long been misconceptualised

as a 'reward, pleasure or reinforcement system'. Instead, it appears to be a general-purpose neuronal system that coaxes animals and humans to move energetically from where they are presently situated to the places where they can find and consume resources needed for survival. It permits learning by readily assimilating predictive reward relationships in the world. A critically important chemical in this system is dopamine. Dopamine circuits can energise and coordinate the functions of many higher brain areas that mediate planning and foresight and that promote normal states of anticipatory eagerness and apparent purpose in both humans and animals.

The RAGE/Anger System

For literature overview see Panksepp and Zellner (2004) and Siegel (2005). Working in opposition to SEEKING is a system that mediates anger. RAGE is aroused by frustration and attempts to curtail an animal's freedom of action. It has long been known that one can enrage both animals and humans by stimulating very specific circuits of the brain that lie rather close to the trajectory of the FEAR system discussed next. The RAGE system invigorates aggressive behaviours when animals are irritated or restrained and also helps animals defend themselves by arousing fear in their opponents (Figure 43.3). Human anger may get much of its psychic energy from the arousal of this brain system; there are a number of well-documented cases where humans stimulated in these brain regions have exhibited sudden, intense anger attacks, with no external provocation. Key chemistries in

Figure 43.3. The RAGE System in action (reprinted Fig 10.2 in Panksepp, J. (1998) *Affective Neuroscience*, with the permission of Oxford University Press).

Figure 43.4. The FEAR System in action (reprinted Fig 11.2 in Panksepp, J. (1998) *Affective Neuroscience*, with the permission of Oxford University Press).

this system are the neuropeptide Substance P and glutamate, which activate the system, and endogenous opioids, which inhibit the system, but these chemistries (especially glutamate and opioids) also participate in many other emotional responses. Specific medicines to control angry behaviour in humans and animals could presumably be developed through further detailed understanding of this brain circuitry.

The FEAR/Anxiety System

For literature overview, see Panksepp et al. (2010). A coherently operating FEAR circuit was designed during brain evolution to help animals reduce pain and the possibility of destruction. When stimulated intensely, the circuit leads animals to flee as if they are extremely scared. With much weaker stimulation, animals exhibit a freezing response (Figure 43.4), which is also common when animals are placed back into an environment in which they have been hurt or frightened. Humans stimulated in these same brain regions report being engulfed by an intense free-floating anxiety that appears to have no environmental cause. Key chemistries that regulate this system are Neuropeptide Y and Corticotrophin Releasing Factor (CRF); specific anti-anxiety agents such as the benzodiazepines inhibit this system.

The LUST/Sexual Systems

For literature overview, see Pfaff (1999). Sexual urges are mediated by specific brain circuits and chemistries that are overlapping but also quite distinct for males and females (Figure 43.5). They are aroused by male and female sex hormones, which control many brain chemistries including two neuropeptides whose synthesis is strongly controlled by sex hormones: Oxytocin transmission is promoted by oestrogen in females and vasopressin transmission by testosterone in males. These brain chemistries help create gender-specific sexual tendencies. Oxytocin promotes sexual readiness and acceptance postures in females and vasopressin promotes assertiveness, and perhaps jealous behaviours, in males. Distinct male and female sexual circuits are constructed very early in life, and are activated by maturation of gonadal hormones at puberty. Because brain and bodily sex characteristics are independently organised, it is possible for animals that are externally male to have female-specific sexual urges and, likewise, for some to be female in external appearance but to have male sexual urges. Some of the chemistries of sexuality, for instance oxytocin, have been re-used to mediate maternal care – nurturing and social bonding – suggesting that there is an intimate relationship between female sexual rewards and maternal motivations.

The CARE/Maternal Nurturance System

For literature overview, see Numan and Insel, (2003). Brain evolution has provided safeguards to ensure that

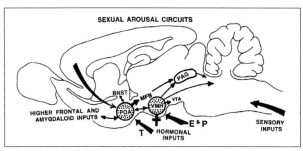

Figure 43.5. Schematic summary of male and female LUST Systems on a saggital depiction of the rat brain. Maternal CARE circuits are anatomically very similar, but sufficiently distinct at a fine neuronal level, suggesting that maternal CARE evolved from pre-existing sexual LUST circuits. (reprinted Fig 12.5 in Panksepp, J. (1998) *Affective Neuroscience*, with the permission of Oxford University Press).

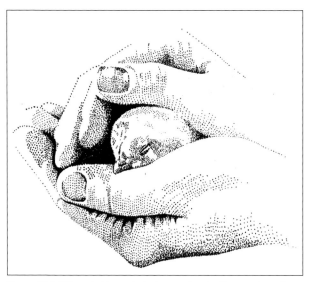

Figure 43.6. When held gently in human hands, distressed newborn chicks exhibit a comfort response consisting of the cessation of vocalisations and eye closure. This social comfort response is partly mediated by release of endogenous brain opioids, since it can be inhibited by administration of opiate receptor antagonists (reprinted Fig 14.9 in Panksepp, J. (1998) *Affective Neuroscience*, with the permission of Oxford University Press).

parents usually the mother take care of offspring. The massive hormonal changes at the end of pregnancy (declining progesterone and increasing oestrogen, prolactin and oxytocin) set the stage for the activation of maternal urges a few days before the young are born. This symphony of hormonal and neurochemical changes, especially the heightened secretions of oxytocin and prolactin, facilitate maternal moods which ensure strong social bonding with the offspring. Similar neurochemicals, especially oxytocin and endogenous opioids, promote infant bonding to the mother. These changes are foundational for one variant of love.

The PANIC/Separation Distress System

For literature overview, see Nelson and Panksepp (1998) and clinical implications in Watt and Panksepp (2009). All young mammals are dependent on parental care, especially maternal care, for survival. Young animals have a powerful emotional system to indicate they are in need of care, as reflected in their intense crying when left in strange places by themselves. These separation calls alert caretakers, mothers typically, to seek out, retrieve and attend to the needs of the offspring. The alleviation of separation distress in young animals can be easily achieved simply by holding them (Figure 43.6). The separation distress system has now been mapped in several species; it is powerfully inhibited by endogenous opioids, oxytocin and prolactin – the major social-attachment, social-bonding chemistries of the mammalian brain. These basic

separation-distress circuits are also aroused during human sadness, which is accompanied by low brain opioid activity. Sudden arousal of this system in humans may contribute to the psychiatric disorder known as 'panic attacks.'

The PLAY/Rough-and-Rumble, Physical Social-Engagement System

For literature overview, see Pellis and Pellis (2009) and clinical implications in Panksepp (2007). Young animals have strong urges for physical play. This takes the form of pouncing on each other, chasing and wrestling (Figure 43.7). These actions can seem outwardly aggressive but they are accompanied by positive affect – an intense social joy. During these activities, rats make abundant high frequency (~50 kHz) chirping sounds that have many features resembling human laughter. It is interesting to note that there seem to be similarities between the subcortical brain circuits that mediate human laughter and play-induced chirping in rats. The most powerful evidence for an evolutionary relationship between positive affect and chirping is the fact that if humans tickle rats, these vocali-

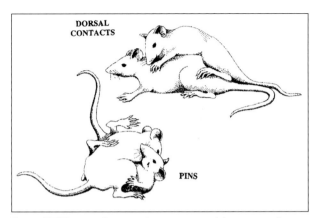

Figure 43.7. Two very frequent play postures in adolescent rats that can be used to quantify the amount of rough-and-tumble play. In carnivores and omnivores, the play is very heavily somatosensory (wrestling), suggesting it prepares animals for adult hunting and energetic social encounters, while in herbivores play is characterised more by running and prancing (reprinted Fig 15.2 in Panksepp, J. (1998) *Affective Neuroscience*, with the permission of Oxford University Press).

sations often go up to maximal levels, and young animals rapidly return to the individual human and attempt to solicit more tickling. In contrast to positive affect, when negative feelings are aroused, animals begin to exhibit 22-kHz 'complaint' type vocalisations and play temporarily ceases. A key function of the social play system is to facilitate the natural emergence of social dominance. Play helps young animals to acquire more subtle social interactions that are not genetically coded into the brain but must be learned. Thus, the play urge may be one of the major emotional forces that promote the epigenetic construction of higher social brains. This system, like all the other emotional systems, is concentrated in specific subcortical regions of the brain.

The primary evidence for the existence of such executive brain systems for basic emotions is our ability to artificially activate various kinds of emotional patterns by applying the appropriate kinds of chemical or electrical stimulation to specific subcortical regions of the brain. Radical decortication (surgical elimination of the dorsal cerebral mantle) generally leaves all of the above emotional-instinctual urges relatively intact, even though the capacity to learn new behaviour patterns is severely impaired. The existence of feeling states is based on the ob-servation that animals are never neutral about such kinds of physical stimulation of their brains. They are attracted to circumstances where the outwardly positive emotions are aroused (SEEKING, LUST, CARE and PLAY) and they avoid the arousal of negative emotions (RAGE, FEAR and PANIC). For instance, all brain sites that activate 50 kHz ultrasonic chirps also support self-stimulation behaviour. Those that provoke FEAR responses also provoke escape behaviours. Thus, raw affective feeling states that accompany emotional arousal are constituted, in part, from the neurodynamics that generate instinctual emotional responses. Without these systems, and various other affect-generating systems such as hunger, pain and thirst, animals could not survive for long. They are ancestral tools for living.

All the affects are intrinsic value systems that inform animals how they are faring in the quest to survive. Feelings are critical for guiding learning. The positive affects indicate that animals are returning to 'comfort zones' that support survival, and the negative affects reflect 'discomfort zones' that indicate animals are in situations that may impair survival. Indeed, the intrinsic affective states generated by ancient brain regions may be the first kinds of experiences that existed on the face of the earth. Without them, consciousness may not have emerged in brain evolution.

Whether other animals also have more subtle emotional feelings such as jealousy, shame, guilt or a sense of humour – feelings that are created by the interrelations of basic emotions with higher cognitive processes – remains an open issue. Subtle analysis of animal behaviour in natural environments certainly suggests that other animals do have more subtle emotions built upon the basic seven described above. However, we have no clear experimental methodologies to study those. We also have no clear evidence that other animals cognitively reflect on their own feelings or the mental states of other animals. Thus, we do not know if they can exhibit cognitive forms of suffering – prolonged and intensified psychological pain because of their ongoing thoughts about their feelings. Those aspects of mind have less distinct behavioural indicators than the basic emotions.

What Difference does it Make whether Animals have Emotional Feelings or Not?

The simplest answer to this question is that it surely makes a difference to the animals having such experiences. Just as we care about how we feel, animals surely care whether they feel good or bad. Since affective feelings are the source of all satisfactions and sufferings, as well as many behavioural choices, the scientific resolution of the existence of feelings in other animals and the brain mechanisms for those feelings is of momentous importance for our understanding of all psychological well-being issues in animals. Feelings inform animals where they stand in terms of health and other survival issues. Since all vertebrates, whether humans or other species, have some capacity for emotional feelings, such issues have implications for how we ethically treat other animals. Indeed, much of basic animal research raises many ethical issues, too subtle to consider here, but it is noteworthy that many of the properties of the basic emotional systems can be studied in anesthetised animals. However, the resulting implications for human behaviour are complex and debatable, and have been well covered elsewhere.

In sum, it is now clear that affective mechanisms are concentrated in ancient subcortical brain regions that are anatomically and neurochemically, and hence, evolutionarily, similar in all mammalian species. However, we do not know how members of different species cognitively respond to such feelings. Because there are no instinctual indicators, it is much harder to decipher the cognitive contents of animal minds than it is to decipher their emotional feelings. That will require more subtle behavioural analyses of more complex behaviour patterns. In any event, the dramatic similarities across mammals, with concordant work in humans, indicate that the basic emotional mechanisms are very ancient in brain evolution and ancestrally related in all mammals. These remarkable evolutionary continuities provide a coherent scientific approach for understanding how basic emotional feelings are created in animal as well as human brains.

Contemporary Issues in Farm Animal Housing and Management

44

Cattle Housing and Welfare

David Arney and Andres Aland
Estonian University of Life Sciences, Tartu, Estonia

Introduction

In most dairy systems cows are housed at some point during the year and in many cases in zero-grazing systems throughout the year. The reasons for housing an animal that is adapted to environmental conditions covering a range of climates is principally ease of management, but also to prevent poaching of grassland and protection from poor weather conditions. Housing has traditionally been designed to ease management and husbandry, in tandem with the demands for increased production, with little regard to the needs of individual animals, or indeed the herd as a whole. The housing facility, of whatever type, should provide protection from adverse weather, and allow ease of movement, with provision of dry, comfortable and clean lying space. Increasing herd size further increases the social stress induced by large numbers of unfamiliar animals, and reduces the attention that the stockman can pay to individual animals. Social space requirements for the dairy cow are not well defined, but should be of concern when grouping animals and designing housing. The housing of beef cattle and of young stock is treated separately at the end of this chapter.

Declining Space

Increases in the size of animals in recent years, through intensified breeding for higher producing animals, have resulted in housing and furniture becoming more and more poorly suited to the cattle housed. This includes: length and breadth of cubicle space, leading to dunging in the cubicle instead of the passageway and an inability to lie down or stand comfortably, partition design impeding comfortable lying, inadequate space in passageways, and restricted access to feed and water. Each of these can affect not only the welfare of the animals, but their feed intakes, levels of production, health and fertility. The opportunity to lie comfortably in a clean area should not be neglected; cows show a strong motivation to lie down (Wierenga and Hopster, 1990; Cooper et al., 2007): dairy cattle lie down for ~7-10 h during the day and night period; individual lying periods are on average 1.5 h long (Figure 44.1). If a comfortable and easily accessible lying area is not available, cows may spend more time lying or standing in dirty passageways (Figure 44.2), which is likely to lead to health problems – udder infection and leg injury in particular.

Figure 44.1. Resting cows in loose housing. Photo: A. Pavlenko.

Figure 44.2. Cow lying on a dirty passageway. Photo: A. Nõmmeots.

Flooring

Lameness is becoming an increasingly important factor affecting the health and welfare of the dairy cow. Usually the flooring is of concrete, which with time, and especially when covered with slurry, becomes slippery. Cows have to alter their gait on lower friction flooring (Phillips and Morris, 2000) and this can lead to injury and a disinclination to walk, making them less inclined to visit the feed barrier despite motivation to do so, possibly reducing feed intake and production. Rubber mats have been found to improve the locomotion of both non-lame and lame dairy cows (Telezhenko and Bergsten, 2005). These are expensive, but other methods can be used to reduce the problem. The flooring should be treated to increase friction, by scoring or a pattern of grooves, slurry should be removed regularly and efforts should be made to keep the floor dry. These strategies would also reduce contamination of the floor surface by pathogenic bacteria that can cause hoof problems.

Types of Housing

Modern housing systems, at least in production systems in the developed world, tend to be of either the cubicle or loose straw yard type, or tied stalls. The choice of system is usually dependent on the availability and cost of straw or other bedding material. Higher stocking rates can be supported in the cubicle compared with the straw yard system. A 600 kg cow requires a total area of 9 m² in the straw yard system and a loafing area of 3 m² in the cubicle system (DEFRA, 2006). There should be sufficient cubicle allowance for at least 5% more than the number of cows housed to facilitate the free choice, movement and preferences of the cows. Considerations of health and welfare have been reported extensively for the different housing types. It may be that if management is good, with due regard for the well-being of the cattle, the welfare of the animals need not be dependent on the type of housing system. In short, mastitis problems have been reported more frequently in straw yards than in cubicles, whereas lameness is more likely to be a problem in cubicles. Lameness has been found to be higher in cubicles than in tied stalls (Cook, 2003), and higher in cubicles than in loose housing (Phillips and Schofield, 1994). Within cubicles, the use of straw or rubber mats has no effect on behaviour, but the former type causes less hoof damage (Wechsler et al., 2000). Comparing rubber mats with bare concrete flooring, cows spend significantly more time lying in the cubicles, appear to be more comfortable and show less difficulty getting up and lying down in the former (Haley et al., 2001). Somers et al. (2003) reported a lower incidence of claw disorders in straw yards, though still rather high at 60%, compared with over 80% on concrete flooring.

UK farmers are advised that straw yards should ideally be rectangular, to give more wall area, which cows preferentially lie against, and the back wall should be no more than 10 m from the feeding area (DEFRA, 2006).

In the same source, different cubicle designs and dimensions are reviewed extensively.

Whichever system is used, cows should have unimpeded access to feeding and drinking facilities, with neither next to the bedding area, as this can lead to soiling and poor cleanliness, with concomitant health and welfare problems.

Drinking Water

Dairy cows require large amounts of drinking water, often in excess of 100 kg per day. This is affected by milk production, dry matter intake, ambient temperature (Murphy et al., 1983), stage of gestation and lactation, age, breed and size of the cow, and salt in the diet (Fraser and Broom, 1997). As with feeding, there are likely to be peak periods of intakes during the day, such as after milking. There should therefore be sufficient access to water so that at these times cows are not restricted in their consumption. Such an impediment to cows drinking fresh water when thirsty would have an adverse effect on their welfare, particularly of subordinate cows, but also on their level of milk production. Intakes can be further affected if the water is not clean.

Feeding Area

The feeding area should have a sufficient face so that all of the cows can feed simultaneously – at high stocking rates feeding times are reduced and displacements of animals from the feeding barrier are increased, and the use of a barrier at the feed face can reduce competition (Huzzey et al., 2006). It has been suggested that for a 600 kg cow this accessible face per cow should be at least 0.67 m (DEFRA, 2006).

Cleanliness

Cleanliness and a suggested scoring system to assess the cleanliness of cows are reviewed by Hughes (2001). Animal cleanliness is affected by the cleanliness of the bedding, feeding areas and passageways, stocking rate, cubicle design and dimensions, type of bedding, health and diet of the cows (and so firmness of the faeces), and ventilation (reducing humidity). This ought to be better in cubicle housing, but not if the cows are lying in passageways, or standing in slurry for long periods. Self-operated cleaning brushes can be provided for the cows, which

Figure 44.3. Self-cleaning brush in use. Photo: R. Leming.

they seem inclined to use if given the opportunity (Figure 44.3). Cleanliness not only affects the health, including lameness, mastitis and metritis, and welfare of the cows, but dirty cows increase the burden on the milking staff, who will have to spend more time cleaning the animals prior to milking, and also increases the likelihood of contamination of the milk.

Ventilation

Ventilation has in the past been neglected, but is now integral to the design of buildings. Old buildings may need to address this problem, and ventilation can be improved with the use of fans, which will need to be well maintained, in cases where there is insufficient natural ventilation. Good ventilation in the housing improves the means of providing appropriate air movement, reduces humidity, reduces heat, and reduces the build-up of dust, noxious gases, principally ammonia and carbon dioxide, and microorganisms. If ventilation is poor a range of health problems can result: heat stress, respiratory diseases and mastitis in particular. In addition, the health of the farm workers and the surrounding environment can be adversely affected. Phillips et al. (1998) reviewed and suggested means of measuring emissions and ventilation rates in livestock buildings.

Lighting

Lighting should be sufficient for the cows to confidently move and explore their surroundings; cows have shown an aversion to darkened passageways (Phillips et al., 2000). There should be provision of a greater intensity of light, available at all times, for the accurate observation of stock by the stockperson. The provision of light should follow the normal daily rhythm of light as much as possible, although increased yields have been observed from increasing the day length through artificial lighting (Dahl and Peticlerc, 2003). The spectrum and intensity of light should also be considered.

Heat and Cold Stress

Cattle are more temperature-tolerant than other farm animals. Their thermoneutral zone is generally wide, and often extends to quite low temperatures. The range of thermal neutrality varies between breeds and individuals with different productivity. At ambient temperatures higher than 25°C, cows show increased stress (Wise et al., 1988) and reduced production (Berman et al., 1985), feed intake, condition and fertility (Wilson et al., 1998). Detection of discomfort from heat stress includes increased respiration rates and increased drinking. Heat stress can be minimised, and feed intake increased, with the use of misters or sprinklers and fans (Lin et al., 1998) and shading exposed areas. The use of water for cooling ought to be used only in the collecting area or passageways, as wetting the bedding will have adverse consequences on the quality and microbial contamination of the bedding material. Cold stress should not be disregarded, but the dairy cow is a cold-hardy animal, with an estimated lower critical temperature of -20°C for the cow in peak lactation, although increased metabolic rate for the production of heat requires a higher maintenance energy, and the flow of digestion is increased (Young, 1981). The lower critical temperature is also affected by the level of activity and locomotion.

Calf Housing

Housing calves represents something of a welfare conflict. Rearing them in individual pens is better for their health, while rearing them in groups reduces the suffering of social isolation in what is a herd animal. Socially housed calves have more space, engage in normal social behaviour – both while calves but also into their adult lives. There may also be reduced labour costs in cleaning out one large pen rather than several individual pens.

However, in early life calf mortality is caused primarily by digestive disorders and, slightly later, by respiratory problems. The commonest cause of these is infection from conspecifics, so keeping them separated makes sense from a health and economic point of view. It is also easier for the stockman to notice problems with calves, including feed intake, if he observes them in isolation and provides the feed and water individually. Most intensive units continue to keep calves in individual pens for these reasons. However, strategies to balance these demands are also common. Many units house calves individually, but then move them into group pens after around a week, by which time the greatest risk of disease is thought to have passed. A further refinement has been suggested by Chua et al. (2002) whereby calves are housed in pairs. This has no adverse effects on scouring or feed intakes, and the range of normal behaviours is higher than in individually housed calves. Whatever the system, the pens should be spacious, the calf should at least be able to turn around even in an individual pen, secure and safe, and they should be frequently cleaned with dry bedding provided. Calves should have easy access to water and feed, not always possible with automatic feeding devices. Calves are more vulnerable to cold temperatures and the pens should be well protected from draughts and from precipitation.

Beef Cattle

Beef production in the Baltic Sea region is relatively small compared with other parts of Europe and particularly the American continent. However, where beef animals are kept they are increasingly kept outdoors, and the cool and wet climate in this region might be a cause of stress to these animals. The welfare of animals kept in these conditions has been thoroughly reviewed by Ekesbo (2009). Outside, in a cool climate, is perhaps as close to their natural environment as such a thing is likely to be, at least for northern European breeds (Figure 44.4). Cattle, but not newborn calves, are unlikely to suffer from cold stress as the rumen is a source of considerable heat, they are able to acclimatise to cooler temperatures, and grow thicker coats and lay down an insulating layer of subcutaneous fat for the winter, at least as long as they are dry. Insulation of the coat is much reduced when wetted, so animals housed outdoors should have some shelter

Figure 44.4: Beef cattle outdoors in winter. Photo: R. Leming.

Conclusions

Dairy cattle spend at least some of their time indoors, and some herds can be housed throughout the year. The housing is usually either in cubicles or in loose housing with straw yards. In terms of the relative merits of these systems, cow health is probably better in the former system and cow welfare and likelihood of injury is probably better in the latter system, although much depends on the local stockmanship and management rather than the system itself. Particular problems include the fact that cows have become larger animals in recent years, outgrowing the space and furniture of their housing. The expense of updating the furniture to make housing more suitable is often too great and the cows suffer stress as well as health and injury problems, and production can be reduced as a result. Drinking water and feed availability, cleanliness, ventilation, lighting and control over the internal climate are all considerations.

Calves are usually housed indoors either individually or in groups. Again, there is a conflict between health and welfare; individually housed calves are less likely to become infected with contagious agents, whereas group-housed calves are able to behave more normally and this improved normalcy is carried on into their adult behaviour. Beef cattle are somewhat different and in the Baltic region spend most, if not all, of their time outdoors. This is on the whole fine, as the cow has evolved to thrive in such conditions, but shelters should be provided, for wet and windy weather in particular. The cows should know where these shelters are, should know how to use them, and they should have sufficient dry area in which all of the herd is able to lie down comfortably.

that provides a dry environment. If a coniferous wooded area is included in the area available to the cows they are able to use this cover, but in the long term such repeated usage can damage the roots and the trees and kill them, reducing the protection available. Constructed structures are most likely to be used. The design of these shelters should be such that precipitation and wind in combination, the worst situation, do not reach the lying area. Wind screens alone do not offer sufficient protection. There should be enough space in the shelter so that all the cows can fit inside it, and they should know where it is. The flooring should be well drained. Cows prefer to lie on a dry surface, and if forced to lie down on a damp floor will lose heat rapidly. Problems are more likely to arise from poor management rather than the system itself. Simply covering the floor lightly with straw, or worse no covering at all, on a poorly-drained surface will not suffice. This will soon become a mudbath. The shelter should be clearly accessible, and the cattle may need to be taught to use it. Introducing a novel temporary shelter at the beginning of the winter is no strategy, as learning to use a shelter in bad weather is considered an acquired behaviour in cattle (Ekesbo, 2009). However, this is quite simply done by offering hay in the shelters to encourage their use and familiarity.

Contemporary Issues in Farm Animal Housing and Management

Swine

45

Bo Algers

Swedish University of Agricultural Sciences
Skara, Sweden

Introduction

During recent decades, there has been a debate about whether farrowing sows need access to nest-building material and space to be able to perform nest building. Studies on the natural behaviour of sows, as well as on physiology, have shown that sows do have a strong motivation for nest building before farrowing and that this to a large extent is internally regulated (for a review, see Algers and Uvnäs-Moberg, 2007). A recent report from EFSA (2007a) concluded that:

- Housing of sows in farrowing crates severely restricts their freedom of movement which increases the risk of frustration. It does not allow them, for instance, to select a nest site, to show normal nest-building behaviour, to leave the nest site for eliminative behaviour or to select pen areas with a cool floor for thermoregulation.
- Sows' nest-building behaviour is triggered by internal hormonal factors. Thus, the motivation for nest building is high in spite of if housing conditions allow for nest building or not. As a consequence, lack of nesting material is very likely to cause stress and impaired welfare.

- The level of piglet welfare and mortality on farms remains a major problem. Great variation in piglet mortality in different systems makes it difficult to draw a general conclusion about the influence of the farrowing systems on piglet mortality.
- Piglet mortality is a multi-factorial issue. The causes of piglet mortality may differ significantly between the different farrowing systems. The primary cause of piglet mortality is often unknown; however mortality due to crushing has been reported to be higher in loose housing systems.
- In a recent large-scale study on indoor loose farrowing and crate systems, no difference in total piglet mortality was observed.
- Risk Assessment of poor welfare ranked frustration and stress due to insufficient space and due to lack of foraging and nest-building material (sows in farrowing crates and pens which are too small) as major risk factors for farrowing sows.

The purpose of this section is to describe some housing systems that are in line with the conclusions stated above and also how recent national regulations highlight some of these aspects, using Sweden as an example, but also to describe some housing systems for fatteners in relation to their need for straw and social stability.

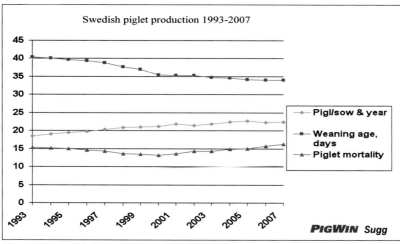

Figure 45.1. Swedish piglet production 1993-2007.

Changes in Regulations

Since 2007, new regulations on the keeping of farrowing sows apply in Sweden. These new regulations emphasise the importance of the sow being able to perform nest-building behaviour and have access to straw (Swedish regulations DFS 2007:5 (L100), Chapter 3):

§3 'A nursing sow's freedom of movement may be confined during the first days after farrowing by the use of a gate or similar construction if she shows aggressive or abnormal behaviour which forms a threat to injure her piglets. A gate or corresponding equipment may also be used during management procedures if the behaviour of the sow poses a threat of injury to staff or during handling of the sow for care and treatment. Group-housed sows and gilts may be confined in stanchions at feeding or when handled for care and treatment' (author's translation).

§8 'During the week before farrowing sows and gilts must have access to litter which allows them to carry out nest building behaviour' (author's translation).

§10 'At least ¾ of the lying area in a pen with litter for a nursing sow must be flooring which is not drained. This part of the lying area must be a homogeneous rectangular area covering the whole width of the pen. The other part of the lying area may be a drained floor with a slot width of maximum 11 mm and a slat width

of minimum 11 mm. If the drained floor is made of concrete, the slat width should be minimum 80 mm' (author's translation).

§11 'Before farrowing, sows and gilts must be able to use the area in the farrowing pen so that they can perform nest-building behaviour' (author's translation).

§19 'Minimum area for farrowing pen: Lying area 4 m², total area 6 m²'.

Recent Trends in Piglet Production in Sweden

Today, farmers commonly choose to use drained flooring on 25% of the lying area, often made from cast iron, which is considered to have the advantages of a more stable surface, which the sow is more willing to tread on, and which is easier to clean. The disadvantage is that it is more abrasive to the piglets' feet and front knees. Recent and ongoing studies suggest that by the use of large quantities of straw, these disadvantages can be limited. Common problems facing the pig producer today are piglet mortality, feet and leg injuries in piglets and their consequences, as well as shoulder lesions in sows.

In piglet production, piglet mortality decreased between 1993-2000 but has since increased (PigWin, 2008) (Figure 45.1). The introduction of sow crating on some farms has not positively affected piglet mortality.

There is considerable variation between farms in production records (PigWin, 2008), showing a potential for improvements through the introduction of better housing and management (Table 45.1).

Housing Systems

Below, some housing systems that comply with the biology of sows in the sense that they allow for group living, nest building and manipulation of nest material are described.

Table 45.1. Piglet production in Sweden – average values.

In total 68,008 sows	2007		
	2007	Best 25%	Worst 25%
Average no. of sows and gilts	234	251	178
Produced piglets/sow and year	22.4	24.8	19.0
No. of litters/sow and year	2.19	2.25	2.06
Proportion of gilt litters, %	25.9	22,4	29.2
Liveborn/litter	12.3	12.8	12.0
Stillborn/litter	0.90	0.91	1.0
No. of weaned/litter	10.3	10.9	9.6
Weaning age, days	34.0	33.4	36.2
Piglet mortality, birth-weaning, %	16.2	14.4	19.5
Returns, %	9.0	6.2	12.2
Daily growth from weaning-delivery, g	426	463	407

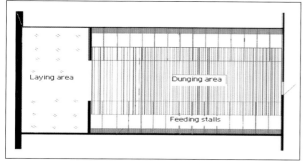

Figure 45.2. Group housing system for sows with individual feeding stalls and communal laying and dunging area.

Group Housing of Dry Sows

In group housing conditions, sows form a strong hierarchy within the group. This is especially seen during feeding, when less dominant sows will give way to dominant individuals. Dry sows are typically fed a relatively small amount of a concentrate diet in one or two daily meals. This has influenced the design of group housing facilities where use of individual feeding stalls is recommended to reduce aggression. Several different group housing systems exist.

a) Group Housing with Individual Feeding Stalls
Individual feeding stalls confine the sows temporarily during feeding, preventing dominant individuals chasing off less dominant sows in order to get access to extra feed

rations. Feeding stalls are slightly smaller than ordinary stalls, 0.4-0.5 x 1.9-2.0 m. The gate closing behind the sow can either be operated by the sow herself or by working staff. The feeding stalls are often combined with communal lying (solid floor with limited use of bedding material) and dunging areas (slatted flooring). Design varies with group size, which is highly variable (5-40). One example is seen in Figure 45.2. Feeding stalls can also be used in combination with deep straw bedding (Figure 45.3, left). Total free space available (excluding feeding stalls) is commonly 2.25-2.8 m² per sow depending on group size. If stall width is a minimum of 60 cm and sows have free access, the stalls may be used for both feeding and resting, reducing the total space needed.

b) Group Housing with Electronic Sow Feeder (ESF)
In ESF systems each sow carries a transponder (ear tag or collar), allowing passage to a feeder station. A precisely measured individual ration of food is then dispensed to that animal and she is protected while eating by a specialised feeding stall with gates operated by the sow herself or by the feeding computer. A single feeding station can be shared by up to 70 sows. In this system sows are often kept in large dynamic flocks (50-300 sows) with communal dunging and lying areas (Figure 45.3, right).

Farrowing and Lactation
Sows are typically moved from dry sow to farrowing accommodation 3-7 days before the expected farrowing date (115 days after service).

In outdoor systems, farrowing and lactating sows are housed in either individual or group paddocks, with access to individual farrowing huts (Figure 45.4).

The use of individual pens for the farrowing/lactating sow and litter is common only in countries where farrowing crates are no longer allowed. These may be simple pens of approximately 2.0 x 3.0 m with anti-crush rails around the walls and a heated creep area for the piglets (Figure 45.5, left.). Traditionally the pens had access to a dunging alley with scrapers, but in newer systems the floor is mostly partly slatted. Beneath the slatted flooring, scrapers or liquid manure systems are used. The type of manure handling system influences the possibility to use straw during farrowing. Slats are either made of concrete, iron or a plastic material. These pens sometimes contain a

Figure 45.3. Left: Group housing of sows with individual feeding stalls in combination with deep straw bedding. Right: Group housing of sows with electronic sow feeders. Photo: R. Westin.

Figure 45.4. Farrowing huts for free-range sows. Photo: B. Algers.

temporary crate structure made by moving a partition into place at the time of farrowing (Figure 45.5, right.) This reduces the total space available when the sow is loose.

In the mid 1980s, there was a trend to introduce a change from confinement systems to group housing of lactating sows. Indoor group-farrowing systems are still in use in commercial practice but only to a small extent. This is because as these systems operate very different-ly compared with conventional ones, in matters such as identifying the maternal characteristics of sows to cull for poor maternal abilities or finding new practical means of identifying and catching piglets in a large group in large pens, farmers had to find their own ways of coping with

these challenges as advisors were not trained to help. Thus, many who did not find practical ways of managing the herd re-converted to conventional systems, but those who found out how to manage stayed on. The knowledge required to manage the system is different from that for conventional systems, as is the need for large quanti-ties of straw (1,000- 1,500 kg per sow and year; Algers, pers. comm.) so there is no 'natural' spread of the use of these systems. There has been a knowledge transfer on the operation of such systems to the USA (Halverson, pers. comm.) and many such systems now are used in the US. In these systems, 5-10 sows are kept in groups where each sow has access to an individual farrowing nest and a communal resting area, often on deep straw bedding (Figures 45.6-7). In this system the sows are moved to the big pen some days before farrowing and a cubicle for each sow is erected along the walls. The cubicle is about 1.75 by 2.40 m and has an entrance for the sow with a 40 cm high threshold with a 15 cm wide roller on top to protect the udder of the sow but also to prevent the piglets from leaving the cubicle during the first week. There are no rails, creep area or heat lamp in the cubicle as it can distort the interaction between the sow and piglets during the nest phase. Piglets remain in the deep bedded system until they reach approximately 25-30 kg.

These systems are described in detail by Algers (1991), Braun and Algers (1993) and Halverson (1997). The nest boxes are taken out when the piglets have left

Figure 45.5. Left: Farrowing pen with anti-crush rails. Right: Farrowing pen with gates that can be used for contemporary confinement of the sow. Photo: R. Westin.

the nest, usually 10-14 days after farrowing. Data collected from 469 sows on four Swedish deep-bedded system farms (Marchant, 1996) showed an average production of 21.8 pigs/sow/year based on a 92% farrowing rate, 11.2 pigs born alive per litter, preweaning mortality of 11.5% and weaning 21.8 pigs per/sow/year at 6-week weaning. Hultén (1997) found that when mixing sows without their litters, lactational ovulations occurred more frequently in group-housed sows than in single-housed, and piglet mortality was higher in group-housed sows. Nowadays, this practice of mixing sows without their litters has been abandoned by farmers as a result of this. Algers (1991) found a lower incidence of MMA in sows kept together during farrowing in a group housing system in comparison to traditional single, loose housing of sows.

Ebner (1993) noted that grouping sows before farrowing caused considerably less aggression that grouping after farrowing. Wülbers-Mindermann (1992) found that cross-suckling occurs in group-housed sows with litters and that this does not cause any detrimental effects as regards mortality or piglet growth, but it could be stressful to some sows when forced to give milk to many demanding piglets. It has been shown that piglets develop different strategies for their cross-suckling and that such strategies are of adaptive value (Braun, 1995).

A large-scale study of group housing systems for lactating sows commercially used in Sweden was performed by Mattsson (1996). The study comprised 49 herds with group housing and 296 control herds where sows were kept loose but singly, in individual pens. The study concluded that group-housed sows had slightly higher piglet production per sow and year on average, that piglet mortality was similar in both groups, that returns were less in the group-housed sows and that the piglets in the group-housed group reached 25 kg on average 5.3 days earlier (see Table 45.2). This is probably due to the significantly lower incidence of weaning diarrhoea in group-housed sows (Table 45.3).

A number of the farms with group housing successfully produced 22-25 piglets per sow and year, which shows the potential of the system. It should also be borne in mind that these production results are maintained using the normal practices in Sweden of weaning at 5-6 weeks, without the regular use of antibiotics in weaner feed and without the use of any hormones for synchronisation of the breeding.

Although the data in the two tables above (Mattsson, 1996; Holmgren and Lundeheim, 1994) were obtained from many farms, there might be confounding factors that at least partly contribute to the effects shown. The data should therefore be interpreted mainly to show the production levels that are possible in group housing systems.

Fattening Pigs
Behaviour of the Growing Pig
Being generalists, i.e. having an innate capability to adapt to various habitats, pigs have a natural tendency to ex-

Table 45.2. Herd average comparisons: The Swedish deep-bedded group housing system for lactating sows versus loose housing of single sows. (Mattsson, 1996).

	Group housing	Single housing
Number of herds	49	296
Av. no of sows per herd	95.2	77.9
Conception rate, %	91.1	87.6
Liveborn per litter	11.0	11.0
Stillborn per litter	0.7	0.9
Piglet mortality until weaning	14.7	14.9
Weaned pig/sow and year	19.9	19.1
Weaning, days	38.9	40.2
Age at 25 kg, days	80.7	86.0
Working hours per sow	18.1(a)	28.9(b)

(a= data from 7 herds, b= data from 42 herds)

Table 45.3. Incidence of weaning diarrhoea and consumption of antibiotics and chemotherapeutics in different pig weaning systems (Holmgren and Lundeheim, 1994).

	Group housing	One unit pen	Weaning pen
No of herds	14	18	17
% treated piglets	21a	59b	71b
Kg medicated feed/sow and year	78a	278b	277b
Differences a-b, p<0.05.			

plore (Wood-Gush and Vestergaard, 1991). Exploration is shown by all pigs, allowing the individual to be prepared for effective food acquisition, response to danger from predators, attack by conspecifics and response to other adverse conditions or needs. Exploration is therefore not only linked to nutritional needs or foraging motivation. In barren environments, pigs redirect exploratory behaviour at the body of pen mates (Algers, 1984; Fraser et al., 1991). Exploration will be difficult if there is insufficient space available and if the environment is barren. All pigs are motivated to explore by digging and manipulating with their nose and mouth.

Apart from adult boars and sows around parturition, pigs are social animals associating and interacting in a friendly way much more than in an aggressive way (e.g. Stolba and Wood-Gush, 1989). Sleeping in pigs is often a social activity, in that pigs prefer to rest near or alongside other pigs. Pigs naturally live in stable groups and lack of social contact causes poor welfare in pigs. However, mixing of unfamiliar pigs always results in aggressive interactions to establish dominance relationships (Turner et al., 2001). In order to avoid further aggression, subdominant animals avoid dominant animals. Moreover, a restriction in access to important resources, such as the number of feeding places, results in increased levels of aggression (Spoolder et al., 1999).

Even when pigs are fully supplied with their daily nutrient requirements for good health and performance, they may have other needs relating to the quantity or form of the diet. Foraging behaviour accounts for up to 75% of the daily activity of pigs kept in a semi-natural enclosure and they show a wide range of various behaviours to investigate and manipulate the environment (Stolba and Wood-Gush, 1989). In addition to the need to feed, pigs therefore need permanent access to a sufficient quantity of material to enable proper investigation and manipulation activities. There is a close relationship between foraging and exploration needs. Pigs are highly motivated to work for access to foraging material such as straw or wood shavings (Ladewig and Matthews, 1996). Insufficient provision of foraging material increases the incidence of tail-biting in fattening pigs (Day et al., 2002; Moinard et al., 2003) and stereotypical behaviour in sows (Spoolder et al., 1995; Whittaker et al., 1998).

Fattening Pig Housing

When piglets reach approximately 30 kg live weight they are usually moved to further accommodations for finishing their growth prior to slaughter. This is currently done in various intensive housing systems and only marginally in outdoor facilities in the EU. Housing system designs are affected by a number of factors including climate, legislation, economics, etc.

Individuals are usually selected to fill pens in the fattening sheds based on live weight, so members of different litters may become pen mates in the fattening pens. This mixing will provoke the establishment of new social hierarchies, resulting in antagonistic behaviour. If not castrated, males become sexually mature at this stage and aggressive behaviour may be intensified (Rydhmer et al.,

Figure 45.6. Left: Group-farrowing system with sows and piglets in their individual nest boxes on deep straw bedding. Right: Group-farrowing system with sows gathering nest material from the straw bedding. Photo: B. Algers.

2006). There are a few incidences where pigs are housed together during the entire rearing period from weaning to slaughter. Ekkel et al. (1996) reported that health, production and welfare were improved when pigs were kept in these housing systems without being mixed or transported. Such systems are most often seen in straw-based housing systems in Scandinavia.

Indoor systems can be divided into three categories based on the manure-handling system adopted: deep-litter systems, scraped systems and slatted systems. Some of these systems provide different climatic zones where the pig can choose its microclimate for various activities (i.e. for resting in kennels or under thermo-boards). The latter systems may provide supplementary heating only in the lying area, which reduces the overall energy input for the building. The various systems are briefly described below. For further details, see the EFSA (2007b) report on animal health and well-being in fattening pigs.

Figure 45.7. Group-farrowing system where the individual nest boxes have been removed. Photo: B. Algers.

Weaners

A variety of housing systems are used for weaned piglets. Piglets are typically housed in highly controlled environments with supplementary heating in partly or fully-slatted pens, or raised on flat decks, in groups of varying sizes (10-40 kg). They may be moved from the first stage weaner accommodation to larger, second stage accommodation after 2-4 weeks, or remain in the same pen until they are 10 weeks of age (30-40 kg) or, in a few instances, until slaughter. The pen area per pig varies from 0.2 (< 20 kg) to 0.3 m² per pig (< 30 kg). Weaner pigs are typically fed ad libitum (dry) or restricted (liquid).

Grower/Finisher Pigs

Accommodation for fattening pigs may be fully-slatted, partly-slatted, minimally bedded with scraped dunging area or deep bedded with straw or sawdust. Although there are national differences, housing with fully or partly-slatted flooring (typically on concrete slats with 17-20 mm slot spacing) with a pen floor area of 0.7 m² at the end of the finishing period predominates within the EU (Figure 45.8-9).

Figure 45.8-9. Pens for fattening with feeding trough at the front of the pen and a separate dunging area along half of the rear part of the pen (8) or with feeding trough along the side wall of the pen and dunging area the whole rear side of the pen (9). Photo: R. Westin.

Feed can be provided either wet or dry. Feed is increasingly distributed automatically to sensor-controlled liquid feeders or slop feeders (semi-liquid). Dry feed is often given ad libitum from one or more hoppers, although feed may be restricted in the later stages to prevent excessive fatness of unimproved genotypes or with very heavy slaughter weights (>120 kg). Traditionally, fattening pigs are housed in groups of 10-15, but recently the use of units with larger group sizes on perforated floors has increased. Large group sizes are also typical for deep litter systems.

Kennels are typically used in cold non-insulated buildings or outdoors providing a sheltered separate resting area

Fully Slatted Floor

Slatted housing systems are widely used in the industrialised world. In these systems, slats cover the entire pen area, usually to maintain hygiene. Foraging material, if used, is small in quantity. One vital component for the successful use of slatted flooring is the proportion of the floor solid/slot dimensions in relation to the dimensions of the feet of the pig at any given age. Furthermore, sharp edges may cause injuries when the loading force exceeds the strength of the digits (e.g. Webb and Nilsson, 1983).

Partly Slatted Floor

Partly-slatted flooring may reduce emissions of ammonia and other gases released from urine and faeces and, if correctly designed and well-drained, can lower emissions considerably. Partly-slatted floor systems, preferably with a raised level of the slatted part, make it possible to use sufficient supplies of straw.

Solid Floor

Solid concrete floors are often used for both the resting and defecating areas. The manure is scraped, manually or by mechanical scrapers, at frequent intervals and the urine usually drained separately. A dry concrete floor can easily be warmed and it retains heat quite well, but it exacerbates the harmful effects of low temperatures if floors or bedding are cold or damp. Therefore, solid floors are found to need either insulation or a floor heating system (warm water pipes or electric cables), whether used with or without small amounts of bedding materials.

The straw-flow system is used for growing pigs from 10 weeks (20–30 kg) to slaughter (90–150 kg). The straw-flow pen system is characterised by sloping concrete floors, where the lying area has a curved surface, with a slope of 5-7% towards the dunging area. The resting area is sometimes levelled about 5 cm above the manure area, which has a slope for allowing the manure to flow down into a manure channel. The group size in straw-flow systems is about the size of a litter and having more than 30 individuals is not recommended (Jackisch et al., 1996).

Surplus straw is as favourable for health and welfare as in the deep-bedding systems. However, the use of straw is much lower and the area per pig cannot be increased significantly because of the system itself. For the flow function of the pen, an amount of 50 grams of straw per pig and day is satisfactory; the amount should not exceed 100 grams to avoid clogging or flow malfunction if short straw is used. With longer straw, however, quantities may be substantially increased. Uninsulated floors need a bedding depth of at least 75 mm for the weaned pig to achieve a thermal resistance to the floor above about 0.5 °C/W (Bruce, 1990).

Deep bedding with materials such as straw, sawdust, wood chips, peat, etc. usually has a solid concrete floor underneath (Figure 45.10), although sometimes a slatted floor is used for drainage of the litter bedding. The deep litter system has disadvantages in that it increases the emissions of ammonia, nitrous oxide, nitrogen and methane (Groenestein and Van Faassen, 1996).

In insulated buildings, especially when the bedding is 'fermenting' and producing a large amount of heat, the temperature may rise and may cause thermoregulatory problems for the pigs, resulting in heat stress and decreased performance unless the pigs have access to a cooler lying place (van den Weghe et al., 1999) or unless ventilators and other means of climate regulation are used.

Outdoor Rearing Systems

Outdoor rearing systems can be seen in many various forms. In outdoor rearing either the pigs are provided with a large paddock and a simple shelter, or they are confined within an outdoor hut-and-run system.

The stocking rate suggested in paddock systems is 40-50 finishing pigs/ha (Brownlow et al., 1995). Housing for free-range pigs usually comprises corrugated iron arks or wooden sheds, although tents have recently been developed in Denmark. The housing is generally flexible, so that the shelters can be moved and each new batch of pigs can begin in a clean paddock. In systems with huts, the pigs are provided with a hut and small outdoor run area bounded by solid fencing and bedded with straw to maintain hygiene. The hut often has an adjustable ventilator as well as a feed hopper. It is moved to fresh ground for each new batch of pigs.

Figure 45.10. Deep litter hoop barn for fatteners. Photo: R. Westin.

Conclusions

Mixing of pigs causes aggression and injury. Pigs have a strong innate motivation for exploration and in the case of the sow, for nest building before farrowing. Farrowing systems as well as systems for weaners and fattening pigs should allow for the handling of destructible nest material to enable investigation and manipulation activities. They should also allow the sow's nest-building behaviour to be expressed and sows and fatteners to be kept in stable groups.

Contemporary Issues in Farm Animal Housing and Management
Poultry Well-being

46

Ruth C. Newberry
Washington State University
Pullman, Washington, USA

Introduction

The world is populated with vast numbers of domesticated birds collectively known as poultry including, at any one time, over 16 billion broiler chickens raised for meat, 5 billion laying hens raised for egg production, a quarter of a billion turkeys, and lesser numbers of ducks, geese, quail, pheasants, guinea fowl, and various species of ratite. The world market for poultry is growing, with the highest production currently occurring in the USA, China and Brazil. From an evolutionary perspective, close association with humans has made the domestic fowl *Gallus gallus domesticus* (comprising broiler chickens and laying hens), the most abundant and thus most successful of all birds.

Human survival depends upon consumption of nutrients obtained from other species, be they from poultry or other animal or plant prey. Due to intense genetic selection, housing and management, poultry products are relatively cheap, plentiful and appetising sources of nutrients to meet our needs. Nevertheless, there are some externalities associated with this massive success in human-poultry mutualism that are difficult to condense into numbers in an economic analysis but nevertheless need to be considered in evaluating the sustainability of poultry production practices. These include:

- Environmental pollutants emanating from poultry facilities, such as ammonia
- Carbon footprint for poultry production
- Use of land and energy/protein sources to produce poultry rather than other crops, or as a bioreserve
- Poultry acting as vectors of diseases (e.g. avian influenza) to humans and other animals, including endangered species
- Occupational hazards related to working at poultry farms, hatcheries and poultry processing plants
- Use of antibiotics to enhance poultry production, contributing to the development of antibiotic resistance
- Human obesity and associated health problems, as a consequence of over-consumption of readily available, low-cost food products including poultry
- Impacts on poultry well-being – the focus of the current article.

The ethic of animal care leads us to strive to keep animals in a manner that minimises suffering and contributes to a positive sense of well-being. Although it may be easier for us to care about sheep and cows than chickens and turkeys, we should remember that birds have a highly developed nervous system that is, essentially, homologous to that of mammals. Their small brains and seemingly expressionless faces should not be construed as evidence of a lack of thoughts and feelings.

Evolution has prepared birds to cope with the vagaries of the natural environment in a flexible manner through learning and subsequent recall; learning that is made salient by association of events with sensations such as pain, fear and separation distress. Based on evidence from brain and behaviour research, we can infer that birds have the ability to experience both positive and negative feelings, and to use memories of specific sensations occurring in specific situations as a foundation for future behaviour. Although domestication has altered the thresholds for expression of some behaviours, poultry species still retain the same basic behavioural repertoires of their wild relatives.

This knowledge leads us to reflect upon the impact of current commercial production systems on poultry well-being. The following discussion identifies the issues surrounding some controversial housing and management practices. As we shall see, scientific knowledge can inform decisions but value judgements are also involved when weighing up the relative merits of different options.

Induced Moulting

Let us start by considering the controversial practice of induced (forced) moulting of laying hens, whereby moulting is induced through feed withdrawal for up to two weeks. Egg producers have argued that this is an appropriate practice since birds moult in nature. Induced moulting is conducted after hens have been laying eggs at a high rate for approximately one year, and has the benefit of rapidly rejuvenating the bird, leading to improved hen survival rates, egg production and egg shell quality during a subsequent laying period. These benefits to subsequent health depend upon the hen losing abdominal fat that has accumulated over the lying cycle.

On the other hand, research assessing the level of motivation to eat during moulting indicates that these benefits come at a cost to the birds of strong hunger during the initial period of feed withdrawal, followed by fatigue and depressed behaviour. If weight loss is too great, feed withdrawal can lead to anorexia and death. Under commercial conditions, where the ratio of birds to caretakers is high, weight loss is monitored based on sampling of a proportion of birds rather than close monitoring of each individual bird. As a consequence, birds that are lighter than average at the start of moulting have an elevated risk of dying during the feed withdrawal period.

One can, therefore, contemplate whether it would be better from an animal welfare perspective to terminate the lives of the hens at the end of the first production cycle, when their egg production rate and egg shell quality have declined to uneconomic levels, than to subject them to a moult. Fortunately, research has shown that it is economically feasible to moult hens under commercial conditions by feeding them low nutrient feedstuffs such as wheat middlings or low sodium diets instead of withdrawing feed completely for 14 days. Producers can thus obtain the benefits of moulting on post-moult health and productivity without severe adverse consequences for the birds during the moulting process.

The complete feed withdrawal moulting procedure has therefore been outlawed in the European Union and, more recently, abandoned in the US through industry adoption of voluntary animal care standards. This approach to solving the animal welfare concerns surrounding induced moulting means that the same number of eggs can be produced with fewer hens than would be needed if flocks were terminated after a single laying cycle and extra pullets had to be raised to replace the flock every year. It also avoids the environmental impact associated with housing, feeding and disposing of manure from additional pullets.

The story does not end here, however. We always face the difficulty of deciding how far we should go towards accommodating poultry well-being. Although the use of low nutrient moulting diets enables birds to fill their gut and provides birds with an outlet for foraging behaviour, these diets do not appear to create a pleasant feeling of satiety, and may promote increased aggression in lines of poultry predisposed towards aggressive behaviour. Use of certain pharmacological appetite suppressants may be more humane than feeding low nutrient feedstuffs, thereby reducing feed inputs and manure outputs, but this approach would not be acceptable to consumers concerned about the naturalness of their food. For increased sustainability, we should also be considering increasing the longevity of hens beyond two laying cycles, even if this can only be achieved by reducing the hens' rate of egg production per cycle.

Problems Associated with Rapid Growth

Weight control is also relevant to the production of broiler chickens and turkeys being raised for breeding purposes rather than for meat production. Genetic selection and management of broilers and turkeys for rapid growth comes at a cost of increased risk for heart attacks and leg deformities that make walking painful, while the prodigious appetite of these birds necessitates continual feed restriction of parent breeding stock to facilitate survival and reproduction. This long-term feed restriction results in hunger and can lead over time to the development of oral stereotypies such as spot pecking. Poultry breeding companies are now applying increased selection pressure against cardiovascular and skeletomuscular problems in these birds, primarily by selecting for somewhat slower growth during early development. The health of broilers and turkeys can also be improved by using short daylengths to limit early growth rate, and hunger in feed restricted breeders can be alleviated to some extent by feeding high-fibre diets.

Bone Fractures

Genetic selection of laying hens for high egg production can also create welfare concerns if insufficient emphasis is placed on concurrent selection for bone strength. The consequence is hens that tend to have fragile bones at the end of lay. This is a problem when hens are caught for transport to a processing plant because they can acquire painful bone fractures when handled. A related problem is that few poultry plants are interested in processing meat from hens, due in part to concerns about food safety created by bone fragments in meat as a result of bone fractures. As a result, hens may face long transportation distances to slaughter, facing an elevated risk of dying in transit.

Due to difficulties in marketing end-of-lay hens in the US, they are increasingly killed on the farm using carbon dioxide gas. Because the hens are killed almost immediately following catching, the duration of suffering from any bone fractures sustained during catching is brief. However, the carcasses must then be disposed of by rendering, incineration or composting, which is wasteful of a potential human food source.

Hen bones are more fragile when hens get little exercise due to confinement in cages. However, the risk of bone breakage in caged hens is low until they are handled at the end of lay. By contrast, although uncaged hens in aviaries and free range systems have stronger bones, they nevertheless can have high rates of keel bone fracture during the laying cycle, possibly due to crash landings and collisions. In either case, broken bones represent a serious animal welfare concern. Fortunately, it is possible to reduce the risk of fractures through improved housing design and gentler handling methods, and to increase bone strength through increased selection pressure for this trait (Figure 46.1). A question is how much to favour bone strength through genetic selection if this benefit comes at a cost of reduced egg production, thereby increasing the number of hens that must be kept to obtain the same number of eggs.

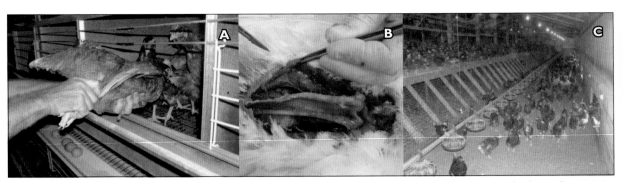

Figure 46.1. (a) Laying hens must be handled carefully to avoid bone fractures; (b) Fractured keel bone; (c) Housing must be designed to minimise the risk of bone fractures when hens move between locations. Photo: R. Newberry.

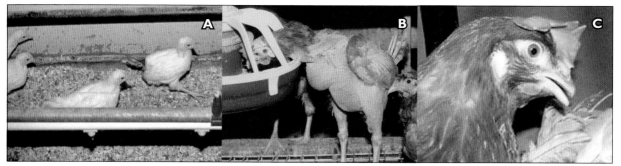

Figure 46.2. (a) Cannibalistic attack; (b) Feather pecked hen; (c) Beak trimmed hen. Photo: Photo: R. Newberry.

Cannibalism

Cannibalism and feather pecking are pervasive welfare problems in poultry (Figure 46.2). The incidence is sometimes very high in hens with intact beaks, especially when hens are kept in large groups and even a single cannibalistic bird has access to many potential victims. In addition to causing welfare problems, feather pecking results in denuded birds that need to eat more feed to stay warm. Beak trimming is a minor surgical procedure used to control these behaviours. Beak trimming also makes manipulation of feed more difficult, resulting in less feed being thrown on the floor and wasted. Beak trimming is, however, a painful procedure and may reduce the ability of hens to remove parasitic mites through preening.

Beak trimming has been banned in Sweden, and some other countries are considering a similar ban. As a result, producers must use management techniques that reduce the risk of cannibalism such as rearing pullets with perches, which increases the likelihood that they will use the nest boxes for egg laying as adults. There is also increased demand for hens of genetic lines in which strong selection pressure has been applied to reduce cannibalistic tendencies. Nevertheless, the debate about beak trimming continues because, if properly done, it is reliably effective in minimising the risk of cannibalism, whereas cannibalism can otherwise emerge unpredictably. An alternative approach might be to permit beak trimming but find effective methods for controlling the pain from the procedure.

Behavioural Restriction

Probably the most hotly debated issue concerning the welfare of poultry is the behavioural restriction that results from the housing of laying hens in unfurnished cages. The European Union is phasing out the use of conventional cage housing systems for laying hens by 2012 by requiring that hens be provided with a nest, perch and foraging/dust bathing substrate. The intention is that these enrichments, whether provided in furnished cages or in aviaries, pens with litter and slatted areas, or free range systems, allow hens to perform more natural behaviour (Figure 46.3). In the US, animal advocacy groups are pressing for legislation to ban the use of cage housing systems where hens are unable to spread their wings without touching cage walls or other birds. In addition, there is increasing consumer demand for eggs from non-cage systems and especially for free range eggs and poultry meat, and consumers are showing a willingness to pay more for poultry products with some form of humane certification. Although increased behavioural freedom is a laudable goal, it is not a simple matter to define and implement welfare standards for non-cage housing that produce an overall net benefit for poultry welfare while at the same time being sustainable in other ways.

For example, what constitutes an adequate perch for a hen (Figure 46.4)? Should a rod a few centimetres off the cage floor count as a perch? It would help to increase leg bone strength but do hens feel safer as a result of sitting on such perches? This may be the case at night when it is dark but not in the daytime when there is an increased risk of being cannibalised while sitting on low perches. What

Figure 46.3. Laying hens are kept in a wide range of housing systems, each with benefits and costs for hen well-being. Photo: Photo: R. Newberry.

if higher perches are required, resulting in birds that are calmer and safer from cannibalism but with an increased incidence of keel bone fractures as a result of crash landings when jumping off perches? If a slatted floor allows birds to wrap their feet around the slats, should the slatted area be counted as perch space? What if birds do not use the perches that are provided to meet an auditing requirement? This may occur if perches are specified in legal requirements for the housing of adults only and the birds are not given the opportunity to obtain early experience in the use of perches. Genetic background and body weight can also influence propensity to use perches. Furthermore, depending on their design and placement, perches can affect the use of nest boxes, the frequency

of cracked eggs, the ease of keeping the facilities clean, the likelihood of faeces falling on birds below, the risk of foot lesions, and a host of other interrelated factors. As a consequence, a simple decision to require that hens be provided with perches to enable natural behaviour turns out to have many implications, depending upon how the requirement is implemented and audited.

Similar questions can be asked about appropriate substrates for promoting foraging, exploration and dust bathing behaviour, the amount of space that should be covered with these substrates, and the amount of time that they should be available to the birds. Porous floors allow faeces to fall through and be separated from the birds, thereby reducing the risk of faeces-born pathogens

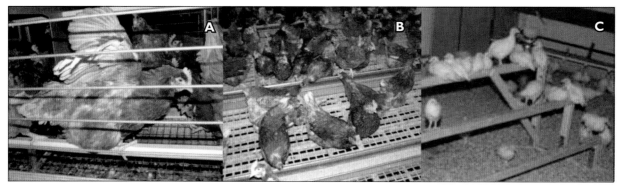

Figure 46.4. (a) Hen on perch in furnished cage; (b) Slatted floor 'perch space'; (c) Providing perches during rearing enables pullets to learn to move in 3-dimensional space. Photo: Photo: R. Newberry.

and parasites. When a particulate substrate is provided, it must be managed carefully to avoid problems with ammonia, dust and painful foot pad dermatitis.

Access to free range can potentially provide the greatest degree of environmental enrichment for the birds, especially when there is woodland cover that provides a sense of security relative to open space. However, it also comes with risks such as predators, soil-borne parasites, and exposure to wildlife providing potential for disease transmission. In addition, manure must be managed to avoid environmental pollution. Products from such systems are more expensive due to greater land use, higher feed consumption, and sometimes higher mortality. Nevertheless, it is likely that the future will bring increased consumer demand for pasture-based production systems and use of less productive but more robust breeds of poultry.

ness and damage to the environment. Ethical review of poultry production practices incorporating the latest scientific knowledge and taking into account the hierarchy of public values can help to identify improvements and avoid unanticipated adverse consequences for both people and poultry.

Conclusions

The health and well-being of poultry in different housing and management systems can range from good to poor depending on the genetic stock used, previous rearing conditions of the birds, specifics of the housing design and management, and husbandry skills and empathy of poultry caretakers. Sustainable solutions are needed that promote poultry health and well-being while at the same time maintaining the affordability and safety of poultry products, ensuring worker safety, and avoiding wasteful-

Humane Transport and Slaughter of Farm Animals

47

David Arney and Andres Aland
Estonian University of Life Sciences, Tartu, Estonia

Introduction

For most animals transport is at the most infrequent and probably a unique experience ending at the slaughterhouse, except perhaps for some intrafarm movement of young stock (Figure 47.1). They are therefore likely to find the experience alarming and stressful, but the process can be managed to minimise discomfort and distress. Increased lengths of journeys for animals, as slaughterhouses become reduced in number and therefore further from the sites of production, add to the problem. Nevertheless, we should consider the animals' needs and reduce the stress experiences insofar as this is possible. This applies from an animal welfare perspective, but also from a strictly economic one; stress and mechanical damage from injury reduce both the quality and quantity of useable meat produced at the end of the operation. This section considers warm-blooded farm animals. Those wishing to consider the issues regarding the transport and slaughter of fish are recommended to access the Humane Slaughter Association's website listed below in the recommended reading section.

Transport

Broom (2000) reviewed the welfare problems associated with the transport of farm animals. EU legislation regard-

Figure 47.1. Moving young calves within a farm. Fine for a very short trip but hardly suitable for a longer journey. Photo: H. Jaakson.

ing the transportation of animals covers regulation of the design and maintenance of vehicles, and is designed to ensure that personnel involved are sympathetic to the needs of the animals under their temporary care, that they are properly trained, that the stress experienced by transported animals is minimised and thereby welfare conditions are optimised.

Measures used to estimate the welfare of animals during transport include physical measures: weight loss (particularly in poultry; Mitchell et al., 2003), incidence of injuries, bruising, mortality, evidence of morbidity, panting/shivering and assessment of carcase quality. Behavioural measures might include a decrease in time spent ruminating and lying and physiological indicators might include heart rate and analysis of cortisol and fatty acids in serum. Assessment of the suitability of the transport should also be included in any audit of the welfare of the transport process; is it clean, likely to cause injury, does it have sufficient ventilation and is it appropriate? In this last regard, low-volume animals, such as wild boar, ostrich and deer, have been reported to be transported in unmodified trailers designed for other stock (Bornett-Gauci et al., 2006). Transport facilities designed for the purpose of such species are at best much less easily available than those for more familiar livestock species.

Inappropriate handling during the entire transport operation (loading, journey time and unloading) can result in poorer meat quality (Voisinet et al., 1997), and this can be more stress-inducing than the transportation itself (Waas et al., 1999). Impairment of meat quality is not only through mechanical damage to the carcase, but also the chemical changes in the meat, such as reduced pH, (a value higher than 6 leads to dark cutting meat) and the consequence of high levels in the meat of cortisol, which is released during periods of stress (Smith and Dobson, 1990). Poultry are at particular risk during loading. In many European broiler systems they are picked up from the floor by the legs in handfuls of up to eight per person (Mitchell and Kettlewell, 2004). The working conditions (low light, dusty, high volumes of bird removal, 1,000 birds per man hour expected) and poor pay are not conducive to an appreciation of the birds' welfare. Mechanical collection devices have been developed which are increasingly being used on production units. While there is some evidence that stress to the chickens can be reduced with these, there is also evidence that physical damage to the chickens can be increased (Ekstrand, 1998).

Consideration of the transport process should include loading and unloading (including personnel handling skills, conditions, widths of approach passageways and the angle of the ramp – this should not be steep), as well as the actual journey. All chutes and other facilities for loading animals should be designed to minimise stress to the animal as they proceed through the loading process. The flooring around the loading area should provide sufficient traction for the animals to avoid slipping. Factors to consider during the journey include the length, road type (road surface, topology and the number and severity of curves; Jago et al., 1997), vehicle type, how the animals are grouped, where they are positioned in the vehicle and the quality of the driving, which should be smooth and steady with no unnecessarily sharp braking or acceleration; Tarrant (1990) found that a third of floored animals during transport were caused by sharp cornering. For the transport of poultry it has been proposed that the greatest threat to their welfare is heat stress (Mitchell et al., 1998), even in conditions where the external temperature is sub-zero (Knezacek et al., 2000).

Regarding the extent of journey time, findings in the literature differ, but there is evidence that longer journeys increase the welfare problems for transported animals linearly, for poultry (Carlyle et al., 1997; Nijdam et al., 2004) as well as for mammal species (Dalin et al., 1993; Waas et al., 1999). There is also evidence of habituation by animals to transport events.

Animals should preferably be transported in groups that are familiar, or at least with animals of the same size, to reduce aggression. Animals ought not to be moved during the sensitive part of their sexual cycle, and if possible single species should be moved together. If the numbers of animals being transported are high, stress is increased and this can lead to mortality in poultry (Nijdam et al., 2004). However if there are too few animals being transported this increases the chances of individual animals losing their balance and falling over. There should be enough room for the animals to lie down if they choose. Guidance figures for cattle have been suggested by Tarrant (1990) of: 0.77 m^2 for a 250 kg animal, 1.13 m^2 for a 450 kg animal and 1.63 m^2 for a 650 kg animal. It has been recommended that when deer are being transported there should be a space allowance of at least 0.4 m^2 per animal (Waas et al., 1997), somewhat lower than the previous figures. Higher numbers will increase the need for sufficient ventilation for all animals, and this is of particular importance for poultry (Mitchell and Kettlewell, 2004). Regarding the position in the vehicle, higher heart rates have been found in animals at the back of the vehicle (Waas et al., 1997). It can be assumed that this is because of more movement, both horizontal and vertical, experienced at the rear, so if possible animals should be loaded towards the front.

Less commonly transported animals may be at more risk of welfare problems through unfamiliarity with their needs (Bornett-Gauci et al., 2006), and the use in practice of equipment and vehicles designed for other species. Consequently, on-farm slaughter of animals such as deer is probably preferable to transport to an abattoir; comparison of animals shot in the field with those transported for slaughter has shown that cortisol and incidences of dark cutting meat in the carcase both increased (Pollard et al., 2002).

Different animal species are affected differently by transport and handling. More domesticated species are generally less disturbed, while low-volume farm animals such as deer, wild boar, ostrich and wild animals that have not been habituated to transport events are more likely to suffer from the experience (Bornett-Gauci et al., 2006). Broom (2000) has suggested that, of domesticated animals, sheep are least affected, cattle are sometimes affected, pigs are always affected and poultry handled by humans are always severely affected. There may also be breed differences within species.

Figure 47.2. Pigs being misted while awaiting slaughter. Photo: A. Tänavots.

Lairage

This is the time and place spent between arrival at a slaughterhouse and the beginning of the slaughter operation, a period that should be kept to a minimum, although there should be sufficient time allowed for recovery from the stress of the journey – three hours for pigs (Warriss et al., 1998). It is a stressful environment that is strange, with unfamiliar sounds and smells. The vocalisations of stressed animals, combined with human shouting, which is thought to be particularly abhorrent to animals (Weeks, 2008), can make this a particularly stressful auditory environment, especially as the auditory thresholds of these animals are thought to be lower than that of humans (Heffner and Heffner, 1983). Personnel should be sympathetic and trained to recognise problems and to move animals calmly and quietly. The longer the time that animals spend in lairage, the more bruising is to be found on the animals (Warriss et al., 1998), the more broiler chickens found dead before the slaughter process begins (Nijdam et al., 2004), and the greater the increase in physiological stress indicators (at least in rabbits; Liste et al., 2009). Behavioural welfare indicators, including vocalisations, suggest that the welfare of animals in lairage can be improved by dim

lighting, misting (Figure 47.2) and large pen size. Weeks (2008) has suggested minimum space allowances of 1.7 m^2 for cattle, 0.56 m^2 for sheep and 0.42 m^2 for pigs, in ideal conditions, with a short lairage period.

The area should be well ventilated. This is true for all animals, but poultry are at particular risk of heat stress while in lairage (Hunter et al., 1998). There should be access to drinking water at all times, and to feed and appropriate bedding if kept overnight. Ideally, animals should not be kept next to other species and not next to unfamiliar conspecifics. If different species need to be kept in close proximity while at lairage the types of species mixed should be considered. For example in the case of deer at lairage the presence of pigs was found to be the cause of more stress than cows. Aggressive animals should be separated. There should be a designated casualty pen for animals that are sick or injured, and animals that are unable to walk should be slaughtered *in situ*.

Slaughter

The slaughter of animals commonly involves stunning (rendering unconscious), rapidly followed by sticking (exsanguination), which should rapidly lead to death. Carried out correctly this should involve as little pain and suffering to the animals as possible. Welfare problems arise if something goes wrong in this process, either the animals are insufficiently stunned or the period between stun and stick is so long that the animal regains consciousness. Signs of effective stunning include a tonic phase: collapsed animal, no regular breathing, fixed and dilated pupils with no corneal reflex, a relaxed jaw with the tongue hanging out and a clonic phase: muscle relaxation, involuntary kicking, eyeballs drift downwards and urination or defecation. These signs are not common to all methods of stunning, which can lead to inaccurate estimation by personnel who are more familiar with one system.

Methods of stunning are commonly either mechanical concussion of the central nervous system or electrical stunning. Larger animals, such as cattle, are stunned with a captive bolt to the head. Sheep and pigs are usually stunned by electrodes applied to the head, and poultry have their heads immersed and electrocuted in water baths. The design of the water baths, and the birds' entry, should be such as to reduce the likelihood of an electric shock prior to effective stunning of the bird. Animals, pigs and poultry particularly, may also be stunned using carbon dioxide in gas tunnels, but there is concern that although the stunning may be effective this may be more stressful than the other methods (Hänsch et al., 2009).

Prior to slaughter, animals should be moved calmly along the race, which should ensure easy passage, with no sharp angles. Poultry have a more complicated pre-stunning procedure as they need to be shackled. This can lead to wing flapping, pain for the birds, and downgrading of the carcase quality. Stress can be reduced at shackling by holding the bird's legs for 1-2 seconds afterwards (Wotton and Wilkins, 2003). As there is wide variation in the electrical resistance of birds (between and within species), the current required to effectively stun birds also varies (Wotton and Wilkins, 2003). As birds are commonly stunned in groups of more than 10, this means that in any group of birds some may not be stunned, while others may be stunned but suffer impairment to their meat quality (Gregory and Wilkins, 1989). The method of stunning with gas is becoming more widely used, particularly for poultry. It removes the need for uncrating after transportation, removes the necessity of handling and shackling of birds while they are conscious, and all birds in a crate are stunned at the same time, avoiding the problem de-

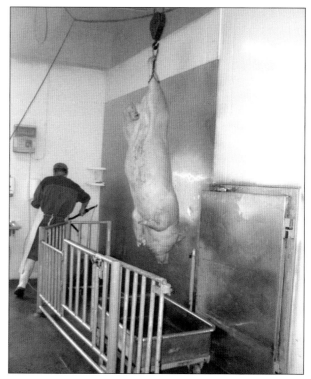

Figure 47.3. A pig that has been stunned and suspended ready for sticking, an interval that should be as short as possible. Photo: A. Tänavots.

scribed above of individuals in a group remaining conscious (Hänsch et al., 2009). These are all positive welfare benefits.

Appropriate handling is important at slaughter too. Both stunning and sticking procedures need to be correctly and quickly applied (Anil et al., 2000). It is particularly important that the stun to stick interval is as short as possible (Figure 47.3). With electric water bath stunning for poultry, the current applied is very important for welfare; too high and the meat will be damaged, too low and the bird will not be stunned. In light of the welfare problems associated with transport, it might improve welfare if animals could be slaughtered on-farm. Indeed this is the case with animals that are wild or recently domesticated, and which comprise a small proportion of total livestock, such as deer, which can be shot in the field or slaughtered in mobile abattoirs. Although the former sounds crude it is probably much the best method in terms of welfare:

shooting with a rifle is accurate up to a range of 40 m, and up to 10 individuals can be shot without noticeably disturbing the rest of the group (MAFF, 1989). However, deer are still transported to distant abattoirs for slaughter, because of concerns about hygiene standards, legislative restrictions, cost-effectiveness and the aversion that some farmers have to killing animals that they have reared themselves (Bornett-Gauci, 2006).

Religious Slaughter

This is a subject heavily loaded with controversy. Muslim (*Halal*) and Jewish (*Shechta*) slaughter involves the sticking of an animal without it having been previously stunned. The animal is handled and stuck while still conscious. It is believed by defenders of this method that this ensures a thorough bleed-out of the animal, leads rapidly to unconsciousness and is painless. Opposition to this method is based on the belief that without stunning the animal is more likely to endure pain and distress. Many would say that the experience of being held and stuck, even with a sharp knife as its defenders claim, is undoubtedly stressful and painful. Work by Anil et al. (2004) on sheep slaughter suggests that stunning, by captive bolt or electrical electrodes, has no impairment on the bleed-out efficiency, and some Muslim groups accept that animals that have been stunned before being bled can be regarded as *Halal* slaughter. We can use science to estimate the suffering endured by animals in any slaughter method, but as individuals and as societies, we need to address whether to permit the freedom for people to follow religious imperatives or to recognise the importance of animal welfare, which in this case probably conflict.

Conclusions

Transport is a rare event in the life of most farm animals, usually to slaughter, but we should not neglect the fact that this can be a serious welfare problem. Not only this, but poorly designed and executed handling and transport can also cause economic losses, the quality of meat can be impaired by stress and injury, and the amount of recovered meat for human consumption can also be reduced in quantity. There are a range of factors to be addressed when considering optimal transport conditions, including handling, loading and unloading procedures, and selection of animals to be transported, in addition to the design of the vehicle and details of the journey, not only the length but also the smoothness of the ride. Lairage is also potentially stressful, an unfamiliar environment with, probably, strange animals and even species in close proximity. The length of time spent in lairage should be short, as longer duration leads to more physical damage in addition to welfare concerns, but should be sufficiently long to allow the animal to recover. The slaughtering process usually involves an initial stunning before the animal is killed by sticking. The animal should not regain consciousness between these two events, and so the stun-stick interval should be as short as possible. Slaughter that is carried out differently, e.g. in accordance with Jewish and Muslim religious codes, involves no stunning prior to sticking, so the animals are conscious when stuck. It is believed that this leads to a more through bleed-out of the slaughtered animal, although this has been disputed. And that the suffering endured by the animal is no different, which is also disputed.

Monitoring Animal Welfare at Slaughterhouses

48

Charlotte Berg
Swedish University of Agricultural Sciences
Skara, Sweden

It is often debated whether official control of animal welfare should focus on prevention of suffering, based on minimum requirements related to housing and management, or whether it is better to focus on the outcome, i.e. trying to determine if there are any signs of suffering by evaluating the status of the animals. In most cases scientists, veterinarians and animal welfare inspectors would agree that a combination of the 'input' based approach and the 'outcome' based approach would be necessary to safeguard animal welfare. Does this apply also to the slaughterhouse situation?

A Slaughterhouse is Not Just Another Farm

Monitoring animal welfare at a slaughterhouse is somewhat different to the situation on the farm. The throughput numbers can be very high, and there is no possibility to know the individual history, background or habits of each animal. The animals are unfamiliar to the staff, and the staff are unfamiliar to the animals. There are obvious time constraints and the environment is of course completely novel to the animals, with lairage areas not necessarily designed to minimise noise or visual distraction. Furthermore, most animals will be unknown to each other even if they may be delivered in groups or batches, and it is not rare to see mixing of completely unfamiliar animals. All in all, the risks of stress are high, even though the duration of the stay at the abattoir is normally short.

If monitoring of animal welfare is to be carried out at abattoirs, tailor-made protocols for this specific purpose will be required. Such protocols have, for example, recently been developed within the Welfare Quality project (Sandström et al., 2008).

Design to Facilitate the Handling of Live Animals at Slaughterhouses

Sub-optimal handling of animals can unfortunately be seen at many slaughterhouses, where animals are coerced in a rough manner, using sticks or prods and loud voices to make the animals move fast enough in the direction desired. Within the European Union the use of electric prods is limited by legislation (93/119/EC), but nevertheless the use of such equipment is frequent in some Member States. This will inevitably result in poor animal welfare. By designing unloading areas, lairage pens and passageways in a way that makes it possible to use the animals' natural exploratory behaviour when moving them forward, the need for coercion can be minimised. For example, our commonly slaughtered species are all flock animals, and it is therefore quite difficult to move one single animal away from the flock. By keeping a small group of animals intact as long as possible, i.e. up to the entrance of the stun box or even into the stunner – depending on stunning method – the entire process will become much smoother for both animals and staff, compared with when individual animals are singled out at an early stage.

By minimising noise from metal gates and other equipment, using solid wall passageways to prevent visual distraction, avoiding sharp bends, dazzling light or sudden reflexes, a more calm and steady flow of animals can be achieved (Grandin, 2006).

Training of Staff

Layout and design is crucial, but the knowledge and training of staff is just as essential (Grandin, 2006; Wotton and Wittington, 2008). Well-designed basic construction will give the staff possibilities to do a good job, but proper training and instructions are also necessary. This should include knowledge about normal animal behaviour for all species concerned, how the flight zone works and how it can be used to move animals forward without violent coercion, how to identify and handle injured or sick animals in the lairage area or passageways, and also knowledge about how rough handling will affect animal welfare and product quality. Avoiding stress or bruising is in the interest of the food business operator, to keep downgradings and rejections to a minimum and meat quality traits optimal, apart from the obvious animal welfare aspects.

Operator Responsibility and Monitoring Systems

Whose responsibility is it to safeguard animal welfare at slaughterhouses? Basically, it is always the operator who is responsible for complying with all types of legislation in the field, both in designing and in managing the facilities and the equipment. The operator should ensure that all staff members handling live animals, from unloading to the point when bleeding is completed and the animal is dead, have the necessary knowledge and training. There have to be clear instructions and guidelines to staff, and preferably standard operating procedures (SOP). Such SOPs will be requested in the future in accordance with the upcoming EU regulation (EC No 1099/2009). There should, for example, be no doubt about the maximum number of animals allowed per pen for animals waiting for a few hours or kept overnight in lairage. Technical equipment, such as stunning equipment or restraint devices, should be accompanied by clear instructions for proper use from the manufacturer. Written and oral information must, of course, be given in a language which can be understood by the staff involved.

The management level at each slaughterhouse has to develop a system for quality control, to be able to guarantee that animal welfare legislation is not violated during the daily work at the abattoir. One aid in this work is the use of different types of standard operating procedures; another is the use of lists for signing when a task has been carried out according to instructions. For example, it is advisable to let the person performing the daily cleaning, maintenance and function control of the stunning equipment put his or her signature on a sheet of paper, where the management can then easily verify that these tasks have been carried out according to the set procedure at set intervals. Such a system also helps in making it clear where the responsibility lies and trace-back in the case of failure. By having a third party auditor verifying the accuracy of this type of documentation, credibility towards both authorities and customers can be even further improved.

In several countries it is already common to have one person, employed by the operator, appointed to be in charge of animal welfare issues at the slaughterhouse. This is important in order to make it easy for staff to know whom to contact in the case of problems or questions, and this person will then have a unique overview of the implementation of legislation and procedures in the slaughterhouse. However, it is crucial that this person has the required technical expertise, is knowledgeable about animal behaviour and health and is well informed about current legislation. He or she must also be authorised to demand immediate action or to intervene if animals are being handled in an unacceptable way. Such a person is often referred to as an 'animal welfare officer'. This term is slightly misleading, however, as this is not a government official but an employee of the slaughterhouse operator. In the upcoming EU regulation on animal welfare at the time of killing (including slaughter), designating such a person will be a requirement for larger slaughterhouses (EC No 1099/2009). However, also for smaller enterprises it can certainly be useful to ensure that one person is clearly given the task of monitoring animal welfare.

Official Control of Animal Welfare at Slaughterhouses

Although, as stated above, the responsibility for animal welfare lies with the business operator, animal welfare is seen as an area where the authorities have an obligation to perform official controls to verify compliance with existing legislation. In most countries – especially within the European Union – everyday animal welfare monitoring is carried out by the official veterinarians, who also have other tasks, mainly in the area of food safety (EC No 854/2004). The official veterinarians can inspect all incoming animals to ensure that they are fit for slaughter. If this is not the case, whether for animal welfare or food hygiene reasons, the animal in question should be immediately euthanised and destroyed. Furthermore, the official veterinarian can inspect animals in lairage and live animal handling when moving animals from lairage to the point of stunning. Finally, the official veterinarian can perform regular on-the-spot checks of stunning efficacy and bleeding procedures. He or she can also supervise how the staff are monitoring stun quality and the results of these operator responsibility checks, including actions taken when results have been unsatisfactory.

Practical Aspects of Slaughterhouse Audits

It is inherently difficult to monitor live animal handling at slaughterhouses (Sandström et al., 2008). Although the buildings should be constructed to facilitate supervision, this is rarely the case. Space is restricted; it is difficult to find somewhere to stand to get a good overview without disturbing the flow of animals, standing where it is meaningful can be dangerous, and so on. Furthermore, people who know that they are being watched can easily change their behaviour, sometimes because they know that what they normally do is not quite acceptable but sometimes just through becoming nervous. It can be foreseen that in the future video surveillance cameras (CCTV) will be used to a much larger extent than today, to monitor the handling of animals. Small, well-placed video or web cameras will not disturb the animals or the staff, and can still provide a lot of information about how animals are handled, and can be a useful tool to identify problem areas in the slaughterhouse. While video surveillance can never be a substitute for the physical presence of an auditor – whether an operator-employed animal welfare officer, a third party auditor or an official veterinarian – it can certainly be a useful complement.

To Demonstrate Compliance and High Ethical Standards

In summary: By involving veterinarians and others with animal welfare expertise when designing new abattoir facilities, many problems can be avoided already at the drawing-table. If the design of an already existing slaughterhouse is sub-optimal, this can – but only to some extent – be compensated for by skilled and patient staff with clear guidance from the management. A modern slaughterhouse operator will need to be able to demonstrate not only compliance with minimum legal requirements with respect to animal welfare, but also high ethical standards in general. To do this, both transparent internal monitoring systems and external audits are necessary.

Can Farm Animal Welfare Standards be Compatible with Free Trade?

49

Michael C. Appleby

*World Society for the Protection of Animals,
London, United Kingdom*

Introduction

In the livestock agriculture of developed countries a predominant tendency over the last 50 years has been a drive for cost efficiency – for cutting the cost of producing each egg or unit of meat or milk. One result has been the development of intensive farming and other practices causing problems for animal welfare, and this is also now occurring in many developing countries. But meanwhile there has been increasing concern in many countries for the welfare of farm animals. This has restricted practices deleterious to welfare or conversely led to standards for the protection or promotion of welfare, albeit very unevenly. Are such standards compatible with the increase in international trade and competition between countries, which tends to increase the pressure for cheap food production?

Production Cost and Welfare

The decline in cost of food production in developed countries was initiated by public policies in favour of more abundant, cheaper food. However, in recent years it has acquired its own momentum. Continuing decline in food prices is sometimes attributed to pressure from consumers, but it would be more accurate to say that it now primarily results from competition between producers and between retailers.

This competition sometimes causes problems for animal welfare, but does not always do so. First it must be noted that some producers claim that the welfare of their animals is satisfactory almost by definition, because poor welfare would be associated with poor production and hence self-defeating. This indicates an emphasis on those physical aspects of welfare that are associated with production. However, people vary in their attitude to welfare, emphasising physical aspects, mental aspects, naturalness, or a combination of these (Figure 49.1; Fraser et al., 1997), and these do not all correlate with production.

Furthermore, profit from a group of animals often does not correlate with welfare of its individual members. So there are many instances where measures to increase profit have caused welfare problems, for example decreasing space allowances for rearing pigs (Figure 49.2). One of the main effects of competition has been intensification of livestock farming: in the case of pigs, keeping them indoors, increasing stocking densities, using crates and stalls, selecting for growth rate and reducing weaning age.

It is true, of course, that emphasis on production does militate against severe mistreatment or neglect of animals,

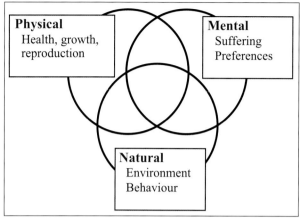

Figure 49.1. Different approaches to welfare overlap, but not completely (Appleby, 1999).

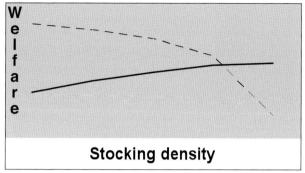

Figure 49.2. Profit from a group of animals often does not correlate with welfare of its individual members. In this hypothetical diagram the broken line represents growth rate and welfare of individual piglets as their stocking density is increased, while the solid line represents profit from the house.

and that conversely there are many instances where measures to reduce costs will improve welfare, for example measures to prevent disease and mortality. Nevertheless, a focus on efficiency has not always identified the best methods even to achieve its own aims. It took an alternative approach, aimed at reducing problems for the animals concerned, to identify the fact that humane treatment of livestock by workers improves growth rate and reproduction (Table 49.1; Hemsworth, 2004). A similar approach showed that understanding animal behaviour can improve design of handling systems and hence efficient use of labour in handling livestock (Grandin, 2004). In both cases the unit cost of producing or handling animals can be reduced, after an initial investment in worker training or facilities, while also improving animal welfare. So a positive attitude to welfare may benefit both animals and producers despite a competitive market. However, people do not always recognise or act on such opportunities, needing education and help to do so, partly because there may be a requirement of short-term expenditure to achieve long-term benefit.

A positive attitude to welfare by individual farmers may thus produce a degree of protection of farm animal welfare that is completely compatible with, and potentially even promoted by, competition, including that from free trade. This is in some sense a basic farm animal welfare standard, but most discussions of standards concerns more formal, agreed guidelines for animal welfare.

Farm Animal Welfare Standards

Standards for farm animal welfare – or for other aspects of food production – operate at a number of levels of authority. Some are informal agreements among, say, a number of producers. Some are more formal agreements. Some involve assurance, with measures for verification (usually by independent assessors) that the standards are being met. A further level is legislation, which should also involve verification and enforcement.

Standards may also be categorised by the type of entity setting them up, as follows.

Producer group
In a number of countries, farmers or production companies form associations, which may agree on standards of

Table 49.1. Gentle treatment of pigs, compared with rough treatment, reduces cortisol (which indicates stress), decreases their fear of humans, as indicated by the speed with which they approach a person, increases pregnancy rates in young sows (gilts) and accelerates maturation in boars (from Hemsworth et al., 1993).

	Handling		
	Gentle	Minimal	Rough
Blood cortisol (ng/ml)	1.7	1.8	2.4
Time to touch person (s)	48	96	120
Pregnancy in gilts (%)	88	57	33
Age of mating by boars (d)	161	176	193

Table 49.2. Topics covered by the Swine Welfare Assurance Program of the US's National Pork Board (2005) encourage producers to review their practices that affect welfare but do not introduce any new criteria for housing systems.

1	Herd health and nutrition
2	Caretaker training
3	Animal observation
4	Body condition score
5	Euthanasia
6	Handling and movement
7	Facilities
8	Emergency support
9	Continuing assessment and education

good practice to safeguard and promote their behaviour, reputation and sales. In recent years these have responded to public opinion by including consideration of welfare, although they vary in how much they actually raise standards above customary practice. For example, in the US the National Pork Board has set up the Swine Welfare Assurance Program, which encourages producers to review their practices that affect welfare but does not introduce any new criteria for housing systems (Table 49.2). By contrast the American Veal Association announced in 2007 that its members would phase out individual crates for veal calves.

Production, processing or retailing company
Companies are also responsive to public opinion and in the US several large companies have introduced standards. In 2000 the McDonalds Corporation started requiring its suppliers to provide laying hens with the same space allowance as in Europe, and not to practise forced moulting. Other fast food chains followed suit, and subsequently the National Council of Chain Restaurants (NCCR) and the Food Marketing Institute (FMI, which represents the major supermarket chains) developed a collaborative programme, producing husbandry guidelines for their suppliers of animal products. More recently some large production and processing companies have acted similarly: for example in 2007 Smithfields, the world's largest pork production and processing company, decided to phase out gestation crates for sows on all its farms.

More stringent standards are being developed by a company that emphasises ethical issues of food, the US/UK chain of food stores Whole Foods Market. Its Animal Compassionate Standards will, for example, prohibit bill trimming in ducks.

Speciality producers
Some producers also address consumer concerns about food production methods by developing niche markets, obtaining higher selling prices to offset their higher production costs – if, indeed, their production costs are really higher, which is often a matter of debate. They do this either because they share consumer concerns, or for business reasons, or both. As well as welfare, such concerns include the following, and production methods that take these into account may also improve the welfare of livestock: the environment (especially organic production) (Appleby, 2005), food safety and quality, food security, local food production, family farms, farm workers, rural communities and developing countries. Standards that specifically address animal welfare are generally endorsed and verified by welfare organisations: in the UK, the Royal Society for Prevention of Cruelty to Animals; in North America, the American Humane Association, Humane Farm Animal Care, the Animal Welfare Institute and the British Columbia SPCA.

States and countries
In some countries, individual states can pass their own legislation, and there are instances of legislation favouring animal welfare. In the US, Florida banned gestation crates for sows in 2002 and California legislated in 2004 to phase out force feeding of poultry for *foie gras* production. However, market forces militate against such legislation because there is resistance to any measures that reduce competitiveness with other states.

Many countries are developing legislation for animal welfare. This varies from codified lists of actions that are prohibited to simple statements that animals must not be ill-treated. Both may be backed by more detailed advisory codes. In European countries, however, legislation is increasingly subject to the wider groupings discussed in the next section.

Groups of Countries

The European Union (EU) has more comprehensive legislation for animal welfare than anywhere else in the world. This is partly influenced by the wider grouping of the Council of Europe, with 47 countries and the EU as members. This has stated that 'the humane treatment of animals is one of the hallmarks of Western civilisation'. The EU passes Directives, which then have to be translated into national legislation. In the current context there are two particularly relevant Directives. A Directive on husbandry systems for laying hens was passed in 1999. It included provisions for a review in 2004 taking into account 'the socio-economic implications of the various systems,' but at the time of writing that review has still not been produced. A Broiler Directive was passed in 2007. This was weaker than earlier drafts, apparently because of concerns over the pressure of imports of chicken meat and the threat to the industry of avian influenza.

There are some moves to include consideration of animal welfare in other groupings, such as Free Trade Areas. The EU is including measures for animal welfare in bilateral trade agreements, for example with Chile: primarily those that overlap with measures to protect food hygiene, such as controls over handling and slaughter methods.

Intergovernmental Organisations

On a worldwide scale, the World Organisation for Animal Health (OIE) has recognised that animal health is affected by other aspects of animal welfare. It has therefore established the first global animal welfare standards, starting with transport and slaughter practices (OIE, 2005) and following up with consideration of husbandry. These have been agreed by the 167 member countries, but many countries have not yet made progress on implementation.

Other intergovernmental organisations are recognising the contributions of animal treatment and animal welfare to economics and to poverty and hunger reduction. For example, the International Finance Corporation, part of the World Bank Group, has issued guidelines on 'Creating business opportunity through improved animal welfare' and on 'Animal welfare in livestock operations.'

Are Standards Compatible with Free Trade?

The multiplicity of standard-setting agencies and standards outlined in the previous section suggests that the

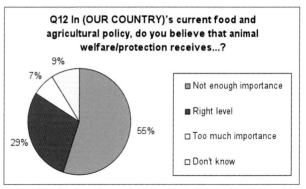

Figure 49.3. Public concern for animal welfare in developed countries continues to grow. The illustration analyses 24,708 replies from the countries of the EU to one of the questions in a survey by Eurobarometer in 2005.

answer to whether such standards are compatible with increasingly competitive trade is not simple, but is nevertheless in many or even most cases positive. The main motivation for creation of standards is increasing public concern for farm animal welfare, in both developed countries (Figure 49.3) and developing countries (as evidenced by the unanimous support for standards from all member countries of the OIE). As such, few standard-setting agencies will back down in the face of competition, in a business environment that is increasingly requiring corporate responsibility and accountability for ethical matters including animal welfare. Thus a senior executive of Burger King commented in 2002 that their customers expect them – the restaurant company – to ensure that the animals supplying them with food are properly looked after. Indeed, the fact that corporate decisions on animal welfare are based on consumer attitudes means that they are based on broad market considerations rather than on narrow accounting of only the cost of food animal production (which is anyway just a small component of final product price) (Appleby et al., 2004). This grounding in consumer preferences means that availability of information on the welfare of food producing animals is often important, whether by product labelling or by other means such as company or national websites.

Some standards are neutral for production costs – although it has to be said that this includes some anodyne 'standards' that do little or nothing more than codify existing practices rather than actually improving welfare.

Some reduce costs – and it is important to note that, as with the work by Hemsworth (2004) and Grandin (2004) described above, this may be a surprise. When the US group United Egg Producers started to phase in larger space requirements for hens in cages in 2002, many producers introduced the final target space allowance rapidly rather than slowly. Contrary to their expectation that housing the maximum number of hens per cage would maximise profits, they found that reducing stocking density improved production and feed conversion efficiency by individual hens, saved on feed costs and improved profit overall.

Some standards do increase costs, but will survive for various reasons. Some generate greater income, particularly in niche markets, and there is every indication that speciality markets will continue to grow, including for high-welfare products, becoming less of a minority 'niche.' As noted above, standards for welfare also overlap with those for other criteria such as organic production. This is important both for niche sales and because wider welfare standards will be protected and even promoted by the fact that they have common characteristics with other imperatives such as environmental protection and food hygiene (Appleby et al., 2003).

Trade is thus not wholly free, and this is particularly true of international trade. A country's own animal food products, produced to certain welfare standards, may be promoted by its authorities (by advertising, use of tariffs etc.) and favoured by its citizens both because of those standards themselves and for other reasons such as local food security. There are also practical factors supporting in-country production, notably transport costs and hygiene controls – although these certainly do not always overwhelm other factors. Thus egg production in Europe is subject to competition from imports (partly because of costs associated with higher welfare, but more because of other costs such as labour and feed being greater than in competitor countries). This will probably have little impact on sales of European-produced whole eggs, but more on those of liquid and dried egg products, which are both more easily transported and sterilised.

Where restrictions on international trade exist, not directly warranted by the World Trade Organisation, they may be challenged under that authority, and the precedents for welfare safeguards being permitted are not

good. However, no challenges on welfare grounds have yet been made, and one possible defence increasingly mentioned is Article XX of the General Agreement on Tariffs and Trade, which says:

'Nothing in this agreement shall be construed to prevent the adoption or enforcement by any contracting party of measures (a) necessary to protect public morals [or] (b) necessary to protect human, animal or plant health.'

Nations faced with imports from countries with lower welfare standards could argue that protecting the welfare of their farm animals was important for public morals and both human and animal health.

It remains true that the pressure of increased trade, both domestic and international, makes creation, strengthening or even maintenance of animal welfare standards even more difficult than in a less competitive market. Some standards may prove incompatible with an increasingly free market, although the arguments presented above suggest that these will be few. Perhaps the strongest effect of freer trade will be a reduction in the creation of new standards, or a weakening of any created – as with the European Broiler Directive discussed earlier.

Yet free trade does not occur in a vacuum: it could be argued that other changes in the environment within which food production occurs are equally important, such as information exchange. Increased communication about animal welfare is maintaining the upward trend in international awareness. People concerned for animals hope, with some justification, that the positive effects of such awareness on farm animal welfare and on welfare protection standards are accelerating (Turner and D'Silva, 2006).

Conclusions

Programmes setting standards for farm animal welfare have increased markedly in recent years, varying in strength from cosmetic to demanding, and in the agencies establishing them from individual farmers to intergovernmental organisations. The main motivation is increasing public concern for farm animal welfare, which overlaps with other concerns for food hygiene and environmental protection. Most will therefore survive the pressure of increasingly free trade: indeed, some prove in practice to reduce costs or to increase or protect income in other ways. Increasing competition may prevent or weaken creation of standards in future, but the impetus for high food quality (in a broad sense, including its provenance and effects) will continue to increase worldwide, thus requiring any further freeing-up of trade to be compatible with continuing standards for farm animal welfare and other aspects of food production.

An Opinion on the Role of Ethics in Modern Animal Production Systems

Bernard Rollin
Colorado State University
Fort Collins, Colorado, USA

Industrial Agriculture

Industrialised animal agriculture, also known as confinement agriculture, intensive agriculture, factory farming (an appellation not favoured by the industry), and CAFOS (confined animal feeding operations), is a creature of the second half of the 20th century. Before that time, agriculture was extensive and pastoral, with the animals primarily housed under open, pastoral conditions. The industrialisation of animal agriculture was a major break from the agricultural systems that had prevailed since the earliest domestication of animals. It is thus fair to affirm that the majority of animal agriculture changed more during the second half of the 20th century than it did during the preceding millennia.

The key to traditional agricultural success was good husbandry of the animals. (The term is supposedly derived from the Old Norse phrase hus/bond – bonded to one's household.) Husbandry meant placing the animals into the optimal environment best meeting their biological and psychological needs and natures, and then augmenting their natural abilities to survive and thrive by provision of food during famine, water during drought, help in birthing, medical attention, protection from preda-

tion, etc. Since the producer did well if, and only if, the animals did well, the imperative for good husbandry was sanctioned by the most effective human concern – self-interest. It is thus reasonable to refer to husbandry agriculture as embodying an ancient contract between humans and animals, wherein both parties fared better by virtue of the contract than they would have done outside of it.

The most powerful articulation of the ethic of husbandry may be found in the 23rd psalm: The Lord is my shepherd: I shall not want. He leadeth me to green pastures; he maketh me to lie down beside still waters; he restoreth my soul.

In other words, when the Psalmist seeks a metaphor for God's ideal relationship to humans, he can do no better than the shepherd. As we know from the Bible, a lamb on its own would not long survive predation by hyenas, wild dogs, lions, eagles and other predators; with a shepherd it lives well. Animals benefit from the ministrations of the shepherd; humans benefit from the animals' products and sometimes their lives, but while they live, they live well.

In the mid-20th century, the value of husbandry as the basic value for animal agriculture was replaced by industrial values of efficiency and productivity. This was the result of the confluence of many factors. In the first place, the US public had lived through the Great Depression and the Dust Bowl, and for the first time in American history, the spectre of insufficient food, non-affordable food, and starvation loomed as viable possibilities. Second, many people who had worked in agriculture sought better jobs and security from the vagaries of nature by moving to cities and as cities grew, urban encroachment on agricultural land became a factor to be reckoned with.

Furthermore, demographic experts predicted a sharp rise in population – more mouths to feed. The two World Wars further exposed many young soldiers to more exciting venues than e.g. rural America. As a post-World War I song put it, 'How you gonna keep 'em down on the farm now that they've seen Paree?' Finally, the success of industrialisation in business and manufacturing reinforced the belief that it was a template for success in all areas.

The convergence of all of these mutually reinforcing vectors probably made the industrialisation of agriculture inevitable. In a telling, emblematic move, academic departments of Animal Husbandry changed their names to Animal Science, defined as the 'application of industrial methods to the production of animals.' The traditional agrarian values of stewardship, husbandry and way of life ever increasingly gave way to the values of efficiency and productivity.

It is fitting to tether our discussion to a pair of anecdotes experienced by the author that evoke both our balanced past and our tenuous future in the area of animal agriculture.

About three years ago, I was visiting a rancher friend in Wyoming, and having dinner at his home along with a dozen other ranch people. I asked the dinner guests how many of them had ever spent more money on medical treatment for their cattle than the animal was worth in economic terms. All replied in the affirmative. One woman, a fifth generation rancher, asked, with something of an edge, 'What's wrong with that, Buster?' I replied 'Nothing from my perspective. But if I were an agricultural economist, I would tell you that one does not spend $25 to produce a widget that one sells for $20.' She fairly spat her reply: 'Well that's your mistake, Buster. We're not producing widgets, we're taking care of living beings for whom we are responsible!'

Virtually every rancher I have encountered – and I have lectured to around 15,000 across the US and Canadian West – would respond in a similar vein. Even if they do not spend cash, ranch people often sit up all night for days with a marginal calf, warming the animal by the stove in the kitchen, and implicitly valuing their sleep at pennies per hour! Children of ranch families often report that the only time their father ever blew up at them was when they went to a dance or a sporting event without taking care of the animals. These ranchers represent the last large group of agriculturalists in the US still practicing animal husbandry.

In contrast to this elevating anecdote, consider the story told to me by one of my colleagues in Animal Science at Colorado State University. This man told of his son-in-law who had grown up on a ranch, but could not return to it after college because it could not support him and all of his siblings. (Notably, the average net income of a Front Range (i.e. eastern slope of the Rocky Mountains) rancher in Colorado, Wyoming, or Montana is about $35,000!) He reluctantly took a job managing a feeder pig barn at a large swine factory farm. One day he reported a disease that had struck his piglets to his boss. 'I have bad news and good news,' he reported. 'The bad new is that the piglets are sick. The good news is that they can be treated economically.' 'No,' said the boss. 'We don't treat! We euthanise (by dashing the baby pigs' heads on the side of the concrete pen.)' The young man could not accept this. He proceeded to buy the medicine with his own money and clock in on his day off, and treated the animals. They recovered, and he told the boss. The boss's response was 'You're fired!' The young man pointed out that he had treated them with his own time and money, and was thus not subject to firing. He did, however, receive a reprimand in his file. Six months later he quit and became an electrician. He wrote to his father-in-law: 'I know you are disappointed that I left agriculture, Dad. But this ain't agriculture!'

Initially, it appeared that industrialised animal agriculture had delivered on its promises. Productivity increased dramatically, driving the price of animal-based food down to the lowest in history relative to income. Those areas of animal agriculture that changed most dramatically were poultry, eggs, pork and dairy, with the beef industry moving to concentrated animal feeding units – feed lots – as the place where cattle were 'finished' with grain. (Cheap and plentiful grain came from a parallel industrialisation of crop agriculture known as the Green Revolution.)

The key to the industrialisation of animal agriculture was the concentration of large numbers of animals in small spaces, usually (except for cattle feed lots), indoors. Capital replaced labour, and 'animal smart' people schooled in husbandry of the type of animal in question were replaced by untrained minimum wage workers with 'the intelligence being in the system' as one manager put it to me.

Initial optimism about confinement agriculture chilled to the point that the consequences of such an agriculture were viewed as highly problematic in many dimensions first in Europe and, beginning in the 1990's, in the US as well. In the first place, agriculture became dominated by large vertically integrated multi-national corporate entities, causing the extinction of small independent producers. This is dramatically illustrated in the pork industry wherein, in four decades, beginning in the 1960s, the vast majority of small swine producers went out of business (by 2002 there were 87.8% fewer farms than in 1980), and five companies produced some 90% of the pork raised. Small rural communities that thrived when small producers dominated became ghost towns.

With husbandry people being largely unwilling to work in 'animal factories', the labour pool required to man factory farms came to be drawn from unskilled, sometimes illegal immigrant labour being paid minimum wage, resulting often in a clash of cultures with local people.

Traditional agriculture was 'sustainable' by its own internal logic. Animals consumed pasture, and then manure nourished the soil. If one exceeded the carrying capacity of the land, the animals would starve and forage would be destroyed. The result was a 'balanced aquarium' with production limited by available resources and few additional 'inputs' required. In other words, domestic animals became part of the ecosystem in a largely benign manner, as still occurs in properly managed Western US cattle ranching.

In contradistinction, confinement agriculture requires major expenditures ('input') of energy, fossil fuel, and water, to increase productivity beyond the inherent carrying capacity of an area. The animals in confinement are fed not on forage, but on grains produced in giant monocultures highly dependent on chemical fertilisers and pesticides, which cause ecosystemic problems of erosion, aquifer contamination, depredation in soil quality. The manure produced by confined animals (a pig, for example, produces ten times as much waste manure as a human) leads to problems of waste disposal and eutrophication of waterways by nitrogen leaching into water. The presence of thousands of animals in relatively small confined areas produces air quality issues as well, which in turn affects quality of life of persons in the area and respiratory health of workers, and citizens.

The use of 'technological sanders', to force animals into environmental conditions they could not have survived in without technology, as it were square pegs into round holes, creates major problems as well. If we had attempted to raise 100,000 chickens in one building 100 years ago, all would have died of disease spread in three weeks. Today we can control these diseases by antibiotics and vaccines. Yet it is now clear that such use of antibiotics endangers human health by driving antibiotic resistance of pathogens.

Such forcing of animal square pegs into round holes leads to the most egregious moral problem of confinement agriculture – animal welfare. With the animals still biologically 'meant' for extensive conditions, confinement systems proliferate welfare problems. Sows, for example, weighing up to 600 pounds are confined in 0.5 x 1 x 2 m 'gestation crates' (and farrowing crates when they give birth) for their entire productive life, unable to move or even turn. Laying hens are kept in tiny cages, with very little space. Dairy cows never see pasture. Broilers are kept in groups of thousands on restricted floor space. In addition, 'production diseases' – diseases that would not be a problem except for the method of production –proliferate, for example liver abscesses in feedlot cattle fed a high calorie and low roughage unnatural diet. Workers are no longer 'animal smart'. The animal's basic biological and psychological needs and natures are no longer met.

The founders of confinement agriculture made one fatal conceptual error regarding animal welfare. They assumed that animals' welfare was assured if the animals were productive, by and large true under extensive husbandry conditions. However they illegitimately assumed that productivity in industrial conditions still guaranteed welfare, which is not true, given the 'technological sanders' mentioned earlier. These animals may produce economically, yet are not well off, as measured by a variety of parameters, including behavioural anomalies and preference tests 'asking' the animals what they prefer.

In Europe, many of the most severe systems have been legally banned. In the US, a consumer and citizen revolution began in the first decade of the 21st century to create a more animal and environmentally friendly animal agriculture. Niche producers raising animals under more natural conditions have proliferated, as have restaurants and grocery shops specialising in such products. Citizen-initiated referenda banning high confinement have begun to appear, and public concern was recognised by Smithfield, the world's largest pork producer, when the company announced early in 2007 that it would phase out sow stalls.

For all the reasons detailed above, one can affirm that unrestricted industrial agriculture in its current form represents an experiment that failed. While it is unlikely that totally extensive agriculture can be fully restored, it is likely that a new agriculture, melding considerations of sustainability, animal welfare, human and animal health, and social concern for workers and rural communities, will emerge for the future.

Risk Assessment Methodology and Identification of Animal-based Indicators to Assess Animal Welfare at Farm Level

51

Oriol Ribó
European Food Safety Authority (EFSA), Parma, Italy
Harry Blokhuis
Swedish University of Agricultural Sciences, Uppsala, Sweden

Introduction

The Treaty of Amsterdam (EU, 1997), through its Protocol on the Protection and Welfare of Animals, obliges the European Institutions to pay full regard to animal welfare requirements when formulating and implementing European Union (EU) legislation. The key area of action of the Community Action Plan on the Protection and Welfare of Animals (2006-2010) (EC, 2005) is to promote policies for high animal welfare standards in the EU and at international level. The introduction of standardised animal welfare indicators was identified as one of the main areas of action, together with the upgrading of existing minimum standards for animal protection and welfare in line with new scientific evidence and socio-economic assessments. In this context, the future Strategy on Animal Health for 2007-2013 (EC, 2006) will address the promotion of farm practices which comply with animal welfare standards.

The main mission of the European Food Safety Authority (EFSA) is to provide comprehensive scientific and technical support for the Community legislation on the safety and other aspects of the whole food and feed supply chain, including animal health and animal welfare (EC, 2002). In response to questions posed by various European Commission services, the European Parliament, EU Member States or as a result of self-mandates, EFSA provides independent information regarding risks associated with food and feed, plant health, environment, animal health and animal welfare. EFSA follows, whenever possible, a Risk Assessment (RA) approach. Another task of the Authority is to promote and coordinate the development of harmonised risk assessment methodologies in the above-mentioned fields.

Since its creation in 2003, the EFSA Panel on Animal Health and Animal Welfare (AHAW) has adopted a total of 36 Scientific Opinions on animal welfare, dealing with among others laboratory animals, stunning and killing methods, animal transport, the welfare of calves, the welfare risks of the import of captive birds, the welfare of pigs, fish welfare, welfare aspects of fish stunning and killing, dairy cow welfare, genetic selection of broilers and harvesting feathers from live geese (Ribó et al., 2009; 2010).

The use of animal-based measures to assess animal welfare is relatively new (Blokhuis et al., 2003). Several research projects have been working on the development of animal-based measures and such measures are also considered in various assessment schemes. The outcomes of the Welfare Quality® Project provide the methodology for assessing animal welfare and a standardised way to assign farms a welfare grade from poor to excellent (Blokhuis et al., 2010). The welfare assessment protocols (Welfare Quality®, 2009a,b,c) give the procedures and requirements for the assessment of welfare in cattle, pigs and poultry according to this methodology.

This paper reviews the work done by the EFSA Panel on AHAW on the development and use of the risk assessment approach for the formulation of Scientific Opinions on animal welfare. The approach for assessment of animal welfare in the EU-supported project Welfare Quality® is also described. Finally, the EFSA's current work on the development of animal-based welfare indicators at farm level, as presented in the Welfare Quality® assessment protocols, and in the light of the outcomes of the EFSA Scientific Opinions on animal welfare, is also presented.

EFSA Approach on Animal Welfare Risk Assessment (AWRA)

Animal welfare is nowadays a real concern and there is common agreement that standards for animal welfare assessment and a reliable monitoring system need to be established. The main constraint on the development of an overall welfare assessment is that some welfare aspects are not easily assessed in an objective way, either qualitatively or quantitatively (Müller-Graf et al., 2008; Blokhuis et al., 2008).

The Risk Assessment (RA) methodology has been commonly used to describe and quantify the risks of introduction of infections, toxi-infections or residues of veterinary medicines, or risks resulting from the import of live animals and their products in the animal food chain (Müller-Graf et al., 2008), for which specific international guidelines - produced by the World Health Organization (WHO, 1999) and by the World Organization for Animal

Health (OIE, 2004) - have become available. For Animal Welfare-related Risk Assessment (AWRA) purposes, OIE and Codex Alimentarius Commission (CAC, 2001; 2002) definitions have been considered in the EFSA Scientific Opinions on animal welfare (www.efsa.europa.eu).

The Risk Assessment approach applied to animal welfare is a methodology under ongoing development. The major advantage of RA methodology is transparency, since scientific data are provided through documented risk pathways, assumptions are defined, and the associated level of scientific evidence is reported. Due to the limited amount of quantitative data on the adverse effects of hazards on animal welfare, a qualitative or semi-quantitative risk assessment has been developed, mainly based on expert opinion.

The AWRA approach followed by EFSA has evolved consistently since the first EFSA Scientific Opinions (EFSA, 2004a, b), when the RA was limited to the listing of hazards which may compromise animal welfare and the definition of risk pathways. Further developments in the AWRA methodology included estimation of the magnitude of adverse effects (depending on their severity and duration) associated with the presence of the hazard and the probability of its occurrence in a specific animal population, which allowed the calculation of a risk estimate. Table 51.1 shows the animal welfare scientific opinions adopted since 2003 and the evolution in RA methodology. In the recently adopted scientific opinions on dairy cow welfare (EFSA, 2009b, c, d, e, f), conclusions and recommendations were based on both the data presented in the scientific report and the outcomes of the semi-quantitative RA approach (Ribó and Serratosa, 2009).

The current AWRA approach used to rank the risk estimates and hazard magnitudes does not give a precise numerical estimate of the risk attributed to certain hazards. It helps to identify major risks affecting each of the animal categories and may be used to rank risk factors within a certain animal population (Figure 51.1). This allows the identification of priority areas of intervention (risk management) and issues that need to be further clarified through future research (recommendations for future research) (Müller-Graf, et al., 2008; Ribó et al., 2008; Candiani et al., 2009).

Mandates requesting scientific assessments on animal welfare received by the EFSA included very broad ques-

Table 51.1. Evolution of the AWRA approach amongst the AHAW Opinions (2003-2009) (Ribó and Serratosa, 2009).

AHAW Opinion on Animal welfare	Year	RA	HI	Qual. RA	Semi-Qt RA
Welfare of animals during transport	2004	-	-	-	-
Welfare aspects of various systems of keeping laying hens	2004	-	X	X	-
Impact of the current housing and husbandry systems on the health and welfare of farmed domestic rabbits	2005	-	X	X	-
Welfare of weaners and rearing pigs: effects of different space allowances and floor types	2005	-	X	X	-
Biology and welfare of animals used for experimental and other scientific purposes	2005	-	X	X	-
Welfare aspects of the main systems of stunning and killing applied to commercially farmed deer, goats, rabbits, ostriches, ducks, geese and quail	2006	-	X	X	-
The risks of poor welfare in intensive calf farming systems	2006	X	X	-	X
Animal health and welfare risks associated with the import of wild birds other than poultry into the European Union	2006	X	X	-	X
Welfare of pigs (Sows and boars, Fattening pigs and Tail biting) (3 scientific opinions)	2007	X	X	-	X
Stunning and killing methods for seals	2007	X	X	X	-
Welfare of fish (Salmon, Trout, Eel, Sea Bass-Sea Bream, Carp) (5 scientific opinions)	2008	X	X	-	X
Stunning and killing methods of fish (Salmon, Trout, Eel, Sea Bass-Sea Bream, Carp, Turbot and Tuna) (7 scientific opinions)	2009	X	X	-	X
Assessment of Dairy Cow Welfare (Leg and locomotion, udder, metabolic and reproductive and behaviour) (5 SOs)	2009	X	X	-	X

HI =hazard identification; Qual RA: qualitative RA; Semi-Qt RA: semi-quantitative RA;

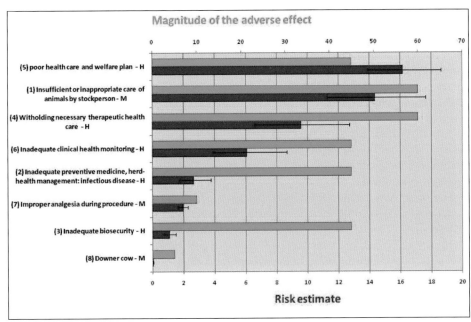

Figure 51.1. Risk estimate and magnitude of the adverse effect of hazards affecting dairy cows (EFSA, 2009b).

tions (i.e. welfare of pigs, welfare of fish, welfare of dairy cows). The quantitative assessment of welfare is therefore a problem, as quantitative data are only available for certain animal categories and hazards and not for all. Future mandates on animal welfare should include narrow and precise risk questions in terms of the welfare components to be considered and animal categories, life stages and husbandry systems, in order to allow more precise and concise AWRA to be carried out (Algers, 2009).

In December 2005, the EFSA Scientific Colloquium '*Principles of Risk Assessment of Food Producing Animals: Current and Future Approaches*' was held in Parma to discuss the state of the art regarding risk assessment in food-producing animals (EFSA, 2006). The main objectives of this Scientific Colloquium were to have an open scientific debate on how to conduct risk assessments (i.e. on essential components of RA for animal health and welfare) and to explore options for making guidelines in these areas. The risk assessment methodology, the need for reliable data, the need for setting up data collection systems, ways to identify the necessary expertise and other resource requirements and the best options to communicate the results of a risk assessment were discussed.

Methodological aspects of animal welfare risk assessment were also debated, notably: i) how to include in such RA exercises the different aspects of animal welfare (including health); ii) how the concept 'hazard' should be interpreted in this context, and iii) the need to identify parameters ('indicators') for measuring animal welfare that are specific for animal species, breed, age, physiological state and production system. In relation to the data needs, it was agreed that to assess animal welfare appropriately, it should be measured directly in a quantitative way on the animals (EFSA, 2006).

One of the main conclusions of the Colloquium was that although different approaches exist for risk assessment related to food microbiology (WHO, 1999) and animal health issues (OIE, 2004 a,b), "no specific standardized methodology exists in the field of the Animal Welfare Risk Assessment". The Colloquium recommended that the EFSA consider developing guidelines in this area and pointed out that it would be worthwhile setting up a working group to further investigate methodologies for risk assessment of animal welfare (EFSA, 2006).

Following this recommendation, an EFSA workshop on 'RA methodology in Animal Welfare' was held in Vienna in June 2007, during which past and current experiences in the development of risk assessments in animal welfare were reviewed, with the final objective of identifying gaps in the current AWRA methodology and options for its further improvement and development. Main issues discussed during the workshop were i) the use and validation of expert opinion, ii) the interaction between hazards and their cumulative adverse effect on the animal, and iii) possible consideration of the positive effects of factors (welfare promoters) on animal welfare. The workshop concluded that the use of the risk assessment approach for the purposes of formulating scientific opinions on animal welfare should be considered wherever appropriate, and that a systematic AWRA methodology would increase the validity and reliability of animal welfare assessments.

In September 2007, EFSA launched a self-mandate for the development of an EFSA Guidance document on risk assessment for animal welfare. This Guidance should define a comprehensive harmonised methodology to evaluate risks in animal welfare, taking into consideration the various procedures, management and housing systems and the different animal welfare issues, with reference to the methodologies followed in the previous EFSA Scientific Opinions on various species. The methodology should include terminology for the assessment of risks, defined strictly in terms of animal welfare. The defined methodology for assessing risks in animal welfare should take into account and adapt current risk assessment methodologies, for example those for animal diseases and food safety, and also the complex range of measurable welfare outcomes. The guidance document should concisely define the generic approach for working groups addressing specific areas of assessment of risks in AW. The development of a Risk Assessment methodology applied to animal welfare may support the scientific prioritisation of welfare issues for the further implementation of animal welfare standards. The EFSA Guidance on risk assessment for animal welfare is foreseen to be released by 2011.

Animal Welfare Assessment Protocols

Quantification of how animal production processes affect animal welfare is essential to provide transparency to all stakeholders (public, industry, government, etc.) and to implement and evaluate appropriate improvement strategies. It is also crucial to provide quantitative input to AWRA processes. This requires on-farm standardised assessment systems to determine the welfare status of the animals, as well as a standard way of converting science-based, welfare-related measures into information that is applicable and easily understood by stakeholders (Blokhuis et al., 2003, 2008, 2010).

The EU-funded Welfare Quality® project aimed to deliver such on-farm welfare assessment and information systems for several species. In the Welfare Quality® system, the welfare assessment related to a specific animal unit is based on the calculation of welfare scores from the information collected on that unit. The published assessment protocols (Welfare Quality®, 2009a,b,c) contain standardised descriptions of the measures relevant for the species and an explanation of what data should be collected, and in what way. The protocols address animals at different stages of their lives and/or in various housing systems. It can cover rearing, production, or the end of life of the animal. At the moment, there are no measures that are carried out during the actual transport process (Welfare Quality®, 2009).

The focus within the Welfare Quality® project was to measure parameters at the animal level that reflect the actual welfare state of the animals. Such animal-based measures (e.g. related to health and behaviour) include the effects of variation in farm management systems as well as the effects of specific system-animal interactions. Obviously, the set of measures to assess welfare must address all important welfare criteria. Welfare Quality® scientists identified four main welfare principles, divided into 12 independent welfare criteria (see Table 51.2) (Keeling and Veissier, 2005; Veissier and Evans, 2007; Blokhuis et al., 2010). In general, the principles and criteria chosen are relevant for different species and throughout an animal's entire lifespan.

Whenever possible, the final Welfare Quality® assessment measures have been evaluated with respect to their validity (does the measure reflect some aspect of the actual welfare of animals), reliability (acceptable inter- and intra-observer repeatability and robustness to external factors, e.g. time of day or weather conditions) and their practical feasibility. A further important aspect of this data collection is that value judgements are mini-

Table 51.2. Welfare principles and criteria identified in welfare quality (adapted from Veissier and Evans, 2007).

Welfare principle	Welfare criteria	Meaning
Good feeding	1. Absence of prolonged hunger 2. Absence of prolonged thirst	Animals should not suffer from prolonged hunger Animals should not suffer from prolonged thirst
Good housing	3. Comfort around resting 4. Thermal comfort 5. Ease of movement	Animals should be comfortable, especially within their lying areas Animals should be in a good thermal environment Animals should be able to move around freely
Good health	6. Absence of injuries 7. Absence of disease 8. Absence of pain induced by management procedures	Animals should not be physically injured Animals should be free of disease Animals should not suffer from pain induced by inappropriate management
Appropriate behaviour	9. Expression of social behaviours 10. Expression of other behaviours 11. Good humane animal relationship 12. Positive emotional state	Animals should be allowed to express natural, non-harmful, social behaviour Animals should have the possibility of expressing other intuitively desirable natural behaviours, such as exploration and play Good humane animal relationships are beneficial to the welfare of animals Animals should not experience negative emotions such as fear, distress, frustration or apathy

mised through appropriate training of assessors. For some criteria, it has been necessary to include resource-based measures (e.g. details of water provision) or management-based measures (e.g. breeding strategies and health plans) because no animal-based measure was available or sufficiently sensitive or satisfactory in terms of validity, reliability, or feasibility.

Once all the measures have been performed on an animal unit, a standardised procedure is followed to produce an overall assessment of animal welfare on that particular unit: First, the data collected (i.e. values obtained for the different measures on the animal unit) are combined to calculate criterion scores; then criterion scores are combined to calculate principle scores; and finally the animal unit is assigned to one welfare category according to the principle scores it obtained. Four welfare categories have been defined:

- Excellent: The welfare of the animals is of the highest level.
- Enhanced: The welfare of the animals is good.
- Acceptable: The welfare of the animals is above or meets minimal requirements.
- Not classified: The welfare of the animals is low and considered unacceptable.

Welfare assessment protocols are structured to present: 1) the measures collected on farms, 2) the measures collected at slaughter that apply to welfare assessment on-farm, 3) the calculation of scores needed for overall assessment, and 4) the measures collected at slaughter that apply to assessment of the welfare of the animals during transport and slaughter.

It should be emphasised that scientific research continues to refine measures and assessment methodologies. It is therefore essential to exchange knowledge between ongoing research projects in order to prevent duplication of work and to update the Welfare Quality® protocols in the light of new knowledge. To facilitate this, former partners in the Welfare Quality® project have established the Welfare Quality Network (www.welfarequalitynetwork.net). The collaboration agreement underlying this Network defines the following main areas of activity:

- Management of the system and support instruments (including training in their use by Network partners)
- Maintenance of the system
- Upgrading the system
- Promoting stakeholder involvement
- Prioritising and facilitating research

Evaluation of Animal-based Measures to Assess the Welfare of Animals

EFSA has been explicitly requested by the European Commission to include measurable welfare indicators, whenever possible, in the conclusions and recommendations of the future EFSA Scientific Opinions on animal welfare. Within this context, EFSA has been recently requested to identify how animal-based measures could be used to ensure the fulfilment of the recommendations of the EFSA Scientific Opinions on animal welfare and how the assessment protocols suggested by the Welfare Quality® project cover the main hazards identified in EFSA scientific Opinions and vice-versa. In addition, possible relevant animal welfare issues that cannot be assessed using animal-based measures and the main factors in the various husbandry systems which have been scientifically proven to have negative effects on the welfare of animals should be identified and listed.

This work will be based on, and linked to, the risk assessments of the previous EFSA Scientific Opinions on animal welfare. In 2009, the Animal Health and Welfare Panel of EFSA released a Scientific Report on the effects of farming systems on dairy cow welfare and disease (EFSA, 2009a), and a Scientific Opinion on an overall assessment of the effects of farming systems on dairy cow welfare and disease (EFSA, 2009b). Therefore, EFSA has been requested to start evaluation of the welfare indicators for dairy cows, which should be followed by an evaluation of indicators for pigs and poultry, as these species have also been considered by the Welfare Quality® assessment protocols. The Scientific Opinion on the use of animal-based indicators for the welfare of dairy cows should be released by summer 2011.

The outcomes of the risk assessment methodology together with the identification of scientific indicators for welfare will be useful for the establishment and implementation of welfare control and monitoring plans at farm level, detection of poor welfare situations and application of improvement measures. Harmonised reliable indicators for the welfare of food-producing animals could also be used by the European Commission for possible future legislation establishing surveillance systems at Member State level.

In Conclusion

Welfare research provides the scientific basis for reliable and feasible welfare assessment systems and standardised tools for the conversion of welfare measures into accessible and understandable information. EU legislation based on scientific evidence and systematic risk assessment is important to support the further improvement of animal welfare in Europe.

There is an important role for the foreseen European Network of Centres of Excellence on Animal Welfare, to harmonise, update, manage and implement standardised systems for welfare assessment. The results of the implementation of the assessment systems should be used to take appropriate measures to improve welfare.

These results should also provide crucial quantitative data to be used in future animal welfare risk assessments developed by EFSA, which is in charge of providing scientific advice for the Community's legislation on animal health and welfare. The results of the EFSA's risk assessment will support the further development of animal-based welfare indicators for welfare assessment at farm level.

Legislative provisions based on appropriate scientific evidence should include animal-based welfare indicators or assessment systems for the control and monitoring of animal welfare at farm level.

Part H

Biological Diversity

Authors: Gert Berger, Alexander Fehér, Michael Glemnitz, Iryna Herzon, Lydia Končeková and Holger Pfeffer

Coeditor and Coordinating Author: Alexander Fehér

Maintaining and Promoting Biodiversity

52

Alexander Fehér and Lydia Končeková
Slovak University of Agriculture, Nitra, Slovakia
Michael Glemnitz, Gert Berger and Holger Pfeffer
Leibniz-Centre for Agricultural Landscape Research, Muenchenberg, Germany
Iryna Herzon
University of Helsinki, Finland

Introduction

Human activity is a considerable transformative force affecting natural environments and biodiversity. Since the Neolithic period, this activity has been creating a new type of landscape which continues to evolve (Figure 52.1). Anthropogenic changes are often irreversible, for instance forests turned into xerothermic shrubs in the Mediterranean region can not regenerate naturally, or once steppes and forest steppes encroached the lowland areas of the Carpathian Basin and the Northern Black Sea Coast they have been persisting for thousands of years. Diversity of species has been changing according to land use.

The more we study biodiversity, the more we come to realise its importance for maintaining essential ecological functions. A diversity of microorganisms below and above ground, plants and animals is required to maintain essential functions such as decomposition, nutrient cycling, soil formation, detoxification, natural pest regulation and pollination. Considerable value of biodiversity may come from supporting resistance and resilience of ecosystems in the face of perturbations. This is true for both agricultural production and natural ecosystems (MA, 2003). Although agricultural fields are greatly simplified in comparison with natural ecosystems, they are still de-

pendent on complex natural interactions and processes driven by organisms. However, the amount of biodiversity needed for the continued resilience and productivity of arable systems remains a scientific challenge.

In Europe with its high proportion of land under agriculture – around 5 million square kilometres compris-

Figure 52.1. During the past 4,000 years the fields shown in this picture have had different character and use: they were covered by the Baltic Sea, later by terrestrial wet meadows, then small fields combined with meadows and after drainage they were turned into intensively used farmland (Gamla Uppsala, Sweden. Photo: A. Fehér).

ing nearly half the continent's total land area – and long history of environmental modification, there are often no boundaries between food production areas, cultural landscapes and wildlife habitats. At the European scale farmland encompasses a dazzling variety of habitat types as different as dry steppe grasslands and rice fields, vineyards and mountainous pastures. This variety supports rich farmland biodiversity over the continent (Benton et al., 2003). It is more considerable than in, for example, the USA, which has much larger areas of monotopes (higher homogeneity). In fact, farmland has the highest overall species richness of birds of any habitat type in Europe (Tucker and Evans, 1997), and the total number of vascular plants regularly occurring on arable land exceeds one thousand. At least 10-15% of all vascular plants use arable land as their main habitat.

Agricultural land use is one of the key pressures on biodiversity in Europe and around the world. The impact of agriculture on biodiversity is attributed to, first of all, conversion of natural ecosystems (e.g. wetlands) to crop fields, but also fragmentation of natural habitats and effects on neighbouring ecosystems such as excess nutrients and pollutants, or diversion of water to crops. On the other hand, agriculture benefits many wild species by providing novel ecotones and a diverse mosaic of habitats, as well as plentiful foraging resources (grain for insects, birds and rodents), and a suitable disturbance regime (for annual plants) (Benton et al., 2003).

managed wheat field, an artificial monoculture force-fed on nutrients, with suppressed competitors and predators.

The steppes of south-east Europe are regarded as the primary origin of the majority of species associated with farmland (Baker, 1974). Recent theories suggest, however, that forest-steppe mosaics were more characteristic of Europe than previously assumed, because the post-Holocene mega fauna created and maintained forest clearings. Other naturally open habitats such as flood plain meadows were also important sources of farmland species.

Nowadays, some farmland species occur exclusively or mainly in farmland as a substitute or remnant for their former natural habitats in Europe – for example great (*Otis tarda*) and little bustard (*Tetrao tetrix*). For another larger group of species farmland is the predominant habitat of occurrence, due to its sheer vastness, e.g. skylark (*Alauda arvensis*) and yellowhammer (*Emberiza citrinella*). Within a study watershed in north-east Germany, 23% of all vascular plants occurred on arable land, and 14% were strictly limited to it (Figure 52.2). Finally, some species, for example curlew (*Numenius arquata*), lapwing (*Vanellus vanellus*) and most of the perennial vascular plants, readily colonise fields but suffer high mortality rates there.

A considerable, though still little studied, portion of biodiversity in agroecosystems is that dwelling below ground: microbial, micro- (for example, protozoa), mezo- (nematodes), macro- (insects) and mega-fauna (earthworms). We do not know most of the species of be-

Characteristics of Agricultural Landscapes and their Communities

Agroecosystems are fundamentally natural systems artificially kept at early successional stages, so that a large proportion of the primary production can be harvested by man. Cultivated crops also structure the habitat conditions for wildlife species on the fields and landscape. On the whole, agricultural land provides very specific ecological conditions characterised by frequent changes in the 'structural species' (crops), relative openness, periodic disturbances, a high resource availability and extensive exchange with neighbouring habitats. At the extreme end of agroecosystem modification is a modern intensively

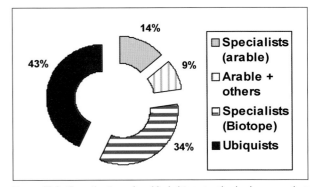

Figure 52.2. Contribution of arable habitats to the herbaceous plant species diversity at the landscape scale (occurrence of species in different habitats, in 11 biotopes of the Quillow watershed in north-east Germany; Glemnitz and Wurbs, 2003).

low-ground communities: the number of known soil microbe species is over 110,000, which is just 3-10% of the estimated total. However, it is certain this fauna controls agricultural productivity by driving nutrient cycling, soil formation and other essential processes.

From the agronomic point of view, wildlife species occurring on arable fields are divided into groups of non-wanted 'noxious species' or 'pests' and 'non-target' species. Most of natural plant and animal species associated with farmland do not cause harm to food production. Considerable effort has been devoted to elimination of noxious species from the field. The unsolved basic problem is that every control measure also affects 'non-target' species and selects 'target' species according to their tolerance of the measure. Only recently, the idea of weed vegetation also having important ecosystem functions has been recognised (Marshall et al., 2002; Booth et al., 2003). What is called by weed vegetation in fact contributes to many abiotic processes, such as storage of nutrients and prevention of their leaching, and control of soil erosion, carbon storage, water balance and soil structure. Plants also perform important biotic functions, such as providing direct or indirect resources for higher taxa (e.g. phytophagous species and birds), supporting pollinating insects and species beneficial for pest control and creating microclimate and regulating invasions through interspecific competition (Naeem et al., 2000).

Farmland as Habitat

Generally speaking, agricultural land provides habitats for the associated organisms in two major ways: i) structural effects by providing ecotones between different forested, wet or other non-farmed habitats and open field areas represented by grassland and cropland; and ii) qualitative effects by providing conditions within a particular arable or grassland habitat patch. Agricultural land use affects biodiversity by changing the landscape structure, reducing small-scale structural heterogeneity and through disturbances within a patch. However, the former (structural) and latter (qualitative) effects often have to be considered separately, because they are driven by different forces and species have different response capabilities to

them. While the structural effects are strongly correlated with geomorphological background and land use history, the habitat quality of the patch is the result of a recent cropping regime.

Furthermore, the habitat of soil organisms cannot be forgotten. Soil in arable land creates special environmental conditions for organisms living underground (edaphic organisms). These organisms, such as microorganisms, fungi and animals of different taxa, participate in positive physical and chemical processes in soil (excluding pests and pathogens). The edaphic organisms are the main agents of promoting nutrient turnover (nitrogen, etc.) in agroecosystems (these processes are discussed in detail in other chapters of this book).

Influence of Landscape Structure

Structural complexity of the whole agricultural landscape is essential for diverse communities of all taxa (see review in Benton et al., 2003). The presence of various non-cropped patches and structures, such as isolated woodlands, hedges, semi-natural grasslands, ponds or streams imbedded into a matrix of agricultural fields considerably enhances biodiversity (Figure 52.3). Many species are most abundant in these non-cropped patches. For example, only very few species of birds, such as skylark (*Alauda arvensis*), meadow pipit (*Anthus pratensis*) and partridge (*Perdix perdix*), breed and feed exclusively within arable fields. The presence of non-cropped elements is critical for a diverse community of farmland birds (Herzon and O'Hara, 2007). Proximity of non-farmed habitats to crops enhances ecosystem functions performed by native species, such as pollination and pest control (Kremen, 2004).

The composition of plant and animal species inhabiting linear landscape elements differs essentially from that of both open arable fields and enclosed woodlands. Variation within any type of non-cropped habitat (hedge height and density, cut or non-cut margin) also enhances populations of species. Most farmland species make extensive use of field margins, which provide relatively undisturbed habitats and overwintering sites for invertebrates, overwintering sites, safe nesting and resource-rich foraging patches for birds, and movement corridors for small mammals.

In a study comparing eight agricultural landscapes of 400 ha size each, with a different amount of semi-natural linear and non-linear structures in east-northeast

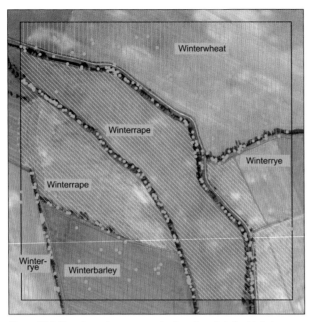

Figure 52.3. Density and arrangement of nesting plots for birds in agrarian landscapes (bird survey at Brandenburg State, Germany 2005; every dot is a nesting plot. Lutze et al., 2007).

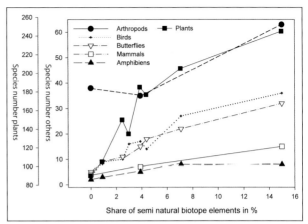

Figure 52.4. Species richness of eight different organism groups in relation to the amount of linear and non-linear semi-natural biotopes in agrarian landscapes (comparative study performed in eight regions of East Germany; Kretschmer et al., 1995).

Germany, Kretschmer et al. (1995) confirmed a general correlation between the relative proportion of semi-natural biotopes in landscapes and the species richness of herbaceous plants, arthropods, birds, butterflies, mammals and amphibians (Figure 52.4). The areal effects of the structural elements are enhanced by the heterogeneity within each habitat type. With increasing area, the variety of habitat conditions within the biotope types also increases. The types of biotopes within a landscape are largely pre-defined by its geomorphological heterogene-

ity and partly by historical land use patterns, such as land inheritance practices or field-delineating traditions, e.g. with stone walls or hedges (Table 52.1). The last four areas listed in Table 52.1 have a similar total amount of semi-natural structures, different biotope types are dominant or, as in the last area, the distribution of different biotope types is balanced. The contribution to the overall diversity is highest in the last area in Table 52.1, where a variety of different biotope types occur and their area is relatively evenly distributed. Every biotope type provides habitats for a number of species with high biotope loyalty (Figure 52.5).

Since the potential for specific habitat functions of a landscape is predefined by the landscape heterogeneity and the geomorphological background, the options for active restructuring of a landscape are often limited to

Table 52.1. Proportion of different semi-natural biotopes within the agricultural landscape – comparison of different ecoregions in north-east Germany (values as % of the total area).

Name of the ecoregion*	Reeds	Wetlands	Slightly fresh meadows	Dry grasslands	Biotope Sum
Uckertal Valley	**10.0**	**7.1**	2.5	0.0	21.4
Neustrelitz Lakeland	1.2	1.4	2.4	**4.9**	12.9
Oder-Alluvial	2.0	**7.3**	3.6	0.1	13.9
Randow Glacial Valley	0.2	2.1	**5.3**	0.1	11.8
Schorfheide Woodland	**2.3**	**2.8**	4.6	**1.5**	13.0

*1 according to the classification of Marcinek and Zaumseil (1993) for Northeast Germany

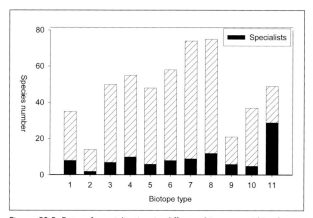

Figure 52.5. Rate of specialisation in different biotopes within the agricultural landscape, proportion of species limited in occurrence to a specific biotope type (landscape monitoring in the Quillow watershed in north-east Germany in 11 different biotopes: 1 – reeds, 2 – shallow water swards, 3 – wetlands, 4 – ruderalised wetlands, 5 – slightly fresh meadows, 6 – ruderalised meadows, 7 – field margins, 8 – old fallows, 9 – dry grasslands, 10 – young fallows, 11 – arable land).

Figure 52.6 a,b. Two examples of the configuration of agrarian landscapes with natural or semi-natural habitats. The first picture shows a homogeneous landscape with small amount of biotopes included, the second picture a heterogeneous landscape with lots of biotopes inbedded into agricultural land (Slovakia and the Czech Republic). Photo: A. Fehér.

the establishment of field margins, hedges and other anthropogenic biotopes. The agreement between landscape abiotic and biotic heterogeneity can be used as an indicator of landscape health or biotic integrity. Homogeneous and heterogeneous landscapes can be easily contrasted (Figure 52.6a,b). In a heterogeneous landscape, biotope remnants often are placed in the middle of the fields. These biotopes occupy sites with some extreme stress factors (caused by water, soil structure or elevation), which cannot be utilised economically for agricultural production. In the homogeneous landscape there is only a little site potential for semi-natural biotopes such as dry grasslands, wetlands or peat lands. Species related to any kind of extreme site conditions (water stress, extreme pH, lack of nutrients), which are typical target species for species protection efforts, cannot be expected in most of the fertile agrarian landscapes. Despite the fact that few species of conservation value can persist in a homogeneous landscape, the addition of non-cropped elements enhances a number of ecosystem services provided by associated species such as pollination and others. These elements are often added as field margins, flower strips or other 'artificial' structural landscape elements. We still do not have robust criteria on the amount of such structures needed for effective functioning.

Local forest habitats or their fragments also contribute to the biodiversity of an agricultural landscape and support its stability (e.g. FAO, 2006b).

Influence of Cropping in Arable Field Habitats

The number of plant species that inhabit arable fields, at least as temporal habitats, seems to be much higher than used to be assumed. In a European survey the regional weed species diversity varied between 405 species in the south of Italy and 126 in the middle of Finland (Figure 52.7) (Radics et al, 2000; Glemnitz et al., 2006). Other organism groups also show very high species richness and abundance on arable land. A study in north-east Germany

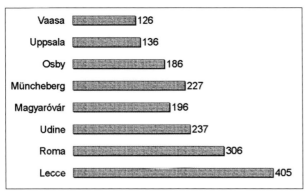

Figure 52.7. Species richness of weeds in eight different regions of Europe ranked in accordance to increasing average annual temperature. Every region has an area of 250-300 km² and there are 27 individual fields (Radics et al., 2000).

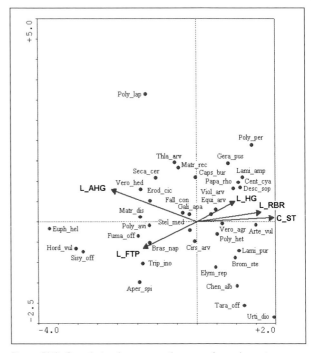

Figure 52.8. Correlation between soil type and weed species occurrence (results of the arable field monitoring in the Quillow watershed in north-east Germany between 2000-2004, N= 43 fields; Legend: L_ AHG - anhydromorphic soils, L_FTP - loamy soils, L_RBR- sandy soils, L_HG - hydromorphic soils, C_ST – substrate type according German soil classification, correspondence analysis, every dot is a weed species, abbreviations are used for species names).

described 86 carabid beetle species of nearly 5000 individuals occurring on arable fields in one year, which was nearly 4 times more species with 15 times more individuals than in forests (20 species, 346 individuals) in the same period. Of spiders, 107 species were found with 3800 individuals on arable fields, which was 25% more species and 33% more individuals compared with forest sites (84 species with 2450 individuals) (LUA, 2006).

The biodiversity on arable land is influenced by three main factors: heterogeneity of site conditions, climate and management practices. The more diverse the available ecological niches, the higher the diversity of regional species. Some species inventory is adapted to specific site conditions as shown in Figure 52.8 for weed species assemblages from north-east Germany. Another group of species has large amplitude in their site requirements and frequent and dominant species typical of arable fields belong to this. For this reason, indicators focusing on site adaptation, rarity or specialisation in general do not meet the needs and specifications of agrarian ecosystems.

Climate impact is of special importance in arable landscapes due to the short period for population recovery. With regular soil tillage, plant communities encounter the habitat conditions in the early stages of secondary succession. The majority of the plants on arable fields can survive and recover only with seeds as therophytes. Germination and first growing stages are highly sensitive to temperature and water availability. Animals should be able to sur-

vive on bare ground. For this reason, the effect of annual climate on species composition and population size is much stronger than in semi-natural habitats. Species composition of communities can differ strongly between wet and dry, cold and warm, sunny or cloudy as well as years with long or short reproduction periods. For weeds, it was found that half the regional species richness occurred only once or twice within the six-year study period, while on the other hand only 30% of all species occurred every year or in at least five of the six years (Figure 52.9).

A mixture of different habitat types, as well as crop types, in the landscape can provide habitats for species with different ecological profiles (Heikkinen et al., 2004). The cropping sequence itself is one of the main factors affecting the quality of an arable habitat. Albrecht (2005) found that the composition of the seed bank in soil is

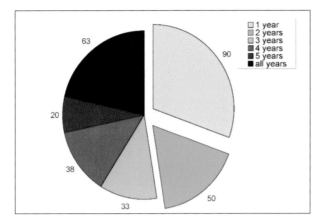

Figure 52.9. Constancy in temporal occurrence of weed species (number of weed species, results of the arable field monitoring in a watershed in north-east Germany between 2000-2006, N= 43 fields, overall species number was 295 = 100%).

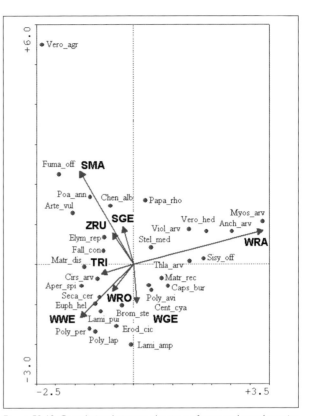

Figure 52.10. Correlation between the type of crop and weed species occurrence (results of the arable field monitoring in a watershed in north-east Germany between 2000-2004, N=43 fields, Legend: SMA - maize for silage, SGE – summer barley, ZRU – sugar beets, TRI – Triticale, WRO – winter rye, WWE – winter wheat, WEG – winter barley, WAR – winter oilseed rape, correspondence analysis, every dot is a weed species, abbreviations are used for species names).

mostly dependent on crop selection. In practice, habitat conditions vary between hibernating dense and slightly high winter cereals, dense summer cereals with an early but short vegetation period, dicotyledeons, flowering summer annual crops, late annual sparse but tall crops (maize), perennial crops and short-term cover crops (Figure 52.10). Monocultures do not provide resources through the whole life cycle of wild organisms. For example, curlew and lapwing both attain highest densities in an open landscape, where crop fields are combined with grass patches of at least 35 ha. Many granivorous birds are dependent on stubble rich in weed and crop seeds for winter survival and declines in stubble seriously impede winter survival of a group of species.

Variation within a crop stand is an important determinant of its value as a nesting and feeding habitat for birds with differing foraging and anti-predator behaviours and lengths of breeding cycle (see review by Wilson et al., 2005). For nesting, most ground-nesting birds prefer patchy vegetation cover with short and sparse spots surrounded by higher swards. Under intensive management, such variation is not available in either crops or grassland during the breeding period. Foraging is also more effective when food is accessible in sparse or heterogeneous swards of both arable crops and grasses.

Land use intensification has contributed substantially to the increase in food production over the past 50

years. However, it impacted on the agricultural landscape through homogenisation of the landscape structure, simplification of crop rotations, use of high-yielding crop varieties, fertilisation, irrigation and pesticide use. These altered the biotic interactions, the patterns of resource availability and the habitat quality of the ecosystems (Matson et al., 1997). The species decline in farmland birds, weeds and the serious reduction in biotic functionality, such as pollination, are related to intensification of agricultural production (e.g. Donald et al., 2001). Species that are most dramatically affected are often specialists, for example, plants adapted to chalky, acidic and wet soil conditions. Intensive agricultural land use is driving selection towards species-poor communities with highly adapted, flexible species, which will be even more difficult to control. The extreme example is a monoculture wheat or maize field with multiple pesticide use, high application of nutrients, poor in species and with limited inter-specific regulation (e.g. food webs).

There remains an unresolved debate on the relative importance of two characteristics of an agricultural landscape responsible for support of associated biodiversity: complex farmland structure versus extensive management of crops. The question has high relevance in practice: to what extent can intensification in field management (e.g. increase in inputs) accelerate without major effects on wildlife if a high level of farmland heterogeneity is retained?

Abundance of Species and their Interactions within Habitats

Typical for different taxa in agricultural landscapes is that only a few numbers of species reach high abundances, while most remain at low population densities. The abundant species are often flexible in site requirements, best adapted to the crops and their management. Despite the fact that most of them have been targets of weed or pest management for decades, they have survived keeping their dominances. These dominant species are 'unloved' by land users as well as by nature protectionists, but all processes and functions related to biomass are carried out by these species (e.g. erosion protection and nutrient storage). El Titi (1986) noted that the reduction in the total weed biomass below a certain level resulted in modifications within the food webs that led the phytophageous insects to move from weeds to the crops and become pests.

Various types of fallow fields are particularly important for many taxa (see review by Van Buskirk and Willi, 2004). They enhance these areas with species of infrequent and unstable occurrence (Figure 52.11). Most of the plant species with limited regional occurrence are found on fallows (75%) or extensive fields (61%) (Glemnitz et al., 2006). Arable plants prefer young and rotational set-aside, while most invertebrate species and ground-nesting birds especially benefit from long-term set-aside.

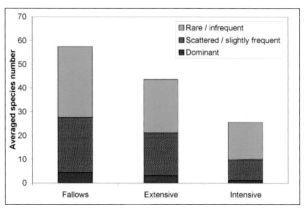

Figure 52.11. Species richness of weeds on different field types (results of an European transect survey, eight regions, every with an area of 250-300 km², in total 210 fields, Glemnitz et al., 2006).

A Special Case: Organic Farming and Biodiversity

Many studies have compared conventional intensive farming systems with organic systems that omit some of the 'intensive' features of the former (e.g. high chemical inputs and simplified crop rotations). The results are mixed and depend on the taxa studied and the scale of the research.

The positive effects of organic farming compared with conventional or integrated farming (se e.g. review by Hole et al., 2005) are the combined effect of the lack of disturbance caused by omitting pesticide use, the more varied crop rotations (higher crop diversity) and the less homogenisation of soil conditions caused by fertilisation or chemical soil improvement. Some researchers claim that the key reason for the greater species diversity in organic farms is an inherently higher level of heterogeneity because of crop rotations (Weibull et al., 2004; Roschewitz et al., 2005). Variation in fields may compensate for biodiversity losses caused by local management intensity by providing non-cropped refuges from which species eliminated from the crop can recolonise fields (Tscharntke et al., 2005). Finally, it has also been demonstrated that a higher level of insect diversity can be achieved within large fields under low intensity compared with smaller but intensively managed fields (see review by Büchs, 2003).

Only in organic farming can weed composition be explained by site conditions, while in conventional fields it is driven by specific management. Chemical weed control, firstly, reduces the number of infrequent species. These are usually the site-adapted, specialised species.

Noxious Associated Species

Weeds, Pests, Pathogens

All species of plants, animals and microorganisms are functional and valuable for an ecosystem, but some of them are classified as noxious or harmful (yield losses, allergy, vectors of disease) from a human point of view (ecosystem service). Not all colonisers are undesirable if they are pioneers in succession (from an ecological viewpoint). Invaders are introduced, so exotic, alien, non-native species (biogeographical viewpoint) and weeds, pests and pathogens interfere with the objectives of people (anthropogenic viewpoint).

Pest organisms and pathogens, if not controlled, considerably reduce the yield (biomass) and quality of products directly. The (potential) negative effects of weeds in agricultural areas are: competition with crops for resources, increase in production costs, reduction in crop and animal quality and human health, decreased land value, reduced crop variety and in some cases also aesthetic value. However, weed species play their role in ecosystem processes such as erosion control, microclimate support, provision of pollination and pest control. Many of them can also be used as edible plants, ornamental plants, traditional ceremonial plants, animal feed, or in the production of pharmaceutical drugs and natural colours. Although the direct value of insect pests is difficult to appreciate, many of the minor pests are important food for higher taxa, for example, birds, and support stable populations of predators and parasitoids, which keep more difficult pests under control. In most cases, tolerating a certain level of weed and pest populations is by far more economically viable and ecologically sensible than attempting to eliminate them totally.

The plant communities of agroecosystems include cropped 'target' species and weeds. In weed associations we can distinguish different life strategies: **ruderals** are adapted to conditions of huge disturbance and low stress (e.g. annual weeds), **stress tolerators** live in high environmental stress, low disturbance environments (e.g. drought, low pH, high soil moisture) and **competitors** live under conditions of low stress and low disturbance and have good competitive abilities (perennials, species with relatively high growth rate). A plant with generalised weed characteristics is called an **ideal weed**. It would

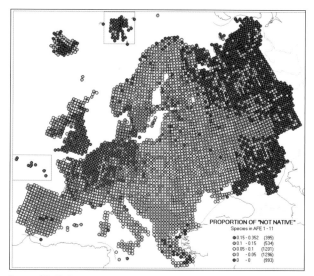

Figure 52.12. Proportion of non-native species in the overall diversity of vascular plants in Europe [Committee for Mapping the Flora of Europe and Societas Biologica Fennica Vanamo (1972-1999): Atlas Florae Europaeae. 12 Volumes, Academic Bookstore & Bookstore Tiedekirja, Helsinki (http://www.fmnh.helsinki.fi//map/afe/E_afe.htm).

have such traits as the ability to germinate in a wide range of environmental conditions, long-lived seeds with discontinuous germination, rapid growth from vegetative to flowering stage and propagules (seeds), and adaptation to short- and long-distance dispersal (Baker, 1974). Of course, every weed species usually has only a selected set of these features. Similarly to weeds, most successful pests are characterised by rapid population growth once established in the crop, good dispersal ability and they can be both generalists and specialists on crops.

Biological Invasions

Species composition, space structure and physiognomy of the vegetation in Europe are significantly modified due to the activities of man (agriculture, transportation, etc.) including expansion of non-native (allochtonous, exotic or alien) species (Figure 52.12). The occurrence of invasive plant species is most abundant near bio-corridors, mainly along watercourses, roads and railways. Plant invasiveness is neither a life form nor a taxonomic issue, but a set of properties of species enabling growth in certain habitats. We have only a few generalisations on

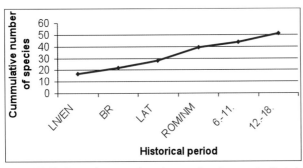

Figure 52.13. Cummulative number of non-native plant species (including species of doubtful origin) found in archaeobotanical findings in the Nitra River Basin, Slovakia. Abbreviations: LN/EN – Late Neolithic and Early Neolithic (4000-1900 B.C.), BR – Bronze Age (1900-700 B.C.), LAT – La Tène (420-0 B.C.), ROM/NM – Roman Age and Nations Migration (0-6. cent. A.D.), 6.-11. – 6.- 11. cent., 12.-18. – 12.-18. cent. (Fehér, 2007).

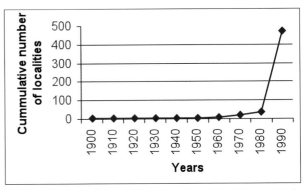

Figure 52.14. Cummulative number of localities of the 14 most distributed neophytes in the Nitra River catchment area (in the 20th century; Fehér, 2007).

the invasiveness of plants or on their attributes (if they do exist) and usually we cannot predict biological invasions. According to some authors (e.g. Crawley, 1997), there is no sense in searching for traits of 'invasive' and 'non-invasive' species because the ability to 'increase when rare' (the invasion criterion) is exhibited by all species in their native habitats, i.e. all plant species are invasive under certain environmental conditions.

According to the European strategy on invasive alien species, an alien species is a species, subspecies or lower taxon introduced outside its natural past or present distribution; this includes any part (seeds, eggs, etc.) of such species that might survive and subsequently reproduce. An invasive alien species is an alien species whose introduction and/or spread threaten biological diversity. In this chapter we consider 'invasive' (naturalised) plants alien species, the distribution and/or abundance of which in the wild is in the process of increasing regardless of habitat. **Archeophytes** are species introduced before 1500 (sometimes considered native species) and **neophytes** are naturalised aliens introduced since 1500 (Figures 52.13-14). Expanding native species (**apophytes**) are not considered invasive alien species. The most important invasive plants in the Baltic countries, for example, are the North American daisy (*Aster novi-belgii* agg.), Japanese and Czech knotweed (*Fallopia japonica, F. x bohemica*), Jerusalem artichoke (*Helianthus tuberosus*), giant and Sosnowski`s hogweed (*Heracleum mante-*

gazzianum, H. sosnowskii), Himalayan and small balsam (*Impatiens glandulifera, I. parviflora*), rugosa rose (*Rosa rugosa*) and the Canadian and early goldenrods (*Solidago canadensis, S. gigantea*, Figure 52.15). Several invasive plant species occur almost exclusively as weeds in arable land or at other sites with frequent disturbances, e.g. Canadian horseweed (*Conyza canadensis*), annual fleabane (*Stenactis annua*), common ragweed (*Ambrosia artemisiifolia*), etc.

Animals can be invasive too, but their area borders are more flexible and in some cases they occur only casually (e.g. some bird species). One of the insect examples is the sweet potato whitefly (*Bemisia tabaci*), which consumes crop plants and transmits plant viruses and fungi. In freshwater in farmland, the zebra mussel (*Dreissena polymorpha*), which threatens water supply, is increasing in occurrence. There are also invasive mammals that threaten yields of crops and may spread diseases.

Pathogens can also behave invasively (e.g. disease in agriculture). They are often vectored by other organisms, for example insects. In these cases the vector should be monitored and, if possible, regulated or eradicated.

There are several prevention possibilities to stop (control, regulate) biological invasions, e.g. **interception** (regulations and their enforcement with inspections and fines), **treatment** (treatment of goods and their packing) and **prohibition** (trade prohibition based on international regulations). There is a Global Invasive Species Database that is managed by the international Invasive Species Specialist Group. The Global Invasive Species Program

Figure 52.15. The native European Goldenrod (*Solidago virgaurea*) can be spontaneously crossed with the invasive alien Canadian Goldenrod (*S. canadiensis*). The new hybrid (in the picture) is called *S.* x *niederederi* (southern Sweden), Photo: A. Fehér.

outlines the eradication programme for invasive aliens as follows: it has to be scientifically based, directed at small, geographically limited populations of non-indigenous species that are easiest to eliminate; the eradication technique should be such that all individuals of the population must be susceptible to them; and monitoring to confirm the success is essential (Wittenberg and Cock, 2001).

The basic **direct field methods** of management of biological invasions are biological control (bio-pesticides, pathogens for control), mechanical control (mowing, grazing, hand-weeding etc.), chemical control (herbicides, etc.) and habitat management (by changing the

environmental conditions – grazing, burning, changing abiotic factors, hunting, etc.). Integrated pest management is recommended.

The **European strategy on invasive alien species** was endorsed in 2003. It states that invasive alien species are the second main cause of global biodiversity loss after direct habitat destruction, and have adverse environmental, economic and social impacts. Some of the European countries have prepared legislation and/or their own national strategies on biological invasions. The lists of invasive plants are under preparation or are ready (the Czech Republic, Poland, Lithuania etc.). In several countries (Switzerland, the USA, New Zealand, etc.) there are 'black lists' which are interlinked with legislation. It is forbidden to introduce or release species that are on the black list.

Rare and Threatened Species and their Conservation

By far the largest proportions of the species associated with agriculture do not have an adverse impact on productivity and, on the contrary, support it. Many species occurring in farmland also have considerable cultural value and aesthetic appeal. Spontaneous flora and fauna is taken to include all the wild plant and animal species from fields (except crops), meadows and other semi-natural grasslands, abandoned fields, riparian and road-

Figure 52.16. The formerly common weed, corncockle (*Agrostemma githago*), is now very rare or only casual. Photo: A. Fehér.

side habitats, farmyards, etc. The spontaneous vegetation often contains rare, endangered or vulnerable plant species and/or their associations (Figure 52.16). These species and their communities are threatened by intensive land use (mechanical regulation, chemical treatments, etc.) and expansion of invasive plants. Trends in agricultural management contributing to loss of (widened) biodiversity include:

a) Loss of non-agricultural habitats due to land reclamation, drainage projects or indirect pollution.
b) Agricultural 'improvement' of low-intensity farmland, through the application of fertilisers and lime, upgrading of drainage schemes, higher stocking densities and ploughing and reseeding of grasslands, including eutrophication of soils.
c) Disappearance of structural elements in the agricultural landscape such as hedgerows, field verges or grass tracks.
d) Loss of diversity on productive agricultural land through intensification, better tillage and harvesting techniques, intensive irrigation systems, increased use of fertilisers and pesticides, simplified management methods, uniformed and simplified crop rotations.
e) Marginalisation and abandonment of farmland, especially on marginal sites and extensive land use.
f) Introduction of new invasive species.

Despite the importance of farmland in providing habitats for a diverse wildlife, the awareness of biodiversity conservation within agroecosystems is relatively new, and there are several detailed case studies (c.f. Flade et al., 2006). In Europe, this development was triggered by the unprecedented decline in species that began with modernisation of the food production industry. Dramatic decreases in floral diversity in farmland have been observed throughout Europe. In some regions, more than one-third of the entire farmland flora is categorised as extinct, endangered or rare. Red lists of rare and endangered species have been developed for threatened weeds. In Sweden, 11 vegetal weeds probably disappeared and 35 species are endangered, in Poland 103 threatened weeds are known, four of which are considered extinct. From almost 350 plant species which can be classified as arable weeds in the Czech Republic, 98 species are endangered or already extinct. Of animal taxa, bird declines are particularly well

Figure 52.17. Two Eurasian buzzards (*Buteo buteo*) indicating a healthy agroecosystem: this predator is on the top of the food-chain. Photo: A. Fehér.

documented (Donald et al., 2001). In the UK, populations of such typical farmland species as corn bunting (*Miliaria calandra*), partridge (*Perdix perdix*), and skylark (*Alauda arvensis*) have declined by as much as 60-80 %. A startling 66 % of farmland habitat bird species in Europe have an unfavourable conservation status – for example, their populations are in either rapid or long-term steady decline – the highest proportion of any habitat. Research on other groups of animals suggests that the conspicuous decline in bird populations represents just the tip of an iceberg of biodiversity collapse on farmland (Figure 52.17). Populations of many insects, on which birds depend, have suffered drastic declines and many formerly common species are now rare (Benton et al., 2003; see examples for wild bees in Biesmeijer et al., 2006).

Management Options for Linking Biodiversity Protection and Modern Agricultural Land Use

Nature conservation measures in landscapes dominated by arable land can be divided into two major types:

a) Measures conducted within the agricultural production process, i.e. modified cultivation procedures and systems with respect to nature conservation goals, yet mainly aimed at the production of agricultural goods: e.g. reduced fertilisation or modified soil cultivation (**integrative pathway**).

b) Measures conducted separate of the production, mainly on areas not being used for crop production, often exclusively aimed at nature-orientated goals (**segregative pathway**).

Integrative Pathway

The most important ways of biodiversity management in conditions of intensive agricultural production (integrative path) are:

- High structural diversity of farmland in space (e.g. diversity of crops) and time (e.g. wide crop rotations) on different levels, in special cases with local fallow.
- Mixed farming, which incorporates grazing livestock with arable cropping.
- Sustainable production measures (minimum tillage, lower crop density, casual mechanical weed control, delayed or rotational mowing on some part of productive grassland, etc.).
- Lowered inputs of plant protection chemicals (herbicides, pesticides etc.) and reduction of preservative applications that do not exceed the economically viable thresholds and the capacity of the system to break them down.
- Reduction and splitting of fertiliser doses (mainly of nitrogen and phosphorus) by better targeting at crop needs, and mitigation of nutrient leaching from the fields.
- Implementation of site-adapted management, beginning with adjusting field size to soil heterogeneity or land management by using precision agriculture.
- Direct methods of biodiversity protection, e.g. delayed or adapted timing of management (fertilisation, plant protection) to breeding of farmland birds, biodiversity protection in vineyards by focusing mainly on geophytes (plants overwintering by bulbs and tubers) by no-tillage during winter and establishment of vegetated strips between rows in vineyards and orchards.
- Avoidance of drastic and large-scale changes in the landscape.

Because of the inevitable trade-offs between achieving high crop productivity on one hand and environmental and conservation goals on the other, the above options can best be achieved under certain farming systems. The wide variety of management options directed at preservation, enhancement and restoration of associated flora and fauna, especially rare species, within farmland can be implemented within any farming system, including the most intensive.

There are different farming systems providing special benefits to biodiversity. Below we list only few of these:

1. *Extensive and/or traditional land use.* Small-scale, well structured landscape is mixed with ecologically valuable plots (so-called biocentres such as woods, ponds, managed grasslands, etc.) and connections between them (so-called bio-corridors such as tree-rows, hedges, brooks, etc.). Small land areas, traditional farming practices and rational crop rotations, cultivation of old crop species and varieties (that have been the result of long-term selection, adapting to the local environmental conditions) and fallow are expected. Vineyards and orchards can be included, with mechanical weed regulation and anti-erosion measures (grass undergrowth, etc.). Priorities in animal husbandry are: traditional breeds, animal welfare and recycling of nutrients and animal waste into crop production.

2. *Permaculture, organic farming, farming with integrated pest control, agro-forestry.* These farming systems put the main emphasis on the understanding and utilisation of ecological cycles, self-regulation and multi-purpose exploitation of goods in agricultural production. Soil protection, promotion of biodiversity (including spontaneous flora, fauna and microorganisms), avoiding pollutants to the environment and production of high-quality, chemical-free green products are declared objectives for these farming systems.

3. *Additional activities, aquaculture (fish, etc.), apiculture, reed cultivation, etc.* Additional activities diversify the land use and make it more sustainable. Energy plants (e.g. willow) provide biomass for energy production from a renewable resource (this is likely to become highly successful in the Nordic countries, e.g. in Sweden). Research on the effects of their cultivation on biodiversity is under way

Segregative Pathway

The basic concepts in biodiversity management in the segregative approach are:

- Maintaining and preserving the proportion of natural or semi-natural vegetation (forests, tree groups, semi-natural grasslands and pastures, etc.) within the landscape.
- Creating additional new habitats (stone piles, hedges, etc.) within the fields either by using plots of extreme soil quality (wet hollows, dry hill tops, acid areas, etc.) or by direct establishment of habitat plots (field margins, bad spots, etc.), establishment and protection of field margins and field corners as disturbance refuges, overwintering habitats, nectar and pollen resources, foraging sites, wet features such as ditches, ponds and wet depressions, management of groundwater so as to promote conditions for wildlife, wild flower strips, which include rare weed species, beetle banks, bird seed mixtures, etc.
- Keeping buffer zones around sensitive biotopes, protected areas and semi-natural biotopes of every kind to protect them from nutrient and pesticide runoff.
- Setting up a scheme for environmental set-aside or requiring a proportion of fields to be under extensive use on each farm.
- Vegetal flora reserves (animal-powered shallow ploughing, hand-sowing of traditional grain varieties, no use of agrochemicals, late hand-harvest, grazing of stubble and fallow, wind-cleaning of grains, use of own seeds).

These segregative measures are often combined with specific funding.

Conservation of Local Varieties of Cultivated Plants and Local Animal Breeds

Conservation and management of broad-based genetic diversity within domesticated species have been improving agricultural production for 10,000 years. The local plant and animal species are adapted to the local climate, site and natural (e.g. pest and disease) conditions. These local genetic sources can be extremely important for breeding.

The Leipzig Declaration on Conservation and Sustainable Utilization of Plant Genetic Resources for Food and Agriculture focuses on the following priority activity areas (LD, 1996):

1. In situ conservation and development, e.g. surveying and inventorying plant genetic resources for food and agriculture; supporting on-farm management and improvement of plant genetic resources for food and agriculture, promoting in situ conservation of wild crop relatives and wild plants for food production.
2. Ex situ conservation, e.g. sustaining existing ex situ collections; regenerating threatened ex situ accessions; supporting planned and targeted collecting of plant genetic resources for food and agriculture.
3. Utilisation of plant genetic resources, e.g. expanding the characterisation, evaluation and number of core collections to facilitate use; promoting development and commercialisation of under-utilised crops and species; developing new markets for local varieties and 'diversity-rich' products.
4. Institution and capacity building, e.g. building national programmes; promoting networks for plant genetic resources for food and agriculture; constructing comprehensive information systems for plant genetic resources for food and agriculture; expanding and improving education and training; promoting public awareness of the value of plant genetic resources for food and agriculture conservation and use.

Similarly, the Global Strategy for the Management of Farm Animal Genetic Resources provides a technical and operational framework for assisting countries, comprising an intergovernmental mechanism for direct government involvement and policy development and a country-based global infrastructure to help countries draw up cost-effective plans and implement and maintain national strategies for the management of animal genetic resources (FAO, 2006a). The genetics of local wild animals need more research if this is to be utilised effectively in farm animal breeding.

Balance Between Agricultural Production and Biodiversity Conservation

Biodiversity brings both costs and benefits to agriculture. The expense of reducing weeds and other pests to maintain yields is a large fraction of the variable costs of arable farming in most countries. Any crop variety or agronomic practice that reduces the variable costs, increases yield or makes life easier is welcomed. Biodiversity in the form of predators of insect pests or crop/weed canopies that impede fungal epidemics can reduce costs, but this is very seldom quantified as a positive asset (TEEB, 2008). Pollination studies indicate a considerable economic value of such services from wildlife: the value of crop pollination in Europe was estimated at a staggering 5 billion euros per year in Europe. Although most pollination is performed by domesticated bees (*Apis mellifera*), wild pollinator communities provide valuable backup in times of troubles with beekeeping, as has been the case in recent years. A diverse farmed landscape with a variety of wildlife can also provide opportunities for additional income by improving the aesthetic, recreational and educational appeal of a farm.

Examples of Integrating Biodiversity Conservation into Agricultural Land Use

Precision Farming and Nature Conservation (Integrative Pathway)

The use of precision farming techniques for achieving nature conservation goals is an example of the integrative pathway. Precision farming, a data- and knowledge-driven and comparably new technology, allows the execution and the modification of specific measures of cultivation within crop fields with spatial variability and respect to nature conservation goals. For example, specific parts of crop fields with a higher potential for achieving nature values can be managed separately and appropriately (e.g. less fertilisers and pesticides).

Areas with specific site conditions for rare weed species, for example those depending on calcareous sites, e.g. love-in-a-mist (*Nigella arvensis*) and annual yel-

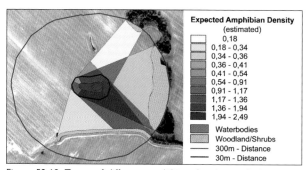

Figure 52.18. Zones of different amphibian abundances during migration periods from or to breeding ponds. Within the migration corridors (high presence of individuals), applications of fertilisers harmful for amphibians can be omitted by precision farming technology.

low-woundwort (*Stachys annua*), or those depending on very sandy soils combined with a low alkalinity, e.g. lamb's succory (*Arnoseris minima*), smooth cat's-ear (*Hypochaeris glabra*), shepherd's cress (*Teesdalia nudicaulis*), parsley-piert (*Aphanes microcarpa*) and annual vernal-grass (*Anthoxanthum aristatum*) can be left untreated with herbicides, often on very small areas within intensively managed fields. On these plots other measures that are harmful to specific valuable species, such as nitrogen fertilisation and/or liming, can be omitted locally. The localisation of areas with particular biotic potential and sensibility, based on GPS technology, is e.g. important for omitting fertilisation within migration corridors of some groups of animals, e.g. amphibians, to which these agents are toxic (Figure 52.18). During spring, amphibians migrate across crop fields in high densities to their breeding ponds. If there is a certain amount of nitrogen fertiliser, e.g. calcium ammonium nitrate, on the soil, a massive die-off of migrating individuals can occur, with a high risk of considerable population decline. This can be avoided e.g. by applying precision agriculture.

At the moment the development of sensors to control agricultural operations is not focusing on nature protection goals. However, there is great potential for protecting plants and animals which depend on, and are restricted to, specific site conditions, as well as those which are directly jeopardised by cultivation measures. Within crop fields, nests of lapwings and skylarks as well as sites of newborn brown hare (*Lepus europaeus*) or roe deer (*Capreolus capreolus*) can be recognised and by online processing,

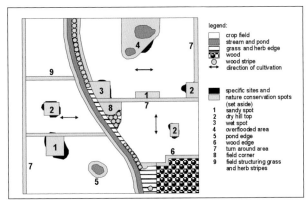

Figure 52.19. Design principle of small-scale structuring of arable landscapes by using nature conservation set-aside: modified land use on arable sites which have a high ecological potential, e.g. extreme sites spots and areas adjacent to biotopes (Berger et al., 2003).

Figure 52.21. Nature conservation set-aside along water bodies: water ponds are protected against input of fertilisers and pesticides. Amphibians such as fire-bellied toad (*Bombina bombina*), which usually lives close to these ponds, find suitable and minimally disturbed habitats (Photo: G. Berger).

Set-aside of Subareals of Arable Land (Segregative Pathway)

For nature conservation purposes, the most valuable parts of crop fields are characterised by low productivity because of technological or natural constraints. Wood or water edges, poor sandy spots, steep hill tops, head land, field corners etc. belong to such patches. We can say that:

Figure 52.20. Goal-orientated management of nature conservation set-aside consisting of cultivation subparts (e.g. soil cultivation in autumn in the area next to the crop field and sowing a site-specific herb grass mixture in the strip next to the wood edge) leads to a rich structured and flowering area with a high habitat value and complexity (Photo: G. Berger).

- the species of nature conservation interest (rare or vulnerable species) are more or less dependent on specific site conditions with often extreme site characteristics and
- they often need more than one type of habitat elements, e.g. vegetation structure, or
- they often live in complex habitats consisting of several biotope types and/or in ecotone situations, and
- the extreme sites in arable situations are very often in close proximity to sites with non-extreme conditions, which is advantageous for a wide range of species.

the cultivation machinery can be operated without harming or damaging these animals. In the same way, operative interruptions of herbicide spraying could be conducted by image recognition of specific species of herbs that are scattered and vulnerable in crop fields. The above makes precision farming a potentially promising technology for protecting biodiversity in agriculturally used landscapes.

Because these parts of crop fields are less valuable for production, it is fairly easy to adapt their management for conservation purposes. Subsidy schemes favouring such environmental set-asides will promote farmers' interest in them. Such sites under appropriate management can develop into areas with a high nature value (Figures 52.19-21).

A wide range of plants and animals such as weeds, grassland vegetation, wild bees, butterflies, grasshoppers, birds, mammals, amphibians benefit from these habitats (Van Buskirk and Willi, 2004). Such environmental set-asides in intensively managed farmland also contribute to a network of biotopes. If set adjacent to other valuable biotopes, they may act as buffers against drift of agro-chemicals (Figure 52.21).

Biodiversity management in agricultural landscapes of Europe should be a part of healthy production and a pil-lar of agroecosystem stability. Considering the value of farmland for biodiversity in Europe, halting biodiversity decline is impossible without considerable enhancement of biodiversity within agricultural landscapes. All the EU countries currently financially support a variety of the management options targeted at conservation in agro-landscapes through agroenvironmental programmes. For many farmers, conservation work has become a valuable source of income and a matter of pride.

Questions:

1. What are the main values of biodiversity for agricul-ture?
2. How can farming practices influence the biological diversity of plants and animals in a landscape?
3. Can you list several animal species that occur almost exclusively in farmland habitats?
4. What are the effects of the structural elements of landscape on the biodiversity of spontaneous flora and fauna?
5. What are the three main factors that affect the biodi-versity on the arable land?
6. How does the organic farming support the local biodiversity?
7. Can you describe the main properties of an 'ideal weed' species?
8. Do you know invasive plant or animal species from your country/region?
9. Why do we need to conserve or protect rare weed species?
10. How can we maintain local varieties of plants and local animal breeds?
11. Do you know good examples of biodiversity conser-vation in an agricultural landscape?

Part I

Occupational Health and Safety in Agriculture

Authors: Bob Aherin and Markus Pyykkönen

Coordinating Editor: Christine Jakobsson

Occupational Health and Safety in Agriculture

53

Markus Pyykkönen
Ministry of Social Affairs and Health, Helsinki, Finland
Bob Aherin
University of Illinois, Urbana-Champaign, Illinois, USA

Introduction

The total number of work-related farm fatalities on United States farms in 2008 as reported by the US Bureau of Labour Statistics (2009) was 661. In several European countries and the United States the fatal accident rate in agriculture is double, or more than double, the average for all other industries (Forastieri, 2001). For example the fatal accident rate for the agriculture, forestry, fishing and hunting industry in the United States was 29.4 per 100,000 workers in 2008 (US Bureau of Labour Statistics, 2009), which was 7.5 times the national average of 3.7 for all US industries and was ranked as being the highest fatality rate of any industry. Together with mining and construction, agriculture is one of the most dangerous sectors of the economy in both industrial nations and in developing countries. Depending on the countries studied, the ranking of the most dangerous sectors of the economy varies, but agriculture is usually mentioned among the four or five most dangerous. The Safework Programme of the International Labour Organisation (ILO) gives the following examples of dangerous sectors of the economy:

- Agriculture
- Mining
- Construction
- Fishing
- Shipbreaking
- Transport.

The variability in working conditions, including even drastic changes in external circumstances, is a feature shared by all these activities.

The great variety of tasks performed in agriculture makes it impossible to provide a complete list of risks. Some risks are specific to one particular area of agriculture, or even to a particular workplace. Machinery, falling objects and falls are consistently the leading causes of work-related fatalities (Saari, 2001; Myers, 2001). Furthermore, animals and chemicals constitute a significant source of hazards in agriculture (Suutarinen, 2003).

Agriculture

In the context of occupational safety and health, the term 'agriculture' is generally used in a broad sense including all activities directly related to cultivating, growing, harvesting and primary processing of agricultural products, animal and livestock breeding including aquaculture, and agroforestry. The term also refers to all agricultural undertakings, irrespective of size. A somewhat open question is whether subsistence farming should be included in agriculture. ILO does not include subsistence farming in agriculture but ISSA (International Social Security Associations) more or less includes it. The borderline between agriculture and forestry is not always clear and well defined.

The variable working conditions in agriculture can be compressed into some specific features, which increase the risk of occupational accidents (adapted from Forastieri, 2001):

- The work is carried out in the open air, exposing the workers to climatic conditions.
- The work is of a seasonal nature and certain tasks are urgent in specific periods.
- A variety of tasks must be performed by the same person.
- There is great variation in working postures and the length of the tasks performed.
- Contact with animals and plants brings exposure to bites, infections, allergies and other heath problems.
- There is contact with chemical and biological products.
- A variety of machines are used.
- The work is often performed in isolation out of sight of others.
- Emergency services are often delayed in time of accidents due to the remoteness of a high percentage of the work sites.
- The worker's home is often embedded in the farm for a high percentage of farm populations, increasing the risk of farm-related accidents to children.
- There are high proportions of young and old workers.

The average farm size is increasing in the EU and North America but the number of farms, workplaces, is still rather high. In Finland, almost 70,000 farms are spread out over the country (TIKE, 2006). The units are small and on many farms the work is done by the farmer and his family. Some farms employ seasonal workers, especially for harvesting fruit and vegetables. There are of course also industrialised farms with permanent staff and occasional seasonal workers. In the United States there are 2.1 million farms (Hoppe and Korb, 2005). There is a wide range of farm sizes today in the United States, from the large capital-intensive units that rely on scale of size to utilise input resources more efficiently compared to small farms that focus on niche production of high-value commodities (Midwest Center for Agricultural Research, Education, and Disease & Injury Prevention, 2002). The largest 7% of farms account for 75% of total US sales of agricultural products (USDA, 2002).

Risk Management

Risk management principles are not widely used in agriculture. Scientific contributions on the application of formal safety management theories or practices in family farming are not commonly available (Suutarinen, 2003; Murphy, 1992). Abstract and theoretical methods tend to reduce acceptance among farmers and a practical approach is needed when risk management systems are implemented. The methods used should be practical and economically feasible to achieve a high degree of acceptance among farmers.

It is known from workplace inspection, accident investigation and social science research that the key issues to address in improving risk management are:

- A deep-seated culture of unwise risk-taking.
- Farmers' resistance to officialdom and their perceptions that regulations and bureaucracy unduly burden the industry and that utilising risk management principles to effectively manage risk will lessen the need for safety regulations.
- Health and safety is not yet universally regarded as integral to good farm business management (HSE, 2007).

There are four primary components of a risk management programme (US Department of Labor, 2007):

1. Management Commitment
2. Work Analysis or Risk Assessment
3. Hazard Prevention and Control
4. Training of Employees, Supervisors and/or Managers

1. Management Commitment. The first step in addressing injury risk is a commitment by the farm operator/manager. This is equally true for the small farm with just one operator as for the large farm with hundreds of employees. It is important to make reducing injury risk a top priority in order to preserve life and to enhance profitability.

2. Risk Assessment of the Work Environment. The key to improving safety and health in agriculture is to manage risks by assessing them systematically and to implement preventive actions based on the assessment. It is sometimes difficult to explain to farmers that a risk assessment is nothing more than a careful examination of what could cause harm to workers, and to make decisions on whether the precautions taken are adequate or whether more should be done to prevent harm. The aim is to make sure that no one gets hurt or becomes ill. A risk assessment involves identifying the hazards present in any undertaking and then evaluating the extent of the risks involved, taking into account existing precautions (EASHW, 2007; U.S. Department of Labor, 2002).

Key points in a risk assessment are:

- Identifying the different risks that could cause harm in the workplace.
- Considering who may be harmed and how, including temporary and part-time staff, as well as workers in specific risk groups such as children, adolescents and elderly persons.
- Evaluating measures that are already in place to control these risks, and deciding what further action needs to be taken.
- Recording all findings and sharing these with workers and their representatives (EASHW, 2007).

Detailed descriptions on how to perform a risk assessment are given in national standards e.g. BS 8800 and guidelines and in the United States Department of Labor's Job Hazard Analysis publication OSHA 3071 (STM, 2003; U.S. Department of Labor, 2002).

3. Hazard Prevention and Control. Farmers often have limited resources but once identified, some risks require minimal direct cost. Once risks are identified and prioritised, a plan can be developed to use available resources to address the greatest need first. Ideally the aim is to eliminate hazards, but often that is not practical. However the farmer can make sure e.g. that machinery has adequate guards and that personal protection equipment is readily available for essential risk reduction activities such as noise and dust exposure.

4. Training of Employees, Supervisors and/or Managers. It is also important to make sure that workers are familiar with the risk they are working with or ex-

posed to. Today there are a number of agricultural training resources readily available, particularly on the internet, and mostly at no cost to users.

In risk management, the health and safety attitude of the farmer is quite important, as some research results show an involvement of personal or environmental risk factors. McCurdy et al. (2004) found that multiple injury events in the same individual occurred more frequently than predicted by chance and Harrell (1995) showed that individuals incurring a farming-related injury scored higher on a measure of personal risk-taking and believed that accidents were inevitable, whereas specific safe farming practices e.g. wearing protective clothing and operating machinery safely, were associated with a lower likelihood of injury.

The general profitability of agriculture is low and on many farms there are no possibilities for investments in new and safe machinery or for improving the working conditions. The use of ageing machines with inadequate safety engineering constitutes a constant source of hazards, as operations involving high numbers of disturbances, e.g. machinery breakdowns, have a higher accident probability (Suutarinen, 2003). According to Loringer and Myers (2008), between 1992 and 2005 a total of 1412 workers died from tractor overturns on farms in the United States. Those authors conducted a national study in 2004 to identify the prevalence of rollover protective structures (ROPS) in the US and found that 49% of tractors were not equipped with a ROPS. A study in Iowa found that only 4% of tractor operators wore the seatbelt installed on tractors with ROPS (Sanderson et al., 2006). Old tractors without ROPS and seatbelts are also a serious problem in the European Union.

Workforce

The workforce meeting the variable working conditions of agriculture has unique characteristics compared with most other sectors of the economy. Production is often based on family-owned and operated enterprises or family farms. Family members younger and older than the conventional workforce take part in farming operations.

Elderly people, children and adolescents are quite often involved in farm accidents (Suutarinen, 2003). In the US, 22.9% of the workforce in the production agriculture industry consists of workers aged 55 or older. No other industry employs more workers in this age group. In addition, 25% of farm operators are aged 65 or older (Peters, 2007). Myers et al. (2007) reported that farm workers over the age of 54 in the US had a fatality rate of 45.8 deaths per 100,000 workers compared with the average farm work fatality rate of 25.5 deaths. Tractors were by far the leading cause of these deaths, accounting for 46%, with trucks being second with 7%. Elderly people are often not sufficiently aware of the onset of the physical and mental ageing process. They often fail to recognise or underestimate potential new hazards because of their habits and routines. The most frequent causes of accidents among older agricultural workers are slips, trips and falls.

Family farms predominate in American and European agriculture and as a result young people are significantly exposed to significant work-related hazards on the farms where they live. According to the National Children's Center for Rural and Agricultural Health and Safety (2010), over 1.12 million young people under the age of 20 live on farms in the US. During the period 1995-2002, an estimated 907 young people died as a result of an accident on US farms. The three leading sources of fatal injuries to young people involved machinery (23%), motor vehicles including All Terrain Vehicles (19%) and drowning (16%). In 2006, approximately 3,600 children were injured while performing farm work. Young people who live on livestock farms had significantly higher injury rates (19.2 injuries/1,000 young people) than those who live on arable farms (12.1 injuries/1,000 young people). For European farm children, agricultural vehicles are the most common cause of injury, with 65% of those involving the child being run over. Other causes include unprotected machine components, falls, drowning and suffocation and contact with animals. Adolescents are a particular risk group because they readily do all kinds of machine work and are eager to try new machines even if they lack the proper training for the work (Rautiainen, 2004). Injuries to young people on farms occur while they are doing any one of three general activities of working, observing and playing in the agricultural work environment (Donham and Thelin, 2006). Young workers are much more likely to suffer non-fatal serious accidents than their older colleagues. The average incidence rate of non-fatal accidents on farms in the EU is at least 50% higher among workers aged 18-24 than in any other age category (ILO, 2005).

Agriculture is a significant employer of women and many women also contribute in farming as wives or partners. Temporary, casual seasonal work, for example during the harvesting season, is an important feature of women's work in this sector. There is likely to be considerable task segregation by gender. Women are concentrated in elementary jobs in agriculture and in animal production. They more often take care of animals rather than performing field work. Reed et al. (1999) found that about 50% of over 1600 rural women from farm households surveyed in Kentucky and Texas described themselves as homemakers, yet they were regularly involved in work with farm animals for about 40% of their time and spent about 30% of their time driving a farm tractor. It could be anticipated that the occupational injury and illness experiences of men and women on farms would differ due to the significant differences in tasks they perform on farms. Generally, women working in agriculture are exposed to the same hazards and risks as male workers, but their frequency of exposure differs. Dimich-Ward et al. (2004) reported that the most common fatal machinery injuries for males involved tractor rollovers (32%) and being run over by farm equipment (20%), whereas for females the most common machinery-related causes of fatalities were being run over (45%) and tractor rollovers (24%). The most common cause of farm accidents in general for males was being struck by an object (33%) or animal (14%). For females the most common farm accidents involved animals (37%) or being struck by an object (32%). Women face further risks, particularly to reproductive health from pesticides and biological agents (EASHW, 2007). Lower extremities are the most frequently injured body parts for women (Carruth et al., 2001).

A six-year study in the US found approximately 11 times as many agriculture-related fatalities in males compared with females (Dimich-Ward et al., 2004). A greater number of males were injured regardless of how the occurrence of injury was categorised. This also holds true in Finland, where 75% of those injured in farm accidents are men (Karttunen, 2006). Servicing and maintenance of machines is the most risky task, followed by construction of farm buildings. The relative incidence rate of injuries in maintenance of machines is 3.1 and in construction of farm buildings 2.1 when the relative incidence rate for livestock work is set to 1.0. The relative incidence rate for field work is 0.6 (Karttunen et al., 2006).

The main farmer may have a secondary occupation, which can lead to excessive burdens on the farmer or the farmer's spouse. Part-time farming can result in long working hours and inadequate rest, for example during the harvesting season. Haste, fatigue or stress is often mentioned as the primary contributing factor in most injuries (Rautiainen et al., 2004). Farmers tend to have good occupational training in production methods and technologies, but not in safety and health questions or in personnel management. In Ireland, only 13% of farmers are trained in occupational safety and health (McNamara et al., 2006). Farmers in the US mainly receive this training in adult learning programmes through University Land Grant Extension programmes, their farmers' organisation, high school vocational agricultural programmes and through regional rural medical centres. There are a few courses in agricultural safety and health offered at a few select universities. The University of Illinois offers the only minor in agricultural safety and health for undergraduate students in the country. The University of Iowa offers the only MSc and PhD programmes specifically in agricultural safety and health.

The productivity of agriculture is significantly enhanced in many Western countries by the labour and assistance provided by migrant workers. The number of migrant workers has steadily increased due to the expansion of labour-intensive crops, particularly in the area of fruit and vegetables. There are no exact figures available on the number of migrant workers in European agriculture. The number of seasonal and migrant farm workers has been estimated to be about 4.5 million, of whom nearly 500,000 come from outside the EU-15 member states (Renault, 2002). Farms in the United States hire approximately 2.5 million seasonal and migrant farm workers (ILO, 2004). These workers work for a short period of time, e.g. for the harvesting season, and start their work after a very short introduction to the job. Information on health and safety is sometimes given in a language not understood or only poorly understood by the workers. Common injuries experienced by European migrant

workers are cuts, falls and slips. Sometimes these injuries are associated with fatigue, most usually brought about by long working hours (McKay et al., 2006). Snake and insect bites are common among young migrant workers during summer, and they affect the upper limbs during manual work close to the ground (Alex et al., 2003). According to Donhan and Thelin (2006), one of the most common work-related injuries experienced by up to 40% of some migrant worker populations in the United States is eye injuries. The causes of these eye injuries include scratches to the cornea, chemical eye irritation and ultraviolet sunlight exposure resulting in damage to the retina and cornea. Other common injuries include back injuries, lung irritation and related illnesses from exposure to organic and inorganic dusts.

Incidence Rates

Comparing health and safety levels in agricultural work over time and between countries is problematic. Absolute accident figures are misleading. Instead, accident figures should be used in relation to some measure of exposure, such as work hours or size of working population (Suutarinen, 2003). The official data on the incidence of occupational accidents and diseases are imprecise and underestimated in agriculture, irrespective of the level of development of the country (Forastieri, 2001). This situation is more evident for occupational diseases. There are different arrangements for reporting occupational accidents and occupational diseases. Accidents can be identified at the moment they occur, but there are differences in how well the accidents of self-employed farmers are reported. Occupational diseases require medical diagnosis and not all work-related diseases are registered as occupational diseases. Occupational diseases often have contributing exposures outside the work environment that make the exact causes difficult to identify and quantify.

The following are examples of the incidence of accidents among European farm workers with more than three days' absence (per 10,000 persons employed) (EUROSTAT, 2005; Spirgys et al., 2005; Mikheev, 2004):

EU-15	516
Denmark	154
Finland	535
Sweden	119
United Kingdom	194
Norway	262
Lithuania	24
Russia	72

There has never been a comprehensive national surveillance system for non-fatal farm injuries in the United States. This is a long-term goal identified by agricultural occupational health and safety professionals, but has yet to come to fruition. Most significant studies focused on determining injury incidence rates have been conducted by stratified national, regional or state level self-reported random sample surveys conducted by such agencies as the National Institute for Occupational Safety and Health (NIOSH), the National Safety Council (NSC) or state Land Grant Universities. A disabling injury in the US includes injuries that range from permanent impairment to those that prevent normal work for at least a full work day. The NSC has estimated that the total number of agricultural work-related disabling injuries each year in the period 1993-2004 ranged from 130,000 to 150,000 (NSC 1993, 1994, 1995, 1996, 1997, 1998, 1999, 2000, 2001, 2002, 2003, 2004). This is an injury rate ranging from 330 to 400 per 10,000 persons.

Based on figures collected by ILO, the incidence of a fatal accident in the EU-15 is 0.8 per 10,000 farm workers (ILO, 2005, EUROSTAT, 2006). The corresponding incidence rate for the mining and construction industry is 0.5 in the EU-15. In 2003, the incidence rate of fatal accidents was 1.1 in the Czech Republic, 0.9 in Poland and 2.5 in Lithuania (Spirgys et al., 2005).

Only 1.9% of the US labour force work in agriculture (Dimitri et al., 2005), which involves approximately 1.8 million full-time workers (CDC, 2010). NSC (2004) reported that the mean fatality rate for the US agricultural industry from 1992 to 2002 was 2.23 deaths per 10,000 farm workers compared with 0.39 per 10,000 workers for all US industries.

In Ireland only 6.5% of the workforce work in agriculture, but it gives rise to 30% of fatal work-related accidents (McNamara et al., 2006). Over the past 10 years, there were on average 49 fatalities per year on farms in the United Kingdom (HSE, 2007). Of the 45 people killed in 2005/06, 23 were farmers or self-employed workers, 13 were employees and 9 were members of the public, of whom 6 were children. This gives a fatal incidence rate of 0.88 per 10 00 workers. The main causes of accidents were (HSE, 2007):

- Transport (including vehicle overturns), 36%.
- Falling from a height, 13%.
- Livestock-related (contact with animal), 13%.
- Contact with moving machinery, 11%.
- Being struck by a moving or falling object (e.g. trees, bales), 9%.

Machines such as tractors and harvesters have the highest frequency and fatality rates of injury. Exposure to pesticides and other agrochemicals constitutes another major occupational risk causing poisoning and death.

Despite technological development and mechanisation, musculoskeletal disorders caused by awkward working postures and demanding physical work are still common. Other hazards are biological agents such as dusts, which give rise to allergies and respiratory disorders and lung diseases. Farmers also have a high incidence of melanoma from sun exposure.

Occupational diseases are generally more expensive than occupational accidents. Rautiainen (2002) studied compensation data for Finnish farmers and found that the mean cost of the 830 compensated occupational diseases was 6,636 euros, while for the 10,092 occupational injuries it was 1,340 euros. Occupational diseases had a higher risk than injuries of leading to a permanent disability pension. In the US, the average direct and indirect cost of a occupational disabling injury is approximately $74,000 and the average cost of a work-related fatality is more than $94,000 (Brown et al., 2001).

According to Walker (2001), about 80% of the workers in agriculture have a musculoskeletal disorder at some time and approximately 40% suffer from noise-induced hearing loss. Respiratory problems in agricultural workers are double the average for the general population. The incidence of dermatitis in the industry is not known, but there are about 450 cases per year in British horticulture.

Lower back pain is a common problem for farmers, with e.g. 41% of British farmers reporting pain each year. The figure in Sweden is slightly higher, with 47% of farmers experiencing pain each year. In the United States, 50% of adults of working age employed in agriculture experience lower back pain episodes each year and more than 10% seek medical care for their back problems (Donham and Thelin, 2006). In Finland, pain in the neck and shoulders is slightly more common than lower back pain, with 67% of farmers reporting pain in the neck and shoulders and 64% reporting back pain each year (Cowie et al., 2005; Perkiö-Mäkela et al., 2006). In Sweden, 82% of the men and 86% of the women working on dairy farms report some kind of musculoskeletal symptoms each year (Lundquist et al., 1997).

In Finnish agriculture the incidence (calculated per 10,000 workers) of different occupational diseases is: respiratory diseases 15, diseases caused by exertion 13, dermatitis 10, noise-induced hearing problems 4 and others 4.

A comparison of occupational diseases between countries is even more difficult than the comparison of injuries. First of all, there are different definitions of occupational diseases and different compensation systems and generally only compensated diseases are recorded as occupational diseases. The following Table 53.1 gives an idea of the problem, with the incidence calculated per 10,000 employees (Spirgys et al., 2005; Mikheev, 2004; Rautianen & Reynolds, 2001):

The differences in incidence are probably due to the definitions of occupational diseases and differences in the compensation system, and not to differences in the health risks in the actual work.

Table 53.1. Reported incidence of occupational diseases in some countries (Spirgys et al., 2005; Mikheev, 2004; Rautianen & Reynolds, 2001).

Finland	45.6
Czech Republic	7.3
Poland	0.4
Lithuania	1.2
Russia	2.2
United States*	43

* Data limited to farms with 11 or more employees, which represent less than 10% of US farms. Corresponding data not available for other segments of the farm population.

Legislation

Agriculture is covered by different kinds of legal instruments such as international and national laws, regulations and rules, technical standards and similar documents. More than 20 ILO Conventions and Recommendations concern health and safety issues relevant to agriculture or deal with aspects of agricultural workers' working conditions. It seems that agriculture is not highly prioritised by the ILO member countries, as only five countries have so far ratified ILO Convention 184, published in 2001, on Safety and Health in Agriculture. Convention 129, published in 1969, on Labour Inspection in Agriculture has been ratified by 43 member countries.

Occupational protection laws often apply generally to all sectors of the economy, including agriculture. The general objectives are often very abstract and the rules have only limited effect, unless they are accompanied by more practical implementing regulations. Problems also arise from the fact that legislation often only covers employees, whereas there are no protective provisions for self-employed farmers and their family members.

In the EU there are two types of safety and health directives. Directive 89/391/EEC on the introduction of measures to encourage improvements in the safety and health of workers in the workplace belongs to the first category. This directive is designed to secure a minimum level of safety and health at work and states that it is the duty of the employer to take care of the safety of his/her employees. Other examples of this category are the directives on noise (2003/10/EC) and vibration (2002/44/EC), giving exact limits on the maximum exposure.

The second category of directives aims to guarantee the safety of machines placed on the market. The machinery directive (98/37/EC) and the tractor directive (2003/37/EC) are examples of this category. The technical specifications of machines are given in harmonised standards and the specifications of tractors in separate directives listed in the annex to Directive 2003/37/EC. According to these directives, the manufacturer is responsible for the safety of a machine placed on the market. A certain minimum level of safety is ensured, and unsafe machines cannot exist on the market if the market surveillance is working properly. The main problem for the user is to keep the safety of machines on the farm unchanged during their technical life span. Directive 89/655/EEC on the minimum safety and health requirements for the use of work equipment by workers in the workplace is the connection between machines and risk management as described in Directive 89/391/EEC.

The directives and standards regulating the safety of new machines represent quite a high level of safety, and improving the safety of the machines further by developing the directives will be difficult. For example when rollover protective structures were made compulsory on tractors in Finland, the number of fatalities in tractor rollovers decreased from 1.6 per 10,000 farmers to 0.2 per 10,000 farmers, in absolute figures two cases per year. It is not quite clear whether these fatalities could be prevented by introducing safety belts in tractors. In most machine and tractor accidents the users and their decisions play a key role. Machines may not be correctly used or protective equipment may be defective or rendered inoperative. More weight should be given to the maintenance of machines and their safety components.

In the United States, farmers have traditionally opposed most mandatory regulations. The Occupational Safety and Health Act (OSHA), which came into law in 1971, initially included essentially all places of public employment, including all farm operations. However, after strong lobbying efforts by farm organisations, an amendment was passed in 1976 that did not allow the expenditure of federal dollars to inspect or enforce these regulations of farms with 10 or fewer employees (Donham and Thelin, 2006). This amendment essentially excluded approximately 90% of all US farms. Most agricultural safety professionals favour including all of agriculture under OSHA regulations. However, with the vast majority of US farms being small in nature and geographically dispersed, enforcement of these regulations would be extremely difficult. Nevertheless, with the strong liability risk that farm operators face in the US, a growing number of farmers are recognising that they must try to comply with established safe work procedures to minimise injury and liability risk. The OSHA regulations contain several standards specific to agriculture, including standards on tractors, safety guards on agricultural machines, anhydrous ammonia, field sanitation, use of the Slow Moving Vehicle emblem on farm equipment transported on public roadways, etc. (Langley

et al., 1997). The American Society of Agricultural and Biological Engineers (ASABE) has developed and published a variety of safety design standards. While these are consensus standards and are not mandatory for farm equipment manufacturers, most comply because of the liability risk. There are specific standards related to the safe application of agricultural restricted-use pesticides and the employment of young people on farms.

Prevention

All those working on a farm, employees and self-employed, permanent and seasonal workers, should enjoy the same level of safety and health protection. Enforcement is not always the best way of improving occupational health and safety in agriculture, as the number of safety inspectors is generally small compared with the number of farms. The effect of enforcement is limited by the fact that legislation often covers only employees, whereas there are no protective provisions for self-employed farmers and their family members.

In Finland the occupational health service provides individual advice and regular health checks for farmers and farm workers and 41% of Finnish farmers are members of the farmers' occupational health service (FOHS). The work of FOHS is mainly preventive but curative activities may also be included. The tasks of FOHS include:

- Analysis of working conditions by regular farm visits.
- Assessing and monitoring of work-related health hazards.
- Surveillance of health through medical check-ups.
- Drawing up proposals to improve working conditions.
- Adjusting work tasks according to the employee's capabilities.

Farmers in Norway who use FOHS are quite satisfied with the results, but the membership of FOHS is low, only 8,300 or less than 15% of farmers (Brunes, 2006). In Sweden, 37% of farmers use the occupational health service, mainly for regular monitoring of their health (Danielson, 2006). An attempt to trial such a service has been implemented in portions of the states of Iowa and

Nebraska in the United States. This programme is titled Certified Safe Farm (Donham and Thelin, 2006). The concept is that those farmers who volunteer to participate in the programme must adhere to most of the interventions listed for the FOHS. If they successfully comply, they receive about a 10% rebate on their total insurance costs. The rebates to date have mostly been funded by government grants, but the intention is that insurance companies will see the value of the programme and will eventually be willing to provide approximately a 10% insurance policy cost rebate. To date, insurance companies have been reluctant to become involved in this type of intervention.

The farmers' occupational health service is one way to promote occupational safety and health but it should not be the only method, as FOHS seems to have certain difficulties in reaching the majority of farmers. Other methods used are information campaigns and training activities, either for specialised groups or general training for all farmers. Sweden has started an information campaign to prevent injuries to children on farms. The model is adapted and developed from the North American Guidelines for Children's Agricultural Tasks (www.nagcat.com). The idea is to assist parents and other adults in assigning appropriate and safe farm jobs for children and adolescents (Svennefelt and Lundqvist, 2006).

In addition, Sweden has two different training programmes available, one providing specialist training in the safe use of chain saws and one general training programme on safe farming. The safe farm programme includes one day of training every third year, followed by a farm walk-through by an expert that includes a check of children's safety if appropriate for the farm. Joining the programme gives the farmer 30% lower insurance fees (Danielsson, 2006).

Most of the intervention efforts in the United States have historically focused on various types of educational initiatives. The primary organisations involved include the Land Grant Universities located in each state through their extension programmes, farm organisations, and regional agricultural safety and health research and outreach centres. In 1990, a major new national focus on agricultural safety and health issues was initiated as a result of a series of national conferences that led to the publication of a report titled '*Agriculture at Risk: A Report to the Nation*'. In addition, a series of major articles were published in the national media regarding the growing problem of farm accidents, and a new national grass roots organisation called Farm Safety Just-4 Kids was formed by a mother in Iowa who had lost a child in a farm accident (Murphy, 2003). Since the early 1990s, the US Congress has appropriated approximately 24 million dollars each year for agricultural safety and health research, establishment of nine agricultural safety and health centres, and establishment of a national agricultural child injury prevention centre. These efforts have significantly increased the scientific knowledge about health and safety issues facing the agricultural industry and the development of more effective interventions.

In many countries a code of practice, which usually means a risk assessment document or programme, has been developed. In Ireland and Finland, farmers are trained to use the risk assessment because according to surveys, farmers' abilities to identify the risks on their own farm are variable (McNamara et al., 2006; Murtonen, 2006). Some farmers are not able to define even the most critical risks or are not willing to discuss those issues, whereas others describe the risks very analytically but certain risks may be underestimated.

The Health and Safety Executive (HSE) in the United Kingdom has chosen another approach by leaving out the training and developing interactive software to help farmers carry out a comprehensive health and safety assessment of their farms. The software is available on the HSE website and is aimed at all farmers and farm managers who are responsible for health and safety.

Features of the self-assessment software include (HSE, 2007):

- A downloadable application, which can be installed on the farm computer and completed off-line at the farmer's leisure.
- A configuration screen that tailors the questions to those relevant for the individual farm.
- A series of questions on key health and safety topics.
- A benchmark for each question of the minimum standards that should be attained to comply with legal requirements and the reasoning behind it.
- The ability to order relevant free HSE guidance.
- A facility for the farmer to add additional risks to his/her assessment on issues/hazards that are either

not covered by the questions or that are unique to the particular farm.

- A facility to allow separate assessments to be produced for more than one farm/holding.
- Outputs in the form of a prioritised list of identified actions.

A more demanding approach is to integrate occupational safety and health into the quality management system of the farm. Theoretically, this seems to be an ideal solution. The problem is that the quality of products is highly prioritised by farmers and the development of the quality management system is finished as soon as the product quality part is done. Some farmers continue by including environmental quality into the system, but few have the endurance to include occupational safety and health. Despite these difficulties, strong efforts have been made, at least in Norway, Sweden and Finland, to include occupational safety and health as an integral part of the quality management system of farms. Academic training efforts in the US have begun to focus more on training farm operators how to develop and implement safety and health risk management plans. Courses have been developed at major agricultural universities such as the University of Illinois and Penn State University that focus on training future agricultural professionals in the basic principles of risk management.

Intervention studies seem to be quite effective in changing the safety behaviour of farmers. In an intervention study in Denmark, Rasmussen et al. (2003) showed a substantial reduction in the number of farm injuries and measures of safety behaviour revealed significant improvements. The intervention effect was estimated to be a 30% reduction in the rate of all injuries and a 42% reduction in medically treated injuries. These results suggest that appropriate training followed by a farm walk-through by an expert could substantially improve the effectiveness of self-assessment systems.

If the farmer is motivated, simple checklists can provide a good start in improving farm safety. The US Occupational Safety and Health Administration (OSHA) has produced a list of simple rules to remind farmers of important safety issues. By following these rules, most accidents could be avoided but the problem is that the rules are very general and are only intended to be remind-

ers of major safety risks and provide basic intervention recommendations. Farm operators and workers would need to seek out other sources to more fully understand the issues and how to implement appropriate intervention measures. The steps recommended by OSHA to improve the safety of farms are:

- Read and follow instructions in equipment operator's manuals and on product labels.
- Inspect equipment routinely for problems that may cause accidents.
- Discuss safety hazards and emergency procedures with workers.
- Install approved rollover protection structures or protective frames on all tractors.
- Make sure guards on farm equipment are replaced after maintenance.
- Review and follow instructions in material safety datasheets and labels that accompany chemical products and communicate information on these hazards to workers.
- Take precautions to prevent entrapment and suffocation caused by unstable surfaces of grain storage bins, silos, or hoppers.
- Be aware that methane gas, carbon dioxide, ammonia and hydrogen sulphide can form in unventilated grain silos and manure pits and can suffocate or poison workers or explode.
- Take advantage of safety equipment, such as bypass starter covers, power take-off master shields, and slow-moving vehicle emblems (OSHA, 2007).

Conclusions

Occupational safety and health work in agriculture has to respond to the needs of diverse farm types, e.g. small farms with part-time farming and large farms with permanent and/or seasonal workers.

Larger farms usually have larger and more modern machinery and therefore less machinery injuries. New animal confinement buildings are generally better in terms of air quality and working conditions. However, the increasing farm size may bring longer work exposure times and increase the risk of chronic diseases. Stress is also often reported as a major problem among farmers.

The introduction of safety measures depends on the technical, economic and social development of the agricultural industry. Integrating safety into quality systems and the planning of new production processes and buildings is a great challenge for all concerned –farmers, safety organisations, professional associations, extension services and administrations. However, this is a challenge that must be met in order to protect the most valuable asset that the agricultural industry has, namely its people.

Part J

Counteracting
Climate Change Effects

Authors: Lars Andersson, Henrik Eckersten, Fredrik Holstein, Stig Karlsson, Elisabet Lewan, Birgitta Mannerstedt Fogelfors, Roland Sigvald and Bengt Torssell

Coordinating Author: Henrik Eckersten

An Evaluation of Climate Change Effects on Crop Production

54

CASE STUDY
Sweden

Henrik Eckersten, Lars Andersson, Fredrik Holstein,
Birgitta Mannerstedt Fogelfors, Elisabet Lewan,
Roland Sigvald, Bengt Torssell and Stig Karlsson
Swedish University of Agricultural Sciences
Uppsala, Sweden

The aim of this chapter was to summarise the effects of climate change on specific areas of crop production within Swedish agriculture, based on climate change scenarios from the Rossby Centre, SMHI (dated October 2006). The criterion for the sub-areas selected was that they could be expected to be negatively affected by climate change and thus require some form of adaptation. However, the overall ambition was to keep the analysis of various sub-areas neutral and to report also positive effects. The section on land use is an analysis of results from two major scientific research projects on climate change and use of agricultural land, and concerns the effects of other climate scenarios, i.e. not specifically those from SMHI. This chapter presents results from a study (SOU, 2007) in which future projections were based on scientifically tested methodologies (mechanistic, empirical and analogy models) when available, otherwise based on expert judgements.

Land Use

The need for land to grow crops for food and feed is in several studies considered to be decreasing in Europe as a whole for the type of society in which we live at present, i.e. a world with a strong growth-orientated economy and a world that sets regional (e.g. EU versus USA) interests in the foreground. The major reason for the decreased requirement for arable land for these purposes is primarily the assumption of strongly increasing productivity per hectare, which is mainly explained by continued technological developments within agriculture at a pace based on that since the middle of the 1900s. For Europe as a whole, the effects of climate change on productivity are expected to be small in comparison with those of improved technology. In one estimate, climate change up to ~2050 will cause a ±5-10% change in the average yield per hectare in Europe, and in another estimate an approx. 25% increase compared with the current position. This can be compared with an 85-160% increase due to technological developments. The evaluations of technological developments lack

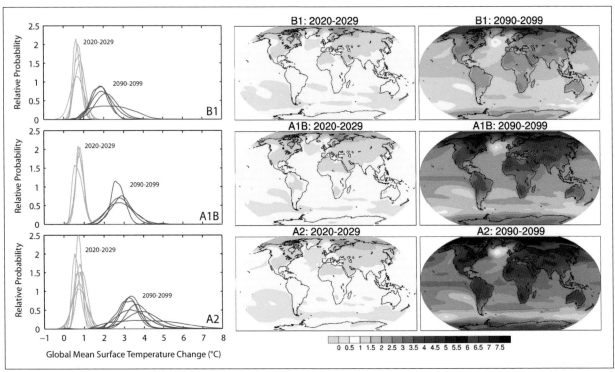

Figure 54.1. Projected surface temperature changes for the early and late 21st century relative to the period 1980–1999. The central and right panels show the AOGCM multi-model average projections for the B1 (top), A1B (middle) and A2 (bottom) SRES scenarios averaged over the decades 2020–2029 (centre) and 2090–2099 (right). The left panels show corresponding uncertainties as the relative probabilities of estimated global average warming from several different AOGCM and Earth System Model of Intermediate Complexity studies for the same periods. Base: A1; Higher population growth: 1->2; Sounder technological solutions: A->B. Some studies present results only for a subset of the SRES scenarios, or for various model versions. Therefore the difference in the number of curves shown in the left-hand panels is due only to differences in the availability of results (IPCC, 2007: Summary for Policymakers, Fourth Assessment Report, AR4).

a concrete explanatory foundation and are mainly based on empirical experiences of changes in productivity. The reasons for the differences in the technology factor between scenarios are unclear, but the evaluations differ so much that the effect of these uncertainties on the requirement for arable land is quite significant in comparison with the actual predicted decrease in the land requirement. Another uncertainty factor is societal (socio-economic) development. Alternative societal developments with less strong technological developments and more environment-orientated policy (the B2 scenario, the effect of the technology factor on productivity approx 10-25%) also affect the evaluation of the areal requirement to a considerable extent. See IPCC Climate Change 2007 Synthesis report, or IPCC Special Report on Emission Scenarios (SRES, 2000). In addition, the climate model used to calculate the

climate scenarios influence the results. Together, all these uncertainties give a low credibility to the land use scenarios. However, the evaluations presented in this chapter were made possible by the fact that the models are transparent, which in turn provides the potential for them to be refined and the reasons for differences in the results to be identified. In summary, a general trend among the scenarios is that in a society that is developing in the direction of strong economic growth, a smaller proportion of Europe's arable area will probably be used for food and feed production than if society were to develop in the direction of increasing environmental protection.

The land use scenarios for Europe were used to produce scenarios for individual countries. The model, which adopts as its starting point the adaptation of profit-maximising farmers to prices, might be regarded as relatively more reliable as regards the relative distribution between countries. On the other hand it is perhaps less reliable on the total European level due to propagation of errors in comprehensive calculations. The scenarios show that climate change alone, i.e. on the assumption that the current socio-economic conditions remain unchanged, would increase the competitive power of Swedish land for food and feed production. All scenarios except that with the least climate change (the B1 scenario) would give an increased use of land area. When changes in socio-economic conditions (cost of inputs, etc.) are also considered, it is only in the scenario with the highest climate impact (A1F1) that Swedish crop production would increase its competitive power. In scenario B2, the Swedish agricultural area decreases strongly and becomes limited mainly to southern Götaland, primarily due to the high costs of inputs and to the fact that the positive effects of climate change are not sufficiently great to compensate for this. It should be pointed out that the results appear to be very sensitive to variations in input data. Tests of the predictions of land use within Sweden have produced very poor results. Even if land use is only controlled to a minor extent by climate, the prevailing regional differences perhaps provide a better picture of the potential changes in land use in Sweden. If Mälardalen were to also acquire the land use of Skåne when it acquires the climate Skåne has today, then winter wheat would generally replace large parts of the oats area. For Västerbotten the corresponding reasoning would mean a large proportion of the cultivated grassland area being replaced by cereal growing, also winter wheat. In southern Sweden up to Mälardalen, the proportion of new crops such as maize and sunflower would increase.

Growing Period

The growing period is generally predicted to be extended, primarily in the spring but also in the autumn, when the period of bare soil from harvest in late summer to autumn sowing may be extended. These evaluations were mainly made with agrarian expertise, but certain empirical data and model runs were also used. For spring-sown crops the start of spring tillage is mainly considered to be determined by drying of the soil, which occurs considerably later than the start of the growing period. Spring tillage in 2085 may start at the beginning of March in the southern and central plains areas of Götaland and at the end of March in the northern plains area and in Svealand. In Norrland, spring tillage will start at the beginning of April in the south and in the latter half of April in the north. Harvest of spring-sown crops is estimated to be approx. three weeks earlier than at present and the differences throughout the country may persist. For spring barley this would mean the latter half of July in the south of Sweden to the latter half of August in northern Norrland. It is uncertain when autumn tillage can occur but in view of the fact that the growing period will be more than a month longer in the autumn, autumn sowing should be delayed. Winter crops will grow until the end of December in both Götaland and Svealand, although quite slowly due to low solar radiation. In southern Norrland, growth will stop in the latter part of November and in northern Norrland in the beginning of November. The increasing temperature will mean that growth in the spring will start in February in Götaland and Svealand, just over a week later in southern Norrland and in the middle of April in northern Norrland, i.e. approx. a month before spring tillage (somewhat less in the north). In the case of e.g. winter wheat, this will be reflected in stages of plant development being brought forward by approx. one month in the beginning of the spring and maturation occurring approx. 3 weeks earlier than at present.

Water Availability

Increased temperature, changed precipitation conditions and increased CO_2 content in the atmosphere will lead to changes in water availability for agriculture. Increased temperature will lead to increased growth and transpiration, mainly in the spring when growth is currently strongly temperature-limited. Precipitation is expected to increase from October to March, remain unchanged in April and be lower than the present level from May to September, but this evaluation is complicated by the fact that the increased CO_2 content will mean that plants will be able to manage water shortage better, i.e. that transpiration can decrease without growth being affected to the same extent. Calculations for fertilised grassland for

~2085 that consider all these factors together indicate that overall, soil water content will decrease from June to October, but that growth will not necessarily become lower than the current level. The calculations are supported by an alternative method where changes in evaporation are taken from climate scenario maps in which the cumulative increase in evaporation will be greatest in the central plains of Götaland (~45 mm), somewhat lower in the rest of Sweden and considerably lower in northern Norrland, where evaporation will only increase by ~15 mm in April-June.

The few simulations that have been carried out indicate that there will be a water deficit and a potential to increase growth through irrigation. For certain locations, this irrigation requirement could be in the order of 15-80 mm/year. The evaluations give no indication of how great the water stress can become for individual extreme years on individual sites or on average. This would require many more simulations. However, it appears that there will generally be drier conditions from the end of July through September. An increased intensity of rainfall indicates that there may be drier conditions locally than shown by the simulations. Winter crops can generally be assumed to have been harvested by the beginning of this dry period, while a larger proportion of grain filling could occur in drier conditions for the corresponding spring crops. This could affect grain yields, mainly through lower harvests and altered protein concentrations, and probably provide a further advantage for winter crops compared with spring-sown crops.

These conditions would also act to the advantage of maize, since it thrives in heat and can withstand moderate drought relatively well. For co-crop and catch crop systems, it is vital that the insown crop has a well-established root system before harvest of the main crop. Grassland may have reduced growth during this period compared with at present, which might create a need for complementary feeding of livestock. For vegetable crops, this dry period would mean an increased irrigation requirement. The majority of vegetable growers already have irrigation systems and the main issue will be whether sufficient water will be available to increase irrigation during these dry periods rather than whether to install new irrigation systems. However, irrigation systems might need to be modified so that the expected increases in precipitation

during other periods of the year can be made available during these dry periods. The extra amount of irrigation that will be required remains to be determined. The individual calculations for fertilised grassland referred to above indicate that an additional quantity of water approximately corresponding to the decrease in summer rainfall caused by climate change may have to be applied in order to utilise the increased growth potential.

Crop Pests

Insect, virus and fungus attacks on crops give rise to considerable crop protection costs, currently amounting to around half the total cost of crop protection chemical inputs within Swedish agriculture. The other half is represented by weed control. Calculations of the damage to crops as a function of climate are complicated and research within this area is working to develop methods for both understanding and predicting the effects of climate on the dynamics of insects and diseases (fungal, viral, bacterial) and on the damage they cause to crops. However, we did not use any quantitative methods but instead attempted to make qualitative evaluations of the potential effects of climate change. Insect and virus attacks on crops can probably be expected to generally increase. The main reason for this is that insects will presumably be favoured by a warmer climate during the winter and will therefore be more numerous in the spring.

The effects of insects on crops are direct since they feed on crops, but indirect damage through the ability of insects to spread various virus diseases is also of great importance. Every region in Sweden will probably experience increased problems with damage caused by insects and virus diseases, but the increase will be greatest in southern Sweden and in drier areas. Insects will be active considerably earlier in the spring than at the present time since the growing period will be extended, which will probably cause increased attacks on spring-sown crops. At present, spring tillage coincides rather well with the start of the growing period, but by ~2085 spring tillage might be delayed by up to a month compared with the growing period. The greater numbers of insects at spring sowing and the fact that spring crops will be exposed to virus diseases at an earlier stage of development would increase the need for pesticides unless there is an increase in other methods such as the use of resistant varieties. The assessment is that this effect will be of equal magnitude in Götaland and Svealand, but less in Norrland.

Insects are also favoured by high temperatures in the summer and pesticide requirements can be predicted to increase here too, for most crops.

Insect and virus attacks in autumn in winter crops are currently limited by the fact that the number of insects is relatively low in the autumn and that there is no bridge between infected spring-sown crops and vulnerable newly-sown winter crops. In a future warmer climate, there will probably be more insects in the autumn, while newly introduced spring-sown crops such as maize that grow long into the autumn could act as a bridge for viruses from spring- to autumn-sown crops and thus virus attacks in winter crops could increase. New species of insects will become established in Sweden, e.g. depending on the types of crops grown, but it is difficult to predict the species involved and a monitoring system is needed to follow developments in this area.

Fungal diseases are favoured by both temperature and moisture. The moisture situation will be altered more irregularly in different parts of Sweden than the temperature. This means that we can expect large differences between regions. In addition, there are fungal diseases that are favoured by high temperature but not specifically by high air humidity. Winter cereals will be particularly vulnerable since they will have a long infection period in the autumn. For spring crops, the effect can be less than at present in areas with a predicted relatively dry early summer period, such as southern areas of the country. In northern Sweden, however, these fungi will probably be of increased importance due to the generally wetter and warmer climate. In potatoes, late blight will probably increase somewhat.

In a future changed climate, seed crops, perhaps particularly seed potatoes, will run a greater risk of being subjected to insect and virus attack than at present. The need may then arise to establish some form of seed reservation area in which ordinary commercial crops with a high proportion of virus-infected plants are restricted. This need may arise for the whole of Sweden. An increased incidence of pests after climate change can be counteracted with an increased use of pesticides, but this is not desirable from a number of perspectives. Improved cropping technology, increased use of resistant varieties and a good crop rotation to decrease the spread of diseases will therefore be of increasing importance.

Weeds

In general, the need for weed control can be expected to increase with climate change. A strong reason for this conclusion is that in countries with a warmer climate than Sweden, the use of herbicides is considerably greater than in Sweden. There are a number of natural explanations for this. A warmer climate will probably give rise to a more species-rich weed flora, e.g. because more species will have time for their reproductive phase in the extended growing period. In addition, crops with poorly competitive stands (e.g. maize with its wide row spacing) will probably increase in scope. An increased proportion of autumn-sown crops, at the expense of spring-sown crops, would increase the propagation of winter annual weeds, which will in turn increase the herbicide requirement. More monotonous crop rotations and thus greater weed control intensity with increased use of herbicides will increase the risk of herbicide resistance, a problem that is predicted to increase with climate change. Strategies for adaptation to climate change mainly involve the development of methods of weed control and planning of cropping systems. There is of course a conflict relationship between weed control and the desire to decrease the use of herbicides, but also the desire to decrease nutrient leaching. Ploughless tillage limits this leaching but at the same time the grower loses an opportunity to control weeds by non-chemical methods.

Quality

The intention in crop production is to produce a product of a certain quality, where each product is defined by a number of different quality parameters. This leads to many conceivable effects of climate change and thus it is

Table 54.1: Projected effects of climate change on areas of Swedish crop production.

Land use:
Reduced requirement for arable land for food and feed production
Uncertainty in calculations, e.g. due to uncertainty in evaluating the effects of technological developments on yields per hectare
Competitive ability of Swedish crop production in Europe is favoured by climate change but hampered by societal development
Winter sowing favoured at the expense of spring sowing, and expansion of new crops
General increase in yields per hectare
Growing period:
Growing period extended mainly in spring but also in autumn
Spring tillage brought forward less than start of growing period
Harvest brought forward
Autumn sowing delayed
Changes occur earlier in south than north
Water availability:
Spring growth favoured by temperatue increase
Growth in July – September possibly restricted by increasing water deficit
Increased irrigation requirement for horticultural crops and potatoes in particular
Water deficit greater locally than regionally, and greater in Götaland and Svealand than in Norrland
Autumn-sown crops favoured compared with spring-sown
Crop pests:
Insect attack generally increase, particularly in southern and eastern Sweden
Spring-sown crops more vulnerable than autumn-sown
New insect species, crops and crop sequences causing new and possibly greater attacks
Fungal infection increased/decreased depending on regional differences in precipitation
Pesticide requirements increased
Weeds:
More weed species establishing in Sweden
Weed incidence generally increased
Increased incidence of winter annual weeds
Herbicide requirements increased
Quality:
Growth, nutrient requirements and nutrient uptake increased, especially in spring
Protein composition of cereal negatively affected by high temperature
Forage cuts brought forward to maintain good quality
Generally more difficult to control quality parameters in crops
Increased fertiliser requirement
Nutrient leaching:
Risk of nutrient leaching generally increase, mainly due to increasing precipitation and nitrogen mineralisation (induced by higher temperature and soil moisture in winter).
Increased leaching possibly dampened by increased plant uptake and removal with crops.
Net load of N to coastal areas will increase but less than gross loads, due to increased retention (N-removal processes in water bodies).
Phosphorus losses – may increase due to increased runoff and higher frequency of intensive rainfall, but may decrease in certain areas due to reduced snow cover and thus less surface runoff at snowmelt.
Changes in land-use due to climate change may increase nutrient leaching – e.g. if grass-leys are replaced by annual crops such as maize.

Table 54.2. Adaption requirements within areas of Swedish crop production due to climate change.

Measure	Aim
Weather-controlled, precision fertilisation	Efficient fertilisation, control of protein content and minimisation of leaching
Weather-controlled, precision crop protection	Decreased use of crop protection chemicals
Climate-controlled design of irrigation systems	Assured irrigation requirements for horticultural crops and potatoes in particular
Climate-driven quality model	Calculation of the effects of climate change on crop quality
Climate-controlled crop production planning	Basis for evaluating the risks and potential of growing new crops in a changing climate
New varieties	Decreased crop chemical requirements, adaption of sowing and harvest times, improved quality and yields per hectare, improved resource utilisation, decreased nutrient leaching
Alternative crop protection methods	Decreased use of crop protection chemicals
Alternative soil tillage	Decreased nutrient leaching
Alternative cropping systems	Decreased use of crop protection chemicals, Improved resource utilisation, improved quality and yields per hectare, decreased nutrient leaching
Optimised crop production planning	Combining environmental and production objectives
Alternative land use	Increased profitability and improved ecosystem services

very difficult to present a general picture. The problems in presenting this picture are exacerbated by that fact that, with few exceptions, there is a lack of methods to predict the effects of given changes in climate. Greater problems can generally be expected with the hygiene quality, since pest attack is generally expected to increase. These difficulties will probably be greater in spring-sown crops than in autumn-sown, and greater in southern Sweden than in northern, since the risk of pest attack is predicted to be greatest in the former. Other factors that can cause changes in quality include changes in overwintering and snow cover conditions, but it is unclear whether this will lead to worse or better quality.

The nutritional quality of crops consists of elements taken up from the soil and air and synthesised in the plant. The protein content in the plant is proportional to the nitrogen content, which is determined by carbon uptake from the atmosphere (growth) and nitrogen uptake from the soil. In a cereal crop, the main amount of nitrogen is taken up during early summer up to the beginning of June whereas the main carbon uptake is shifted more towards summer. Our few calculations for fertilised grassland indicate that plant nitrogen requirements will increase considerably and that the increase in mineralisation will only be able to meet this requirement until the end of March in southern Sweden, while there will be an increasing deficit in April and May. If fertilisation rates are not in-

creased, this will mean lower protein concentrations. The decreasing soil water content in July could limit carbon uptake and give an increase in protein concentration, but the crop will probably be so near maturation at this time that the effect might be small. In the example of malting barley, where the protein content must not be too low or too high, this will exacerbate existing growing problems. Too large a nitrogen dose in the spring can give rise to excessively high protein content in the event of a dry summer. However, a high nitrogen dose is desirable if summer growth is to proceed at a high rate. This type of problem applies to many crops and must also be understood in various cropping systems with different pre-crops and co-crops, which will require comprehensive analysis and synthesis work. In addition, high temperatures during grain filling can affect protein storage and protein composition, and these problems can generally be expected to increase. With climate change, protein storage in crops will also display a tendency to favour autumn-sown crops over spring-sown. Other quality parameters will also be affected by the climate but in most cases there is a lack of methods to evaluate whether the net effect will be positive or negative. However, higher temperatures during grain filling will generally cause increased problems in achieving planned quality standards.

The possibilities for adjustment will probably consist of breeding new crop varieties, both traditional and ge-

Table 54.3. Research requirements for adaption of areas of Swedish crop production to climate change.

General:
Identifying existing effects of climate change on land use, crop access to water, incidence of pests and weeds and their effect on the crop, crop quality and nutrient leaching. Well-documented long-term monitoring systems are important for this.
Development of new crop varieties, to meet a changing balance between the near-arctic light conditions and other climate variables, mainly temperature.
Land use:
Analyses of alternative modelling approaches for land use criteria, soil productivity and climate. Application to Swedish conditions with a dynamic link to European and global conditions.
Analyses and development of cropping systems for optimisation of production and environmental objectives as a function of climatic conditions.
Water availability:
Application of simulation models to evaluate the effects of changing climate and climate variability on crop water status and production at local and regional scale in Sweden. Calibration of these models to experimental data for extreme water conditions, new crops and varieties.
Simulation of irrigation requirements, particularly in horticultural crops and potatoes.
Crop pests/weeds:
Development of methods for tailoring insecticide/herbicide inputs to weather and need.
Analysis and development of cropping methods and cropping systems for decreasing the risk of attack/competition.
Analysis of the use of monitoring and modelling for tactical planning of insecticide/herbicide applications.
Quality:
Development of weather-driven crop models for field conditions that are tested against experimental data.
Development of methods for tailoring fertiliser inputs to weather and need for different crops and varieties.
Evaluation of the effects of an extended growing period on nutrient uptake and growth of different crops.
Nutrient leaching:
Development of of dynamic simulations of crop development and growth and of water and nutrient uptake as a function of climate, linked to existing calculation systems for simulation of nutrient leaching from arable land at regional level.
Calculation and analysis of the effects of increased variability in climate and increased frequency of extreme weather situations for nitrogen and phosphorus leaching from agricultural soil.
Analysis of the potential effects of changes in production level, production specialisation and land use, and analysis of new cropping systems including changes in management practices with regard to plant nutrient leaching.

netically modified, for local growing conditions but also the more quickly available option of changes in cropping methods and systems (when these are known). For example, harvest times for silage maize can be brought forward and ley cuts can be taken more frequently to obtain forage with the correct quality. The need for nitrogen fertilisers will probably increase to produce the same protein concentrations as in the present climate.

Nutrient Leaching

The expected changes in climate will most likely bring about an increase in the leaching of both nitrogen and phosphorus from agricultural land. Quantifications of nitrogen leaching in a future climate have only been carried out for a few individual sites/areas in Sweden, but indicate an increase in leaching from the root zone of 10-70% (depending on site and climate scenario). The increased losses are mainly caused by higher precipitation and increased mineralisation due to higher temperatures and soil moisture during winter. However, climate change may also result in increased retention (N removal processes) in the water bodies. Therefore increased N losses from arable land might to some extent be compensated for by increased N retention, before the water reaches coastal waters. In a catchment study by Arheimer et al. (2005), the annual N load to the sea increased by 10-33%, depending on climate scenario. This tendency should be compared with the National Environmental Objective of decreasing nitrogen leaching from agricultural land to neighbouring water courses by 30% by the year 2015. The potential to decrease leaching in the current climate situation (1980-2000) with current cropping methods has been estimated to be a maximum of 20-25%. Current food and feed production on agricultural land is thus causing a leaching of nitrogen that is at or above the limit for the relevant Environmental Objective. This problem will probably be accentuated by climate change. To achieve the above-mentioned Environmental Objective in the future, changes in both cropping methods and land use will probably be required. A number of land use scenarios (Table 54.3) indicate a decreased need for agricultural land for food and feed production. The Environmental Objective could in those cases to a certain extent be achieved through alternative land uses that are aimed at decreasing leaching.

Adaptation

A large proportion of the adaptation to climate change within agriculture will occur through farmers adjusting the timing of sowing and cultivation measures to the start of the growing period and soil drying, and adjusting the time of harvest to earlier crop ripening. It can become more difficult to predict when autumn sowing should occur than before. Experiences from previous years will then be central. Although the climate varies widely between years, there is a high risk that what worked in the previous years might not work in the coming year, especially when adapting cropping to a progressively warmer climate through introducing new crops, varieties and cultivation methods. Here, research should provide agricultural stakeholders and farmers with support in evaluating the risks associated with new crops and cropping systems and the potential for introducing these in such a way that risk-taking is adjusted to the finances of the entire farm and environmental impacts. In addition, the increased requirement for crop protection chemicals and irrigation and the increasing variability in the weather will probably create an increasing need for requirement-based cropping measures. Research could help farmers by developing methodologies that can simulate e.g. the developments in crops, crop pests and weeds based on weather forecasts.

Alternative uses of arable land (alternatives to annual crops) may be necessary to decrease nitrogen leaching from arable land to a level that meets the specified Environmental Objectives. The most extreme and probably most effective method would be to plant a part of that area with forest. Most land use scenarios predict a considerable proportion of excess land, which could be used for purposes other than agricultural production, except in a strongly growth-orientated society with a high degree of global trade, where Swedish arable land might be more competitive for food and feed production than it is at present. However, we must bear in mind that the land use scenarios showed great uncertainty in the assumptions of both societal development and climate, not least the assumption of productivity increases per hectare caused by technological developments. If technological developments do not prove to be as strong as predicted, it is unclear whether Swedish food and feed production in the event of future climate change would not only be more competitive but also essential for food supply. Therefore in the perspective of these uncertainties, an alternative use of arable land to reduce nitrogen leaching should also consider the possible need for returning this land for use in supplying food. This means that alternative land uses for decreasing nutrient leaching should concentrate on crops that have a high capacity to take up nitrogen throughout the year, that do not have a negative effect on soil fertility and that are relatively simple to remove and replace with food and feed crops. In this perspective, forest is less suitable. Alternatively, or as a complement to altered land use, wetlands and barrier zones could be established to limit phosphorus and nitrogen leaching from agricultural soil. The need for such measures will increase in a climate change situation. Technical advances with the aim of improving crop nitrogen use efficiency through both plant breeding and cropping techniques can also contribute to decreased nitrogen leaching in the future.

Improved cropping techniques, increased use of resistant varieties and improved crop sequences will be required to limit the expected increased use of crop pesticides. This will require research and development of e.g. methods of crop protection tailored to need, development of new varieties tailored to the changing relationship between an unchanging extreme northern light and a changing temperature climate, alternative pest control methods and development of new systems that limit the spread of diseases. Adaptation to limit the expected increased use of herbicides to control weeds will principally involve the same components. A frequently recurring problem in crop production is that a measure to achieve one Environmental Objective often counteracts another Environmental Objective. For example, reduced tillage of the soil to reduce nutrient leaching provides less scope for non-chemical control of weeds. Increased difficulties in simultaneously achieving the Environmental Objectives and production objectives should be counteracted with increased knowledge of how crop production systems can be optimised. Use of existing systems analysis knowledge and technology to optimise planning of crop production systems against certain predetermined objectives will be an essential process that will also provide tools for evaluating the potential benefits of the new potential adaptation measures.

The first adaptation to the expected decrease in water availability during the summer is to accept a moderate level of crop production increases in agriculture and perhaps increased variability between years. To utilise the production potential of climate change to the full, irrigation will probably be required. For horticultural crops and potatoes, the decrease in water availability should be covered by a corresponding increase in irrigation. The magnitude of this requirement could be approximately the same as the decrease in precipitation due to climate change. However, this figure is very rough and derives from individual cases. Model simulations must be performed to provide a measure of the magnitude of the water deficit for individual sites and years and its average value over years and regions. Such simulations will require organised indata for the various growing sites. These tools are available for individual locations and are used within research, but have not been applied in practical crop production in Sweden. Before irrigation measures are planned, the requirement needs to be mapped and the first adaptation measure should be to calculate the water deficit caused by climate change scenarios for different crops on different soil types in different parts of Sweden.

The predicted increase in crop nitrogen requirements to achieve the desired protein concentrations can be met by increased fertilisation and by including more nitrogen-fixing crops in the crop sequence. These adaptation measures will lead to increasing difficulties in fulfilling the Environmental Objective of decreasing nitrogen leaching from arable land, and alternative uses of areas of arable land may be a necessary consequence. Quantification of the additional fertiliser requirement will require extensive calculations of the same type as those required to calculate the decrease in water availability. In general, the nitrogen calculations can be regarded as more complicated. In environmental protection work within agriculture, this type of calculation tool has been used on a relatively large scale in Sweden to assess leaching risks, but has not been linked to modelling of crop dynamics in relation to climate. Corresponding calculations for crop growth dynamics and nitrogen requirement are lacking, but modelling tools for such calculations are available within research. These calculations are strongly linked to the calculations of water requirements.

Increasing problems will probably arise with the hygiene quality of crops. These will probably be counteracted by using alternative cropping systems, new varieties and increased inputs of crop protection chemicals. However, as regards a number of other quality parameters there is a lack of methods to evaluate the effects of climate change, even within research, and it is not possible to determine the net positive/negative effect. The first adaptation measure within research would therefore be to find methods (i.e. weather-driven models) for evaluating the effects of climate on quality parameters. In practical cropping, farmers' experience and knowledge will have to be used to evaluate any patterns in how quality determination appears to react to weather, which probably depends to a high degree on the specific growing conditions on the farm.

Research Requirements

Perhaps the most obvious adaptation measure is to establish and enhance expertise in evaluating the effects of climate change on crop production within agriculture, but also to propose adaptation strategies and implement these. This section deals primarily with the former, but also provides some suggestions for adaptation measures and reveals great deficiencies in methods for evaluating the effects of climate change. For example, the evaluations in this section cannot be regarded as strictly scientific, since appropriate analytical methods and applications were lacking in a number of sub-areas. Within certain areas, research has made great progress in developing analytical methods and there is mainly a lack of systems for application and calibration to Swedish conditions (e.g. water), while in other areas there is still a lack of conceptual models (e.g. quality). Proposals for practical and strategic adaptation measures for crop production within Swedish agriculture thus currently rest on a weak scientific foundation. To strengthen research within this area, there is a need for increased concentration on the development and application of weather-driven and climate-driven models for crop production systems. A central precondition for the applicability of these models for future studies is that they can explain observed variations. Therefore model development must have strong links to observable data. The models can be of very different character depending on the issue. For example, in land use models crop production might need to be represented in a greatly simplified form, while models for evaluation of local water availability and irrigation requirements would require a detailed description of plant and soil characteristics etc. The modelling approach will determine the experimental data that have to be collected. It can be difficult or even impossible to identify climate effects from normal crop yield statistics, but well-documented long-term trials and other experimental series can provide valuable information. To overcome this, new experimental measurements need to be planned for the purposes of model development. From this perspective, our study identified a number of areas with considerable research requirements (Table 54.3).

Part K

Farm Level Economics and How to Change Behaviour

Authors: Valery Belyakov, Galina Bulgakova, Stefan Bäckman, Gennady Fedorov, Svetlana Golovina, Alexandra Izosimova, Christine Jakobsson, Evgene Krasnov, Mikhail Moskalev and John Sumelius

Coeditor and Coordinating Author: John Sumelius

Economic and Business Principles for Farm Management

55

John Sumelius
University of Helsinki
Helsinki, Finland

Introduction

Economics is often defined as the study of how to allocate scarce means among alternative competing ends in order to maximise welfare or some other result. This definition stems from the fact that the material resources and factors of production (labour, capital and land) are scarce and they can be used for alternative competing objectives. The allocation resources need to be carefully considered before making a decision. Economic use of resources implies that a certain amount of production is produced by using as little resources as possible. The prices are central in this respect. Through prices, the production inputs are efficiently allocated.

In this chapter we aim to provide a basic review of the Economic and Business Principles for farm management, i.e. how to manage a farm in an economically sustainable manner. The text is introductory and those interested are encouraged to explore the issues further in other textbooks. Although the principles should be understood as general, the focus of application here is intended to be suited to countries surrounding the Baltic Sea, particularly to agricultural conditions in north-west Russia.

The Farm Environment

A farm manager has to take into account many things in his work. He has to understand and seek information about many factors that influence his work, the results of this and trends in the environment surrounding production and marketing. Olson (2004) describes farm management as having four main components: resources, markets, institutions and technology. We adopt his classification for the purpose of characterising the farm environment below.

Resources

By resources is meant the productions inputs. Inputs are all requisites (seed, fertiliser, fuel, feed, pesticides, lime, etc.), the production animals, machinery, buildings land and labour. Sometimes reference is made only to the classical factors of production capital, land and labour. The production inputs are turned into commodities in a production process. Resources and commodities are normally stored on the farm. The natural conditions of the farm have a high influence on the production. Soil, precipitation and temperature affect choice of crop and yield level. A technically efficient use of resources means that production inputs are combined and organised in such a way that the ratio of production to resources used is high.

An economically efficient use of resources implies that the ratio economic value/resource cost is high.

Technology

There are usually many different ways of producing a commodity. For instance, grassland farming can be accomplished in many ways and with alternative sets of machines. However, technology is more than machines, since it includes biological and physical production processes, new varieties and breeds. Technology choices have to be evaluated based upon goals, restrictions and costs. One task in farm management is to decide upon the use of technology in order to achieve economically and technically efficient production.

Institutions

Institutions create various rules. Through legislation, stipulations on what is forbidden are created. The laws and directives describe what farmers can and cannot do. Environmental regulations, production policy regulation, various quota and land set-aside schemes affect the possibilities that farmers have at their use. Taxes and credit institutions also affect the economic environment. For good management it is essential to know the institutional environment and the rules stipulated by society.

Markets

Although it is important that production is efficient, it is just as important that the products are demanded by consumers and processors. The possibilities to market a product at a certain price, potential buyers and the distance to the market need to be taken into account. James and Eberle (2000) outline some key marketing decisions as the following: What and how much to produce? Where to sell? How to sell? What grade, quality or form? When to sell? When to deliver?

A farm manager has to understand and take into account all these components. When deciding upon how to combine inputs, how to organise resources and what products to produce for which market, he has to make technology decisions and observe the rules laid down by institutions. He has to know some fundamental principles of biology, technology and economics. A farm manager typically acts in a multidisciplinary context.

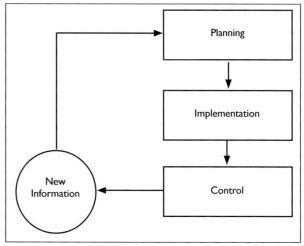

Figure 55.1. Management flow chart according to Kay and Edwards (1999).

Functions of Management

General

The task of the farm manager is to combine ideas, methods and resources to produce and market a product profitably. This involves for instance setting goals, seeking and sorting all kinds of information, analysing alternative ways of action, making decisions and carrying them out, acquiring resources, organising the use of resources, training themselves, marketing the product, recognising problems and opportunities and evaluating results (Olson, 2004). Kay and Edwards (1999) list the functions of management as being planning, implementation and control (see Figure 55.1). James and Eberle (2000) add organisation. A brief description of these functions is provided below.

Planning

Goals

The first thing a farmer has to do is to set *goals*. The clearer and better defined the goals, the easier it will be to decide how to reach them. There may be many goals. Some possible goals for a farm manger are to maximise profit, maximise wealth, avoid debt, reduce labour requirements, improve the environment, contribute to the local community and work in some other occupation at the same time as being a farmer. If goals are written it is easier to remember them. The goals can be put in priority order, i.e. a *goal structure* can be made. Based on higher level goals, lower level goals can be established. The overall aim of a farmer may for instance be to specialise in a certain production line. In order to realise this goal, he has to set some lower level goals: good profitability, good productivity, efficient use of resources, enough free time, etc. Some goals may be contradictory, so listing these in order of priority will help the farmer to balance the goals. A farmer may want to use resources efficiently and to take care of the environment at the same time. He may decide to use buffer zones on steep banks next to a river, thereby making a trade-off between efficient uses of resources and caring for the environment. Often a certain level of income, i.e. return on the labour, capital and land employed, is needed to be able to realise other goals.

Business Plan

In order to achieve the goals some sort of business plan is needed. A plan need not be written, although a written plan certainly helps remembering. The content of a Business plan according to Olson (2004) is presented in Fact Box 1.

A detailed business plan usually starts with describing the farm resources, the farm environment and current production. The following section presents a strategic plan which describes the vision for the future farm, analysing possibilities and threats in the environment. Separate marketing, production plans and financial plans are included.

Important tools in planning include various *budgets*. A budget is a projection of income and expenses in the future. Important budgets are *enterprise budgets*, *partial budgets, whole-farm budgets* and *cash-flow budgets*. An enterprise budget based on Finnish data for winter wheat is presented in Table 55.1.

An enterprise budget such as that in Table 55.1 is a projection of future returns and costs. Costs include operating costs (variable costs), which vary according to the production volume, and ownership costs (fixed costs), which are fixed and do not vary with changing volumes of production. The concepts of variable and fixed costs are explained in Box 2.

Fact Box 1.
Business plan outline

I.   **Executive summary**
II.   **General description of the farm**
  A.   Type of business
  B.   Products and services
  C.   Market description
  D.   Location(s), legal description
  E.   History of the farm and operators
  F.   Owners, partners, operators
III. Strategic plan
  A.   Vision, mission, goals and objectives
  B.   External analysis
  C.   Internal analysis
  D.   Chosen business strategy
  E.   Strategy evaluation and control
IV.   **Marketing plan**
  A.   Target market
  B.   Pricing strategy
  C.   Product quality management
  D.   Inventory and delivery timetables
  E.   Market risk and control management
V.   **Production and operation plans**
  A.   Production process
    1. Product choice
    2. Product and process design
    3. Technology choice
    4. Environmental considerations
  B.   Raw materials, facilities and equipment.
  C.   Location of production
  D.   Management of process quality
  E.   Production risk and control management
  F.   Production and operations schedule
VI.   **Financial plan**
  A.   Financial statements. Historical and projected
    1. Balance sheet
    2. Income statement
    3. Cash flow statement
    4. Ratio analysis
  B.   Capital needed
  C.   Investment analysis
  D.   Financial risk and control management
VII.   **Organisation and staffing plan**
  A.   Personnel need
  B.   Sources of personnel
    1. Owner and other family labour
    2. Hired employees
    3. Consultants
  C.   Structure and responsibilities
    1. Business organisation
    2. Brief job descriptions
  D.   Basic personnel policies
    1. Compensation
    2. Evaluation
    3. Training
  E.   Workforce risk and control management

Table 55.1. Enterprise budget. A combined gross margin budget and production cost calculation for winter wheat per ha, A-area, south Finland Oct. 2007 (Pro Agria 2007).

RETURNS	Unit	Price, euro/unit	Quantity	Euro
Bread grain	tonnes	225	3.60	810
Feed grain	tonnes	190	0.40	76
Farm support, flat rate/ha	ha	239	1	239
Production support	ha	45	1	45
National support	ha	24	1	24
Agri-environmental support	ha	151	1	151
Less favoured area support	ha	169	1	169
Total Returns				1,514
VARIABLE COSTS				
Own seed	kg	0.24	176	42
Purchased seed	kg	0.37	44	16
Fertiliser 1, Y 1	kg	0.25	226	57
Fertiliser 2, Saltpetre	kg	0.21	426	89
Lime	tonnes	35	0.25	9
Pesticides	times	37	1	78
Tractor (variable costs)	h	4.6	8.5	39
Harvest combiner (variable costs)	h	4.6	1.4	6
Dryer machine (variable costs)	kg	0.012	4,000	48
Freight and intermediary test	kg	0.013	3,824	50
Interest on working capital (75%)	euro	5%	448	22
Sum Variable costs				457
Gross Margin I				1,057
Gross margin without support				429
Labour	h	13.05	12.5	163
Gross Margin II				894
Machinery cost				
Tractor (fixed costs)	h	8	8.5	66
Harvest combiner (fixed costs)	h	69	1.4	96
Dryer machine (fixed costs)	ha	41	1	41
Other machines (fixed costs)	ha	133	1	133
Total machinery cost				336
Buildings, dryer	ha	1	68	68
Buildings, machine hall	ha	47	1	47
Total building costs				115
Other costs				60
Machinery, building and other costs				511
Gross margin III				383
Land rent (including pipe draining)	ha	0.05	0.7*7,800	273
(Pipe draining)	ha	138	1	(138)
Total production costs				1,404
NET PROFIT OR LOSS				110

Fact Box 2. Variable costs and fixed costs.

A *variable cost* varies with varying volume of production (Y). Most requisites used on a farm are typically variable, e.g. purchased feed is a variable input (X) and the corresponding cost a variable cost (VC). The more milk a dairy cow yields, the more feed it needs. Fuel is another variable cost. The larger the area cultivated, the more fuel is needed. Fertiliser cost is also variable, since large yields per ha need more nutrients than low yields. Inputs that can be increased or decreased and that will increase or decrease production are variable. If the price of the input X is W, the variable cost can be calculated according to the formula $VC = W * X$.

A *fixed cost* (FC), on the other hand, does not vary with the volume of production and exists even if nothing is produced. Typical fixed costs on farms are the cost of buildings or machinery, which does not depend upon production. Total costs (TC) are the sum of fixed and variable costs: $TC = FC + VC$. The development of the cost curve is illustrated in Figure 55.2.

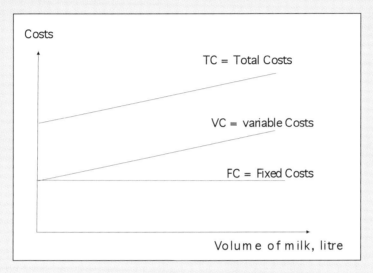

Figure 55.2. Development of variable, fixed and total costs according to the volume of production.

The division of costs into variable and fixed costs is based upon a *short run* planning horizon, e.g. less than a year. The short run can be thought of as a growing season during which no new machinery is bought or buildings built. In the *long run* machinery can be renewed, more land can be bought or more buildings can be built. In the long run all inputs become variable and the division between fixed and variable costs loses its importance.

If returns are bigger than total cost, there is a profit. If total costs equal returns, there is no profit but the returns on labour and capital have been compensated at the calculated hourly wage and interest rate. If total costs are bigger than returns, either labour or capital has not been fully compensated. This may imply that the depreciation of machinery and building has not been compensated.

The *gross margin* budget is the returns less operating expenses (variable costs). The gross margin is the amount of the returns left as compensation for fixed costs (ownership costs). If operating expenses are higher than returns, production is unprofitable in the short run, no returns on

labour or capital have been received and production does not cover variable costs.

A *whole-farm budget* is a budget which estimates expected returns and costs or expected income and expenses for the whole farm, combining all enterprises. It can be used to calculate expected returns on capital, labour and possible profit. It can also be used to compare alternative production lines or technologies. A whole-farm budget can be a good way to communicate credit possibilities with lending institutions. Whole-farm budgets are usually made by extended gross margin or enterprise calculations or by linear programming models (e.g. Barnard and Nix, 1973).

A *cash-flow budget* is a summary of the actual and future cash incomes and expenses for a given period of time, e.g. six months, a year or several years. One major aim of the cash flow budget is to make it obvious when expenses should be paid and when cash will be received. Cash inflows and outflows often do not take place at the same time. On a cropping farm, cash outflows are usually greater during the sowing season, while cash inflows take place after harvest. Because the timing of expenses and incomes is different, a monthly cash-flow budget is needed to permit an analysis of how the cash flow should be arranged. The cash flow is a central tool for analysing the *liquidity* (see section *Measures of Profitability, Solvency and Liquidity*) of the firm.

Implementation

Once the plan has been made it has to be implemented. It is necessary to make decisions and to act. The resources have to be acquired and actions have to be coordinated.

Control

Records

The control function of management includes records of various sorts; financial records, production records, input use, tax payments and other essential records. Based on these records it is possible to make comparisons between current and past results and practices on the farm. Financial records can also be compared against what is expected to be default results on other farms with similar production. Based on the comparison and analysis of results it is possible to take corrective actions. The sequence of the control function is therefore record keeping, comparison, analysis and adjustment. Among the financial accounts, the most important are the income statement and the balance sheet. On the basis of these, it is possible to calculate financial measures for profitability, liquidity and solvency. Insights may also be gained from measures of efficiency and productivity.

Income Statement

The income statement (or profit and loss statement) is a summary of all revenues and expenses over a time period, usually a year. It shows the difference between the gross income and the costs incurred to produce that income, the net farm income. It should show the financial results of the business, if there have been any profits or losses from the activities undertaken. An income statement can be used to compare the results for the same farm in different years. It can also be used to compare the results between different farms with the same production enterprise/s in the same year. With a more detailed analysis it is possible to gain some insights into why the net farm income has been low or high.

According to Kay and Edwards (1999), the income statement can be stated in very condensed form as:

Total revenue
Less total expenses =
net farm income from operations plus or minus
gains and losses from sale of capital assets
= net farm income

The income statement described above is based upon cash revenues and expenses. However, an income statement should include not only cash income but also non-cash income and the value of inventories. It includes depreciation of assets and amortisation of loans. When revenues are received as cash there is no problem, but when revenues are non-cash (e.g. products consumed

---

Fact Box 3. Machine Cooperation

Costs of machinery (as well as buildings) often make up a substantial part of the fixed costs on a farm. Depreciation, maintenance and interest costs of machinery can be very high, particularly if the farm size is small. One way to decrease fixed costs per unit produce is to cooperate with other farmers. Farmers can either own machines in common, or they can hire machines from each other. Hiring of machines may imply that the farmer rents a particular machine and uses it. Alternatively, he may buy the service from another farmer or a machinery contractor who has the machine needed. One possibility is to form machine groups (Swedish *maskinringar*) that list the machines available and the respectively hourly fee for their use. The basic idea behind all of these alternatives is to use machinery more efficiently instead of all owning their own, under-used machines. Because fixed costs are divided over more labour hours or a larger volume produced, it is possible for farmers to lower machinery costs through cooperation. Bulgakova (this volume, *Conditions for effective operating of farms in Russia*) mentions joint purchasing and use of machinery as an important field of cooperative relationships.

Table 55.2. Complete accrual income statement for a hypothetical dairy farm, pig farm and cereal farm in Finland (Euro).

	DAIRY FARM		PIG FARM		CEREAL FARM	
Arable land, ha	33		74		92	
Number of cows	15					
Number of sows			100			
RETURNS						
Sales returns	45,700		112,300		26,500	
Subsidies	26,000		60700		56,600	
TURNOVER		71,700		173,000		83,100
Change of product stocks	5,400		41,800		-3,400	
Internal transfer within the farm (given)	400		130		0	
Investment support, used amount	2,100		0		500	
Other returns from the business	0		800		0	
TOTAL RETURNS		79,600		215,730		80,200
VARIABLE EXPENSES						
Material and requisites	-11,900		-54,000		-15,700	
Change of stocks	60		-3,100		-250	
Internal transfer within the farm (taken)	-260		-120		0	
External services	-1,700		-6,800		-3,800	
Personnel expenses	-2,300		0		0	
Other variable expenses	-2,750		-4,000		-2,000	
SALES MARGIN		60,750		147,710		58,450
FIXED EXPENSES						
Wage claim for the farm family	-34,200		-50,400		-20,000	
Own wages and social costs	0		0		0	
Rents	-1,000		-3,200		-5,500	
Other fixed costs	-10,200		-27,000		-10,600	
GROSS MARGIN		15,350		67,110		22,350
DEPRECIATION						
Depreciation of buildings	-6,900		-3,900		-2,600	
Depreciation of machinery	-3,700		-32,200		-2,900	
Other depreciation	-200		-1,100		-2,200	
OPERATING PROFIT AFTER DEPRECIATION		4,550		29,910		14,650
FINANCING INCOME AND EXPENSES						
Financing income	300		1,400		0	
	-990		-5,700		-20	
PROFIT AFTER FINANCIAL ITEMS		3,860		25,610		14,630
EXTRAORDINARY INCOME AND EXPENSES						
Extraordinary income	580		1,800		0	
Extraordinary expenses	0		0		0	
RESULT BEFORE RESERVATION AND TAXES		4,440		27,410		14,630
Change in depreciation reserve (+/-)	0		0		0	
Direct taxes	-12,400		-22,700		4,700	
PROFIT OR LOSS FOR THE FINANCIAL YEAR		**-7,960**		**4,710**		**19,330**

by the farm household or tractor work done in forestry), it is not always straightforward how to value this income. There are various ways to overcome this problem. Basically, the farmer has to make a choice whether to use a **cash accounting** or **accrual accounting** system. If the farmer chooses a cash accounting system, only cash flow will be recorded. Because such a system does not properly measure the changes in inventory or non-cash transfers, the cash accounting system does not accurately measure the income attributed to a specific year. An accrual accounting system is more appropriate since it will reflect these changes in the correct time period, regardless of when they are paid. According to Kay and Edwards (1999), a cash-basis income statement can be *accrual-adjusted* at the end of each year by taking into account changes in inventory accrual values and accounts receivable. This can be done for the inventories by calculating the changes in inventories at the beginning and end of the year and adjusting the net farm income accordingly. For the accounts receivable the beginning accounts receivable should be subtracted from the cash receipt and the end accounts receivable should be added as cash receipts.

An example of a complete accrual income statement from a hypothetical Finnish dairy farm, pig farm and cereal farm is given in Table 55.2. In the table, the key figures are written in bold text

The accrual income statement above is based on an accounting system similar to that used for conventional non-agricultural firms. The advantage is that it gives a lot of information. The disadvantage is that it demands more accounting skills and work, or the use of a professional accountant. Therefore many firms, especially smaller firms, use simpler accounting systems which are more condensed. Table 55.3 shows a more condensed accrual-adjusted income statement, which is based upon an average of a given number of Farm Accountancy Data Network (FADN) farms in Finland (MTT Agrifood Research Finland).

The adjusted income statement above gives many valuable key figures such as operating margin, operating profit after depreciation, net profit and entrepreneurial profit. Based upon the adjusted income statement it is possible to calculate other key figures such as farm income, as presented in Table 55.4.

In summary, an income statement organises and summarises the incomes and expenses from the financial year. Based upon that, it is possible to compute key figures that can be of use in analysing the results of a particular farm in a particular year. Comparisons with previous years or with farms with a similar production line can be informative.

Balance Sheet
The balance sheet shows the assets and the liabilities on a farm at a given point in time. The balance sheet is a 'snapshot' of the assets used by a farm and the sources of funds used to finance these assets (Turner and Taylor, 1998). Through the balance sheet, measures of the solvency and solvency-based liquidity can be calculated.

The balance sheet presents *the assets* of the farm. The assets are classified into current, intermediate and long-term assets according to how quickly they can be converted into cash. Current assets such as claims and inventories are most easily converted into cash, intermediate assets include breeding animals, whereas real estate, which is difficult to convert quickly into cash without losses, is classified as a long-term asset. The balance sheet also presents how the assets are financed, though *liabilities* or through *owner equity*. The sum of total assets has to correspond to total liabilities and owner equity. All liabilities are listed according to when they are due to be paid. Current liabilities which are due within one year are listed first, next the intermediate liabilities and last the long-term liabilities. The *owner equity* (also called Proprietor's Capital, Net Worth) is calculated last as the difference between total assets and total liabilities. In other words, owner's equity is calculated as a residual.

The balance sheet relating to the complete accrual income statement for the hypothetical Finnish dairy, pig and cereal farms in Table 55.2 is shown in Table 55.5.

The balance sheet in Table 55.5 is a complete balance sheet based on advanced accounting systems similar to those for regular enterprises. It corresponds to the income statement in Table 55.2. However, it is possible to calculate a more condensed balance sheet corresponding to the adjusted income statements in Table 55.3. Table 55.6 presents such a condensed balance sheet. It corresponds to the adjusted income statement for the three farms in Table 55.3.

Table 55.3. Adjusted income statement for a hypothetical dairy farm, pig farm and cereal farm in Finland (Euro) (MTT Agrifood Research Finland).

	DAIRY FARM		PIG FARM		CEREAL FARM	
Number of farms represented	13,600		980		12,800	
Number of FADN-farms	360<n<370		30<n<40		160<n<170	
Arable land, ha	44		51		56	
RETURNS						
Returns from animal production	70,400		128,600		1,350	
Returns from crop production	850		2,320		16,100	
Returns from horticulture	30		0		110	
Other sales returns	1,890		2,880		4,130	
Sales returns	73,170		133,800		21,690	
Subsidies	48,000		54,600		33,300	
TURNOVER		121,170		188,400		54,990
Change of product stocks	460		4,220		1,560	
Internal transfer within the farm (given)	430		190		50	
Investment support, used amount	650		810		180	
Other returns from the business	440		400		1,120	
TOTAL RETURNS		123,150		194,020		57,900
Material and requisites	-31,700		-63,800		-12,900	
Purchase of animals	-1,530		-12,400		-350	
External services	-6,840		-6,230		-1,800	
Personnel expenses	-2,540		-5,300		-820	
Machine rents	-350		-430		-190	
Other variable costs	-3,660		-6,520		-1,460	
Wages	-52,900		-39,900		-12,900	
Rent	-2,160		-4,600		-3,110	
Insurance	-5,490		-7,550		-4,240	
Maintenance	-7,090		-8,650		-3,920	
Other fixed	-5,520		-5,220		-3,290	
OPERATING MARGIN		3,370		33,420		12,920
Depreciation of buildings	-7,470		-15,500		-2,640	
Depreciation of machines	-13,900		-16,800		-9,730	
Other depreciations	-870		-1,120		-1,090	
OPERATING PROFIT AFTER DEPRECIACION		-18,870		0		-540
Net financial expenses	-2,470		-5,220		-1,790	
NET PROFIT		-21,340		-5,220		-2,330
Claims for interest	-11,900		-16,100		-10,100	
ENTERPRENEURIAL PROFIT		-33,240		-21,320		-12,430

Table 55.4. Key figures for a hypothetical dairy farm, pig farm and cereal farm in Finland (Euro) (MTT Agrifood Research Finland).

	DAIRY FARM	PIG FARM	CEREAL FARM
Number of farms represented	13,600	980	12,800
Number of FADN-farms	360<n<370	30<n<40	160<n<170
Arable land, ha	44	51	56
ENTERPRENEURIAL PROFIT	-33,240	-21,320	-12,430
+ Wages	52,900	39,900	12,900
+ Claim for interest	11,900	16,100	10,100
= FARM INCOME	31,560	34,680	10,570
COEFFICIENT OF PROFITABILITY	0.49	0.62	0.46
Returns on labour	6.00	7.70	5.70
Returns on capital, %	2.40	3.10	2.30
Entrepreneurial income	34,700	34,700	10,600
Claims for interest	11,900	16,100	10,100
Earnings from labour	19,700	18,500	430
Labour hours	4,270	3,220	1,040
Earnings from labour per hour	0.40	5.80	4.60
Equity capital	244,500	335,800	208,700
Total capital	328,500	493,300	260,100
Equity ratio	74.4	68.1	80.2
Return on total assets	-18,300	440	-460
Assets during financial year	319,800	483,200	254,200
=Return on total assets, %	-5.7	0.1	-0.1

The interpretation of Table 55.6 is similar to Table 55.5. Once again, the *owner equity* is calculated as the difference between total assets and total liabilities.

Measures of Profitability, Solvency and Liquidity

Rate of return on assets, return on equity and coefficient of profitability

Farm profitability can be measured in many ways. The net farm income and the farm income, which was described in the section on Income Statement is an absolute measure of the compensation to own unpaid labour and management and equity. The farm income for the cereal farm, dairy farm and pig farm based on the adjusted income statement in Table 55.3 was 10,570 euro, 31,560 euro and 34,680 euro respectively (see Table 55.4)

However, it is not a good measure for comparing profitability between farms. In order to measure profitability of different farms the farm income has to be related to the assets or to equity. Here we follow the procedure recommended by Kay and Edwards (1999). The rate of return on assets (ROA) is:

$$Rate\ of\ return\ on\ assets = \frac{Return\ on\ assets}{Average\ farm\ asset\ value}$$

In our example based on the adjusted income statement in Table 55.3, the rate of return on assets was -5.7%, 0.1%. and -0.1% for the dairy, pig and cereal farm respectively.

In addition to ROA, it is possible to calculate a rate of return on equity (ROE). The main difference is that the interest paid to debtors is not added to net farm income from operations. The ROE can be greater or smaller than ROA depending on the rate of interest paid to borrowed capital. If ROA is greater than the interest paid, then ROE will be greater than ROA. If ROA is less than the interest paid, then ROE will be smaller than ROA. We do not present the ROEs for the average sample here.

The coefficient of profitability is used in Finland as a measure of profitability of agriculture. It is defined as:

$$Coefficient\ of\ profitability = \frac{Farm\ income}{Wage\ claim + claim\ for\ interest}$$

In our example based on the adjusted income statement in Table 55.3 the coefficient of profitability was 0.49, 0.62 and 0.46 for the dairy, pig and cereal farm respectively (see Table 55.4). This means the respective farmers received 49%, 62% and 46% of their wage claim and claim for interest.

Solvency may be defined as the ability to survive temporary periods of losses. According to Barry et al. (2000, p. 110), a farm is insolvent if the sale of all assets fails to generate sufficient cash to pay all liabilities. Solvency measures relate to the total structure of assets, liability and equity of the farm. Common measures of solvency that may be calculated from the balance sheet are the following:

$$Debt/Asset\ ratio = \frac{Total\ liabilities}{Total\ assets}$$

Another measure of solvency is the Equity/Asset ratio, which is a similar measure:

$$Equity/asset\ ratio = \frac{Owner\ equity}{Total\ assets}$$

A rule of thumb for farms, based upon circumstances in Finland, is here suggested to be that the solvency is good if the Equity/Asset ratio is above 80%, satisfactory if it is 50-80%, adequate if it is 30-50% and bad if it is below 30%.

Based on the figures in Table 55.6, the Equity/Asset ratio is 74.4% for the dairy farm, 68.1% for the pig farm and 80.2% for the cereal farm.

Liquidity is defined as the ability of a firm to meet its short-term financial obligations as they come due without disrupting the normal operations of the business. Liquidity measures the capacity to generate cash in the amount needed. Problems of liquidity may arise from the seasonal nature of production. Output is generated at harvest time, while inputs are required at concentrated periods at times other than harvest. Provisions for these inputs have to be generated either through saving or borrowing. By having enough *working capital*, the farm ensures its capacity to meet cash obligations for buying inputs.

A solvency-based measure of working capital can be calculated as

$$Working\ capital = Current\ assets - \frac{Short\ term\ loans}{(Current\ liabilities)}$$

The working capital is the oil of the machinery; it is the amount of capital the farm has available to use without restrictions in the short run. Through keeping a *cash-flow budget* the farmer is able to monitor his future incomes and expenses and make a picture of the working capital he has available. Liquidity problems may furthermore arise from unusual events such as crop failure and animal diseases. The working capital in our example for the farms in Table 55.6 is € 17,640, € 44,820, and € 69,700 for the cereal, dairy and pig farm respectively.

A **solvency-based liquidity** measure is the *current ratio*, which is calculated as:

$$Current\ ratio = \frac{Total\ current\ assets}{Total\ current\ liabilities}$$

According to Hallgren (1991), a general rule of thumb is that the current ratio for businesses in general should be at least 2. Leppiniemi 1994 (p. 159) gives the following rule for the current ratio of general businesses: good >1.6,

satisfactory 1.2-1.5, adequate 0.9-1.1 and weak <0.9. James and Eberle (2000, p. 91) state that current ratio values above 2 are safe for most businesses, but note that some loan agencies give loans with current ratios at 1.5 but that the safety of the ratio is dictated by the amount of uncertainty associated with the income.

In the event of a farmer encountering problems with liquidity, he may try the following measures, here suggested in order of preference: 1) Try to postpone payment of bills; 2) try to bring forward claims; 3) change the production plan by changing combination of products, not making small investments, saving certain inputs etc.; 4) keep smaller stocks; 5) use old machines; 6) decrease private consumption; 7) renegotiate loans; 8) find alternative sources of income outside agriculture; 9) sell current assets; and 10) sell long-term assets. In most cases these measures may be associated with some sort of cost.

In addition to the measures of profitability, solvency and liquidity, measures of efficiency and productivity exist. Efficiency and productivity is described by Stefan Bäckman in another chapter of this book.

Organising the Work

In addition to planning, implementation and control, it has become increasingly important to organise the workload itself. This is especially important when a farm is growing into a large unit. For instance, on large expanding livestock farms, the available labour force may be a restriction, at least on privately-owned family farms. Paradoxically, enlargement may imply that the work input per unit of products decreases, while the total labour time increases. Therefore it is important to plan how to use the available labour on a farm. During recent years the time required for farm management, including administration, has also increased, and can make up a significant part of total work time. Since farm management work is time-consuming, it is important to plan the total labour requirement and to organise the work on the farm (Tuure et al., 2007). In Finland a tool has been developed for the time planning on farms, especially large and expanding farms (Kaila and Tuure, 2007).

Table 55.5. Balance sheet for a hypothetical dairy farm, pig farm and cereal farm in Finland (Euro).

ASSETS			DAIRY FARM	PIG FARM	CEREAL FARM
	IMMATERIAL ASSETS				
		Foundation and research expenses			
		Immaterial rights	17,300		
		Business commercial value			
		Other long-term expenses			
		Advance payments			
		Subtotal	17,300	0	0
	MATERIAL ASSETS				
		Land and water areas	42,700	207,500	186,600
LONG-TERM ASSETS		Buildings	49,600	40,300	26,200
		Machinery	26,200	159,400	13,200
		Other material assets	3,300	21,900	41,700
		Advance payments			
		Subtotal	121,800	429,100	267,700
	LONG-TERM INVESTMENTS				
		Shares	1,500		
		Loan claims			
		Other investments			
		Subtotal	1,500	0	0
VALUATION ITEMS		Valuation items	0	0	0
		Subtotal	0	0	0
	MATERIALS AND ANIMALS				
		Materials and requisites	4,100	8,300	8,700
		Intermediary products	8,000	40	2,000
		Ready products	4,300	28,500	13,200
		Domestic animals	16,500	80,000	
		Other materials			
		Advance payments			
		Subtotal	32,900	116,840	23,900
	CLAIMS				
CURRENT ASSETS		Claims for sales			
		Claims for support	2,800	11,500	10,100
		Transfer claims (VAT)	5,600	2,700	6,700
		Other claims			1,400
		Subtotal	8,400	14,200	18,200
	FINANCIAL ASSETS				
		Shares	0	8,000	0
		Other value documents			
		Subtotal	0	8,000	0
	BANK ASSETS AND CLAIMS				
		Bank deposits and cash	0	0	0
TOTAL ASSETS			181,900	568,140	309,800

Table 55.5. Balance sheet for a hypothetical dairy farm, pig farm and cereal farm in Finland (Euro).

LIABILITIES			DAIRY FARM	PIG FARM	CEREAL FARM
OWNER EQUITY					
		Share capital			
		Other own capital	139,900	425,340	305,300
		Losses from earlier periods			
		Profit or loss from the accounting year			
		Subtotal	139,900	425,340	305,300
PROVISION (for reserve)					
		Voluntary provisions			
		Obligatory provisions			
		Balance value of investment support	22,000		4,500
		Subtotal	22,000	0	4,500
VALUATION ITEMS					
		Increases in value	0	0	0
		Subtotal	0	0	0
LOANS					
	LONG-TERM LOANS				
		State loans			
		Loans with supported interest rates			
		Other bank loans	20,000		
		Loans for retirement			
		Other long-term loans		135,000	
		Subtotal	20,000	135,000	0
	SHORT- TERM LOANS				
		Short-term bank loans			
		Loans for retirement			
		Obtained advance payments			
		Purchase loans			
		Financing bills of exchange			
		Transfer loans (VAT)		7,800	
		Other short-term loans			
		Subtotal	0	7,800	0
TOTAL LIABILITIES			181,900	568,140	309,800

Table 55.6. Balance sheet for a hypothetical dairy farm, pig farm and cereal farm in Finland (Euro) (MTT Economics FADN-results 2006, www.mtt.fi/kannattavuuskirjanpito).

	Dairy	Pig	Cereal
Number of farms represented	13,600	980	12,800
Number of FADN-farms	360-370	30-40	160-170
Cultivation area, ha	44	51	56
Intangible assets (Milk quotas)	22,600	0	140
Land areas	72,300	123,000	129,400
Buildings	78,200	159,300	27,700
Machinery and equipment	64,800	80,600	48,400
Pipe drainage	15,500	20,400	20,500
Standing crops	10	0	10
Other noncurrent assets	570	410	90
Tangible assets, subtotal	**231,400**	**383,600**	**226,100**
Long-term investments	**18,100**	**15,500**	**2,210**
Materials and requisites	6,470	10,100	6,020
Work in progress	v9,700	50	200
Ready products and goods	3,300	13,200	12,400
Domestic animals	26,800	57,000	510
Other current assets	250	240	530
Current assets, subtotal	**46,500**	**80,600**	**19,700**
Debtors	**7,180**	**11,200**	**10,700**
Financial assets	**2,710**	**2,320**	**1,290**
ASSETS	**328,490**	**49,320**	**260,100**
Owner equity	244,510	335,820	208,680
of which investment support	5,870	5,710	1,610
Long-term loans	82,300	146,600	49,400
Short-term loans	1,680	10,900	2,020
LIABILITIES	**328,490**	**493,320**	**260,100**

Principles of Planning: Short-term

The section before this reviewed the functions of farm management. This section covers the economic principles for determining the input level, input combinations and product combinations in agriculture. Various cost concepts are also covered. The economic principles can be applied to a single production line or to the whole farm (See e.g. Rasmussen, 2011).

The planning horizon for the economic principles described below is short. It means we assumed the fixed inputs (machinery, building and land) are given. There are three important questions to be decided in the short run:

1. How much of an input to use? (the input-output relation)
2. How to combine inputs, how to replace one input by another? (the input-input relation)
3. How to combine enterprises or products? (the output-output relation).

Input-output Relation

When planning a farm operation the farmer needs to decide how much inputs to use. He has to decide how much feed to give a cow, how much fertilisers or irrigation to apply on one hectare of agricultural land and how many seeds to sow per m². That is, he has to decide upon the *intensity* of production. By intensity is meant amount of one production input unit (X) per amount of another production input. A typical example is the feeding intensity in terms of feed unit/cow or fertiliser intensity in kg/ha.

When deciding upon intensity the farmer also chooses the corresponding production level (Y) that he assumes the input use will result in. He needs some rule to decide which level of intensity will be economically optimal from his point of view. The rule for deciding upon this optimal level is based upon marginal returns and marginal costs:

The production function. The production function is a basic concept in production economics. It shows the relationship between production Y and an input X. Production can be litres of milk per cow or yield per hectare arable land. Table 55.7 shows some results from hypothetical data.

The first column of Table 55.7 shows the units of input X. The corresponding values of production Y are presented in the second column. The third column shows the marginal product ΔY. The marginal product measures the change in production which follows from the use of one more additional input. If, for instance, inputs are increased from two units to three units the additional increase in production is $\Delta Y = 49.05 - 45.5 = 3.55$ units of Y. A graphical illustration of production Y and marginal product ΔY as a function of input X is given in Figure 55.3.

Table 55.7 and Figure 55.3 show the physical relationship between input X and production Y. The maximum production 62.3 Y is obtained for 8 units of input X. We

Table 55.7. Relationship between production and inputs.

X, kg	Y, kg	Δ Y, kg	Δ X, kg	Δ MVP	Δ MIC, euro	Marginal net return, euro
0	40	0	0	0	0	
1	42.5	2.5	1	5	4	1
2	45.5	3	1	6	4	2
3	49.05	3.55	1	7.1	4	3.1
4	52.7	3.65	1	7.3	4	3.3
5	56.15	3.45	1	6.9	4	2.9
6	59.1	2.95	1	5.9	4	1.9
7	61.25	2.15	1	4.3	4	0.3
8	62.3	1.05	1	2.1	4	-1.9
9	61.95	-0.35	1	-0.7	4	-4.7
10	60	-1.95	1	-3.9	4	-7.9

can see that the marginal physical product, *MPP* or Δ*Y*, is initially positive and initially increasing for input levels up to 4. When more than 4 units of input *X* are given the marginal product decreases, i.e. each extra input leads to a higher production level, but the incremental production becomes smaller and smaller. If 9 or more units of *X* are given the marginal product becomes negative, which implies that production is decreasing.

In order to identify the economically optimal intensity level of an input, we need to translate the physical relations into economic relations. The main concepts for this are the marginal value product and marginal input cost. The marginal value product (Δ*MVP*) is simply the marginal physical product multiplied by the price (in the example 2 euro). The marginal input cost (Δ*MIC*) is the additional cost of one unit of input, i.e. the additional price of the input times the input quantity for the increment. In this case it is 1 * 4 euro = 4 euro. We see from Table 55.7 that the marginal net return, the extra net return obtained for an incremental input use, stays positive until 7 units of *X* but turns negative for higher intensity levels. This means that the intensity that will maximise marginal net returns on input use is seven units of *X*. At this level the marginal value product is 4.3 kg, which is roughly equal to the marginal input cost of 4 euro.

To summarise: *Increase the use of an input if the value added by the use of that input is larger than the additional cost.*

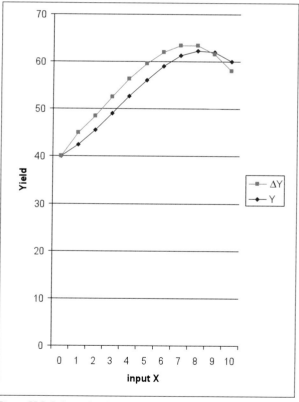

Figure 55.3. Relationship between production Y, marginal product ΔY and input X based upon Table 55.7.

433

Table 55.8. Various combinations of silage feed units/day and grain feed units/day that lead to the same daily growth of beef cattle.

Silage X1	Grain X2	X1	X2	X1/X2	W2/W1
11.0	1.0				
10.00	1.40	-1.00	0.40	-2.50	1.74
9.00	2.00	-1.00	0.60	-1.67	1.74
8.00	2.90	-1.00	0.90	-1.11	1.74
7.00	4.00	-1.00	1.10	-0.91	1.74
6.00	5.20	-1.00	1.20	-0.83	1.74
5.00	6.70	-1.00	1.50	-0.67	1.74
4.00	8.90	-1.00	2.20	-0.45	1.74
3.00	11.00	-1.00	2.10	-0.48	1.74

Input-input Relation

Usually more than one input X is needed to produce a product Y. Moreover, one input X_1 can often replace another input X_2. For instance, in beef production silage or grain can be used as feed, while in pork production barley or oats or rapeseed can be used. A given amount of Y can often be produced with different combinations of X_1 and X_2. The question is which combination of input X_1 and X_2 will minimise the cost of producing a given amount of Y, i.e. what is the most cost-minimising combination of inputs X_1 and X_2? To answer this question we need to know the *substitution ratio* for inputs X_1 and X_2, which is defined as:

$$Substitution\ ratio\ \frac{-X_1}{X_2} = \frac{-Amount\ of\ replaced\ input\ X_1}{Amount\ of\ substituted\ input\ X_2}$$

Experiments with beef cattle have produced the same daily growth through the combinations of silage and grain shown in Table 55.8[1].

From Table 55.8 and Figure 55.4 it is obvious that various combinations of silage and grain lead to the same daily growth. The curve of various combinations is called an *isoquant*. However, the substitution ratio gradually changes. If the input of X_1, silage, is reduced from 11 feed units (FU)/day to 10 FU/day, grain corresponding to 0.4 FU/day is needed. The substitution ratio is -1/0.4 = -2.5. The more silage that is replaced by grain, the more grain is needed. If silage is reduced from 10 FU/day to 9 FU/day, grain corresponding to 0.6 FU/day is needed. The substitution ratio decreases to -1/0.6 = -1.67. Reducing

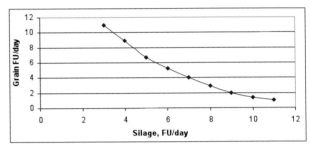

Figure 55.4. Various combinations of silage and grain feed that lead to the same daily growth of beef cattle.

silage more will need more and more grain. For instance, reducing silage in the interval from 7 FU/day to 6 FU/day needs 1.2 FU/day of grain. The substitution ratio is here -1/1.2 = - 0.83. How do we determine the cost-minimising combination of inputs X_1 and X_2? Obviously we need to take into account the cost of inputs X_1 and X_2. Here we assumed that the price the farmer has to pay for silage (W_1) is €0.23/FU and the price of grain (W_2) is €0.4/FU. The rule for the cost-minimising combination is:

$$Substitution\ ratio = \frac{-X_1}{X_2} = \frac{-Amount\ of\ reduced\ input\ X_1}{Amount\ of\ added\ input\ X_2} =$$

$$\frac{Price\ of\ W_2}{Price\ of\ W_1}$$

Since 0.4/0.23 ≈ 1.74, we need to find the combination of X_1 and X_2 which has a substitution ratio corresponding to -1.74. From Table 55.8 we see that the combination of 9 FU/day of silage and 2 FU/day of grain has a substitution

---

1 The values have been somewhat modified based upon real experimental values.

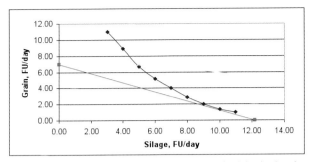

Figure 55.5. Various combinations of silage and grain feed that lead to the same daily growth of beef cattle (black line) and various combinations of silage and grain feed that can be bought for 1 euro (purple line).

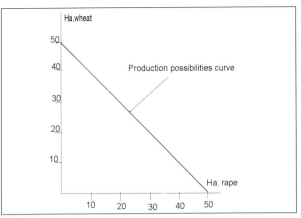

Figure 55.6. Production possibilities curve for two competing products Y_1 and Y_2.

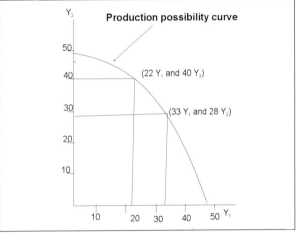

Figure 55.7. Production possibilities curve for two complementary products Y_1 and Y_2.

ratio of -1.67, which is approximately equal to -1.74. This combination of silage and grain will minimise feed costs at this daily rate of growth and at the given price relationship. Note, however, that if the price ratio changes, the cost-minimising combination of silage and grain will also change. A graphical solution is presented in Figure 55.5.

Figure 55.5 presents an isoquant curve which shows the various combinations of silage and grain that lead to the same growth per day. In addition, we have added a curve which shows the various combinations of silage and grain that can be bought for one euro (*the isocost curve*). The least cost combination is given by the point where the isocost curve is tangent to the isoquant curve.

To summarise: *Substitute one input for another if the cost of the substituted input is less than the cost of the input that has been replaced and the production level stays the same.*

Output-output Relation

The third question to decide in the short run is what to produce, given that investments have been made and that some costs are fixed. The farmer has to decide upon a possible combination of products. There may be many alternatives: milk, beef, pork, piglets, eggs, poultry, cereals, root crops, grass and legumes. In deciding upon the combination of enterprises, the first task is to determine the physical relationship between enterprises. There are three main types of relationships, *competitive, complementary* and *supplementary*. By competitiveness is meant that given limited resources, the products compete with each other and that production of one product will de-

crease the production of another, e.g. similar cropping plants such as wheat and barley, or rapeseed and flax, can be seen as competitive. This is illustrated by the production possibilities curve in Figure 55.6.

The production possibilities curve in Figure 55.6 shows the various combinations of two competing products Y_1 (wheat) and Y_2 (rape) that can be produced with a given set of resources, in this case arable land. The farmer can produce for instance 20 ha Y_1 and 30 Y_2 with his given set of resources, 50 ha. Alternatively, he can cultivate 33 ha Y_1 and 17 ha Y_2 with the same resources. The curve

Table 55.9. Two products Y_1 and Y_2, their required inputs X and marginal products MP_1 and MP_2.

Input	Product 1	Marginal Product 1	Input	Product 2	Marginal Product 2
X	Y_1	MP_1	X	Y_2	MP_2
0	0		0	0	
1	5	5	1	7	7
2	9	4	2	13	6
3	12	3	3	18	5
4	14	2	4	22	4
5	15	1	5	25	3
6	14	-1	6	26	1

shows all possible combinations of Y_1 and Y_2 that can be produced. The curve is a straight line, which indicates that the products are competitive.

By complementarity is meant that given limited resources, the production of one product increases production of another product without extra resources. Examples include milk and beef (calves), nitrogen-fixing legumes and cereals, manure-producing livestock and cereals. A graphical illustration is presented in Figure 55.7.

In a similar way, the production possibilities curve in Figure 55.7 shows all combinations of two complementary products, Y_1 and Y_2, that can be produced with a given set of resources. The farmer can produce 22 Y_1 and 40 Y_2 or 33 Y_1 and 28 Y_2 with the same resources. The curve is not a straight line, which indicates that the products are complementary. It means the production of one of the products has a stimulating effect on the production of the other product.

Finally, supplementarity means that production of one product Y_1 does not in any way affect the production of another product Y_2. Examples include crop production and winter labour in forestry. These two enterprises do not compete for the same resources.

Given the physical relationships between various products, how can one decide upon the combination of two products so that profit will be maximised? The most profitable combination of two products is determined by the substitution ratios and their price ratio:

$$Substitution\ ratio = \frac{-\ Amount\ of\ lost\ product\ Y_1}{Amount\ of\ added\ product\ Y_2} = \frac{price\ P_2}{price\ P_1}$$

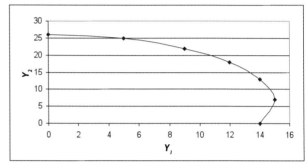

Figure 55.8. Production possibilities curve based on Table 55.9 and $X = 6$.

or $\dfrac{\triangle Y_1}{-\triangle Y_2} = \dfrac{P_{y2}}{P_y}$ which is equal to $\dfrac{\triangle Y_1}{\triangle Y_2} = \dfrac{-P_{y2}}{P_y}$

The rule may be applied to the example in Table 55.9. Two products can be produced with one input. The product levels Y_1 and Y_2 and required input levels are illustrated in the table. The marginal products are also presented.

It is possible to draw a production possibilities curve for $X = 6$ for both products. This production possibilities curve is presented in Figure 55.8.

In order to determine the most profitable combination of Y_1 and Y_2, we need to know the price relationship. Suppose $P_1 = 3$ and $P_2 = 1$. In this case:

$$\frac{P_2}{P_1} = \frac{-1}{3}$$

Consequently we need to find the combination where:

$$\frac{\triangle Y_1}{\triangle Y_2} = \frac{1}{3}$$

This combination is given for $4X$ to Y_1 ($MP_1 = 2$) and $2X$ to Y_2 ($MP_2 = 6$) so consequently if 4 units of X are used for Y_1 and 2 units of X are used for Y_2 we have:

$$\frac{\triangle Y_1}{\triangle Y_2} = \frac{2}{6} = \frac{1}{3} \quad \text{or} \quad \frac{\triangle Y_1}{\triangle Y_2} = \frac{-P_{y2}}{P_{y1}}$$

To summarise: *Substitute one product for another if the value of the product is larger than the value of the product that has been replaced and the total cost stays the same.*

Conclusions

This chapter examined some of the fundamentals of farm management and economic business principles to be applied on farms, with the focus on the functions of farm management and some tools to use. In addition, the basic economic principles to use in short-term planning were briefly reviewed. Due to restrictions on space, enterprise and partial budgeting, whole farm planning, marketing, investment and finance were not discussed. Long-term planning including economies of size and economies of scale were omitted, as was risk and uncertainty. There is ample literature on these issues in English. It is our hope that the reader has acquired some initial insights into the issues involved in farm management and planning.

Questions for review and further thoughts:

1. How is economics defined?
2. Which components describe what farm management should take into account?
3. What are the functions of farm management?
4. What are the main tools the farmer has available for planning?
5. How can the farmer check the economic performance of the farm?
6. With what type of results should the farmer compare the records of his/her farm?
7. For what can he/she use the key figures?
8. What are the three central questions to be decided in the short term?
9. What is the profit-maximising intensity of a variable input?
10. How is the cost-minimising combination of two variable inputs determined?

Conditions for Effective Operation of Farms

56

CASE STUDY
Russia

Galina Bulgakova
St. Petersburg State Agrarian University
Pushkin, Russia

Russia actively began building up its farm network in the mid-1990s. There are currently 255,000 farms with a total land area of 21 million ha (on average 81 ha per farm). Farmers own 19.5% of agricultural land and 14.7% of arable land. They produce 12.5% of total agricultural products in Russia (Smolyaninov, 2004).

Analyses of farm problems should focus on finding ways of development and effective management and economic mechanisms of operating. Particular attention should be paid to optimal farm structure, size, services and cooperation, state support. One of the main conditions for successful farm operation is achievement of optimal production and economic parameters. In contrast to general Western practice, where highly specialised small-scale agricultural enterprises are one of the main factors in increasing production volume and labour productivity, in Russia it is risky to create highly specialised enterprises, because the market is unsustainable, prices for different types of agricultural products are disproportionate, quite often partners break treaty commitments, etc. In every enterprise it is reasonable from a management and economic point of view to have no less than two agricultural enterprises.

Statistics show that small-scale farms (with less than 15 ha of land) stop operating most often. Effective development of farm enterprises is impossible without enlargement. Enlargement is possible by transfer of the land from those enterprises which stopped operating to those which work efficiently, by well developed rent and creation of a regulated market of land (Russian Statistical Yearbook 1998-2008).

An important condition which ensures successful operation of farms is the availability of means of production. In Russia, only 75% of farmers have a tractor, while 68% of farmers have a lorry. Weak supply of materials and technical resources is one of the main problems in farm formation. This problem has two aspects: a) lack of financial resources available for farmers; b) existing disproportion between prices of industrial and agricultural products.

The main financial source for creation of a material and technical base available for farmers is bank credit with favourable rates of interest. Besides this, it is possible to use long-term leasing of both agricultural machinery and processing equipment (primarily for processing products of animal husbandry). Another important condition for effective operating of farms is state support on both federal and regional level (Borhunov and Polyanina, 2004; Smolyaninov, 2004; Sokolova and Chudilin, 2005).

The main activities in the framework of the national project 'Development of Agro-industrial complexes' focused on stimulating development of small-scale agricultural enterprises were:

1. Increase in credit for personal subsidiary plots and farms, as well as cooperatives of small-scale agricultural producers. The main mechanism is to subsidise interest rates for loans taken in commercial banks to the amount of 95% of the refinancing rate of the Bank of Russia;
2. Support a network of agricultural cooperatives of different kinds. The joint-stock company 'Rosselhozbank' provides credit, information and methodical support to the cooperatives. Besides that, Rosselhozbank is an associate member of the cooperatives.
3. Development of borrowing using land as collateral. The main banks that are members of the national project are Rosselhozbank (57% of all concluded treaties and 37% of all credit resources) and the Bank of Savings of the Russian Federation (31% of all concluded treaties and 41% of all credit resources).

Since 2005, lending has increased 10-fold. In 2006 it reached 40.0 billion RUB, whereas in 2005 it was just 3.4 billion RUB. The number of borrowers was more than 130,000 in 2006, compared with 2,500 in 2005. The increase happened thanks to private subsidiary plots. Private subsidiary plots, farmers and cooperatives took 55%, 32% and 13% of loans respectively (Borhunov and Polyanina, 2004).

Foreign experience shows that state interference in the market relationship occurred previously in regulation of prices of agricultural products. Within the EU, the old subsidisation environment is being replaced by a market where the price is increasingly determined by market demand and supply. The agricultural support paid by the EU or its Member States is mainly based on hectares or animal units and only to a smaller extent on producer prices.

Due to the sharp decrease in state purchasing of agricultural products and liberalisation of prices of agricultural products and raw materials in Russia, it is necessary to elaborate an effective mechanism for pricing agricultural products. Customs dues should be fixed on the level that could ensure 40% profitability and cover expenses related to permanent assets.

An important issue in farm activity is the development of cooperatives, not only with farms themselves, but also with other agricultural and industrial enterprises which store, process and sell agricultural products and provide services. Development of cooperative relationships is mostly reasonable in the processing field, as well as in joint purchasing and use of agricultural machinery and marketing and advisory services.

Arguments for organising processing at the place of production are that important economic problems are solved: a) losses are decreased; b) quality is preserved; c) the cost of transport is decreased; and d) joint products are used more effectively. Besides that, social problems are solved: a) the rate of employment is increased; b) seasonal fluctuations in demand for labour are evened out; c) the supply of food is improved.

In 2006, more than 2000 agricultural consumers' cooperatives were formed in Russia. Formation of cooperatives is proceeding more rapidly in the Federal Districts that received more funding in the framework of the National Project. These are the Republic of Mordovia, Belgorod and Orenburg oblast and the Republic of Sakha.

Agricultural Cooperation

From Past to Present

57

CASE STUD
Russ

Svetlana Golovina

Kurgan State Agricultural Academy , Kurgan, Russia

Cooperative practices in Russia have a history of more than a century. New forms of collective activity in the spheres of manufacturing, services and living conditions have been generated because of the necessity to overcome the difficulties caused by a severe climate, features of agricultural production, and extreme economic, political and social conditions. The development of cooperative societies in Russian agriculture usually accelerated during periods when the production was individualised, i.e. at the end of the 19th and the start of the 20th century (Stolypin reform), within the NEP (New Economic Policy) years (the 1920s) and during the last reform (from the end of the 1980s).

Experience of cooperation of people has been collected through centuries. *Obshina* (village community), *artel*[1], *skladchina*[2] and *mutual aid* are among pre-cooperative forms of collective action in Russia. The origin of the first true cooperative societies is connected with such important circumstances as cancelling serfdom (1861) and the advent of legally free peasants. The development of the cooperative movement during the last decade of the 19th century was caused by the growth of industry, banking and trade and expansion of commodity-money relations in villages (Podgorbunskih and Golovina, 2005).

The number of cooperatives in Russia in 1914 reached 32,975, including credit cooperatives (13,839), consumer cooperatives (10,000), agricultural cooperatives (8,576), repair cooperatives (500) and others (60). The number of cooperatives in Russia was only exceeded in one other country, Germany. During the next years Russia was foremost in the world regarding cooperative development; in 1916, cooperative societies numbered 47,000 (Table 57.1).

The October Revolution brought significant amendments to the evolution of cooperation; after land nationalisation, production cooperation was strongly supported by government. Up to 1919 the agricultural communes, in which land and all means of production were socialised and distribution of income carried out equally per head, were the basic economic form of cooperatives.

---

1 *Artel* (from the Tatar *orta* = community, *ortak* = common). A small voluntary association of individuals who come together for a limited or indefinite period for the purpose of performing some economic activity. The members of an artel donate labor, tools, and even capital and divide the profits according to the amount and quality of the labor they contribute.

2 "*Skladchina*," from the verb "skladivat," (collect) which means to put something in common.

Table 57.1. Development of Russian cooperation in the beginning of the 20th century, number of cooperatives (Podgorbunskih and Golovina, 2005).

Type of cooperatives	1901	1917	Growth (times)
Credit cooperatives	837	16,055	19
Consumer societies	600	20,000	33
Agricultural societies	137	6,032	44
Agricultural artels	-	2,100	-
Butter-making artels	51	3,000	59
Handicraft and other artels	-	600	-
Total	1,625	47,787	29

Table 57.2. Number of Russian cooperatives in 1922-1925 (thousands). (Results of Soviet Authority Decades in Figures: 1917-1927, pp. 419-423).

Types of cooperatives	1922	1923	1924	1925
Consumer cooperatives	22.0	17.8	21.1	24.5
Industrial producer cooperative	17.2	7.4	7.7	13.2
Agricultural cooperatives	22.0	31.2	37.9	54.8
including:				
communes	1.9	1.8	1.5	1.8
artels	8.4	6.8	7.4	8.8
joint cultivation of land (TOZ)	5.0	5.3	4.6	4.6
Agricultural subsidiary – production cooperatives	1.8	2.4	3.0	9.1
Association in agricultural production processing and marketing	4.7	4.3	4.3	8.6
Universal agricultural association	7.0	10.4	17.0	21.9
Total	135.9	73.5	91.0	132.1

The purpose of the NEP was to restore agriculture by means of cooperation. It included a number of measures contributing to a transition from command methods of management to economic, which promoted cooperative practices in Russia (Table 57.2).

However, towards the end of the 1920s the curtailment of the NEP policy and complete collectivisation radically changed traditional methods of managing and organisation forms of agricultural production. Collective farms became the basic model for agricultural collective organisations. Other forms of cooperation existing earlier in agriculture were gradually liquidated.

The new stage in cooperative development has come since the second half of the 1980s. The government has recognised the necessity for small producer systems, which could adapt to changes in consumer demand more quickly and more flexibly, satisfy the needs in small-scale production and a wide range of services more operatively and qualitatively, and make better use of labour resources. The result was the law 'About cooperation in the USSR' in 1988.

Now a legal basis for agricultural cooperatives is constituted by the law 'About consumer cooperatives (consumer societies and unions) in the Russian Federation' (1992), clause 116 of the first part of the Civil Code of the Russian Federation (1994) and the Law of the Russian Federation 'About agricultural cooperation' (1995). According to this legislation, the cooperative sector of the Russian economy includes production and consumer cooperative societies (Figure 57.1).

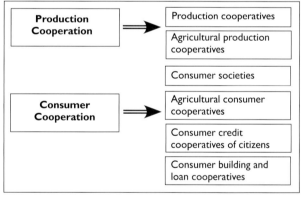

Figure 57.1. Classification of cooperative organisations in the Russian Federation.

Agricultural production cooperatives are commercial organisations uniting citizens for agricultural production within uniform enterprises. The members of the cooperative pool a part of their property or financial resources. The cooperative can cultivate the land, which: 1) is brought by its members in share funds; 2) is transferred to it in rent; or 3) is redeemed by the cooperative society. In the first and third cases the land becomes the property of the cooperative. The members of the cooperative are

Table 57.3. Number of agricultural consumer cooperatives (The report of Minister of Agriculture of Russian Federation November 27th, 2007, http://www.mcx.ru/index.html?he_id=981&news_id=3981&n_page=1).

Types of cooperatives	01.01.2006	According to National Project (plan)	Created according to National project *	Share of working cooperatives in total quantity
Agricultural consumer cooperatives, total	776	2,550	3,576	55.7
including: credit cooperatives	511	1,000	1,075	66.8
processing cooperatives	121	550	689	43.0
supply and sales cooperatives	144	1,000	1,812	53.7

* - during 2006 and 10 months of 2007.

obliged to contribute their labour in the production. The income of the cooperative society is distributed according to labour contributions of its members.

Agricultural consumer cooperatives are non-commercial organisations of people who own small individual farms, peasant farms and legal entities for agricultural product processing and realisation, supplying resources and rendering services.

Agricultural commodity producers can create different kinds of agricultural consumer cooperatives: processing, marketing, servicing, supplying, insurance and credit cooperatives:

- *Processing cooperatives* engaged in agricultural production (manufacture of meat, fish, dairy products, bakery products, vegetable, fruit and berry products)
- *Marketing cooperatives* carrying out sales of products and also the storage, sorting, drying, washing, packaging, packing and transportation of such products
- *Service cooperatives* performing ameliorative, transport, repair and building activities, veterinary services and breeding, work on application of fertilisers and plant protection, consulting and auditor activities
- *Supply cooperatives* organised for purchasing means of production, fertilisers, feed, mineral oil, spare parts, and other goods which are necessary for agricultural and raw material production
- *Insurance cooperatives* carrying out various sorts of service such as personal and medical insurance, insurance of crops, property and land
- *Credit cooperatives* carrying out consumer lending and savings of members' money resources.

The national project 'Development of APK' and other state programmes initiate the formation of cooperative societies of a vertical type in domestic agriculture. However, many newly established cooperatives do not function in reality (Table 57.3).

The establishment of new cooperatives runs very unevenly in various parts of the Russian Federation. Moreover, the dynamics of the creation of processing and marketing cooperative societies differ significantly. According to the last census, the basic kinds of services for owners of individual farms and peasant farms are provided by individual businesses and corporations, and the main sales channel for agricultural products is the collective-farm market, i.e. small markets where farmers sell their produce themselves (Table 57.4).

Table 57.4. Functioning of consumer cooperatives and collective-farm markets in different federal regions of the Russian Federation (Information Bulletin of Minister of Agriculture of Russian Federation, No 11-12, 2006).

Federal region	Number of markets	Number of cooperatives	Share of cooperatives in total number of markets, %
Central	1228	185	15.1
Northwestern	344	18	5.2
South	813	113	13.9
Prevolga	1022	271	26.5
Ural	254	40	15.7
Siberia	745	183	24.6
Far East	306	13	4.2
Russian Federation	**4712**	**823**	**17.5**

Although both the government and agricultural producers have realised the necessity for collective action in the stages before and after farm production, some factors interfere with the development of cooperative societies in Russia (Golovina, 2007):

- Cooperation was discredited during the Soviet period and through the first years of the last reform and, as a consequence, most agricultural manufacturers have a negative attitude to it
- Individual farmers and other small producers have no experience of collective action, its organisation and management
- Formal and informal institutional conditions for cooperatives are created very slowly
- The cooperative movement develops too slowly and the production of more profitable and less risky value-added products are monopolised by investor-orientated firms with capital that originates from outside agriculture. The owners of these firms are not concerned about the problems of the village and rural communities.

However, the government is concerned about the destruction of agricultural production and the degradation of rural territories. It has realised the necessity for collective structures which work in the interests of agricultural producers. The process of cooperative formation is initiated by the development and realisation of particular programmes. Special institutional structures in the Ministry of Agriculture and the regional departments have been created. Nevertheless, the implementation of projects resembles the former administrative procedures (with plans and reports), and it has not yet been realised that cooperative societies created in this way are doomed to a short life. The top-down procedure for establishing cooperatives leads to low involvement from the side of the farmers, but on the other hand, this procedure helps to accelerate the process of cooperative establishments.

World history shows that viable cooperative societies should be created only by certain types of producers; namely producers motivated to agricultural production; well informed on procedures of the establishment of cooperative societies and cooperative principles; trusting other potential members of the cooperative and prepared to be involved in cooperative activity. In Russia, most farmers, with few exceptions, consider agriculture only as a temporary means of survival. Many land owners do not accept cooperation as a way to solve difficulties with deliveries and sales of products and provision of services. Due to economic and social instability, fellow villagers distrust not only government and local authorities, but also neighbours and potential partners. Moreover, the demographic situation of the village, meaning the ageing of the rural population, is not conducive to cooperative development.

The future of agricultural cooperation depends in many respects on which organisational models are created for the cooperatives (Nilsson, 1998). An analysis of the cooperative legislation in Russia and the bylaws developed by the new cooperatives indicates that the internal organisation of the traditional cooperative model is not suitable when modern market strategies are to be introduced and implemented. In such a situation a traditional cooperative society is doomed to be inefficient. The members get weak incentives to invest, poor motivation to participate in the cooperative's activities and in the management, and difficulties in attracting professional managers; moreover problems may arise due to vaguely specified property rights. To avoid waste of resources, time and effort, it is necessary to find the shortest way to create 'new generation cooperatives' (Cook, 1995), which are ready to compete with other organisational forms and which have the potential for effective business and performance of the important social functions. The main attributes of this cooperative model are open membership, tradable delivery rights, differential voting power, individualised ownership and top-qualified leadership.

Agricultural Education and Extension

58

CASE STUD
Russ

Valery Belyakov and Mikhail Moskalev
St Petersburg Agrarian University, St Petersburg, Russia

Alexandra Izosimova
Agro-Physical Research Institute, Pushkin, Russia

Vocational Training in Russia

The Russian system of vocational training consists of several levels: 1) Vocational school, providing senior secondary education; 2) technical college, providing technical training for different professions; 3) vocational college, providing higher level technical training, e.g. farm mechanics; 4) institute, academy, university; and 5) postgraduate applied education (Figure 58.1).

Agricultural Education

There are 62 agricultural Higher Education Institutions (HEIs) and 5 branches thereof, 285 colleges and technical schools, as well as academies and institutes of improvement of professional skills and retraining of personnel in the 88 regions of the Russian Federation. Forms of train-

ing include full-time tuition, extra-mural studies, correspondence training, externships and courses.

The most effective ecological education of students is achieved using a mixed model, with basic ecological knowledge taught through the separate subjects 'ecology' and the ecologically directed content of some closely-related basic subjects (biology, geography, chemistry, physics, etc.). This approach includes organisation of ecological excursions, ecological paths, groups and courses, establishment of ecological department on a school experimental plots, etc.

A degree in agroecology teaches methods for assessing the condition of the agrolandscape; methods of toxicant detection in soils, plants and production; methods of ecological estimation of fertilisation, plant protection and land improvement systems; engineering techniques in action systems for restoration of polluted and disturbed lands; methods of soil-ecological inspection and

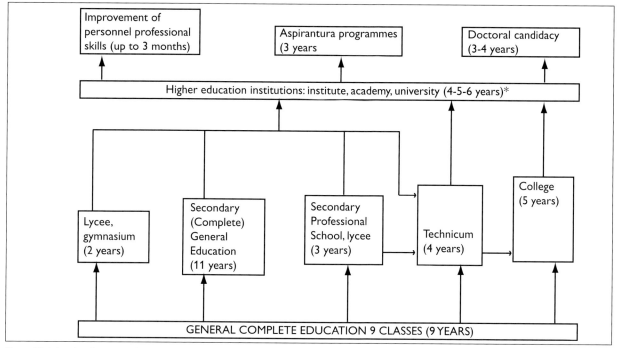

Figure 58.1. Levels of vocational training in the current Russian system.

Note* Since 1992, the following degrees are awarded: Bachelor of Science (4 years); Master of Science (2 years after receipt of Bachelor degree); Expert Diploma (5-6 years of training) – a qualifying degree. The Master of Science and Expert Diploma qualify graduates for postgraduate study.

techniques for agrolandscape research for appropriate use in the agricultural industry; methods of agroecosystem modelling and determination of degree of soil erosion. Graduates are prepared for tasks such as agroecological monitoring, ecological examination, land evaluation and rational use of agrolandscapes, carried out in regional centres for ecological services.

The ecological awareness of students of the leading agrarian HEIs and colleges in the Russian Federation is substantially enhanced through the participation of these educational institutions and their teachers and students in international programmes and projects. Thus during the implementation of the Russian-Swedish project 'Agriculture and Environment in Leningrad Oblast, AELO' in the actions directed at increasing ecological awareness, special attention was given to young people.

At the initial stage of this project, the curricula of various levels of some educational establishments in St. Petersburg and Leningrad region were analysed to assess

the ecological content. The following institutions were involved: St. Petersburg State University (SPSU), St. Petersburg State Agrarian University (SPSAU), Academy of Management and Agribusiness of the Russian Federation Nonchernozem Zone, Besedsky Agricultural College. The technical and methodological potential of these establishments was also analysed. During meetings with representatives of educational institutions, issues regarding the state of vocational training in the field of ecology and agricultural production were discussed, as well as the existing curricula.

The cooperation between the project and the Faculty of Soil Science and Agroecology SPSAU resulted in the organisation of a conference for pupils and students 'Agroecology and scientific and technical advances'. On the basis of conference work, a collection of materials was issued. It comprised contributions from pupils of Polyanskaya comprehensive school of the Vyborg area of Leningrad region, Selsovskaya educational school

Tosno area of Leningrad region, students of Besedsky Agricultural College, Vsevolozhsk Agricultural College, students and post-graduate students of SPSAU, and also information from experts in the project.

Both the AELO project and the succeeding Baltic Sea Programme for the Leningrad Region, uniting six cooperating projects, mainly focused on solving ecological questions regarding the agricultural production. At the same time, great value was placed both in the project and in the Program on interaction with educational institutions, research institutes and local farmers' organisations in preparing and carrying out ecological seminars for heads and experts of agricultural production, organising practical consultations, preparing and implementing ecological components into actual technological projects and increasing ecological awareness in young people.

The international project 'Development of agricultural education in the north-west region of Russia based on the experience of Denmark', which developed and introduced curricula for three special educational institutions in the Leningrad, Novgorod and Kaliningrad areas, has significantly promoted the use of international experience, in particular on questions of ecology, in teaching in agricultural technical schools and colleges. The main educational institutions involved in the project the St. Petersburg Agrarian University and Vsevolozhsk Base Agricultural College of Leningrad region. The project was coordinated by the Danish agricultural consultation centre and funded by the Danish Ministry of Food, Agriculture and Fishery.

Good Agricultural Practice (GAP)

Successful cooperation between Russia and Finland has resulted in creation of a code of Good Agricultural Practice (GAP) in the Leningrad region This code is a system of rules and principles covering all kinds of agricultural activity and protecting the environment from negative influences of agriculture. The Code improves opportunities for farmers, identifies simpler and more effective methods of environmental protection, safeguards the health of humans and animals, and helps preserve rural landscapes and a biodiversity of wild animals and plants. In the EU countries national GAP codes were applied in 1990-2000 using general conditions specified by EU Directives.

Furthermore, the countries bordering the Baltic Sea (including Russia) signed the Convention on Protection of the Marine Environment of the Baltic Sea Area (the Helsinki Convention), which is governed by the Helsinki Commission (HELCOM) and aims to fulfil the transition to ecologically safe agriculture by developing and using GAP throughout the Baltic Sea Region.

Ecological legislation, including a series of laws and normative documents regulating environmental protection in detail, has now been established in Russia. However farmers have difficulties in understanding this legislation and using it in their daily work, so general provisions on the organisation of ecologically safe agricultural production have been clarified taking into account the modern theoretical and practical level and full conformity with Russian legislation, the laws of the Leningrad region and HELCOM recommendations.

In 2005-2006, a group of Russian and Finnish experts prepared and issued the first part of the GAP Code for the Leningrad region: 'Animal husbandry and fodder production' (Semenova, 2006). In 2006-2007 the second part of the Code (Poultry) was prepared and issued (Dzhavadova, 2007). This work was funded by the Ministry of Environment of Finland. The Code is designed for the use of direct agroproducers: farmers, experts, heads of the agricultural enterprises and aviculture farms; experts and heads of control bodies, consultancy services and various service organisations; and HEIs and special agricultural educational institutions. Both parts are issued in Russian and English and are available on the website of the Baltic Sea Program for the Leningrad Region www.eagri.spb.ru

Information-consulting Services (ICS)

In the early 1990s, essential changes connected with the transition to a market economy, including establishment of farmer facilities and creation of agricultural co-operatives and limited liability companies, took place in the Russian agricultural sector. Such organisations were frequently governed by people lacking appropriate education and sufficient professional experience, which led to a need for expert help for training and improvement of professional skills.

Furthermore, advisory services on operating in a market environment were demanded by both skilled managers and experts in agricultural production. This resulted in the creation of information-consulting service (ICS) in the agricultural sector (AS) in Russia to furnish rural producers of all patterns of ownership with scientific and technical knowledge, innovative projects and commercial information. This service was provided within the Ministry of Agriculture of the Russian Federation and consisted of regional, republican, territorial, area and district ICS centres. Experienced staff in agriculture departments and at research organisations were initially employed as consultants. In addition, training-consultation centres were also created under the auspices of higher education institutions and colleges, academies and vocational training institutes.

In order to increase the efficiency of ICS, its functioning and coordination of the activities of regional information-consultation centres, an ICS-AS Council with 35 members including representatives of regional information-consulting services, the Ministry of Agriculture and the Russian Academy of Agricultural Sciences has been established. ICS staff training is provided at Moscow Agricultural Academy (Klimenko, 2000).

The formation and development of ICS in Russia was assisted by a number of domestic and international projects, the most significant of which was the project on support of realisation of reforms in agriculture – ARIS. One of the key international projects in the sphere of agricultural education in north-west Russia was TACISFDRUS 9702 'Strengthening Agricultural Reform through Training', which was mainly dedicated to formation and development of ICS. Within the framework of the project a series of seminars was carried out and a manual 'The Organization of Information - Consulting Service in Agricultural Sector' was prepared and issued. The coordination office of the project in the north-west region was in SPSAU.

At the same time, it is necessary to understand that despite significant organisational efforts, ICS is not as vital for the development of agricultural production of Russia is it is e.g. in Denmark. This can be due in part to the absence of corresponding traditions, since in the planned economy all key positions in agricultural production were occupied by experts with higher/professional secondary education who were obliged to maintain their qualifications. The system of improvement of professional skills and retraining of personnel played, and still plays, a vital role in agricultural education.

Up to the middle of the 1980s, professional skills training for directors and experts in the agricultural sector was carried out at higher education institutions in Russia. At a lower level, a network of academies and institutes specialised in improving professional skills and retraining staff in the agrarian sector. In the 1990s these were drastically reduced, although lately there has been a noticeable growth in this kind of activity in HEIs, and in some cases, vocational training institutes have merged with HEI.

In north-west Russia, vocational training institutes for agriculture are located in Saint Petersburg, Kaliningrad, Novgorod, Petrozavodsk, Vologda, Syktyvkar (Komi Republic) and Pskov. There is also an institute for 'Improvement of Professional Skills and Retraining of the Experts in Natural Resources, Environmental Safety and Protection' in St. Petersburg. In addition, professional public associations, e.g. the Union of Farmers of Leningrad region and St. Petersburg, in partnership with research institutions, plan and organise courses for the general public.

Agriculture in Kaliningrad

59

Gennady Fedorov and Evgene Krasnov

Immanuel Kant State University of Russia
Kaliningrad, Russia

Compared with other regions in north-west Russia, the Kaliningrad region has more favourable conditions for agricultural production. The long vegetation period and mild winter favour grain and fodder crops and cultivation of vegetables. The abundance of rainfall in the lowland plains is the chief cause of drainage requirements. A wide range of economic factors such as the dense road network and numerous cities with rural area management centres give certain advantages. However, soil amelioration infrastructure (drainage systems etc.) requires considerable investments to update it, generating high capital requirements. Poor soils deprived of humus and minerals demand a huge amount of fertilisers. Meanwhile the quantity of organic fertilisers applied per hectare has decreased more than five-fold compared with 1980, and mineral fertilisers by 2.5-fold. Therefore crop yields in the region are much lower than in developed European countries.

The technical equipment in agriculture has halved. For example, in 1990 there were 9,800 tractors but at the beginning of 2001 only 3,300, and the number of combine harvesters has decreased from 1,500 to 710. During the 1990s, capital investment in agricultural all but ceased (chemicals, farm machines, land reclamation, maintenance, etc.).

Animal rearing, particularly of poultry and pigs, is capitalintensive because of the usage of mainly purchased, imported fodder, which gives rise to high production costs. In the sphere of animal breeding, the well-developed fish industry provides animal feed inputs, e.g. less valuable pieces of fish and waste from the canning industry are used as feedstuffs in fur farming. The lack of investment means that farmers are forced to apply outdated technologies.

According to the regulations set in the special economic zone, food items are duty-free. Such conditions mean that the local food industry faces tough competition from cheap imported goods, produced in a quite favourable environment through subsidies on export and manufacturing in the countries of origin. This is the chief cause of the rapid agricultural recession in the region compared with the rest of the country. The agrarian crisis has not been solved yet. Gross output in 2009 totalled only 62% of that in 1990 (in Russia 86%) (see Figure 59.1). Cattle breeding in the region, once successful, has fallen below the average standards.

Total agricultural land makes up 812,700 ha, but arable land 394,600 ha and planted area only 158,300 ha (2008). A total of 129,300 ha of the planted area is the property of the former collective and state farms, which

Figure 59.1. Changes in agricultural production in the Russian Federation and Kaliningrad Region, 1990-2009.

In the 1990s there was a sharp drop in basic agricultural production due to the low efficiency and the decrease in livestock and the cropped area. The cultivation of vegetables, rape and bread grain increased.

The highly profitable branch of breeding animals for furs is experiencing harsh times. Although the number of large breeding farms in Russia has decreased from 250 to 30, the six manufacturing plants in the region are continuing to operate, but the production quantity is less. Numbers of livestock, mainly mink, have fallen by a quarter in the country overall, but the Kaliningrad region produces about one-third of the fur on the Russian market and here the number of animals has been increasing since 2000, and now it exceeds 180,000 head.

In 1990 crop production peaked, mainly such export crops as rape. In 2009 the rape cultivation area was 27,000 ha. The cultivation of vegetables is exceeding the 1990 rate and the range is expanding.

Despite favourable weather conditions, available workforce and demand for food among people, the lack of agricultural production in the Kaliningrad region is apparent. The great majority of the products that could be manufactured in the region are imported. Some enterprises have now adjusted to the new market changes, although clear improvements in the field are not apparent yet. The agricultural complex has become the weak point in the regional economy. It requires additional government support.

A comprehensive successful rural policy aimed at the market must be developed. The steady growth in the agricultural sphere has to proceed into another stage of development, based on the introduction and support of the most recent business owners, up-to-date technologies, taking into the account basic principals of the environ-

in 1990 underwent reorganisation into joint-stock companies of various types. A further 8,500 ha is farmland and 20,500 ha is private land.

The first farms were established in the region at the end of the 1980s. Nowadays about 5,600 farmers own land, but only about 400 of these practise commercial agriculture. Farmers manage 17% of agricultural land, which gives 5% of the gross production, the farming industry output is 48% and private rural sector *(individual holdings)* produces 47% (2009).

Grain, feed and industrial crops are grown by large collective farms and agricultural enterprises. Potatoes and vegetables are produced by farmers and private households. The farmers are less interested in animal breeding. Meat (beef and pork) and eggs are mainly produced by large enterprises rather than small, while the opposite is true for milk.

Table 59.1. Cultivation of the most significant sorts of agricultural products in Kaliningrad from 1990 to 2009 (thousand tonnes).

Item	1990	1995	2000	2003	2004	2005	2006	2007	2009
Milk	546.1	296.1	218.7	188.3	190.5	175.8	165.9	149.8	134.5
Meat (slaughter weight)	67.4	32.8	23.2	28.3	29.4	27.8	28.5	27.8	27.5
Eggs, (million)	333.6	264.9	201	206.3	185.7	257.0	179.9	189.2	134.9
Grain (processed)	489.2	228.4	194.6	220.0	298.1	253.6	145.9	160.6	227.4
Potatoes	204.2	124.9	224.3	153.6	97.2	84.6	86.1	65.3	120.1
Vegetables	57.0	60.7	79.1	92.1	50.9	48.8	51.4	48.3	51.5

mental development. The government ought to maintain the infrastructure development of the farming industry:

- Establishing on a competitive basis repair shops, including a net of tractor repair centres, providing them with some tax benefits (such as exemption for a certain period of time from local taxes, cheap loans, different grants and awards).
- Maintaining the co-operative societies and other institutions manufacturing raw materials, finished commodities and other wholesalers and retail traders through giving preferential terms for the lease of the regional and public property of vertical integration.
- Setting up a chain of agricultural advice centres providing information in the field of farm production for the farmers; establishing public farms spreading the knowledge of the advanced experience, new technologies, foremost machinery, prices and so on.
- Training of personnel; further retraining, on an obligatory basis, for the experts in co-operative societies and the heads of the farms, with partial subsidisation from the regional and federal budget.
- Establishing infrastructure for selling agricultural products and food (agricultural exchanges, wholesale food market).

Funding is also essential for:

- Reclamation and amelioration of agricultural soils.
- Renewing machinery and introduction of new technologies in the sphere of crop farming and animal breeding within the programme of technical renovation of agriculture.
- Regeneration of seed farming and livestock breeding in the region.

Conclusions

Special attention must be paid to the social development of rural areas: the improvement of the rural infrastructure and standards of living.

For future success, the agrarian complex in the region must become a high-tech branch of the economy, based on the large vertically integrated commodity exchange economy, working in the market. The development of the agrarian complex would solve complicated social problems for the people living in the rural and suburban areas in the Kaliningrad region.

How to Change Behaviour
Carrots and Sticks

60

John Sumelius and Stefan Bäckman
University of Helsinki, Finland

Why are Economic Instruments Needed?

The relationship between agriculture and the environment is diverse. Agriculture may have adverse effects for the ecosystem, for instance on the waterways or on the soil. On the other hand, if managed properly it can create value in the form of an aesthetic landscape and a habitat for many birds. The integration of environmental concerns with agricultural policies is therefore important. Integration can be accomplished through the use of economic instruments, educational activities or administrative measures. The type of instrument recommended depends to a large degree on the particular characteristic of the problem. It is important to use an instrument suited for the particular problem in question. We may for instance look at instruments that aim at decreasing nutrient flows to waterways. The relationship between nutrient emissions and cyanobacteria blooms is described in Fact box 1.

Nutrients entering waterways originate partly from non-point sources, partly from point sources (see Fact box 2). The main non-point sources are agriculture, forestry, boat traffic, settlements and deposition from the air, whereas the main point sources are industry and munici-

Fact Box 1. Nutrient Emission and Cyanobacteria Blooms

There is a clear relationship between excessive amounts of nitrogen (N) and phosphorus (P) in the brackish Baltic Sea and cyanobacteria blooms that severely reduce the environmental quality. This relationship has been described by Vaahtera et al. (2007) in the following way '...*eutrophication of the Baltic Sea has potentially increased the frequency and magnitude of cyanobacteria blooms. Eutrophication leads to increased sedimentation of organic material, increasing the extent of anoxic bottoms and subsequently increasing the internal phosphorus loading*'. According to those authors, it is apparent that in order to reduce cyanobacteria blooms, both N and P external loads need to be reduced. Wulff et al. (2007), on the other hand, draw the conclusion that N emissions mainly originate from land runoff, primarily agricultural land, and that human emissions are the major source of P. According to HELCOM (the Helsinki Commission – Baltic Marine Environment Protection Commission), waterborne inputs represented 75% of the main inputs of N and nearly 100% of P inputs to the Baltic Sea in the year 2000. Agriculture and forestry contributed almost 60% of the waterborne N inputs, 28% were from natural background sources and 13% from point sources (see Fact box 2). Of the waterborne P inputs to the Baltic Sea, approximately 50% originated from agriculture, while natural background sources and point sources accounted for approximately 25% each. P from scattered dwellings is also an important source. Point sources are less important than agricultural sources, but are still very important in some regions (HELCOM, 2005).

Fact Box 2. Point Source and Non-point Source Pollution

Pollution from an identifiable source such as residues from an industrial plant or smoke from a pipe is called point source pollution. Pollution from sources which follow indirect and diffuse ways is called non-point source pollution.

Nutrients can enter into waterways in several ways, either as runoff (surface runoff) over the soil surface by rainwater or melting snow, through run-in directly through groundwater or wells, through leaching by percolating rain or through atmospheric deposition.

Non-point source pollution is characterised by uncertainty about the origin of the pollutant and, as a consequence, who is responsible. Measuring the pollution is not possible since the pollution flow is unobservable. Solutions to non-point pollution are still generally highly site-specific. Climatic factors, the physical environment (e.g. soil type and slope and timing) are very important when it comes to non-point source pollution. Point source pollution is technically easier to monitor because measurement is easier (Shortle and Abler, 1997; 2001. See also Part B Reducing Nutrient Losses from Agriculture).

Fact Box 3. Economic, Administrative and Informational Instruments

Economic instruments
1. Taxes and fees
2. Permits, quotas
3. Tradable permits
4. Support

Command and control (administrative instruments)
1. Directives
2. Penalties
3. Legal sanctions
4. Cross compliance

Market-based incentives
1. Labelling

Education, extension and information

---

palities. The economic instruments that can be used for decreasing non-point source pollution, e.g. from agriculture, are different from large point sources of pollution such as factories or municipalities. Therefore, in the design of instruments care has to be taken with regard to the mechanisms of nutrient transport and their origin.

The problems of soil compaction or acidification may look different than eutrophication or reduction in biodiversity. However, the various forms of environmental damage often have one thing in common. Environmental degradation consists of problems that are often not taken care of by the free market mechanism and which imply one type of failure of the market mechanism. In order to correct for market failure, economic instruments or in some cases environmental regulations are needed. Through carrots and sticks created by economic instruments, it is in theory possible to integrate the environmental problem with functioning markets in order to increase social welfare (i.e. improve the situation compared with the free market situation). Instruments can also be administrative (i.e. based on regulations or directives) or informational (i.e. based on education, extension and information). A short list of instruments is presented in Fact Box 3. It is worthwhile noting that these are instruments from the point of view of an environmental planner, not

from an individual manager or producer. An individual farmer, for instance, can influence the environmental problem by management measures, i.e. good agricultural practices. Environmental instruments are those carrots and sticks which the environmental planner uses in order to induce the individual producer to use environmentally sound management measures.

The major advantage of economic instruments in comparison with command-and-control measures is their ability to achieve a given environmental objective at lower cost. Another advantage is the stimulus to adopt new technology. The choice of economic instrument depends on a number of criteria against which it is to be evaluated. Following Weersink and Livernois (1996), some possible alternative criteria are:

1. *Environmental effectiveness.* By environmental effectiveness is meant goal-accomplishment or environmental performance. An instrument must be effective in achieving its environmental goal. A measure which to a larger degree accomplishes the objectives set out is preferable to one that does not accomplish the same objectives (e.g. Braden and Segerson, 1993).
2. *Cost efficiency, cost effectiveness.* By cost effectiveness is meant the ability of an instrument to achieve

its goal in relation to its cost. A certain reduction in emissions might be achieved in several ways and by different instruments. An instrument A might lead to a certain emissions reduction at a lower cost than an instrument B. In this case A is said to be more cost-effective than B. One also has to make a distinction between cost effectiveness on social level and farm level. The cost effectiveness of one instrument need not be the same for the society (consumers, producers and taxpayers) and for the producers. On the other hand, there is a distinction between cost efficiency and cost effectiveness. According to Perman et al. (1996), a cost-efficient instrument achieves a particular target at the minimum overall cost to society, whereas a cost-effective instrument attains some target, but not necessarily the best target, at a minimum cost to society.

3. *Transaction costs for businesses. The introduction of a new economic instrument implies* transaction costs for farmers. The concept of transaction costs was introduced by Ronald Coase (1937), according to whom transaction costs are extra costs in the market for information search, implementation of changes and bargaining. The existence of such transaction costs in agriculture because of changes in regulations has been shown e.g. by Slangen (1997), Vernimmen et al. (2000), Vatn et al. (2002), Perling and Poleman (2004) and Rørstad et al. (2007).

4. *Cost of monitoring.* An economic instrument needs to be monitored and followed-up. Different instruments involve different degrees of monitoring. Transaction costs for the administrators need to be considered.

5. *Incentives to technological change.* Different instruments may have different incentives for farmers to develop and take into use new technology. A regulatory directive, on the contrary, often does not involve similar carrots or sticks for technological change.

6. *Distributional effects.* The introduction of an economic instrument affects the distribution of how social costs are borne between producers and consumers, between production lines, between regions between the industry sector and government (e.g. Weersink and Livernois, 1996).

7. *Flexibility.* The flexibility of the economic instrument may be important when new information is obtained

(see the Stern review on the economics of climate change, 2006).

8. *Consistency with other policies.* Economic instruments need to be consistent with other policy objectives (production policy, income policy, trade policy, fiscal policy).

Finally, it is worth noting that economic instruments can be used for many different agricultural problem settings. Different problems may need different policy design. It is therefore possible to make a distinction between policy instruments for nutrient pollution reduction from point sources and non-point sources (see Fact Box 2), for soil erosion, for pesticides, for biodiversity, for landscape and for greenhouse gases.

Theory of Externalities

The basic economic theory behind economic instruments is the theory of externalities. Arthur Cecil Pigou was the first to propose the use of a tax to correct the market mechanism for externalities. He made a distinction between private and social marginal net benefits. He also claimed that the government can correct the market mechanism for market failures through imposition of taxes or subsidies, i.e. he claimed externalities can be internalised with the markets through the use of a tax or a subsidy. The most well-known work of Pigou is the book 'The Economics of Welfare' (1920), in which he developed these ideas. An external cost exists when two conditions prevail: 1) An activity by one agent causes a loss of welfare to another agent; and 2) the loss of welfare is uncompensated. Both conditions need to be fulfilled. If the loss of welfare is compensated, the externality is said to be internalised (Pearce and Turner, 1991). Another way to express the phenomenon according to Baumol and Oates (1988) is that an externality is present when two conditions are fulfilled:

> '*Condition 1.*
> *An externality is present whenever some individual's (say A's) **utility** or **production** relationships include real (nonmonetary) variables, whose val-*

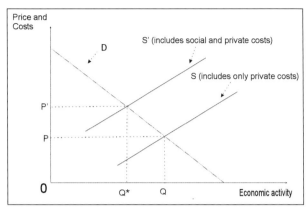

Figure 60.1. Social and private costs in the paper market according to Goodstein (1999, p. 33).

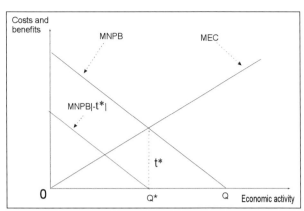

Figure 60.2. Optimal tax on the externalities according to Pearce and Turner (1991, p. 86).

ues are chosen by others (persons, corporations, governments) without particular attention to the effects on A's welfare.....

Condition 2.

The decision maker, whose activity affects others' utility levels or enters their production functions, does not pay (receive) in compensation for this activity an amount equal in value to the resulting costs (or benefits) to others'.

If the producer of the externality is forced to compensate the victims for the damage imposed, the external costs are said to be *internalised,* or in short the externality is internalised (Baumol and Oates, 1988).

We may think of an example modified after Goodstein (1999). Let us imagine a paper factory discharging emissions that pollute a stream so that most fish are dying and bathing is becoming impossible. Obviously the factory is causing a negative externality (social costs) both for fishermen and for people using the river for recreation. The factory does not compensate the fishermen or the swimmers. Both conditions for an externality are met. This implies that the full social and private costs of the factory are different. Figure 60.1 illustrates this.

Both the demand D and supply curves of paper are illustrated in the figure. The supply curve S including only private costs (excluding social costs) leads to too low a price on paper and a higher quantity of paper produced (Q) than the social optimum. The intersection between the demand curve and supply curve, which takes into account the full social costs S', leads to a production corresponding only to Q*. The social and the private optimum differ in this case. Obviously the social optimum can be reached by imposing a tax $t = (P'–P)$ on the paper itself (or on some of its inputs or the emissions). It is important to note that this does not imply zero pollution. If we look at costs alone, we would like them to be as low as possible, but there is a trade-off between costs and production.

Environmental Taxes

Using the theory of externalities, it has been shown that a tax on the externality (e.g. a tax on a point-source discharge to a watercourse) can optimise social welfare when markets are competitive and information is complete. This is illustrated by Figure 60.2.

In Figure 60.2 the marginal externality curve MEC is shown. In general, the negative externalities which follow from economic activity and production increase with increasing activity. For example, waterways may be able to tolerate a modest amount of emissions. If the intensity of emissions increases, the self-purifying capacity of a river or a lake may be exceeded or the total carrying capacity may be in danger. This implies rising marginal externalities for each marginal unit of production. The curve MNPB, on the other hand, shows the marginal net private benefits from production for the polluting pro-

Fact Box 4. Tax on Fertilisers

Rougour et al. (2001) have compiled experiences with fertiliser taxes in Europe. According to this compilation, the price elasticity of demand for fertilisers in Austria, Finland and Sweden varied between -0.1 and -0.5. In Finland, taxes on nitrogen (N) fertilisers were in use between 1 July 1976 and 1 July 1994 and on phosphorus (P) fertiliser between 1 January 1992 and 1 July 1994. The tax on N varied between FIM 0.03/kg and FIM 2.90/kg. For P-fertilisers the tax was FIM 1.70/kg (Sumelius, 1994; Bäckman, 1999). These taxes were abolished when Finland joined the European Union, but Swedish farmers have paid taxes on artificial fertilisers since 1 July 1984.

Some estimates of the cost efficiency of these fertiliser taxes exist. A distinction between the social cost efficiency and the private cost efficiency has been made in many cases. The social abatement cost for Finnish fertiliser taxes, which are compensated for by an acreage subsidy, was estimated at FIM 24.7 (EUR 4.15) per abated kg N leaching using a Danish leakage function (the reduction in leaching was simulated to be 30%). According to the results, the use of buffer zones was a more cost efficient way to reduce leaching than fertiliser taxes (Lankoski and Ollikainen, 1999). In Norway, Vatn et al. (1997) estimated the corresponding social marginal abatement cost to be about NOK 4/kg abated N leaching. The social average cost was estimated at NOK 20/kg reduced N leaching (the variation was NOK 13-37/kg abated N leaching). The private cost for the farmers varied between NOK 96-138/kg abated N leaching (EUR 12.8-18.4). The difference between private and social costs in this case depends on the fact that the agricultural support has been deducted from the social costs. Sumelius et al. (2005) estimated marginal abatement costs of an N fertiliser tax and an N quota in Croatia which aims to prevent NO_3 levels from rising. On a sample of maize-producing farms the marginal social costs were found to be negative (i.e. a social return). The average abatement cost of both N taxes and a quota was estimated at EUR 0.921/mg NO_3 l^{-1}, (EUR 0.208/mg N l^{-1}). None of the studies cited took account of transaction costs or monitoring costs.

be achieved if a tax t* corresponding to the difference between the MNPB and the MEC curves is levied on the economic activity.

However, there are several weaknesses connected with the theory of Pigou:

1. In order to determine the right tax, *perfect information* is needed. This is rarely the case in real life. Imperfect information is more of a rule than of an exception. It is hard to establish individual sources and amount of discharges for non-point source pollution. Assymetric information is also common. This implies that the environmental planner and a producer do not have access to the same information.
2. Externalities are *difficult to measure*, so one needs to use proxies instead such as nutrient loading. In the case of non-point source pollution, even the proxies are difficult to measure. It is therefore hard to target instruments (Horan and Shortle, 2001). A tax on an externality may imply an emission fee, an ambient fee, an input fee or a product fee. In real life taxes have often been levied on inputs (e.g. fertilisers), which is not a very close proxy for an externality (see Fact Box 4 for some studies on fertiliser taxes).
3. The theory does not solve the problem of *spatial and temporal heterogeneity*, which is particularly important when it comes to non-point source pollution.

The Coase Theorem

The discussion on the need to regulate an externality has not gone undisputed. According to Nobel Prize winner Ronald Coase (1960), if a polluter and the victim can *bargain* about the outcome of how much of the externality (social cost) should be allowed and what the compensation to the victims should be, negotiation should lead to an efficient outcome regardless of the initial property rights. In other words, let the victims and the polluter negotiate instead of imposing taxes or other instruments from the outside. It has been shown that the theorem only holds under limited restrictions (no transaction costs for negotiations, perfect information, and small number of victims).

ducer (marginal benefits minus marginal costs for one unit of production). The marginal private net benefits are decreasing. This means the net value of each extra unit of production is decreasing. According to profit-maximising behaviour, the polluter is producing an amount of the goods corresponding to Q in the diagram. The external cost for each unit produced is again increasing with increasing production. The optimal point which shows the combination of marginal private net benefits is given by Q* in the diagram. At this level of production the benefits from increased production correspond to the marginal external cost. According to Pigou, such an optimum can

Permits and Quotas

One possibility to regulate undesired emissions is to establish emissions permits or quotas (an emission standard) for pollution sources. A precondition for such a system is that it is possible to measure the emissions. This is not always possible. However, it is possible to use a quota for the inputs, e.g. for fertilisers. Production quotas are common in many countries (e.g. for milk and sugar within the EU). Denmark has established quotas for nitrogen fertilisers and since 2002 it is possible to sell and buy such N quotas, which have been tightened within a certain time period. The N quotas are set according to the crop: In cereal production the quota is 105 kg N/ha, in other crop cultivation 145 kg N/ha; within dairy production 122 kg N/ha and within pork production 106 kg N/ha. The system of N quotas has reduced the use of N fertilisers by 22%. The average price of an N quota is DKK 28/kg N, although the variation is large: DKK 7.9-85/kg N. The average marginal value is in most cases below DKK 10/kg N, which means that farmers selling N quotas have received a good price for them (Jacobsen, 2004). The total reduction in N leaching as a consequence of N quotas is 4 tons of N. According to Grant and Waagepetersen (2003), the overall reduction in N leaching from agriculture is estimated to be 143,000 tonnes (from 311,000 tonnes in the middle of the 1980s to 168,000 tonnes in 2002), so the quota system accounts for a small proportion. Note, however, that these estimates on reduced N leaching include a high degree of uncertainty. A problem with most studies on quotas is that the costs of monitoring may be substantial. Alternatively, monitoring may be done in a less costly way, but enforcement may then pose problems.

Marketable Emission Permits

Instead of regulating the price of the externality with charges or taxes, it is also possible to regulate the quantity of the externality by setting a total level standard S and then letting the polluters bargain about emission permits. Such an economic instrument is called a system of *marketable emission permits*, (also called *emission trading permits*, or *tradeable permits*). The first one to propose

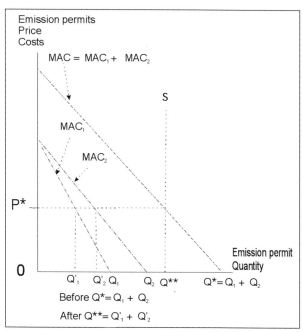

Figure 60.3. Minimisation of costs with marketable emission permits, modified after Pearce and Turner (1991).

such a system was Martin L. Weitzman in his seminal article in 1974. According to Weitzman, whether emission taxes or emission permits are more effective depends on the curvature of the marginal cost curve. Emission permits are recommended when the aim is to achieve a certain reduction in emissions, ΔQ, at least cost, and when the quantities of emissions can be measured. The reduction in emissions will be achieved cost-effectively if permissions to emit are traded freely once such a level has been established. While it must be possible to measure or approximate the emissions, it is not necessary for the social planner to know the cost curves of reduction (marginal and average control cost curves). According to the theory, the initial distribution of pollution rights will not affect the end outcome. The market mechanism will guarantee that a cost-efficient distribution of marketable emission permits develops. Every polluter will decrease its pollution to the point where the marginal abatement cost is equal to the marginal control costs (marginal abatement cost) (Baumol and Oates, 1988). This is illustrated in Figure 60.3 for a market with only two polluting companies.

Company 1 initially emits an amount Q_1 and company 2 a somewhat higher amount, Q_2 so that the total amount of emissions is $Q^* = Q_1 + Q_2$. The social planner decides that the total level of emissions can be S at maximum and a corresponding amount of permits $S = Q^{**}$ is issued so that both companies can buy based upon best offer. The companies can also trade these permits with each other after initial purchase. From Figure 60.3 it is evident that company 1 has lower marginal abatement costs (control costs) MAC_1 than company 2, which has marginal abatement costs MAC_2. Company 1 will reduce its emission to Q'_1 because this is less expensive than buying emission permits. However, it is more expensive to reduce emissions to a higher degree than $Q_1 - Q'_1$ than buying permits. Therefore company 1 will buy emission permits corresponding to Q'_1. Company 2 will correspondingly reduce its emissions by an amount corresponding to $Q_2 - Q'_2$ and buy Q'_2 permits. The total amount of emission will correspond to Q^{**} and the reduction in emissions $\Delta Q = Q^* - Q^{**}$ will be achieved cost efficiently. When implemented in this way the major advantage with a system with marketable emission permits is cost efficiency. However, in order to implement such a system emissions need to be determined and followed-up. The *Emission Trading Programme* (ETS) for greenhouse gases of the European Union is based on marketable emission permits.

A system of marketable emissions is of limited relevance for non-point source pollution, since emissions according to definitions are diffuse and emissions cannot generally be measured.

Trading programmes based on emissions-for-estimated loadings have been proposed, as well as emissions-for-input trading in order to overcome the problem (Horan and Shortle, 2001).

Subsidies, Agri-environmental Schemes

Subsidies are common economic instruments for reducing agricultural pollution. The purpose is often to change agricultural practices in an environmentally friendly manner and to lower the cost of these technologies. The subsidy is in this case cost-sharing. Practical examples of implementation are various agri-environmental schemes where annual farm level costs of implementing good agricultural practices are lowered through an area-based payment (see e.g. Sumelius, 1999). Such agricultural practices typically may be buffer strips or zones, reduced tillage, animal density restrictions, restricted fertiliser doses and timely restriction of manure spreading. Such agri-environmental schemes have been implemented in Finland since 1995. Partly because of the scheme, partly because of changes in the input-output price relationship, average fertiliser doses have decreased, from 101.6 kg N/ha and 20.0 kg P/ha in the cropping year 1994/05 to 73.9 kg N/ha and 8.6 P kg/ha in 2005/2006 (Yearbook of Farm Statistics, 2006). However, in two follow-up studies of the agri-environmental schemes in four watersheds, no significant changes in leaching of nutrients as a consequence of the agri-environmental schemes were found (Palva et al., 2001; Pyykkönen et al., 2004). One possible explanation is that natural factors such as soil type, slope and precipitation have such a large influence that the scheme is too rough an instrument for directing practices on problematic parcels. Another possible explanation is that old practices persist and some fields are still overfertilised. A third explanation is that animal husbandry has become more and more concentrated and that manure is spread on the same parcels from year to year.

Another common application is subsidies for organic agriculture (e.g. Reeder, 2005; Pietola and Lansink, 2001). Investment support for manure facilities is also common. Subsidies for design-based technologies are another typical example. According to Horan and Shortle (2001, p. 24-25), if authorities are willing to use subsidies at levels that will have an impact, one can expect an impact from input base incentives.

Subsidies have some drawbacks. They are not in accordance with the Polluters Pays Principle, which is somewhat problematic, especially in the case when emissions can be measured. Subsidies may also increase the probability of entry decisions of polluting companies, so total loading may increase. However, sharing the cost of measures for good agricultural practices and best management practices has been advocated in order to increase the probability of farmers adopting measures for which the social benefits exceed the costs (Carpentier, 1996). Subsidies can be designed so that they induce farmers to adopt environmentally sound agricultural measures.

Such measures and their farm level cost efficiency are presented in Table 60.1, which is taken from a Danish study (Jacobsen, 2004).

According to the table, the most cost-efficient measure on farm level seems to be tightened requirements on utilisation of N in animal manure, followed by wetlands, better utilisation of feed, decreased recommended doses for fertilisation and catch crops. Transaction costs for the businesses and the administrative costs of monitoring were not taken into account. Note also that most of these measures were probably not subsidised.

Penalties, Liabilities

A liability rule is classified as an ambient-based incentive. An individual who can be proved to have spoilt the assets or health of some others may be ordered to pay a penalty. For instance, a producer or pesticide dealer contaminating groundwater with pesticides may be given fines and ordered to pay damages. The liability rule is ambient-based, since the sanctions are only imposed after the damage has been done. In this way it is supposed to serve as an *ex ante* incentive, preventing high levels of pesticides in groundwater (Shortle and Abler, 1997; Horan and Shortle, 2001).

Command and Control (Administrative Instruments)

The most common type of environmental policies is based on some sort of *standard* or *direct regulation* (Hodge, 1995). This approach is called 'command and control', or administrative instruments. It can take various forms. For instance, it can be a stipulation that manure storage has to correspond to a certain minimum volume in order not to spread manure in winter time; it may concern time of spreading manure; it may be a certain maximum limit on animal density; or it may be cross-compliance conditions in order to be eligible for a certain programme such as the cross-compliance measures within the European Union. The major advantage with command and control

Table 60.1. Cost efficiency on farm level of the water environmental plan II (Vandmiljøplan II) (Jacobsen, 2004).

	Annual costs	Cost efficiency
	Million DKK	DKK/kg N
Wetlands[1]	5	7
Environmentally Sensitive Areas directives	57	81
Plantation of forests[1]	35	44
Organic agriculture	104	28
Better utilisation of feed	43	11
Tightened requirements on animal density[2]	11	78
Catch crops (6%)	48	16
Tightened requirements on utilisation of N in animal manure (15%)	50	5
Decreased recommendations for fertilisation (10%)	170	13
Total	523	15

1) Calculated with a 4 % interest rate
2) For dairy cows from 2.3 animal units (AU)/ha to 1.7 AU/ha, for pigs and plant cultivation farms from 1.7 AU/ha to 1.4 AU/ha and for other farms from 2.0 AU/ha to 1.4 AU/ha

measures according to Hodge is that they are easy to introduce and administer. However, the problematic issue with command and control measures relates to the fact that they are often not very cost-effective. The amount of information to be collected for command and control measures to be effective is often substantial because of a diversity of conditions characterising operating firms (e.g. agricultural enterprises). For instance, a regulation stipulating maximum fertiliser doses may come into force. Leaching and surface runoff, on the other hand, depend upon the soil type, the crop, the timing and the yield level, factors which involve individual information not only on farm but on field level. In order to be cost-effective, the regulation would have to be able to account for all these factors, not only on each farm but in each field of every single farm. Costs of implementing a standard on emissions differ substantially between different businesses. Because of this, a uniform standard regulation seldom minimises costs. On the other hand, it seems plausible that most farmers have more detailed information on their own farm than the regulator. It would be better to use an instrument that can make use of this information. The kind of information that is needed in that case is described in two other chapters of this book. Gustafson (this volume) outline the factors influencing leaching of nitrogen and the complexities connected to soil and climate, while Ulén et al. (this volume) discuss phosphorus management and best management practices in order to reduce phosphorus losses.

Those variables are typically site-specific and are likely to be better known by the farmer who is cultivating the fields.

When are regulations generally preferred? According to Horan and Shortle (2001), such a situation exists when the societal cost of the use of an input or process exceeds the expected benefits for any level of use. Hazardous pesticides are a clear example. Another may be the social desirability to avoid long-term soil compaction due to high axle load traffic (Håkansson and Petelkau, 1994; Alakukku 1997).

Some of the most important international regulations from the Baltic Sea point of view are the Nitrate Directive, the Water Framework Directive and the Baltic Sea Action Plan. Increased concern that NO_3 leaching was becoming a significant problem led to the Nitrate Directive addressed to EU Member States in 1991. The main objective of the Nitrate Directive is to reduce water pollution resulting from, or induced by, the NO_3 that comes from agricultural sources, and to prevent further such pollution. The Nitrate Directive recognises ground- and surfacewater containing more than 50 mg NO_3 l^{-1} as being situated in vulnerable zones (Directive 91/676/EEC). A more recent EU Directive, the Water Framework Directive, requires the state of surface waters to be sustained and improved by controlling the input of nutrients, the aim being for all surface waters to have a good ecological status by 2015 (Directive 2000/60/EC, Ekholm et al., 2007). The Baltic Sea Action Plan is a plan signed by all the countries around the Baltic Sea which aims at reducing losses of nitrogen and phosphorus in 2008. It allows the countries to develop national programmes to achieve the reductions in a cost-effective way. The measures may include reduction in agricultural inputs, including manure, as well as improvement in the treatment of wastewater. In accordance with the relevant parts of this Convention, the Contracting Parties must apply the measures and take into account Best Environmental Practice (BEP) and Best Available Technology (BAT) to reduce the pollution from agricultural activities. These measures concern animal density, storage of manure, location and design of farm animal houses, application of manure and application rates for nutrients and other factors influencing losses of nitrogen and phosphorus (HELCOM, 2007, 2008).

Labelling

Labelling of food is one way of providing information to consumers about technologies used by farmers and possible environmental, animal welfare or other effects. A label may provide a guarantee for consumers that a product is produced in an environmentally friendly way. Possible higher costs of production are passed on to consumers in order to prevent undesired effects of technologies. In this way consumers are made aware about the effects of their consumption decisions. Labels typically may be organically produced products, local products or animal products where a given husbandry method has been used to take care of animal welfare (e.g. producing free range eggs). Labelling is usually put in practice by the food trading chains and retailers. Appropriate legislation about what are correct labelling practices is therefore important.

Conclusions

This chapter reviewed a number of carrots and sticks for internalising external effects of agriculture, typically linked to an environmental issue. Many of the instruments described have a theoretical foundation. However, all instruments rest on some assumptions. These assumptions are adequate for some situations but less adequate for others. The environmental tax is suitable when externalities can be measured, which is rarely the case. A somewhat good proxy would be emissions from point sources. Because of spatial and temporal heterogeneity, measurement is not feasible for non-point sources. Instead, input taxes are being applied. Taxes on inputs have the disadvantage that inputs are taxed regardless of intensity level. On low intensity level, a tax on an input on a non-leaching soil may be quite a different thing from a tax on a negative externality. The assumption of perfect information by the regulator is often not valid. Information is also often assymetrical. Tradeable permits can only be used when emissions can be measured. Command and control measures, on the other hand, are usually quite costly rough measures. Given these shortcomings, well-designed instruments particularly suitable for the problem at hand should be employed.

Focus on Nutrients
Advisory Service, Training and Information

61

Christine Jakobsson
Uppsala University, Uppsala, Sweden

Introduction

The advisory and information project Focus on Nutrients (in Swedish Greppa Näringen) was introduced in 2001 by the Swedish Board of Agriculture in collaboration with the Federation of Swedish Farmers (LRF), county authorities and agricultural advisory organisations. It offers free environmental advice to farms of more than 50 hectares and/or more than 25 animal units*. The aims are to reduce emissions of greenhouse gases from agriculture, to reduce nitrogen and phosphorus losses from agriculture in a cost-effective way and to promote the safe handling of crop protection products. Focus on Nutrients is funded by the Swedish Government, the EU and reinvested environmental taxes. In recent years around 2.9 million Euros have been spent annually, of which three-quarters went to the individual advice sessions that are provided free of charge to farmers.

The project takes the form of a campaign to provide training and advice and aims to encompass the entire flow of

* animal unit: 1 cow, 1 horse, 3 sows, 10 slaughter pigs, 100 poultry

nutrients on the farm. The background to the project is the Swedish national environmental quality objectives (EQO). Farmers are expected to voluntarily implement measures to reach the goals as a result of the advisory service. They can choose between approximately 20 different advisory modules suitable for the different production specialisations on farms and, together with the advisor, develop concrete solutions that benefit both the environment and farm profits.

Table 61.1. Swedish environmental quality objectives and areas covered by the Focus on nutrients project.

Swedish EQO	Area covered by Focus on Nutrients
Zero Eutrophication	Phosphorus losses, nitrogen leaching, ammonia volatilisation
Natural Acidification Only	Ammonia volatilisation
Good-Quality Groundwater	Nitrogen leaching
Reduced Climate Impact	Nitrous oxide emissions (nitrogen leaching)
A Non Toxic Environment	Handling of plant protection chemicals

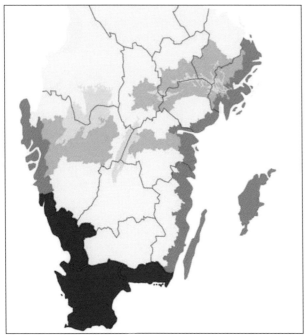

Figure 61.1. Map of Sweden showing environmentally sensitive areas in terms of the EU Nitrate Directive (SBA, 2006).

Resources Directed to Where the Need is Greatest

Focus on Nutrients started in Southern Sweden, where agriculture is more intensive, the environmental impact is larger and environmental protection measures have the greatest effect. Advisory work was extended in stages to include all the plains of Götaland and Svealand (Central Sweden), a region identified as being nitrate-sensitive according to the EU Nitrate Directive (Figure 61.1) as well as since 2010 to several bordering counties (Jonköping, Kronoberg, Dalarna, Värmland and Gävleborg). The reasons for this are that advisory service on climate change is recently offered and some of the waterbodies in these counties are not classified as good ecological status according to the EU Water directive. Northern Sweden is still not included, mainly due to its very extensive agriculture leading to a smaller impact on the environment. The county authorities procure advisory services from advisory firms or organisations.

There are many different ways to reduce nutrient leaching, some of which are more important than others. The most critical are:

- Adapt animal feeding strategies to the animals needs of nitrogen and phosphorus (do not overfeed with protein).
- Decreasing nitrogen emissions from animal houses to a minimum.
- Decreasing nutrient losses from manure storage and during spreading to a minimum.
- Spreading farmyard manure when there is little risk of nutrient losses.
- Having fewer occasions when more than the optimal amount of nutrients is applied to crops.
- Decreasing fertilisation for a high protein content in crops.
- Carrying out as much soil tillage as possible in spring or late autumn.
- Increased cultivation of catch crops.
- A larger area of wetlands.

Sequence of Advisory Modules

The advisor applies the EQO at the level of the individual farm and goes through all the possible ways of decreasing nutrient losses to the atmosphere and water. The need for advice varies from farm to farm and is tailored accordingly. The advice offered is divided into different modules, some of which apply to all farms, e.g. nutrient balance. Each farm is unique and many farms have already drawn up a nutrient balance. After that, the advice required is tailored according to the specialisation and type of livestock on the farm. Advice is provided by different local advisors and it is up to the farmer to choose. The service starts with a single farm visit and relies on the advisor returning to monitor the outcome of the advice given. To help in this process, different key environmental indicators are calculated. These are documented so that the progress in improvements can be traced. Below the modules in Focus on Nutrients are listed. A later addition is the module on climate change and it should also be mentioned that all modules are climate secured.

- Start – planning advisory needs
- Basic nutrient balance
- Repeat nutrient balance
- Nitrogen strategy
- Phosphorus strategy
- Soil compaction
- Handling of plant protection chemicals

- Planning wetlands
- Grass crop strategy
- Animal housing environment
- Planning of buildings
- Inspection of feeding plan for dairy cows
- Inspection of feeding plan for beef cattle
- Grazing strategy
- Feed consumption recording for piglets
- Feed consumption recording for fattening pigs
- Climate change strategy

More Information Pathways Used

Towards the end of this ten-year period, 7,250 farmers are receiving recurrent advisory services. Some 700 have received advisory services but are no longer farmers. 1,350 have received advice about wetlands or water protection and some 750 have signed up to use calculation services on the website. This corresponds to a total participation of 10,050 farmers. The advisory services have had the greatest uptake in the county of Skåne, in the south of Sweden, where more than 60% of the arable land belongs to farms within Focus on Nutrients. All members receive a membership letter twice a year. The project website www.greppa.nu is an information channel directed at both farmers and advisors. Environmental news, assessment of manure and calculation of nutrient balances are examples of functions used by farmers visiting the website. Advisors obtain material for their advisory work via a special link. Training courses are provided for advisors.

Benefits of the Project

Information is collected from the first visit and is stored in a database. This provides a description of cropping practices and plant nutrient balances and how they have changed after the advisory service. Other evaluation methods include postal questionnaires on environmental attitudes, protection measures and opinions on the project.

Nutrient Leaching

A plant nutrient budget for nitrogen, phosphorus and potassium is calculated on many farms. The inflow of nitrogen to the farm occurs through purchased products, i.e. feed and fertilisers, deposition and nitrogen fixation. The outflow of nitrogen takes place through products, e.g. crops and livestock (meat and milk). What remains is called sur-

plus, of which a small fraction is transformed to increase the soil humus content, but the majority is lost as ammonia emissions, leaching and denitrification. On a Swedish arable farm, the nitrogen use efficiency is often around 70%, which means that 30% of the nitrogen supplied is lost. The surplus is often between 30 to 50 kg per hectare. Nitrogen use efficiency on livestock farms varies between 25 and 70% depending on animal species and number of animals per hectare. On an intensive dairy farm, the nitrogen surplus is often around 150 kg per hectare in southern Sweden. The conversion of plant products to animal products leads to unavoidable losses (Figure 61.2). On 35

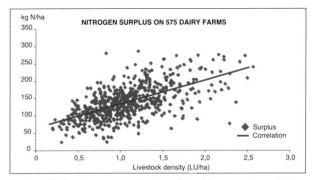

Figure 61.2. The nitrogen surplus is explained by ammonia emissions, nitrogen leaching, nitrogen gas emissions and some storage in the soil. The surplus increases with increasing the surplus on many farms. Data from Focus on Nutrient farms (SLU).

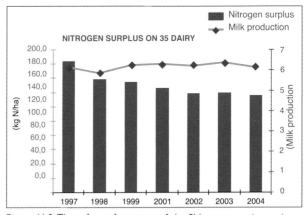

Figure 61.3. These farms form part of the Skåne creameries environmental bonus programme and have continuous balances from 1997 with the exception of the year 2000. Milk production has remained fairly constant (~ 6,000 kg milk/hectare) but the nitrogen surplus has decreased over time (SLU).

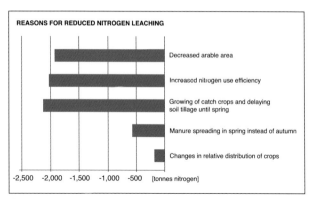

REASONS FOR REDUCED NITROGEN LEACHING

Decreased arable area

Increased nitrogen use efficiency

Growing of catch crops and delaying soil tillage until spring

Manure spreading in spring instead of autumn

Changes in relative distribution of crops

-2,500   -2,000   -1,500   -1,000   -500   [tonnes nitrogen]

Figure 61.4. Calculations show that nitrogen leaching from agriculture has decreased by 12% (7,000 tonnes) over eight years (1995-2003) (SLU).

Figure 61.5. Injector machine for incorporation of slurry, which reduces ammonia losses (SBA, 2007).

milk-producing 'environmental bonus farms' that were monitored over a long period, the nitrogen surplus decreased by over 45 kg per hectare from 1997, with a 7 kg decrease in the period 2001-2004 (Figure 61.3), showing that it is possible to decrease surpluses and that long-term work produces rewards. The decrease in nitrogen leaching from Swedish fields is mainly explained by farmers growing considerably more catch crops, nitrogen use efficiency being improved, a decrease in the area of arable land and delayed soil tillage (Figure 61.4). The decrease in leaching depends to a lesser extent on changes in livestock numbers and in the time of manure spreading.

Concrete Measures

Changes in cropping practices such as reducing manure spreading in early autumn and performing soil tillage, especially ploughing of ley, to a larger extent in the spring can lead to decreased nitrogen leaching. Agriculture is dependent on the weather and therefore there have to be certain margins in cropping, as variations between years remain. In very dry or wet years it is difficult to get high yields, which leads to poorer returns on nitrogen and greater losses. One way to decrease the flow of nitrogen that continues to leach out despite preventive measures is the establishment of wetlands. Conversion of nitrate nitrogen to nitrogen gas and increased biological diversity are both benefits created by wetlands. Almost 3,700 hectares of new wetlands were established in Sweden in the period 2000-2005.

Better Manure Handling Decreases Ammonia Emissions

Ammonia losses have decreased on many farms, partly due to increased precision in manure spreading, such as more incorporation of manure (Figure 61.5). A positive development is that many farmers are converting from a solid manure system to slurry, but if the manure is not quickly incorporated into the soil the entire nutrient gains can be lost. On livestock farms in particular, there are many ways to reduce emissions. Ammonia emissions represent 25% of the nitrogen surplus on dairy farms and nitrogen gas emissions 20%. Nitrogen gas emissions are a loss for the farmer but are not an environmental problem, although small amounts of the greenhouse gas nitrous oxide are emitted. The most critical deciding factors in decreasing ammonia emissions are appropriate storage and spreading of manure. Losses during storage can be avoided through good

Table 61.2. Phosphorous surplus more than halved. Repeated nutrient balance calculations on 64 pig farms (SBA, 2009).

Difference per hectare between inflow and out-flow of phospho-rus with:	First balance year 2002	Balance year 2004	Difference between balances
Feed	27.1	25.2	-1.9
Fertiliser, bedding	0.6	0.6	0.0
Animal products	-8.2	-9.7	-1.5
Vegetable products	-11.8	-13.5	-1.7
Surplus	7.7	2.6	-5.1

covering and thus decreased air exchange, which is easiest for slurry. Spreading of manure on open soil is decreasing and spreading in ley and other growing crops is increasing. The project has shown so far that farmers nowadays seldom spread manure during unsuitable weather conditions such as warm and windy weather, while increasing numbers are incorporating manure more promptly.

Animal Diet and Housing Important for Ammonia Emissions

Another important measure to reduce the nitrogen content in urine and faeces produced by livestock is to supply the correct diet and not overfeed animals with protein. On 575 dairy participating farms, a 4-6% reduction in the inflow of protein-rich concentrate has been observed in recent years but milk production has still increased due to more efficient forage production and feeding strategies.

Additional measures to prevent ammonia emissions often involve high costs, for example conversion of livestock housing and manure containers, and can often only be implemented in new buildings or if the investment is heavily subsidised. Such measures include cooling manure in manure tanks, installing efficient urine separation, decreasing the manure area in houses and building roofs over manure containers.

Increasing Efforts for Phosphorus

Efforts are now being increased to obtain knowledge and produce new advice regarding phosphorus. The improved Greppa Näringen prevention programme for phosphorus losses involves:

- Decreasing the amount of phosphorus that can be lost
- Decreasing the risk of phosphorus leaving the field
- Capturing the phosphorus lost from fields.

Both dairy and pig production farms have similar surplus in their plant nutrient balance and in the case of phosphorus this is mainly a question of avoiding overfeeding the animals, as a large proportion of the phosphorus supplied to animals via the diet ends up in the manure. It is also important for farmers to have an up-to-date soil map of their fields so that they can refine their fertilisation strategy. Phosphorus fertilisation can often be decreased on many farms with potato crops. Focus on Nutrients has found that on most farms phosphorus fertilisation is well adjusted to crop requirements but on livestock farms there are still gains to be made by applying manure to all fields on the farm and not only in the vicinity of the animal housing (Table 61.2).

Appropriate Tillage and Barrier Zones Stop Field Losses

To decrease the risk of phosphorus leaving the field, it is necessary for the farmer to know their fields well, to know how water moves and where it collects in hollows and to prevent phosphorus dissolved on soil particles from reaching the water environment. Careful soil tillage gives rapid infiltration, which decreases the risk of phosphorus being lost in surface runoff. Environmental subsidies are available for the creation of riparian zones along watercourses and lakes and for establishing wetlands on suitable sites in the agricultural landscape. Wetlands do not decrease the amount of phosphorus, but prevent it from leaching out into sensitive watercourses. They can be seen as a filter and the material they capture is collected in the bottom sediment and must be removed on occasion. Barrier zones are frequently implemented. In one of the latest environmental target reviews, 88% of farmers reported that they had established such zones along watercourses. In addition, 63% are now growing grass on land prone to flooding and many of those who have surface water wells in arable fields have ensured that there is grass growing around them.

Safer Handling of Crop Protection Products

Around 90% of farmers surveyed in Focus on Nutrients fill their crop sprayers on impermeable slabs or similar and thus decrease the risk of crop protection chemicals leaking out into lakes and watercourses. The project motivates farmers to improve their handling of crop protection chemicals and over 1,000 advice sessions on safer crop protection have been provided. Apart from filling crop sprayers on an impervious surface where water is collected – or on a biobed – around 90% also test the function of their crop sprayers regularly nowadays. The use of glyphosate (Roundup) in conjunction with weed control on farm yards and other paved areas has decreased compared with previously.

The Vemmenhög Project led by Jenny Kreuger at SLU shows that it is possible to decrease the occurrence of pesticide residues in watercourses by 90%, despite almost no changes being made to the amounts of crop protection chemicals used (described in Chapter 24). This is achieved through safer handling of crop protection chemicals, a measure that has been promoted in advisory work in Swedish agriculture in recent years. In addition to the work on avoiding point sources of emissions, this is increasingly a question of choice of chemical.

Losses of glyphosate can be particularly large on clay soils, while other pesticides leach more readily from sandy soils. The intrinsic leaching properties of different crop protection chemicals and the timing of application have a great impact on the occurrence of chemical residues in watercourses. Fewer autumn sprayings are recommended, since these carry a greater leaching risk. The soil is often saturated with water at this time of the year, while crop uptake and evaporation are minimal. Therefore excess water in the soil goes towards filling the groundwater reserves or runs out via the drainage system and the risk of undesirable transport of chemical residues increases.

Epilogue

Sustainable Agriculture – Cross-cutting Themes, Truly Multidisciplinary.

We hope that the reader has gained an appreciation of the themes and approaches of Sustainable Agriculture. Naturally it is up to each reader to decide on their own definition and picture of Sustainable Agriculture for the future, which will probably differ depending on the individual and the specific case. In this series of books we attempt to highlight the importance of an ecosystem approach as regards sustainable agriculture. We strongly recommend that readers study the other two volumes in this educational series:

> *Rural Development and Land Use (ed. Ingrid Karlsson and Lars Rydén)*

> *Ecology and Animal Health (ed. Leif Norrgren and Jeffrey Levengood)*

Sustainable agriculture is an approach to securing the necessary resources for safeguarding global food produc-tion, biodiversity reserves, recreation needs, water quality and well developed rural areas and wildlife areas. It can also be an effective means of poverty reduction and of achieving the Millennium Development Goals, as well as means of mitigating climate change. It is also about health, welfare, respect and ethics regarding both animals and man, as well as quality of food and feed.

We would also like to thank all the scientists and experts that have contributed to these books as well as our financiers, SIDA, SEPA and SI. Without all of your sustained support and interest, the project would not have been possible.

Uppsala, 2011-08-15

Christine Jakobsson, Leif Norrgren, Jeffrey Levengood, Ingrid Karlsson and Lars Rydén

References

Chapter 1

Helsinki Commission. 1998. *Agenda 21 for the Baltic Sea Region, Sustainable Development of the Agricultural Sector in the Baltic Sea Region*, Baltic Sea Environment Proceedings No. 74, SOU 2003:72. *Ocean- time for a new strategy*

Chapter 2

Johansson, S. 2005. *The Swedish Foodprint. An Agroecological Study of Food Consumtion*. Doctoral Thesis. Swedish University of Agricultural Sciences. Uppsala. Acta Universitatis Agriculturae Sueciae

Johansson, S., Doherty, S. and Rydberg, T. 2000. Sweden Food System Analysis 1996. In: Brown, M.T. (Ed.). *Emergy Synthesis: Theory and Applications of the Emergy Methodology*. First Biennial Emergy Analysis Research Conference. Gainesville, FL.

Odum, H.T. 2007. *Environment, power, and society, for the twenty-first century the hierarchy of energy*. Colombia University Press, New York

WWF, 2008. *Living Planet Report 2008*. (Ed. In Chief, Chris Halls., Eds. Sarah Humphrey, Jonathan Loh and Steven Goldfinger) WWF International Avenue du Mont.Blanc, Gland, Switzerland.

Chapter 3

Ahlgren, S., Baky, A., Bernesson, S., Nordberg, Å., Norén, O. and Hansson, P-A. 2009. Ammonium nitrate fertilizer production based on biomass – environmental effects from a life cycle perspective. In: *Bioresource Technology* 99, pp 8034-8041.

Åslund, Y. 1965. *Hjalmar Lundbohm. Lapplands okrönte kung*. 2. Upplagan. LT: Förlag Stockholm.

Becker, P. 1989. *Phosphates and Phosphoric Acid – Raw materials, Technology and Economics of the Wet Process*. Second Edition. Marcel Dekker Inc. New York.

Bertilsson, G., Kirchmann, H., and Bergström, L. 2008. Energy analysis of conventional and organic agricultural system. In: Kirchmann, H. and Bergström L. (Eds.).*Organic Crop Production – Ambitions and Limitations*, Springer, Dordrecht, The Netherlands, pp 173-188.

Bryne, C., Divekar, S.D., Storchan, G.B., Parodi, D.A. and Martin, M.B. 2009. Cadmium – a metallhormone? In: *Toxicology and Applied Pharmacology* 238, pp 266-271.

Buckingham, D.A. and Jasinski, S.M. 2006. *Phosphate Rock Statistics, Historical Statistics for Mineral and Material Commodities in the United States, Data Series* 140 US Geological Survey. Assessed 14.03.2011, available from http://minerals.usgs.gov/ds/2005/140/

Cohen, Y., Kirchmann, H. and Enfält, P. 2011. Management of phosphorus resources – historical perspective, principal problems and sustainable solutions. In: Kumar, S. (Ed) *Waste Management. Book 2*, ISBN 978-953-307-447-4. Intech Open Access Publisher.

Cordell, D., Drangert, J-O. and White, S. 2009. The story of phosphorus: global food security and food for thought. In: *Global Environmental Change*, Vol. 19, pp 292-305.

Driver, J., Lijmbach, D. and Steen, I. 1999. Why recover phosphorus for recycling, and how? In: *Environmental Technology* 20, pp 652-662.

EasyMining. 2011. EasyMining Sweden AB. Assessed 14.03.2011, available from http://www.easymining.se

EFSA, European Food Safety Authority. 2009. Scientific Opinion of the Panel on Contaminants in the Food Chain on a request from the European Commission on cadmium in food. In: *EFSA Journal* 980, pp 1-139.

Energy Information Administration. 2010. *International Energy Outlook 2010*. Assessed 31.03. 2011, available from http://www.eia.doe.gov/oiaf/ieo/index.html

Eriksson, J. 2009. *Strategi för att minska kadmium-belastningen i kedjan mark-livsmedel-människa (Strategi for reduction of cadmium load to the soil-food-human chain in Sweden)*. Swedish University of Agricultural Sciences, Report MAT21 No. 1/2009, Uppsala, Sweden.

FAO. 2008. *Agriculture*. Assessed 10.4.2011, available from ftp://ftp.fao.org/docrep/fao/011/i0765e/i0765e08.pdf

GeoHive. 2010. *Population statistics for agglomerations over 750,000 inhabitants*. Assessed 14.03.2011, available from http://www.geohive.com/earth/cy_aggmillion2.aspx

Greaves, J., Hobbs, P., Chadwick, D. and Haygarth, P. 1999. Prospects for the recovery of phosphorus from animal manures: a review. In: *Environmental Technology* 20, pp 697–708.

Gregory, P.J., Ingram, J.S.I., Andersson, R., Betts, R.A., Brovkin, V., Chase, T.N., Grace, P.R., Gray, A.J., Hamilton, N., Hardy, T.B., Howden, S.M., Jenkins, A., Meybeck, M., Olsson, M., Ortiz-Monasterio, I., Palm, C.A., Payn, T.W., Rummukainen, M., Schulze, R.E., Thiem, M., Valentin, C., and Wilkinson, M.J., 2002, Environmental consequences of alternative practices for intensifying crop production. In: *Agriculture, Ecosystem and Environment* 88, pp 279-290.

Grimm, N.B., Faeth, S.H., Golubiewski, N.E., Redman, C.L., Wu, J., Bai, X. and Briggs, J.M., 2008. Global change and the ecology of cities. In: *Science* 319, pp 756-760.

Haygarth, P.M., Jarvis, S.C., Chapman, P. and Smith, R.V. 1998. Phosphorus budgets for two contrasting grassland farming systems in the UK. In: *Soil Use and Management* 14, pp 1–9.

Heffer, P., Prud'homme, M., Muirhead, B. and Isherwood, K.F. 2006. *Phosphorus fertilization: issues and outlook*. Proceedings 586, International Fertilizer Society, York, UK.

References

IFA. 2010a. The International Fertilizer Industry Association (IFA). *Online production and international trade statistics: production, exports, imports by region from 1999 to 2008.* Assessed 14.03.2011, available from http://www.fertilizer.org/ifa/Home-Page/STATISTICS/Production-and-trade

IFA. 2010b. The International Fertilizer Industry Association (IFA). *SurfIFADATA The IFA database – which contains historical fertilizer production, trade and consumption statistics.* Assessed 07.04.2011, available from http://www.fertilizer.org/ifa/ifadata/search

IFDC. 2010. *World Phosphate Rock Reserves and Resources.* International Fertilizer Development Center. Technical Bulletin T-75.

Joseph, P. 2009. Mechanisms of cadmium carcinogenesis. In: *Toxicology and Applied Pharmacology* 238, pp 272-279.

Järup, L. and Åkesson, A. 2009. Current status of cadmium as an environmental health problem. In: *Toxicology and Applied Pharmacology* 238, pp 201-208.

Kemira Oy. 1980. Kemira exploits low-grade phosphate deposit at Siilinjärvi. In: *Phosphorus and Potassium* 108, pp 31-34.

Kirchmann, H. 1998. Phosphorus flows in Swedish society related to agriculture. In: *Kungliga Skogs- och Lantbruksakademiens Tidskrift* (KSLAT) 135, pp 145-156.

Kirchmann, H., Nyamangara, J. and Cohen, Y. 2005. Recycling municipal wastes in future – from organic to inorganic forms? In: *Soil Use and Management* 21, pp 152 – 159.

Kuligowski, K. and Poulsen, T.G. 2010. Phosphorus dissolution from thermally gasified waste ash using sulphuric acid. In: *Bioresource Technology* 101, pp 5123-5130.

McLaughlin, M.J., Tiller, K.G., Naidu, R. and Stevens, D. 1996. The behaviour and environmental impact of contaminants in fertilizes. In: *Australian Journal of Soil Research* 34, pp 1-54.

Rockström, J., Steffen, W., Noone, K., Persson, Å., Chapin, F.S., Lambin, E.F., Lenton, T.M., Scheffer, M., Folke, C., Schellnhuber, H.J., Nykvist, B., de Wit, C.A., Hughes, T., van der Leeuw, S., Rodhe, H., Sörlin, S., Snyder, P.K., Costanza, R., Svedin, U., Falkenmark, M., Karlberg, L., Corell, R.W., Fabry, F.J., Hansen, J., Walker, B., Liverman, D., Richardson, D., Crutzen, P. and J. A. Foley. 2009. A safe operating space for humanity. In: *Nature* 461, pp 472-475.

SCB. 1982-2010. *Yearbooks of Agricultural Statistics. Official Statistics of Sweden.* SCB, Örebro, Sweden.

Smil, V. 2001. *Enriching the Earth: Fritz Haber, Carl Bosch, and the Transformation of World Food Production.* MIT Press, Cambridge, MA, 338 pp.

Smil, V. 2002. Nitrogen and food production: proteins for human diets. In: Ambio 31, pp 126-131.

Stewart, W.M., Hammond, L.L. and van Kauwenbergh, S.J. 2005. Phosphorus as a natural resource. In: Sims, T.J. and Sharpley, A.N. (Eds.). *Phosphorus: Agriculture and the Environment.* American Society of Agronomy, Madison, Wisconsin, USA, pp 3 – 22.

Swedish EPA. 2002. *Action plan for increased recycling of phosphorus from sewage.* Swedish Environmental Protection Agency, Report 5214. Stockholm, Sweden, ISBN 91 620-5214-4.

United Nations. Department of Economic and Social Affairs, Population Division, 2009 *World Population Prospects: The 2008 Revision,* New York.

United Nations. Department of Economic and Social Affairs, Population Division, 2010. *World urbanization Prospects. The 2009 Revision.,* New York.

USGS. 2008. U.S. *Geological Survey, Mineral Commodity Summaries, January 2008.*

USGS. 2011a. *U.S. Geological Survey. Mineral Commodity Summaries, January 2011.* Assessed 14.03.2011, available from http://minerals.usgs.gov/minerals/pubs/commodity/phosphate_rock/mcs-2011-phosp.pdf

USGS. 2011b. *U.S. Geological Survey, Mineral Commodity Summaries, January 2011.* Assessed 07.04.2011, available from http://minerals.usgs.gov/minerals/pubs/commodity/sulfur/mcs-2011-sulfu.pdf

Watson, C.A., Atkinson, D., Gosling, P., Jackson, L.R., and Rays, F.W., 2002. Managing soil fertility in organic farming systems. In: *Soil Use Management* 18, pp 239-247.

William, C., Burnett, M., Schultz, K and Hull, C. D. 1996. Radionuclide flow during the conversion of phosphogypsum to ammonium sulfate. In: *Journal of Environmental Radioactivity* 32, pp 33-51.

Zhang, Y. and Muhammed, M. 1990. An integrated process for the treatment of apatite obtained from dephosphorization of iron ore. In: *Journal of Chemical Technology and Biotechnology* 47, pp 47-60.

Chapter 4

Claesson, S. and Steineck, S. 1996. *Plant nutrient management and the environment.* Special Report 41, Uppsala: Swedish University of Agricultural Sciences. 69+24 pp.

Granstedt A., Seuri P. and Thomsson O. 2004. *Effective recycling agriculture around the Baltic Sea. Background report.* Ekologisk Lantbruk Nr. 4 1, Uppsala: Swedish University of Agricultural Sciences. pp 48.

Jakobsson, C. 1999. Ammonia Emissions -Current legislation Affecting the Agricultural Sector in Sweden. In: *Proceedings from an international conference on regulation of animal Production in Europe in Wiesbaden, Germany, 9-12 May, 1999.* KTBL, Germany

Jakobsson C., Andersson R., Lund S. and Sundell, B. 1998. *Sustainable development of the agricultural sector in the Baltic sea region.* Baltic Sea Environment Proceedings No. 74, Helsinki Commission. 123 pp.

Löfgren, S., Steineck, S. and Carlson, G. 1997. Analysis of environmental impact by two hypothetical agricultural production systems in Sweden, Denmark and Lithuania by the years 2010 and 2030. In: *Baltic Sea Agenda 21. Appendix*, 12 pp.

Swedish Board of Agriculture. 2007. *Manure and environment. Storage and spreading of manure, autumn and vintergreen land* 106 pp. Article nr: OVR141

Chapter 5

Aksomaitienė, R., Gužys, S. and Petrokienė, Z. 2004. Dissolved inorganic nitrogen and phosphate cycles in different crop rotations. In: *Transactions of Lithuanian University of Agriculture and Water Management Institute of Lithuanian University of Agriculture,* 1(4).

Altieri, M.A. 1995. *Agroecology. The science of sustainable agriculture.* Boulder: Westview Press.

Askergaard, M. 1999. Nutrient management in organic crop production. In: *Nordisk Jordbrugsforskning* 81, pp 91-99.

Baltramaitytė, D. 2001. *Ekologinės, tausojančios ir intensyvios žemdirbystės sistemų ir augalininkystės produktų kokybinis vertinimas glėjiškame karbonatingame išplautžemyje.* Daktaro disertacijos santrauka.- 40 p.

Bahman, E. 2003. Leaching of phosphorus fractions following manure or compost application. In: *Communications in Soil Science and Plant Analysis* 34 (19&20): pp 2803-2815.

Barrow, N.J. 1979. The description of desorption of phosphate from soil . In: *European Journal of Soil Science* 30 (2), pp. 259–270.

Bergström, L. and Johnsson, H. 1988. Simulated nitrogen dynamics and nitrate leaching in a perennial grass ley. In: *Plant and Soil* 105: pp 273-281.

Bokhorst, J.G. 1989. The organic farm at Nagele. In: *Development of farming systems. Evaluation of five-years period*, pp.57-65.

Breeuwsma, A., Reijerink, J.G.A. and Schoumans, O.F. 1995. Impact of manure on accumulation and leaching of phosphate in areas of intensive livestock farming. In: Steele, K. (ed.) *Animal waste and the land-water interface.* Boca Raton, FL:CRC/Lewis, pp 239-249.

Bučienė, A., Antanaitis, Š., Mašauskienė A. and Šimanskaitė, D. 2007. Nutrients N, P losses with drainage runoff and field balance as a result of crop management. In: *Communications in Soil Science and Plant Analysis* Vol. 38, Issue 15 & 16, September 2007, pp 2177-2195.

Bučienė, A. 2003. *Žemdirbystės sistemų ekologiniai ryšiai, monografija.* Klaipėda: Klaipėdos universitetas, Lietuvos Žemdirbystės institutas, pp. 9-14.

Bučienė, A., Šlepetienė, A., Šimanskaitė, D., Svirskienė, A. and Butkutė, B. 2003. Changes in soil properties under high and low-input cropping systems in Lithuania. In: *Soil use and management,* 19, pp 291-297.

Bučienė, A., Švedas, A. and Antanaitis, Š. 2003. Balances of the major nutrients N, P and K at the farm and field level and some possibilities to improve comparisons between actual and estimated crop yields. In: *Europ. J. Agronomy* Special Issue 20 (1-2): pp 53-62.

Bundinienė, O. 2003. Žemdirbystės sistemų įtaka augalų ir dirvožemio produktyvumui bei maisto medžiagų nuostoliams. In: *Žemdirbystė. Mokslo darbai,* 1, 81, pp 24-33

Conway, G.R. 1987. The properties of agro-ecosystems. In: *Agricultural systems* 24: pp 95–117.

Daniel, T.C., Sharpley, A.N., Edwards, D.R., Wedepohl, R. and Lemunyon, J.L. 1994. Minimizing surface water eutrophication from agriculture by phosphorus management. In: *Journal of Soil and Water Conservation* 49: pp 30–38.

Ežerinskas, V. 1998. Augalų maisto medžiagų išplovimas įvairių Lietuvos regionų dirvožemiuose. In: *Žemdirbystės instituto užbaigtų tiriamųjų darbų konferencijos pranešimai.* Nr. 30.-Akademija, pp. 31-32.

Friedel, J.K. and Gabel, D. 2001. Nitrogen pools and turnover in arable soils under different durations of organic farming: In: *Journal of Plant Nutrition and Soil Science* 164, pp 415-419.

Giampietro, M. 1994a. Sustainability and technological development in agriculture: A critical appraisal of genetic engineering. In: *BioScience* 44(10):677–689.

Giampietro, M. 1994b. Using hierarchy theory to explore the concept of sustainable development. In: *Futures* 26(6):616–625.

Giampietro, M. 1997. Socioeconomic pressure, demographic pressure, environmental loading and technological changes in agriculture. In: *Agriculture, ecosystems & environment* 65: pp 201–229.

Gomiero, T., Giampietro, M. and Mayumi, K. 2006. Facing complexity on agro-ecosystems: a new approach to farming system analysis. In: *International Journal of Agricultural Resources, Governance and Ecology,* Volume 5, Number 2-3 / 2006: pp 116 – 144.

Gužys, S. and Arlauskienė, E.A. 2001. Žemdirbystės intensyvumo ryšys su agroekosistemos produktyvumu ir medžiagų migracija. In: *Lietuvos žemės ūkio universiteto ir Lietuvos vandens ūkio instituto mokslo darbai,* 16 (38), pp 94-110.

Gužys, S. 2001. Drenažo vandens nuotėkis, cheminių elementų migracija ir balansas biologinės ir intensyvios žemdirbystės sąlygomis Vakarų Lietuvos dirvožemiuose. In: *Žemdirbystė. Mokslo darbai,* 74, pp. 53-69.

Gužys, S. 1999. *Žemės ūkio augalų derliaus ryšio su žemdirbystės sistemomis, dirvožemio ir vandens rodikliais analizė.* Daktaro disertacijos autoreferatas, Lietuvos žemdirbystės institutas, Dotnuva-Akademija.- 24 p.

Hart, R.D. 1984. The effect of interlevel hierarchical system communication on agricultural system input-output relationships. International Association for Ecology Series Study. In: *Options Mediterraneennes Ciheam IAMZ*-84-1.

Ikerd, J.E. 1993. The need for a system approach to sustainable agriculture. In: *Agriculture, ecosystems & environment* 46:147–160.

Indiati, R. and Sequi, P. 2004. Phosphorus intensity-quantity relationships in soils highly contrasting in phosphorus adsorption properties. In: *Communications in Soil Science and Plant Analysis* 35 (1 & 2): pp 131-143.

Jankauskas B. 1989. *Tręšimas ir aplinkos tarša,* Vilnius.-85 p.

Kirchmann, H. and Bergström, L. 2001. Do organic farming practices reduce nitrate leaching? In: *Communications in Soil Science and Plant Analysis* 32 (7&8): pp 997-1028

Krauss, A. 2000. Potassium, integral part for sustained soil fertility. In: Potassium and phosphorus: fertilisation effect on soil and crops. In: *Potassium and phosphorus: fertilisation effect on soil and crops.* Proceed. of the Regional IPI Workshop, October 23-24, 2000. Dotnuva-Akademija pp 7-19.

Kutra, G., Gaigalis, K. and Šmitienė, A. 2006. Land use influence on nitrogen leaching and options for pollution mitigation. In: *Žemdirbystė / Agriculture,* vol. 93, No. 4 , pp. 119-129.

Larsson, M. and Johnsson, H. 2003. Simulation of nitrate leaching using a modeling system with automatic parameterization routines. In: *Soil Use and Management* 19: pp 172-181.

Liu, Y.J., Laird, D.A. and Barak, P. 1997. Release and fixation of ammonium and potassium under long-term fertility management. In: *Soil Science Society of America Journal* 61, pp 310-314.

Lowrance, R., Hendrix, P. and Odum, E. 1986. A hierarchical approach to sustainable agriculture. In: *American journal of alternative agriculture* 1: pp 169–173.

References

Løes, A.K. and Øgaard, A.F. 1999. Soil nutrient content after long-term organic farming. In: *Nordisk Jordbrugsforskning* 81, 120-124.

Marcinkonis, S. and Karmaza, B. 2007. Fosforo akumuliacijos duomenų vizualizacija potencialios taršos židiniuose. In: *Žemdirbystė. Mokslo darbai*, 1, 94 : pp 64-73

Mažvila, J., Vaišvila, Z., Radžiūnas, V. and Adomaitis, T. 1992. *Ilgalaikio tręšimo mineralinėmis trąšomis įtaka derliui, dirvožemio agrocheminėms savybėms, maisto medžiagų išplovimui.* Kn: Antropogeninių veiksnių įtaka dirvožemio derlingumui, Vilnius, p.52-57.

Mažvila, J., Pekarskas, J. and Arbačiauskas, J. 2003. Ekologinės žemdirbystės ūkių dirvožemių agrocheminės savybės ir jų kaita. In: *Žemdirbystė. Mokslo darbai*, 3, 83: 66-76.

Mishina, I.J. 1984. *Rastitelnyje ostatki kak faktor plodorodija dernovo-podzolistych pochv.* Avtoreferat dissertaciji, Moskva.-14 p. (in Russian).

Pekarskas, J. 2005. *Ekologinio ūkininkavimo įtaka dirvožemio agrocheminėms savybėms ir augalų mitybos problemų sprendimas.* LR Žemės ūkio ministerija, Lietuvos mokslų akademijos Žemės ūkio ir miškų mokslų skyrius, Lietuvos žemės ūkio universiteto Bandymų stotis, LŽŪU Žemės ūkio mokslo ir technologijų parkas, Akademija, Kauno r.: 40-43.

Pupalienė, R. and Stancevičius, A. 2003. Įvairaus intensyvumo žemdirbystės sistemų poveikis dirvožemio agrocheminėms savybėms. In: *Žemdirbystė. Mokslo darbai*, 3, 83, 19-30.

Raupp, J. 1995. The long-term trial in Darmstadt: mineral fertiliser, composted manure and composted manure plus all biodynamic preparations. In: Raupp, J. (ed.) *Main effect of various organic and mineral fertilization on soil organic matter turnover and plant growth.* Proceedings of the first meting Concerted Action Fertilization Systems in Organic Farming 5. Darmstadt, Germany: Institute for Biodynamic Research. pp 28-36.

Romanovskaja, D. and Tripolskaja, L. 2003. Įvairių organinių trąšų naudojimo priesmėlio dirvožemyje agroekologinis įvertinimas. In: *Žemdirbystė. Mokslo darbai*, 4, 84, p. 3-22.

Scow, K.M., Somasco, O., Gunapala, N., Lau, S., Venette, R., Ferris, H., Miller, R. and Shennan, C. 1994. Transition from conventional to low-input agriculture changes soil fertility and biology. In: *California Agriculture* 48, pp 20-26.

Sharpley, A.N., Chapra, S.C., Wedepohl, R., Sims, J.T., Daniel, T.C. and Reddy, K.R.1994. Managing agricultural phosphorus for protection of surface waters: issues and options. In: *J. Environ. Qual.* 23: pp 437–451.

Shatokhina, S.F. and Khristenko, S.I. 1998. The effect of agricultural chemicals on the biological activity of Southern Chernozem. In: *Eurasian Soil Science* 31, pp 867-872.

Švedas, A. and Antanaitis, Š. 2000. Aplinkos veiksnių ryšys su drenažo nuotekų ir išplaunamų nitratų kiekiu. In: *Žemės ūkio mokslai* 4, 24-31.

Švedas A. 1990. *Žemdirbystės ekologija.*-Vilnius. 115 p.

Tyla, A., Rimšelis, I. and Šleinys, R. 1997. *Augalų maisto medžiagų išplovimas iš įvairių dirvožemių.* - Dotnuva-Akademija. - 25 p.

Tripolskaja, L. 2004. Ilgalaikio trąšų naudojimo įtaka dirvožemio savybėms lizimetriniuose įrenginiuose. In: *Žemdirbystė. Mokslo darbai*, 1, 85, pp 17-27.

Tripolskaja, L. and Romanovskaja, D. 2001. *Trąšų poveikis cheminių elementų migracijai.* Lietuvos žemės ūkio universiteto ir Lietuvos vandens ūkio instituto mokslo darbai, 17(39), Kaunas.

Wolf, S.A. and Allen, T.F.H. 1995. Recasting alternative agriculture as a management model: The value of adept scaling. In: *Ecological economics* 12: pp 5–12.

Zarina, L. 2000. Soil potassium and phosphorus in different crop rotation by influence of fertilisation system. In: *Potassium and phosphorus: fertilisation effect on soil and crops.* Proceed. of the Regional IPI Workshop, October 23-24, 2000, Lithuania. Dotnuva-Akademija. pp 202-205.

Chapter 6

De Buck, A.J., van Rijn, I., Roling, N.G. and Wossink, G.A.A. 2001. Farmers' reasons for changing or not changing to more sustainable practices: an exploratory study of arable farming in the Netherlands. In: *J. Agr. Educ. and Exten.* 7(3), pp. 153-166.

Helander, C.A. 1997. The Logarden project: development of an ecological and integrated arable farming systems. In: van Ittersum, M.K. and de Geijn, S.C. (eds.) *Proceedings of the 4th ESA Congress.* Elsevier, Amsterdam. pp. 309-317.

Hunek, T. 2004. Convergence of Agriculture in The Market Oriented Economy. In: Rosner A. (ed.): *Problems of village and agriculture during market reorientation of the economy.* Warsaw: IRWiR PAN pp. 45-59.

Lantinga, E.A. and Rabbinge, R. 1997. The renaissance of mixed farming system: a way towards Sustainable agriculture. In: Jarvis, S.C. and Pain, B.F. (eds.). *Gaseous nitrogen emissions from grasslands.* Willingford, UK: CAB International pp. 408-410.

Oomen Ormowski, J.M., Lantinga, E.A., Goewie, E.A. and Van der Hoek Ormowski, W. 1998. Mixed farming systems as a way towards a mere efficient use of nitrogen in European Union agriculture. In: *Env. Poll.* 102, pp. 697-704.

Prus, P. 2008 Sustainable development of individual farms based on chosen groups of farmers. In: *EJPAU* 11(3), #06.

Chapter 7

Danilov-Daniljan, V.I. and Losev, K.S. 2000. *Environmental challenge and sustainable development.* M.: Progress-Tradicion Press.

Mathematics Encyclopaedic Glossary. - M., 1988.

Moiseev, N. N. 1995. Recent anthropogenesis and disruptions of civilization//In: *Voprosy filosofii.* №1, P. 5-22.

Oldak, P.G. 1983. *Balanced nature usage. Economist point of view.* - Novosibirsk: Nauka Press. 128 c.

Rudsky, V.V. and Sturman, V.I. 2007. *Fundamentals of nature usage.* - M.: Aspect Press.

Sundstrom, T. and Ryden, L. 2003. The prospect of sustainable development. In: Rydén, L., Migula, P. and Andersson, M. (eds.) 2003 . *Environmental science.* Uppsala: Baltic University Press. pp. 764-800.

Valyansky, S.I. and Kaljuzhny, D.V. 2002. *Third way of civilization.* - M.: Algoritm.

World Commission on Environment and Development. 1987. *Our common future.* Report of the World Commission on Environment and Development. [The Brundtland report] Oxford:.Oxford University Press.

Chapter 8

Aronsson, H., Torstensson, G. and Bergström, L. 2007. Leaching and crop uptake of N, P and K from a clay soil with organic and conventional cropping systems. In: *Soil Use and Management* vol. 23 71-81

Baltic Nest Institute (http://nest.su.se/)

Claesson, S. and Steineck, S. 1996. *Plant nutrient management and the environment*. SLU.

De Clercq, P., Gertsis, A.C., Jarvis, S.C. and Neeteson, J.J. 2001. *Nutrient management legislation in European countries*. Wageningen: Wageningen Pers.

EEA, 2005. *EEA web site*, http://www.eea.europa.eu

EU, 1991. *Nitrate directive*. http://ec.europa.eu/environment/water/water-nitrates/index_en.html

EU, 2000. *Water framework directive* http://ec.europa.eu/water/water-framework/index_en.html

Fleischer, S., Gustafson, A., Joelsson, A., Pansar, J. and Stibe, L. 1994. Nitrogen removal in created ponds. In: *Ambio*, 23, 1994 pp. 349-357.

Gustafson, A. 1983. *Leaching of nitrate from arable land into groundwater in Sweden*. Environmental Geology, Vol. 5, No 2, pp. 65-71

Gustafson, A. 1987. *Simulation of Nitrate Leaching from Arable Land in Southern Sweden*. Acta Agriculturae Scandinavica, 38, pp. 13-23.

Gustafson, A., Kyllmar, K. and Ulén, B. 1999. Leakage of nitrogen and phosphorous. In: Lundin, L-C. (ed.) *Water use and management*. Uppsala: The Baltic University Programme. pp. 111-123.

Gustafson, A., Fleischer, S. and Joelsson, A. 2000. A catchment oriented and cost-effective policy for water protection. In: *Ecological Engineering*, 14, pp. 419-427.

HELCOM, 2007. *Baltic sea action plan* (adopted on 15 November 2007 in Krakow, Poland). http://www.helcom.fi/BSAP/ActionPlan/en_GB/ActionPlan/

Humborg, C., Mörth, C.-M., Sundbom, M. and Wulff, F. 2007. Riverine transport of biogenic elements to the Baltic Sea – past and possible future perspectives. In: *Hydrol. Earth Syst. Sci. Discuss.*, 4, pp. 1095-1131.

Johansson, G. and Gustafson, A. 2008. *Observation fields on arable land. Discharge and nutrient losses for the agro-hydrological year 2006/07 and a long term review*. Technical report no. 121. Uppsala: Swedish University of Agricultural Sciences. (In Swedish) http://www-mv.slu.se/Vv/jrk/obs/obs_result.htm

Johnsson, H., Larsson, M., Mårtensson, K. and Hoffmann, M. 2002. SOILNDB: a decision support tool for assessing nitrogen leaching losses from arable land. In: *Environmental Modelling & Software*, 17, pp. 505-517.

Johansson, S., Wulff, F. and Bonsdorff, E. 2007. The MARE Research program 1999-2006: Reflections on Program Management. In: *Ambio*, 36, No. 2-3. pp. 119-122.

Iital, A. Stålnacke, P., Deelstra, J., Loigu, E. and Pihlak, M. 2005. Effects of large-scale changes in emissions on nutrient concentrations in Estonian rivers in the Lake Peipsi drainage basin. In: *J. Hydrol.*, 304, pp. 261-273.

Kirchmann, H. et al. 2007. Comparison of Long-Term Organic and Conventional Crop-Livestock Systems on a Previously Nutrient-Depleted Soil in Sweden. In: *Agronomy Journal* 99:960-972. doi:10.2134/agronj2006.0061.

Kronvang, B., Jeppesen, E., Conley, D.J., Sondergaard, M., Larsen, S.E., Ovesen, N.B. and Carstensen, J. 2005. Nutrient pressures and ecological responses to nutrient loading reductions in Danish streams, lakes and coastal waters. In: *J. Hydrol.*, 304, 274-288.

Kyllmar, K., Carlsson C., Gustafson A., Ulen B. and Johnsson H. 2006. Nutrient discharge from small agricultural catchments in Sweden – Characterisation and trends. In: *Agriculture Ecosystems & Environment* vol 115, pp. 15-26

Kynkäänniemi, P. and Kyllmar, K. 2008. *Nutrient losses in small agricultural catchments 2006/07*. Ekohydrologi nr 101. Uppsala: Swedish University of Agricultural Sciences. (In Swedish) http://www-mv.slu.se/Vv/publ/Ekohydrologi_101.pdf

Larsson, M.H. and Jarvis, N.J., 1999. Evaluation of a dual-poporosity model to predict field-scale solute transport in a macroporous soil. In: *Journal of Hydrology* 215, pp. 153-171.

MARE NEST model, http://nest.su.se/nest/

Torstensson, G., Aronsson, H. and Bergström, L. 2006. Nutrient use efficiency and leaching of N, P and K of organic and conventional cropping systems in Sweden. In: *Agronomy Journal*, Vol 98, p 603-615.

Vagstad, N., Stålnacke, P., Andersen, H.E., Deelstra, J., Gustafson, A., Ital, A., Jansons, V., Kyllmar, K., Loigu, E., Rekolainen, S., Tumas, R. and Vuorenmaa, J. 2001. *Nutrient losses from agriculture in the Nordic and Baltic countries. Results of measurements in small agricultural catchments and national agro environmental statistics*. TemaNord 2001:591. 74 pp

Willer, H. and Yussefi, M. (eds.) 2007. *The world of organic agriculture – Statistics and emerging trends 2007*. International Federation of Organic Agriculture Movements (IFOAM), DE-Bonn and Research Institute of Organic Agriculture, FiBL, CH-Frick.

Chapter 9

Antikainen, R., Lemola, R., Nousianen, J.I., Sokka, L., Esala, M., Huhtanen, P. and Rekolainen, S. 2005. Stocks and flows of nitrogen and phosphorous in the Finnish food production and consumtion system. In: *Agriculture, Ecosystems & Environment*, Vol 107, Iss. 2-3 Pp 287-305.

Astover, A., Roostalu, H., Lauringson, E., Lemetti, I., Selge, A., Talgre, L., Vasilier, N., Mõtte, M., Tõrra, T. and Penu, P. 2006. Changes in agricultural land use and in plant nutrient balances of arable soils in Estonia. In: *Archives of Agronomy and Soil Sciences* 52(2): pp. 223-231.

Baker, D.B. and Richards, R.P. 2002. Phosphorus budgets and riverine phosphorus export in northwestern Ohio watersheds. In: *Journal of Environmental. Quality*. 31:1, pp. 96–108.

Beegle, D. and Lanyon, L. 2006. *Phosphorus balance*. SERA 17. Minimizing phosphorus losses from agriculture. (http://www.sera17.ext.vt.edu/SERA_17_Publications.htm)

Brandt, M., Ejhed, H. and Rapp, L., 2006. *Nutrient loads to the Swedish marine environment in 2006*. Swedish Environmental Protection Agency.

Braskerud, B., Tonderski, K., Wedding, K., Bakke, A.G., Blankenberg, B., Ulén, B. and Koskiaho, J. 2005. Can constructed wetlands reduce the diffuse phosphorus loads to atrophic water in cold temperature regions? In: *Journal of Environmental. Quality* 34, pp. 2145-2155.

Bučienė, A., Antanaitis, Š., Mašauskienė A. and Šimanskaitė, D. 2007. Nutrients N, P losses with drainage runoff and field balance as a result of crop management. In: *Communications in Soil Science and Plant Analysis* Vol. 38, Issue 15 & 16, September 2007, pp. 2177 – 2195.

Calvert, D.V. 1975. Nitrate, phosphate, and potassium movement in drainage lines under three management systems. In: *Journal of Environmental Quality* 4, pp. 183-186.

Csathó P., Sisák, I., Radimszky, L., Lushaj, S., Spiegel, H., Nikolova, M.T., Nikolov, Y.N., Čermák, P., Klir, J., Astover, A., Karklins, A., Lazauskas, S., Kopiński, J., Hera, C., Dumitru, E., Čuvardić, M., Bogdanović, D., Torma, S., Leskošek, M. and Khristenko, A. 2007 Agriculture as a source of phosphorus causing eutrophication in central and eastern Europe. In: *Soil Use and Management* 23, Suppl., 1, pp. 36-56.

Djodjic, F., Börling, K. and Bergström, L. 2004. Phosphorus leaching in relation to soil type and soil phosphorus content. In: *Journal Environmental Quality* 33, pp. 678-684.

Djodjic, F., Bergström, L. and Ulén, B. 2002. Phosphorus losses in relation to tillage practices on a structured clay soil. In: *Soil Use and Management* 18, pp. 79-83.

Djodjic, F. and Bergström, L. 2005. Conditional phosphorus index as an educational tool for risk assessment and phosphorus management. In: *Ambio* 34, pp. 296-300.

Egnér, H., Riehm, H. and Domingo, W. R. 1960. Untersuchungen über die chemische Bodenanalyse als Grundlage für die Beurteilung de Nährstoffzustandes der Böden. II. *Kung.l Lantbrukshögskolans Annaler* 26, 199-215.

Eriksson, J. Andersson, A. and Andersson, R. 1997. *Current Status of Swedish arable soil.* Swedish Protection Agency report 4778.

Gaynor, J.D. and Findlay, W.I. 1995. Soil and phosphorus loss from conservation and conventional tillage in corn production. In: *Journal Environmental Quality* 24, pp. 734-741.

Henriksson, A. 2006. *Actions against phosphorus losses from agriculture in the countries around the Baltic Sea.* Report Food 21 www-mat21.slu.se

Isermann, K. 2007. *Phosphorus balances in Europe and implications for diffuse pollution policy.* Extended abstract International Phosphorus Workshop 5, Silkeborg Denmark 3-7 Sept 2007.

Ivanov, P. 1984. *New acetate-lactate method for determination of plant-available phosphorus and potassium in soil.* (in Bulgarian).

Johansson, G. and Gustafson, A. 2005. *Observation field on arable land.* Technical report 107, Div. Water quality Management, SLU. 38 pp.

Johansson, G. and Gustafson, A. 2008. *Observationsfälten på åkermark.* Teknisk rapport 121, Avd. Vattenvårdslära SLU. 38 pp

Jongbloed, A.W. and Kemme, P.A. 1990. Apparent digestible phosphorus in the feeding of pigs in relation to availability, requirement and environment: 1. Digestible phosphorus in feedstuffs from plant and animal origin. In: *Netherlands Journal Agriculture Science* 38, pp. 567-575.

Karklins, A. 1998. Plant available phosphorus in Latvian soils and trends in fertiliser use. In: *Bibliotheca Fragmenta Agronomica Tom.* 3, pp. 310-316.

Končius, D. 2007. The effect of periodical liming and fertilization on the forms of phosphates and on the chantes in its fractional composition in the soil. In: *Zemdirbyste-Agriculture.* Vol. 94, No. 1, pp. 74-88.

Kopinski, J., Tujaka, A. and Igras, J. 2006. Nitrogen and phosphorus budgets in Poland as a tool for sustainable nutrient management. In: *Acta agriculturae Slovenica*, 87, pp. 173-181.

Leinweber, P., Meissner, R., Eckhardt, K.V. and Seeger, J. 1999. Management effects on forms of phosphorus in soil and leaching losses. In: *European Journal of Soil Sciences* 50, pp. 413-424.

Leinweber, P., Turner, B.L. and Meissner, R. 2002. Potential source of water pollution: phosphorus. In: Haygarth, P.M. and Jarvis, S.C. (eds.) *Agriculture, Hydrology and Water Quality.* CABI International, Oxon, UK and New York, USA, pp 29-55.

Lipiński, W. 2005. The content of available phosphorus in soils of Poland. In: *Nawozy i Nawożenie* (Fertilisers and Fertilization), Nr. 2(23). Polish Fertiliser Society – CIEC, Puławy 2005. pp. 49-54.

Lundekvam, H., and Skøien S., 1998. Soil erosion in Norway. An overview of measures from soil loss plots. In: *Soil Use and Management* 14, pp. 84-89.

McDowell, L.L. and McGregor, K.C. 1984. Plant nutrient losses in runoff from conservation tillage corn. In: *Soil & Tillage Research* 4, pp. 79-91.

McDowell, R.W. and Monaghan, R.M. 2002. The potential for phosphorus loss in relation to nitrogen fertilizer application and cultivation. In: *New Zealand Journal Agriculture Research* 45, pp. 245-253.

Marcinkonis, S. and Karmaza, B. 2007. Visualisation of phosphorus accumulation data in potential pollution sources. In: *Zemdirbyste-Agriculture.* Vol. 94, No. 1, pp. 64-73..

Mažvila, J. and Adomaitis, T. 2005. Judriuju fosforo ir kalio liekiu kaita Lietuvos žemės ūkio naudmenu dirvožemiuose. In: *Zemdirbystè Mokslo darbai*, 3,9, pp. 3-36.

Mechlich, A. 1984. Mechlich 3 soil test extractant: a modification of Mechlich 2 extractant. In: *Communications in Soil Science and Plant Analysis* 15, pp. 1409-1416.

Miller, M.H., Beauchamp, E.G. and Lauzon, J.D. 1994. Leaching of nitrogen and phosphorus from the biomass of three cover crop species. In: *Journal Environmental Quality* 23, pp. 267-272.

Neyrod, J-A. and Lischer, P. 2003. Do different methods used to estimate soil phosphorus availability across Europe give comparable results? In: *Journal Plant Nutrition Soil Science* 166, pp. 422-431.

Olsen, S.R., Cole, C.V., Watanabe, F.S. and Dean, L.A. 1954. *Estimation of Available Phosphorus in Soils by Extraction with Sodium Bicarbonate.* USDA Circular No. 939. 19 pp. Washington, DC., U.S.

Petersen, C.T., Hansen, S. and Jensen, H.E. 1997. Tillage-induced horizontal periodicity of preferential flow in the root zone. In: *Soil Scence. Society. Amercan Journal* 61, pp. 586-594.

Peters, J., Combs, S., Hoskins, B., Jarman, J., Kovar, J., Watson, M., Wolf, A. and Wolf, N. 2003. *Recommended Methods of Manure Analysis.* University of Wisconsin Extension Publ., Madison, WI. (http://www1.uwex.edu/ces/pubs/pdf/A3769.pdf; http://www1.uwex.edu/ces/pubs/pdf/A3769.pdf)

Reimann, C., Siewers U., Tarvainen, T., Bityukova, L., Eriksson, J., Gilucis, A., Gregorauskiene, V., Lukashev, V.K., Matinian, N.N. and Pasieczna, A. 2003. *Agricultural soils in northern Europe. A geochemical atlas.* Hannover: E. Schweizerbartsche Verlagsbuchhandlung,

Richards, J.E., Bates, T.E. and Sheppard, S.C. 1985. The effect of broadcast P applications and small amounts of fertilizer placed with seed on continuously cropped corn (*Zea mays* L.).In: *Fertilizer Research*. 6, pp. 269-277.

Riehm, H. 1943. Bestimmung der laktatlöslichen Phosphorsäure in karbonathaltigen Böden. *Phosphorsäure* 1, pp. 167-178.

Schüller, H. 1969. Die CAL-Methode, eine neue Methode zur Bestimmung des pflanzenverfügbaren Phosphates in Böden. In: *Zeitschrift für Pflanzenernährung und Bodenkunde* 123, 48-63.

Sharpley, A.N., Chapra, S.C., Wedepohl, R., Sims, J.T., Daniel, T.C. and Reddy, K.R. 1994. Managing agricultural phosphorus for protection of surface waters: Issues and options. In: *Journal Environmental Quality* 23, pp. 437-451.

Thomas, G.W. and Phillips, R.E. 1979. Consequences of water movement in macropores. In: *Journal of Environmental Quality* 8, 149-152.

Timmons, D.R., Holt, R.F. and Latterall, J.J. 1970. Leaching of crop residues as a source of nutrients in surface runoff water. In: *Water Resources Research* 6, pp. 1367-1375.

Tripolskaja, L. 2004. Ilgalaikio trąšų naudojimo įtaka dirvožemio savybėms lizimetriniuose įrenginiuose. In: *Žemdirbystė. Mokslo darbai*, 1, 85, pp. 17-27.

Turtola, E. and Jaakola, A. 1995. Loss of phosphorus by surface runoff and leaching from a heavy clay soil under barley and grass ley in Finland. In: *Acta Agriculturae Scandinavica*, Section B 45, pp. 159-165.

Turtola, E. and Paajanen, A. 1995. Influence of improved subsurface drainage on phosphorus losses and nitrogen leaching from a heavy clay soil. In: *Agricultural Water Management*. 28, pp. 295-310.

Ulén, B. 1995. Episodic precipitation and discharge events and their influence on losses of phosphorus from tile-drained arable fields. In: *Swedish Journal Agriculture Research* 25, pp. 25-31.

Ulén, B. 1997. Nutrient losses by surface runoff from soils with winter cover crops and spring-ploughed soils in the south of Sweden. In: *Soil & Tillage Research* 44, pp. 165-177.

Ulén, B. and Mattsson, L. 2003. Losses of different forms of phosphorus and of nitrate from a clay soil under grass and cereal production. In: *Nutrient Cycling in Agroecosystems* 65, pp. 129-140.

Ulén, B. 2003. Concentrations and transport of different forms of phosphorus during snowmelt runoff from an illite clay soil. In: *Hydrological Processes* 17, pp. 747-758.

Ulén, B. 2004. Size and settling velocities of phosphorus-containing particles in water from agricultural drains. In: *Water Air and Soil Pollution* 157, pp. 331-343.

Ulén, B. and Jakobsson, C. 2005. Critical evaluations of measures to mitigate phosphorus losses from agricultural land to surface waters in Sweden. In: *Science of Total Environment* 344, pp. 37-50.

Uusi-Kämppä, J., Braskerud, B., Jansson, H., Syversen, N. and Uusitalo, R. 2000. Buffer zones and constructed wetlands as filters for agricultural phosphorus. In: *Journal of Environmental Quality* 29, pp. 151-158.

Uusitalo, R., Turtola, E., Grönroos, J., Kivistö, J., Mäntylathi, V., Turtola, A., Lemola, R. and Salo, T. 2007. Finnish trends in phosphorus balances and soil test phosphorus. In: *Agricultural and Food Science Finland*, 16, pp 301-316.

Vuorinen, J. and Mäkitie, O. 1955. *The method of soil testing in use in Finland*. Agrigeological Publication 63, pp. 1-44.

Withers, P.J A., Hodgkinson, R.A., Bates, A. and Withers, C.L. 2007. Soil cultivation effects on sediment and phosphorus mobilization in surface runoff from three contrasting soil types in England. In: *Soil & Tillage Research* 93, pp. 438-451.

Chapter 10

Baker, D.B. and Richards, R.P. 2002. Phosphorus budgets and riverine phosphorus export in northwestern Ohio watersheds. In: *J. Environ. Qual.* 31:1, pp 96–108.

Carpenter, S.R., Caraco, N.F., Howarth, R.W., Sharpley, A.N. and Smith, V.H. 1998. Nonpoint pollution of surface waters with P and nitrogen. In: *Ecol. Applic.* 8: pp. 559–568.

Clark, G.M., Mueller, D.K. and Mast, M.A. 2000. Nutrient concentrations and yields in undeveloped basins of the United States. In: *Journal of the American Water Resources Association*. 36:4, pp 849-860.

Dove, A. and Warren, G. 2008. Phosphorus concentrations and loadings. In: *State of the Great Lakes*, Environment Canada and U.S. and Environmental Protection Agency, pp 70-73. Available on-line: http://www.epa.gov/solec/

Duvick, D.N. 2005. The contribution of breeding to yield advances in maize (Zea mays L.). In: *Advances in Agronomy*, 86 pp 83-145.

Elmi, A.A., Madramootoo, C.A., Egeh, M., Liu, A. and Hamel, C. 2002. Environmental and agronomic implications of water table and nitrogen fertilization management. In: *J. Environ. Qual.* 31: pp 1858-1867.

Fixen, P.E. and West, F.B. 2002. Nitrogen fertilisers. Meeting contemporary challenges. In: *AMBIO: A Journal of the Human Environment*. 31: 2, pp. 169–176.

Frankenberger J., Kladivko E., Sands G., Jaynes D., Fausey N., Helmers M., Cooke R., Strock J., Nelson K. and Brown L. 2006. *Drainage Water Management: Questions and Answers about Drainage Water Management for the Midwest*. Bulletin WQ-44, Purdue University, W. Lafayette, Ind.; 8 pp.

Fuller, K., Shear, H. and Wittig, J. (eds.) 1995. *Great lakes environmental atlas and resource book* (3rd Edition). Government of Canada and US Environmental Protection Agency. Available on line http://www.epa.gov/glnpo/atlas/index.html

International Plant Nutrition Institute. 2008. *Crop nutrient balances in Ontario 1950-2007*. http://www.ipni.net/ppiweb/canadae.nsf/$webindex/article=4EC4F7DF8525740A006843D6F653DBC5

McCabe, G.J., Palecki, M.A. and Betancourt, J.L. 2004. Pacific and Atlantic Ocean influences on multidecadal drought frequency in the United States. In: *Proceedings of the National Academy of Sciences USA* 101:12, pp. 4,136-4,141.

McIsaac, G.F. and Hu, X. 2004. Net N input and riverine N export from Illinois agricultural watersheds with and without extensive tile drainage. In: *Biogeochemistry* 70:2, pp 251-271.

McIsaac, G.F., David, M.B. and Mitchell, C.A. 2010. *Miscanthus* and switchgrass production in central Illinois: impacts on hydrology and inorganic nitrogen leaching. In: *Journal of Environmental Quality* 39:1790-99.

Myers, D.N., Thomas, M.A., Frey, J.W. , Rheaume, S.J. and Button, D.T. 2000. Water quality in the Lake Erie-Lake Saint Clair drainages Michigan, Ohio, Indiana, New York, and Pennsylvania, 1996–98.

In: *U.S. Geological Survey Circular 1203*, 35 p., on-line at http://pubs.water.usgs.gov/circ1203/

National Oceanographic and Atmospheric Administration (NOAA). 2010. *Great Lakes Environmental Research Laboratory Great Lakes Monthly Hydrologic Data*. Available on line http://www.glerl.noaa.gov/data/arc/hydro/mnth-hydro.html

Oquist, K.A., Strock, J.S. and Mulla, D.J. 2007. Influence of alternative and conventional farming practices on subsurface drainage and water quality. In: *J. Environ. Qual.* 36:4, pp 1194-1204.

Randall, G.W. and Mulla, D.J. 2001. Nitrate nitrogen in surface waters as influenced by climatic conditions and agricultural practices. In: *J. Environ. Qual.* 30:2, pp 337–344.

Richards, R.P. and Baker, D.B. 2002. Trends in water quality in LEASEQ rivers and streams (Northwestern Ohio), 1975-1995. In: *J. Environ. Qual.*, 31:1 pp 90 - 96.

Roberts, P., Shaffer, R. and Nanney, R. 2008a. Nutrient management plans. In: *State of the Great Lakes*, Environment Canada and U.S. and Environmental Protection Agency, pp 259-61. Available on-line: http://www.epa.gov/solec/

Roberts, P., Shaffer, R. and Nanney, R. 2008b. Sustainable agriculture practices. In: *State of the Great Lakes*, Environment Canada and U.S. and Environmental Protection Agency, pp 233-35. Available on-line: http://www.epa.gov/solec/

Sharpley, A.N., Daniel, T., Sims, T., Lemunyon, J., Stevens, R. and Parry, R. 2003. *Agricultural phosphorus and eutrophication*, 2nd ed. U.S. Department of Agriculture, Agricultural Research Service, ARS–149, 44 pp.

Smith, R.A., Schwarz, G.E. and Alexander, R.B. 1997. Regional interpretation of water-quality monitoring data. In: *Water Resources Research* 33: 12, pp 2781-2798.

Smith, R.A., Alexander, R.B. and Schwarz, G.E. 2003. Natural background concentrations of nutrients in streams and rivers of the conterminous United States. In: *Environ. Sci. Tech.* 37:14, pp 2039-2047.

Valero, C.S., Madramootoo, C. and Stampfli, N. 2007. Water table management impacts on phosphorus loads in tile drainage. In: *Agricultural Water Management* 89:1-2, pp 71-80.

Chapter 11

Holdren, C. 1997. NALMS looks at greater national focus, welcomes board members. In: *Lakeline*. Vol. 17. No.2. North American Lake Management Society, Madison. WI.

NALMS (North American Lake Management Society). 1992. *Developing Eutrophication Standards for Lakes and Reservoirs*. A Report Prepared by the Lakes Standards Subcommittee. NALMS, Madison, WI.

Terrene Institute. 1995. *Local ordinances. A user's guide*. Alexandria, VA.

Terrene Institute. 1996. *A watershed approach to urban runoff. Handbook for decisionmakers*. Alexandria, VA.

U.S. Environmental Protection Agency (EPA) 1993. *A commitment to watershed protection: A review of the Clean Lakes Program*. EPA-841-R-93-001. Office of Wetlands, Oceans, and Watersheds, Washington, D.C.

U.S. Environmental Protection Agency. 1995. *Source water protection: Protecting drinking water across the nation*. EPA-813-F-95-005. Office of Water, Washington, D.C.

Chapter 12

Gužys, S. 2001. The runoff of drainage water, migration and balance of chemical elements in the conditions of biological and intensive cropping systems in the soils of Western Lithuania. In: *Žemdirbystė: mokslo darbai/Agriculture: Scientific articles*. LIA, LUA, Akademija. 74, pp 53-69 (in Lithuanian with summary in English).

Kairiūkštis, K. and Rudzikas, Z. 1999. *Lietuvos ekologinis tvarumas istoriniame kontekste*. Vilnius, pp 19-33 (in Lithuanian).

Lietuvos žemės ir maisto ūkis / Agriculture and food sector in Lithuania 2008. Lithuanian Institute of Agrarian Economics (LIAE). Vilnius, pp 121-125 (in Lithuanian with summary in English).

Mašauskas, V. and Mašauskienė, A. 2005. The impact of long-term application of superphosphate as sulphur containing fertilizer on the yield of crops in the rotation. In: *Žemdirbystė: mokslo darbai / Agriculture: Scientific articles* LIA, LUA. Kėdainių raj., Akademija, 92 (4), pp 36-51 (in Lithuanian with summary in English).

Mažeika, R., Cigienė, A., Mašauskas, V., Bernotas, S., Rainys, K., Mašauskienė, A., Repšienė, R. and Rudokas, V. 2008. Azoto trąšų su kizeritu efektyvumas lauko augalams rudžemyje, balkšvažemyje ir išplautžemyje. In: *Nitratinių trąšų tobulinimas, naujų sukūrimas ir jų efektyvumo įvertinimas*. Stock company 'Achema', LIA, LUA, LIH. Jonava, pp 170-193 (in Lithuanian).

Mažvila, J., Vaišvila, Z., Lubytė, J. and Adomaitis, T. 2007. The changes in sulphur content in the soil and plants as affected by long-term fertilisation. In: *Zemdirbyste / Agriculture*. LIA, LUA, 94 (1), pp 51-63 (in Lithuanian with summary in English).

Mažvila, J. (eds.) 1998. *Lietuvos dirvožemių agrocheminės savybės ir jų kaita / Agrochemical properties of Lithuanian soils and their change*. Lithuanian Institute of Agriculture (LIA). Kaunas, pp 123-129 (in Lithuanian with summary in English).

Spencer, K. and Freney, J.R. 1980. Assessing the sulphur status of field-grown wheat by plant analysis. *Agronomy Journal*: 72, pp 469-472.

Šiaudinis, G. 2007. *The effect of sulphur and nitrogen on spring wheat and spring rape yield and yield components. Summary of doctoral dissertation*. LIA, LUA. Akademija, 22 p.

Šidlauskas, G. and Bernotas S. 2003. Some factors, affecting seed yield of spring oilseed rape (*Brassica napus* L.). In: *Agronomy research*, 1(2) pp 229-243.

Šileika, S.A., Haneklaus, S., Gaigalis, K. and Kutra, S. 2003. Impact of the agrarian reform on nutrient run-off in Lithuania. In: *FAL Agricultural research* 53 (2/3), pp171-179.

Staugaitis G., Mažvila J., Vaišvila Z., Arbačiauskas J. 2009. Sieros reikšmė augalams. In: *Mano ūkis.*- LŽŪKT, Nr.1.

Tyla, A., Rimšelis, J. and Šleinys, R. 1997. *leaching of nutrient matter of plants in different soils*. LIA, Dotnuva-Akademija, 21 p (in Lithuanian with summary in English).

Velička, R. 2002. *Rape. Monography*. Kaunas, Lututė, 320 p. (in Lithuanian with summary in English).

Velička, R., Rimkevičienė, M. and Trečiokas, K. 2001. Influence of the rape area in the crop rotation on the content of sulphur in the soil and plants. In: *Žemdirbystė: mokslo darbai / Agriculture: Scientific articles*. LIA, LUA. - Akademija, vol. 73, p. 91-103 (in Lithuanian with summary in English).

Zhao, K.J., McGrath, S.P., Blake-Kalff, M.M.A., Link, A. and Tucker, M. 2003. Crop responses to sulphur fertilization in Europe. In: *Proceedings of the International Fertiliser Society*: 504, pp 26-51. International Fertiliser society, York, UK.

Chapter 13

Bujnovsky, R. and Igras, J. 2001. Nutrient balances (NPK) for representative farms in Czech Republic, Latvia, Poland and Slovak Republic In: *Nawozy i nawozenie / Fertilizers and Fertilizatio.* IUNG, (III), No. 2(7), pp 53-65.

Feizienė, D. Feiza, V., Lazauskas, S., kadžienė, G. Šimanskaitė, D. and Deveikytė I. 2007. The influence of soil management on soil properties and yield of crop rotation. In: *Zemdirbyste/Agriculture*. LIA, LUA. Kedainiu r., Akademija, 94 (3), pp 129-145.

Gužys, S. 2001. The runoff of drainage water, migration and balance of chemical elements in the conditions of biological and intensive cropping systems in the soils of Western Lithuania. In: *Žemdirbystė: mokslo darbai/Agriculture: Scientific articles*. LIA, LUA. Akademija: 74, pp 53-69 (in Lithuanian with summary in English).

Maikštėnienė, S., Krištaponytė, I. and Masilionytė, L. 2008. The effects of long-term fertilization systems on the variation of major productivity parameters of gleyic Cambisols. In: *Zemdirbyste/Agriculture*. LIA, LUA. Kedainiu r., Akademija, 95 (1), pp 22-39 (in Lithuanian with summary in English).

Mašauskas, V. and Mašauskienė, A. 2006. Dynamics of Potassium Offtake and Active Potassium in Soil. In: *Vagos: mokslo darbai/Vagos: research papers*. LUA, Akademija, 68 (21), pp 20-29.

Matusevičius K. 2005. Lietuvos agrocheminė tarnyba (1965-2005) / Lithuanian Service of Agrochemistry (1965-2005). Lithuanian Institute of Agriculture, 167 p. (in Lithuanian).

Mažvila, J., Antanaitis, A., Arbačiauskas, J., Lubytė, J., Adomaitis, T., Mašauskas, V. and Vaišvila, Z. 2004. Kalio tyrimai skirtingais metodais ir jų tinkamumas Lietuvos dirvožemiams / Potassium tests using different methods and their suitability for Lithuanian soils / In: *Žemdirbystė: mokslo darbai/Agriculture: Scientific articles*. LIA, LUA. Akademija: 87 (3), pp 12-29 (in Lithuanian with summary in English).

Mažvila, J., Vaišvila, Z., Arbačiauskas J., Adomaitis, T. and Antanaitis, A. 2007. Dependence of agricultural crop yield and its quality on long-term fertilization on sandy loam soils. In: *Zemdirbyste/Agriculture*. LIA, LUA. Kedainiu r., Akademija, 94 (3), pp 3-17 (in Lithuanian with summary in English).

Šileika, S. (ed.) 2001. *Code of good Agricultural Practices for Lithuania. Rules and recommendations.* Vilnius, 64 p.

Chapter 14

Bäckman, S. 2008. *Intensity, productivity and efficiency in agriculture in Finland and implications for N and P fertiliser management.* University of Helsinki. Department of Economics and Management, Publications 45, Agriculture Economics.

Coelli, T., Prasada Rao, D.S. and Battese, G.E. 1999. *An Introduction to Efficiency and Productivity Analysis.* Kluwer Academic Publishers. p.275.

Chapter 15

Claesson, S. and Steineck, S. 1996. *Plant nutrient management and the environment.* Swedish University of Agricultural Sciences, SLU, Special Report 41, Uppsala, 69+24 pp.

Jakobsson C. and Lindén B. 1991. *Nitrogen effects of manure on clay soils.* Swedish University of agricultural Sciences, Dept. of Soil Sciences, Div. of Soil Fertility, Report 190, 41 pp.

Chapter 16

Claesson, S. and Steineck, S. 1996. *Plant nutrient management and the environment.* Swedish University of Agricultural Sciences, SLU, Special Report 41, Uppsala, 69+24 pp.

Integrated pollution prevention and control (IPPC). *Reference document on best available techniques for intensive rearing of poultry and pigs.* (BREF). European Commission. http://www.epa.ie/downloads/advice/brefs/name,14520,en.html (Retrieved 2010-07-30)

Jakobsson C. and Lindén B. 1991. *Nitrogen effects of manure on clay soils.* Swedish University of agricultural Sciences, Dept. of Soil Sciences, Div. of Soil Fertility, Report 190, 41 pp.

Chapter 17

Albihn, A. 2009. Infectious waste management. In: Moselio Schaechter (Ed.) *Encyclopaedia of Microbiology.* Oxford: Elsevier, pp. 500-512.

Bagge, E., Sahlström, L. and Albihn, A. 2005. The effect of hygienic treatment on the microbial flora of biowaste at biogas plants. In: *Water Res.* 39, 4879-4886.

Bean, C.L., Hansen, J.J., Margolin, A.B., Balkin, H., Battzer, G. and Widmer, G. 2007. Class B alkaline stabilization to achieve pathogen inactivation. In: *Int. J. Environ. Res. Public Health* 4, 53-60.

Bemrah, N., Sanaaa, M., Cassin, M.H., Griffiths, M.W. and Cerf, O. 1998. Quantitative risk assessment of human listeriosis from consumption of soft cheese made from raw milk. In: *Prev. Vet. Med.* 37, 129-145.

Bennet, D.D., Higgins, S.E., Moore, RW, Beltran, R, Caldwell, DJ, Byrd, J.A. and Hargis, B.M. 2003. Effects of lime on *Salmonella enteritidis* survival in vitro. In: *J. Appl. Poult. Res.* 12, 65-68.

Cassin, M.H., Lammerding, A.M., Todd, E.C.D., Ross, W. and McColl, R.S. 1998. Quantitative risk assessment for *Escherichia coli* O157:H7 in ground beef hamburgers. In: *Int. J. Food Microbiol.* 41, 21-44.

Elving, J., Ottoson, J.R., Vinnerås, B. and Albihn, A. 2010. Growth potential of faecal bacteria in simulated psychrophilic/mesophilic zones during composting of organic waste. In: *J. Appl. Microbiol.* 108, 1974-1981.

References

Emmoth, E. 2010. *Virus inactivation – evaluation of processes used in biowaste management.* Dissertation. Swedish University of Agricultural Sciences, Uppsala, Sweden. ISBN 978-91-576-9001-2.

Feachem, R.G., Bradley, D.J., Garelick, H. and Mara, D. 1983. Sanitation and disease; Health aspects of excreta and wastewater management. In: *World Bank Studies in Water Supply and Sanitation 3*, Pitman Press, Bath, GB.

Gajadhar, A.A. and Allen, J.R. 2004. Factors contributing to the public health and economic importance of waterborne zoonotic parasites. In: *Vet. Parasitol.* 126, 3-14.

Heaton, J.C. and Jones, K. 2008. Microbial contamination of fruit and vegetables and the behaviour of enteropathogens in the phyllosphere: a review. In: *J. Appl. Microbiol.* 104, 613-626.

Himathongkham, S., Bahari, S., Reimann, H. and Cliver, D. 1999. Survival of *Escherichia coli* O157:H7 and *Salmonella typhimurium* in cow manure and manure slurry. In: *FEMS Microbiol. Lett.* 178, 251-257.

Hutchison, M.L., Walters, L.D., Moore, A., Crookes, K.M. and Avery, S.M. 2004. Effect of length of time before incorporation on survival of pathogenic bacteria present in livestock wastes applied to agricultural soil. In: *Appl. Environ. Microbiol.* 70, 5111-5118.

Kühn, I., Iversen, A., Finn, M., Greko, C., Burman, L.G., Blanch, A.R., Vilanova, X., Manero, A., Taylor, H., Caplin, J., Dominguez, L., Herrero, I.A., Moreno, M.A. and Möllby, R. 2005. Occurrence and relatedness of vancomycin resistant Enterococci in animals, humans and the environment in different European regions. In: *Appl. Environ. Microbiol.* 71, 5383-5390.

Mas-Coma, S., Valero, M.A. and Bargues, M.D. 2008. Effect of climate change on animal and zoonotic helminthiases. In: *Climate Change: Impact on the Epidemiology and Control of Animal Diseases.* De La Rocque, S., Hendrickx, G. and Morand, S. (Eds), *Rev. Sci. Tech. Off. Int. Epiz.* 27, 443-458.

Mitscherlich, E. and Marth, E.H. 1983. *Microbial survival in the Environment: Bacteria and Rickettsiae Important in Human and Animal Health.* Springer Verlag, Berlin, Germany.

Nordin, A. 2010. *Ammonia sanitation of human excreta – treatment technology for production of fertilizer.* Doctoral thesis. Swedish University of Agricultural Sciences, Uppsala, Sweden. ISBN 978-91-576-7512-5.

Nyberg, K.A., Vinnerås, B., Ottoson, J.R., Aronsson, P. and Albihn, A. 2010. Inactivation of *Escherichia coli* O157:H7 and *Salmonella* Typhimurium in manure-amended soils studied in outdoor lysimeters. In: *Appl. Soil Ecol.* 46, 398-404.

Sahlström, L., Bagge, E., Emmoth, E., Holmqvist, A., Danielsson-Tham, M.L. and Albihn, A. 2008. A laboratory study of survival of selected microorganisms after heat treatment of biowaste used in biogas plants. In: *Bioresour. Techn.* 99, 7859-7865.

Sumpter, J.P. and Johnsson, A.C. 2005. Lessons from endocrine disruption and their application to other issues concerning trace organics in the aquatic environment. In: *Environ. Sci. Technol.* 39, 47-54.

Vinnerås, B., Winker, M. and Clemens, J. 2008. Non-metallic contaminants in domestic waste, wastewater and manures: constraints to agricultural use. In: *International Fertiliser Society, Proceedings* 640, York, UK.

Yen-Phi, V.T., Clemens, J., Rechenburg, A., Vinnerås, B., Lenßen, C. and Kistemann, T. 2009. Hygienic effect of plastic bio-digesters under tropical conditions. In: *J. Water Health* 7, 590-596.

Chapter 18

FGNU Rosinformagrotech. 2005. *Recommendations on removal, transport, storage and preparation for the use of manure for different production and nature-climatic conditions.* – M.:. 180 p.

Chapter 19

The code of environmentally safe agricultural practice in the conditions of Leningrad Oblast. Part 1. Animal breeding and feed production. Saint-Petersburg, 2007.

Khazanov E.E. *Experience of the development of modern milk production technologies* – SPb-Pushkin: SZNIIMESH, 2003. – 44 p.

Kostyaev, A.I. and Surovtsev, V.N. *Organizational and economic factors of the development of dairy cattle breeding in a region (by the example of Leningrad Oblast)* / Proceedings of the Bureau of the Department of economics and land use of the Russian Academy of Agricultural Sciences in Saint-Petersburg, Pushkin, 24-25 September 2003. – SPb-Pushkin: SZNIESH, 2003. – 100 p.

NTP 17-99. *The norms of technological projects of the systems for manure removal and preparation to utilization.*

Surovtsev, V.N., Burkhieva, T.C., Ponomarev, M.A. and Chastikova, E.N. *Recommendations. Ensuring of milk production competitiveness under conditions of increasing environmental requirements.* – SPb, GNU SZNIESH, 2009. – 84 p.

Chapter 20

EU directive on sewage sludge (Directive 86/278/EEC)

European Communities. Report: 'Disposal and recycling routes for sewage sludge, Part 4 - Economic report' (2002)

VA-Forsk report. 2005. 'Regional or Local Sludge Handling in Thirteen Municipalities in South Western Sweden – Technologies, Environmental Impact and Costs' – in Swedish

Chapter 21

Granato, T.C., Pietz, R.I., Knafl, G.J., Carlson Jr., C.R., Tata, P. and Lue-Hing, C. 2004. Trace metal concentrations in soil, corn leaves, and grain after cessation of biosolids application. In: *J. Environ. Qual.* 33,2078-2089, 2004.

McBride, M.B. 1995, Toxic metal accumulation from agricultural use of sludge, are USEPA regulations protective? In: *J. Environ. Qual.* 24,5-18.

North East Biosolids and Residuals Association (NEBRA). 2007. *A national biosolids regulations, quality, end use & disposal survey, 2007.* Available at www.nebiosolids.org.

Pietz, R.I., Sustich, R., Tata, P., Richardson, G. and Lue-Hing, C. 1999. *Improvements in the quality of sewage sludge at the Metropolitan Water Reclamation District of Greater Chicago.* Research and Development Department Report No. 99-20. Chicago, Ill.: Metropolitan Water Reclamation District of Greater Chicago.

Pietz, R.I., Tata, P., Sustich, R., Richardson, G. and Lue-Hing, C. 2002. *Reductions in metal concentrations in sludge and biosolids from water reclamation plants at the Metropolitan Water Reclamation District of Greater Chicago from 1982 through 2000*; Research and Development Department Report No. 02-7. Chicago, Ill.: Metropolitan Water Reclamation District of Greater Chicago;

Sustich, R.C., Lue-Hing, C., Lanyon, R. and Kollias, L. 1997. Chicago's 503 enforcement initiative. A great industrial clean-up experience, In: Residuals and Biosolids Management, *Proceedings of the Water Environment Federation Annual Meetings*, Volume 3, p. 327, Chicago, Ill.: Water Environment Federation.

Tata, P., Lue-Hing, C., Bertucci, J., Sedita, S., Kambhampati, C.R. and Zenz, D. 1997. Class A biosolids production by a low cost conventional technology, In: Residuals and Biosolids Management, *Proceedings of the Water Environment Federation Annual Meetings*, Volume 2, p. 1, Chicago, Illinois.

Tata, P., Lue-Hing, C., Bertucci, J.J., Sedita, S.J. and Knafl, G.J. 2000. Class A biosolids production by a low-cost conventional technology. In: *Water Environ. Res.* 72, pp. 413-422.

Tian, G., Granato, T.C. Pietz, R.I. Carlson, C.R. and Abedin, Z. 2006. Effect of long-term application of biosolids for land reclamation on surface water chemistry. In: *J. Environ. Qual.* 35, pp. 101-113, .

United States Environmental Protection Agency (USEPA). 1993. Part 503-standards for the use or disposal of sewage sludge. In: *Federal Register*, 58(32), 9387.

Chapter 22

Bachmann, S. and Eichler-Löbermann, B. 2009. Fertilizing effect of biogas slurries. In: *More sustainability in agriculture – new fertilizers and fertilization management, 18th Symposium CIEC, Rome, Nov 2009, proceedings*

Codling, E.E., Chaney, R.L. and Scherwell, J. 2002. Poultry litter ash as a potential phosphorus source for agricultural crops. In: *J Environ Qual* 31: pp. 954-961

Dorado, J.; Zancada, M.; Almendros, G.; López-Fando, C. (2003): Changes in soil properties and humic substances after long-term amendments with manure and crop residues in dryland faming systems. In: *J. Plant Nutr. Soil Sci.* 166, 31-38

Eichler-Löbermann, B., Schiemenz, K. and Makadi, M. et al 2008. Nutrient cycling by using residues of bioenergy production - II Effects of biomass ashes on plant and soil parameters. In: *Cereal Res Commun* 36: pp. 1259-1262

Fritsche, U.R., K. Hennenberg, and Hünecke, K. 2010. *The "iLUC Factor" as a means to hedge risks of ghg emissions from indirect land use change.* Darmstadt: Öko-Institut. Retrieved 20.08.2010 from http://www.oeko.de/oekodoc/1030/2010-082-en.pdf.

Gutser, R., Ebertseder, T., Schraml, M., Schmidhalter, U. (2005): Short-term and residual availability of organic fertililzers on arable land. In: *J. Plant Nutr. Soil Sci.* 168, 439-446

Huffman, S. A., Cole, C. V., Scott, N. A. (1996): Soil texture and residue addition effects on soil phosphorus transformations. In: *Soil Sci. Soc. Am. J.* 60, 1095–1101.

Kaur, K., Kapoor, K.K., Gupta, A.P. (2005): Impact of organic manures with and without mineral fertilizers on soil chemical and biological properties under tropical condition. In: *J. Plant Nutr. Soil Sci.* 168, 117-122.

Krejsl, J.A. and Scanlon, T.M. 1996. Evaluation of beneficial use of wood-fired boiler ash on oat and bean growth. In: *J Environ Qual* 25: pp. 950-954

Loria, E.R. and Sawyer, J.E. 2005. Extractable soil phosphorus and inorganic nitrogen following application of raw and anaerobically digested swine manure. In: *Agron. J.* 97: pp. 879–885.

Mokry, M. and Bockholt, K. 2008. Gärreste richtig beurteilen. In: *dlz agrarmagazin*, 3: pp. 52–56.

Mozaffari, M., Russelle, M.P. and Rosen, C.J. 2002. Nutrient supply and neutralizing value of alfalfa stem gasification ash. In: *Soil Sci Soc Am J* 66: pp. 171–178

Muse, J.K. and Mitchell, C.C. 1995. Paper mill boiler ash and lime by-products as soil liming materials. In: *Agron J* 87: pp. 432-438

Odlare, M. 2005. *Organic residues – a resource for arable soils.* Dissertation, Dept. of Microbiology, SLU. Acta Universitatis agriculturae Sueciae vol 2005, 71

Ohno, T. and Erich, M.S. 1990. Effect of wood ash application on soil pH and soil test nutrient levels. In: *Agric Ecosyst Environ* 32: pp. 223-239

Patterson, S.J., Acharya, S.N. and Thomas, J.E. et al. 2004. Integrated soil and crop management: Barley biomass and grain yield and canola seed yield response to land application of wood ash. In: *Agron J* 96: pp. 971–977

Roschke, M. 2003. Verwertung der Gärrückstände. In: *Leitfaden Biogas*, pp. 29–33.

Schiemenz, K. and Eichler-Löbermann, B. 2010. Biomass ashes and their phosphorus fertilizing effect on different crops. In: *Nutr. Cycl. Agroecos.*.87, 471-482

Umetsu, K., Kondo, R., Tani, M. and Hayashi, T. 2001. Fertilizer value of anaerobically co-digested dairy manure and food processing wastes. *Greenhouse Gases and Animal Agriculture, Proceedings*, pp. 331–342.

Van den Bossche, A., De Neve, S., Hofman, G. (2005): Soil phosphorus status of organic farming in Flanders: an overview and comparison with the conventional management. In: *Soil Use and Management* 21, 415-421

Van Reuler, H. and Janssen, B.H. 1996. Comparison of the fertilizing effect of ash from burnt secondary vegatation and of mineral fertilizers on upland rice in south-west Côte d'Ivoire. *Fert Res* 45: pp. 1-11

Chapter 23

Anderson, J.P.E. et al. (Eds.) 1996. Pesticides, soil microbiology and soil quality. In: *Abstr. From the 2nd Int. Symp. On Environmental Aspects of Pesticide Microbiology.* ISBN 90-5607-004-5. 191 pp.

Bergström, L. and Stenström, J. 1998. Environmental fate of chemicals in soil. In: *Ambio* Vol 27:1, pp. 16-23.

Brooks, G.T. and Roberts, T.R. (eds.) 1999. Pesticide chemistry and bioscience. The Food-Environment Challenge. Proc 9th Int. Congress on Pesticide Chemistry. Publ. by The Royal Scociety of Chemistry, Spec. Publ. No. 233. ISBN 0-85404-709-3. 438 pp.

Castillo, M.dP., Torstensson, L. and Stenström, J. 2008. Biobeds for environmental protection from pesticide use. A review. In: *J. Agric. Food Chem*. 56, 6206-6219

Domsch, K.H. 1992. *Pestizide im Boden. Mikrobieller Abbau und Nebenvirkungen auf Mikroorganismen*. VCH, Weinheim and Cambridge. 575 pp. ISBN 3-527-28431-1.

Eijsackers, H. 1998. Soil quality assessment in an international perspective: Generic and land- use based quality standards. In: *Ambio* 27:1, pp. 70-77.

Fomsgaard, I.S. 1999. *The mineralization of pesticides in surface and subsurface soil – in relation to temperature, soil texture, biological activity and initial pesticide concentration*. Ministry of Food, Agriculture and Fisheries, Danish Institute of Agricultural Sciences, Research Centre Foulum, Tjele. Ph. D. dissertation, No. 19 Plant Production . 224 pp.

Helweg, A. 1994. Threats to water quality from pesticides – Case histories from Denmark. In: *Pestic. Outlook*, 5 pp. 12-18

Tomlin, C.D.S. (Ed.) 2005. The pesticide manual. A world compendium. B.C.P.C., ISBN 1-901396-14-2. Also on CD, The e-Pesticide Manual Version 4.1, ISBN 1-901396-42-8.

Torstensson, L., Pell, M. and Stenberg, B. 1998. Need of a strategy for evaluation of arable soil quality. In: *Ambio* Vol 27:1, pp. 4-8.

Torstensson, L. 2000. Experiences of biobeds in practical use in Sweden. In: *Pestic. Outlook*, 11 pp.206-212.

Chapter 24

Kreuger, J. 1998. Pesticides in stream water within an agricultural catchment in southern Sweden, 1990-1996. In: *The Science of the Total Environment* 216: pp. 227-251.

Kreuger, J. and Brink, N. 1988. Losses of pesticides from agriculture. In: *Pesticides. Food and environmental implications. IAEA/FAO International Symposium on Changing Perspectives in Agrochemicals, 24-27 Nov. 1987*. IAEA: Vienna. pp. 101-112.

Torstensson, L. and Castillo, M.dP. 1997. Use of biobeds in Sweden to minimise environmental spillages from agricultural spraying equipment. In: *Pesticide Outlook* 8: pp. 24-27. This article was previously published in *2001 BCPC Symposium Proceedings NO. 78: Pesticide Behaviour in Soil and Water*

Chapter 25

Andersson, B. 1994. *Output from the NEGFRY warning system for potato late blight with various types of weather input data*. Workshop on Weather Information and Plant Protection, models, forecasting methods and information systems, Uppsala, Sweden 9-10 November.

Andersson, B. 2007. *Sexual reproduction in Phytophthora infestans. – epidemiological consequences*. Doctoral Thesis No. 2007:77, Faculty of Natural Resources and Agricultural Sciences,

Acta Universitatis Agriculturae Sueciae. Swedish University of Agricultural Sciences.

Andersson, B., Sandström, M. and Strömberg, A. 1998. Indications of soil borne inoculum of Phytophthora infestans. In: *Potato Research* 41, pp. 305-310.

Grichanov, I.Ya. 2002. *General information about important pests of different crops in NW Russia*. Crop Protection conference – Pests, diseases and weeds in NW Russia, St Petersburg, Pushkin, May 22-30, 2002. Conference Report 01. Uppsala, Swedish University of Agricultural Sciences.

Grichanov, I.Ya. 2010. *Modern information technologies of phytosanitary monitoring*. International conference on databases and information technologies for diagnostics, monitoring and forecasting the major weed, plants, plant pests and diseases. St Petersburg, Pushkin, June 14-17, 2010.

Grichanov, I.Ya. and Ovsyannikova, E.I., 2010. *Climate change and agricultural insect pests in Russia*. NJF Seminar 430: Climate change and Agricultural Production in the Baltic Sea region – Focus on Effects, Vulnerability and Adaption, Uppsala, Sweden. May 4-6, 2010. NJF Report, Vol 6, No1. Website: http://www.njf.nu

Lindblad, M. and Solbreck, C. 1998. Prediction Oscinella frit population densities from suction trap catches and weather data. In: *Journal of Applied Ecology*, 53: pp. 871-881.

Lindblad, M. 1993. Forecasting frit fly damage on oats using meteorological and monitoring data. *Workshop on Computer-based DSS on Crop Protection, Parma, Italy, 23-26 November 1993*.

Lindblad, M. and Sigvald, R. 2004. Temporal spread of wheat dwarf virus and mature plant resistance in winter wheat . In: *Crop Protection* 23 (3), pp. 229-234.

Lindblad, M. and Sigvald, R. 1999. Frit fly infestation of oats in relation to growth stage and weather conditions at oviposition. In: *Crop Protection* 18 (8), pp. 517-521.

Olvång, H. 1991. *Lönsamhet av bekämpning mot utvintringssvampar och stråknäckare vid förändrade spannmålspriser*. 32:a Svenska Växtskyddskonferensen, Uppsala.

Ruesink, W.G. and Irwin, M.E. 1986. Soybean mosaic virus epidemiology. A model and some implications. In: McLean, G. D., Garret, R. G. and Ruesink, W. G. (eds.). *Plant virus epidemics monitoring. Modelling and predicting outbreaks*. p 295-313. Academic Press, Australia

Rufelt, S., 1993. Starka angrepp av rapsjordloppa 1992. Erfarenheter av 18 års prognosundersökningar. In: *34:e Svenska växtskyddskonferensen, Uppsala, 1993*.

Saulich, M.I. and Grichanov, I.Ya., 2010. The database "Pest, Disease and Weed Warning System in Northwest Russia", NJF Seminar 430: Climate change and Agricultural Production in the Baltic Sea region – Focus on Effects, Vulnerability and Adaption, Uppsala, Sweden. May 4-6, 2010.

Sigvald, R. 1984. The relative efficiency of some aphid species as vectors of potato virus Yo (PVYo) In: *Potato Res* 27, pp. 285-290.

Sigvald, R. 1985. Mature plant resistance of potato plants against potato virus Yo (PVYo) In: *Potato Res*, 28 pp. 135-143.

Sigvald, R. 1986. Forecasting the incidence of potato virus Yo. In: McLean, G.D., Garret, R.G. and Ruesink, W.G. (eds.). *Plant virus epidemics monitoring. Modelling and predicting outbreaks*. pp. 419-441. Academic Press, Australia.

Sigvald, R. 1989. Relationship between aphid occurrence and spread of potato virus Yo (PVYo) in field experiments in southern Sweden. In: *J. Appl. Ent.* 108, p. 34-43.

Sigvald, R. 1990. Aphids on potato foliage in Sweden and their importance as vectors of potato virus Yo. In: *Acta Agric. Scand.* 40: pp. 53-58.

Sigvald, R. 1992. Progress in aphid forecasting systems. In: *Neth. J. Pl. Path*, 98, Supplement 2: pp. 55-62.

Twengström, E. and Sigvald, R. 1993. Forecasting sclerotinia stem rot using meteorological and field specific data. *Workshop on Computor-based DSS on Crop Protection, Parma, Italy, 23-26 November 1993.*

Twengström, E., Sigvald, R., Svensson, C. and Yuen, J. 1998. Forecasting Sclerotinia stem rot in spring sown oilseed rape. In: *Crop Protection*, 17:5, pp. 405-411.

Wiik, L. 1993. Väderleken och Septoria Spp. Sambandet mellan några klimatparametrar och skördeförlusten orsakad av Septoria Spp. In: *34e svenska växtskyddskonferensen, Uppsala, 1993.*

Wiik, L. 2009a. Yield and disease control in winter wheat in southern Sweden during 1977-2005. In: *Crop Protection* 28 (1), pp. 82-89

Wiik, L. and Ewaldz, T. 2009b. Impact of temperature and precipitation on yield and plant diseases of winter wheat in southern Sweden 1983-2007. In: *Crop Protection*, (Article in Press).

Wiktelius, S. 1981. *Studies on aphid migration with special reference to the bird cherry oat aphid Rhopalosiphum padi (L.).* Växtskyddsrapporter avhandlingar 5. Sveriges Lantbruksuniversitet, Uppsala.

Yuen, J., Twengström, E. and Sigvald, R. 1996. Calibration and verification of risk algorithms using logistic regression. In: *European Journal of Plant Pathology* 102:847-854.

Chapter 26

Chulkina, V.A., Toropova, E.U., Chulkin, U.I. and Stetsov, G.J. 2000. *Agrotechnical methods in plant orotection.* – Moscow.: (in Rus). *Encyclopedia Britannica*, 1999.

Soroka, S.V. (ed.) 2005. *Integrated Pest Management in agriculture.* Minsk.: 2005 (in Rus)

Chapter 27

Eilenberg, J., Hajek, A., Lomer, C. 2001. Suggestions for unifying the terminology in biological control. In: *BioControl* 46, 387-400.

Chapter 28

Alakukku, L. 2000. Response of annual crops to subsoil compaction in a field experiment on clay soil lasting 17 years. In: Horn, R., van den Akker, J. J. H. and Arvidsson, J. (eds.) *Subsoil compaction. Distribution, processes and consequences.* Advances in Geoecology 32: pp. 205-208.

Alakukku, L. 1999. Subsoil compaction due to wheel traffic. In: *Agricultural and Food Science in Finland.* 8: 333-351.

Alakukku, L., Ahokas, J. and Ristolainen, A. 2002. Response of clay soil macroporosity to stress caused by tracked tractors. In: Pagliai, M. and Jones, R. (eds.) *Sustainable land management. Environmental protection. A soil physical approach.* Advances in Geoecology 35: 319-330.

Alakukku, L., Weisskopf, P., Chamen, W.C.T., Tijink, F.G.J., Van Der Linden, J.P., Pires, S., Sommer, C. and Spoor, G. 2003. Prevention strategies for field traffic-induced subsoil compaction: a review, Part 1. Machine/soil interactions. In: *Soil & Tillage Research* 73: pp. 145-160.

Ansorge, D. and Godwin, R.J. 2007. The effect of tyres and a rubber track at high axle loads on soil compaction, Part 1: single axle-studies. In: *Biosystems Engineering* 98: pp. 115-126.

Arvidsson, J. 1998. Influence of soil texture and organic matter content on bulk density, air content, compression index and crop yield in field and laboratory compression experiments. In: *Soil Tillage Research* 49: pp. 159-170.

Arvidsson, J. 2001. Subsoil compaction caused by heavy sugarbeet harvesters un southern Sweden. I. Soil physical properties and crop yield in six field experiments. In: *Soil Tillage Research* 60: pp. 67-78.

Arvidsson, J. 1999. Nutrient uptake and growth of barley as affected by soil compaction. In: *Plant and Soil* 2008: pp. 9-19.

Arvidsson, J. and Håkansson, I. 1996. Do effects of soil compaction persist after ploughing? Results from 21 long-term field experiments in Sweden. In: *Soil Tillage Research* 39: 175-197.

Arvidsson, J., Trautner, A., Van den Akker, J.J.H. and Schjønning, P. 2001. Subsoil compaction caused by heavy sugarbeet harvesters in southern Sweden II. Soil displacement during wheeling and model computations of compaction. In: *Soil Tillage Research* 60: 79-89.

Ball, B.C., Scott, A. and Parker, J.P. 1999. Field N2O, CO2 and CH4 fluxes in relation to tillage compaction and soil quality in Scotland. In: *Soil Tillage Research* 53: 29-39.

Blackwell, P.S., Graham, J.P., Amstrong, J.V., Warc, M.A., Howse, K.R., Dawson, C.J. and Butler, A.R. 1986. Compaction of a silt loam soil by wheeled agricultural vehicles. I Effects upon soil conditions. In: *Soil Tillage Research* 7: 97-116.

Blake, G.R., Nelson, W.W., Allmaras, R.R., 1976. Persistence of subsoil compaction in a Mollisol. In: *Soil Science Society American Journal* 40: 943-948.

Chamen, T., Alakukku, L., Pires, S., Sommer, C., Spoor, G., Tijink, F. and Weisskopf, P. 2003. Prevention strategies for field traffic-induced subsoil compaction : a review, Part 2.Equipment and field practices. In: *Soil Tillage Research* 73: 161-174.

Chamen, W.C.T., Chittey, E.T., Leede, P.R., Goss, M.J. and Howse, K.R. 1990. The effect of tyre/soil contact pressure and zero traffic on soil and crop responses when growing winter wheat. In: *Journal of Agricultural Engineering Research* 47: 1-21.

Commision of the European Communities 2006. *Proposal for a Directive of the European Parliament and of the Council establishing a framework for the protection of soil and amending Directive 2004/35/EC.* COM (2006) 232 final http://ec.europa.eu/environment/soil/pdf/com_2006_0232_en.pdf).

Ehlers, W. 1982. Die Bedeutung des Bodengefüges für das Pflanzenwachstum bei moderner Landbewirtschaftung. In: *Mitteilungen Deutsche Bodenkundliche Gesellschaft* 34: 115-128.

References

Eriksson, J. 1982. *Markpackning och rotmiljö*. Summary: Soil compaction and plant roots. Swedish University of Agricultural Sciences. Reports Divison of Agricultural Hydrotechnics 126: 1-138.

Etana, A., Håkansson, I., 1994. Swedish experiments on the persistence of subsoil compaction caused by vehicles with high axle load. In: *Soil Tillage Research* 29: 167-172.

Fullen, M.A., 1985. Compaction, hydrological processes and erosion on loamy sands in east Shropshire, England. In: *Soil Tillage Research*. 6: 17-29.

Guérif, J. 1990. Factors influencing compaction-induced increases in soil strength. In: *Soil Tillage Research* 16: 167-178.

Hamza, M.A. and Anderson, W.K. 2005. Soil compaction in cropping systems a review of the nature, causes and possible solutions. In: *Soil Tillage Research* 82: 121-145.

Hanssen, S. 1996. Effects of manure treatment and soil compaction on palnt production of a dairy farm system converting to organic farming practice. In: *Agriculture, Ecosystem and Environment* 56: 173-186.

Horn, R. and Lebert, M. 1994. Soil compactability and compressibility. In: Soane, B. D. and van Ouwerkerk, C. (eds.). *Soil compaction in crop production*. Elsevier Science B.V, The Netherlands. p. 45-70.

Håkansson, I. and Petelkau, H. 1994. Benefits of limited axle load. In: Soane, B.D. and Van Ouwerkerk, C. (eds.) *Soil Compaction in Crop Production. Developments in Agricultural Engineering* 11. Elsevier, Amsterdam, The Netherlands, pp. 479-499.

Håkansson, I. 2005. *Machinery-induced compaction of arable soils. Incidence-consequences-counter-measures*. SLU Department of Soil Sciences. Reports from the Divison of Soil Management. No 109. 153 p.

Kirkham, D. and Horton, R. 1990. Managing soil-water and chemical transport with surface flow barriers. II. Theoretical. In: *Agronomy Abstract* 82: 213.

Kooistra, M.J. and Boersma, O.H. 1994. Subsoil compaction in Dutch marine sandy loams: loosening practices and effects. In: *Soil Tillage Research* 29: 237-237.

Koolen, A.J. and Kuipers, H. 1983. *Agricultural soil mechanics*. Adv. Series Agric. Sci. 13. Springer-Verlag, Berlin Heidelberg, Germany. 241 p.

Lebert, M., Burger, N. and Horn, R. 1989. Effects of dynamic and static loading on compaction of structured soils. In: Larson, W.E., Blake, G.R., Allmaras, R.R., Voorhees, W.B. and Gupta, S.C. (eds.). *Mechanics and related processes in structured agricultural soils*, NATO ASI Series E: Applied Sci. 172, pp. 73-80.

Lipiec, J. and Stępniewski, W. 1995. Effects of soil compaction and tillage systems on uptake and losses of nutrients. In: *Soil Tillage Research* 35: 37-52.

Oldeman, L.R., Hakkeling, R.T.A. and Sombroek, W.G. 1991. *World map of the status of human-induced soil degradation. An explanatory note*. ISRIC, Wageningen, the Netherlands/UNEP, Nairobi, Kenya. 34 p.

Olesen, J.E. and Munkholm, L.J. 2007. Subsoil loosening in a crop rotation for organic farming eliminated plough pan with mixed effects on crop yield. In: *Soil Tillage Research* 94: 376-385.

Pietola, L., Horn, R. and Yli-Halla, M. 2005. Effects of trampling by cattle on the hydraulic and mechanical properties of soil. In: *Soil Tillage Research* 82: 99-108.

Radford, B.J., Yule, D.F., McGarry, D. and Playford, C. 2001. Crop responses to applied soil compaction and to compaction repair treatments. In: *Soil Tillage Research* 61: 157-166.

Rasmussen, K.J. 1985. Jordpakning ved forkelling belating. Summary: Soil compaction with different surface pressure. In: *Tidsskrift för Planteavdelning* 89: 31-45.

Schjønning, P. and Rasmussen, K. 1994. Danish experiments on subsoil compaction by vehicles with high axle load. In: *Soil Tillage Research* 29: 215-227.

Simojoki, A., Jaakkola, A. and Alakukku, L. 1991. Effect of compaction on soil air in a pot experiment and in the field. In: *Soil Tillage Research* 19: 175-186.

Soane, B.D., Dickson, J.W. and Campbell, D.J. 1982. Compaction by agricultural vehicles: A review. III. Incidence and control of compaction in crop production. In: *Soil Tillage Research* 2: 2-36.

Soane, B. and van Ouwerkerk, C. 1995. Implications of soil compaction in crop production for the quality of the environment. In: *Soil Tillage Research* 35: 5-22.

Spoor, G., Tijink, F.G.J. and Weisskopf, P. 2003. Subsoil compaction: risk, avoidance, identification and alleviation. In: *Soil Tillage Research* 73: 175-182.

Tijink, F.G.J. 1994. Quantification of vehicle running gear. In: Soane, B.D. and Van Ouwerkerk, C. (eds.). *Soil compaction in crop production. Developments in agricultural engineering* 11. Elsevier Science B.V., The Netherlands, pp. 391-416.

Wollny, E. 1898. Untersuchungen über den Einfluss der mechanischen Bearbeitung auf die Fruchtbarkeit des Bodens. In: *Forschung Gep Agrikultur Physik* 20: 231-290.

Wu, L., Allmaras, R.R., Gimenez, D. and Huggins, D.M. 1997. Shrinage and water retention characteristic in a fine-textured mollisol compcation uncer different axle loads. In: *Soil Tillage Reseach* 44: 179-194.

Chapter 29

Arvidsson, J., Elmqvist, H., Gunnarsson, S., Johansson, D., Rydberg, T., Salomon, E. and Stenberg, M. 1997. *Results of research in soil tillage in 1996*. Report 91, Division of Soil Management, Swedish University of Agricultural Sciences, Uppsala. (In Swedish, with English summary).

Arvidsson, J., Ehrnebo, M., Etana, A., Gustafsson, K., Keller, T., Löfquist, J., Myrbeck, Å., Rydberg, T., Svantesson, U., Svensson, T. and Trautner, A. 2003. *Research in soil tillage in 2002*. Report 104, Division of Soil Management, Swedish University of Agricultural Sciences, Uppsala. (In Swedish, with English summary). 78 pp

Arvidsson, J. (ed.) 2006. *Research in soil tillage in 2005*. Report 109, Division of Soil Management, Swedish University of Agricultural Sciences, Uppsala. (In Swedish, with English summary). 84 pp.

Etana, A. and Rydberg, T. 2006. *A study on aggregate stability and on the risk for soil P-losses in two long-term tillage experiments*. Nr 51, Bulletins from the Division of Soil Management, Swedish University of Agricultural Sciences, Uppsala. (In Swedish, with English summary).

Myrbeck, Å., Rydberg, T. and Stenberg, M. 2006. Nitrogen efficient soil tillage systems. In: *Proceedings of ISTRO 17, 'Sustainability*

– its Impact on Soil Management and Environment. 28 August – 3 September, Kiel. Germany. On CD-Rom ISBN no: 3-9811134-0-3.

Rydberg, T. 1992. Ploughless tillage in Sweden. Results and experiences from 15 years of field trials. In: *Soil Tillage Res.*, 22, 253-264. Annual reports from the Division of Soil Management at the Swedish University of Agricultural Sciences, http://www.mv.slu.se/JB/jb.htm and www.ffe.slu.se.

Chapter 30

Askinazi, D.L., Ginzburg, K.E. and Lebedeva, L.S. 1963. Mineral phosphorus compounds in soil and methods of its determination. In: *Soil science*, 5, p. 27 (in Rusian).

Chang, S.C. and Jackson, M.L. 1957. *The nature and properties of soils*, 12th ed. Prentice-Hall, Inc., Upper Saddle River, NJ, pp. 175-181.

Lukin, S., Simakov, G. and Shilova, N. 1998. *Nutrient looses upon application of organic manure. Lysimetrics investigations in agrochemistry, soil science, melioration and agroecology*. Moscow-Nemchinovka, p. 96-101 (in Rusian).

Mazvila, J.1998. *Lietuvos dirvozemiu agrochemines savybes ir ju kaita*. Petro ofsetas, Kaunas, pp. 68-69,107-119 (in Lithuanian).

Titova, V.I., Varlamova, L.D. and Trofonov, A.I. 1998. *Some peculiarities of phosphorus compounds migrations in phosphorus-rich soils. Lysimetrics methods of soil study*. Moscow, p. 84-87 (in Russian).

Tripolskaja, L. 2002. Phosphorus changes in a soil at regular application of organic fertilizers. In: Rubio, J.L., Morgan, R.P.C., Asins, S. and Andreu, V. (eds.) *Proceedings of the third International Congress Man and Soil at the Third Millenium*. Geoforma, Ediciones Logrono.

Tripolskaja, L. 2004. The effects of long-term fertilizer use on soil properties in lysimetric stations. In: *Agriculture – proceedings of the Lithuanian institute of Agriculture*, 1, 85: 17-27 (in Lithuanian, abstract in English).

Tripolskaja, L. and Marcinkonis S. 2003. The effect of mineral fertilizing and liming on soil phosphorus regime. In: *LLU Raksti – proceedings of the Latvia University of Agriculture* 8 (303): 22-28.

Chapter 31

Boile M. 2002. Erosion's contribution to greenhouse gasses. In: *Erosion Control*, January/February 2002. http://www.forester.net/ecm_0201_gases.html

Bundiniene O. and Paukšte V. 2002. The work of the Dukstas Research Station of the Lithuanian Institute of Agriculture in 1960-2000. In: *Agricultural Sciences*, Nr. 4. pp. 45-53. (In Lithuanian with summaries in English and Russian).

Feiza V., Malinauskas A. and Putna J. 2004. *Theory and practice of ploughing*. Lithuanian Institute of Agriculture. Akademija. 219 pp. (In Lithuanian with summary in English).

Feiziene, D. 1996. *Differentiation of fertilisers application on the hills in Western Lithuania. Sustainable agricultural development and rehabilitation*. Proceedings of International Symposium, Tallinn, 133-138.

Jankauskas B. 1996. *Soil erosion*. Margi rastai. Vilnius. 168 pp. (In Lithuanian with summary in English).

Jankauskas B. and Fullen M.A. 2002 A pedological investigation of soil erosion severity on undulating land in Lithuania. In: *Canadian Journal of Soil Science* 82: pp. 311-321.

Jankauskas B. and Jankauskiene G. 2003. Erosion-preventive crop rotations for landscape ecological stability in upland regions of Lithuania. In: *Agriculture, Ecosystems and Environment* 95: pp. 129-142.

Jankauskas B. and Kiburys B. 2000. Water erosion as a consequence of tillage erosion in the hilly relief of Lithuania. In: *ESSC Newsletter* 3+4/2000. pp. 3; and http://slide.giub.uni-bonn.de/Events/ESSC/ 4 pp.

Jankauskas B., Jankauskiene G., and Fullen M.A. 2004, Erosion-preventive crop rotations and water erosion rates on undulating slopes in Lithuania. In: *Canadian Journal of Soil Science*, Vol. 84, No 2: – pp. 177-186.

Jankauskas, B., Jankauskiene, G. and Fullen, M.A. 2007. Relationships between soil organic matter content and soil erosion severity on the Albeluvisols of the Žemaičiai Uplands. In: *Ekologija*, Vol. 53. No. 1: pp. 21-28.

Jankauskas, B., Slepetiene, A., Jankauskiene, G. Fullen, M.A. and Booth, C.A. 2006. A comparative study of soil organic matter content in Lithuanian Eutric Albeluvisols and the development of transfer functions for associated analytical methodologies. In: *Geoderma*, Vol. 136: pp. 763-773.

Kiburys, B. 1989. *Mechanical soil erosion*. Mokslas. Vilnius. 174 pp. (In Lithuanian).

Kiburys. B., Jankauskas, B. 1997. The extent and relative importance of tillage erosion as cause of accelerated soil erosion on hilly landscapes. In: *Journal of Soil and Water Conservation*, July-August, pp. 307.

Kudaba, C. 1983. *Uplands of Lithuania*. Mokslas. Vilnius. 186 pp. (In Lithuanian).

Njøs, A. 1991. Soil Erosion - a Problem for Agriculture and Environment in Norway. In: Lilleng, H. and Rognerud, B. (eds.). *Environmental challenges and solutions in agricultural engineering. Proceedings, Seminar of the 1st, 2nd and 3rd Technical Sessions of CIGR*, Ås – Norway, pp. 99–113.

Norgailiene, Z. and Zableckiene, D. 1994. Selection of different maturity of moving and grazing grass-stands for erodible clay loam soils. In: *Agricultural Sciences* 3: pp. 72-76. (In Lithuanian, with English and Russian abstracts).

Oygarden, L., Lundekvam, H., Arnoldussen, A.H. and Borresen, T. 2006. Norway. In Boardman, J. and Poesen, J. (Eds.) *Soil erosion in Europe*. John Wiley & Sons, Ltd. P. 3-15.

Tattari S. and Rekolainen, S. 2006. Finland. In Boardman, J. and Poesen, J. (Eds.) *Soil erosion in Europe*. John Wiley & Sons, Ltd. pp. 28-32.

Ulen, B. 2006. Sweden. In: Boardman, J. and Poesen, J. (eds.) *Soil erosion in Europe*. John Wiley & Sons, Ltd. pp. 18-25.

Chapter 32

Bogdevitch, I.M., Shmigelskaja, I.D., Germanovitch, T.M., Konashenko,Yu. and Kalenik, G. 2005. Dynamika plodorodija pachotnych poch v Belorussiji. In: *Pochvovedenije i agrochimija*, 1:34, pp 167-173.

Chwil, S. 2002. Changes of basic indices of acidification in soil profile as affected by fertilization. In: *Zeszyty problemowe postepow nauk rolniczych*. 482, ss79-85.

Eidukevičienė, M. 1993. *Geochimicheskoje i geograficheskoje obosnovanije optimizirovanija izvestkovanija kislysh pochv Litvy*. The work of doctor habilitatis. Vilnius: Vilniuskij Universitet. 99 p.

Eidukevičienė, M. 2001. *Kalkinimo įtaka dirvožemio cheminėms savybėms*. Lietuvos dirvožemiai. Vilnius: Lietuvos mokslas, Knyga 32, 855-869.

Eidukevichiene, M.J., Ozheraitiene, D.J., Tripolskaja, L.N. and Marcinkonis, S.I. 2001. The effect of long-term liming on the chemical properties of Lithuanian soils. In: *Eurasian Soil Science*, 34:9, pp 999-1005.

Eidukevičienė, M., Ožeraitienė, D., Tripolskaja, L. and Volungevičius, J. 2007. Change of soil pH in the territory of Lithuania: spatial and temporal analysis. *Žemės ūkio mokslai*, T.3, p. 1-8.

Eidukevičienė, M., Volungevičius, J. and Prapiestienė, R. 2006. Dirvožemio pH erdvinių dėsningumų Lietuvoje pagrindimas. In: *Geografija*, 42:2, pp 8-14.

Eidukeviciene, M., Volungevicius, J., Marcinkonis, S., Tripolskaja, L., Karcauskiene, D., Fullen, M.A. and Booth, C.A. 2010. Interdisciplinary analysis of soil acidification hazard and its legacy effects in Lithuania. In: *Nat. Hazards Earth Syst. Sci.*, 10, 1477–1485

Eresko, M. 2005. Bufernost k podkisleniju dernovo-podzolystych pochv razlichnovo granulometricheskovo sostava i stepeni uvlaznenija. In: Pochvovedenije i agrochimija, 1:34, pp 96-99.

Ivanov, A.I. 2000. Nekotoryje zakonomiernosti izmenenija kislotno-osnovnovo sostojanija dernovo-podzolistych pochv pri sielsko-choziaistvennom ispolzovanii. In: *Agrokhimiya*, 10, pp 28-33.

Mažvila, J., Vaičys, M. and Buivydaitė, V. 2006. *Lietuvos dirvožemių makromorfologinė diagnostika*. Akademija: Lietuvos žemdirbystės institutas,. 283 p.

Soil Atlas of Europe. 2005. European Soil Bureau Network European Commission. Luxembourg: Office for Official Publications of the European Communities, p.25-126.

Volungevičius, J., Eidukevičienė, M. and Prapiestienė, R. 2006. Assessment of grain – size composition spatial structure for Lithuania's Pleistocene surface deposits by statistical grid method. In: *Geologija*, 55, pp58-65.

Chapter 33

Andrén, O., Kihara, J., Bationo, A., Vanlauwe, B. and Kätterer, T. 2007. Soil climate and decomposer activity in sub-Saharan Africa estimated from standard weather station data – a simple climate index for soil carbon balance calculations. In: *Ambio* 36:379-386.

International Panel on Climate Change (IPCC). 1997. *The Revised 1996 IPCC Guidelines for National Greenhouse Gas Inventories*. http://www.ipcc-nggip.iges.or.jp/public/gl/invs1.htm

Kätterer, T., Andrén, O. and Jansson, P-E. 2006. Pedotransfer functions for estimating plant available water and bulk density in Swedish agricultural soils. In: *Acta Agric Scand. Sec. B* 56: 263-276.

Kätterer, T., Bolinder, M.A., Andrén, O., Kirchmann, H. and Menichetti, L. 2011. Roots contribute more to refractory soil organic matter than aboveground crop residues, as revealed by a long-term field experiment. In: *Agric. Ecosys. Environ.* 141: 184-192.

Le Quéré et al. 2009. Trends in the sources and sinks of carbon dioxide. In: *Nature Geoscience* 2: 831 – 836.

Smith et al. 2008. Greenhouse gas mitigation in agriculture. In: *Phil. Trans. R. Soc.* B 363: 789-813.

Chapter 34

Lehmann, J. 2007. A handful of carbon. In: *Nature* 447(10):143-144.

Lehmann, J. and Joseph, S. (Eds.) 2009. *Biochar for environmental management*. Earthscan, London, UK and Sterling, VA, USA. 416 pp. http://www.earthscan.co.uk/?tabid=49381

Preston, C.M. and Schmidt, M.W.I. 2006. Black (pyrogenic) carbon: a synthesis of current knowledge and uncertainties with special consideration of boreal regions. In: *Biogeosciences*, 3:397–420.

Chapter 35

Alekseev, Y. 1987. *Heavy metals in soil* and plants. Leningrad: Publishing House Agropromizdat, 142 p /in Russian/

Benson, N.R. 1953. Effect of season, phosphate and acidity on plant growth in arsenic toxic soils. In: *Soil Sci.*, 76, 215, 1953

Bolan, N., Adriano, D. and Curtin, D. 2003. Soil acidification and liming interactions with nutrient and heavy metal transformation and bioavailability. In: *Advances in Agronomy*, Vol. 78: 215-272

Cataldo, D.A. and Garland, T.R., and Wildung, R.E. 1983. Cadmium uptake kinetics in intact soybean plants. In: *Plant Physiol.*, 73, 844.

Cho, J, Han, K. 1996. Comparison of growth and physiological responses in radish for assay of nickel toxicity. I. Growth of radish and adsorption and translocation of nickel. In: *Agricultural Chemistry and Biotechnology*, Vol. 39, Issue 4: 287-292

Dudley, L.M., McNeal, B.I. and Baham, J.E. 1986. Time-dependent changes in soluble organic copper, nickel, and zinc from sludge amended soils. In: *J. Environ. Qual.*, 15,188.

Eriksson, J.E. 1989. The influence of pH, soil type and time on adsorption and uptake of cadmium. In: *Water, air, soil pollut.*, 48,317.

Gorbatov, V. and Zyrin, N. 1987. About choosing of substance for extraction of exchangeable heavy metals kations from soils. In: *Bulletin of Moscow State University, Issue Soil Science* 2, pp 22-26 /in Russian/

Haghiri, F. 1974. Plant uptake of cadmium as influenced by cation exchange capacity, organic matter, zinc and soil temperature. In: *J. Environ. Qual.*, 3,180.

Haq, A., Bates, T. and Soon, Y. 1980. Comparison of extractants for plant-available zinc, cadmium, nickel and copper in contaminated soils. In: *Soil Sci. Soc. Amer.* J. 44: 772-777

Hinesly, T.D., Redborg, K.E., Ziegler, E.L. and Alexander, D.E. 1982. Effect of soil cation exange capacity on the uptake of cadmium by corn. In: *Soil Sci. Soc. Am. J.*, 46, 490. http://www.db-thueringen.de/servlets/DerivateServlet/Derivate-1304/Dissertation.pdf

Kabata-Pendias, A. and Pendias, H. 1992. *Trace Elements in Soils and Plants*, 2nd ed. CRC Press, Boca Raton. 365 p.

Kabata-Pendias, A. 2001. *Trace elements in soils and plants.* 3d ed. CRC Press LLC, USA, 331 p

Knoche, H., Brandt P., Götte-Viereck, L. and Böcken, H. 1999. *Schwermetalltransfer Boden-Pflanze. Ergebnisse der Auswertungen hinsitlich der Koenigswasser- und Ammoniumnitrat-Extraction anhand der Datebank TRANSFER.* Texte 11, Umwelt Bundes Amt, Berlin, ISSN: 0722-186X, 213 p

Kovalskiy, V. and Letunova, S. 1974. *Geochemical ecology of microorganisms.* Tr. Biogeochim. Lab, 13 3.: 15-25 /in Russian/

Marin , A.R., Masscheleyn, P.H., and Patrick Jr., W.H. 1993. Soil redox-pH stability of arsenic species and its influence on arsenic uptake by rice. In: *Plant and Soil.* 152, 245.

Masscheleyn, P., Pardue, J., Delaune, R. and Patrick, J. 1991. Effect of redox potential and pH on As speciation and solubility in a contaminated soil. In: *Environ. Sci. Tech.* 25: 1414–1419

McLaughlin, M. 2002. Heavy metals. In: Lal, R. (eds.) *Encyclopedia of soil science.* pp. 650-653

Miller, J.E., Hassett, J.J. and Koeppe, D.E. 1976. Uptake of cadmium by soybean as influenced by soil cation exchange capacity, pH and available phosphorus. In: *J. Environ. Qual.*, 5, 157.

Mineev, V.G. 1990. *Chemization of agriculture.* Agropromizdat, Moscow P 287.

Ming, D. 2002. Carbonates. In: Lal, R. (eds.) *Encyclopedia of soil science.* pp. 139-142

Morel, J.L. 1997. Bioavailability of trace elements to terrestrial plants. In: Tarradellas, J., Bitton, G. and Rossel, D. (eds.) 1997. *Soil ecotoxicology.* CRS Press, p. 141-176.

Mulla, D.J., Page, A.L. and Ganje, T.J. 1980. Cadmium accumulations and bioavailability in soils from long term phosphorus fertilization. In: *J. Environ. Qual.*, 10, 408.

Nebolsin, A. and Sychev, V. (eds.). 2000. *Ecological-economical recommendations on liming adapted to the certain soil conditions.* Moscow: Publishing House of the Central Institute of Agrochemical Service TSINAO 80 p (in Russian)

Patrick, H., Ronald, D. and Patrick, J. 1990. Transformations of Se, As affected by sediment oxidation–reduction potential and pH. Environ. In: *Sci. Tech.* 24 : 91–96

Reddy, C.N. and Patrick, W.H. 1977. Effect on redox potential and pH on the uptake of cadmium and lead by rice plants. In: *J. Environ. Qual.*, 6, 259

Richards, B., Steenhus, T., Peverly, J. and McBride, M. 2000. Effect of sludge-processing mode, soil texture and soil pH on metal mobility in undisturbed soil columns under accelerated loading. In: *Environmental Pollution* 109: 327-346

Rothbaum, H.P., Goguel, R.L., Johnston, A.E. and Mattingly, G.E.G. 1986. Cadmium accumulation in soils from long-continued application of superphosphate. In: *J. Soil Sci.*, 37, 99,

Schoenbuchner, H. 2005. *Untersuchungen zu Mobilitaet und Boden-Pflanze-Transfer von Schvermetallen auf/in uranhaltigen Haldenboeden.* Dissertation Dr. Ere. Nat., Gemisch-Geowissenschaftlichen Fakultaet der Friedrich-Schiller-Universitaet Jena. Publikation on-line:

Smilde, K.W., van Luit, B. and van Driel, W. 1992.The extraction by soil and absorption by plants of applied zinc and cadmium. In: *Plant and Soil*, 143, 233.

Stevenson, F.J. 1982. *Humus chemistry, genesis, composition, reaction*s. New York: John Wiley& Sons, p. 443.

Tyler, L.D. and McBride, M.B. 1982. Influence of Ca, pH, and humic acid on Cd uptake. In: *Plant and Soil*, 64, 259.

Weyman-Kaczmarkowa, W. and Pedziwilk, Z. 2000. The development of fungi as affected by pH and type of soil, in relation to the occurrence of bacteria and soil fungi static activity. In: *Microbiological Research* 155 2.: pp. 107-112

White, M.C. and Chaney, R.L. 1980. Zinc, cadmium, and manganese uptake by soybeans from two zinc- and cadmium-amended coastal plain soils. In: *Soil Sci. Soc Am. J.*, 44, 308.

Yaron, B, Calvet, R., Prost, R. 1996. *Soil pollution processes and dynamics.* Berlin & Heidelberg: Springer-Verlag 313 p

Zachara , J.M., Smith, S.C., Resch, C.T. and Cowan, C.E. 1993. Cadmium sorption on specimen and soil smectites in sodium and calcium electrolytes. In: *Soil Sci. Soc. Am. J.*, 57, 1491.

Zyrin, D. and Orlov, D. (eds.). 1980. *Physical and chemical investigation of soil.* Moscow: Publishing House of Moscow State University. 382 p /in Russian/

Zyrin, N. and Sadovnikova, L. (eds.). 1985. *Chemistry of heavy metals, Arsenicum, Molibdeum.* Moscow: Publishing House of Moscow State University. P 206

Chapter 36

Anon. 1999. *Norms of radiation safety* (NRS). Ministry of Health Protection, Russian Federation.

Aleksakhin, R. and Korneeva, N. (eds.) 1992. A*gricultural radioecology.* Moscow: Publishing House Ecologia p. 400.

Cigna, A. and Durante, M. (eds.) 2005. *Radiation Risk Estimates in Normal and Emergency Situations: Proceedings of the NATO Advanced Research Workshop on Impact of Radiation Risk Estimates in Normal and Emergency Situations*, Yerevan, Armenia, September 8-11 2005; ed.

Drichko, V. and Tsvetkova, V. 1990. Sorption model of radionuclides transfer from soil to plants. USSR Academy of Science. In: *Soil Science*, Issue 10: pp. 35-40 (in Russian)

Drichko, V., Ponikarova, T. and Efremova, M. 1996. Uptake of 137Cs by grasses from peatsoil under increasing K- and N-fertilization rates. In: *Radiobiology. Radioecology*, Vol. 36, Issue 4: 524-530 (in Russian)

Drichko, V., Izosimova, A., Lisachenko, E., Graschenko, E. and Shamov, V. 2008. Setting normative rates of natural radionuclides in phosphorus fertilizers. In: De Kok, L. J. and Schnug, E. (eds.). *Loads and fate of fertilizer derived uranium.* Leiden: Backhuys Publishers, pp. 203-209.

Firsakova, S., Timofeev, S., Shumilin, V. and Podolyak, A. 2002. Accumulation of 90Sr by grccn crops undcr conditions of ra dioactive contamination of agricultural lands. In: *Radiobiology. Radioecology*, Vol. 42, Issue 3: pp. 345-351 (in Russian)

Nisbet, A.F. and Wodman, R.F.M. 2000. Soil-to-plant transfer factors for radiocaesium and radiostrontium in agricultural systems. In: *Health Phys.* 78(3), pp. 278-279.

References

Yudintseva, E., Zhigareva, T. and Sidorova, E. 1980. Influence of lime application on radionuclides availability for plants. In: *Agricultural Chemistry* 6: pp. 93-98 (in Russian)

Wauters, J., Sweeck, L., Valke, E., Elsen, A. and Cremers, A. 1994. Availability of radiocaesium in soils: a new methodology. In: *Sci. Total Environ.* V. 157. pp. 239-248

Chapter 37

Attra. 1995. An overview of organic crop production. In: *Fundamentals of sustainable agriculture. Appropriate technology transfer for rural areas* (ATTRA), online: http//www.attra.org.

Balzer-Graf, U.R. 1987. Vitalaktivität fon Nahrungsmittel im Spiegel bildschaffender Methoden. In: *Elemente der Naturwissenschaft*, 46, pp 69-92.

Balzer-Graf, U.R. and Balzer, F.M. 1991. Steigbild und Kupferchlor idkristallisation – Spiegel der Vitalaktivität von Lebensmitteln. In: Meier-Ploeger, A. and Vogtmann, H. *Lebensmittelqualität – Ganzheitliche Methoden und Konzepte*. 2. Auflage. Karlsruhe: Verlag C.F. Müller, pp 163-210.

Benbrook, C. 2005. *Breaking the mold. Impacts of organic and conventional farming systems on mycotoxins in food and livestock feed*. Review. Boulder, Co.: The Organic Center.

Boeringa, R. 1980. *Alternative methods of agriculture*. Amsterdam: Elsevier, 160 p.

Brandt, K. and Molgaard, J.P. 2006. Food quality. In: Kristiansen et al., *Organic agriculture. A global perspective*. Clayton South VIC: CSIRO, pp 305-322.

Brandt, K. 2007. Organic agriculture and food utilization. In: *Organic agriculture and food security*, FAO, Italy.Online: http//www.fao. org./organicag/oft/index_en.htm. Accessed 08/11/07.

Canali, S. 2003. Soil quality of organically managed citrus orchards in the mediterranean area. In: *Organic agriculture, sustainability, markets and policies*. CABI Publishing, OECD, pp 115-125.

Carson, R. 1962. *Silent spring*. Boston: Houghton Mifflin Comp.

Dabbert, S. 2003. Organic agriculture and sustainability: Environmental Aspects. In: *Organic Agriculture: Sustainability, Markets and Policies*. OECD, CABI Publishing, pp 51-64.,

Davis, J. and Abbott, L. 2006. Soil fertility in organic farming systems. In: Kristiansen et al. *Organic agriculture. A global perspective*, Clayton South VIC: CSIRO, pp 25-51.

Dlouhý, J. 1990. Quality in ecological agriculture. In: *Alternative agriculture, proceedings*, Uppsala, 5, pp 209-219.

El-Hage Scialabba, N., Grandi, C. and Henatsch, C. 2002. *Organic agriculture and genetic resources for food and agriculture*. FAO, Italy.

El-Hage Scialabba, N. 2007. *Organic agriculture and food security*, FAO, Italy, Online: http//www.fao.org/organicag, Accessed 08/11/2007.

Ewel, J. 1986. Designing agricultural ecosystems for the humid tropics. In: *Annual Review of Ecology and Systematics,* 17, pp 245-271.

FAO. 1999. *Codex OA definition*. Online: http//www.fao.org/do-crep/003/AC116E/ac116e02.htm.

FAO. 2007. *International conference on organic agriculture and food security, Report, Rome*, 11 p. Online:http//www.fao.org/organicag/ofs/index_en.htm, Accessed 08/11/07.

Foereid, B. and Hogh-Jensen, H. 2004. *Carbon sequestration potential of organic agriculture in northern Europe – a modelling approach*. Nutrient Cycling in Agroecosystems 68, pp 13-24.

Hart, M.R., Quin, B.F. and Nguyen, M. 2004. Phosphorus runoff from agricultural land and direct fertiliser effects. In: *A Review, J. Environ. Qual.,* 33, pp 1954-1972.

IFOAM 2009. *The principles of organic agriculture* Online:http//www. ifoam.org/about_ifoam/principles/index.html, Accessed 16/10/09.

IFOAM. 2009. *Global organic agriculture. Continued growth*. Online: http//www.ifoam.org/press/2008, Accessed 10/11/09.

Kasperczyk, N. and Knickel, K. 2006. Environmental impacts of organic farming. In: Kristiansen, P. et al. *Organic Agriculture a Global Perspective*, Clayton South VIC: CSIRO, 259-294.

Kristiansen, P. and Merfield, C.H. 2006 Overview of organic agriculture. In: Kristiansen P. et al. *Organic agriculture. A global perspective*, Clayton South VIC: CSIRO, 1-19.

Lacko-Bartošová, M. et al. 1995. *Ekologické poľnohospodárstvo*, Nitra: EKO, 173 p.

Lacko-Bartošová, M. 2006. Sustainable agricultural systems – production and qualitative parameters. In: *Scientifical papers Agriculture, XXXVIII, Timisoara*, pp 151-154.

Leiber, F., Fuchs, N. and Spiess, H. 2006. Biodynamic agriculture today. In: Kristiansen P. et al. *Organic agriculture. A global perspective.* Clayton South VIC: CSIRO, pp 141-150.

Lotter, D.W., Seidel, R. and Liebhardt, W. 2003. The performance of organic and conventional cropping systems in an extreme climate year. In: *Am. J. of Alternative Agriculture*, 18, 3, pp 146-154.

Lotter, D.W. 2003. Organic agriculture, In: *J. Sustain. Agric. 21* (4).

Mariott, E.E. and Wander, M.M. 2006. Total and labile soil organic matter in organic and conventional farming systems. In: *Soil Sci. Soc. Am J.* 70, pp 950-959.

Mäder, P., Pfiffner, L., Niggli, U., Plochberger, K., Velimirov, A., Balzer, U., Balzer, F. and Besson, J.M. 1993. Effect of three farming systems on yield and quality of beetroot in a seven year crop rotation. In: *Acta horticulturae,* 339, pp 11-31.

Mäder, P., Fliessbach, A., Wiemken, A. and Niggli, U. 1995. Assessment of soil microbial status under long-term low input and high input agriculture. In: *Proceedings: Concerted action AIR 3-CT 94 "Fertilization systems in organic farming". Darmstadt,* pp 24-38.

Mäder, P., Fliessbach, A., Dubois, D., Gunst, L., Padruot, F. and Niggli, U. 2002. Soil fertility and biodiversity in organic farming. In: *Science,* 296, pp 1694-1697.

Nguyen, M.L., Haynes, R.J. and Goh, K.M. 1995. Nutrient budgets and status in three pairs of conventional and alternative mixed cropping farms in Cantenbury. In: *Agriculture, Ecosystems and Environment* 52, pp 149-162.

Niggli, U., Earley, J. and Ogorzalek, K. 2007. Organic agriculture and environmental stability of the food supply. In: *Organic agriculture and food security*, FAO, Italy. Online:http//www.fao.org/organicag/ofs/index_en.htm, Accessed 08/11/07.

OECD. 1997. *Environmental Indicators for Agriculture*. Paris.

Olesen, J., Rasmussen, A. and Askegaard, M. 2000. Crop rotations for grain production. In: *Proceedings 13 International IFOAM Sci. Conference, Basel, 145.*

Padel, S. and Lampkin, N.H. 1994. Farm level performance of organic farming systems, an overview. In: Lampkin, N.H.- Padel, S. *The Economics of Organic Farming.* CAB, UK, pp 201-219.

Pfeiffer, E.E. 1984. *Chromatography applied to quality testing.* Wyoming: Bio-Dynamic Literature pp 1-44.

Pfiffner, L. and Mäder, P. 1997. Effect of biodynamic, organic and conventional production systems on earthworm populations. In: *Biological Agriculture and Horticulture,* 15, pp 3-10.

Pimentel, D. and Hepperly, P. and Hanson, J. and Douds, D. and Seidel, R. 2005. Environmental, energetic, and economic comparisons of organic and conventional farming systems. In: *BioScience* 55, pp 573-582.

Plochberger, K. 1989. Feeding experiments. A criterion for quality estimation of biologically and conventionally produced foods. In: *Agriculture, Ecosystems and Environment,* 27, pp 419-428.

Plochberger, K. and Velimirov, A. 1992. Are food preference tests with laboratory rats a proper method for evaluating nutritional quality? In: *Biological Agriculture and Horticulture,* Vol. 8, pp 221-233.

Popp, F.A. 1988. Biophotonen – Analyse der Lebensmittel. In: Meier-Ploeger, A, Vogtmann, H. *Lebensmittelqualität – ganzheitliche Methoden und Konzepte,* Alternative Konzepte, 66, pp 87-112.

Pretty, J. and Hine, R. 2001. *Reducing food poverty with sustainable agriculture: a summary of new evidence.* Essex, UK: SAFE Res. Project 136 p.

Rembialkowska, E. 2004. The impact of organic agriculture on food quality. In: *Agricultura* 3, pp 19-26.

Ryan, M. 1999. Is an enhanced soil biological community, relative to conventional neighbours, a consistent feature of alternative agricultural systems ? In: *Biological Agriculture and Horticulture* 17, pp 131-144.

Siegrist, S., Staub, D., Pfiffner, L. and Mäder, P. 1998. Does organic agriculture reduce soil erodibility ? The results of a long-term field study on loess in Switzerland. In: *Agriculture, Ecosystems and Environment* 69, pp 253-264.

Stolze, M., Piorr, A., Häring, A. and Dabbert, S. 2000. *The environmental impacts of organic farming in Europe.* Vol. 6, University of Hohenheim, 127 p.

Willer, H., Yussefi-Menzler, M. and Sorensen, N. 2008. *The world of organic agriculture.* Statistics and Emerging Trends 2008, IFOAM and FiBL.

Vogtmann, H. 1992. *Ökologische landwirtschaft,* Stiftung Ökologie und Landbau, Verlag C.F. Müller, 350 p.

Woodward, L. and Vogtmann, H. 2004. IFOAM´s organic principles. In: *Ecology and Farming* 36, pp 24-26.

Younie, D., Taylor, D. and Watson, C.H. 2000. Effect of crop rotation, manure application and site on yield and grain quality of organic oats. In: *Proceedings 13 International IFOAM Sci. Conference, Basel, 146.*

Zundel, C.H. and Kilcher, L. 2007. Organic agriculture and food avaibality. In: *Organic Agriculture and Food Security,* FAO, Italy, Online:http//www.fao.org/organicag/ofs/index_en.htm, Accessed 08/11/07.

Chapter 38

Adams, R.M., Hurd, B.H. and Reilly, J. 1999. *Agriculture and global climate change. A review of impacts to U.S. Agricultural Resources.* Arlington, VA: Pew Center on Global Climate Change.

Anonymous, 2006. Brawn yields to brains. 2006. In: *The Economist,* March print edition.

Azeez, G.S.E. and Hewlett, K.L. 2008. The comparative energy efficiency of organic farming. In: *ISOFAR Proceedings, Modena Italy, June 2008.* pp. 316-319.

Bengtsson, A. Ahnstrom, A. and Weibull, A-C. 2005. The effects of organic agriculture on biodiversity and abundance: a meta-analysis In: *Journal of Applied Ecology* 42: 261–269.

Burnham, A., Wang, M. and Wu, Y. 2006. *Development and applications of GREET 2.7 —The transportation vehicle-cycle.* Argonne National Laboratory.

Bryant, R. and Goodman, M., 2004. Consuming narratives: the political ecology of 'alternative' consumption. In: *Transactions of the Institute of British Geographers* 29 (3), pp 344–366.

Buller, H. and Morris, C. 2004. Growing goods: the market, the state, and sustainable food production. In: *Environment and Planning* 36 : pp1065- 1084

Clay, J. 2003. *World agriculture and the environment. A commodity-by-commodity guide to impacts and practices.* Washington: Island Press.

Curry, P. 2008. *Personal communication.* Prepared for the Illinois Foods Background Report.

D'Angelo, D.J., Webster, R.J. and Benfield, E.F. 1991. Mechanisms of stream phosphorus retention: An experimental study. In: *Journal of the North American Benthological Society* 10: pp 225-237.

De Lind, L.B. 2000. Transforming organic agriculture into industrial organic products: Reconsidering national organic standards. In: *Human Organization.* 59: pp 198-208.

Dimitri, C. and Oberholtzer, L. 2006. EU and U.S. organic markets face strong demand under different policies. In: *Amber Waves.* Volume 4:1.

Donner, S. 2003. The impact of cropland cover on river nutrient levels in the Mississippi river basin In: *Global Ecology and Biogeography* 12: pp 341-355.

Eden, S., Bear, C. and Walker, G. 2008. The sceptical consumer? Exploring views about food assurance. In: *Food Policy.* 33: pp 624-630

Edwards, W.R. 1994. Agriculture and wildlife in the midwest. In: McIsaac, G. and Edwards, W.R. (eds.) *Sustainable agriculture in the American midwest. Lessons from the past, prospects for the future.* . Urbana: University of Illinois Press.

Edwards-Jones, G., Milà i Canals, L., Hounsome, N., Truninger, M., Koerber, G., Hounsome, B., Cross, P., York, E.H., Hospido, A., Plassmann, K., Harris, A.M., Edwards, R.T., Day, G.A.S., Tomos,, A.D. Cowell, S.J. and Jones, D.L. 2008. Testing the assertion that 'local food is best': the challenges of an evidence-based approach. In: *Trends in Food Science & Technology.* 19: pp 265-274.

Farrell, A.E., Plevin, R.J. and Turner, B.T. 2006. Ethanol can contribute to energy and environmental goals. In: *Science* 311: pp 506-8.

Fiskel, J. 2007. Sustainability and resilience: toward a systems approach. Sustainability: In: *Science, Practice & Policy* 2: pp 1-8.

References

French, K. and Gardner, J. 2002. *Feeding ourselves. Strategies for a new Illinois food system*. Canton, MA: Red Tomato.

Gibbon, P. 2008. An Analysis of Standards-based Regulation in the EU Organic Sector, 1991–2007. In: *Journal of Agrarian Change*. 8: pp 553–582.

Guthman, J. 2004. 'The Trouble with 'Organic Lite' in California: A Rejoinder to the 'Conventionalisation' Debate. In: *Sociologia Ruralis*. 44 : pp 301–16.

Hill, J., Nelson E., Tilman D., Polasky S. and Tifany, D. 2006. Environmental, economic, and energetic costs and benefits of biodiesel. In: *PNAS*. 103: pp 11206–11210.

Interlandi, S.J. and Crockett, C.S. 2003. Recent water quality trends in the Schuylkill river, Pennsylvania, USA: a preliminary assessment of the relative influences of climate, river discharge and suburban development. In: *Water Research*. 37: pp 1737-1748.

Huijbregts, M.A.J., Hellweg, S. and Frischknecht R., et al. 2008. Ecological footprint accounting in the life cycle assessment of products. In: *Ecological Economics*. 64: pp 798-807.

Jackson, J.E., Smucker, S., Murphree, L. Yokota, R., Koike, S.T. and Smith, R.F. 2008. Cross-disciplinary analysis of the on-farm transition from conventional to organic vegetable production. In: *ISOFAR Proceedings*, Modena Italy, June 2008. pp. 316-319.

Kim, S. and Dale, B.E. 2005. Life cycle assessment of various cropping systems utilized for producing. In: *Biomass Bioenergy*. 29: pp 426-39.

Larson, G. and Schaetzl, R. 2001. Origin and evolution of the Great Lakes. In: *J. Great Lakes Res*. 27: pp 518-546.

Lass, D, Stevenson, G.W., Hendrickson, J. and Ruhf, K. 2003. CSA *Across the nation: Findings from the 1999 CSA survey*. Madison: Center for Integrated Agricultural Systems, College of Agricultural and Life Sciences, University of Wisconsin - Accessed online at: http://www.cias.wisc.edu/pdf/csaacross.pdf.

Lin, B-H., Smith, T.A. and Huang, C.L. 2008.Organic Premiums of U.S. Fresh Produce. In: *Renewable Agriculture and Food Systems*, 23(3) 2008: pp. 208-216, .

Lipson, M. 2009. Eight (sustainable) objections: Arguments challenging certification and metrics for marketing 'Sustainability' in Agriculture. In: *Organic Farming Research Foundation Commentary*, Jan. accessed online at: http://ofrf.org/policy/090130_sustainability_commentary.pdf .

Lynch, S. and Batie, S.S. (eds.). 2006. *The scientific basis for green payments. Workshop report*. Sponsored by the U.S. Department of Agriculture, CSREES, World Wildlife Fund, and The Elton R. Smith Endowment at Michigan State University.

McIsaac, G.F., David, M.B., Gertner, G.Z. and Goolsby, D.A. 2001. Eutrophication - Nitrate flux in the Mississippi river. In: *Nature*. 414 : pp 166-167.

Mitsch, W.J. and Gosselink, J.G. (eds.) 2000. *Wetlands*. 3rd edition. New York: John Wiley and Sons.

Monfreda, C., Wackernagel, M. and Deumling, D. 2004. Establishing national natural capital accounts based on detailed. Ecological footprint and biological capacity assessments. In: *Land Use Policy*. 21: pp 231-246.

National Agricultural Statistics Service. 1999. *Census of agriculture 1997*. Available on USDA website www.nass.usda.gov/census/.

Nearing, M.A., Pruski, F.F. and O'Neal, M.R. 2004. Expected climate change impacts on soil erosion rates: A review. In: *Journal of Soil and Water Conservation* 59: pp 43-50.

Pascual, U. and Perrings, C.P. 2007. The economics of biodiversity loss in agricultural landscapes. In: *Agriculture, Ecosystems and Environment* 121: pp 256-268.

Raynolds, L. 2004. The globalisation of agro-food networks. In: *World Development*. 32: pp. 725–34.

Root, T.L., Price J.T., Hall K.R., Schneider S.H., Rosenzweig C., and J.A. Pounds. 2003. Fingerprints of global warming on wild animals and plants. In: *Nature*. 421: pp. 57-60

Rosen, S. and Shapouri, S. 2008. Rising food prices intensify food insecurity in developing countries. In: *Amber Waves*, USDA ERS. http://www.ers.usda.gov/AmberWaves/February08/Features/RisingFood.htm.

Robertson, G.P., Dale, V.H., Doering, O.C., Hamburg, S.P., Melillo, J.M., Wander, M.M., Parton, W., Adler, P.R., Barney, J.N., Cruse, R.M., Duke, C.S., Fearnside, P.M., Follett, R.F., Goldemberg, J., Mladenoff, D.J., Ojima, D., Palmer, M.W., Sharpley, A., Wallace, L., Weathers, K.C., Wiens, J.A. and Wilhelm, W.W. 2008. Agriculture-Sustainable biofuels redux. In: *Science*. 322: pp 49-50.

Robins, P., Holmes, R.B. and Laddish, K. 2001. *Bringing farm edges back to life*. 5th Edition. Yolo County Resource Conservation District

Runge, C. and Stuart, K. 1998. *The history trade and environmental consequences of corn (maize) production in the United States*. Report prepared for the World Wildlife Fund. Washington DC: WWF.

Schlich, E.H. and Fleissner, U. 2005. The ecology of scale: Assessment of regional energy turnover and comparison with global food. In: *International Journal of Life Cycle Assessment* 10: pp.219-223.

Schnepf, R. 2004. *Energy use in agriculture: Background and issues*. Congressional Research Service. USDA. Washington DC: USDA.

Selfa, T., Jussaume, R.A. and Winter, M. 2008. Envisioning agricultural sustainability from field to plate: Comparing producer and consumer attitudes and practices toward environmentally friendly' food and farming in Washington State. USA In: *Journal of Rural Studies*. 24: pp. 262-276

Singer, D.K., Jackson, S.T. Madsen, B.J. and Wilcox, D.A. 1996. Differentiating climatic and successional influences on long-term development of a marsh. In: *Ecology* 77 (6): pp. 1765-1778.

United States Department of Agriculture. *Census for agriculture, 2002*. http://www.nass.usda.gov/Census/Create_Census_US_CNTY.jsp

United States Department of Agriculture. *Census for agriculture, 2007*. http://www.agcensus.usda.gov/Publications/2007/Full_Report/index.asp

United States Department of Agriculture. Agricultural Marketing Service. 2006. *2000 USDA Farmer's market statistics*. Accessed online.

United States Department of Agriculture. Agricultural Marketing Service. 2008a. *Community-supported agriculture* (CSAs). Accessed online at: http://www.ams.usda.gov/AMSv1.0/ams.fetchTemplateData.do?template=TemplateL&navID=LearnAboutCSAsLinkWholesaleAndFarmersMarkets&rightNav1=LearnAboutCSAsLinkWholesaleAndFarmersMarkets&topNav=null&leftNav=WholesaleandFarmersMarkets&page=WFMCommunitySupportedAgriculture&resultType=&acct=wdmgeninfo. (Accessed 29 July 2008).

United States Department of Agriculture. Agricultural Marketing Service. 2008b. *Who benefits from farmer's markets?* Accessed online at: http://www.ams.usda.gov/AMSv1.0/ams.fetchTemplate-Data.do?template=TemplateM&navID=WholesaleandFarmersMarkets&leftNav=WholesaleandFarmersMarkets&page=WFMWhoBenefits&description=Who%20Benefits%20from%20Farmers%20Markets?&acct=frmrdirmkt (Accessed 29 July 2008).

United States Department of Agriculture. Agricultural Marketing Service. 2008c. *Farmer's market growth, 1994-2006.* Accessed online at: http://www.ams.usda.gov/AMSv1.0/ams.fetchTemplateData.do?template=TemplateS&navID=WholesaleandFarmersMarkets&leftNav=WholesaleandFarmersMarkets&page=WFMFarmersMarketGrowth&description=Farmers%20Market%20Growth&acct=frmrdirmkt. (Accessed 29 July 2008).

van der Werf, H.M.G., Tzilivakis, J., Lewis, K. and Basset-Mens, C. 2007. Environmental impacts of farm scenarios according to five assessment methods. In: *Agriculture Ecosystems and Environment.* 118: pp. 327-338

Vesterby, M. and Krupa, K.S. 2001. *Major uses of land in the United States, 1997.* Resource Economics Division, Economic Research Service, U.S. Department of Agriculture. Statistical Bulletin No. 973.

Wackernagel, M. and Rees, W.E. 1996. *Our ecological footprint: reducing human impact on the earth.* Gabriola Island, BC, Canada: New Society Publishers.

Wackernagel, M., Schulz, N.B., Deumling, D., Linares, A.C., Jenkins, M., Kapos, V., Monfreda, C., Loh, J. and Myers, N. 2002. Tracking the ecological overshoot of the human economy. In: *Proceedings of the National Academy of Sciences of the United States of America* 99, pp. 9266–9271.

Wackernagel, M., Monfreda, C., Moran, D., Wermer, P., Goldfinger, S., Deumling, D. and Murray, M. 2005. National footprint and biocapacity accounts 2005. The underlying calculation method. Oakland: Global Footprint Network.

Wang, M. and Haq, Z. 2008. *Letter to Science* [on the article'Use of U.S. croplands for biofuels increases greenhouse gases through emissions from land use change by Searchinger et al. in Sciencexpress' February 7, 2008]. Available online at: http://www.biodiesel.org/.../Wang%20Letter%20to%20science%20anldoe%2003-14-08.pd (Accessed 28 July 2010)

Wilcox, D.A. 1995. Wetland and aquatic macrophytes as indicators of anthropogenic hydrologic disturbance. In: *Natural Areas Journal.* 15: pp. 240-248.

Zander, K. 2008. Diversification and specialization as development strategies in organic farming. Cultivating the future based on science. In: *ISOFAR Proceedings*, Modena Italy, June 2008. pp. 316-319.

Zehnder, G., Gurr, G.M., Kuhne, S., Wade, M.R., Wratten, S.D. and Wyss, E. 2007. Arthropod pest management in organic crops. In: *Annual Review of Entomology.* 52: pp. 57-80.

Zinn, J. 2005. Setting the stage. The political context for agriculture and ecosystem policy change. In: Lynch, S. and Batie, S.S. (eds.) *Building the scientific basis for green payments.* A Report on a Workshop sponsored by the U.S. Department of Agriculture, CSREES, World Wildlife Fund, and The Elton R. Smith Endowment at Michigan State University.

Chapter 39

EC 2008. Commission Regulation No 889/2008 of 5 September 2008 laying down detailed rules for the implementation of Council Regulation (EC) No 834/2007 on organic production and labelling of organic products with regard to organic production, labelling and control. In: *Official Journal of the European Union*, No. L 250, 18 September 2008, pp. 1-84

Lund, V. 2006. Natural living. A precondition for animal welfare in organic farming, In: *Livestock Science* 100 (2–3), pp. 71–83

Pryce, J.E., Conington, J., Sørensen, P., Kelly, H.R.C. and Rydhmer, L. 2004. Breeding strategies for organic livestock. In: Vaarst, M., Roderick, S., Lund, V. and Lockeretz, W. *Animal health and welfare in organic agriculture.* Wallingford, UK: CABI Publishing. pp. 357-388

Stolze, M. and Lampkin, N. 2006. *European organic farming policies.An overview.* Joint Organic Congress, Odense, Denmark, May 30-31.

West Virginia University Department of Chemical Engineering. 2009. *Production of dl-Methionine.* http://www.che.cemr.wvu.edu/publications/projects/large_proj/dl-methionine.pdf

Zollitsch, W., Kristensen, T., Krutzinna, C., MacNaeihde, F. and Younie, D. 2004. Feeding for health and welfare. The challenge of formulating well-balanced rations in organic livestock production. In: Vaarst, M., Roderick, S., Lund, V. and Lockeretz, W. *Animal health and welfare in organic agriculture.* Wallingford, UK: CABI Publishing, pp. 329-356

Chapter 40

Frame, J., Charlton, J.F.L. and Laidlaw, A.S. 1998. *Temperate forage legumes.* CAB International. 327 pp.

Frame, J. 1994. *Improved grassland management.* Farming Press, UK, pp. 191-192.

Maastik, A. 1984. *Water pollution control in agriculture.* Tallinn. 296 pp. (in Estonian).

Mattila, P. 2006. *Ammonia emissions from pig and cattle slurry in the field and utilization of slurry nitrogen in crop production* – Doctoral dissertation. Agrifood Research Reports 187, Jokioinen.136 pp.

Mägi, E. 2006. Grazed grasslands as spreaders of ruminant internal parasites and methods for their control. In: Bender, A. (ed.) *Establishment and utilization of type-diverse grasslands.* Tartu, pp. 480-489 (in Estonian).

Turbas, E. 1996. Major lime fertilizers. In: Kärblane, H. (ed.) *Plant nutrition and fertilization. Handbook.* Tallinn. pp. 78-86 (in Estonian).

Viiralt, R. 2007. Grassland nutrition. In: Older , H. (ed.). *Integrating grassland husbandry, livestock breeding and green areas management.* Estonian Grassland Society. Saku, 262 pp. (in Estonian).

Chapter 41

European Commission. 2003. Integrated Pollution Prevention and Control (IPPC). *Reference document on Best Available Techniques for intensive rearing of poultry and pigs.* http://eippcb.jrc.es/pages/FActivities.htm

Frank, B., Persson, M. and Gustafsson G. 2002. Feeding dairy cows for decreased ammonia emission. In: *Livestock Production Science*. 76, pp. 171 – 179.

Reynal, S.M. and Broderick, G.A. 2005. Effect of Dietary Level on Rumen-Degraded Protein on Production and Nitrogen Metabolism in Lactating Dairy Cows. In: *J. Dairy Sci*. 88, pp. 4045 – 4064.

Steinfeld, H., Gerber, P., Wassenaar, T., Castel, V., Rosales, M. and de Haan, C. 2006. *Livestock's long shadow. Environmental issues and options*. http://www.virtualcentre.org/en/library/key_pub/longshad/A0701E00.pdf

Swensson, C. 2003. Relationship between content of crude protein in rations for dairy cows, N in urine and ammonia release. In: *Livestock Production Science*. 84, pp. 125 – 133.

van Duinkerken, G., Andre, G., Smits, M.C.J., Monteny, G.J. and Šebek, L.B.J. 2005. Effect of Rumen-Degradable Protein Balance and Forage Type on Bulk Milk Urea Concentration and Emission of Ammonia from dairy Cow Houses. In: *J. Dairy Sci*. 88, pp. 1099 – 1112.

Chapter 42

Bartussek, H. 2001. An historical account of the development of the animal needs index ANI-35L as part of the attempt to promote and regulate farm animal welfare in Austria. An example of the interaction between animal welfare science and society. In: *Acta Agriculturae Scandinavica* A, vol. 51, suppl. 30, pp.34-41

Broom, D.M. 1986. Indicators of poor welfare. In: *British Veterinary Journal*. Vol. 142, pp. 524–526.

Broom, D. and Johnson, K.G. 1993. Approaching questions of stress and welfare. In: *Stress and animal welfare*. Kluwer Academic Publishers, pp 1-7.

Dawkins, M.S. 1983. Battery hens name their price: consumer demand theory and the measurement of ethological 'needs'. In: *Anim. Behav*. 31, pp. 1195–1205

European Commission 2007. *Animal welfare factsheet*. Director-General for Health and Consumer Protection.

Hursh, S.R. 1984. Behavioural Economics. In: *J. Exp. Anal. Behav*. 42, pp. 435–452.

Wiepkema, P.R., Van Hellemond, K.K., Roessingh, P. and Romberg, H. 1987. Behaviour and abomasal damage in individual veal calves. In: *Applied Animal Behaviour Science*. Vol. 18, p.257.

Further reading

Appleby and Hughes 1997. *Animal welfare*.

Benson and Rollin 2004. *The well-being of farm animals*

Broom and Fraser 2003. *Domestic animal welfare and behaviour*. 4th edition

Martin and Bateson 1993. *Measuring behaviour*.

The following journals:

Animal Welfare, Applied Animal Behaviour Science, Animal.

Chapter 43

Alcaro, A., Huber, R. and Panksepp, J. 2007. Behavioral functions of the mesolimbic dopaminergic system: An affective neuroethological perspective. In: *Brain Research Reviews*, 56: 283-321.

Burghardt, G.M. 2005. *The genesis of animal play*. Cambridge, MA: MIT Press.

Nelson, E.E. and Panksepp, J. 1998 Brain substrates of infant-mother attachment: Contributions of opioids, oxytocin, and norepinephrine. In: *Neuroscience & Biobehavioral Reviews*, 22: 437-452.

Numan, M. and Insel, T.R. 2003. The neurobiology of parental behavior. New York: Springer-Verlag.

Pankscpp, J. 1990. The psychoneurology of fear: Evolutionary perspectives and the role of animal models in understanding human anxiety. In: Roth, M., Burrows, G.D. and Noyes, R. (eds) *Handbook of anxiety*. pp. 3-58 Amsterdam Elsevier/North-Holland: Biomedical Press.

Panksepp, J. 1998. *Affective neuroscience: The foundations of human and animal emotions*. New York: Oxford University Press.

Panksepp, J. 2007. Can PLAY diminish ADHD and facilitate the construction of the social brain. In: *Journal of the Canadian Academy of Child and Adolescent Psychiatry*, 10: 57-66.

Panksepp, J., Fuchs, T., and Iacabucci, P. 2010. The basic neuroscience of emotional experiences in mammals: The Case of subcortical FEAR circuitry and implications for clinical anxiety. In: *Applied Animal Behaviour Science*, in press.

Panksepp, J. and Moskal, J. 2008. Dopamine and SEEKING: Subcortical 'reward' systems and appetitive urges. In: Elliot, A. (ed.) *Handbook of approach and avoidance motivation*, pp. 67-87 Mahwah, NJ.: Lawrence Erlbaum Associates,

Panksepp, J. and Zellner, M. 2004. Towards a neurobiologically based unified theory of aggression. In: *Revue Internationale de Psychologie Sociale/International Review of Social Psychology*. 17, pp. 37-61.

Pellis and Pellis 2009. *The playful brain: Venturing to the limits of neuroscience*. Oxford, UK: Oneworld Pubs.

Pfaff, D.W. 1999. *Drive: Neurobiological and molecular mechanisms of sexual behavior*. Cambridge, MA: MIT Press.

Siegel, A. 2005. *The neurobiology of aggression and rage*. Boca Raton, FL: CRC Press.

Watt, D.F. and Panksepp, J. 2009. Depression: an evolutionarily conserved mechanism to terminate separation-distress? A review of aminergic, peptidergic, and neural network perspectives. In: *Neuropsychoanalysis*, 11, pp. 5-104.

Further Reading

McMillan, F. (ed.). 2003. *Mental Health and Well-being in Animals*. Ames, Iowa: Iowa State University Press.

Panksepp, J. 2003. At the interface of affective, behavioral and cognitive neurosciences: Decoding the emotional feelings of the brain. In: *Brain and Cognition*, *52*, 4-14.

Panksepp, J. 2005. Affective consciousness: Core emotional feelings in animals and humans. In: *Consciousness & Cognition, 14*, 30-80.

Panksepp, J. 2006. Emotional endophenotypes in evolutionary psychiatry. In: *Progress in Neuro-Psychopharmacology & Biological Psychiatry*, *30*, 774-784.

Panksepp, J. 2007. Neuroevolutionary sources of laughter and social joy: Modeling primal human laughter in laboratory rats. In: *Behavioral Brain Research*, *182*, 231-244.

Chapter 44

Berman, A., Folman, Y., Kaim, M., Marnen, M., Herz, Z., Wolfensen, D., Arieli, A. and Graber, Y. 1985. Upper critical temperature and forced ventilation effects for high-yielding dairy cows in a subtropical climate. In: *Journal of Dairy Science*, pp. 1488–1495.

Chua, B., Coenen, E., van Delen, J. and Weary, D.M. 2002. Effects of pair versus individual housing on the behavior and performance of dairy calves. In: *Journal of Dairy Science*. Vol. 85 pp.360-364.

Cook, N.B. 2003. Prevalence of lameness among dairy cattle in Wisconsin as a function of housing type and stall surface. In: *Journal of the American Medical Veterinary Association*, Vol. 223, no.9, pp. 1324-1328.

Cooper, M.D., Arney, D.R. and Phillips, C.J.C. 2007. Two- or four-hour lying deprivation on the behaviour of lactating dairy cows. In: *Journal of Dairy Science*, Vol. 90, pp. 1149-1158.

Dahl, G.E. and Peticlerc, D. 2003. Management of photoperiod in the dairy herd for improved production and health. In: *Journal of Animal Science*, Vol. 81, pp. 11-17.

DEFRA Department for Environment, Food and Rural Affairs. 2006. *Housing the modern dairy cow. ADAS advisory campaigns 2005/6.*

Ekesbo, I. 2009. Impact and demands for health and welfare of range beef cattle in Scandinavia. In: Aland, A. and Madec, F. (eds.) *Sustainable animal production.* Wageningen: Wageningen Academic Publishers. pp.173-188.

Fraser, A.F. and Broom, D.M. 1997. *Farm animal behaviour and welfare.* 3rd Edition, Wallingford, UK: CABI Publishing. p.93.

Haley, D.B., de Passillé, A.M. and Rushen, J. 2001. Assessing cow comfort: effects of two floor types and two tie stall designs on the behaviour of lactating dairy cows. In: *Applied Animal Behaviour Science*, Vol. 71, pp. 105-117.

Hughes, J. 2001. A system for assessing cow cleanliness. In: *In Practice*, Vol. 23, pp. 517-524.

Huzzey, J.M, DeVries, T.J., Valois, P. and von Keyserlingk, M.A.G. 2006. Stocking density and feed barrier design affect the feeding and social behaviour of dairy cattle. In: *Journal of Dairy Science*, Vol. 89, 126-133.

Lin, J.C., Moss, B.R., Koon, J.L., Flood, C.A., Smith, R.C. III, Cummins, K.A. and Coleman, D.A. 1998. Comparison of various fan, sprinkler, and mister systems in reducing heat stress in dairy cows. In: *Journal of Dairy Science*, Vol.14, pp. 177-182.

Murphy, M.R, Davis, C.L. and McCoy, G.C. 1983. Factors affecting water consumption by Holstein cows in early lactation. In: *Journal of Dairy Science*, Vol. 66, pp. 35-38.

Phillips, C.J.C. and Morris, I.D. 2000. The locomotion of dairy cows on concrete floors that are dry, wet or covered with a slurry of excreta. In: *Journal of Dairy Science*, Vol. 83, pp. 1767-1772.

Phillips, C.J.C, Morris, I.D, Lomas, C.A. and Lockwood, S.J. 2000. The locomotion of dairy cows in passageways with different light intensities. In: *Animal Welfare*, Vol. 9, pp. 421-431.

Phillips, C.J.C. and Schofield, S.A. 1994. The Effect of Cubicle and Straw Yard Housing on the Behaviour, Production and Hoof Health of Dairy Cows. In: *Animal Welfare*, Vol. 3, pp. 37-44.

Phillips, V.R., Holden, M.R., Sneath, R.W., Short, J.L., White, R.P., Hartung, J., Seedorf, J., Schröder, M., Linkert, K.H., Pedersen, S., Takai, H., Johnsen, J.O., Groot-Koerkamp, P.W.G., Uenk, G.H., Scholtens, R., Metz, J.H.M. and Wathes, C.M. 1998. The development of robust methods for measuring concentrations and emission rates of gaseous and particulate air pollutants in livestock buildings. In: *Journal of Agricultural Engineering*, Vol. 70, pp. 11-24.

Somers, J.G., Frankena, K., Noordhuizen-Stassen, E.N. and Metz, J.H. 2003. Prevalence of claw disorders in Dutch dairy cows exposed to several floor systems. In: *Journal of Dairy Science*, Vol. 86, pp. 2082-2093.

Telezhenko, E. and Bergsten, C. 2005. Influence of floor type on the locomotion of dairy cows. In: *Applied Animal Behaviour Science*, Vol.93, pp. 183-197.

Wechsler, B., Schaub, J., Friedli, K. and Hauser, R. 2000. Behaviour and leg injuries in dairy cows kept in cubicle systems with straw bedding or soft lying mats. In: *Applied Animal Behaviour Science*, Vol. 69, pp. 189-197.

Wierenga, H.K. and Hopster, H. 1990. The significance of cubicles for the behaviour of dairy cows. In: *Applied Animal Behaviour Science*, Vol. 26, pp. 309-337.

Wilson, S.J., Marion, R.S., Spain, J.N., Speers, D.E., Keisler, D.H. and Lucy, M.C. 1998. Effects of controlled heat stress on ovarian function of dairy cattle. 1. Lactating dairy cows. In: *Journal of Dairy Science*, Vol. 81, pp. 2124-2131.

Wise, M.E., Armstrong, D.V., Huber, J.T., Hunter, R. and Wiersma, F. 1988. Hormonal alterations in the lactating dairy cow in response to thermal stress. In: *Journal of Dairy Science*, Vol. 71, pp. 2480-2485.

Young, B.A. 1981. Cold stress as it affects animal production. In: *Journal of Animal Science*, Vol. 52, pp, 154-163.

Chapter 45

Algers, B. 1984. Early weaning and cage rearing of piglets: Influence on behaviour. In: *Zentralblatt für Veterinärmedizin Reihe A.*, 31, pp. 14-24.

Algers, B. 1991. Group housing of farrowing sows. In: *Health aspects on a new system. Proc. 7th Int. Congr. Anim. Hyg., Leipzig.* pp. 851-857.

Algers, B. and Uvnäs-Moberg, K. 2007. Maternal behaviour in pigs. In: *Hormones and Behavior.*, 52: pp. 78-85.

Braun, S. 1995. *Individual variation in behaviour and growth of piglets in a combined system of individual and loose housing in sows.* Thesis. Dept. of Anim. Hyg., Swed. Univ. Of Agr. Sci., Report 36, 72 pp.

Braun, S. and Algers, B. 1993. Schweden-Stall für grosse Altgebäude. In: *DLG-Mitteilungen/agrar-inform*, 4, pp. 60-61.

Brownlow, M.J.C., Carruthers, S.P. and Dorward, P.T. 1995. Financial aspects of finishing pigs on range. In: *Farm Management* 9, pp. 125-132.

References

Bruce, J.M. 1990. Straw-flow: a high welfare system for pigs. In: *Farm Buildings Progress* 102, pp. 9-13.

Day, J.E.L., Burfoot, A., Docking, C.M., Whittaker, X., Spoolder, H.A.M. and Edwards, S.A. 2002. The effect of prior experience of straw and the level of straw provision on the behaviour of growing pigs. In: *Applied Animal Behaviour Science* 76, pp. 189-202.

DFS, 2007. DFS 2007:5 *Djurskyddsmyndighetens författningssamling*

Ebner, J. 1993. *Group-housing of lactating sows. Studies on health, behaviour and nest temperature.* Thesis. Swed. Univ. Agr. Sci. Dept. of Anim. Hyg. Report 31, 108 pp

EFSA, 2007a. (Algers, B., Sanaa, M., Nunes Pina, T., Wechsler, B., Spoolder, H., Meunier-Salaün, M.C. and Pedersen, L.J.) Scientific report on animal health and welfare aspects of different housing and husbandry systems for adult breeding boars, pregnant, farrowing sows and unweaned piglets. In: *The EFSA Journal* (2007) 572, pp. 1-107.

EFSA, 2007b. (Broom, D., Algers, B., Sanaa, M., Nunes Pina, T., Bonde, M., Edwards, S., Hartung, J., de Jong, I., Manteca Vilanova, X., Martelli, G. and Martineau, G. P.) Scientific report on animal health and welfare in fattening pigs in relation to housing and husbandry. In: *The EFSA Journal* (2007) 564, pp. 1-100.

Ekkel, E.D., Savenije, B., Schouten, W.G. and Tielen, M.J. 1996. Health, welfare, and productivity of pigs housed under specific-stress-free conditions in comparison with two-site systems. In: *J. Anim. Sci.* 74, pp. 2081-2087.

Fraser, D., Phillips, D.A., Thompson, B.K. and Tennessen, T. 1991. Effect of straw on the behaviour of growing pigs. In: *Applied Animal Behaviour Science* 30: 307-318.

Groenestein, C.M. and Van Faassen, H.G. 1996. Volatilization of ammonia, nitrous oxide and nitric oxide in deep-litter systems for fattening pigs. In: *Journal of Agricultural Engineering Research* 65, pp. 269-274.

Halverson, M. 1997. *Swedish deep-bedded group nursing systems for feeder pig production. Sustainable agriculture. Swine system options for Iowa.* Iowa State University. Ames, Iowa. 12 pp.

Holmgren, N. and Lundeheim, N. 1994. Djurhälsomässiga behovet av fodermedelsantibiotika i smågrisproducerande besättningar. In: *Sv. Vet.tidn.* 46: 57-65.

Hultén, F. 1997. *Group housing of lactating sows. Effects on sow health, reproduction and litter performance.* Thesis. Swed. Univ. Agr. Sci. Acta Univ. Agr. Suec. Veterinaria 27, 59pp.

Jackisch, T., Hesse, D. and Schlichting, M.C. 1996. Pen structure related behaviour of fattening pigs in housing systems with and without straw. In: *KTBL-Schrift* (No. 373): pp. 137-147.

Ladewig, J. and Matthews, L.R. 1996. The role of operant conditioning in animal welfare research. Acta Agric. Scand. Sect. A, 27, 64-68

Marchant, J.N. 1996. *Alternatives to confining the farrowing sow.* 1996 Fellowship Report to the Winston Churchill Memorial Trust. 120pp.

Mattsson, B. 1996. *Digivande suggor i grupp.* Slakteriförbundets FoU-grupp Svin. Report no 9, 16pp.

Moinard, C., Mendl, M., Nicol, C.J. and Green, L.E. 2003. A case control study of on-farm risk factors for tail biting in pigs. In: *Appl. Anim. Behav. Sci.* 81, pp. 333-355.

PigWin, *2008*. http://www.svenskapig.se/?id=324 (Accessed 2009-09-07)

Rydhmer, L., Zamaratskaia, G., Andersson, H.K., Algers, B., Guillemet, R. and Lundström, K. 2006. Aggressive and sexual behaviour of growing and finishing pigs reared in groups, without castration. In: *Acta Agric. Scand.*, 56: pp. 109-119.

Spoolder, H.A.M., Burbidge, J.A., Edwards, S.A., Simmins, P.H. and Lawrence, A.B. 1995. Provision of straw as a foraging substrate reduces the development of excessive chain and bar manipulation in food restricted sows. In: *Appl. Anim. Behav. Sci.* 43, pp. 249-262.

Spoolder, H.A.M, Edwards, S.A. and Corning, S. 1999. Effects of group size and feeder space allowance on welfare in finishing pigs. In: *Animal Science*, 69: pp. 481-489.

Stolba, A. and Wood-Gush, D.G.M. 1989. The behaviour in pigs in a semi-natural environment. In: *Animal Production* 48: pp. 419-425.

Turner, S.P., Horgan, G.W. and Edwards, S.A. 2001. Effect of social group size on aggressive behaviour between unacquainted domestic pigs. In: *Applied Animal Behaviour Science* 74: pp. 203-215.

van den Weghe, H.F.A., Kaiser, S., Arkenau, E.F., Winckler, C. and Hartwi, A. 1999. A two compartment deep litter housing system for growing-finishing pigs. An evaluation with respect to animal welfare and production. In: *Landbauforschung Volkenrode*, Sonderheft. 199, pp. 148-156.

Webb, N.G. and Nilsson, C. 1983. Flooring and injury – an overview. In: Baxter, S.H., Baxter, M.R. and McCormick, J.A.C. (eds.) *Farm animal housing and welfare.* The Hague: Nijhoff, pp. 226-259.

Whittaker, X., Spoolder, H.A.M., Edwards, S.A., Lawrence, A.B. and Corning, S. 1998. The influence of dietary fibre and the provision of straw on the development of stereotypic behaviour in food restricted pregnant sows. In: *Applied Animal Behaviour Science* 61, pp. 89-102.

Wood-Gush, D.G.M. and Vestergaard, K. 1991. The seeking of novelty and its relation to play. In: *Animal Behaviour* 42: pp. 599-606.

Wülbers-Mindermann, M. 1992. *Characteristics of cross-suckling piglets reared in a group housing system.* Dept. Anim. Hyg., Swed. Univ. Agr. Sci., report 13, 77pp.

Further reading

EFSA, 2007. (Algers, B., Sanaa, M., Nunes Pina, T., Wechsler, B., Spoolder, H., Meunier-Salaün, M.C. and Pedersen, L.J.) Scientific report on animal health and welfare aspects of different housing and husbandry systems for adult breeding boars, pregnant, farrowing sows and unweaned piglets. In: *The EFSA Journal* (2007) 572, pp. 1-107. http://www.efsa.europa.eu/cs/BlobServer/Scientific_Opinion/ahaw_report_pig_welfare_sowsboars_en,3.pdf?ssbinary=true (Accessed 2009-09-07)

EFSA, 2007. (Broom, D., Algers, B., Sanaa, M., Nunes Pina, T., Bonde, M., Edwards, S., Hartung, J., de Jong, I., Manteca Vilanova, X., Martelli, G. and Martineau, G. .) Scientific report on animal health and welfare in fattening pigs in relation to housing and husbandry. In: *The EFSA Journal* (2007) 564, 1-100. http://www.efsa.europa.eu/cs/BlobServer/Scientific_Opinion/ahaw_report_pig_welfare_fattening_en,3.pdf?ssbinary=true (Accessed 2009-09-07)

EFSA 2007. (Blokhuis, H., Nunes, T., Saana, M., Bracke, M., Edwards, S., Gunn, M., Martineau, G., Mendl, M. and Prunier, A.) Scientific report on risks associated with tail biting in pigs and possible means to reduce the need for tail docking considering the different housing and husbandry systems. *In: Annex to the The EFSA Journal* (2007)

611, 98 pp. http://www.efsa.europa.eu/cs/BlobServer/Scientific_Opinion/ahaw_report_pigwelfare_tailbiting_en.pdf?ssbinary=true (Accessed 2009-09-07)

EFSA 2005 (Broom, D., Gunn, M., Edwards, S., Wechsler, B., Algers, B., Spoolder, H., Madec, F., von Borell, E. and Olsson, O.) The welfare of weaning and rearing pigs: effects of different space allowances and floor types. In: *Annex to the The EFSA Journal* (2005) 268. 129 pp. http://www.efsa.europa.eu/cs/BlobServer/Scientific_Opinion/ahaw_op_ej268_pigwelfare_report_en3,0.pdf?ssbinary=true (Accessed 2009-09-07)

Chapter 46

Further reading

Appleby, M.C., Mench, J.A. and Hughes, B.O. 2004. *Poultry behaviour and welfare*. Wallingford, U.K.: CAB International.

Berg, C. 2002. Health and welfare in organic poultry production. In: *Acta vet. scand. 2001, Suppl.* 95, 37-45.

Council of the European Union, 1999. Council Directive 1999/74/EC of 19 July 1999 laying down minimum standards for the protection of laying hens. In: *Official Journal of the European Communities. L 203/53-57*. http://eur-lex.europa.eu/LexUriServ/LexUriServ.do?uri=OJ:L:1999:203:0053:0057:EN:PDF.

Council of the European Union, 2007. Council Directive 2007/43/EC of 28 June 2007 laying down minimum rules for the protection of chickens kept for meat production. In: *Official Journal of the European Union. L 182/19-28*. http://eur-lex.europa.eu/LexUriServ/LexUriServ.do?uri=OJ:L:2007:182:0019:0028:EN:PDF.

LayWel, 2006. Welfare implications of changes in production systems for laying hens. In: *European Commission, 6th Framework Programme, contract No. SSPE-CT-2004-502315*. http://www.laywel.eu/.

National Chicken Council, 2005. *Animal welfare guidelines and audit checklist*. Washington, D.C.: National Chicken Council. http://www.nationalchickencouncil.org/files/AnimalWelfare2005.pdf.

Perry, G.C. (ed.) 2004. *Welfare of the laying hen*. Wallingford, U.K.: CABI Publishing

United Egg Producers. 2008. *Animal husbandry guidelines for U.S. egg laying flocks*. 2008 Edition. Alpharetta, GA: United Egg Producers. http://www.uepcertified.com/docs/UEP-Animal-Welfare-Guidelines-2007-2008.pdf

Weeks, C. and Butterworth, A. 2004. *Measuring and auditing broiler welfare*. Wallingford, U.K: CABI Publishing

Recommended Reading

Appleby, M., Cussen, V., Lambert, L. and Turner, J. (eds.) 2008. *Long distance transport and welfare of farm animals*. Wallingford. UK: CABI International.

Grandin, T. (ed.) 2007. *Livestock handling and transport*. Wallingford. UK: CABI International.

Humane Slaughter Association, website: http://www.hsa.org.uk

Chapter 47

Anil, M.H., Whittington, P.E. and McKinstry, J.L. 2000. The effect of the sticking method on the welfare of slaughter pigs. In: *Meat Science*. Vol. 55, pp. 315-319.

Anil, M.H., Yesildere, T., Aksu, H., Matur, E., McKinstry, J.L. Erdogan, O., Hughes, S. and Mason, C. 2004. Comparison of religious slaughter of sheep with methods that include pre-slaughter stunning, and the lack of differences in exsanguination, packed cell volume and meat quality parameters. In: *Animal Welfare*. Vol. 13, pp. 387-392.

Bornett-Gauci, H.L.I., Martin, J.E. and Arney, D.R. 2006. The welfare of low-volume farm animals during transport and at slaughter: A review of current knowledge and recommendations for future research. In: *Animal Welfare*. Vol.15, pp. 299-308.

Broom, D.M. 2000. Welfare assessment and welfare problem areas during handling and transport. In: Grandin, T. (ed.) *Livestock handling and transport*, 2nd edition. Wallingford, UK: CABI publishing.

Carlyle, W.W.H., Guise, H.J. and Cook, P. 1997. Effect of time between farm loading and processing on carcase quality of broiler chickens. In: *Veterinary Record*. Vol. 141, p.364

Dalin, A.M., Magnusson, U., Haggendal, J. and Nyberg, L. 1993. The effect of transport stress on plasma levels of catecholamines, cortisol, corticosterol-binding globulin, blood cell count and lymphoctye proliferation in pigs. In: *Acta Veterinaria Scandinavica*. Vol. 34, pp. 59-68.

EFSA 2004. *Opinion of the scientific panel on animal health and welfare AHAW on a request from the Commission related to welfare aspects of the main systems of stunning and killing the main commercial species of animals.* Question number: EFSA-Q-2003-093. Summary, Opinion and Report: http://www.efsa.europa.eu/EFSA/efsa_locale-1178620753812_1178620775454.htm;Report:http://www.efsa.europa.eu/cs/BlobServer/Scientific_Opinion/opinion_ahaw_02_ej45_stunning_report_v2_en1,1.pdf?ssbinary=true

EFSA 2006. *Opinion of the scientific panel on animal health and welfare AHAW on a request from the Commission related with the welfare aspects of the main systems of stunning and killing applied to commercially farmed deer, goats, rabbits, ostriches, ducks, geese .* Question number: EFSA-Q-2005-005. Summary, Opinion and Report: http://www.efsa.europa.eu/EFSA/efsa_locale-1178620753812_1178620773440.htm. Report:http://www.efsa.europa.eu/cs/BlobServer/Scientific_Opinion/ahaw_stunning2_report1.pdf?ssbinary=true

Ekstrand, C. 1998. An observational cohort study of the effects of catching methods on carcass rejection rates in broilers. In: *Animal Welfare*. Vol. 7, pp. 87-96

Gregory, N.G. and Wilkins, L.J. 1989. Effect of stunning current on carcass quality in chickens. In: *Veterinary Record*. Vol. 121, pp. 530-532.

Heffner, R.S. and Heffner, H.E. 1983. Hearing in large mammals, horse *equus caballus* and cattle *bos taurus*. In: *Behavioural Neuroscience*. Vol. 97, pp. 299-309

Hunter, R.R., Mitchell, M.A, Carlisle, A.J., Quinn, A.D., Kettlewell, P.J. Knowles, T.G. and Wariss, P.D. 1998. Physiological responses of broilers to pre-slaughter lairage: Effects of the thermal micro-environment? In: *British Poultry Science*, Vol. 39. pp. 53-54

References

Hänsch, F., Nowak, B and Hartung, J. 2009. Behavioural and clinical response of turkeys stunned in a v-shaped carbon dioxide tunnel. In: *Animal Welfare*. Vol.18 pp. 81-86.

Jago, J.G., Harcourt, R.G. and Matthews, L.R. 1997. The effect of road-type and distance transported on behaviour, physiology and carcass quality of farmed red deer *cervus elaphus*. In: *Applied Animal Behaviour Science*. Vol. 51, pp. 129-141.

Knezacek, T.D., Audren, G.F., Mitchell, M.A, Kettlewell, P.J, Hunter, R.R., Classen, H.L., Stephens, S., Olkowski, A.A., Barber, E.M. and Crowe, T.G. 2000. Temperature heterogeneity and moisture accumulations in trailers transporting broilers under canadian winter conditions. In: *Poultry Science*. Vol. 79, supp.1, p.31

Liste, G., Villaroel, M., Chacon, G., Sanudo, C., Olleta, J.L., Garcia-Belenguer, S., Alierta, S. and Maria, G.A 2009. Effect of lairage duration on rabbit welfare and meat quality. In: *Meat Science*. Vol.82 pp. 71-76.

Ministry of Agriculture, Fisheries and Food MAFF. 1989. *Code of recommendations for the welfare of livestock. Farmed deer*. London, UK: MAFF Publications.

Mitchell, M.A. and Kettlewell, P.J. 2004. Transport and handling. In: Weeks, C.A. and Butterworth, A. (eds.) *Measuring and auditing broiler welfare*. Wallingford. UK: CABI Publishing. pp. 145-160.

Mitchell, M.A., Carlisle, A.J., Hunter, R.R. and Kettlewell, P.J. 2003. Weight loss in transit. An important issue in broiler transportation. In: *Poultry Science*. Vol. 82, supp.1, p.52

Mitchell, M.A., Hunter, R.R., Kettlewell, P.J and Carlisle, A.J. 1998. Heat and moisture production of broilers during transportation. A whole vehicle direct calorimeter. In: *Poultry Science*. Vol. 77, supp.1, p.4

Nijdam, E., Arens, P., Lambooij, E., Decuypere, E. and Stegeman, J.A. 2004. Factors influencing bruises and mortality of broilers during catching, transport and lairage. In: *Poultry Science*. Vol.83 pp. 1610-1615.

Pollard, J.C., Littlejohn, R.P., Asher, G.W., Pearse, A.J.T., Stevensen-Barry, J.M., McGregor, S.K., Manley, T.R., Duncan, S.J., Pollock, K.L. and Prescott, J. 2002. A comparison of biochemical and meat quality variables in red deer *cervus elaphus* following either slaughter at pasture or killing at a deer slaughter plant. In: *Meat Science*. Vol.60. pp. 85-94.

Smith, R.F. and Dobson, H. 1990. Effect of pre-slaughter experience on behaviour, plasma cortisol and muscle pH in farmed red deer. In: *Veterinary Record*. Vol.126, pp. 155-158

Tarrant, P.V. 1990. Transportation of cattle by road. In: *Applied Animal Behaviour Science*. Vol.28, pp. 153-170.

Voisinet, B.D., Grandin, T., O'Connor, S.F., Tatum, J.D. and Deesing, M.J. 1997. *Bos indicus* cross feedlot cattle with excitable temperaments have tougher meat and a higher incidence of borderline dark cutters. In: *Meat Science*. Vol.46, pp.367-377.

Waas, J.R., Ingram, J.R. and Matthews, L.R. 1997. Physiological responses of red deer *cervus elaphus* to conditions experienced during road transport. In: *Physiology and Behaviour*. Vol. 61, pp. 931-938

Waas, J.R., Ingram, J.R. and Matthews, L.R. 1999. Real-time physiological responses of red deer *cervus elaphus* to translocations. In: *Journal of Wildlife Management*. Vol. 63, pp. 1152-1162.

Warriss, P.D., Brown, S.N., Edwards, J.E. and Knowles, T.G. 1998. Effect of lairage time on levels of stress and meat quality in pigs. In: *Animal Science*. Vol. 66, pp. 255-261

Weeks, C.A. 2008. A review of welfare in cattle, sheep and pig lairages with emphasis on stocking rates, ventilation and noise. In: *Animal Welfare*. Vol. 17 pp.275-284

Wotton, S. and Wilkins, L.J. 2003. Primary processing of poultry. In: Weeks, C.A. and Butterworth, A. (eds.) *Measuring and auditing broiler welfare*. Wallingford, UK: CABI Publishing. pp. 161-180.

Chapter 48

93/119/EC *Council Directive of 22 December 1993 on the protection of animals at the time of slaughter or killing*

EC No 854/2004 *Regulation of the European Parliament of the Council of 29 April 2004 laying down specific rules for the organization of official controls*

EC No 1099/2009 *Council Regulation of 24 September 2009 on the protection of animals at the time of killing*

Grandin, T. 2006. Progress and challenges in animal handling and slaughter in the U.S. In: *Applied Animal Behaviour Science* 100: 129–139

Sandström, V., Wotton, S.B., Berg, C. and Algers, B. 2008. *Proposal of monitoring system for the assessment of cattle welfare in abattoirs*. Welfare Quality sub project 2, WP 2.3, Report December 15th, 55 pp

Wotton, S. and Wittington, P. 2008. Capacity building & training for animal welfare: slaughter. In: Algers, B., Blokhuis, H. and Keeling, L. (eds.) *Proceedings 'Animal welfare at slaughter and killing for disease control – emerging issues and good examples', Sweden, 2008.* Pp 48-52.

Chapter 49

Appleby, M.C. 1999 *What should we do about animal welfare?* Oxford: Blackwells.

Appleby, M.C. 2005 Sustainable agriculture is humane, humane agriculture is sustainable. In: *Journal of Agricultural and Environmental Ethics* 18, 293-303

Appleby, M.C., Cutler, N., Gazzard, J., Goddard, P., Milne, J.A., Morgan, C. and Redfern, A. 2003 What price cheap food? In: *Journal of Agricultural and Environmental Ethics* 16, 395-408

Appleby, M.C., Mench, J.A. and Hughes, B.O. 2004. *Poultry behaviour and welfare* (including chapter on Economics). Wallingford, UK: CAB International.

Fraser, D., Weary, D.M., Pajor, E.A. and Milligan, B.N. 1997 A scientific conception of animal welfare that reflects ethical concerns. In: *Animal Welfare* 6, 187-205

Grandin, T. 2004 Principles for the design of handling facilities and transport systems. In: Benson, G.J. and Rollin, B.E. (eds.) *The well-being of farm animals: Challenges and solutions*. Ames: Blackwell. pp. 145-166

Hemsworth, P.H. 2004 Human-livestock interaction. In: Benson, G.J. and Rollin, B.E. (eds.) *The well-being of farm animals: Challenges and solutions*. Ames: Blackwell. pp. 21-38

Hemsworth, P.H., Barnett, J.L. and Coleman, G.J. 1993. The human-animal relationship in agriculture and its consequences for the animal. In: *Animal Welfare* 2, 33-51

National Pork Board. 2005. *Swine welfare assurance program.* Available at www.porkboard.org/SWAPHome

OIE (World Organisation for Animal Health). 2005 http://www.oie.int/eng/press/en_050602.htm

Turner, J. and D'Silva, J. (eds.) 2006 *Animals, ethics and trade: The challenge of animal sentience.* London: Earthscan.

Chapter 50

Benson, G.J. and Rollin, B.E. (eds.) 2004. *The well-being of farm animals: Challenges and solutions.* Ames, IA: Blackwell Publishing.

Rollin, B.E. 1995. *Farm animal welfare* (Ames, Iowa: Iowa State University Press.

Chapter 51

Algers B., 2009. A risk assessment approach to animal welfare. In: Smulders, F.J.M and Algers, B. (Eds.). Food safety assurance and veterinary public health, Vol. 5, Welfare of production animals: assessment and management of risks. Wageningen Academic Publishers, the Netherlands, 223-237.

Blokhuis, H.J., Jones R.B., Geers R., Miele M. and Veissier I., 2003. Measuring and monitoring animal welfare: transparency in the food product quality chain. Animal Welfare, 12, 445-455.

Blokhuis H. J., Keeling L. J., Gavinelli A., Serratosa J., 2008. Animal welfare's impact in the food chain. Trends in Food Science & Technology, 19 (1), S75-S83.

Blokhuis, H.J., Veissier, I., Miele, M. and Jones, R.B., 2010. The Welfare Quality® project and beyond: safeguarding farm animal well-being. Acta Agriculturae Scandinavica A, Animal Science, 60, 129-140.

CAC, 2001. Codex Alimentarius Commission. Food Hygiene, Basic texts, FAO/WHO, Rome, Italy.

CAC, 2002. Codex Alimentarius Commission. Principles and Guidelines for the Conduct of Microbiological Risk Assessment. Document CAC/GL 30.

Candiani, D., Ribó , O., Afonso, A., Aiassa, E., Correia, S., De Massis, F., Pujols, J; Serratosa, J., 2007. Risk assessment challenges in the field of animal welfare. In: Proceedings of the XIII international congress in animal hygiene, ISAH, June 17-21, Tartu, Estonia. 587-581.

Candiani D., Ribó O., Barbieri S., Afonso A., Grudnik T., Berthe F., Serratosa J., 2009. Development of a risk assessment methodology for animal welfare in EFSA's scientific opinions. In: Sustainable Animal Production. The challenges and potential developments for professional farming. Eds. Andres Aland and Francois Madec. Wageningen Academic Publishers, pp. 421-434.

EC, 2002. European Commission. Regulation (EC) No. 178/2002 of 28 January 2002, laying down the general principles and requirements of food law, establishing the European Food Safety Authority and laying down procedures in matters of food safety. Official Journal L31, 1/2/2002, p. 1-24.

EC, 2005. European Commission. Community Action Plan on the Protection and Welfare of Animals (2006-2010). http://ec.europa.eu/food/animal/welfare/actionplan/actionplan_ en.htm

EC, 2006. European Commission. Future Strategy on Animal Health for 2007-2013 http://ec.europa.eu/food/animal/diseases/strategy/final_report_en.htm

EFSA, 2004a. European Food safety Authority. Opinion of the Scientific Panel on Animal Health and Welfare related to the welfare of animals during transport. The EFSA Journal (2004) 44, 1-36.

EFSA, 2004b. European Food Safety Authority. Scientific Opinion of the AHAW Panel on the welfare aspects of the main systems of stunning and killing the main commercial species of animals. The EFSA Journal (2004) 45, 1-29.

EFSA, 2006. European Food Safety Authority. Scientific Colloquium "Principles of Risk Assessment of Food Producing Animals: Current and future approaches" http://www.efsa.europa.eu/en/science/colloquium_series/no4_animal_diseases.html

EFSA, 2009a. Scientific Report on the effects of farming systems on dairy cow welfare and disease. Report of the Panel on Animal Health and Welfare. Annex to the EFSA Journal (2009) 1143, 1-38

EFSA, 2009b. Scientific Opinion on the overall assessment of dairy cows welfare. Scientific Opinion of the Panel on Animal Health and Animal Welfare. The EFSA Journal (2009) 1143, 1-38.

EFSA, 2009c. Scientific Opinion on the impact of housing, nutrition and feeding, management and genetic selection on leg and locomotion problems in dairy cows. Scientific Opinion of the Panel on Animal Health and Animal Welfare. The EFSA Journal (2009) 1142, 1-57.

EFSA, 2009d. Scientific Opinion on the impact of housing, nutrition and feeding, management and genetic selection on udder problems in dairy cows. Scientific Opinion of the Panel on Animal Health and Animal Welfare. The EFSA Journal (2009) 1142, 1-60.

EFSA, 2009e. Scientific Opinion on the impact of housing, nutrition and feeding, management and genetic selection on metabolic and reproductive problems in dairy cows. Scientific Opinion of the Panel on Animal Health and Animal Welfare. The EFSA Journal (2009) 1140, 1-75.

EFSA, 2009f. Scientific Opinion on the impact of housing, nutrition and feeding, management and genetic selection on behavioural problems in dairy cows. Scientific Opinion of the Panel on Animal Health and Animal Welfare. The EFSA Journal (2009) 1139, 1-66.

EU, 1997. European Commission. Treaty of Amsterdam - Protocol on protection and welfare of animals. Official Journal C 340, 10/11/1997, p. 110.

Keeling, L. and Veissier, I., 2005. Developing a monitoring system to assess welfare quality in cattle, pigs and chickens. In: A. Butterworth (Ed.) Science and society improving animal welfare.
Welfare Quality conference proceedings 17/18 November 2005, Brussels, Belgium, 46-50.

Müller-Graf C., Candiani C., Barbieri S., Ribó O., Afonso A., Aiassa E., Have P., Correia S., De Massis F., Grudnik T., Serratosa J., 2008. Risk assessment in animal welfare – EFSA approach. AATEX 14, Special Issue, March 31, 789-794.

OIE, 2004a. Handbook on Import Risk Analysis for Animals and Animal Products. Volume 1. Introduction and qualitative risk analysis. pp. 57.

OIE, 2004b. Handbook on Import Risk Analysis for Animals and Animal Products. Volume 2. Quantitative risk assessment. pp. 126.

Ribó O., Serratosa J., 2010. Papel de la EFSA en la estrategia de la Unión Europea en Salud y Bienestar Animal. SUIS nº 72, Noviembre 2010, 58-64.

Ribó, O., and Serratosa, J., 2009. History and procedural aspects of the animal welfare risk assessment at EFSA. In: Smulders, F.J.M and Algers, B. (Eds.). Food safety assurance and veterinary public health, Vol. 5, Welfare of production animals: assessment and management of risks. Wageningen Academic Publishers, the Netherlands, 305-335.

Ribó O., Candiani D., Barbieri S., Grudnik T., Afonso A., Berthe F., De Massis F.,Dhollander S., Correia S., Have P., Serratosa J., 2008. EFSA approach on risk assessment in animal welfare for the identification of scientific indicators in different livestock species. OIE, 2nd Global Conference on Animal Welfare, Cairo, Egypt, 20-22 October 2008. Poster.

Ribó O., Candiani D., Serratosa J., 2009a. Role of the European Food Safety Authority (EFSA) in providing scientific advice on the welfare of food producing animals. Ital. J. Anim. Sci. vol. 8 (Suppl. 1), 9-17, 2009.

Serratosa, J., and Ribó, O., 2009. International context and impact of EFSA activities in animal welfare in the European Union. In: Smulders, F.J.M and Algers, B. (Eds.). Food safety assurance and veterinary public health, Vol. 5, Welfare of production animals: assessment and management of risks. Wageningen Academic Publishers, the Netherlands, 275-303.

Veissier, I. and Evans, A., 2007. Rationale behind the Welfare Quality® assessment of animal welfare. In: I. Veissier, B. Forkman and B. Jones (Eds), Assuring animal welfare: from societal concerns to implementation, Second Welfare Quality stakeholder conference, 3-4 May 2007, Berlin, Germany, 9-12.

Welfare Quality®, 2009a. Welfare Quality® assessment protocol for poultry. Welfare Quality® Consortium, Lelystad, Netherlands, 114 p.

Welfare Quality®, 2009b. Welfare Quality® assessment protocol for pigs. Welfare Quality® Consortium, Lelystad, Netherlands, 122 p.

Welfare Quality®, 2009c. Welfare Quality® assessment protocol for cattle. Welfare Quality® Consortium, Lelystad, Netherlands, 182 p

WHO, 1999. Codex Alimentarius Commission (CAC). http://www.who.int/foodsafety/publications/micro/cac1999/en/

Chapter 52

Albrecht, H. 2005. Development of arable weed seed banks during the 6 years after the change from conventional to organic farming. In: *Weed Research* 45: pp. 339-350.

Baker, H.G. 1974. The evolution of weeds. In: *Annual Review of Ecology and Systematics*, 5: pp. 1-24

Benton, T.G., Vickery, J.A. and Wilson, J.D. 2003. Farmland biodiversity: is habitat heterogeneity the key? In: *Trends in Ecology & Evolution*, 18(4): pp. 182-188.

Berger, G., Pfeffer, H. Kächele, H., Andreas, S. and Hoffmann, J. 2003. Nature protection in agricultural landscapes by setting aside unproductive areas and ecotones within arable fields ("Infield Nature Protection Spots"). In: *Journal for Nature Conservation*. 11 (3. 221-233.

Biesmeijer, J.C., Roberts, S.P., Reemer, M., Ohlemüller, R., Edwards, M., Peeters, T., Schaffers, A.P., Potts, S.G., Kleukers, R., Thomas, C.D., Settele, J. and Kunin, W.E. 2006. Parallel declines in pollinators and insect-pollinated plants in Britain and the Netherlands. In: *Science*. 313(5785): 286.

Booth, B.D., Murphy, S.D., Swanton, C.J. 2003. *Weed ecology in natural and agricultural systems*. Wallingford: CABI Publishing, 303 p.

Büchs, W. 2003: Biodiversity and agri-environmental indicators. General scopes and skills with special reference to the habitat level. In: *Agriculture, Ecosystems & Environment*, 98: pp. 35-78.

Crawley, J.M. 1997. Biodiversity. In: Crawley, J.M. (Ed.) *Plant ecology*. Oxford: Blackwell Science, pp. 595-632.

Donald, P.F., Green, R.E. and Heath, M.F. 2001. Agricultural intensification and the collapse of Europe's farmland bird populations. In: *Proc. R. Soc. Lond. B*; 268, pp. 25-29.

El Titi, A. 1986. Unkrautkonkurrenz im Zuckerrübenanbau und ihre praktische Ausnutzung. In: *Zeitschrift für Pflanzenkrankheiten und Pflanzenschutz* 93: pp. 136—145.

FAO, Food and Agriculture Organization of UN, 2006a. *Animal genetic resources*. Rome: FAO. http://www.fao.org/AG/cgrfa/AnGR.htm

FAO, Food and Agriculture Organization of UN. 2006b. *Global forest resources assessemnt 2005. Progress towards sustainable forest management*. FAO Forestry Paper 147. Rome: FAO, ISBN 92-5-105481-9

Fehér, A. 2007. *Historical reconstruction of expansion of non-native plants in the Nitra river basin (SW Slovakia)*. Kanitzia 15: 47-62

Flade, M., Plachter, H., Schmidt, R. and Werner, A. (ed.) 2006. *Nature conservation in agricultural ecosystems. Results of the Schorfheide-Chorin research project*. Quelle & Mezer Verlag. 706 p.

Glemnitz, M., Radics, L., Hoffmann, J. and Czimber, G. 2006. Weed species richness and species composition of different arable field types – A comparative analysis along a climate gradient from south to north Europe. In: *Journal of Plant Diseases and Protection*, Sonderheft XX, pp. 577-586.

Glemnitz, M. and Wurbs, A. 2003. Zusammenhänge zwischen der Standortheterogenität und der potenziellen Biotopausstattung in verschiedenen Naturräumen. In: Bastian, O., Grunewald, K., Schanze, J., Syrbe, R.-U. and Walz, U. (Eds.) Bewertung und Entwicklung der Landschaft. In: *IÖR-Schriften*, Vol. 40, 141-153.

Heikkinen, R.K., Luoto, M., Virkkala, R. and Rainio, K. 2004. Effects of habitat cover, landscape structure and spatial variables on the abundance of birds in an agricultural–forest mosaic. In: *J. of Applied Ecology*, 41(5): pp. 824-835.

Herzon, I. and O'Hara, R.B. 2007. Effects of landscape complexity on farmland birds in the Baltic States. In: *Agriculture, Ecosystems & Environment*, 118: pp. 297-306.

Hole D.G., Perkins, A.J., Wilson, J.D., Alexander, I.H., Grice, P.V. and Evans, A.D. 2005. Does organic farming benefit biodiversity? In: *Biological Conservation* 122: pp. 113–130.

Kremen, C., Williams,N.M., Bugg, R.L., Fay, J.P. and Thorp, R.W. 2004. The area requirements of an ecosystem service: crop pollination by native bee communities in California. In: *Ecology Letters*, 7: 1109–1119.

Kretschmer, H., Pfeffer, H., Hoffmann, J., Schrödl, G. and Fux, I. 1995. *Strukturelemente in Agrarlandschaften Ostdeutschlands. Bedeutung für den Biotop- und Artenschutz*. ZALF-Bericht 19, Müncheberg, 164p.

LD, Leipzig declaration on conservation and sustainable utilization of plant genetic resources for food and agriculture. 1996. http://www.fao.org/FOCUS/E/96/06/more/declar-e.htm

LUA, Brandenburg State Office for Environment. 2006. *Brandenburg 2006 - Environmental information*, http://www.mluv.brandenburg.de/cms/media. php/2320/udat5_06.pdf

Lutze, G., Voß, M., Wuntke, B., Kiesel, J., Wieland, R., Hoffmann, J., Strauß, D. and Schultz, A. 2007. *Operationalisierung eines Indikators mit dem Hauptelement der Entwicklung von Vogelbeständen für die regionalisierte und gegliederte Abbildung der Artenvielfalt in Agrarlandschaften : als Beitrag zur Abbildung der Umweltqualität mit naturräumlichem Bezug (Vogelindikator - BMELV), final report*, ZALF Müncheberg, 121 p.

MA, 2003. *Millennium ecosystem assessment. Ecosystems and human well-being. A framework for assessment*. WRI (World Resources Institute). Washington, D.C.: Island Press, p. 245.

Marcinek, J. and Zaumseil, L. 1993. Brandenburg und Berlin im physisch-geographischen Überblick. In: *Geographische Rundschau* 45(10. 556–563.

Marshall, E.J.P., Brown, V.K., Boatman, N.D., Lutman, P.J.W., Squire, G.R. and Ward, L.K. 2002. The role of weeds in supporting biological diversity within crop fields. In: *Weed Research* 43: pp. 77-89.

Matson, P.A., Parton, W.J., Power, A.G. and Swift, M.J. 1997. Agricultural intensification and ecosystem properties. In: *Science* 277(5325): pp. 504 – 509.

Naeem, S., Knops, J.M.H., Tilman, D., Howe, K.M., Kennedy, T. and Gale, S. 2000. Plant diversity increases resistance to invasion in the absence of covarying extrinsic factors. In: *Oikos* 91: pp. 97–108.

Plachter, H. and Janssen, B. 2004. *Managementsystem für den ortsschpezifischen Pflanzenbau*. Verbundprojekt *pre agro*, Abschlussbericht (final report), KTBL, 163-195.

Radics, L., Glemnitz, M., Hoffmann J. and Czimber, G. 2000. Comparative investigations on weed flora composition along a climatic gradient in Europe as basis for climate research efforts. In: *XI.-th International Conference on Weed Biology*. INRA Annales 2000. Dijon: 191- 202.

Roschewitz, I., Gabriel, D., Tscharntke, T. and Thies, C. 2005. The effects of landscape complexity on arable weed species diversity in organic and conventional farming. In: *Journal of Applied Ecology*, 42: pp. 873–882.

TEEB. 2008. *The economics of ecosystems and biodiversity – An interim report* – European Communities.

Tscharntke, T., Klein, A.M., Kruess, A., Steffan-Dewenter, I. and Thies, C. 2005. Landscape perspectives on agricultural intensification and biodiversity ecosystem service management. In: *Ecology Letters*, 8: pp. 857–874.

Tucker, G.M. and Evans, M.I. 1997. *Habitats for birds in Europe. A conservation strategy for the wider environment*. Cambridge, UK BirdLife International.

Van Buskirk, J. and Willi, Y. 2004. Enhancement of farmland biodiversity within set-aside land. In: *Conservation Biology*, 18(4): pp. 987-994.

Weibull, A.C., Östman, Ö. and Granqvist, Å. 2004. Species richness in agroecosystems: the effect of landscape, habitat and farm management. In: *Biodiversity and Conservation* 12(7): pp. 1335-1355.

Wilson, J.D., Whittingham, M.J. and Bradbury, R.B. 2005. The management of crop structure: a general approach to reversing the impacts of agricultural intensification on birds. In: *Ibis*, 147:453-463.

Wittenberg, R. and Cock, M.W.J. (eds.) 2001. *Invasive alien species: a toolkit of best prevention and management practices. Global invasive species programme (GISP)*. Wallingford: Cab International Publishing,

Chapter 53

Alex, D.M., Petridou, E., Dessypris, N., Skenderis, N. and Trichopoulos, D. 2003. Characteristics of farm injuries in Greece. In: *J Agric Saf Health*. 9(3): pp. 233-40.

BS 8800. 2004 *Guide to occupational health and safety management systems*. British Standard Institution.

Brown, C.M., Lehtola, C.J. and Becker, W.J. 2001. *Preventing injuries from slips, trips and falls*. National Ag Safety Data Base, University of Florida. http://nasdonline.org/document/208/d000006/preventing-injuries-from-slips-trips-and-falls.html

Brunes, O. 2006. Status of occupational health, working environment and safety in Norway. In: *Nordic Meeting on Agricultural Occupational Health. Kuopio, August 21-23.2006*. http://www.ttl.fi/Internet/English/Thematic+pages/Agriculture+and+health/

Carruth, A.K., Skarke, L., Moffett, B. and Prestholdt, C. 2001. In: *J Am Med Womens Assoc*. 56(1):15-8.

CDC. 2010. *NIOSH safety and health topic. Agricultural safety*. National Institute for Occupational Safety and Health. http://www.cdc.gov/niosh/topics/aginjury/

Cowie, H.A., Soutar, C.A., Graveling, R.A., Cattermole, T.J., Cherrie, J.W., Graham, M.K. and Mulholland, R.M. 2005. *Baseline incidence of ill health in agriculture of Great Britain*. HSE Research Report 370.

Danielsson, A. 2006. The current situation of farmers' OHS in Sweden. In: *Nordic Meeting on Agricultural Occupational Health. Kuopio, August 21-23. 2006*. http://www.ttl.fi/Internet/English/Thematic+pages/Agriculture+and+health/

Dimich-Ward, H., Guernsey, J.R., Pickett, W., Rennie, D., Hartling, L. and Brison, R.J. 2004. Gender differences in the occurrence of farm related injuries. In: *Occup Environ Med*. 61(1): pp. 52-56.

Dimitri, C., Effland, A. and Conklin, N. 2005. The 20th century transformation of U.S. agriculture and farm policy. In: *USDA Electronic Information Bulletin* Number 3, June 2005.

Donhan, J.D and Thelin, A. 2006. Agricultural Medicine: Occupational and Environmental Health for the Health Professions. Ames, IA: Blackwell.

EASHW, 2007. European Agency for Safety and Health at Work. http://osha.europa.eu/good-practice/sector/agriculture/

Eurostat, 2005. http://epp.eurostat.cec.eu.int.

Eurostat, 2006, http://epp.eurostat.cec.eu.int.

Forastieri, V. 2001. Challenges in providing occupational safety and health services to workers in agriculture. In: *Afr. Newslett. on Occup.Health and Safety*. 11: pp. 33-38.

Harrell, W. 1995. Factors influencing involvement in farm accidents. In: *Percept Mot Skills*. 81(2): pp. 592-594.

References

Hoppe, R.A. and Korb, P. 2005. Large and small farms: trends and characteristics. In: *Structural and financial characteristics of U.S. farms. 2004 farm report*. Washington, D.C.: United States Department of Agriculture – Economic Research Service.

HSE, 2007. Health and Safety Executive. http://www.hse.gov.uk/agriculture/

ISSA. [199?] *Prevention strategy. Safety and health protection in small agriculture and forest enterprises. Problems and solutions.*

ILO. 2004. *Towards a fair deal for migrant workers in the global economy*. Geneva: International Labour Office.

ILO. 2005.*World day of safety and health at work*. http://www.ilo.org/public/english/protection/safework/index.htm

Karttunen, J. 2006. Relative accident risks in farm work. In: *Nordic Meeting on Agricultural Occupational Health. Kuopio, August 21-23.2006*. http://www.ttl.fi/Internet/English/Thematic+pages/Agriculture+and+health/

Karttunen, J., Suutarinen, J., Leppälä, J., Louhelainen, K. and Tuure, V-M. 2006. *Suhteellisesti vaarallisimmat maataloustyöt – töiden organisoinnilla turvallisuutta ja tehokkuutta maitotiloille* (Summary: Relative accident risk in farm work). Työtehoseuran julkaisuja 397.

Langley, R.L., McLymore, R.L. Meggs, W.J. and Roberson, G.T. 1997. *Safety and health in agriculture, forestry and fisheries*. Rockville, MD: Government Institutes.

Loringer, K.A. and Myers, J.R. 2008. Tracking the prevalence of rollover protective structures on U.S. farm tractors: 1993, 2001 and 2004. In: *J Saf Research*. 39(5): pp. 509-517.

Lundquist, P., Stål, M. and Pizke, S. 1997. Ergonomics of cow milking in Sweden. In: *J. Agromed* 4: pp. 169-176.

McCurdy, S.A., Farrar, J.A., Beaumont, J.J., Samuels, S.J., Green, R.S., Scott, L.C. and Schenker, M.B. 2004. Nonfatal occupational injury among California farm operators. In: *J Agric Saf Health*. 10(2): pp. 103-119.

McKay, S., Craw, M. and Chopra, D. 2006. *Migrant workers in England and Wales*. HSE Books. http://www.hse.gov.uk/

McNamara, J., Laffey, F., Griffin, P., Morahan, A. and Phelan, J. 2006. Development of a Code of Practice based OHS Training course for Farmers in Ireland. In: *Nordic Meeting on Agricultural Occupational Health. Kuopio, August 21-23.2006*. http://www.ttl.fi/Internet/English/Thematic+pages/Agriculture+and+health/

Midwest Center for Agricultural Research, Education, and Disease and Injury Prevention. 2002. *North American agriculture 21st century: Implications for protecting the health and safety of persons exposed to agricultural hazards*. Marshfield, WI: The National Farm Medicine Center-Report of the Advisory Board to the Midwest Center for Agricultural Research, Education, and Disease and Injury Prevention, August, 2002.

Mikheev, M. 2004. Occupational health and safety in agriculture in Russia – a country report. In: *Tenth annual meeting of the Baltic Sea Network on occupational health and safety. 21-22 October, Copenhagen, Denmark.*

Murphy, D.J. 1992. *Safety and health for production agriculture*. St. Joseph, MI: American Society of Agricultural and Biological Engineers.

Murphy, D.J. 2003. *Looking beneath the surface of agricultural safety and health*. St. Joeseph, MI: American Society of Agricultural and Biological Engineers.

Murtonen, M. 2006 In: *Nordic Meeting on Agricultural Occupational Health*. Kuopio, August 21-23.2006. <http://www.ttl.fi/Internet/English/Thematic+pages/Agriculture+and+health/

Myers, J.R. 2001. *Analysis of the national traumatic occupational fatalities 1992-1997*. Department of Health and Human Services, Centers for Disease Control and Prevention, National Institute for Occupational Safety and Health (Unpublished).

Myers, J.R., Layne, L.A. and Marsh, S.M. 2007. National injury and fatality data for aging farmers. In: *Proceedings of The Aging Farm Community Using Current Health and Safety Status to Map Future Action, March 6-8, 2007*. Indianapolis, IN.: University of Illinois.

National Children's Center for Rural and Agricultural Health and Safety. 2010. *Fact sheet: Childhood agricultural injuries.*

NSC. 1993. *Accident facts, 1993* edition. Itasca, IL: National Safety Council.

NSC. 1994. *Accident facts, 1994* edition. Itasca, IL: National Safety Council.

NSC. 1995. *Accident facts, 1995* edition. Itasca, IL: National Safety Council.

NSC. 1996. *Accident facts, 1996* edition. Itasca, IL: National Safety Council.

NSC. 1997. *Accident facts, 1997* edition. Itasca, IL: National Safety Council.

NSC. 1998. *Accident facts, 1998* edition. Itasca, IL: National Safety Council.

NSC. 1999. *Injury facts, 1999* edition. Itasca, IL: National Safety Council.

NSC. 2000. *Injury facts, 2000* edition. Itasca, IL: National Safety Council.

NSC. 2001. *Injury facts, 2001* edition. Itasca, IL: National Safety Council.

NSC. 2002. *Injury facts, 2002* edition. Itasca, IL: National Safety Council.

NSC. 2003. *Injury facts, 2003* edition. Itasca, IL: National Safety Council.

NSC. 2004. *Injury facts, 2004* edition. Itasca, IL: National Safety Council.

OSHA, 2007.U.S. *Department of labor. Occupational Safety and Health Administration* http://www.osha.gov/OshDoc/data_General_Facts/farm-fact-factsheet.html

Perkiö-Mäkelä, M., Jokela, P. and Manninen, P. 2006. Pitkäaikaissairastavuus ja oireet. In: Rissanen, P. (ed.) *Työterveys ja Maatalous Suomessa 2004*. työterveyslaitos. Helsinki.

Peters, K.E. 2007. *Implications of the aging process: Opportunities for prevention*. Proceedings of The Aging Farm Community Using Current Health and Safety Status to Map Future Action, March 6-8, 2007. Indianapolis, IN: Published by the University of Illinois.

Rasmussen, K., Carstensen, O. Lauritsen, J.M., Glasscock, D.J., Hansen, O.N. and Jensen, U.F. 2003. Prevention of farm injuries in Denmark. In: *Scand J Work Environ Health* 29(4): pp. 288-296.

Rautiainen, R. 2004. Children are the future. Psychosocial behaviour of children. In: *International colloquium of ISSA. Prevention in agriculture. 31 August - 2 September, 2004.*

Rautiainen, R. 2002. *Injuries and occupational diseases in agriculture in Finland. Cost, length of disability, and preventive effect of a non-claims bonus*. University of Iowa.

Rautiainen, R., Lange, J.L., Hodne, C.J., Schneiders, S. and Donham, K.J. 2004. Injuries in the Iowa safe farm study. In: *J Agric Saf Health*. 10(1): pp. 51-63.

Rautiainen, R.H. and Reynolds, S.J. 2001. *Mortality and morbidity in agriculture in the United States*. Conference proceedings Using Past and Present to Map Future Actions. Baltimore, MD: March, 2001 published by University of Illinois. http://www.uic.edu/sph/glakes/agsafety2001/

Reed, D.B., Westneat, S.C. and Browning, S.R. et al. 1999. The hidden work of the farm homemaker. In: *J Agric Saf Health* 5: pp. 317–327.

Renault, A. 2002. *Migrants in European agriculture – the new mercenaries?* ILO. http://www.ilo.org/public/english/dailogue/

Saari, J. 2001. Successes and failures in occupational injury prevention. Injury Prevention. 7:1-2. Safework Programme. http://www.ilo.org/public/english/protection/safework/index.htm

Sanderson, W.T., Madsen, M.D., Rautiainen, R., Kelly, K.M., Zwerling, C., Taylor, C.D., Reynolds, S.J., Stromquist, A.M. Burmeister, L.F. and Merchant, J.A. 2006. Tractor overturn concerns in Iowa: perspectives from the Keokuk county rural health study. In: *J Agric Saf Health*. 12(1): pp. 71-81.

Spirgys, A., Sarlauskas, A. and Vilkevicius, G. 2005. *The state of occupational safety and health in agriculture in some new member states*. osha.europa.eu/sector/agriculture/state_osh_agriculture.doc

STM, 2003. Riskien arviointi. Sosiaali- ja terveysministeriö. Työsuojeluoppaita ja –ohjeita 14.

Suutarinen, J. 2003. *Occupational accidents in Finnish agriculture – Causality and managerial aspects for prevention*. Agrifood Research Reports 39.

Svennefelt, A.C. and Lundqvist, P. 2006. Swedish guidelines for children´s agricultural tasks. Part II In: *Nordic Meeting on Agricultural Occupational Health. Kuopio, August 21-23.2006*. http://www.ttl.fi/Internet/English/Thematic+pages/Agriculture+and+health/

TIKE. 2006. *Yearbook of farm statistics*. Maa-ja metsätalousministeriön tietopalvelukeskus. Helsinki.

United States Department of Labor. 2005. *Occupational safety and health administration small business handbook* OSHA 2209-02R 2005. http://www.osha.gov/Publications/smallbusiness/small-business.pdf

United States Department of Labor, 2002. *Job hazard analysis*. Occupational Safety and Health Administration, OSHA 371. http://www.osha.gov/Publications/osha3071.pdf

United States Department of Labour Bureau of Labour Statistics. 2009. *Injuries, illnesses and fatalities* http://www.bls.gov/iif/

United States Department of Labor. 2007. *National census of fatal occupational injuries in 2006*. Summary printed in "News" Thursday, August 9, 2007 by Bureau of Labor Statistics, United States Department of Labor http://www.bls.gov/news.release/pdf/cfoi.pdf

United States Department of Agriculture. 2002. *Census of Agriculture, United States, Summary and State Data*. Washington, DC.

Walker, G. 2001. *Occupational health priorities in agriculture*. Report of a conference on occupational health in agriculture. HSC and RASE. Stoneleigh. 11th October.

Chapter 54

Arheimer, B., Andréasson, J., Fogelberg, S., Johnsson, H., Pers, C.B. and Persson, K. 2005. Climate change impact on water quality: Model results from Southern Sweden. In: *Ambio*, Vol 34, No 7: pp. 559-566.

Eckersten, H., Andersson, L., Holstein, F., Mannerstedt Fogelfors, B., Lewan, E., Sigvald, R., Torssell, B. and Karlsson, S. 2008. *An evaluation of climate change effects on crop production in Sweden*, Report from the Department of Crop Production Ecology (VPE) • No. 6, Swedish University of Agricultural Sciences (SLU), ISSN 1653-5375, ISBN 978-91-576-7237-7

IPCC Climate Change 2007: Synthesis report.

IPCC Special report on Emission Scenarios, SREC. 2000.

Further Reading

Andersson, L., Arheimer, B., Kallner Bastviken, S., Johnsson, H., Kyllmar, K., Larsson, H., Pers, C., Rosberg, J., Ståhl-Delbanco, A. and Tonderski, K. 2006. VASTRA-modeller i vattenplaneringscykeln. In: Jöborn, A., Danielsson, I. and Oscarsson, H. (eds.) *På tal om vatten*. VASTRA rapport 6:149-172.

Eckersten, H., Blombäck, K., Kätterer, T. and Nyman, P. 2001. Modelling C, N, water and heat dynamics in winter wheat under climate change in southern Sweden. In: *Agriculture, Ecosystems and Environm*. 86: pp. 221-235.

Johnsson, H,, Mårtensson, K,, Larsson, M. and Mattson, L. 2006. *Beräkning av kväveutlakning vid förändrad gödsling för höstvete och vårkorn*. Teknisk Rapport 106. Avd Vattenvårdslära, Inst Markvetenskap, SLU. Uppsala. 20 pp.

Larsson, M., Kyllmar, K., Jonasson, L. and Johnsson, H. 2005. Estimating reduction of nitrogen leaching from arable land and the related costs. In: *Ambio*, Vol 34, No 7: pp. 538-543.

IPCC reports, 2007, 2008 and 2009

Rounsevell, M.D.A., Berry, P.M. and Harrison, P.A. 2006. Future environmental change impacts on rural land use and biodiversity: a synthesis of the ACCELERATES project. In: *Environmental Science & Policy* 9 (2), 93-100.

Rounsevell, M.D.A., Ewert, F., Reginster, I., Leemans, R. and Carter, T.R. 2005. Future scenarios of European agricultural land use II. Projecting changes in cropland and grassland. In: *Agriculture Ecosystems & Environment* 107 (2-3), 117-135.

SOU 2007. *Sverige inför klimatförändringarna - hot och möjligheter*, SOU 2007:60 (summary in English) (http://www.regeringen.se/sb/d/8704/a/89334)

Spratt, D. and Sutton, P. 2008. *Climate Code red*. Friends of the Earth.

Stern, N. 2006. *The Stern review on the economics of climate change*.

Chapter 55

Banard, C.S. and Nix, J.S. 1973. *Farm planning and control*. Cambridge University Press. 530 p.

Barry, P.J., Ellinger, P.N., Hopkin, J.A. and Baker, C.B. 2000. *Financial management in agriculture*. Sixth edition. Interstate publishers, inc. USA 622 p + annexes.

References

Hallgren, Ö. 1991. *Finasiell metodik*. 8. ed. Värnamo: Studentlitteratur. 330 p.

James, S.C. and Eberle, P.R. 2000. Economic & business principles In: *Farm Planning & Production*. Iowa State university Press. USA. 405 p.

Kaila, E. and Tuure, V-M. 2007. *TTS-manager – Tool for the labour time planning on farms*. pp 43-44, NJF report Vol 3 Nr.2. NJF 23rd Congress.

Kay, R.D. and Edwards, W.M. 1999. *Farm management*. McGraw-Hill, 4. ed. USA. 465p.

Leppiniemi, J. 1994. *Rahoitus*. WSOY. Juva.163 p + annexes

MTT Agrifood Research Finland. Economydoctor. www.mtt.fi/kannattavuuskirjanpito Olson, K. 2004. Farm management. Principles and strategies. Iowa state press. 370 p + annexes.

Olson, K. 2004. *Farm management*. Principles and strategies. Iowa state press. 370 p + annexes.

Pro Agria 2007. *Mallilaskelmia maataloudesta 2007*. (Model Calculations of agriculture. Calculations of production costs. Agricultural support 2005-2007, in Finnish). 46 p. ISBN 978-951-808-154-1. Kurikka, Finland.

Rasmussen, Svend. 2011 *Production Economics The Basic Theory of Production Optimisation*. Springer-Verlag. ISBN 978-3-642-14609-1

Turner, J. and Taylor, M. 1998. *Applied farm management*. ISBN 0-632-03603-6. 387 s. + appendices. Blackwell Science. 387 p.

Tuure, V-M., Kaila, E. and Karttunen, J. 2007. Labour time in farm management work. pp. 668-672 In: *Proceedings, part II from XXXII CIOSTA-CIGR Section V Conference 'Advances in labour and machinery management for a profitable agriculture and forestry, 17-19 September, Slovak University of Agriculture, Nitra, Slovakia*.

Chapter 56

Borhunov, N and Polyanina, M., 2004. Public finance and agriculture. In: *Journal Agricultural Economics of Russia*. № 3 – 20 p. (In Russian).

Liner, A. and Tolstov, M., 2007. *Economic monitoring businesses of Agroindustrial comlex*, Moscow: Kolos, 362 p. (In Russian).

Russian Statistical Yearbook 1998-2008 years (In Russian).

Smolyaninov, S., 2004. *Interaction of the budgetary system of agriculture in the Russian Federation* St. Petersburg:,St.Petersburg State University of Economics and Finance, 278 p. (In Russian).

Sokolova, T. and Chudilin, M., 2005. *Economic analysis and diagnosis of agricultural enterprises*. Moscow: Russian Statistics, 192 p. (In Russian).

Chapter 57

Cook, M.L. 1995. The future of U.S. agricultural cooperatives. In: *American Journal of Agricultural Research* 77: 1153-1159.

Golovina, S. 2007. *Institutional approach to the selection of agrarian enterprises forms*. Kurgan: Kurtamysh printing house. (In Russian)

Information Bulletin of Minister of Agriculture of Russian Federation, No 11-12, 2006

Nilsson, J. 1998. The emergence of new organizational models for agricultural cooperatives. In: *Swedish Journal of Agricultural Research,* 28: 39–47.

Podgorbunskih P. and Golovina, S. 2005. *Theory and practice of agricultural enterprises development: From the classics to institutionalism*. Kurgan: Zauralie. (In Russian).

The report of Minister of Agriculture of Russian Federation November 27th, 2007 (http://www.mcx.ru/index.html?he_id=981&news_id=3981&n_page=1)

Results of Soviet Authority Decades in Figures: 1917-1927, pp. 419-423

Chapter 58

Dzhavadova, E.D. 2007. *The Code of Good Agricultural Practice in Leningrad region part 2: Poultry*. St-Petersburg - Helsinki, 61 p.

Klimenko, JU.I. 2000. *The organization of information – consulting service in agricultural sector*. The manual to seminars. MSHA 335 p.

The international project 'Development of agricultural education in Northwest region of Russia with use of experience of Denmark'. Section. Operative administration of business: the curriculum on speciality 'Farmer-manager' developed for agricultural colleges of Northwest region of Russia based on the experience of Denmark.' ('An agricultural education Programme developed for the North-West Region of Russia focusing on operational farm management'.

Semenova, V.A. 2006. *The Code of Good Agricultural Practice in Leningrad region of Russia. Part 1: Animal husbandry and fodder production*. St Petersburg, 2006, 68 p.

Chapter 59

Dedkov, V. and Fedorov, G. 2006. *Spatial, territorial and landscape planning in Kaliningrad Region*. Kaliningrad: Publ. Immanuel Kant State University of Russia (Monograph in Russian). – 184 p.

Klemeshev, A., Kozlov, S. and Fedorov, G. 2002. *The island of cooperation*. Kaliningrad: Publ. Kaliningrad State University (Monograph in Russian with English summary). – 326 p.

Orlyonok, V. and Fedorov, G. 2005. *Regional geography of Russia: Kaliningrad region*. Kaliningrad: Publ. Immanuel Kant State University of Russia. – 259 p. (In Russian)

Chapter 60

Alakukku, L. 1997. *Long-term soil compaction due to high axle-load traffic*. Academic dissertation. Agricultural Research Centre of Finland. Institute of Crop and Soils Science. ISBN 951-729-485-9 Vammala

Baumol, W.J. and Oates, W.E. 1988. *The theory of environmental policy*. Second edition. Published by Cambridge University press. Printed in USA. 296 p.

Braden, J.B. and Segerson, K. 1993. Information Problems in the Design of Nonpoint-Source Pollution Policy. In: Russell, C.S. and Shoegren, J.F. (eds.). *Theory, Modelling and Experience in the Management of Nonpoint Source Pollution*.

Bäckman, S. 1999. Literature Review on Levies and Permits: pp. 41-62. In: red van Zeijts, H. (ed.) *Economic Instruments for Nitrogen Control in European Agriculture*. CLM 409, Utrecht, 246 p

Carpentier, C.L. 1996. Economic instruments to control soil erosion: a review. In: Weersink, A and Livernois, J. (eds.), [1996] *Exploring alternatives. Potential application of economic instruments to address selected environmental problems in Canadian agriculture*, pp. 77-109. Agriculture and Agri-food Canada

Coase, R.H, 1937. The nature of the firm. In: *Economica* (4): pp. 386-405.

Directive 91/676/EEC. Council Directive of 12 December 1991 concerning the protection of waters against pollution caused by nitrates from agricultural sources.

Directive 2000/60/EC of the European Parliament and of the Council of 23 October 2000 establishing a framework for Community action in the field of water policy. Official Journal L 327 , 22/12/2000 P. 0001 - 0073.

Ekholm, P., Granlund, K., Kauppila, P., Mitikka, S., Niemi, J., Rankinen, K., Räike, A. and Räsänen, J. 2007. In: *Agricultural and Food Science*, Vol 16, No (4): pp. 282-300.

Farmer, M., Swales, V. Kristensen, L., Nitsch, H., Osterburg, B., and Poux, X. 1997. *Cross compliance. Practice, lessons and recommendations. A research paper of the cross compliance network.* Deliverable 24. Sixth Framework Programme. SSPE-CT-2005-022727. 63 p. http://www.ieep.eu/projectminisites/crosscompliancenetworkproj/index.php.

Goodstein, E.S. 1999. *Economics and the Environment.* 2nd ed. John Wiley & Sons, Inc. USA. 544 p.

Grant, R. and Waagepetersen, J. 2003. *Vandmiljøplan II – slutevaluering,* Danmarks Miljøundersøgelser Miljøministeriet, Danmarks Jordbrugsforskning Ministeriet for Fødevarer, Landbrug og Fiskeri. ISBN: 87-7772-776-2. 32 p.

HELCOM 2005. Nutrient pollution to the Baltic Sea in 2000. Helsinki Commission. Baltic Marine Environment Protection Commission. In: *Balt Sea Environment Proceedings No. 100.* 22 p.

HELCOM 2007. *Baltic Sea action plan.* 101 p.

HELCOM 2008. http://www.helcom.fi/BSAP/en_GB/intro/. Page used Aug 14. 2008

Hodge, I. 1995. *Environmental economics.* 198 p. Malaysia.

Horan, R.D. and Shortle, J.S. 2001. Environmental Instruments for Agriculture. In: Shortle. J.S. and Abler, D. (eds.). *Environmental Policies for Agricultural Pollution Control*, UK: CABI Publ. p. 19-65.

Håkansson, I. and Petelkau, H. 1994. Benefits of Limited axle Load. Pp.479-499. In: Soane, B. D. and van Ouwerker, C. (eds.) *Soil compaction in crop production.* Elsevier.

Jacobsen, B.H. 2004. *Økonomisk slutevaluering af vandmiljøplan* II. Fødevareøkonomisk Institut. Rapport nr. 169 116 p.

Lankoski, J. and Ollikainen, M. 1999. The environmental effectiveness of alternative agri-environmental policy reforms: theoretical and empirical analysis. In: *Agric. and Food Science in Finland* 8:321-331

Palva, R., Rankinen, K., Granlund, K., Grönroos, J., Nikander, A. and Rekolainen, S. 2001. *Maatalouden ympäristötuen toimenpiteiden toteutuminen ja vaikutukset vesistökuormitukseen vuosina 1995–1999.*

Mytvas-projektin loppuraportti. Suomen ympäristökeskus. Suomen ympäristö 478. Helsinki. 92 p

Pearce, D.W. and Turner, R.K. 1991. *Economics of natural resources and the environment.* John Hopkins University Press. 378 p.

Perling, J. and Poleman, N. 2004. Wildlife and landscape services production in Dutch dairy farming; jointness and production costs. In: *ERAE* Vol 31(4): pp. 427-449.

Perman, R. Ma, Y. and McGilvray, J. 1996. *Natural resource & environmental economics.* 388 p. Singapore. 0-582-25727-1

Pietola K. and Oude Lansink, A. 2001. Farmer response to policies promoting organic farming technologies in Finland. In: *ERAE* Vol 28(1): pp. 1-15.

Pigou, A.C. 1920. *The economics of welfare.* Re-Published 2002 Transaction Publishers ISBN 0765807394 900 pages

Pyykkönen, S., Grönroos, J., Rankinen, K., Laitinen, P., Karhu, E. and Granlund, K. 2004. *Ympäristötuen mukaiset viljelytoimenpiteet ja niiden vaikutukset vesistökuormitukseen vuosina 2000-2002.* Suomen ympäristö 711. Helsinki. 119 p.

Reeder, H. 2005. Production Cost of Organic Milk. A case study of a dairy farm in Sweden. Pp. 8-2. In: Sumelius, J. (ed.) *Possibilities for and Economic Consequences of Switching to Local Ecological Recycling Agriculture.* Baltic Ecologic recycling Agriculture and Society (BERAS) Nr. 3. Ekologiskt lantbruk Nr 43. SLU Swedish University of Aghricultural Sciences. Centrum för uthålligt lantbruk. CUL. 68 p.

Rørstad, P.K., Vatn, A. and Kvakkestad, V. 2007 Why do transaction costs of agricultural policies vary? In: *Agricultural Economics* 36 (2007): pp. 1–11.

Shortle, J.S. and Abler, D.G. 1997. Nonpoint pollution. In: Folmer, H. and Tietenberg, T (eds.) *The International Yearbook of Environmental and Resource Economics 1997/1998. A Survey of Current Issues.* Cheltenham, UK: Edward Elgar. p. 114-155.

Shortle, J.S. and Abler, D. (eds.) 2001. *Environmental Policies for Agricultural Pollution Control.* CABI Publ.: UK 211 p

Slangen, L. 1997. How to organise nature production by farmers? In: *ERAE* Vol 24: 508 - 529.

Stern Review on the economics of climate change. 2006. HM treasury http://www.hm-treasury.gov.uk/independent_reviews/stern_review_economics_climate_change/stern_review_report.cfm

Sumelius, J. 1994. Controlling nonpoint source pollution of nitrogen from agriculture through economic instruments in Finland. In: *Agricultural Economics Research Institute Res. Publ.*74. 62 p.

Sumelius, J.1999. EU agri-environmental programmes – can Central and East European countries learn anything from the Finnish experiences? In: *Zemědělská ekonomika (Agricultural Economics)* 1999(4):163-167.

Sumelius, J., Mesić, M., Grgić, Z., Kisic, I. and Franić, R. 2005. Marginal abatement costs for reducing leaching of nitrates in Croatian agriculture. In: *Agricultural and Food Science*, Vol 14, No (3): pp. 293-309.

Vaahtera, E. Conley, D., Gustafsson, B.G., Kuosa, H., Pitkänen, H., Savchuk, O.P., Tamminen, T. Viitasalo, M., Voss, M. Wasmund, N. and Wulff, F. 2007. Internal ecosystem feedbacks enhance nitrogen-fixing cyanobacteria blooms and complicate management in the Baltic Sea. In: *Ambio* Vol 36(2-3): pp. 186-194.

References

Vatn, A., Bakken, L. R., Lundeby, H., Romstad, E., Rørstad, P. K., Vold, A. 1997. Regulating nonpoint source pollution from agriculture: An integrated modelling analysis. In: *European Review of Agricultural Economics* 24: 207-229.

Vatn, A., Kvakkestad, V. and Rørstad, P.K. 2002. *Policies for multifunctional agriculture. The trade-off between transaction costs and precision.* Report 23, Agricultural University of Norway, Dep. Economics and Social Sciences. 81 p. Ås.

Vernimmen, T., Verbeke W., and Huylenbroeck, G. 2000. Transaction costs analysis of outsourcing farm administration by Belgian farmers. In: *ERAE* Vol 27(3): pp. 325-345.

Weersink, A. and Livernois, J. 1996. Introduction. In: Weersink, A. and Livernois, J. (eds.), [1996] *Exploring alternatives. Potential application of economic instruments to address selected environmental problems in Canadian agriculture*, pp. 77-109. Agriculture and Agri-food Canada

Wulff, F., Savchuk, O.P., Sokolov, A. Humborg, C. and Mörth. C-M. 2007. Management options and effects on a marine ecosystem: Assessing the future of the Baltic. In: *Ambio* Vol 36(2-3): pp. 243-249

Yearbook of Farm Statistics 2006. Information Centre of Ministry of Agriculture and Forestry. Official Statistics of Finland. 267 p. Vantaa

Chapter 61

Swedish Board of Agriculture, SBA. 2006. *Plan of Action against Plant Nutrient Losses from Agriculture.* 11 p. http://www.jordbruksverket.se/blanketterochtrycksaker.4.5954014612 l0ae2d58980003322 5.html

Swedish Board of Agriculture, SBA. 2007. *Greppa näringen* (Focus on Nutrients) Working effectively towards our environmental objectives! A report on environmental protection work in agriculture from Greppa Näringen. http//www.greppa.nu

Swedish Board of Agriculture, SBA. 2009. *Focus on Nutrients* - a project run jointly by the Swedish agricultural industry, the Swedish county administrative boards and the Swedish Board of Agriculture.

List of Authors

Name of author	Current position	University/Affiliation	Email address
Bob Aherin	Program Director	University of Illinois Urbana-Champaign	raherin@uiuc.edu
Laura Alakukku	Professor of Environmental engineering in Agriculture	University of Helsinki	laura.alakukku@helsinki.fi
Andres Aland	Associate Professor at Institute of Veterinary Medicine and Animal Sciences	Estonian University of Life Sciences	andres.aland@emu.ee
Ann Albihn	Associate Professor/Head of Section	National Veterinary Institute	ann.albihn@sva.se
Bo Algers	Professor at Department of Animal Environment and Health	Swedish University of Agricultural Sciences	bo.algers@hmh.slu.se
Lars Andersson	Professor at Department of Crop Production Ecology.	Swedish University of Agricultural Sciences	lars.andersson@slu.se
Michael C. Appleby	Chief Scientific Advisor	World Society for the Protection of Animals	michaelappleby@wspa-international.org
David Arney	Associate Professor at Institute of Veterinary Medicine and Animal Sciences	Estonian University of Life Sciences	david.arney@emu.ee
Johan Arvidsson	Professor at Department of Soil & Environment	Swedish University of Agricultural Sciences	johan.arvidsson@mark.slu.se
Valery Belyakov	Professor at Department of Automobiles and tractors	Saint-Petersburg State Agrarian University	valery.belyakov@gmail.com
Charlotte Berg	Professor at Faculty of Veterinary Medicine and Animal Science	Swedish University of Agricultural Sciences	lotta.berg@slu.se
Gert Berger	Doctor at Institute of Land Use Systems	Leibniz Centre for Agricultural Landscape Research	gberger@zalf.de
Harry Blokhuis	Professor at Department of Animal Environment and health	Swedish University of Agricultural Sciences	harry,blokhuis@slu,se
Angelija Buciene	Associate Professor at Department of Geography	Klaipeda University	abuciene@yahoo.com
Galina Bulgakova	Professor. Dean of the Economics Faculty	St. Petersburg State Agrarian University	bulgakova1@mail.ru
Tujana Burkhieva	Dr.	North-West Research Institute of Economics and Organization of Agriculture	
Stefan Bäckman	Doctor at Department of Economics and Management	University of Helsinki	stefan.backman@helsinki.fi
Yariv Cohen	Researcher at Department of Soil and Environment	Swedish University of Agricultural Sciences	yariv.cohen@slu.se
Albert E. Cox	Environmental Soil Scientist	Metropolitan Water Reclamation District of Greater Chicago	albert.cox@mwrd.org
Thomas E. Davenport	National NPS Expert and Regional Agricultural Advisor	US Environmental Protection Agency	davenport.thomas@epamail.epa.gov
Faruk Djodjic	Researcher at Department of Aquatic Sciences and Assessment	Swedish University of Agricultural Sciences	faruk.djodjic@slu.se
Henrik Eckersten	Professor at Department of Crop Production Ecology	Swedish University of Agricultural Sciences	henrik.eckersten@slu.se
Marina Efremova	Ass. Prof. at Dept. of Agrochemistry and Agroecology	St. Petersburg State Agrarian University	marina_efremova@mail.ru
Bettina Eichler Löbermann	Professor habil. Doctor	University of Rostock	bettina.eichler@uni-rostock.de
Marija Eidukevičiene	Professor habil. Doctor	Klaipeda university	mariae@takas.lt
Patrik Enfält	CEO Agr.	Easy Mining Sweden AB	

Ararso Etana	Researcher at Dept. of Soil and Water Management	Swedish University of Agricultural Sciences	ararso.etana@slu.se
Gennady Fedorov	Professor	Immanuel Kant State University of Russia	gfedorov@kantiana.ru
Alexander Fehér	Associate Professor	Slovak University of Agriculture in Nitra	alexander.feher@uniag.sk
Michael Glemnitz	Doctor	Leibniz-Centre for Agricultural Landscape Research	
Svetlana Golovina	Pro-rector	Kurgan State Agricultural Academy	s_golovina@yahoo.com
Thomas C. Granato	Assistant Director of R&D	Metropolitan Water Reclamation	thomas.granato@mwrd.org
Arne Gustafson	Professor Emeritus	Swedish University of Agricultural Sciences	arne.gustafson@telia.com
Borje Gustafsson		University of Illinois Urbana-Champaign	
Folke Günther	University Lecturer/ Researcher	Lund University	folke@holon.se
Irina Herzon	Doctor, Researcher	University of Helsinki	herzon@mappi.helsinki.fi
Fredrik Holstein	Doctoral student	Swedish University of Agricultural Sciences	fredrik.holstein@slu.se
Lars D. Hylander	Researcher at Department of Earth Sciences	Uppsala University	lars.hylander@hyd.uu.se
Alexandra Izosimova	Senior Scientist	Agro-Physical Research Institute	alexandra.izosimova@gmail.com
Christine Jakobsson	Director of Baltic University Programme Cooperation Coordinator	Uppsala University and Swedish University of Agricultural Sciences	christine.jakobsson@slu.se
Benediktas Jankauskas	Habil. Doctor	Kaltinenai Research Station of Lithuanian Institute of Agriculture	kaltbs@kaltbs.lzi.lt
Allan Kaasik	Scientist at Institute of Veterinary Medicine and Animal Sciences	Estonian University of Life Sciences	allan.kaasik@emu.ee
Uladzimir Kapitsa	Head of Environmental Management Sub-department	International Sakharov Environment University	v_kapitska@yahoo.com
Stig Karlsson	Professor Emeritus	Swedish University of Agricultural Sciences	
Holger Kirchmann	Professor at Dept. of Soil and Environment	Swedish University of Agricultural Sciences	holger.kirchmann@slu.se
Louis Kollias	Scientist	Metropolitan Water Reclamation District of Greater Chicago	louis.kollias@mwrdgc.dst.il.us
Lydia Končeková	Scientist	Slovak University of Agriculture in Nitra	
Evgeny Krasnov	Professor	Kaliningrad State University	ecogeography@rambler.ru
Jenny Kreuger	Senior research officer at Department of Soil and Environment	Swedish University of Agricultural Sciences	jenny.kreuger@slu.se
Thomas Kätterer	Professor at Department of Soil and Environment	Swedish University of Agricultural Sciences	thomas.katterer@slu.se
Magdaléna Lacko-Bartošová	Professor	Slovak University of Agriculture in Nitra	magdalena.lacko-bartosova@uniag.sk
Ragnar Leming	Associate Professor at Institute of Veterinary Medicine and Animal Sciences	Estonian University of Life Sciences	ragnar.leming@emu.ee
Elisabet Lewan	Assistant Professor at Department of Soil and Environment	Swedish University of Agricultural Sciences	lisbet.lewan@slu.se
Birgitta Mannerstedt Fogelfors	Scientist at Department of Crop Production Ecology	Swedish University of Agricultural Sciences	birgitta.mannerstedt.fogelfors@slu.se
Audrone Mašauskiene	Dr	Lithuanian Institute of Agriculture	audrone.masauskiene@lzi.lt
Gregory McIsaac	Associate Professor at Department of Crop Sciences	Science University of Illinois at Urbana Champaign	gmcisaac@uiuc.edu
Vytas Mašauskas		Lithuanian Institute of Agriculture	vytas.masauskas@lzi.lt
Mikhail Moskalev	Professor, head of Department Marketing in agribusiness	Saint-Petersburg State Agrarian University	moskalev_market@mail.ru
Åsa Myrbeck	Research Assistant	Swedish University of Agricultural Sciences	asa.myrbeck@slu.ee
Ruth C. Newberry	Associate Professor	Washington State University	rnewberry@wsu.edu

Julia Nikulina	Dr	North-West Research Institute of Economics and Organization of Agriculture	
Eskil Nilsson	Consultant	VISAVI AB/SYDEK	eskil.visavi@sydek.se
Karin Nyberg	Dr/Researcher	National Veterinary Institute	karin.nyberg@sva.se
Jakob R. Ottoson	Associate Professor/Researcher	National Veterinary Institute and Swedish University of Agricultural Sciences	jakob.ottoson@sva.se
Ola Palm	Research & Development Manager	JTI – Swedish Institute for Agricultural and Environmental Engineering	ola.palm@jti.se
Jaak Panksepp	Adjunct Professor	Washington State University	jhheiss@wsu.edu
Holger Pfeffer	Scientist	Leibniz-Centre for Agricultural Landscape Research	tkalettka@zalf.de
Mikhail Ponomarev	Researcher	North-West Research Institute of Economics and Organization of Agriculture	m.a.ponomarev@gmail.com
Piotr Prus	Dr at Department of Economics and Advising in Agribusiness	University of Technology and Life Sciences in Bydgoszcz	prus@utp.edu.pl
Markus Pyykkönen	Head of Development	Ministry of Social Affairs and Health Department of Occupational Safety and Health	markus.pyykkonen@stm.fi
Oriol Ribó	Director	European Food Safety Authority (EFSA), Parma, Italy	oriol.ribo@efsa.europa.eu
Bernard Rollin	Professor	Colorado State University	bernard.rollin@colostate.edu
Tomas Rydberg	State agronomist, AgrD	Swedish University of Agricultural Sciences	tomas.rydberg@slu.se
Torbjörn Rydberg	Instructor at Department of Rural development	Swedish University of Agricultural Sciences	torbjorn.rydberg@slu.se
Are Selge	Associate Professor at Institute of Agricultural and Environmental Sciences	Estonian University of Life Sciences	are.selge@emu.ee
Roland Sigvald	Senior Research Officer, AgrD	Swedish University of Agricultural Sciences	roland.sigvald@entom.slu.se
Staffan Steineck	Research Manager	The Swedish Institute of Agricultural Engineering	staffan.steineck@jti.slu.se
John Sumelius	Professor at Department of Economics & Management	University of Helsinki	john.sumelius@helsinki.fi
Vladimir Surovtsev	Dr	North-West Research Institute of Economics and Organization of Agriculture	
Bengt Torssell	Professor Emeritus	Swedish University of Agricultural Sciences	bengt.torssell@evp.slu.se
Lennart Torstensson	Professor Emeritus	Swedish University of Agricultural Sciences	lennart.torstensson@mikrob.slu.se
Peter Tóth	Scientist	Slovak University of Agriculture	petery@nextra.sk
Liudmila Tripolskaja	Professor habil. Doctor	Lithuanian Institute of Agriculture	sk@lzuu.lt
Barbro Ulén	Researcher at Department of Soil and Environment.	Swedish University of Agricultural Sciences	barbro.ulen@slu.se
Michelle Wander	Associate Professor	University of Illinois	mwander@illinois.edu
Rein Viiralt	Professor Emeritus at Institute of Agricultural and Environmental Sciences	Estonian University of Life Sciences	rein.viiralt@emu.ee
Björn Vinnerås	Associate Professor/Researcher	National Veterinary Institute and Swedish University of Agricultural Sciences	bjorn.vinneras@sva.se
Hava Zaburaeva	Docent	Department Ecology and Nature Use at State Oil Institute, Grozny, Russia	